RED ROCKS
A Climber's Guide
Second Edition
by Jerry Handren

© 2016 by Jerry Handren. All rights reserved.
No part of this book may be reproduced in any form without permission in writing from the author.
ISBN: 978-1-4951-8204-4
Printed in China.

Warning! Read before using this book.

Climbing is an extremely dangerous activity. Always use judgement rather than the opinions represented in this book. The author assumes no responsibility for injury or death resulting from the use of this book. The information in this book is based on opinions gathered from a variety of sources. Do not rely solely on the information, descriptions or difficulty ratings as these are entirely subjective. If you are unwilling to assume complete responsibility for your safety, do not use this book.

The author and publisher expressly disclaim all representations and warranties regarding this guide, the accuracy of the information herein, and the results of your use hereof, including without limitation, implied warranties of merchantability and fitness for a particular purpose. The user assumes all risk associated with the use of this guide.

The ultra-thin crux on Pitch 7 of Dreefee. Page 186.

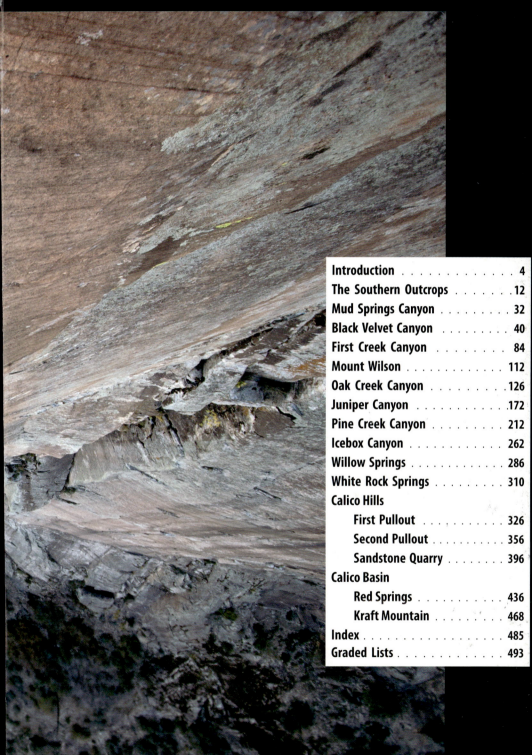

About this Guidebook

This is a comprehensive guide to the rock climbs found in Red Rock Canyon National Conservation Area, twenty miles to the west of the famous Las Vegas Strip in Southern Nevada. Red Rocks offers the climber everything from sport routes to big aid walls and long free routes. The reliable weather, beautiful surroundings and great climbing make Red Rocks one of North America's best and most popular destinations during the fall, winter, and spring.

This book provides detailed information on over 2300 rock climbs, using full written descriptions, maps, topos and photodiagrams. This new edition includes over 400 previously unpublished routes. Recent developments include the addition of a large number of entry-level and moderate sport routes in the Calico Hills; it is probably true to say that Red Rocks now has one of the biggest collections of such climbs in the country. At the other end of the difficulty spectrum, the free ascents of old, big-wall aid climbs in the canyons has resulted in the addition of a batch of fantastic long, free routes.

One of the most notable developments in recent years has been the emergence of Red Rocks as a world class bouldering area. All the bouldering is documented in Tom Moulins' superb guidebook, "Southern Nevada Bouldering".

If the routes in the photographs throughout this book seem unfamiliar, that's because I have made a deliberate attempt to shoot new and/or obscure routes. In order to save some space, the updated history of climbing in Red Rocks, as well as the historical essays that appeared in the previous edition have now been moved to the website (www.redrocksguide-book.com.)

In the next few years the BLM is going to be making a series of improvements to the basic infrastructure of Red Rocks. This is going to include expansion of the existing parking areas and possibly the addition of several new ones. Also, it seems likely that there is going to be some sort of return option from the Sandstone Quarry parking area, either making the existing road to that point two way or building an entirely new road back to the Visitor Center. It is worth keeping track of these developments as they will have an effect on some of the information in this book.

Jerry Handren, February 2016.

The Land, Rules and Regulations

The climbing in Red Rocks lies within the boundaries of the Red Rock Canyon National Conservation Area. The land received this designation in 1990 to protect and preserve what was then recognized as a resource of national importance. The land is managed by the Bureau of Land Management, from the Las Vegas District Office, (702 515 5000).

There are two wilderness areas within Red Rock National Conservation Area, Rainbow Mountain Wilderness area, which includes all the canyons, and La Madre Mountain Wilderness which includes the Kraft Mountain area of Calico Basin.

Scenic Loop Hours	
November 1 to February 28/29	6:00 A.M. to 5:00 P.M.
March 1 to March 31	6:00 A.M. to 7:00 P.M.
April 1 to September 30	6:00 A.M. to 8:00 P.M.
October 1 to October 31	6:00 A.M. to 7:00 P.M.

Most of the northern half of Red Rocks is accessed from the Red Rock Scenic Drive. This is a gated 13-mile-long, one-way loop road which requires an entrance fee, and has restricted access hours.

As of 2020 the entrance fee was $15 per car, but this seems to be steadily increasing every few years. Also available are Red Rock annual passes which are usually worth buying if you are spending more than a couple of days in the area in any given year. The America The Beautiful pass that works for Yosemite, Joshua Tree and all the other national parks will also get you into the Red Rock Scenic Drive.

In recent years the Red Rock Scenic Drive has become extremely busy, with tourists as well as climbers. On certain popular weekends and holidays many of the parking areas can be completely full, and when this happens the BLM will sometimes close the Scenic Drive for a few hours. During busy times of year it is best to get an early start, even if you are just planning a casual day of cragging in the Calico Hills.

Vehicles left inside the Scenic Drive after hours are subject to a heavy fine ($120 in 2016). Please note that this includes the parking area beside the fee station at the Scenic Drive entrance.

Late exit permits are available to provide an additional two hours after the normal closing time. These permits are available only for multi-pitch routes, not for the climbing in the Calico Hills or Willow Springs.

Take note that as of January 1, 2020 the late exit permit process has changed. Permits are now processed online at www.recreation.gov. Search for Red Rock Canyon National Conservation Area and click on the "Buy a Pass" button. Late exit permits are free, but a 50-cent processing fee will be charged. The website requires your license place number.

If you have additional questions or comments feel free to call a climbing ranger (Monday to Friday 8 a.m. to 4:30 p.m.) at 702 515 5000.

For multi-day routes it is also possible to get an overnight permit. These are issued for the following walls only:

Mt. Wilson (1-2 nights)
Eagle Wall (1 night)
Rainbow Wall (1-2 nights)
Buffalo Wall (1-3 nights)
Hidden Wall (1-3 nights)
Bridge Mountain (1 night)

For updates on permits, entrance fees etc. check the news in the updates section of www.redrocksguidebook.com.

With the exception of the Red Springs parking area in Calico Basin, all the areas outside the Scenic Drive are not subject to the same time restrictions.

Camping is not allowed anywhere in the National Conservation Area. In particular, this includes the network of dirt roads, accessed from route 160, which provide access to Black Velvet Canyon and the other areas at the southern end of the range. The rangers regularly patrol this area looking for campers, and the fines are stiff.

There are several other rules that relate directly to climbers.
1. It is prohibited to chip, glue, chisel or scar the rock.
2. Climbing is not allowed within 50 feet of any Native American rock art site.
3. It is prohibited to place bolts in either of the wilderness areas. This includes all the canyons and also the Kraft Mountain area of Calico Basin. The fine is $300 per instance, so if you are unsure about the status of your proposed route contact the climbing rangers.

An important development in May 2007 was the release of the Preliminary Action Plan. This plan was created by the BLM in cooperation with various interested groups, including the Climbers Liaison Council. It includes a proposal for a permit system for new routes that would allow for the addition of new bolts, with certain provisions. As of 2020 this plan is still unratified with no resolution in sight.

The BLM runs a visitor center just inside the Scenic Drive entrance, there is an exhibit which provides interesting historical and geological background information on Red Rocks. This is where you can get current information about the National Conservation Area.

The activities of climbers are under close scrutiny in the Red Rock Canyon National Conservation Area. It is very important that climbers treat Red Rocks with the utmost care. This means using Leave No Trace Ethics, treating other users with respect, and observing the rules and regulations.

There is a twenty-four hour limit to parking along route 159. If you are planning to park here for a multi-day objective you will want to make sure that this is ok with the rangers.

Access Map

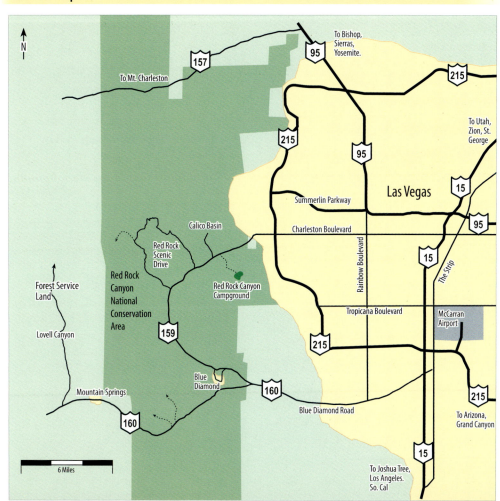

The Rock

Red Rocks is composed of a three-thousand-foot thick escarpment of Aztec Sandstone, which has weathered into a series of ten major canyons which drain from west to east. This rock is generally quite well-bonded, being more solid than that found in the other great sandstone areas of the west, such as Zion or Canyonlands. Another major difference is that much of the rock is covered with a thin layer of desert varnish which, on many of the faces, has partially weathered to leave behind a sea of good incut edges. It is these edges which allow routes like Dream of Wild Turkeys, Eagle Dance, and Crimson Chrysalis to climb such impressive features at a reasonable standard. In general, the unvarnished white and red rock can be soft, sandy and rounded in its natural state, although it cleans up well on popular routes to give very enjoyable climbing. The varnished rock provides superb climbing, especially on some of the north-facing walls where the varnish has resisted weathering and there are far fewer face holds. On these walls the long, clean, crack and corner systems provide some of the best routes in Red Rocks.

The edges that are the hallmark of so much of the climbing in Red Rocks can be quite fragile in their natural state. On popular climbs the loose holds and fragile lips are gradually cleaning up, but even on these routes it is not uncommon to pop a foothold or two. Some of the more recent and/or less travelled routes can feel very fragile and require careful climbing. Climbers also have to be aware of larger blocks and flakes which crop up from time to time and can be amazingly unstable.

By far the most important factor affecting rock quality is precipitation. The Aztec Sandstone is porous and easily absorbs water; when waterlogged the rock becomes much weaker, causing holds to break with alarming ease. During long stretches of dry weather the rock will dry out in a few hours after an isolated rainstorm. However, after a long spell of heavy rain, it can take up to three days for the rock to dry out. In fact, during a wet "El Nino" year the rock can feel snappy all winter long. It is important to stay off routes when the rock is wet, especially in the Calico Hills where the rock is particularly soft after rain, and the loss of a crucial hold can easily destroy a classic route for good.

Despite these words of doom, the rock in Red Rocks is generally superb and a joy to climb, many of the classic routes rank with the best of their grade anywhere in the world.

Luke Olson enjoying the immaculate varnish of Saracen. Page 321.

The Weather

The numbers say it all: Red Rocks is often blessed with perfect climbing conditions for months on end, with the spring and fall each usually having three months of perfect weather.

Average temperature 66.3 degrees (19 degrees centigrade). Average yearly rainfall 4.13 inches (10.64 centimeters). Average daily humidity 29 percent. 211.5 clear days annually, 82.4 partly cloudy days, 71.3 cloudy days.

Month	Average Daily Low (°F)	Average Daily High (°F)	Sunny Days	Average Rainfall (inches)
January	33	56	24	0.5
February	37	67	22	0.46
March	42	68	25	0.41
April	49	77	26	0.22
May	59	87	27	0.22
June	68	98	28	0.09
July	75	104	27	0.45
August	73	101	26	0.54
September	65	94	28	0.32
October	53	81	27	0.25
November	41	66	24	0.43
December	33	67	24	0.32

Red Rocks is one of the few areas that can genuinely claim to offer year-round climbing. It is possible to find reasonable climbing conditions on all but a few of the hottest days of the year, when temperatures creep up towards 110°F or more.

Nevertheless, during the hottest and coldest times of year, comfortable climbing depends on making good choices and being prepared to adapt your objectives to suit the prevailing weather of the day. In particular, warm weather climbing takes some getting used to; sunny approaches must be tackled early in the morning and climbing is not feasible until your chosen route goes into the shade. Climbing in the canyons during colder weather also requires some thought. The difference between sun and shade is often dramatic, 30°F or more. It is quite common to be comfortable in the parking area and freezing on the route. The temperature in the canyons is usually at least 10°F colder than town and can feel a lot colder yet if there is any wind. A windshell is almost always a good idea. By contrast, the south-facing walls in the Calico Hills can feel hot on all but the coldest days, so bring plenty of water and some light clothing.

Wind is an important factor to consider at all times of year. The reason is not so much how it affects the climbing as what it does to rappel ropes. The sharp flakes that cover many of the faces are always a problem when rappelling, but with the wind whipping the ropes all over the wall, the chances of a snagged rope are greatly increased. Some of the taller walls in Red Rocks are very exposed, and if your chosen route involves a rappel descent, strong winds can pose a serious hazard. Walls such as the Eagle Wall and Crimson Chrysalis are best avoided under these conditions.

It is worth remembering that the weather data are only averages. During El Nino years, when a huge bubble of warm water shows up in the Western Pacific, Red Rocks will often have a miserable wet winter. During any winter, snowstorms can happen any time from October until April, with the snow sticking around for many days in the canyons. In the summer, a sudden storm can cause very cold conditions on long backcountry routes, and any canyon can flash flood without warning.

A winter storm, February 2008.

Staying in Red Rock Canyon

Transport
Although some hardy individuals do without, a car is pretty much essential for climbing at Red Rocks. There is no public transportation system, and the distances involved are just too great for walking to be a reasonable option. Las Vegas is one of the least expensive places in the country to rent a car.

Camping, Groceries, Showers Etc.
At present, there is only one campground close to Red Rocks. It is in a good location, close to the Scenic drive entrance, but isn't the prettiest campground in the world. It is located at the end of a one mile long spur road on the southeast side of route 159. The spur road is called Moenkopi, and is on the right 1.9 miles east of the Scenic Drive entrance, and 0.5 miles east of the Calico Basin Road. Alternatively, if you are driving west out of town along Charleston Boulevard, it is on the left, 3.2 miles west of the Charleston/215 interchange.

It is a relatively primitive campsite with pit toilets, picnic tables and a water tap. The sites can be booked online. Go to www.recreation.gov and search for Red Rock Canyon Campground. There is a 14 day limit. Individual sites are available up to 6 months in advance, group sites up to one year in advance. The Campground is closed June, July and August.

Within five miles from the campsite, and getting closer every year, the west end of Charleston Boulevard is one of the main suburban shopping areas in Las Vegas with all manner of grocery stores, coffee shops, casinos etc.

Showers are available for $4.00 at the Red Rock Climbing Center, 8201 W. Charleston Blvd. Phone: 702 254 5604

Free wireless Internet service is provided at Desert Rock Sports, located at 8221 W. Charleston Blvd., a few doors up from the Red Rock Climbing Center. As well as being a retailer of all things climbing, this store often puts on special events such as slide shows and film screenings.

There is dispersed camping in Lovell Canyon, the canyon to the west of the Red Rock range. It is accessed from route 160 by taking a right at the bottom of the hill to the west of Mountain Springs. There are no facilities, and it's a long drive (25 miles from the Scenic Drive), but there are some nice spots to spend the night in a pinch. Stays are limited to 14 days.

Climbing Alternatives
If soggy rock is curtailing climbing at Red Rocks, there is a lot of limestone sport climbing all around Las Vegas which can be climbable as soon as the rain stops. There are no in-print guidebooks available to these areas but some information is available online.

If the local Limestone sport climbing doesn't appeal, then it is a very reasonable drive (2½ hours) to Joshua Tree. The weather in Joshua Tree is similar to Red Rock Canyon, but the granitic rock is very quick drying.

If the weather really craps out you can stay fit at one of the three excellent gyms in town; Red Rock Climbing Center, The Refuge, and Origin.

Notes on the use of this Guide

Layout
The routes described in this guidebook are generally grouped in chapters according to the main canyon from which they are accessed, or in the case of the Calico Hills, the parking area from which they are accessed.

Within each chapter most routes are grouped into areas which correspond to either particular crags or major topographical features.

The chapters are arranged from south to north, starting with the Southern Outcrops and finishing with Kraft Rocks.

In the canyons, the main areas are described from south to north going clockwise around the walls.

Route Descriptions

Route Number
Some routes within an area are assigned a route number. This number is used to identify the route on any photodiagrams, plan maps, or topos of that area. In most cases routes are on the same page as their photodiagram. In certain sections, where the route descriptions are spread over several pages, the photodiagram will always be within that section.

Route Names
Generally the route names are those given by the first ascent party. However, Red Rocks has many mystery routes with no

established name. Rather than having numerous "Unknowns" I have taken the liberty of providing a name for every route in the guidebook. In future guidebook editions some route names will undoubtedly change as their real names come to light. Hopefully the confusion that this causes is the lesser of two evils.

Length
This is the actual climbing length of the route rather than the vertical height gained. It takes the place of the commitment grade (I,II,III,IV, etc.) since along with the description, it gives a pretty accurate idea of the scale of the undertaking.

Grade
The standard rating system is used: 5.0 to 5.14 with the grades from 5.10 up subdivided into a,b,c and d. In a few cases I have used seriousness ratings R and X. But generally, where a route is known to be serious for some reason, this will be mentioned in the description. Do not assume that a route is safe just because there is no seriousness rating or any mention of danger in the description.

Star Rating
This guidebook uses a three-star system to rate the quality of the routes. Obviously this is a very subjective undertaking and these ratings should be taken with a grain of salt. Certain

personal biases no doubt crept into the assessment. So, for the record, I should say that clean, varnished rock, sweeping natural lines, and sustained climbing are factors that will push a route up the scale. Flaky rock, dirt, and a wandering or contrived line will push a route down.

I have tried to be very conservative in doling out stars so that the really good routes stand out; this is mostly to point visiting climbers at the very best routes. The fact that a route has no stars does not mean that it is not worth doing; instead I have tried to mention in the text if a route is really poor quality.

The sport climbing in the Calico Hills posed a little bit of a problem because there is a lot of similarity from one route to the next. Generally, even the best routes would not be considered world class in the same way the best canyon routes definitely are. With this in mind, the star ratings for sport climbs and trad climbs are not really comparable. Generally, in the Calico Hills I have tried to give the extra stars to routes with particularly nice moves, good rock, or some other special feature that makes them stand out from the crowd.

Symbols

❸ A sport climb. A route that is protected exclusively by closely spaced bolts, with a fixed anchor at the top.

❶ Old bolts. Many of the old ¼ inch bolts have been replaced with solid ⅜ inch bolts, but a few still remain. These bolts are not reliable and should be backed up wherever possible.

† The dagger symbol is used for routes where I have been unable to track down a definitive description, the given route description should be treated as a very rough guide at best.

First Ascent Details

Where possible I have included the names of the first ascent team. Many of the more recent routes were submitted anonymously and so this information is not available. There are also many older routes whose origin is unknown.

Bolt-Free Ascents

Red Rocks pioneers have often had a fairly liberal attitude towards placing bolts, tending to err on the side of making routes fun and enjoyable and putting bolts in if there was any doubt. Improvements in modern protection gizmos have also made many older bolt placements redundant. In order to get a bit more challenge out of older routes, climbers are sometimes re-climbing established routes without clipping the bolts. I have made note of such ascents in the descriptions. Sometimes this includes an adjusted grade due to the extra effort involved in fiddling in gear instead of just clipping and going.

GPS

When preparing this book, I had every intention of providing GPS information for routes, approaches, parking etc. However, as I collected the data it became apparent that in many parts of Red Rocks GPS is not 100% reliable. The problem appears to be associated with signal getting reflected and/or blocked by the tall canyon walls. Because of this I was then faced with the dilemma of whether to include information that was usually useful, but, occasionally, potentially misleading. Since this book provides more than enough information to find every route without GPS, I decided not to include GPS data with this edition.

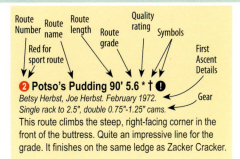

❷ Potso's Pudding 90' 5.6 * † ❶
Betsy Herbst, Joe Herbst. February 1972.
Single rack to 2.5", double 0.75"-1.25" cams.
This route climbs the steep, right-facing corner in the front of the buttress. Quite an impressive line for the grade. It finishes on the same ledge as Zacker Cracker.

Equipment Recommendations

Where possible I have tried to include a recommended gear list. This is a very rough guide to what a climber comfortable at the grade might need to protect a particular climb.

> Single rack to 3"

This would be a full set of wires, and a full set of cams from #00 TCU to #3 Camalot. It would also include a number of biners and slings and/or quickdraws appropriate for the particular type of climb.

Cam Size	Metolius	BD Camalots	Wild Country Friends	CCH Aliens	Trango Big Bro
0.4"	00	0.1		Black	
0.5"	0	0.2	00	Blue	
0.6"	1	0.3	0	Green	
0.75"	2	0.4	0.5	Yellow	
1"	3	0.5	1	Grey	
1.25"	4	0.75	1.5	Red	
1.5"	5	1	2	Orange	
1.75"	6	2	2.5	Violet	
2"	7	2	3	White	
2.5"	8	3	3.5		
3"	9	3 to 4	4		
3.5"	10	4	4 to 5		1
4"-5"		5	5		2
5"-7"		6	6		2 to 3
8"-12"					4
11"-18"					5

Pitch Numbers

On many of the multi-pitch routes (e.g. on the Black Velvet Wall), adjacent climbs will often share the first several pitches. Where this is the case, the pitch numbers of a route that break off from the main line reflect the number of pitches required to reach that point. For example, Ancient Futures starts at the third belay of Epinephrine; so the first pitch number is 4.

Maps, Topos and Photodiagrams

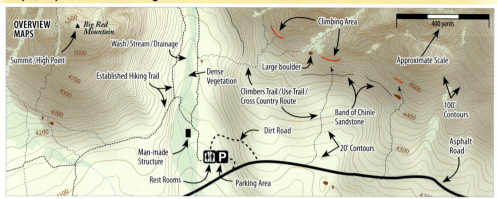

OVERVIEW MAPS

5300

▲ Big Red Mountain

5000

Summit/High Point

4700

Wash/Stream/Drainage

Established Hiking Trail

4500

↓ Dense Vegetation

4300

4200

Man-made Structure

Rest Rooms

Parking Area

Climbing Area

Large boulder

Approximate Scale

400 yards

Climbers Trail/Use Trail/ Cross Country Route

4600

Band of Chinle Sandstone

4400

100' Contours

Dirt Road

20' Contours

4300

Asphalt Road

4200

5100

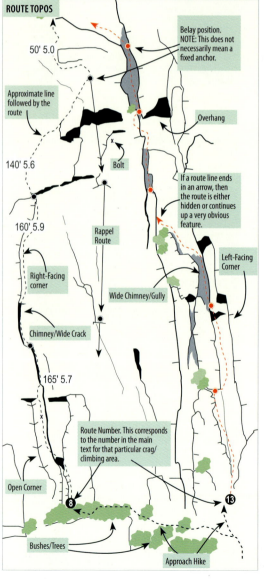

ROUTE TOPOS

50' 5.0

Belay position. NOTE: This does not necessarily mean a fixed anchor.

Approximate line followed by the route

Overhang

140' 5.6

X

Bolt

If a route line ends in an arrow, then the route is either hidden or continues up a very obvious feature.

160' 5.9

Rappel Route

Left-Facing Corner

Right-Facing corner

Wide Chimney/Gully

Chimney/Wide Crack

165' 5.7

Route Number. This corresponds to the number in the main text for that particular crag/ climbing area.

Open Corner

8   13

Bushes/Trees

Approach Hike

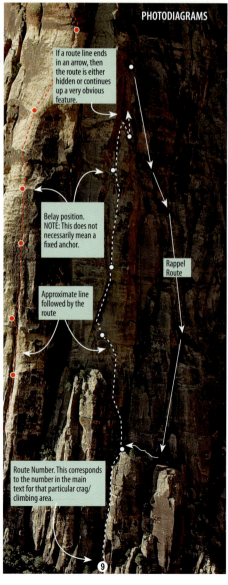

PHOTODIAGRAMS

If a route line ends in an arrow, then the route is either hidden or continues up a very obvious feature.

Belay position. NOTE: This does not necessarily mean a fixed anchor.

Rappel Route

Approximate line followed by the route

Route Number. This corresponds to the number in the main text for that particular crag/ climbing area.

9

Overview & Access Map

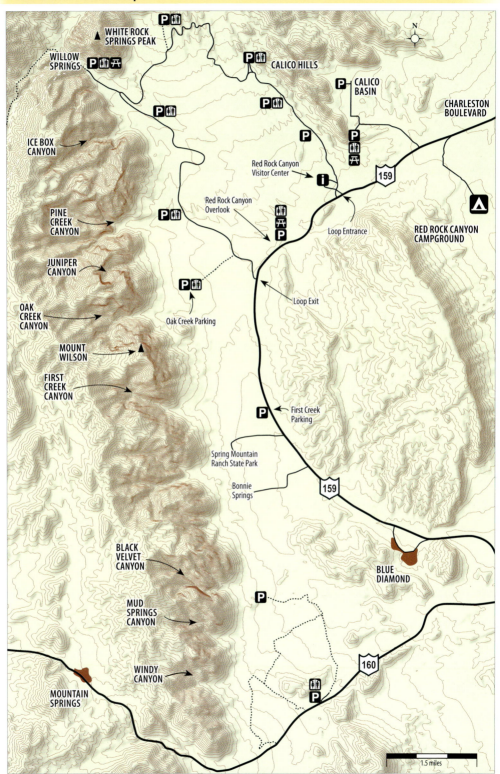

White Rock Springs Peak

Willow Springs

Calico Hills

Calico Basin

Charleston Boulevard

Ice Box Canyon

Red Rock Canyon Visitor Center

Pine Creek Canyon

Red Rock Canyon Overlook

Loop Entrance

Juniper Canyon

Oak Creek Canyon

Oak Creek Parking

Loop Exit

Mount Wilson

First Creek Canyon

Red Rock Canyon Campground

First Creek Parking

Spring Mountain Ranch State Park

Bonnie Springs

Black Velvet Canyon

Blue Diamond

Mud Springs Canyon

Windy Canyon

Mountain Springs

1.5 miles

Chocolate Rocks

Disappearing Buttress

Illusion Crags

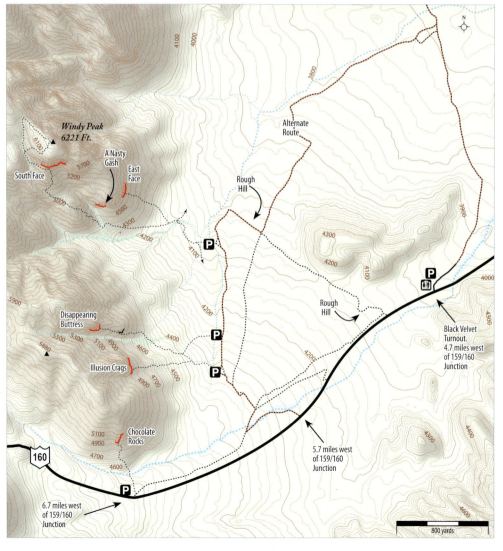

Windy Peak
6221 Ft.

A Nasty Gash

East Face

South Face

Alternate Route

Rough Hill

Rough Hill

Black Velvet Turnout.
4.7 miles west
of 159/160
Junction

Disappearing Buttress

Illusion Crags

Chocolate Rocks

160

5.7 miles west
of 159/160
Junction

6.7 miles west
of 159/160
Junction

800 yards

WINDY PEAK

Windy Peak,
South Face

Windy Peak,
East Face

A Nasty Gash

This chapter covers Chocolate Rocks, Illusion Crags and Disappearing Buttress, three isolated outcrops at the southern end of the range, and also Windy Canyon, the most southerly of the major canyons. These crags are seldom visited nowadays and have quite a quiet and secluded atmosphere. Interestingly, this area was one of the first to be explored in Red Rocks. In fact, Jubilant Song on the south face of Windy Peak was one of Red Rocks pioneer Joe Herbst's first major routes in the area.

The access roads are fairly rough and can get washed out after heavy rains. However, there are several possible alternate routes into the area and at least one is usually passable. The BLM would prefer if climbers visiting the area stuck to the designated access routes, as described in this book.

The big traverse on pitch 4 of Jubilant Song. Page 25.

Chocolate Rocks

This small, sunny outcrop is located at the extreme southern end of Red Rocks, on the rocky hillside overlooking Route 160 to Pahrump. It faces southeast and gets sun until late afternoon. Although it sees very little traffic, this crag has a decent collection of moderate traditional routes on nice, varnished rock. A good option for a cold day.

Access: The parking area for Chocolate Rocks is located about 6.7 miles west of the 159/160 junction. Look for a paved entrance on the right as you drive west, immediately before the beginning of a crash barrier. Park on the side of the entrance, which is blocked by a locked gate.

Approach: From the parking area, go though the gate and follow a dirt track on the left which leads down into the wash. On the opposite side of the wash is a small conglomerate cliff band split by a wide open gully. A faint trail, marked by cairns, starts at the base of the gully. Follow the trail up and left across the hillside onto a red dirt ridge. At the top of the ridge is a small cliff band. Go left under this for 40 yards, then over a short step and into an easy gully. Go up the gully to reach the bottom of a band of dark rock which slants up the steep, broken hillside. 0.4 miles, 450' elevation gain, 15 to 20 minutes.

The routes are described from left to right.

The first four routes are at the left end of the cliff, on a square buttress with an obvious varnished wall on its right side, and a pine tree on top. To descend from these routes, use either the tree above Minute Maid or the anchor of Shortcake.

❶ Combination Corner 50' 5.8
Mark Moore, Joe Herbst. March 1973.
Single rack to 3".
On the front face of the square buttress is a steep crack. This route climbs the right-facing corner just to the left of the crack. Climb the corner to a small roof. Move left and climb steeply past the roof to an easier crack which leads to a large platform.

❷ Spinach 50' 5.10c
Joe Herbst. January 1972.
Double 2"- 3" cams.
The steep crack in the front of the buttress has a couple of wide sections, but the hard climbing consists of steep, athletic hand jamming.

❸ Shortcake 40' 5.9
Joe Herbst. November 1972.
Single rack to 1.25".
Start around to the right of the previous two routes, below the varnished face on the right side of the buttress. Climb straight up the face to an anchor.

❹ Minute Maid 70' 5.6
Joe Herbst. November 1972.
Single rack to 2". Large cams optional.
Climb the wide crack to the right of Shortcake to the edge of a large platform. Move right and climb up to a large pine tree with rap rings.

❺ The Gallows 30' 5.10b
John Long, Joe Herbst. March 1973.
Single rack to 1.25".
Scramble up onto the top of the block beside Minute Maid. On the right side of the recess above is a thin corner. Climb

this corner to a big roof. Move right, around the roof, and finish with a short easy wall.

About 50 yards to the right of the previous routes, the cliff turns slightly to the east and forms the side wall of a steep, blocky gully. The next two routes are on the steep buttress at the base of the gully, where the cliff changes direction.

❻ Zacker Cracker 80' 5.9

Joe Herbst. November 1972.
Double 6"- 8" cams.
In the left side of the buttress is an impressive varnished offwidth in the back of a big left-facing corner. Climb the offwidth past a big roof, which goes much more easily than anticipated. The route finishes on a blocky ledge with a thread anchor.

❼ Potso's Pudding 90' 5.6 *

Betsy Herbst, Joe Herbst. February 1972.
Single rack to 2.5", double 0.75"-1.25" cams.
This route climbs the steep right-facing corner in the front of the buttress. Quite an impressive line for the grade. It finishes on the same ledge as Zacker Cracker.

The following three routes are on the left wall of the blocky gully. To descend scramble down behind the cliff to the rappel tree of Minute Maid. The first route climbs a big left-facing corner above a flat spot 30 yards up the gully.

❽ McCracken 60' 5.7

Matt McMackin, Nanouk Borche, Richard Harrison, John Long. March 1973.
Climb the corner to a roof. Move left around the roof and continue up the crack to the ledge where Zacher Cracker finishes. Either stop here, or continue up the chimney on the right to the top.

❾ P,B & J 80' 5.9+ *

Joe Herbst, David Hop. January 1973.
Single rack to 8".
This route starts at another flat spot 30' higher up the gully from the previous route. Climb blocky cracks to a roof. Awkward jamming leads over the roof to a rest, then continue up the offwidth to the top.

❿ The Little Engine 60' 5.7

H. Booth, D. Hop, Joe Herbst. January 1973.
Single rack to 6".
Climb the chimney to the right of the previous route, threading a white chockstone at the top.

Matt Kuehl on PB&J. Page 15.

Illusion Crags

These outcrops consist of a series of broken buttresses of decent, varnished rock on the east flank of the formation to the south of Windy Canyon. Most of the routes face northeast and lose the sun by mid-morning, making this a good location for warm weather cragging on traditional routes. However, on the left side of the cliff, the buttress containing Arm Forces faces southeast and holds the sun for an extra hour or two.

Access: The approach as described is usually suitable for regular passenger vehicles, although the wash occasionally gets washed out after a lot of rain, the alternative routes (marked on the access map) could be better under these conditions. Drive 5.7 miles west from the 159/160 junction, and turn right onto a road. This is about 1 mile west of the more obvious road to Black Velvet Canyon. The dirt road heads west at first, up a broad wash, then after 0.34 miles it loops back in a northeasterly direction. At 0.47 miles from Route 160 there is a four way junction. Take the road on the left and follow it to a rough spot where it splits and rejoins beyond a gully, take the option on the left. Continue to a small loop on the left which is 0.8 miles from where you leave Route 160. Park here. There is an access map to the area on page 12.

Approach: From the parking spot, head down into the wash. Look for a boulder with a cairn on the bank of red soil on the far side of the wash. The cairn marks the start of a trail that winds up through a series of shallow gullies and across ridges, eventually zig-zagging up the broad ridge that passes to the left of the red cliff band below the wall. The trail is a little hard to follow in places but is marked with cairns the entire way. 0.6 miles, 600' elevation gain, 20 to 25 minutes.

Nice wall climbing on Spell Me. Page 19. Photo: Matt Kuehl.

Illusion Crags - Left side

The routes are described from left to right. The first routes face southeast, across the shallow drainage to the left of the cliff. A short distance above the drainage, is a buttress split by two big right-facing corners. There is a sturdy pine tree about 20 feet up, below the left-most corner. To descend from the top of the buttress, do a short rap, then scramble down the gully to the right of the buttress.

❶ French Bulges 70' 5.7
Nanouk Borche, Joe Herbst. February 1973.
Single rack to 3".
Climb the right-facing corner above the pine tree to a bushy ledge. Belay here then scramble off left and down a gully.

❷ Arm Forces 120' 5.9 *
Joe Herbst, Nanouk Borche. February 1973.
Single rack to 4", double 2"- 3".
A nice climb up the big corner on the right. The corner is initially quite low-angled with a very thin crack. After a small roof continue to a rest below a short slot. Climb the slot to a big roof which is passed by a few burly pulls. The final roof is avoided on the left by easy face climbing to reach a bolt anchor at the top.

❸ Mirage 140' 5.7
Betsy Herbst, Joe Herbst, Joanne Urioste. Fall 1976.
Single rack to 4".
An impressive looking line for the grade. This route climbs the wide crack splitting the wall to the right of Arm Forces. Start 15' to the right of Arm Forces below a white crack system. Climb the crack, past a slot/roof, to the top.

❹ Corner's Inquest 140' 5.7
John Wilder, Larry DeAngelo. January 2006.
Single rack to 1.5".
This route climbs the blunt arete to the right of Mirage, joining that route for the last few moves to the belay ledge.

Where the southeast and northeast faces meet there is a large blocky buttress. This feature is called the Chameleon Pinnacle. The next two routes start below an obvious overhang at the base of the south face of the pinnacle.

❺ Morph Out 75' 5.7
Donette Swain, Todd Swain. April 1994.
This route climbs the loose left-facing corner that passes the right side of the overhang. Continue to a ledge with a thread anchor.

❻ Chameleon Pinnacle 75' 5.4
Bill Lowman, Betsy Herbst, Joe Herbst, Matt McMackin, Nanouk Borche, Howard Booth. February 1973.
From the base of Morph Out, move out right onto an easy slab which is climbed to the ledge and communal thread anchor. It is possible to continue, wandering around blocks and slabs to the top of the pinnacle. Descend down the gully to the west.

❼ Changeling 75' 5.6
Donette Swain, Todd Swain. April 1994.
Start below the right arete of the formation, about 30' to the right of Morph Out. Climb the blocky arete to the ledge and communal anchor.

Illusion Crags - Right side

The following routes are on the east-facing wall well to the right of Chameleon Pinnacle. They start in the vicinity of a large pine tree below the obvious, curving offwidth of Who Deany. This is about 70 yards to the right of the arete of Changeling. There is a flat, open area with an old fire ring beside the tree.

❽ Smoke and Mirrors 90' 5.9 R
Todd Swain. November 1993.
Start just left of the tree, around the left side of an arete. Climb a shallow corner system and the easier bulges above to reach a ledge and communal anchor.

❾ David Copperhead 90' 5.8+
Todd Swain, Bobby Knight. November 1993.
Start 15' right of the tree, below an obvious wide crack. Climb the crack for 15', then follow a horizontal left for 15' to a little niche in the arete. Climb a short crack and continue up the arete, over a small bulge, to the ledge and communal anchor.
Variation: 5.10b Climb direct to the end of the traverse.

❿ Who Deany 90' 5.8
Cams to 8".
This route climbs straight up the curving wide crack at the start of the previous route to reach the ledge and communal anchor.

⓫ First Lady of Magic 110' 5.9 *
Todd Swain, Donette Swain. November 1993.
Single rack to 2".
This route climbs up the long, varnished wall to the right of the previous routes. Start 5' right of Who Deany. Climb a curving left-facing corner for 15', then step right over the corner onto

the face. Continue up the face (b) then up and a little right to a small ledge. Continue up to a crack which leads to an anchor on a ledge.

⓬ Deez Guys 140' 5.8+
Todd Swain, Bobby Knight. November 1993.
Single rack to 2.5", double 0.4"- 0.75", extra wires.
This route climbs the face to the right of the previous route to reach the long thin crack which splits the upper wall. Start 40' to the right of the pine tree, just to the left of a loose and blocky crack system. Climb the varnished face to a small right-facing corner at 40'. Climb the face above to reach the base of a long, thin crack which is climbed to a large ledge.

⓭ Con Jurors 110' 5.7
Raleigh Collins, Brandt Allen. October 1994.
Double rack to 3".
Start 90' to the right of Deez Guys and 40' to the left of a pine tree which is just left of a big, ugly chimney. Scramble up to a ledge at 20', then move left and follow a crack to a slung chockstone. Move right and follow a right-leaning crack to a ledge with an anchor. A single rope rappel reaches the ledge, and an easy down-climb reaches the ground.

⓮ Sore Sirs 110' 5.8
Bobby Knight, Todd Swain. November 1993.
Single rack to 3", double 0.4"- 1", extra wires.
Follow the previous route to the ledge at 20'. Climb straight up the varnished face to the anchor of Con Jurors.

About 120 feet to the right of Sore Sirs is a prominent varnished buttress which is slightly to the right of the center of the cliff. The next two routes climb cracks to the left of this buttress, starting from a high, bushy ledge tucked into the corner on the left side of the buttress.

⑮ Lady in Question 160' 5.11b *
Joe Herbst. Fall 1978.
Double rack to 3".
The top pitch is a good splitter crack. Start below a curving right-facing corner, to the left of the main corner.
1. 100' 5.8 Climb the curving corner, past a couple of bulges, to reach a ledge. Move left along the ledge dropping down to a bushy ledge below a steep corner crack.
2. 60' 5.11b Climb the crack to a bush anchor on a ledge.

⑯ Hanging Tough 150' 5.8
Joe Herbst, Betsy Herbst. Aug. 1973.
Follow the previous route to the ledge. Move right and climb the big left-facing corner to the top.

The next routes start from the same bushy ledge as the previous routes and climb the nice, varnished wall on the southeast side of the prominent buttress.

⑰ Spell Me 80' 5.11b *
Bobby Knight, Todd Swain. November 1993.
Single rack to 1.25", double tiny cams, Rp's, one 2" cam.
A nice, sustained wall climb with a serious start. Begin at the left edge of the south facing wall of the buttress. Climb an easy, left-leaning crack to a small ledge then step right and climb the wall with tricky, thin protection to reach the first bolt. Pass the first bolt on the left then continue up and right (2 b's) to reach a left-leaning crack at the top (2" cam). Continue easily to a thread anchor on top of the buttress.

⑱ Illusions of Grandstaff 80' 5.11b (Tr.)
Todd Swain, Bobby Knight. November 1993.
From the block anchor of Spell Me, toprope straight up the wall to its right.

⑲ Petite Deceit 80' 5.8
Bobby Knight, Todd Swain. November 1993.
Start just right of Spell Me. Climb the short, left-facing corner to a stance. Step right and continue up the face just left of the arete. Finish straight up the varnished wall above a left-leaning crack to reach the huge ledge. Rappel from the communal block anchor on top of the buttress.

The next routes start down and right of the previous routes, below the northeast face of the buttress.

⑳ Shell Game 140' 5.9
Todd Swain, Donette Swain, Bobby Knight. April 1994.
Single rack to 4".
Start beside a big pine tree which sits below a large, smooth roof at the base of the northeast face. Climb a varnished pillar which leads up to a ledge below the left edge of the roof. Move right and pull the roof as for Sweet Little Whore, then move back left towards the arete. Continue up the arete (3 b's) to a shallow corner. Climb the corner to a belay in an alcove. Traverse right and rappel from the anchor of False Perception.

㉑ Sweet Little Whore 130' 5.9
Joe Herbst, Tom Kaufman. 1973.
Start 5' to the right of the pine tree. Climb the blocky, wide crack up to the left edge of the roof. Follow the crack over the roof and continue to a belay in an alcove at 120'. Traverse right and rappel from the anchor of False Perception.

There is no record of an ascent of the crack that goes through the right edge of the roof. The next two routes are on the tall varnished face to the right.

㉒ Skinny Mini 120' 5.9 **
Joe Herbst. March 1973.
Double rack to 4".
Start below a thin crack in the left edge of the varnished face. Climb the finger crack which jogs left then widens. At the top move right to the anchor of False Perception.

㉓ False Perception 120' 5.11a **
Todd Swain, Donette Swain. November 1993.
Single rack to 1.75".
Start just right of Skinny Mini. Climb the varnished face (5 b's) to a bulge. Pull over the bulge and continue to a beautiful thin crack which leads to an anchor.

The next two routes are on a short but nicely-varnished buttress at the right end of the cliff, about 100 yards down and to the right of the previous routes, and just to the left of the low point of the cliff band.

Sensual 60' 5.7
John Long, Joe Herbst, Richard Harrison. 1973.
Single rack to 3", double 1"- 2".
Start about 30' to the left of the low point of the rocks, at the base of a tight, right-facing corner. Finger and hand jamming leads up the nice crack in the corner to a ledge.

Sensible 50' 5.7
Stephanie Petrilak, Betsy Herbst, Joe Herbst. 1973.
The crack to the right of Sensual.

Disappearing Buttress

Just north of Illusion Crags, a small canyon cuts into the escarpment. On the north side of this drainage, about half way up, is a five-hundred-foot buttress which is called Disappearing Buttress. The routes on this buttress were first documented in the late 2000's, but it seems very likely that there had been some prior exploration, especially since quite a few signs of passage (old slings etc.) were found on the recorded first ascents.

The buttress is slightly broken and vegetated, but there is some good rock and several nice, moderate lines. Most of the routes face due south and since the opposite side of the canyon has rather low sidewalls, the cliff holds the sun until late in the afternoon. The walls are also quite sheltered from the prevailing westerly winds, making this a reasonable out of the way venue for climbing some multi-pitch moderates on a cold winters day.

Access: Drive in as for Illusion Crags. The approach as described is usually suitable for regular passenger vehicles, although the wash occasionally gets washed out after a lot of rain, the alternative routes (marked on the access map) could be better under these conditions. Drive 5.7 miles west from the 159/160 junction, and turn right onto a road. This is about 1 mile west of the more obvious road to Black Velvet Canyon. The dirt road heads west at first, up a broad wash, then after 0.34 miles it loops back in a northeasterly direction. At 0.47 miles from Route 160 there is a four way junction. Take the road on the left and follow it to a rough spot where it splits and rejoins beyond a gully, take the option on the left. Continue to a small loop on the left which is 0.8 miles from where you leave Route 160. This is the Illusion Crags parking area. Continue to a small turnout 300 yards further north, 1 mile total from route 160. There is an access map to the area on page 12.

Approach: Head across the desert toward the mouth of the canyon. The route goes generally up and over the small ridgelets keeping to the south of the main wash. As you approach the mouth of the canyon there is a vague trail which is marked by a line of cairns. This trail leads through the broad wash to its north bank where the trail becomes more distinct. Continue up the north side of the canyon, passing below a small, varnished outcrop where the canyon narrows. The trail then continues up the more open slopes, through blocky talus to the base of the buttress.
0.85 miles, 800' elevation gain, 35 to 45 minutes.

Descent: From the shoulder at the top of the buttress a long, spacious ledge system angles west beneath another tier of cliffs. Walk and scramble along this, crossing a couple of very minor ridges, to a wide, slabby gully. Go down the gully to the slopes below. From this point it is probably easiest to pass right (south) of the small outcrop, then contour east toward the toe of the buttress.

The routes are described from left to right.

The approach trail reaches the cliff at the low point of the rocks. There is a small, square-cut buttress here with a clean corner in its front face.

No Country for Young Men 400' 5.8
Maurice Horn, Andrew Carson. Feb. 11, 2009.
Single rack to 3".
This route starts about 80 yards up and left of the toe of the buttress. At this point there is a 60' high pinnacle in front of the main face, separated from the main wall by a short gully. Start on some blocks in a little alcove at the top of the gully. On the wall above are two left-slanting cracks.
1. 180' 5.8 Step into the right most crack and follow it to a small bush at 60'. The continuation crack shoots up a steep varnished wall and has some distinctive white patches on its left side. Climb this crack, pulling past a loose block to reach a comfortable belay ledge.
2. 190' 5.6 Move to the left end of the ledge and climb a crack, clipping a ring piton. Continue up enjoyable rock with several short headwalls to a belay just below the top.
3. 30' 5.5 Climb a short pitch to easy ground and the top.

❶ Ms. Management 600' 5.8
Sendi Kalcic, Larry DeAngelo. March 2010.
Single rack to 3".
This route climbs a crack system to the left of Prime Rib, it has some nice climbing in places but also patches of fragile and blocky rock.
Start just left of the toe of the buttress.
1. 120' 5.5 Climb up a short wall to get onto a bushy ledge system just to the left of the square-cut buttress at the toe of the cliff. From the upper left corner of the ledge, climb a steep corner and turn a large chockstone on its left, belay on the large ledge above.
2. 120' 5.8 Above the left end of the ledge is a big right-facing corner guarded by a bulge at its base. Climb through the bulge into the corner and continue up the corner to a good ledge.
3&4 360' 5.7 Continue up the crack system for a few hundred feet. It deepens into a gully which becomes blocked by a short, narrow chimney. Climb the chimney. At the top of the chimney, move left onto the face and continue (unprotected) to the top.

❷ Prime Rib 500' 5.7 *
Maurice Horn, Andrew Carson, Bill Hotz, Jorge Urioste. Jan. 10, 2009.
Single rack to 3".
This is probably destined to be the most popular route on the buttress. An airy, enjoyable climb up the broad rib directly above the low point of the cliff.
1. 70' 5.4 Start by scrambling up into the gully to the right of the small square-cut buttress at the low point of the rocks. Go up the gully to a large ledge.
2. 130' 5.7 Climb to the left of a small pine tree, following a line of cracks close to the crest of the buttress. Pass to the left of a small, square-cut roof and belay at a good stance a short distance higher.
3. 120' 5.7 Continue slightly right of the ridge crest, following a curving crack, then trend left and back to the crest. Follow the crest more or less directly upwards. Belay at a small stance beside an old pin.
4. 130' 5.7 Climb on the crest, or slightly right of it, to a final headwall. Climb this from the right to a comfortable ledge.
5. 50' 5.5 A short pitch leads up and right to the top.

There are several clean corner systems on the east face of the buttress. The most prominent is a very large smooth-walled corner about 100' up and right from the toe of the buttress, which is climbed by the route Adam's Rib. The next route climbs the long, right-arching crack in the left wall of this corner. To reach the next four routes, scramble up and right on easy ledges to the base of the big corner.

❸ Pricks and Ticks 495' 5.9

Dyan Padagas, Kevin Hogan, Jason Martin. March 2010.
Double cams to 3.5".
Start from the ledges below the long, curving crack in the left wall of the corner.
1. 160' 5.9 Climb the arching crack to a ledge. Most of

the crack is 5.7, but as it squeezes down and traverses, it becomes 5.9. Belay at a double-bolt anchor.
2. 100' 5.7 Climb onto the bushy ledge above. Above the left side of the ledge is a varnished rib. Climb the rib on nice varnish at first, then as the rock quality deteriorates, step left onto a ledge and belay.
3. 75' 5.5 Climb up a chimney up and right. Continue to a traverse right to a belay ledge at the base of a large corner.
4. 160' 5.7 A nice, exposed pitch on good rock. Climb the corner to the summit.

The tricky crux of Adam's Rib.
Page 23. Photo: Matt Kuehl.

Disappearing Buttress

❹ Adam's Rib 140' 5.11b
Single rack to 4".
Start at the base of the big, smooth corner. Climb the corner, initially on poor rock, to a bulge. Undercling left (b) then turn the corner and make some thin face moves up to and over a small roof (b, crux). Continue up the widening finger crack in the back of the main corner, then layback up the flake on the left to an anchor.

❺ Vanishing Act 480' 5.9– *
Maurice Horn, Joanne Urioste, Bill Hotz, Andrew Carson. Jan. 17, 2009.
Single rack to 4".
Above and right of the large, smooth-walled corner of Adam's Rib is a pair of attractive, slender corners starting from a ledge 100' up. This route climbs the left of the two corners. From the toe of the buttress scramble up and right for 100' to the highest ledges below the large, smooth-walled corner.
1. 100' 5.4 Traverse out right to an easy crack system which is followed to a ledge below the twin corners.
2. 190' 5.9– A varied, beautiful pitch. Climb a corner just left of the main leftmost dihedral for about 40', then step right into the dihedral as it widens into a chimney. Layback/chimney up the corner to a roof blocking progress and undercling/stem left to pass the roof. Continue up easier ground, going right to a belay at a big pine with a nice ledge on the crest of the buttress.
3. 190' 5.8 Climb the steep white face above the ledge, then continue up the varnished face. Above this black face, follow a finger crack in the white slab to a steepening headwall. Surmount a bulge at the base of the headwall and follow cracks leading to the left edge of the buttress and the top. The route finishes at the same point as Prime Rib.

❻ Into Thin Air 190' 5.10b
Joanne Urioste, Dave Sorric. February 2009.
Single rack to 2", Rp's, double to 1.75".
This route climbs the long, snaking corner to the right of pitch 2 of Vanishing Act; the rock is fragile. Stem up the start, then 12' up, move onto the left arete and make a few crux moves before stepping back into the main corner. Continue up the corner to the pine tree belay above pitch 2 of Vanishing Act.

The next route starts up an obvious clean-cut chimney about 200' up and right of the toe of the buttress. From the toe of the buttress, scramble around to the right, going around a rock band below the main wall. Once above the rock band scramble back left through ledges and bushes to the base of the obvious chimney.

❼ Missing Nothing 560' 5.8+
Matt Clarke, John Wilder. 2010.
Single rack to 5".
Overall not a very good route, but with a few nice sections.
1. 50' 5.8 Climb the chimney to a ledge.
2. 80' 5.8 Climb straight up the crack, crossing two short face sections until you reach another crack. Climb this to a nice ledge.
3. 100' 5.6 Head up and right, aiming for the very nice looking seam on an orange headwall. Pass it on the right, going up a ramp to a dead tree on a nice ledge.
4. 130' 5.8+ This pitch is quite poorly protected. Climb up and left onto another ledge, then ascend the face in front of you to another sloping ledge. From here, head up the seam in the middle of the face, continuing straight up when it runs out. Follow the face to a crack, then follow the crack up through a steep section to a nice ledge.
5. 200' 5.2 Fight through the scrub oak to a ledge above, then head up and right to the top.

On the far right side of the buttress is a clean slab of black and white rock. Below the left side of the slab is a steep, clean left-facing corner of black-streaked orange rock. The next route starts 40' right of this feature. From the toe of the buttress scramble around to the right, going around a broken rock band below the main wall. Once above the rock band continue up the broad gully then scramble up and left to ledges below the base of the slab.

❽ Sunday Cruise 500' 5.6
Matt Clarke, Alex Henson. March 2010.
Single rack to 3".
About 40' to the right of the orange corner is a shallow left-facing corner with a finger crack just to its right.
1. 180' 5.6 Start up the featured finger crack and continue up and left to a belay at a large tree.
2. 200' 5.6 Traverse out right from the anchor and continue on on good holds to the base of a corner. Climb this corner to the base of an obvious corner higher up. Start up the corner, then swing out left on good holds and up to an another tree anchor. Watch for rope drag on this pitch.
3. 120' 5.3 Easier climbing leads to the top of the buttress.

The next route is passed on the descent from the top of the buttress and makes for a good way to finish the day. From the top of the buttress, walk along the right (north) side of the ridge for 100 yards to an obvious face split by a crack.

Maraschino Crack 200' 5.9
George Wilson, Larry DeAngelo. March 2010.
Single rack to 5", double 3"- 5".
Start below and right of the main crack, then climb it to the top.
Descent: Scramble west and down from a big pine tree to rappel slings on a smaller tree overlooking a gully. Do a single rope rappel and scramble back to the base of the route.

The next route can be reached from the descent route. Instead of dropping down the wide, slabby gully, continue west on the ledge system, contouring north around the base of the buttress and up the hillside. At the top of the hillside is a gully and high on its right side is a beautiful, clean-cut corner/crack. Some 4th class is required to get to the spacious belay ledge at the base of the corner. It is also possible to reach this climb by hiking up the main drainage system from the toe of the buttress, at the top of the drainage the corner is obvious, up and to the right.

Haul for Nothing 35' 5.10d *
Matt Clarke, John Wilder. Feb 2010.
Single rack to 1.75", triple 0.75"- 1", double 1.25".
A short but superb corner/crack. Climb the corner to a ledge, save a large nut and the 1.75" cam for the anchor. Descend climbers left from the ledge.

WINDY CANYON

WINDY PEAK

Descent

South Face

Joanne of Arch

A Nasty Gash

East Face

This is a pretty canyon which has quite a remote feel, despite the fact that it's fairly easy to access. Perhaps the maze of dirt roads on the approach adds to the feeling of seclusion. It certainly seems to help keep the crowds down. It is not at all unusual to have the canyon to yourself; a rare treat in Red Rocks nowadays.

Access: The approach as described is usually suitable for regular passenger vehicles, although the wash occasionally gets washed out after a lot of rain, the alternative routes (marked on the access map) could be better under these conditions. Drive

5.7 miles west from the 159/160 junction, and turn right onto a dirt road. This is about 1 mile west of the more obvious road to Black Velvet Canyon. The dirt road heads west at first, up a broad wash, then after 0.34 miles it loops back in a northeasterly direction. At 0.47 miles from Route 160 there is a four way junction. Take the road on the left and follow it to a rough spot where it splits and rejoins beyond a gully, take the option on the left. Continue to a small loop on the left at 0.8 miles. This is the parking area for Illusion Crags. Continue along the road to another loop on the left at 1.5 miles from Route 160. Park here. There is an access map to the area on page 12.

Windy Peak - South Face

As you are driving along Route 160 to Pahrump, this 1000' high wall dominates the view of the southern end of the Red Rocks range. It is a very sunny wall with a relatively straight-forward approach and a fast descent, making it an ideal choice for doing a long route during the winter months. The wall faces straight south and gets sun until late afternoon. It is high and exposed and will catch any wind that is blowing.

Approach: From the parking spot go down into the wash and pick up a trail on the other side. It leads west across the desert towards an unusual mound of dark red, conglomerate boulders. Take a left when the trail splits near the crest of the boulder mound. The trail then heads down into the main wash and crosses to the north side. From here, the trails lead up the canyon. Continue to a very obvious, bushy gully which runs all the way down from the cliffs below the main south face. Don't try and go up this gully. Instead, cross to its west side where the trail leads up the long, steep hillside, passing through a small notch to a pretty meadow. Cross to the back of the meadow then scramble up and left, then back up and right to

a ridge below the main face. Depending on which climb you're heading for, climb up one of several easy breaks in the slab above to reach a ramp directly under the face. 1.4 miles, 1500' of elevation gain, 1-1.5 hours.

Descent: There are two ways to descend from the summit. Option 2 is faster, but involves some rock walking which could be tricky if there is much snow and/or ice around, a distinct possibility during the coldest months.

Option 1: From the summit, head northwest along the ridge to the limestone. From a small col, a gully filled with trees and bushes heads back to the south. Follow the gully, which descends very gently at first, then more steeply. Go down the gully to a point where there are some large boulders. From here, if you look off to the left (east), you can see a prominent cairn on a small col on the skyline. Leave the gully and scramble over to the cairn on the col. The base of Jubilant Song is a short distance down the easy rock ridge on the other side of the col. 30 minutes, 0.7 miles.

Option 2: From the summit head 60 yards southwest to a big pine tree. Below the pine tree is a shallow rock gully. Go down the gully for about 70 yards until above a drop off into a little bushy slot. Go right then back left to a boulder with a cairn. This is at the top of a slabby rock ledge which leads down to the northwest onto a bushy talus slope. Go down the talus slope to join Option 1 in the gully about 90 yards above the large boulders. 20 minutes, 0.5 miles.

❶ Marion's Melody 700' 5.9
George Urioste and others. 2005.
Single rack to 4".
Start immediately to the left of Jubilant Song.
1. 105' 5.7 Climb the face past a few bolts to an anchor.
2. 105' 5.7 Continue up the face to an anchor at good ledge at the base of a left-facing dihedral.
3. 110' 5.7 Climb the dihedral to an anchor at its top.
4. 30' 5.9 Step left, then climb a corner past some protection bolts to an anchor. (For many years this was the route's high-point, the result of a blizzard-induced epic retreat.)
5. 150' 5.7 Go up, then right, eventually following a small crack to a hanging belay beneath an overhanging headwall.
6 & 7 200' 5.9 Climb the short headwall (5.9), then follow easy climbing on the path of least resistance for a pitch or two to the top of the wall.

❷ Jubilant Song 770' 5.8 **
Joe Herbst, Terry Schultz. December 1972.
Single rack to 3.5", double 1.75"- 3".
A great route up a high, exposed wall, with a beautiful summit and a fast descent. This route is popular but, surprisingly, seldom crowded.
On the left side of the south face is a huge right-facing corner system. Two parallel cracks lead up into the main corner. Start below the crack on the left, which begins as a right-facing corner.
1. 80' 5.7 Climb the easy corner to a small roof. Pull over the roof (5.7) and continue to a ledge with a bush.
2. 150' 5.7 A sustained pitch on nice rock leads up the same crack system to a belay beside blocks.
3. 150' 5.5 Climb the easy chimney above, then move out right and climb up into the right-facing corner below the huge roof. Climb the corner to a belay on a small ledge with a good crack a short distance below the huge roof.
4. 60' 5.7 Climb up to the roof then traverse right. To keep the rope drag manageable, set up an awkward hanging belay in a small left-facing corner capped by a triangular roof, below the right edge of the huge roof.
5. 60' 5.8 Pull over the roof above the belay, move right and make a thin move up a small corner to reach lower-angled rock which leads right into a gully. Continue to a belay beside a bush. **Variation:** The hardest moves can be avoided by easier friction climbing on the right (5.5).
6. 100' 5.7 Go up the easy chimney above to a bush, then move right and pull up (b) into a rounded, water-washed groove, which is followed to a ledge on the left.
7. 100' 5.8 Move back into the water-washed groove and follow it to an exit left onto a ledge. Protection is decent but spaced on this section. Continue up the big corner to a ledge.
Variation: 5.4 From the belay ledge go up and left on the black face to avoid the water-washed groove.
8. 70' 5.5 Easier climbing leads to the top.

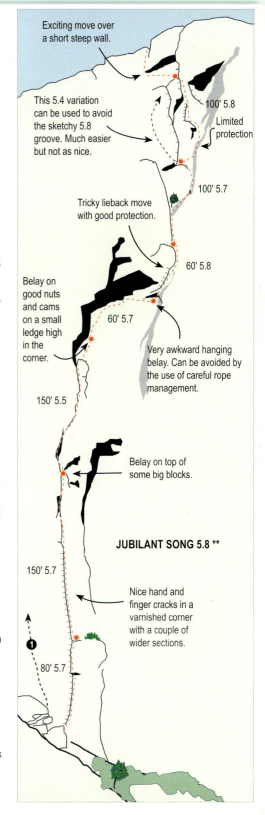

Exciting move over a short steep wall.

This 5.4 variation can be used to avoid the sketchy 5.8 groove. Much easier but not as nice.

100' 5.8
Limited protection

100' 5.7

Tricky lieback move with good protection.

60' 5.8

Belay on good nuts and cams on a small ledge high in the corner.

60' 5.7

Very awkward hanging belay. Can be avoided by the use of careful rope management.

150' 5.5

Belay on top of some big blocks.

**JUBILANT SONG 5.8 **

150' 5.7

Nice hand and finger cracks in a varnished corner with a couple of wider sections.

❶

80' 5.7

Windy Peak - South Face

❸ A Song & A Prayer 900' 5.10a R
Larry DeAngelo, John Wilder. February 2005.
Single rack to 4" plus a set of Ballnutz and double 0.33"- 0.5".

This route has some bold climbing and is wildly exposed in a few places. Start just to the right of Jubilant Song.

1. 80' 5.7 Climb up easy rock to the large, bushy belay ledge.

2. 180' 5.8 Continue straight up a thin crack splitting the narrow facet of rock about 15 feet to the right of the main Jubilant Song dihedral. Continue to the base of a chimney below some roofs. Move left and set up a belay on Jubilant Song. A #4 Camalot gives a good anchor in the crack.

4. 190' 5.10a A bold pitch up the steep pillar to the left of the big, arching corner of Jubilant Song. Move left onto the arête and continue up an easy crack to a sloping ledge. Move left to a thin, right-leaning seam, the left most of two. The seam is steep and thinly-protected at first (this is where the Ballnutz are used) but gets easier and better protected. Set up a hanging belay below a white corner.

5. 200' 5.9 Make a few moves up the soft white rock of the corner, then exit right as soon as possible to a crack in dark, varnished rock. This exposed position is directly above the huge Jubilant Song roof. Climb the crack then pull a small bulge and angle up left to the top of the varnished section. Continue up easy, blocky ground and belay in a small alcove.

6. 50' 5.6 Climb a varnished crack to a huge ledge.

7. 200' 4th Class Scramble up easy ground until you can make a 4th class switchback to the right and belay on the ledges above. 30 feet of third class allow you to exit right onto the summit plateau.

❹ Western Swing 370' 5.10b
John Wilder, Larry DeAngelo. 2005.
Single rack to 7".

A variation start to Jubilant Song which can be finished in a variety of ways. Start about 40 feet down and right from the start of Jubilant Song, below another right-facing corner.

1. 100' 5.8 Climb this corner to a ledge with a tree.

2. 140' 5.10b A good pitch. Continue up the corner to a bush at the base of a flared chimney. Climb the chimney until it squeezes down and arches to the right, then make a difficult swing move into the upper corner. Layback up the corner to a hanging belay a short distance above.

3. 130' 5.9 Traverse up and right across a poorly-protected face to below a slot in the overhangs, Follow the slot through the roofs, then climb up and left over easier rock to a belay at the beginning of the big roof on Jubilant Song.

❺ Crocodile Rock 400' 5.9
John Wilder, Ryan McPhee, Larry DeAngelo. 2006.
Single rack to 3". Extra small wires.

Start about 30 feet right of Western Swing.

1. 70' 5.7 Face climb up and right, passing to the right of a bush, to a small left-facing corner in an area of white rock.

2. 90' 5.9 Start by climbing up to a small roof, then move left and cross the roof (5.9) onto the varnished rock above. Easier rock leads to a belay stance.

3. 200' 5.7 Continue up the dramatically corrugated buttress (rough, like a crocodile's back!) for about 200 feet to a belay near Windy Corner.

Climb up about 40 feet and join Windy Corner where it moves right out of the main dihedral system. Continue to the top on either the upper pitches of Windy Corner or Hot Fudge Thursday which is just a few feet to the right.

❻ Windy Corner 850' 5.7
Jorge Urioste, Joanne Urioste. January 1977.
Single rack to 5".

This route climbs a left-slanting, left-facing corner system up the front of a buttress to the right of Jubilant Song. It joins Jubilant Song just above the giant roof.

Start in the bushes about 60' to the right of Western Swing below a thin crack in a black slab.

1. 120' 5.5 Climb the thin crack to a blocky ledge. Move up the ledge to the right and belay close to the main corner.

2. 160' 5.6 Climb the chimney in the back of the main corner and continue up the face to the left to belay on top of a pillar.

3. 100' 5.5 Climb the black corner above to a ledge on the left.

4. 120' 5.4 Go up the black face to a large ledge.

5. 130' 5.7 Go up a corner, until 30' below an overhang with a water trough. Step right onto the face, then continue to join Jubilant Song, belaying at the bush at the end of pitch 5. The route finishes up Jubilant Song.

6. 100' 5.7 Go up the chimney above to an oak tree, then move right into a rounded, water-washed groove, which is followed to a ledge on the left.

7. 100' 5.8 Move back into the water-washed groove and follow it up a smooth face to an exit left onto a ledge. **Variation:** From the ledge go up and left on the black face to avoid the water-washed groove (5.5).

8. 70' 5.5 Easy climbing leads to the top.

❼ Hot Fudge Thursday 930' 5.9 *
Jorge Urioste, Joanne Urioste. January 1977.
Single rack to 3", extra small wires.

An airy and enjoyable route. Start at the right end of the bushy ledge below the black slab at the base of the cliff, about 40' to the right of Windy corner, and just to the left of a large pine tree at the base of a long, right-leaning ramp.

1. 165' 5.8 Start up a thin crack system, passing just to the left of a little arch at 40', then traverse right and go up and right, following a long, thin crack to an anchor

2. 170' 5.9 Continue up the slabby wall (5 b's) to an anchor on a nice ledge at the base of a big, slabby bowl.

3. 190' 5.8 Climb up and left onto a slabby face, up this (2 b's) to the base of the crack in the steeper headwall, up the crack to a bolt then move left onto the steep, black face. Go up the face to a bolt at its top and continue to a good ledge with an anchor.

4. 160' 5.6 Zig-Zag around a couple of steep sections, then climb up easier cracks and shallow grooves to an anchor.

5. 110' 5.9 Climb a thin, intermittent seam in the fragile face above (2 b's), to reach a crack that leads to a slanting ledge with an anchor below the summit roofs.

6. 50' 5.9 Traverse left, making a tricky step past a bolt then moving into the big corner. Go up the corner to a belay in an exposed notch.

7. 70' 5.5 Easy rock to the top.

The next routes start about 150' below and right of the tree of Hot Fudge Thursday, at various points along a low-angled right-leaning access ramp. If you are climbing these routes it is best to use a different approach. Cross the band of slabs in front of the wall about 100' below the break used to approach Jubilant Song, 4th or easy 5th class.

To the left of the access ramp is a smooth, low-angled slab.

❽ Slabotomy 150' 5.9

A good quality slab climb with some long runouts. Start at the base of the access ramp. Climb straight up the slab (3 b's), staying to the left of the corner of Ain't no Saint.

❾ Ain't no Saint 960' 5.10b

Danny Rider, Luis Saca. Winter 1997.
Single rack to 4".
A wandering line with a couple of nice sections.
Start by scrambling up the access ramp and setting up a belay below a shallow, left-slanting corner in the slab to the left.
1. 160' 5.9 Climb the corner and the face to its right to some ledges at the top of the corner. Traverse left and move up to the upper ramp. Belay beside a bush.
2. 150' 5.9 Continue up the ramp for 40' to reach a steep crack which slants leftwards up the wall on the left. Climb the crack, past a wide section, to a belay on a small ledge.
3. 100' 5.10a Thin face moves out right (3 b's) lead to the base of a corner which is climbed to a sloping ledge.
4. 100' 5.10a Climb the steep corner above to a roof. Pull through the roof into a crack which soon branches. Follow the right branch to blocky ledges which lead right, then back left to a stance below and to the right of a steep crack. Poor anchor placements on the ledge, but if you climb up a bit there are good pieces in the start of the crack.
5. 150' 5.10b Climb the steep crack past an awkward exit onto the slab above. Continue up into a corner which is followed over a couple of roofs until it is possible to exit right and climb the easy face to a huge ledge with a tree
6&7 300' 5.6 From the left end of the terrace climb over a short steep wall onto a slab. Continue up the slab with poor protection, eventually moving left into a water-washed groove which is followed to the top.

❿ Thriller 1000' 5.9

John Wilder, Larry DeAngelo. 2006.
Single rack to 7".
Start on the access ramp, halfway between the starts of Ain't no Saint and Saint Stephen.
1. Climb up and left to an easy ramp.
2. Go up easily to a belay beneath a steep section of the ramp.
3. Climb the steep section, then a crack system on the main wall to your left. A short rappel leads to a good belay position in the gully at the base of a varnished wall.
4. Sustained climbing along the left crack leads to a belay in the broken rock above.
5&6. Route-find up and left for two pitches, aiming for the left end of the large overhang capping this section of the face.
7. Go left around the overhang and climb a long friction pitch with scarce protection, setting up an anchor when you can.
8. Continue up the water streak and move right when reaching a headwall. Belay on a small perch just below the summit ridge. Scramble to the top.

⓫ Saint Stephen 960' 5.8

Joe Herbst, Larry Hamilton. January 1974.
Single rack to 7".
This route starts up the lower ramp then wanders up the face to the left of the huge pillar in the upper wall, eventually joining the last part of Ain't no Saint. Start by scrambling up the lower ramp for a rope length. At this point twin cracks go up the dark slab on the left.
1. Climb the parallel cracks to a series of steep, short corners which are followed to a large ledge on the left.
2. Go left into a large, smooth corner, which is harder than it looks. Climb the corner to a ledge.
3. Left of the main corner system is an obvious crack which slants out left, and gradually widens. It leads to a large terrace.
4&5 Easier climbing leads up and left to a terrace with a tree.
6&7 300' 5.6 From the left end of the terrace climb over a short steep wall onto a slab. Continue up the slab with poor protection, eventually moving left into a water-washed groove which is followed to the top.

Joanne of Arch 260' 5.9

Jorge Urioste, Joanne Urioste. February 1977.
Single rack to 3".
On the far right hand side of the south face of Windy Peak is a varnished wall. In the middle of the wall is a big left-facing corner which arches left at its top. The route starts on top of a triangle of white rock below the big arch. This is above the bottom end of the huge ramp which slants up and left underneath the whole wall. To reach the start, scramble up and left up the ramp which forms the right side of the triangle of white rock.
1. 100' 5.8 From the top of the triangle, climb straight up a crack. At its top traverse 20' to the right to a ledge.
2. 80' 5.9 From the ledge, climb up to the left-facing corner which is followed to a belay beside a bolt near its top.
3. 80'. 5.6 Face climb out left, then pull through the apex of the arch. Belay shortly afterwards.
Descent: Although the route continues, it is best to rappel from this point.

The following route is on the lower part of the south face of Windy Peak. It is on the lowest cliff band to the right of the deep gully leading up to the south face of Windy Peak. It is about 30 minutes from the parking spot. At the far right end of the cliff band is a very impressive left-facing corner which widens from tips to offwidth in 110 feet.

A Nasty Gash 110' 5.11c **

Single rack to 7", double 0.4"- 0.75".
An excellent varied crack climb.
1. 50' 5.11c After pulling over the initial roof, climb the nice tips crack in the back of the corner to an anchor on a good ledge on the left.
2. 60' 5.11b Lieback and stem up the sharply overhanging wide crack above the belay, pulling through the final roofs to an anchor on the right, just below the top.
Descent: A 60m rope just makes it down.

Ian Teixeira on pitch 2 of Hot Fudge Thursday. Page 27.

Windy Peak - East Face

These walls are on the shoulder of Windy Peak facing due east. They are seldom visited, but have some nice rock and a relatively easy approach. The walls lose the sun by about 1pm.

Approach: From the parking spot go down into the wash and pick up a trail on the other side. It leads west across the desert towards a mound of dark red, conglomerate boulders. Take a left when the trail splits near the crest of the boulder mound, it then heads down into the main wash and crosses to its north side. The trail heads up beside the wash for a short distance before leading up onto its north bank. From here, cut off to the north and head for a red dirt ridge. A gradually improving trail, marked by cairns, leads up the slope on the right side of the ridge. It reaches the cliff in the vicinity of the descent gully. 0.74 miles, 600' elevation gain. 35 to 45 minutes.
The routes are described from left to right.

Blockade Runner 120' 5.8 *
Single rack to 3", double 1"- 2".
This route climbs the clean, left-facing flake/corner on the left side of the buttress to the left of the descent gully.
Start up a finger crack to reach a ledge below the corner. Climb the corner, past a booming block at it's top, then con-

tinue up the face to the top.
Descent: A 100' rappel leads down into the gully behind the buttress. Scramble down the gully to the starting ledge.

Three routes in the 5.5 to 5.6 range climb cracks in the left sidewall of the descent gully. They share the anchor of Blockade Runner.

The most prominent feature on the cliff is a flat, slabby wall topped by a huge roof. A gully to the left provides a descent route from the top of the wall. The next two routes climb the clean brown buttress to the right of the bottom of the descent gully. Look for a flared, varnished stembox with clean, thin cracks in either corner.

❶ The Free Crack 140' 5.8 *
Joe Herbst 1973.
Single rack to 6".
Start up the stembox and continue up the left-hand finger crack which soon leads to some blocks. Move out left around the corner to a wide crack which leads to the top of the formation. In order to keep the rope drag down, it makes sense to split this into two short pitches.

Windy Peak - East Face

❷ The Aid Crack 80' 5.10b **
Joe Herbst. February 1973.
Single rack to 1.75", double cams to 0.75".

Good rock and interesting climbing. Start up the stembox and continue up the right-hand finger crack. Sections of tricky tips laybacks are separated by stem rests. At the top, step right to an anchor on a ledge.

To the right, the base of the cliff is guarded by a short, steep cliff band. Scramble around this obstacle on the right to reach a ledge system under the main wall. To reach the next route make an awkward, bushy traverse along this ledge system.

❸ Jackass Flats 200' 5.6 *
Joe Herbst, Matt McMackin. February 1973.
Double rack to 3".

This route climbs the very prominent, curving crack in the center of the flat, slabby wall, ending on a ledge just below the left end of the huge roof. This route has enjoyable crack climbing despite some suspect rock. Start on the approach ledge below the obvious crack system.

1.80' 5.6 Climb the crack, past some loose blocks, to a good ledge.

2. 120' 5.5 Continue up the curving crack to a ledge below the left end of the huge roof.

Descent: Traverse left to an anchor. Make a 100' rappel down into the gully to the left of the wall. Scramble down the gully to the base of the cliff.

❹ Action by Knight 300' 5.10b
Betsy Herbst, Joe Herbst. April 1974.

This route climbs the right edge of the wall to the huge roof. Start 80' to the right of Jackass Flats, below a right-facing corner.

1. 80' 5.6 Climb blocky corners up and left to belay on a large ledge at the base of the corner.

2. 80' 5.8 Climb the corner and belay on top of a block.

3. 100' 5.10c Follow a left-leaning ramp for 20' then head straight up until just below the huge roof. Traverse left (b) to the left end of the roof.

❹ₐ Variation. This makes the route a worthwhile 5.8

3a. 70' 5.6 From the belay, go over the overhang and climb up and right (unprotected but easy) to a bushy ledge at the base of a right-facing corner.

4a. 90' 5.8 Step right and follow the cracks straight up the steep black face to the top.

Descent: A rappel leads into the gully to the left of the wall. Scramble down the gully to the base of the cliff.

❺ Diet Delight 330' 5.9 **
Jorge Urioste, Joanne Urioste. February 1977.
Double rack to 3", single 3.5", three 0.75".

This route climbs a nice series of cracks and corners up the long, clean sweep of rock to the right of the Jackass Flats wall. In the center of the wall, about 250' up, is an obvious scrub oak. Start directly below the scrub oak, beside a big flake leading to a thin crack.

1. 130' 5.9 Climb the crack on the right side of the flake then follow the thin crack above to its top. Follow small corners up and left and belay at the base of a right-facing corner.

2. 90' 5.9 Climb flakes up the face to the right of the corner, with a hard section past a bolt and pin. Continue to a ledge then up the corner above to belay beside the scrub oak.

3. 60' 5.8 Continue up the crack system, up then right to a belay.

4. 50' 5.8 Continue up the steep corner finishing on the steep arete to the left, then scrambling up to a belay at some boulders.

Descent: Scramble up for a rope length then around to the top of the descent gully. Scramble down the gully to the base of the cliff. The anchor of The Lovely Bones is a short distance up and right from the finish. If you can find it, this makes for a fast and easy alternative descent.

❻ The Lovely Bones 315' 5.11a *
Single rack to 2", double 0.33"- 1.25", Rp's.

This route climbs straight up the attractive varnished face to the right of Diet Delight. It was probably first done in the early 1990's, but it has languished in obscurity for many years and a description appears here in print for the first time. This is a very good route with a lot of good quality climbing and several technical crux sections. The protection is generally good, but requires a bit of guile in several places, and overall the route feels a little bold. Start in the bushes 20' right of Diet Delight, below a short, open corner.

1. 115' 5.11a Climb the corner and the thin crack above. When the crack fades, make thin moves up to better holds. Clip a bolt and continue up a delicate and slightly runout face (crux) to a rest below a smooth, shallow right-facing corner. Climb just right of the corner, joining it towards its top. Decipher another tricky sequence then move up and left to an anchor.

2. 100' 5.10a Step right past a bolt and follow good holds to some protection in a right-facing flake. Move left then back right to a groove in the steeper rock above. Climb the groove, then step right to a lovely finger crack which leads to an anchor under a small A-frame roof.

3. 100' 5.10c Move out left to a right-leaning crack. Follow the crack, with tricky protection at its top, to reach a bushy ramp on the right. Make a balancy pull past a bolt onto an exposed rib. Climb the rib to a small roof (2" cam) step right and make a move up to a thin horizontal (small cams) step right again and climb straight up the face to the left of a left-leaning, varnished corner to reach an anchor just below the top.

Descent: 3 raps with a single 70m rope.

🔴 Michelin Man 80' ???
To the right of the flat face containing the previous two routes is a steep buttress with a bulging front face. Start 20' up on the left side of the buttress. Climb a short corner to its top. Pull onto the bulge above and continue up the arete and face to an anchor (7 b's).

The Black and White Crack 300' 5.3
Jorge Urioste, Joanne Urioste. February 1977.

Around the corner, about 80 yards to the right of the previous routes, is a long chimney in the back of a big, left-facing corner. The right wall of the corner is white, the left wall is black varnish. The chimney starts about 80' up the cliff in the back of an alcove. To the left of the start of the chimney is a huge, flat roof. Scramble up into the alcove from the left and belay at the base of the huge chimney/corner system. Climb the corner in two, long, enjoyable pitches, passing numerous chockstones along the way.

Descent: It is possible to make a non-technical descent by scrambling off to the north.

Mountain Skills guide Jay Foley on A Man of the People. Mud Spring Wing. Page 37.

Introduction

This remote canyon is probably the least visited in Red Rocks, although the route Chuckwalla is somewhat popular. The Mud Spring Wing also has some very good short routes which are reasonably close to the Black Velvet parking area.

Access

For most of the routes, with the possible exception of A Midsummer Nights Scheme, the canyon is best approached from the Black Velvet Canyon parking area.

From the 160/159 junction drive west on Route 160 for 4.7 miles and turn right on a road which goes past a large parking area on the left after 100 yards. Follow this road, staying to the right. After 2 miles the road is blocked by a gate. Take a left here and continue for another 0.8 miles to the Black Velvet Canyon parking area, 2.8 miles total from route 160. This road is quite rough in places but is usually suitable for passenger vehicles.

Approach

From the parking area follow the old road towards Black Velvet Canyon for a couple of hundred yards. At this point the road swings to the south while the main Black Velvet trail cuts straight west through the desert. Stay on the road, which soon turns into a mountain bike trail. After half a mile or so the trail passes a huge boulder. At this point, cut southwest across the desert towards the mouth of the canyon.

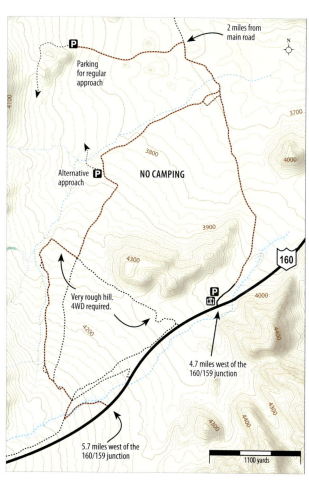

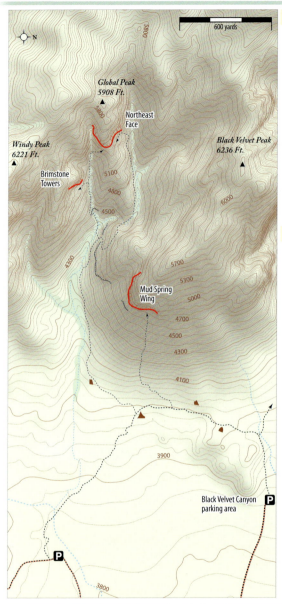

The huge, broken wall that forms the left side of the entrance to Mud Spring Canyon is the north face of Windy Peak. It is climbed by the following route.

Midsummer Night Scheme 1800' 5.7 †

Joe Herbst, Mark Moore. Mid 1970's.

This is a mountaineering style route with a few fifth class sections. From the base of the canyon, scramble up to a bushy gully which leads up and right, underneath the wall for a few hundred yards. Follow the gully to a wide crack system which begins easily but eventually steepens and includes a few 5th class sections along with a lot of 4th class. The gully ends on easy ground below the summit of Windy Peak. **Descent:** Follow the Windy Peak descent.

Brimstone Towers

To the north and west of the north face of Windy Peak are some varnished 500' high cliffs, the Brimstone Towers. The following route climbs the Waffle Wall which is the shiny black face to the left of the highest point of the Brimstone Towers.

Approach: Reaching the Brimstone Towers is long and involved, making this a serious route. From the main canyon follow the gully between Brimstone Towers and Global Peak until a ramp leads back left (east) to the base of the wall. There are several 5th class sections.

Los Frijoles Humanos 570' 5.8 ●

Joanne Urioste, Jorge Urioste. April 1979.

The route starts at a crack, just left of a large chimney which borders the right edge of the Waffle Wall.
1. 100' 5.6 Climb to the top of a white slab leaning against the main wall.
2. 165' 5.8 Go up and left for 30', then head straight up past a couple of steep sections (2 b's) to a thin crack. Follow the crack until a short traverse left leads to an anchor in a scoop.
3. 165' 5.7 Climb up to an overhang. Traverse left and pull over the overhang. Continue up the face (2 b's) to an anchor.
4. 120' 5.6 Go straight up to the summit.
Descent: Rappel the route with two ropes.

Global Peak - Northeast Face

This 800' high dome is tucked way in the back of the canyon. It is the large pyramid of smooth rock which sits on top of the more broken buttress that divides the main canyon into north and south branches. The routes are on the smooth and impressive northeast face.

Approach: Walk up the main canyon, following faint trails to the right of the creek. As you proceed up the canyon, there is a red band on the right. When the red band fades at its west end scramble up onto a terrace at its top. Cut back right on the terrace, looking for a bushy ledge/ramp which slants up to the west (cairns). Follow the ramp to a small saddle with a view of the peak. From the saddle drop down, following the right side of a ledge system down into the main wash. Continue up the main canyon which soon becomes a narrow slot. A couple of blockages require 5th class climbing. Eventually follow a bushy ramp out left for a couple of hundred yards to the base of the wall. The most obvious feature of the wall is a large, left-facing corner system which leans to the right. This is the line of Sidewinder. 2.9 miles, 1300' elevation gain, 2 to 3 hours.

❶ The Sidewinder 860' 5.7

Jorge Urioste, Joanne Urioste. May 1978.

This route climbs the most obvious feature of the wall, a large left-facing corner system which leans to the right.
1. 150' 5.7 Climb the face past two ledges to reach a short left-

facing corner. Up this, then the crack above to a good ledge.

2. 5.5 Climb cracks up to the right side of the roof above. Step left and climb past loose slabs to a belay.

3. Follow a short lieback and a 4th class ramp.

4. 5.6 Go up to a roof and climb its left side. Face climbing leads to a stance.

5. 5.6 Follow a lichenous ramp to a platform.

6&7 5.5 Continue up the crack system and face to the summit.

Descent: Rappel Chuckwalla with two ropes.

❷ Chuckwalla 815' 5.9 *

Jorge Urioste, Joe Herbst, Joanne Urioste. June 1978.
Single rack to 3", doubles 0.6"- 1", extra wires.

Exposed climbing, an adventurous approach and an isolated, lonely summit make for a great day out.

Start 40' to the left of Sidewinder at the base of a low-angled, left-leaning ramp.

1. 150' 5.9 Climb the ramp, then make a couple of bold steps up to a small right-facing corner. From the top of the corner, go left, then straight up the wall (3 b's) to an anchor. A heady lead.

2. 155' 5.9 Continue up the wall (10 b's) to an anchor below a right-facing corner.

3. 110' 5.8 Climb the corner for 20', then make a delicate traverse left (b) to a left-facing corner. Climb the corner and step out right to an anchor level with the roof.

4. 160' 5.8 Face climb (b) up to a finger crack. Climb the finger crack (5.8) until it is possible to move right into a trough which is followed to an anchor on the left.

5. 120' 5.5 Continue up the corner above to a slabby area. Continue up the runout and fragile face (b) in the back of a broad scoop to a bushy ledge with an anchor on the left.

6. 120' 5.4 Continue up the easy corner to the top.

Descent: Rappel the route with two ropes.

❸ Horn-Carson Route 660' 5.8

Maurice Horn, Andy Carson. May 2006.

This route climbs the left side of the east face of Global Peak. The approach, which is different than Chuckwalla, is extremely complex and convoluted. The South Fork of Mud Spring canyon is blocked by a massive headwall. To avoid it, just after entering the South Fork, go steeply up left through brush, scramble across low-angle slabs and climb up through narrow slots. Descend a few feet to the start of a traverse across the wall (exposed, low 5th class). After the traverse, climb steeply up through brush and descend 170 feet through brush back into the South Fork above the massive headwall. Go up the South Fork about 600 feet to where it becomes possible to climb out right through thick brush. Climb a difficult 15' high slot using a knotted, fixed line. Two gullies are available, go up the right hand gully, which is much less brushy, and continue to the base of the wall. The route starts up a dogleg crack in the varnished face to the right of a huge right-facing flake at the base of the wall.

1. 100' 5.8. Climb the crack to the dogleg, then traverse left to another crack which is followed to a belay above a small tree.

2. 90' 5.7 Start up a right-facing corner then traverse right to a left-facing corner. Follow this corner to a pedestal, then traverse right to belay at a good crack.

3. 150' 5.7 Continue up the crack, finishing up a 30' chimney to a ledge below a right-facing corner. There is an off-route bolt in the face out to the left of the middle of this pitch.

4. 160' 5.7 Instead of climbing the corner, step left and climb the beautiful face to a "V." below an overhang.

5. 160' 5.7 Climb the left side of the "V." and step left to a moderate face which leads to a belay.

500' of easy scrambling leads to the top.

Global Peak - Northeast Face.

The first pitch and a half of the Horn/Carson Route is hidden behind a large buttress in front of the main formation.

The Mud Spring Wing

This is the name given to the heavily varnished crags on the north side of the entrance to the canyon. This cliff is seldom visited, but it is a worthwhile cragging area with a good spread of grades and some very good rock. In the past The Schwa was the only route that received any attention, but there are quite a few other excellent routes that deserve to be more popular. The first routes described face south across the canyon and get the sun until mid-afternoon. The routes from Mito northward, face east and lose the sun by 1pm.

Approach: From the Black Velvet Canyon parking area, follow the old road towards the canyon. Stay on the road, which swings south and becomes a mountain bike trail. After half a mile or so the trail is getting close to a huge, pyramid-shaped boulder. At this point cut across the desert towards a long, straight gully which comes down from the right side of the cliff. Follow a trail up the ridge to the left of the gully to reach the base of the cliff close to the obvious off-width corner of Schwalette. 1 mile, 800' elevation gain, 45- 50 minutes.

Mud Spring Wing — Left side

The routes are described from left to right. A prominent feature is a gigantic roof at the base of the prow where the east and south facing walls meet. 100 yards to the left (west) of the roof is a very impressive steep buttress at the top of a broad, open gully. The buttress is split by a prominent zigzag crack.

Rhonestone Cowboy 500' 5.10c
Dave Anderson & Friend. Fall 1976.
Bring some big gear.
This is a good-looking route. Start at the top of the approach gully below the left of two corners.
1. 120' 5.9 Climb the corner, past a bush and into a slot. Continue up the finger and hand crack to a ledge on the right.
2. 150' 5.10b Step left and climb up to a roof. Exit left around the roof and follow the long, zigzag crack system up and left to a belay on a ledge below a slanting corner.
3&4 Climb the corner, then move left and climb a crack which leads up into an alcove. Climb the alcove to a ledge above and follow a right-facing corner to easier ground.

❶ Schwallow 90' 5.7
Single rack to 2".
Get onto a block to the left of Hangman's House. Continue up the slender corner in the arete above. At the top, step right to the anchor of Hangman's House.

❷ Hangman's House 90' 5.12d *
3 sets of cams to 0.5". Single rack to 3".
This is the left of two gorgeous, clean-cut, black corners just to the left of the huge roof. The blocky lower corner leads to a stem rest below a smooth, arching corner with a tips crack. Desperate corner shenanigans lead to an easing of the angle. Stem the upper corner to an anchor at its top.

❸ Gadgers Edge 75' 5.12c *
The scalloped arete to the left of The Long Riders. Climb a hand crack in a short corner to get onto a ledge below the arete proper. Interesting moves on really nice rock lead to a bulge at the top. The route finishes with a wild boulder problem up the upper arete (6 b's).

❹ The Long Riders 75' 5.12a **
Paul Van Betten, Jay Smith. 1983.
Single rack to 1.75", four 0.33", single 3"& 4", Rp's.
The right hand corner is a superb varied climb. There is a large white scar to the left of the corner about 40' up. Climb the corner for 40', then make a few moves up the left wall. Rejoin the corner just below an obvious fist slot. Use this to pull over the bulge to a rest. The upper corner starts with a hard boulder problem to a good finger lock. Athletic stemming and laybacks lead up the remainder of the corner to an anchor over the lip.

To the right of the roof are two crack systems. The Last Hurrah climbs the crack on the left, Mito climbs the crack on the right.

❺ The Last Hurrah 270' 5.10a
Start under the right end of the huge overhang.
1. 80' 5.10a Start up a tricky, thin corner to reach the roof. Traverse right (b) and mantle up into a little niche. Layback up the steep corner above and exit left to good holds. Continue up the easier crack to an anchor.
2. 90' 5.8 Continue up the hand crack above, then a steeper, flakier crack to reach an anchor where the angle eases.
3. 80' 5.7 Follow the crack/chimney to an anchor at the top.
Descent: Three single rope rappels.

❻ Mito 240' 5.8
Tom Kaufman, Joe Herbst. December 1973.
Single rack to 4", double 1.5" to 4".
Start directly below the crack on the right. This is about 20' right of the right end of the huge roof.
1. 100' 5.8 Climb broken rock past a ledge at 40' and continue up the curving crack to a small ledge.
2. 70' 5.8 Continue up the crack for 50'. When the rock quality deteriorates and the crack veers right, head up and left for 15' to another wide crack, then step left to the ledge above pitch 2 of The Last Hurrah. Either finish up the last pitch of The Last Hurrah or make two single rope rappels to the ground.

The next five routes are based around a huge, left-facing corner which starts above a ledge system 90' up the cliff. From the base of Mito, scramble up and right over short cracks and ledges to the big platform at the base of the corner (5.4). To the left of the big corner is a beautiful, varnished wall.
Descent: It is possible to rap back to the platform from the anchor of Man of the People with a 70m rope. With a 60m rope it is possible to swing over to the anchor above Schwalli, and then rap back to the platform from there. From the platform, scramble down 50' to a tree with rap slings and do a short rappel back to the base of the cliff from here.

❼ Spirit Air 125' 5.11c **
A spectacular climb up a wildly exposed arete. Start left of the platform, below the arete (gear anchor, 0.75" - 1" cams). Climb up and left onto the left arete of the wall. Continue more or less straight up the arete, with several thin sections separated by good rests. Above the last rest, continue up the slabby, white face just left of the arete then traverse right to the anchor of Man of the People (12 b's). It is not possible to lower off this route with a 70m rope. Either lower off with an 80m rope, or belay at the top and rap straight back down from the anchor.

❽ Fingers in the Honeypot 115' 5.12c *
Small wires, 3 sets of medium/large Rp's, small cams to 1.25".
A great route, straight up the center of the varnished wall. Thin, sustained climbing (5 b's, crux) leads to better holds. Continue up the face (5.12a at first, then easier) fiddling lots of good gear into the thin cracks, at one point making a short traverse left to a hairline crack for protection. From the hairline crack, step back right and move up to reach a horizontal at 85'. Follow the horizontal up and right to finish up the last 3 bolts of Man of the People.

❾ Man of the People 110' 5.11a **
A nice, well-protected wall climb straight up the right side of the tall, varnished wall, starting up a shallow left-facing offset. Lots of thin, technical cruxes separated by decent rests (11 b's).

❿ Schwalli 80' 5.9 *
Triple 2"- 4" cams.
The big corner is an impressive looking pitch for the grade, but a lot of well-placed footholds on either side allow most of the crack to be avoided by casual stemming. Finally, towards the top, some nice hand-jamming leads to a ledge with an anchor.

⓫ The Jagged Edge 60' 5.11b
A pumpy and enjoyable climb. In the right arete of the overhanging wall to the right of Schwalli is a slender corner. Climb up and right to reach the corner, then follow it to an anchor at its top (6 b's).

100 yards to the right of the huge roof is a striking crack in an orange wall, starting 80' up the cliff, the line of The Schwa. The next route climbs the long, twisting corner down and left of The Schwa.

⑫ Beautiful Bastard
125' 5.10d ✦✦
Single rack to 3", double 0.6"-1". Rp's.
A nice, varied climb with an exciting finale. Start 30' left of the corners of the direct start to The Schwa, below the long, twisting corner system.

1. 80' 5.9 Climb up past a scary-looking block, which is actually reasonably solid, to some ledges. Step right into a lovely, clean corner with a finger crack. Follow the corner and the right-leaning crack above to a shelf at its top. Traverse left 10' to an anchor at a small ledge.

2. 45' 5.10d This pitch climbs the impressive thin crack in the headwall above. The holds and pro-tection are better than they appear, but it's an exciting and exposed lead. From the anchor, climb up and right to reach the thin crack at a small niche. Continue up the crack, over a bulge (large brass offset), to an anchor at the top.

⑬ Gorgeous George
60' 5.12d ✦✦
An enjoyable route with good rock and varied movement. It's rounded and pumpy low down then powerful and crimpy towards the top. Start at an anchor on the shelf to the right of the finish of pitch 1 of Beautiful Bastard. Step right and palm up a shallow corner to a horizontal. Move up to a sloping pocket and make a fingery series of moves up the steepening headwall to an anchor over the lip (7 b's).

Bob Goodwin on pitch 2 of Beautiful Bastard. Page 38.

⓮ The Schwa 200' 5.10d ✱✱
Joe Herbst. 1977.
Single rack to 7", triple 3"- 4".
An obscure-but-beautiful, pure crack climb. This route climbs an attractive widening crack which splits the red wall to the right of a corner.
1. 110' 5.7 Climb a bushy gully on the right, to the base of the red wall. Traverse left behind a bush, then along a narrow ledge to the base of the crack.
1a. Direct Start 5.11b. A good pitch with a hard crux. Start at the base of a wide, low-angled corner directly below the upper crack. Climb the lower corner then move left and go up a little slot. Hard moves up the thin crack springing from its apex lead to the belay ledge.
2. 90' 5.10d Climb the finger and hand crack to a rest on a big diving board. Continue up the fist crack to a ledge. The crux is getting through a short offwidth pod in the middle of the final crack. Move right to an anchor.
Descent: Rappel with two ropes.

Apostrophe 90' 5.9+
Joe Herbst. 1977.
The clean corner to the left of pitch two of The Schwa, finishing on the big diving board. To descend it is possible to scramble over to the left and rap off the anchor above Schwalli.

The next two routes climb an obvious, slabby pyramid of black rock about 100 yards to the right of the Schwa.

⓯ Once upon a Time 180' 5.10a ✱
Single rack to 3", Rp's, double 0.6"- 1.25".
A nice, varied climb. Start below the bottom left side of the slab at the base of the formation.
1. 90' 5.8 Climb the slab, easily at first, to some ledges. Go up to a bolt and continue up to a thin crack (good protection). Traverse right and move up to an anchor at the base of a right-facing corner.

2. 90' 5.10a Layback and stem up the finger crack in the right-facing corner. When things get hard, swing left onto the left arete and continue up the easy face to a ledge. Continue up the cracks in the left-facing corner above to reach the top.
Descent: A complicated scramble leads down to the north.

⓰ High Plains Drifter 100' 5.11b
Paul Crawford, Jay Smith. 1981.
Single rack to 3", double ropes.
A challenging climb up the left-leaning crack in the upper wall of the pyramid. Start at the anchor of Once upon a Time. Traverse out right to a left-leaning flake. Climb the flake to a ledge. Move right past a bolt and make a hard move up. Easier but runout moves lead up and right to the base of the crack. Climb the steep crack, past a small roof (b), then up into a little alcove. Move left and climb an easier crack to the top.

Drifter Direct 90' 5.10c (Tr?)
2 Sets of Rp's.
It is unclear if this pitch has been led, but there are a few small cracks for protection in the face. Start slightly to the right of center at the base of the slab. Climb straight up the face to the bottom of the left-leaning flake of the regular route.

Further to the right, around a corner, is a striking off-width dihedral.

⓱ Schwalette 80' 5.10a
Big cams for the initial corner, then double 0.75"- 1".
If you've lugged a bunch of big cams up the hill to do The Schwa, then you might as well do this route too. An enjoyable pure crack climb.
Struggle up the smooth offwidth, past a chockstone, then on to the base of the big, arching chimney. Move right and layback and jam up a nice, clean corner with a perfect 1" crack to reach the top.

Mud Spring Wing – Right side

Glenda Huxter on pitch 4 of Mustang Cracks. Page 83.

BLACK VELVET PEAK

WHISKEY PEAK

BURLAP BUTTRESS

THE MONUMENT

Introduction

The tall walls of Black Velvet Canyon house a dense concentration of classic multi-pitch routes on some of the best rock in Red Rocks. As an added bonus the approaches are mostly short and easy to follow. Since the entire area lies outside the loop road there are no time restrictions, making it possible to get very early starts for the longer routes.

Most of the routes in the canyon face north, and are best during the spring and fall. However, for some of the harder routes, the colder temperatures of winter can provide superb friction. Conversely even in the heat of summer, temperatures can be reasonable once the walls go into the shade, or even downright comfortable with a little wind.

Access

From the 160/159 junction drive west on Route 160 for 4.7 miles. Turn right on a paved road. After 100 yards, the road goes past a large parking area on the left, and turns to dirt. Follow this road, staying to the right at forks. After 2 miles the road is blocked by a gate; take a left here and continue for another half mile to the parking area. This road is quite rough in places but is usually suitable for passenger vehicles, although it sometimes gets washed out after heavy rains.

Camping is not allowed anywhere in the area.

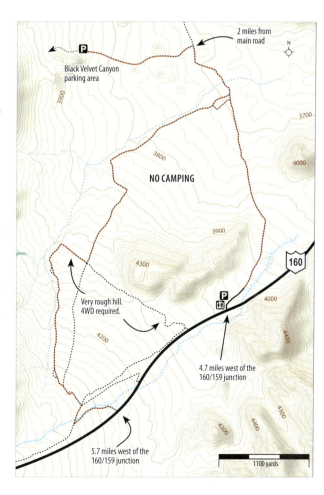

2 miles from main road

N

Black Velvet Canyon parking area

3900

3800

3700

4000

NO CAMPING

3900

160

4300

4000

Very rough hill. 4WD required.

4200

4.7 miles west of the 160/159 junction

5.7 miles west of the 160/159 junction

4300

4400

4300

1100 yards

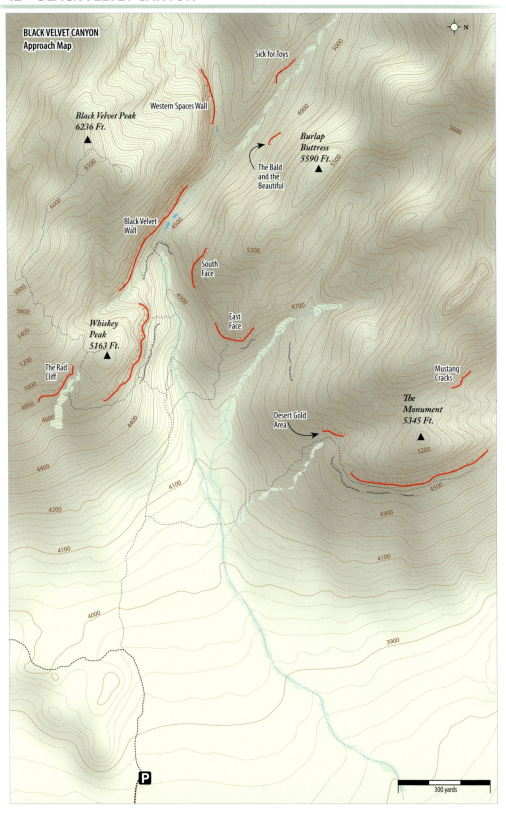

BLACK VELVET CANYON
Approach Map

N

Sick for Toys

Western Spaces Wall

5000

4900

5600

Black Velvet Peak
6236 Ft.

Burlap
Buttress
5590 Ft.

The Bald
and the
Beautiful

6100

6000

5500

Black Velvet
Wall

4500

5200

South
Face

4300

East
Face

4700

5800

Whiskey
Peak
5163 Ft.

Mustang
Cracks

5600

5400

The
Monument
5345 Ft.

The Rad
Cliff

5200

5000

4800

4600

Desert Gold
Area

5200

4400

4100

4500

4200

4300

4100

4100

4000

3900

P

300 yards

Brian Bowman about to launch into the pitch 7 crux of The Shuffle. Page 68. Photo: Tom Moulin.

WHISKEY PEAK

Whiskey Peak is the small sub-peak on the south side of the entrance to the canyon. It is separated from the main mass of Black Velvet Peak by a gully which provides a quick and convenient descent. The routes here face north-northeast and receive very little sun for most of the year. Even in late spring the sun is gone by late morning. The climbing on Whiskey Peak is characterized by cracks and corners, with the 5.10 grade being very well represented. However, in typical Red Rocks style, there are often plenty of face holds around to lessen the impact of poor crack technique.

Approach: From the parking area walk towards the canyon on a rough road. When the road swings south, continue straight, on a good trail. Eventually the trail splits, with one branch heading down into the wash and the other heading up the hill on the left. Follow the trail up the hill, skirting the left side of a red cliff band in front of the main wall. Once on top of the red cliff band, a trail leads rightward along the slope underneath the wall. All routes are easily accessed from this trail. 1 mile 600' elevation gain, 30-45 minutes.

Whiskey Peak – North face
To the Rad Cliff
Lazy Buttress
Frogland Buttress
Ixtlan Buttress
Wholesome Fullback Buttress

The Rad Cliff

This is the name given to the outcrops on the south side of the gully that drops down towards the east from the saddle that separates Whiskey Peak from the main mass of Black Velvet Peak. These routes face northeast and are in the shade by late morning.

Approach: Follow the Whiskey Peak approach to the top of the red cliff band, then contour around to the left and scramble up into the base of the Whiskey Peak descent gully. 40 minutes.

The routes are all on the left side of the gully and are described from left to right. At the left end of the cliff, well to the left of the entrance to the Whiskey Peak gully, is a tall, slim buttress, the Phoenix Buttress. This is split into upper and lower sections by a large platform. The following routes climb the upper buttress. The lower buttress has several easy fifth class routes.

❶ Ravenclaw 120' 5.5

From the platform, scramble up a gully which leads up and left. When the gully steepens, follow a crack on the right past an overhang then continue up easier rock to the top of the buttress. **Descent:** Scramble down to a gully to the south of the buttress. Go down the gully then take a left and go through a tunnel and on down to the starting ledge.

❷ Fright of the Phoenix 160' 5.7 *

Larry DeAngelo, Jason Fico. Mid 2000's.
Single rack to 2", extra wires.
From the right side of the platform, start up a crack then continue up the face to the top of the buttress, an airy piece of climbing. Use the Ravenclaw descent.

❸ Azkaban Jam 140' 5.9 *

Single rack to 4".
An excellent route up the long, steep crack on the right side of the Phoenix Buttress. Belay at the top of the crack then traverse right and rappel from the Dementor tree.

❹ Rita Skeeter 120' 5.9

Xavier Wasiak, Larry DeAngelo. Mid 2000's.
Single rack to 2", Rp's.
The sporty arete to the right of the previous route.

❺ Moaning Myrtle 120' 5.9

Larry DeAngelo. Mid 2000's.
Single rack to 2.5", double 0.6"- 1.25".
This route climbs the corner to the right of the Phoenix

The Rad Cliff – Left side

Rappel Tree

Buttress, with a short detour on the left to get past the steep section, a long reach helps here. From a belay on top, traverse right and rappel from the Dementor tree.

The next three routes are 100 feet to the right of the Phoenix Buttress where there is a prominent curving rib, called the Basilisk Fang.

❻ The Dementor 100' 5.10b
Larry DeAngelo, Paul Crosby. Mid 2000's.
Single rack to 4", Double 1.75"- 2.5".
This route climbs the huge corner to the left of the Basilisk Fang, going through the impressive bomb bay roof. Start by scrambling up 50' (4th class) to a small ledge below the impressive roof. A crack leads up into the roof. Chimney out and down until it is possible to pull around the lip. Easy, loose rock leads to the rappel tree. A single 70m rope makes it to the ground from here.

❼ The Basilisk Fang 150' 5.7
Jason Fico, Larry DeAngelo. Mid 2000's.
Climb the curving rib. Rappel from the Dementor tree.

❽ The Chamber of Secrets 180' 5.7 *
Larry DeAngelo, Jason Fico. Mid 2000's.
Single rack to 3", double 2.5".
This route climbs the superb, clean-cut corner/crack to the right of The Basilisk Fang. Rappel from the Dementor tree.

Get Rad 180' 5.8 *
Matt Kuehl, Jason Molina. November 2012.
Single rack to 8", double 3 & 4 Big Bros.
Get Rad follows the impressive wide crack splitting the left wall of the initial corner of The Chamber of Secrets, it makes for a much better start for that route. Squeeze up the chimney for about 75' before the crack narrows and forces an exit. Continue up the superb hand crack/flare of Chamber of Secrets to finish.

The next routes are located at the very bottom of the Whiskey Peak gully, about 150 feet to the right of the previous routes. Cadillac Crack is unmistakable, a superb wide crack in the back of a clean-cut right-facing corner. There is a two-pitch 5.7 up the flaky face to the left of the corner around to the left of Cadillac Crack.

Cadillac Crack 130' 5.9 *
Joe Herbst, Randal Grandstaff. 1975.
Double 3.5"- 4" cams, bigger cams optional.
Climb the corner/crack, past a bolt, to a ledge with an anchor.

Dark Arts 130' 5.9
Larry DeAngelo, Jorge Urioste. Mid 2000's.
Single rack to 2.5".
Start on top of a white pillar leaning against the base of the black slab to the right of Cadillac Crack. Go up and left to a thin ledge which is followed leftwards for 20' until it is possible to go straight up (2 b's) on good holds to reach a shallow left-facing corner. Up this, then join Cadillac Crack, which is followed to the anchor.

Diagon Alley 130' 5.7
Single rack to 3".
Start just right of Dark Arts and climb a right-slanting crack to a ledge. Either rappel from the dubious looking tree or scramble up and left to the Cadillac Crack anchor.

The next two routes are a couple of hundred feet further up the gully. They start above a bushy terrace on the left side of the gully. Back to Basics climbs an obvious right-facing flake/corner above a white boulder.

Back to Basics 100' 5.7
Wendell Broussard, Ed Prochaska. 1992.
Single rack to 5".
Make a crux move to get established in the corner then continue up and left, up the huge flake/corner to an anchor on top.

First Grader 100' 5.7
Wendell Broussard, Ed Prochaska. 1992.
Single rack to 1.75".
Start 15' to the right of Back to Basics. Start up a right-leaning finger crack and continue up the face to another crack which leads to an anchor under a roof.

Lazy Buttress

The following routes are at the far left end of the north face of Whiskey Peak, almost directly above the point where the approach trail goes through the left end of the small, pink cliff band underneath the main wall. The most obvious feature is an S-shaped crack which is the first pitch of Lazy Buttress. This is a nice area which is seldom crowded and has a few pleasant moderate routes. A good option for some end of day climbing or if Frogland is too crowded.

Descent: Many of these routes finish on Lovers' Ledge. A big ledge about 100' below the top of the buttress. From here, it is possible to finish up the rather loose last pitch of Lazy Buttress. In order to avoid this pitch, go climbers' left along Lovers' Ledge then down into a gully. Scramble up the gully for 150' until it is possible to drop down to the left into the main Whiskey Peak descent gully.

❶ Shaken, Not Stirred 380' 5.9
Paul Crosby, Larry DeAngelo. Mid 2000's.
Single rack to 3".
This route begins just around the corner to the left of the small face with Schaeffer's Delight and Lazy Buttress. The short first pitch goes up a square-cut, somewhat loose corner to a good ledge, level with the start of the above-mentioned climbs. The second pitch goes straight up on face climbing to a belay niche in a flared slot, about fifteen feet up and left from a prominent bush. The third pitch continues up the slot and then ascends the dark headwall above. The climb ends with a short, easy pitch to a big ledge at the top of pitch 3 of Lazy Buttress, called Lovers' Ledge.

The next route climbs the deep right-facing corner system to the left of Lazy Buttress, merging with that route 150' up.

❷ Microbrew 150' 5.6
Single rack to 3", double 1"- 1.25".
Start at the left end of the ledge underneath the wall. Climb the chimney (b) then the face to its right, pulling around a roof into a crack. Up this, then follow a sandy corner up and right to the communal anchor.

❸ Schaeffer's Delight 350' 5.8 **
Mike Petrilak, Mike Ward, Jorge Urioste. September 1984.
0.6"- 1.25" for pitch 1. Up to 3" if continuing.
The first pitch is usually done as an end in itself, although the entire route makes for a nice, varied climb. Start just to the left of the obvious S-shaped crack of Lazy Buttress.
1. 150' 5.7 Excellent wall climbing up the face between the two crack systems. A runout start over a bulge then a move left leads onto a black wall. Up this (7 b's) to the communal anchor.
2. 100' 5.7 Go straight up past a bolt, then up the slab to a low angled corner. Climb the corner to a belay ledge.
3. 60' 5.8 Continue up the main corner for 25', then move left into a clean, square-cut corner. Climb the corner to a big ledge at its top. **Variation:** The clean cut corner can be avoided by staying to the right; 5.7 but loose.
4. 40' 5.2 A short scramble leads to Lovers' Ledge.

❹ Lazy Buttress 490' 5.7
Matt McMackin, Nanouk Borche, Joe and Betsy Herbst. October 1973.
Single rack to 3", double 0.6"- 1.25".
This route climbs the obvious S-shaped crack in the center of the buttress.
1. 150' 5.7 Wide chimneying and stemming with scarce protection and some hollow rock lead up the crack, past a couple of small roofs. At the top, a short traverse left across the face leads to the communal anchor.
2. 160' 5.6 Move up and around to the right to get into a big right-facing corner. Climb the corner until forced out right onto an easy but unprotected face. Climb the face to a big ledge.
3. 90' 5.6 Climb up and left around the roof above. Then go left up the face and continue to Lovers' Ledge.
4. 90' 5.7 There is some poor rock on this pitch. Continue up the headwall, climbing the crack on the right. Move up to a roof (b) which is passed to reach easier but runout climbing. Belay at a big ledge.
Descent: Scramble left and up to the 'summit' then drop down into the standard descent gully.

❺ Ballantine Blast 300' 5.7 *
Single rack to 3", double 1"- 1.25".
This route starts up the left-facing corner to the right of Lazy Buttress. The first two pitches have good rock and good protection, a good introductory lead. The third is runout.
1. 60' 5.6 Climb the corner to an anchor.
2. 60' 5.7 Continue past an awkward flare to an anchor.
3. 180' 5.7 Climb up about fifteen feet to a slightly bulging headwall. A 5.7 move over the right side of the overhang leads to beautiful and easy face climbing. The knobby face leads upward to two overhangs. The easiest route passes the lower overhang on the left and continues up the slab to a good belay ledge on Lazy Buttress.
Follow pitch 3 of Lazy Buttress up to Lovers' Ledge.

❻ Gentle Ben's Afternoon Delight 450' 5.8+
John Wilder, Brandon Arens. August 2005.
Single rack to 4".
This route starts about 150' to the right of Lazy Buttress and about 50' left of Crown Royal, at the base of a gully system that leads up to an obvious crack in a right-facing dihedral, about a rope length above.
1. 180' 5.7 Start in a nice right-facing corner, then head up easy ground to a belay at the base of the crack (two fixed stoppers).
2. 100' 5.8+ Climb the crack, exiting to the right, then traversing left to a nice stance at the base of another dihedral.
3. 100' 5.5 Head left and up, aiming for an obvious ledge that comes into view after about 15'. This pitch only gains about 40' of height, but traverses about a half of a rope length. Belay on the ledge with a huge boulder on it, which is the large ledge at the top of the second pitch of the Lazy Buttress.
4. 70' 5.7 Head up and left, through a slot, then head straight up to Lovers' Ledge.

To the right of Lazy Buttress is a well-defined rib with an attractive varnished wall on its right side.

❼ Crown Royal 620' 5.8

Single rack to #4 Camalot.

This route climbs a series of cracks and corners up the left side of the big varnished rib.

Start below a small corner in the flat face at the base of the rib.

1. 100' 5.8 Climb the corner and the cracks above to a belay stance on the left, level with a big roof.

2. 80' 5.7 Move left into the main corner and climb the chimney to a belay on a ledge

3. 140' 5.8 Jam the crack above to the roof. Move right and continue easily up the wide crack above to a bushy ledge.

4 & 5. 300' 5.6 Wander up the same general line to the top.

❽ Thirty Something 500' 5.11a †

Dave Wonderly, Jenny Richards. Late 1980's.

A bit of a mystery route which follows an impressive looking line up the crest of the rib.

Start at a large flake to the right of the rib.

1. 180' 5.11a Climb the flake and continue up thin cracks above to the arete proper (3 b's). Continue up the arete to an anchor which is just right of a roof.

2. 160' 5.9+ Continue up the arete, passing some big scoops, to a large ledge.

3. 160' 5.7 Continue up the arete above the ledge to easier ground.

Frogland Buttress

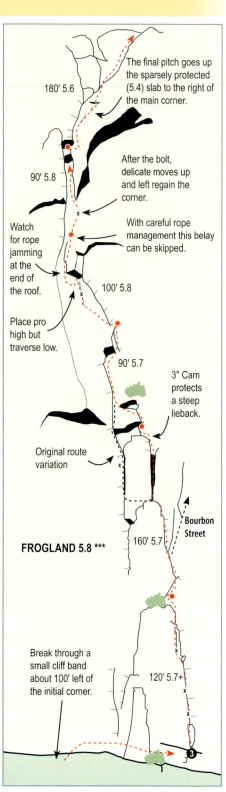

The final pitch goes up the sparsely protected (5.4) slab to the right of the main corner.

180' 5.6

90' 5.8

After the bolt, delicate moves up and left regain the corner.

With careful rope management this belay can be skipped.

Watch for rope jamming at the end of the roof.

100' 5.8

Place pro high but traverse low.

90' 5.7

3" Cam protects a steep lieback.

Original route variation

Bourbon Street

FROGLAND 5.8 *

160' 5.7

Break through a small cliff band about 100' left of the initial corner.

120' 5.7+

❶ Bourbon Street 710' 5.8+ *
Larry DeAngelo, John Wilder. May 29, 2005.
Double cams to 3", single 3.5" and 4".
This route starts to the left of Frogland, then after joining Frogland at the top of the first pitch, it climbs a series of cracks up the right edge of the Frogland Buttress. There are several low-quality routes which climb in the same general vicinity, but Bourbon Street is the best of the bunch. Even then, care is needed to avoid dropping rocks on climbers on Frogland. Start 50' left of Frogland in a corner with a good looking finger crack.
1. 120' 5.7 Climb the corner, over a bulge, to a ledge with some bushes. From here, step right and continue up another corner to the first belay of Frogland.
2. 120' 5.8+ The best pitch on the route. Start up the right-leaning ramp of the second pitch of Frogland, but instead of moving left, climb the left hand of two cracks on the right hand wall. About 70' up, this crack ends. Step right to gain the upper part of the other crack and follow this to a belay on a bushy ledge.
3. 180' 5.7 Climb blocky corners above the ledge then move out left and climb a smooth face, with better holds and protection than it would first appear. The face leads to a hanging belay below a big, right-arching corner with a slabby right wall.
4. 70' 5.7+ This pitch looks harder than it is. From the belay move up and right, until it is possible to step left onto the lip of the buttress above the belay. Follow the ramp above, up and left until it ends. Pass a small bulge and climb the right-facing corner above to a series of small ledges.
5. 150' 5.6 Climb the short finger crack, just left of belay then step onto a right-leaning ramp and follow it to a large horn. From here, head straight up the beautiful face until an arete is reached. Step right and follow the ramp up and left toward a weakness in the summit overhangs. Belay on a ledge below an improbable looking corner on the left.
6. 35' 5.7 Move left into the corner and climb the face to its left. Continue to a large ledge.
7. 35' 5.5 This is best done separate from the previous pitch due to rope drag possibilities. Climb the face just to your right as you arrive at the ledge. Follow this up to the summit.
It is possible, but not as good, to avoid the middle part of the route by climbing easier cracks to the right, starting a short distance up the third pitch.

❷ Rain Dance 120' 5.10a *
Dave Wonderly, Don Wilson. Spring 1990.
Single rack to 1".
An enjoyable pitch up the excellent rock on the front of the small buttress to the left of the first pitch of Frogland. Start 20' to the left of Frogland. Make a few moves up the wall (b) to the base of a thin, right-facing flake which is followed (2 b's) to a ledge. Step left and continue up a thin, left-facing flake (b) to a ledge with a tree.

❸ Frogland 770' 5.8 *
Mike Gilbert, Joanne Urioste, Jorge Urioste. May 1978.
Single rack to 3".
Frogland is an enjoyable and varied route with sustained climbing at the grade. Given its quality and easy access it is not surprising that it is one of the most popular routes in Red Rocks.
There is a huge white scar on the left side of the north face of Whiskey Peak. To the right of this scar is a long corner system

which is dirty and vegetated in its lower portion. About 50' to the right again is a clean, varnished left-facing corner leading to a bushy ledge at 120'. The route starts up this corner. Start on a ledge a few feet above the base of the cliff, below a 30' high, white flake which blocks the base of the corner.
1. 120' 5.7+ Bear hug carefully up the booming flake, then continue up the corner (3 b's) to a tree ledge.
2. 160' 5.7 Start up a right-leaning ramp then continue up the clean, varnished crack on the left to a ledge. Climb the obvious chimney/flake directly above, pulling over the bulge at its top to reach a ledge.
3. 90' 5.7 Pull over a bulge above the belay then traverse back left under a small roof into the deep, varnished corner. Climb the corner then exit out right and pull over a bulge to an anchor on a small blocky ledge.
Variation: 5.7. This was the way this section was climbed on the first ascent. After belaying on the ledge halfway up pitch two, traverse out left (b) to a wide crack. Continue up the crack (runout 5.7) into an easier corner above. Climb a crack through a bulge to join the deep, varnished corner of pitch three. Continue up this to the anchor.
4. 100' 5.8 Face climb out left on beautiful rock to reach a ledge. Continue up a small corner (b) towards the roof. The goal at this point is to traverse left to a thin crack in the arete. It is easier to traverse lower rather then higher. Once on the arete, a few very exposed moves lead past the roof to easier cracks. Continue to a belay on a small ledge.
5. 90' 5.8 Climb up to a bolt on the right in white rock. With the bolt at your heels, make a few thin moves (crux) up and left into the main corner. Continue up the stembox in the corner, tunneling under the huge chockstone and belaying on its top.
6. 180' 5.6 Pull over the bulge on the right to get into a huge, low-angled corner. After a few moves in the main corner, continue up the runout face to the right, using thin cracks to pass a small roof. From the ledge above, continue up a blocky, slanting corner to the top.
Descent: Scramble down to the col at the top of the gully that separates Whiskey Peak from the main mass of Black Velvet Peak. Follow the broad gully down to the east. From the base of the gully a short walk leads back west to the base of the route. 30 minutes.

❹ As the Toad Turns 240' 5.10d
Nick Nordblom, Jenni Stone, Jay Smith. 1989.
Start at the base of Frogland.
1. 150' 5.10d Climb the initial flake of Frogland, then move right to a bolt in the corner on the arete. Up this for a few moves, then move right to the arete and continue up the black face (b) to a stance on the arete.
2. 90' 5.9 Continue up the narrow, black face, moving left into Bourbon Street and finishing in the vicinity of the second belay.
Descent: Two rappels with two ropes.

❺ Romance is a Heart Breakin' Affair 150' 5.10a
Nick Nordblom, Richard Harrison, Brad Ball. 1989.
A long, sparsely protected pitch up the arete and face to the right of the previous route.
Start around to the right of Frogland. Climb a thin, sandy crack, moving left to the arete. Continue, passing a large hole, then up and right across the black face to ledges and the belay. Rappel from slings which will probably need some backup.

The central portion of the north face of Whiskey Peak is a very impressive buttress split by many long, clean, crack and corner systems. In the middle of the buttress is a very obvious crack which starts about 70 feet above the ground and slices up a smooth, tan-colored wall. The crack widens to offwidth and splits a roof 200 feet above the ground. This is the line of Ixtlan.

At the base of the cliff on the left side of this buttress is a large roof 25 feet above the ground.

❶ Kenny Laguna 250' 5.10d *
Richard Harrison, Paul Crawford, Paul Van Betten, Sal Mamusia. 1983. Single rack to 3", double small, medium wires, Rp's.

This route breaks through the large roof to gain an obvious deep, varnished corner. Start on top of a block 15' above the ground, below a corner leading up to the roof.

1. 65' 5.10d Climb the corner, stem over a slight bulge, then traverse right around the roof. This is the crux, which is a little scary for both leader and second. Continue the easy wide crack to a belay at the base of the main corner.

2. 185' 5.10c Stemming leads up the nice tips crack in the back of the deep varnished corner for 100'. Continue more easily around a roof, then up a hand crack to the rap anchor.
Descent: Two rappels with two ropes.

❷ Perplexity 150' 5.10d
Todd Swain, Donette Swain. October 1984. Single rack to 1.75", Rp's, Z1, Z2 Wild Country cams useful.

Start at the base of The Misunderstanding. Climb the tricky varnished wall to the left of The Misunderstanding (2 b's) to a narrow ledge. Move left (b) along the ledge then easily up to the base of the obvious right-slanting corner. There used to be two pegs at the start of this corner, but the pegs are long gone, leaving some tricky Rp placements and small cams as the only protection for the crux moves. Continue up the corner, making liberal use of the left arete. At the top of the corner, a short traverse right leads to the anchor of The Misunderstanding.

To the right of the large roof is a blocky recess above which is a beautiful left-facing corner with a fist crack.

❸ The Misunderstanding 150' 5.9 **
Dave Anderson, Randal Grandstaff. Fall 1975. Single rack to 4", triple 3"- 4".

Start at the back of the recess.
1. 70' 5.9 Climb the right crack in a stembox into a down-sloping roof. Move awkwardly left around the roof and up to a ledge with an anchor.
2. 80' 5.9 Continue up the beautiful corner to a ledge. Move right around a roof then up to an anchor on the left.
Descent: Two single rope rappels.

❹ Miss Conception 225' 5.10c *
Todd Swain, Donette Swain. June 1995. Single rack to 2", double 1.75" - 2".

An exciting route up the arete to the right of The Misunderstanding. Start below below a left-leaning corner.
1. 75' 5.9 Climb the corner to a white ceiling. Move left, then back right above the ceiling (2 b's) to an anchor.
2. 80' 5.10a Continue up the arete into a shallow corner (7 b's).
3. 90' 5.10c Climb the face above on good holds then go up a technical varnished wall. After the last bolt, move left and finish up a short crack to an anchor on a ledge (10 b's).
Descent: 3 single rope rappels.

❺ Return to Forever 220' 5.10d *
Richard Harrison, Paul Crawford, Paul Van Betten, Sal Mamusia. 1983. Single rack, double 4"-9".

This route climbs the obvious long offwidth that splits the small buttress to the left of the smooth face of Ixtlan. A chockstone behind the huge block at the start of the crack is a good place to belay.

1. 180' 5.10d Climb the long crack, through a yellow roof about 160' up (crux). Set up a hanging belay about 20' above the roof, where the crack jogs horizontally left. **Variation**: it is possible to finish the route early by traversing left to the anchors of Miss Conception from just below the crux bulge, (10b.)
2. 40' 5.9 From the belay move right 5' and climb a nice finger crack, then follow a slight ramp up and left to the anchor.
Descent: Rappel with two ropes.

❻ Mazatlan 110' 5.10d *
Dave Anderson, Randal Grandstaff. 1978. Single rack to 3", Rp's, double 1" to 2.5".

This is the deep right-facing corner to the left of the smooth face of Ixtlan. Start at the base of the corner. The first 20' of the crack is very thin and is bypassed by technical stemming, with adequate Rp's for protection. After the start, the climbing continues up the steep corner with great hand and finger cracks leading to an anchor on the left.

❼ Ixtlan 655' 5.11c ***
Jorge Urioste, Joanne Urioste, Dan Goodwin. June 1981. Single rack to 3".

A classic varied climb. Usually only the first three pitches get done, but the climb continues up the wide crack system for another five pitches. The route goes up the obvious widening crack on a smooth wall, which starts 70' above the ground. Start below and left of the crack at the base of a small right-facing corner.

1. 60' 5.11c Climb the corner past a bouldery section at its top. Move up and right across the wall to an anchor at the base of the crack (7 b's).
2. 60' 5.10a Climb the crack on beautiful splitter rock to a hanging belay below the offwidth.
3. 60' 5.10d Climb the offwidth (4 b's) to an anchor just above the roof. For once a true offwidth with no face holds around it. Three single rope rappels to the ground from here, or...
4. 80' 5.9 Continue up the offwidth (8 b's) to an anchor where it widens into a chimney.
5. 80' 5.8 Climb the chimney to its top. There is an anchor in a comfortable alcove.
6. 30' 5.5 Traverse right (2 b's) to belay on a good ledge.
7. 120' 5.9+ Climb the crack (2 b's) that leads to the left side of the tower above. Belay on a blocky ledge just to the left of the bottom of the tower.
8. 165' 5.10a Move right and climb a shallow corner (3 b's) to easier ground.
Easier climbing leads to the summit of Whiskey Peak.
Descent: Scramble down to the col at the top of the gully that separates Whiskey Peak from the main mass of Black Velvet Peak. Follow the broad gully down to the east. From the base of the gully a short walk leads back west to the base of the route. 30 minutes.

❽ Matzoland 60' 5.12a *
Dan McQuade. 1999.
Start 20' to the right of Ixtlan, below a shallow left-leaning corner capped by a roof.
This is an excellent pitch with technical moves in the lower corner and a pumpy finish leftwards across the final wall to the anchor of Ixtlan (6 b's).

❾ Cabo San Looseness 225' 5.10c
Single rack to 2". Rp's.
This climbs the arete between Matzoland and Sand Felipe.
1. 115' 5.10c Climb the right-facing corner just left of the arete, pumpy with tricky gear, then continue up the arete (b) to an anchor 10' below a small roof.
2. 110' 5.10a Climb up to the roof (unprotected), then continue up the corner to its right. Follow thin cracks above, passing the right edge of the Ixtlan roof to some fixed gear, traverse left into Ixtalan and down climb 10' to the anchor above the roof.

❿ Sand Felipe 160' 5.10a.
Around to the right of Ixtlan is a high face of lightly varnished rock, covered in small holds. This is an enjoyable sport route up the center of the wall. There are two anchors, one at 100' and one at 160' (20 b's).

⓫ Sandblast 320' 5.10a *
Paul Van Betten, Nick Nordblom. 1987.
Single rack to 3.5", double 0.4"- 1", Triple 2.5"- 3".
Start below a left-facing chimney/flake about 20' to the right of the obvious bolt line of Sand Felipe.
1. 160' 5.10a Climb the chimney/flake to a ledge. There are two cracks above the ledge, Climb the long thin crack on the left for 60' to a bolt, then move right to a wider crack. Follow this crack to the anchor above pitch 2 of Triassic Sands.
2. 160' 5.9+ Traverse out left to a thin seam. Follow the seam, staying to the left of the hand crack of Triassic Sands, to reach a ledge. Continue up the wide crack above to a big ledge on Triassic Sands.

⓬ Triassic Sands 730' 5.10b ***
Joe Herbst, Larry Hamilton. May 1972. FFA. Augie Klein, Tom Kaufman, Randal Grandstaff, Chris Robbins, Joe Herbst. Spring 1979.
Single rack to 3", triple 2"- 3".
This long, elegant crack system is one of Red Rocks' oldest and most classic routes. It is most often done by climbing the first three pitches, then rappelling. However, it is worth continuing up the excellent fourth pitch, which also has a rappel anchor. The route follows a left-leaning crack, which is the right-most of several possible crack systems, up the wall about 100' to the right of Ixtlan.
Start below an obvious fist crack in a darkly varnished corner which leads up to a ledge below the left-leaning crack of the second pitch.
1. 50' 5.7 Climb the corner/crack to the ledge.
2. 120' 5.10b Move left and make an athletic series of moves over the bulge at the base of the crack (crux). Continue up the long hand crack to a bolted anchor above a big booming block.
3. 160' 5.8 Continue up the hand and fist crack to an anchor on a good ledge at the base of a beautiful corner.
4. 100' 5.10a Pull past a loose flake into the clean-cut corner above the ledge. Up this, exiting left near its top. A short distance higher is a ledge with a bolted anchor.
5. 300' 4th Class. Broken corners lead to the top.

⓭ Cole Essence 60' 5.11c **
Charles Cole, Randal Grandstaff. 1990.
Single rack to 2", double 0.4"- 0.6".
A superb and sustained pitch with a variety of corner problems on smooth rock. Protection is reasonable, but strenuous to place and the demise of the original pin has left the finish quite sporty. Start on the ledge above the first pitch of Triassic Sands. Climb the light-colored left-facing corner to an anchor on the right arete.

⓮ Archaeopteryx 450' 5.11a ❶
Nick Nordblom, Lynn Robinson. Fall 1988.
Double rack to 2", single 3".
The right edge of the buttress containing Ixtlan, Triassic Sands etc. forms a very impressive arete. Archaeopteryx climbs this arete in three long pitches. Old bolts, fragile rock and long runouts on pitch two make for a serious route.
Start in the gully/corner below and to the right of the arete, about 20' to the right of Triassic Sands.
1. 190' 5.10a Climb the gully to a bush, then move into a crack in the face to the left. Follow the crack, passing the Cole Essence anchors, and continue up the thin crack and face (b) until it is possible to move left around the arete and climb up to an anchor.
2. 160' 5.10a Continue up the left side of the arete (b) past a roof. Continue up the arete (2 b's) switching sides a couple of times (b) before moving right and climbing past a bolt on a ledge to a higher ledge below a thin crack. Small cams for the belay.
3. 100' 5.11a Climb the thin crack (crux) above the ledge with small Tcu's for protection. Continue up the crack which leads left around the arete then widens, and finally ends on a very loose, sloping ledge with a block anchor.
Descent: Either rap climber's left off the block to the anchor above the pitch 4 corner of Triassic Sands, or traverse left and downclimb to the same place. Rappel Triassic Sands with two ropes.

The next two routes are on a small shield of beautiful brown rock about 100' above the base of the cliff, midway between the Ixtlan Buttress and the buttress containing Wholesome Fullback. Scramble up a vegetated left-facing corner/gully and belay on the highest ledge beneath the wall. Both routes rappel from slings around some boulders on the ledge on top of the slab.

⓯ Off the Lip 80' 5.10d
Start below a short right-facing corner at the base of the slab. Climb the corner and continue up the left edge of the slab (3 b's) to the top.

⓰ Desert Wave 80' 5.11b
Follow Off the Lip to the first bolt, then head up and right (4 b's) to the top. Good rock and technical moves.

Mike Lorenzo on The Delicate Sound of Thunder, pitch 2. Page 55.

Wholesome Fullback Buttress

This is the buttress at the far right end of the north face of Whiskey Peak. The most obvious feature is a 200' high pillar with a dramatic arete up its center. This is the line of The Delicate Sound of Thunder. There are obvious crack systems on either side of this pillar. The one on the left is Wholesome Fullback, the one on the right is Our Father.

Approach: As well as the approach described in the introduction to Whiskey Peak, these routes can also be reached by dropping down into the wash when the approach trail splits. Continue up the wash until a dusty trail heads up the hillside on the left, skirting the right edge of the red cliff band and reaching the base of the wall in the vicinity of Wholesome Fullback. 40 minutes.

❶ Amber 475' 5.10c *

Single rack to 3.5", double 1.25"- 3".

This route starts up Wholesome Fullback, then moves left and climbs a long series of cracks to the top of the cliff.

1. 50' 5.10a Climb Wholesome Fullback to the base of the hand crack. From here, move left to a ledge with an anchor.

2. 160' 5.10c Start up the hand crack of Wholesome Fullback, then move out left and climb a face (3 b's) to reach a big left-facing flake. Climb the flake/chimney (b) then continue up cracks to the right of a big, varnished flake system. From the top of the flake, traverse left (b) to an anchor in a big corner.

Variation: From the belay, climb straight up the bolted face to the flake/chimney. 5.12b

Amber belays here

3. 130' 5.9 Climb the crack on the right, passing to the left of the obvious roof. Continue up cracks and small ledges until face climbing leads left (2 b's) to an anchor.

4. 135' 5.8 Follow a thin crack which ends below a small roof. Climb over the roof (b) and continue up the face (b), heading up and right to the arete. Climb the face to the left of the arete, staying to the left of a big crack. Continue to an anchor on top. **Descent**: Rappel the route with two ropes.

❷ Wholesome Fullback 250' 5.10b **
Carl Folsom, Lars Holbek. May 1975.
Single rack to 3.5", triple 1.75"- 3".
Start at a small clearing at the base of the crack system on the left side of the pillar. This is about 100 yards to the right of Triassic Sands. A superb crack climb.

1. 180' 5.10b Climb a tips crack (10a) up a gray slab to a ledge. Go up through some steep blocks into a perfect splitter hands crack which leads to a small roof. Traverse right under the roof to a thin crack. Make a few awkward moves up this crack (crux), then continue up the long, perfect hand crack above. Belay below a slot.

2. 70' 5.7 Continue up the crack to a chimney behind the top of the pillar. Chimney up to the top of the pillar then step down to an anchor on a ledge on the opposite side of the pillar. **Descent**: 3 single rope rappels down Our Father.

❸ Jay Smith Route 220' 5.10d †
This route wanders up the face between Wholesome Fullback and The Delicate Sound of Thunder.

❹ The Delicate Sound of Thunder 240' 5.11b ***
Dave Wonderly, Marge Floyd, Dave Evans. November 1988.
Single rack to 1.75".
This route finds an improbable line up the front of the pillar. Start below a smooth, varnished face in the center of the pillar.

1. 140' 5.11b Climb the face (3 b's) to a thin ledge (b) then make a technical traverse out right to the arete. Make bold moves (5.10c) 15' out from the bolt, pulling over a slight bulge onto a wall which leads up to a small roof. Pull over the roof and continue to a stance at the base of a short crack.

2. 100' 5.11a Climb the crack and pull onto the superb arete above. Continue up the arete to the top of the pillar (5 b's).

❺ Our Father 240' 5.10d **
R. Wheeler, Joe Herbst, R. Grandstaff, Vern Clevenger. Spring 1977.
Single rack to 2.5", double 1.25"-2.5".
This route climbs the crack system on the right side of the pillar. The final pitch is a burly hand and finger crack with little in the way of footholds, not your typical Red Rocks corner at all. Start below an obvious right-leaning corner/crack in dark rock.

1. 70' 5.7 Climb the nice corner/crack to a tree.

2. 95' 5.9 Climb the slab above (2 b's), then make delicate moves up and left into a corner (a little runout but not too scary). Continue up the corner to a blocky ledge on the right.

3. 75' 5.10d Climb the corner to an anchor just below the top. **Descent**: 3 single rope rappels with a 60m rope.

❻ Fuck God 80' 5.12d *
Tom Moulin, Chad Umbel. Fall 2008. After practice.
Single rack to 3", Rp's, double 0.33"- 1", small Lowballs.
This route climbs the impressive thin seam and offset system to the right of the final corner of Our Father. Start at the anchor above pitch 2 of Our Father. The seam starts with a very hard (V6/7) and reachy boulder problem with tricky, thin protection.

After the start, better holds and good slots lead to another tricky section (11d) just before a ledge.

❼ Tales from the Gripped 285' 5.11c *
Todd Swain, Elaine Mathews. November 1990.
Single rack to 2", Rp's.
Start 20' to the right of Our Father, below a dark slab.

1. 70' 5.11c Climb a short crack onto the slab. Very thin slab climbing (3 b's) leads to a roof. Move right, through the roof, then up to a ledge. Tree and bolt anchor.

2. 110' 5.10b Go left up a ramp, then up an arete (2 b's) (5.10b). Move right, into a long right-facing corner. Up this then out right across the face (2 b's) to an anchor.

3. 105' 5.11c Climb past an overlap (5.10c), then up and left to a right-facing corner. Just before reaching the corner, move back right to a seam, go up this (5.11c) to the anchor (7 b's). **Descent**: 3 rappels with a 70m rope.

❽ Geriatrics 280' 5.12a *
Single rack to 1", double to 0.75", Rp's. One #4 camalot for pitch 3.
This is an excellent and exposed route up the right edge of the wall. Start about 30' up and left of the base of the rounded arete that forms the right edge of the wall.

1. 90' 5.12a A great pitch with very thin and sustained climbing. Climb a thin, right-leaning crack then go straight up the face (6 b's) until a traverse right (b) leads to a move up to the anchor.

2. 80' 5.11d An awkward and hard sequence off the anchor (3 b's) leads to easier face climbing. Continue over a small roof (3 b's) and move up to an anchor in a scoop.

3. 110' 5.12a Climb up the face above (3 b's), moving left to the base of a steep, varnished scoop. A great piece of climbing leads up the scoop (3 b's) and onto the slab above. Move up and right into a short corner formed by a big roof *(#4 Camalot)*. Pull over and climb up and left (b) to an anchor. **Descent**: 3 rappels with a 70m rope.

❾ Only the Good Die Young 340' 5.11b/c *
Jorge Urioste, Joanne Urioste, Mike Ward, Bob Findlay. 1984.
Single rack to 3", double 0.6"- 1.25".
This route is tucked away, a short distance up the gully on the right hand side of the wall. It is reached by a bushy and blocky scramble around to the right from the base of Our Father. The route goes up a beautiful series of ramps and corners which slice through a very impressive wall. Start below a steep left-facing corner/crack which is the first real break in the overhanging wall as you go up the approach gully.

1. 50' 5.10d After a burly start (b) the corner leads to an anchor.

2. 70' 5.11a Climb through a roof on the right (4 b's) into a nice corner. Up this to an anchor below a beautiful ramp.

3. 70' 5.10b Climb the exposed ramp (3 b's) to an anchor.

4. 50' 5.11b/c Move up, then negotiate a bouldery traverse (crux) to the right side of the roof. Pull right onto the slab and continue up to a big, sloping ledge (7 b's).

5. 100' 5.7 Continue up the slabby corner to easier ground. **Descent**: Exposed scrambling leads across to an obvious slabby ledge. Follow this towards the gully then scramble down to a tree. A 70' rappel from the tree leads into the gully.

❿ Closed on Monday 50' 5.9+ *
Joe Herbst, Stephanie Petrilak. May 1978.
This route climbs a lovely thin crack to the left of an obvious black left-facing corner 100' up the hill to the right of Only the Good Die Young.

BLACK VELVET WALL – LEFT SIDE

The north face of Black Velvet Peak is a huge sweep of varnished rock, whose velvety appearance gives the canyon its name. This tremendous wall provides a host of world-class routes on superb rock. These routes are real toe-crunchers which generally climb up endless ladders of small edges. There are very few ledges anywhere on the wall and so almost all the belays are hanging on most of the routes. For most of the year this wall is shady, however, in late spring with the sun creeping high in the sky, it faces east just enough that it bakes in the sun until late morning. Once it goes in the shade, climbing can be very comfortable even with temperatures in the 90s in Las Vegas. The wall is surprisingly sheltered, but is best avoided when a west wind is whistling straight through the canyon. Not surprisingly, these routes are very popular although the scary ones see few ascents.

Approach: From the parking area walk towards the canyon on a rough road. When the road swings south, continue straight, on a good trail. Eventually the trail splits, with one branch heading down into the wash on the right, and the other heading up the hill on the left. (There are two trails on the right, both will work but the second makes for easier hiking.) Head down into the wash and follow it all the way into the canyon. Below the big roofs on the right side of Black Velvet Wall, the wash is blocked by boulders. About 100' before the blockage, follow a trail leftwards into the bushes. This leads to the base of a small cliff band. 50' of 4th class leads through the cliff band to the broad ramp below the wall. 1.2 miles, 600' elevation gain, 40-50 minutes.

Benny Benson on pitch 6 of Sour Mash. Page 60.

The first three routes are located about 200 yards up and left from where the approach trail tops out on the small cliff band. A useful landmark is a 15' high obelisk which leans against the base of the cliff, forming a small archway.

❶ Spark Plug 100' 5.10b *
Paul Van Betten, Sal Mamusia. 1983.
Single rack to 2.5", triple 0.75", double 1".
This route starts up a nice right-facing corner with a finger crack in its back, located about 60' left of the Obelisk. Start below the corner. Make a powerful pull up a steep finger crack which leads into the corner. Continue up the corner to a big ledge on the left. Climb over a bulge into the continuation crack and follow this to an anchor.

❷ Cutting Edge 120' 5.11b **
Danny Meyers. 1987.
Double 0.75"- 1", one 4", wires .
A brilliant hand traverse on beautiful, smooth rock. Climb Spark Plug to the ledge above the initial corner. Traverse out right to the base of a spectacular hand rail which slants up and right across the smooth wall. Follow the hand rail past three well-spaced bolts to the anchor. A race against the pump. One 60m rope is sufficient to lower off.

❸ Smooth as Silk 320' 5.10d
Jay Smith, Paul Crawford, Randal Grandstaff, Dave Diegleman. 1981.
Single rack to 3", double 0.75"- 1.5", Rp's.
A stout and not overly protected first pitch, leads to some nice, splitter crack climbing on the second. Start just to the right of the obelisk.
1. 160' 5.10d Follow a line of thin right-leaning cracks, with the crux in a short, smooth right-facing corner. Above this, continue more easily into a huge corner which is followed to an anchor on the right.
2. 160' 5.10a Continue up the huge corner, using an excellent splitter crack in the right wall. Above the steep section, continue up the corner system to an anchor on the left.
Descent: 2 double rope rappels.

❹ Refried Brains 2000' 5.9 *
Joanne Urioste, Jorge Urioste, Stephanie Petrilak. November 1979.
Single rack to 4", extra medium wires, optional 5" piece.
This route finds a line up the left hand side of the huge, sheer wall. The lower pitches have good rock and interesting climbing. Higher up the rock is not as good and the route finishes with over 1000' of steep 4th class terrain leading to the summit of Black Velvet Peak. Below the left hand side of the huge, smooth wall is a large block; start 50' to its left, below a short right-leaning seam.
1. 150' 5.8+ Follow the right-leaning seam, making a delicate step (b) to reach a deeper, vertical crack. Up this (b) to an anchor on the left .
2. 150' 5.8+ Step left and climb a thin crack system into a big, right-facing corner. The corner deepens into a gully which is followed to the top of a pillar. Belay beside a tree on top of the pillar.
3. 160' 5.9 Traverse out right, passing a rap anchor, to reach a steep, varnished crack. Up this, past a couple of wide sections, to an anchor above a small tree. A superb pitch.
4. 140' 5.9 Climb a blocky gully (b) then go up and left over blocky terrain to an anchor on the left arete of the huge corner. Continue past the anchor, climbing the face (4 b's) to the left of the arete, to a higher anchor.

This is probably the best place to begin a rappel descent since the rock quality starts to deteriorate at this point, and the fixed anchors above are very dicey.
5.150' 5.8 Continue straight up steep cracks to a hanging belay. Poor fixed anchors.
6. 80' 5.7 Go up and left to a small, black corner (b). Step left onto a ledge with a bolt anchor.
7. 130' 5.8 Go straight up (2 b's) a thin, steep crack to a large ledge with an anchor.
8. 80' 5.7 Climb the corner to trees.
1200' of 4th class leads up the east ridge of Black Velvet Peak to the summit.

❺ The Flesh 2000' 5.10d †
Richard Harrison, Jay Smith. 1984.
This route follows a series of corners just to the right of Refried Brains.
1. 140' 5.9 Follow the first pitch of Refried Brains to a hole. Climb the shallow corner on the right and belay beside a bolt.
2. 180' 5.10d Continue up the thin crack above, then move right and climb the face up and right (this section may be in common with pitch two of American Ghostdance) to reach a good ledge on a huge flake system.
3. 80' 5.10b Continue up the huge flake system occasionally, using the face on the right, to the anchor at the top of pitch 3 of Refried Brains.
4.100' 5.9 The route continues up the right hand of the two huge corner systems above. Belay on top of a big flake which comes in from the right.
5. 180' 5.10d Continue up the corner system and belay below a huge roof.
6. 90' 5.10d Continue up the crack system through the roofs and on to a belay.
After one more pitch the route joins the upper part of Refried Brains and continues with 1000' of third and fourth class climbing.

❻ American Ghostdance 1200' 5.12a *
Jordy Morgan, Kevin Fosberg. November 1988.
The first pitch of this route is a beautiful, technical wall climb which follows random features through a band of very smooth, dark varnish. Above the first pitch, the route continues straight up the wall to the right of Refried Brains.
Start 40' to the right of Refried Brains, behind the huge block. Look for a bolt below a right-slanting finger traverse.
1. 130' 5.12a Climb past the bolt and follow the finger traverse rightwards into the varnish. Sustained climbing leads past 4 bolts. From the 4th bolt traverse left and make more hard moves (b) to get out of the varnished band. Easier (10a), but runout climbing (2 b's), leads to the anchor (8 bolts total).
2. 180' 5.10c Climb up the wall, passing to the left of a small roof (4 b's.) Continue into a crack which is followed to a ledge in a huge right-facing corner system.
3. 150' 5.10c From the right end of the ledge, climb up the wall (6 b's) to reach an anchor.
4. 150' 5.9 Climb up the face (3 b's) into a crack. Climb the crack to an anchor.
5. 100' 5.9 Continue up the crack, then face climb up and left (2 b's) to a right-facing corner. Belay at a bolt.
6. 100' 5.10c Climb up and left (2 b's) and over a roof to an anchor on a ledge.
Descent: Rappel with two ropes.

❼ Sandstone Samurai 730' 5.11a ❶
Paul Van Betten, Nick Nordblom. Spring 1988.
This is a very serious route with many long runouts, especially on the first and second pitches.
Start 30' to the left of an obvious, easy-looking crack, the first pitch of Dream of Wild Turkeys. This is just to the right of a low ceiling and left of a short corner formed by a pillar.
1. 140' 5.11a Climb 40' up white rock to a left-leaning white ramp (b). Traverse right on the white slab, then diagonal up and left (2 b's) to a smooth, varnished wall. Hard moves up the wall lead to a bolt and then the anchor.
2. 140' 5.10a. Go up a short seam, protect, then make a runout to a bolt 50' above the belay. Continue up and slightly right to the anchor.
3. 150' 5.10a Head up and left to a short seam. Above the seam continue to a larger crack system, climb this and the face above heading towards another crack. There is an anchor just to the left of the base of this crack.
4. 150' 5.10a Climb up and left to a tiny left-leaning crack which ends at a fixed anchor.
5. 150' 5.11a Climb up and left across a water streak (5 b's) to an anchor to the right of a right-facing corner.
Descent: Rappel the route with two ropes.

❽ Rock Warrior 900' 5.10b *
Richard Harrison, Jay Smith, Nick Nordblom. Fall 1983.
Single rack to 2", Rp's, extra wires.
In doing this route, the first ascent crew made every effort to keep bolting to a minimum. Spying out a line of subtle features and drilling a few bolts to fill in the blanks, they were able to weave a magnificent natural line up this huge chunk of rock. Sometimes runout but seldom really dangerous, the route quickly became a renowned test of trad climbing skills, and for a few years was climbed regularly. It now receives fewer ascents in a year than Prince of Darkness gets on an average day. Start 30' to the left of an obvious, easy-looking crack, the first pitch of Dream of Wild Turkeys. This is just to the right of a low ceiling and left of a short corner formed by a pillar.
1. 150' 5.10b Perhaps the neckiest pitch on the route, with the first bolt at 60' and some hefty runouts. Climb up and right on white rock to a slab (b). Move up then traverse right until below the anchor. Up the wall (b) to the anchor.
2. 150' 5.10b Climb up and left to a bolt then straight up the face to a shallow left-facing corner (b). Make difficult moves up the arete of the corner to a seam which is followed up and right (b) to an anchor.
3. 150' 5.10a Go slightly left (b) then up (pin) to a ceiling. Over the ceiling then up the wall (b) to the anchor.
4. 150' 5.9 Up the face (3 b's) to an anchor at the base of a short corner.
5. 150' 5.9 Climb the corner then up the face (3 b's) to an anchor.
6. 150' 5.10a Climb up to and over a roof (b), then follow thin cracks and seams up and right to an anchor around the corner.

❾ Prince of Darkness 665' 5.10c **
Jorge Urioste, Joanne Urioste, Bill Bradley, Mike Ward. Fall 1984.
Single rack to 1.25".
The first ascent of Prince of Darkness was completed almost a year later than Rock Warrior and couldn't have been more different in style. The goal with this climb was to create a direct and safe route blasting straight up the most impressive part of the wall. With bolts every few feet, it provides climbers with

limited trad skills a way to experience a spectacular route up a huge, open wall. It is by far the most popular route on the wall, although nowhere near the best, since the climbing lacks the variety and interest of some of the others.
1. 75' 5.7 The first pitch of Dream of Wild Turkeys. Climb up to the base of a right-facing corner. Climb up a crack in the left arete to an anchor.
2. 110' 5.10b Follow a line of bolts past a delicate crux to an anchor (14 b's).
3. 130' 5.10a Continue up the wall, passing a short crack which requires some gear placements. Continue up the wall on beautiful rock to an anchor (15 b's).
4. 130' 5.9 Continue, following 14 bolts to the anchor.
5. 120' 5.9 Climb a thin seam on the left (8 b's) to the anchor.
6. 100' 5.10c Above the belay, a thin crack through a smooth, varnished slab is the crux of the route. Above, continue more easily to the anchor (13 b's).
Descent: Rap any of the routes in the vicinity with two ropes, if possible avoiding rapping through other parties.

❿ Dream of Wild Turkeys 1000' 5.10a **
Jorge Urioste, Joanne Urioste. June 1980.
Single rack to 4".
Dream of Wild Turkeys follows the line of least resistance up the huge shield of rock in the lower left hand corner of the Black Velvet Wall. The route connects superb cracks and corners with sections of spectacular face climbing. You'll be hard pressed to find a better climb at the grade anywhere. The two 5.10a cruxes are short and bolt-protected. Start about 60' to the left of the huge arch at the base of the wall. Slabby, white rock leads up into a small, right-leaning corner about 40' up.
1. 75' 5.7 Climb up to the base of the corner then move out to a crack in the left arete. Up this to the anchor. This pitch is shared with Prince of Darkness.
2. 150' 5.9 Move right and up (2 b's) into the base of a long right-slanting crack which is followed to an anchor on a tight little ledge.
3. 80' 5.10a Up the steep, varnished crack above for 40', then follow a traverse right (5 b's), leading across to a comfortable ledge at the base of a huge corner.
4. 180' 5.10a Thrash up the wide crack in the corner which gradually narrows. At the very top of the corner, a delicate slab (2 b's) leads to a hanging belay.
5. 60' 5.9+ Delicate climbing leads out left across the slab (5 b's) to the base of a corner.
6. 140' 5.9 Move up and right on a ramp. At the top of the ramp, climb up then back left into the corner (7 b's). Continue to an anchor a few feet higher.
Variation: After the first 30' of pitch 5 climb straight up (3 b's) to join pitch 6. A 200' pitch.
7. 110' 5.9 Climb a delicate, low-angled seam, then face climb (5 b's) to a big ledge in a large bowl.
Many parties rappel from here, although the next few pitches are well worth doing.
8. 80' 4th class. Go up and right up the bowl, then cut up and left on ramps and ledges to a good ledge with a bolt anchor at the base of a steep wall.
9. 140' 5.9 Climb a thin crack in the back of the beautiful right-facing corner to a good ledge with a bolt anchor (7 b's).
10. 150' 5.9 Climb past 4 bolts into a crack on the left. Follow this to a ledge with a bolt anchor.
Descent: Rappel with two ropes.

Black Velvet Wall – Left side

⑪ Yellow Brick Road 630' 5.10c *
Jorge Urioste, Joanne Urioste, Bill Bradley, Mike Ward. Fall 1985.
Single rack to 2".

This route is a direct variation on Dream of Wild Turkeys. It provides two pitches of superb wall climbing on bulletproof rock. The route starts at the top of pitch two of Dream of Wild Turkeys.

3. 130' 5.10c Start up the varnished crack of pitch 3 of Dream of Wild Turkeys, but instead of traversing right across the face, continue up the dwindling crack. The Uriostes kindly left a plaque with directions here, for the route-finding impaired. When the crack ends, continue up the steep, varnished face to an anchor (7 b's).

4. 120' 5.10a Continue up the gradually easing wall to the anchor at the end of the traverse on pitch 5 of Dream of Wild Turkeys.

Descent: Rappel with two ropes.

⑫ The Gobbler 290' 5.10a **
Jorge Urioste, Joanne Urioste. July 1980.
Single rack to 2".

This route is a direct start to Dream of Wild Turkeys. It is a beautiful, varied climb, well worth doing as an end in itself. Start below a smooth, gray slab dotted with a zig-zag line of bolts. This is just to the left of the huge, arching roof.

1. 120' 5.9 Technical climbing up the uncharacteristically smooth slab (7 b's) leads an anchor at the base of a right-slanting chimney/corner.

2. 90' 5.9 Climb the crack to the right of the main corner to a bolt. Move up, then make an awkward step left into the main corner. Continue up the crack to an anchor on the right.

3. 80' 5.10a Climb the steep face above (7 b's) to the comfortable ledge above pitch 3 of Dream of Wild Turkeys.

Descent: Rappel with two ropes.

⑬ 18 Year Mcallen 120' 5.11d
Randy Marsh, Pier Marsh. 1994.

This route starts at the top of the second pitch of The Gobbler. Climb the face to the right of the third pitch of the Gobbler. Continue up and slightly right, staying to the right of the big corner of Dream of Wild Turkeys, then after the last bolt move left to an anchor (7 b's).

⑭ Fiddler on the Roof 820' 5.10d ***
Dave Wonderly, Warren Egbert, Jennifer Richards. November 1990.
Single rack to 2", Rp's, extra wires.

Many people think that this is the best route on the wall, and I'm not inclined to disagree. It starts up the first two pitches of the Gobbler, then continues with a spectacular traverse right above the huge roof, finishing up the wall directly above. The situations and climbing are consistently amazing.

Start from the belay above pitch 2 of The Gobbler.

3. 100' 5.10c Move out right and go up a crack for 20', until a long traverse leads to the right, above the lip of the huge roof (3 b's). The crux comes early in the traverse, and although the protection is good, it is a little spaced. The climbing is more runout for the follower than the leader.

4. 150' 5.10d Climb straight up the fabulous wall above (4 b's). This pitch has a bold feel despite being quite well-protected. Holds and protection are hard to see from below, but keep appearing just when you really need them.

5. 150' 5.10b A long pitch of great face climbing with some healthy runouts leads to an anchor below a slight swell (7 b's).

6. 100' 5.10b Move leftwards over the swell (2 b's), then up to a ledge. Continue up the face (b) and just when you thought it was over, fret and worry past a thin move (9+) way out from protection before reaching the belay ledge.

7. 100' 5.9+ Climb past two bolts to Turkey Ledge.

Descent: Rappel with two ropes. 60m ropes needed for the rap over the huge roof which goes down to an anchor on a ledge 40' up the first pitch of Sour Mash.

The following routes climb the wall below the huge roof system on the right side of the wall.

⑮ The Fiddler Roof 180' 5.10c
Dan Goodwin, Joanne Urioste. June 1981.
Double 4"- 7" cams.

This route climbs the right-arching crack which forms the left side of the roof system. A very nice, clean crack climb.

Easy rock leads up to the base of a wide, left-facing corner/crack to the right of the main arch. Climb the corner/crack (2 b's) to a small roof at its' top, then traverse left into the main arch. Layback up the arch to an anchor under the huge roof. A bolted second pitch out the huge roof remains unclimbed.

⑯ Overhanging Hangover 220' 5.10a *
Jorge Urioste, Joanne Urioste, Dan Goodwin. 1981.
Single rack to 2".

A superb short route which uses an inset slab to break through the huge roofs. Start almost directly below the inset slab in the roof. From the ground, scramble up and left on a ramp to a ledge below the left hand of two bolted lines up the black rock.

1. 90' 5.10a Climb up past a thin crack to reach the bolt line. Thin, slabby climbing leads to the anchor (10 b's).

2. 120' 5.10a Continue past a bolt into a nice finger and hand crack. Follow the crack (b) to an optional anchor below the roof. A delicate traverse right across the inset slab (4 b's) leads to an anchor on the lip.

Descent: Rappel with two ropes.

⑰ Johnny Come Lately 115' 5.10d *
A few small to medium nuts optional.

This route climbs the bolt line to the right of Overhanging Hangover, getting quite close to that route in one or two places. Start by scrambling up onto a ledge below the wall. Climb beautiful, dark rock (8 b's) to an anchor.

⑱ Early Times 5.10c
Bob Finlay. 1980s.

Early Times starts at the last anchor of Overhanging Hangover and climbs up and left crossing Fiddler on the Roof and trending up and left across a smooth wall to join pitch 4 of Dream of Wild Turkeys.

⑲ Sour Mash 695' 5.10a **
Jorge Urioste, Joanne Urioste. July 1980.
Single rack to 3", double 0.5"- 1.25".

This route follows a long crack system that skirts the right edge of the huge, arching roof, then slants leftwards up the wall above. It is another excellent climb, but unlike most of the routes on the wall, it is primarily a crack climb, albeit with several bolt-protected cruxes.

Start below the right end of the huge roof and a short distance left of a buttress of white rock.

1. 100' 5.8 Climb up slabby rock for 40' to a nice lieback crack which leads to the ledge below a triangular black wall hemmed in by corners on either side.

2. 70' 5.9 Climb the corner on the right, moving left and face climbing up to the apex of the black triangle (4 b's). Continue up the crack above for 30' to a belay beside a tree.

3. 170' 5.8 Move out right and climb a rib (b), then over a bulge to a second bolt. Move around to the right into a crack which diagonals up and right (b) to an anchor. Climb the crack above (2 b's) to a ledge. Move left along the ledge (b) and go up a short corner to a higher ledge with a bolt anchor.

4. 60' 5.7 At this point there are three parallel crack systems on the wall. Climb the central crack (b) to an anchor.

5. 130' 5.9 Climb the long left-slanting crack on excellent rock, stepping left into a parallel crack and following this to an anchor.

6. 90' 5.10a Continue up the crack (5 b's) to a stance below a steep, shallow corner. Lieback up this, and over the bulge at its top (3 b's) moving right to reach an anchor at the right edge of a white roof.

7. 75' 5.9+ Step left over the roof and go up a thin crack until it ends and a delicate sequence of moves leads up into a left-facing corner, up this then move right to an anchor (6 b's).
Descent: Rappel with two ropes.

To the right of the upper pitches of Sour Mash, two very obvious corner and crack systems slice through the steep, dark rock above a bowl. My Little Pony is the corner on the left. Velveeta is the corner on the right. Both routes are usually approached by climbing the first three pitches of Sour Mash. Near the top of pitch 3, instead of stepping left along a ledge to a bolt in a right-facing corner, step right to a cold shut bolt on a ledge. Small cams and nuts for the anchor.

⑳ My Little Pony 640' 5.11d
Paul Van Betten, Richard Harrison, Shelby Shelton. Summer 1990. Single rack to 3", Rp's. Double 2"-3".
3. 120' 5.8 Climb up and right along a shallow ramp (good but spaced gear) then straight up to a tree belay in the bowl.
4. 80' 5.11d Climb up into a low-angled corner which is followed to a steepening at the top. Make a hard series of moves past a bolt and continue to a single bolt anchor on the right (1"- 1.75" cams for the anchor).
5. 100' 5.11b A very airy pitch with some flaky rock but excellent climbing. Wide stemming leads up the corner (2 b's) to an exciting exit right and a delicate semi-rest (b). Climb the hand crack above (2"- 3" cams) and the face to its left to reach a narrow ledge with a bolt anchor.
6. 120' 5.10a Continue up the crack to a ledge.
Descent: Either... rappel down the route from the top of pitch 5. Start with a 195' diagonal rap to the anchor above pitch 4 of Sour Mash... Or... continue up and traverse right and rappel Epinephrine. Either option requires two ropes.

㉑ Velveeta 710' 5.11d *
Richard Harrison, Wendell Broussard. Summer 1990. Single rack to 4", Rp's.
3. 200' 5.8 Climb up and right along a shallow ramp (good but spaced gear) then straight up to a tree in the bowl. Climb up and right and belay on top of a huge block below the right most of the two corners.
4. 150' 5.11d An excellent pitch. Climb the corner to a bolt. Step left and make crux moves before rejoining the corner and continuing to an anchor.
5. 150' 5.10d Continue up the corner (old bolt) and crack system until a ramp leads out right to a tree. Continue right to

a better ledge and belay here.
Descent: Scramble out right to join Epinephrine below the Elephants' Trunk. Rappel down Epinephrine with two ropes.

BLACK VELVET WALL- RIGHT SIDE

The right hand side of the Black Velvet Wall is one of the tallest sweeps of rock in Red Rocks. The rock is a little different here, much smoother and with far fewer face holds than is usual in Red Rocks, but very clean and solid.

Approach: Approach as for the main Black Velvet Wall, but once above the small cliff band go down and right, back into the main wash above the blockage. About 150 feet up canyon is a bolted gray slab almost directly below the right edge of the huge Black Tower. This is the start of Epinephrine. 1.25 miles, 600' elevation gain, 50-60 minutes total.

Descent: From the huge tree at the end of the Epinephrine ramp, scramble 300' up to a small saddle between a subsidiary summit and the main summit of Black Velvet Peak. Scramble up onto the main summit and then follow the ridge southeastwards for about half a mile. At this point there are several cairns close together on the ridge, and you are looking almost straight down into the notch behind Whiskey Peak. The cairns mark the start of a descent which leads down the steep hillside. When close to the bottom of the slope, the trail leads leftwards (west) for about 100 yards to a slabby break in the cliff band that forms the side wall of the descent gully for Whiskey Peak. Go down this break into the Whiskey Peak descent gully and follow this back to the parking lot. 1.5 - 2 hours. This descent is fairly easy and fast, but requires care. The most common mistake is to descend from the summit ridge too early. Scoping out the descent from the parking area prior to going into the canyon is very helpful.

Black Velvet Peak descent

BLACK VELVET PEAK

Do not go down this gully

Whiskey Peak

Matt Kuehl on pitch 6 of Epinephrine. Page 64.

❶ Chalk is Cheap 700' 5.10d

Mike Ward, Mike Clifford, Eric Sutton. Fall 1989.

This route climbs the front face of the Black Tower. There is a lot of fragile rock, as well as several serious runouts. Start 50' to the left of Epinephrine, at the base of a left-slanting ramp up the lowest tier of cliff. Scramble left along the ramp, then up either of two cracks to a bushy ledge. Belay below a left-facing corner that leads to a ceiling.

1. 140' 5.9 Climb the left-facing corner and step out right onto a scary face which leads to a right-slanting corner. Follow this into a large left-facing corner. Belay on blocky ledges below a crack in a corner.

2. 120' 5.8 Climb the crack and follow it out left. Just before the crack ends, move right to a V-groove, up this and the easy corner above to belay on top of a pillar.

3. 140' 5.10d Climb the left edge of the brown wall above, moving out right to a pin. Follow a vertical seam up to the center of a ceiling. Pull over the ceiling and follow an easy ramp leftwards. Belay at a short, vertical crack.

Variation: 5.10a Very Serious. From the top of the pillar, go left then out right on big holds to a vertical seam. Climb the seam to a right-facing flake/corner. Up this to a good stance. Angle left to rejoin the regular route at the seam leading to the center of the ceiling.

4. 160' 5.10c The wall above is split by four parallel cracks. Climb either of the two cracks on the left.

Variation: 5.10a Climb up and left then back right to the third crack from the left. Climb this to its end and belay. Very serious.

5. 50' 5.6 Easy rock leads to the top of the Black Tower.

Descent: Rappel Epinephrine with two ropes.

❷ Malicious Mischief 700' 5.10a

Joe Herbst, Stephanie Petrilak, Mike Gilbert. May 1978.
Single rack to 6", double to 2", Extra wide (big bros, valley giants).

This route starts up Epinephrine, then moves left around the base of the Black Tower and climbs the crack on its left side.

1. 60' 5.8 Climb the gray slab to a bushy ledge (4 b's).

2. 110' 5.7 Climb a left-facing corner over a small roof onto a slab. Climb the slab (b), climbing over a small roof then moving left (b) into a corner which slants back right. Follow this to an anchor.

3. 150' 5.8 Climb up into the deep chimney above. Follow it until a move out right leads onto an easy face. The face leads up to a ledge at the base of the main chimney. Before reaching the chimney, traverse left and up to a large ledge below the center of the Black Tower.

4&5 200' 5.6 Easy ground leads up the left side of the pillar to a sloping ledge at the base of the ominous, clean-cut offwidth on the left side of the Black Tower.

6. 100' 5.10c A serious and scary pitch which starts as a 10" down-flaring offwidth that gradually eases and leads to a hanging belay.

7. 80' 5.8+ Face climbing leads up to the top of the pillar.

Descent: Rappel Epinephrine with two ropes.

❸ Velvet Wall - Original Route 2000' 5.9 *

Joe Herbst, Tom Kaufman. December 1973.

The original ascent of the wall. It climbed the chimneys of what was later to become Epinephrine to the top of the Black Tower. From the top of the tower it climbed up and slightly left to the very bottom of the exit ramp at the top of Epinephrine. It then followed the ramp to the top.

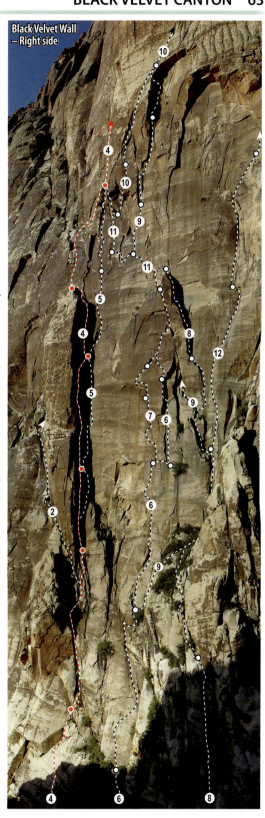

Black Velvet Wall – Right side

❹ **Epinephrine 2240' 5.9 *****
Jorge Urioste, Joanne Urioste, Joe Herbst. August 1978.
Single rack to 5", double 1"- 3".

In an area known for classic, middle-grade routes, Epinephrine is one of the best. The chimneys leading up to the top of the Black Tower are not typical for Red Rocks, being smooth-walled, intimidating, and demanding of good technique. Higher up, the route climbs pitch after pitch up a magnificent exposed dihedral before cutting out right on an easier exit ramp which leads up close to the summit. With superb climbing the entire way, a beautiful direct line and, for once, a summit, this is a route not to miss.

Start at the base of the gray slab, below some new bolts.

1. 60' 5.8 Climb the gray slab to a bushy ledge (4 b's). **Variation**, the original start climbs the slab 10' to the right (3 b's).

2. 110' 5.7 Climb a left-facing corner over a small roof onto a slab. Climb the slab (b) past a small roof then move left (b) into a corner which slants back right. Follow this to an anchor.

3. 150' 5.8 Climb up into the deep chimney above. Follow it until a move out right leads onto an easy face. The face leads up to a ledge at the base of the main chimney.

4. 110' 5.9 Climb the chimney to an anchor on the right.

5. 150' 5.9 Continue up the chimney. Above an old anchor make a short detour on the left, then follow a good crack in the right wall to a comfortable ledge below an overhang.

6. 120' 5.9 Move back left into the airy chimney. Up this (2 b's) to the top of the Black Tower.

7. 180' 5.7 Climb up the face above (2 b's) and pull through a small overhang. Continue up to big ledges, which lead around to the right, to the base of a big pile of hollow-sounding blocks, called the Elephants' Trunk. Set up an anchor at the base of this.

8. 80' 5.9 Climb to the top of the Elephants' Trunk and continue up the face, climbing thin cracks (2 b's) to a small, exposed ledge.

9. 120' 5.9 Continue up the steep corner (5 b's) to an anchor.

10. 160' 5.7 Continue up the long corner/crack to an anchor.

11. 140' 5.9 Continue up the easier corner till it is blocked by a huge roof. Face climbing on delicate holds leads right across the wall and up to the edge of the roof and some protection. Continue on big holds to an anchor in an alcove.

12. 160' 5.7 Continue up the long left-facing corner above, which eventually tops out at an anchor on a huge right-leaning ramp.

13-16 700' 5.4 Follow the ramp up and right past a few very exposed steps. After going round an exposed corner, the ramp becomes almost horizontal and leads slightly up and across towards a huge tree on the Northwest ridge of Black Velvet Peak. Unrope here, then follow the descent described on the previous page.

❺ **Ancient Futures 750' 5.12a ****
Dan McQuade, Randal Grandstaff. 1997.
Single rack to 3".

This route follows an elegant line of corners immediately to the right of the chimneys of Epinephrine. The crux sections are short and bolt-protected, and the climb as a whole is quite varied and enjoyable. The route starts up the first 3 pitches of Epinephrine, to the base of the main chimneys.

4. 110' 5.11b Follow the corners on the right into a deep V-groove. Stem up the V-groove, and where it constricts, stem out to a hidden bolt on the left edge of the chimney. Pull up

past the bolt to an anchor shared with Epinephrine.

5. 140' 5.12a Climb up a thin seam (b) above the anchor, then make a tricky step right to a flake. Lieback up this, then move left to a short corner. Make thin face moves to the right of the corner (2 b's) before stepping back into the corner (crux). Continue past a 5.9 offwidth to a comfortable ledge.

6. 140' 5.12a Technical moves (2 b's) up the slanting V-slot above lead to a rest below a roof. Pull over the roof (11b) and up to a left-facing corner. Climb the face to the left of the corner and up the wall above (7 b's) to an anchor.

7. 150' 5.10d Climb the face above past a short flake (5 b's) and climb leftwards into right-leaning corner. Follow this to reach Epinephrine at the Elephants' Trunk.

Descent: Rappel with two ropes.

A prominent feature of the face to the right of Epinephrine is a huge flake plastered to the middle of this wall, called Texas Tower. All the routes here end up passing through the top of Texas Tower.

❻ **Texas Tower Direct 800' 5.12d *****
John Rosholt, et al. June 1997.
FFA: Jerry Handren, Josh Horniak. Feb. 2006.
Single rack to 3".

This great route climbs straight up the wall to Texas Tower. A technical testpiece on bulletproof rock and with excellent protection. When combined with the upper pitches of Texas Hold'Em, it makes for a classic long route.

Start 100' to the right of Epinephrine, and below and to the left of a long left-facing corner.

1. 120' 5.8 Go up on some steep ledges, then move right and follow a flake up and right to where a few face moves on fragile rock lead into the base of the large left-facing corner. Follow the corner over a bulge, then 20' higher move left and up to an anchor on a bushy ledge.

2. 150' 5.9 Climb straight up the easy slab above into the huge left-leaning corner. Continue up the corner to a bolt on the right wall. Traverse to the right, staying low, then step up and make a final pull over a slight bulge (5.8 R) to reach a good ledge.

3. 160' 5.12a An amazing pitch of wall climbing. Start by climbing left then up to a short right-facing corner (a few nuts and small cams). Once the corner is reached, follow the bolt line (11 b's) above, ignoring an anchor which is for rappelling only. Belay at the base of an impressive left-facing corner.

4. 20' 5.12b A very tricky boulder problem traverse (b) leads to an anchor on the right.

5. 110' 5.12d Another superb pitch. Climb the lovely right-facing flare, which leads into a desperate sequence up a small right-facing corner (crux.) Continue into a bigger corner (1.75"-2" cams), then move onto the left arete which leads up to an anchor (9 b's).

Variation: The mossy face to the right (5 b's) moving back left into the corner above the crux. 5.11c.

6. 160' 5.12a Face climb (4 b's) up then left into a short crack. Make a hard move to a small roof, then follow the flakes above to another roof. Move right over the roof then follow the steep corner above (4 b's), finishing up a thin crack to a big ledge just below the top of Texas Tower.

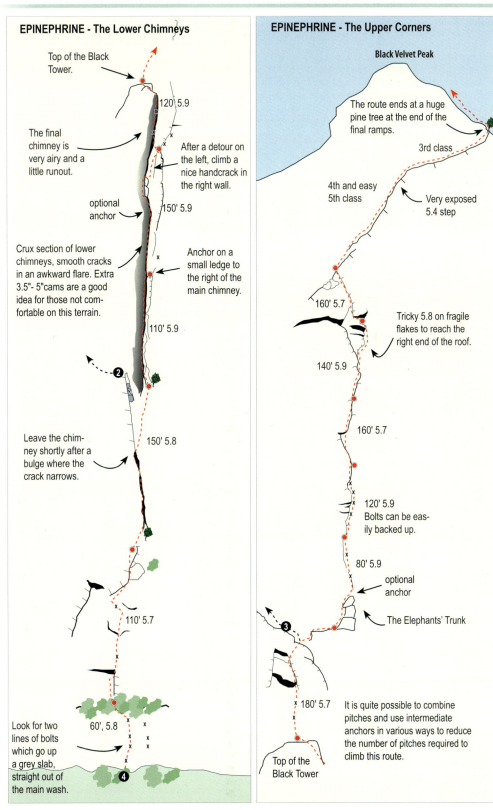

EPINEPHRINE - The Lower Chimneys

Top of the Black Tower.

120' 5.9

The final chimney is very airy and a little runout.

After a detour on the left, climb a nice handcrack in the right wall.

optional anchor

150' 5.9

Crux section of lower chimneys, smooth cracks in an awkward flare. Extra 3.5"- 5"cams are a good idea for those not comfortable on this terrain.

Anchor on a small ledge to the right of the main chimney.

110' 5.9

2

Leave the chimney shortly after a bulge where the crack narrows.

150' 5.8

110' 5.7

Look for two lines of bolts which go up a grey slab, straight out of the main wash.

60', 5.8

4

EPINEPHRINE - The Upper Corners

Black Velvet Peak

The route ends at a huge pine tree at the end of the final ramps.

3rd class

4th and easy 5th class

Very exposed 5.4 step

160' 5.7

Tricky 5.8 on fragile flakes to reach the right end of the roof.

140' 5.9

160' 5.7

120' 5.9 Bolts can be easily backed up.

80' 5.9

optional anchor

The Elephants' Trunk

3

180' 5.7

Top of the Black Tower

It is quite possible to combine pitches and use intermediate anchors in various ways to reduce the number of pitches required to climb this route.

❼ The Velvet Tongue 290' 5.12d ***

This route was bolted at the same time as Texas Hold'Em but had to wait nearly a decade before its first ascent.
FFA. Jerry Handren, Jarret Hunter. April 2006.

This route climbs the obvious left-facing corner in the front face of Texas Tower. It provides one of the most beautiful pitches in all of Red Rocks. Follow Texas Tower Direct for three pitches to the base of the impressive left-facing corner.

4. 90' 5.12d Start up the corner (gray, purple Tcu) then make a delicate step onto the left wall, which is climbed to a hard move back into the corner. (Crux, much easier for the tall.) Continue up the corner to an anchor (8 b's).

5. 60' 5.12c Continue up the corner to the roof. Make a wild traverse left, hand traversing the lip of the roof for 20' until it is possible to pull over and continue up the face to a small ledge and anchor (5 b's). Either rap from here or...

6. 140' 5.11c Make a delicate traverse right to join pitch 6 of Texas Tower Direct just above its crux. Continue up the Direct to the top of Texas Tower.

❽ Yellow Rose of Texas 670' 5.11a

Joe Herbst, Jorge Urioste, Joanne Urioste. September 1978.
Single rack to 7".

This route finds a meandering line to the top of Texas Tower. The last couple of pitches climb the crack on the right side of the flake that forms Texas Tower. Not very high quality but an important route since it provides access to Lone Star and Texas Tower Connection.

Start above a big pool in the floor of the canyon, about 200' to the right of Epinephrine.

1. 90' 5.10a Climb a crack (b) up to a ledge with bushes.
Variation: 5.7 Climb the east-facing chimney which is about 120' to the right of Epinephrine, and just to the right of the start of Texas Hold'em.

2. 85' 5.8 Go up a thin crack in black rock to a bushy platform with a bolted anchor.

3. 140' 4th Class Scramble up and left to a gully. Belay on a ledge below right most of two thin cracks.

4. 100' 5.8 Go up the thin crack to a ledge with a bolted anchor.

5. 60' 5.7 Go left, up a wide crack to a good ledge

6. 60' 5.11a Make a technical traverse right (4 b's) to reach the flake forming the right side of Texas Tower. Up this to a good ledge.

7. 140' 5.10a A superb pitch. Climb the wide crack to the top of Texas Tower.

Descent: Rappel with two 60m ropes. The best option is to do a 15' rappel down the left side of the tower to the anchors of Texas Hold'em and to rappel that route.

❾ Texas Hold'Em 1090' 5.11c **

John Rosholt, Bob Conz. June 1997. The pitch 7 variation was free climbed by Brad Gobright & Cameron Casey. March 28, 2019.
Single rack to 3", double 1.5"- 2.5".

A big route with a superb finish up the wall above Texas Tower. The route shares the first two pitches with Texas Tower Direct. Start on the ledge above the second pitch of Texas Tower Direct.

3. 130, 5.7 Climb a short corner on the right, then scramble up and right along bushy ledges to the base of the right most of two thin cracks.

4. 160' 5.8 Follow the crack system past an anchor at 100' to a higher anchor on a good ledge. (Pitches 4&5 of Yellow Rose of Texas.)

5. 180' 5.10d. The next pitch climbs the long left-angling crack above, which starts as fists but gradually narrows. After passing an overhang the route joins the last part of pitch six of Texas Tower Direct, climbing a steep seam (4 b's) to reach the big ledge just below the top of Texas Tower.

6. 90' 5.10a There are several thin left-slanting cracks on the wall above the ledge. Follow the crack directly above the anchor for 35', then traverse 10' left into the left-hand crack; follow this with poor protection to an anchor on the left. This pitch is the first pitch of Texas Tower Connection.

7. 90' 5.11c Step right and climb up a crack until it is possible to exit right onto an awkward ramp (2 b's). Climb up the ramp, then up to the left end of a roof. Climb the steep corner to the left of the roof (3 b's) to a cramped stance at the base of a beautiful flare.

Variation: 180' 5.12d This is an amazing pitch which climbs directly up from the initial crack on pitch 6 and eventually joins pitch 7 at the left end of the roof. Climb the thin left-slanting crack above the anchor. After 60' pull left over a steep bulge (3 b's) into a left-facing corner. The corner turns into a shallow stembox and excruciatingly wide stemming leads to a small roof. A hard boulder problem leads over the roof (V7), then make a series of moves to the left end of the roof above. Pull up the short corner (2 b's) to an anchor at the base of a beautiful flare.

8. 100' 5.11c. Climb the flare (3 b's), then traverse into a corner on the right. Up this to a ledge below huge roofs.

9. 70' 5.10d Follow the crack under the roof around to the right and up to another huge roof. This roof is avoided by a traverse left on a ledge. Once past the roof a short face leads to an anchor. Leave the rappel line fixed on this pitch for the descent, otherwise no amount of swinging will get you back to the anchor.

Descent: Rappel with two 60m ropes.

❿ Lone Star 2090' 5.11a **

Richard Harrison, Paul Crawford, Paul Van Betten, Paul Obenheim. April 1984.
Double rack to 3", single 3.5"- 5".

Lone Star is one of the longest climbs in Red Rocks. It starts on top of Texas Tower and follows a line through the wall and the overhangs above to reach the base of a prominent right-slanting ramp. The ramp is followed to a huge left-facing corner system. Above, more cracks lead up and right, finishing at the top of the exit ramp of Epinephrine.

This route is a major undertaking. The traversing pitches above the huge overhangs 1000' up the wall make retreat from high on the route a tough proposition. The pitches beyond this point are not trivial.

Start by climbing the Yellow Rose of Texas to the top of Texas Tower. From the top make a 20' rappel down the left side of the Tower to the large ledge with a bolted anchor. The route then continues up Texas Tower Connection for three pitches. Start from the anchor above the third pitch of Texas Tower Connection.

11. 90' 5.11a From the anchor traverse right to a bolt. Make a couple thin face moves (5.10d/11a) up and right around a roof into a dihedral with fragile rock. Continue up the dihedral (5.9) to a bolt and Rp nest belay.

12. 130' 5.10d Continue up the dihedral, then trend right pulling over some small roofs on suspect patina crimps (runout.)

Velveeta

My Little
Pony

Work around a bulge (5.10) and onto a right-trending ramp, then continue 30' up the ramp to a bolted belay.

13. 200' 5.5 Continue up the ramp (easy/moderate fifth class) to a ledge system below a large cleft.

14. 80' 5.10a Follow the chimney/crack system on the right of the cleft to small ledges in the chimney.

15. 70' 5.10a Continue up this crack system (5.10a) for about 30', then move right through a small corner onto a ledge.

16. 50' 5.5 Climb through ledges, trees, and large blocks, to a belay on top of the highest large block.

17. 80' 5.10b Traverse right into a corner/crack and climb this to a large scrub oak. Climb through the tree and traverse right along a ledge to a belay.

18. 100' 5.10a Climb straight up from the belay on a well featured face with much lichen. Follow the obvious right-slanting crack to a ledge up and right.

19. 100' 5.6 Traverse up and right around an arête to a large corner and ledge; belay.

20. 220' 5.9 Head up and right with hollow patina crimps (5.9 runout) and over a bulge with more crimps, aiming for a large pine tree. Belay in an alcove with large blocks.

21. 70' 5.7 From the alcove step left and climb to the pine tree at the top of the final ramp of Epinephrine.

⑪ Texas Tower Connection 900' 5.10a *
Jorge Urioste, Joe Herbst, Joanne Urioste. Fall 1980.

This route connects the top of Texas Tower with the Elephants' Trunk of Epinephrine.

Start by climbing the Yellow Rose of Texas to the top of Texas Tower. From the top make a 20' rappel down the left side of the Tower to the large ledge with a bolted anchor.

8. 90' 5.10a There are several thin left-slanting cracks on the wall above the ledge. Follow the crack directly above the anchor for 35', then traverse 10' left into the left-hand crack, follow this with poor protection to an anchor.

9. 60' 5.9 Make a 40' traverse left; this is runout for the follower. Start the traverse by moving down and left for 10', then up for 15' until it is possible to traverse straight left (2 b's) to the belay.

10. 80' 5.10a Continue up a shallow corner (7 b's) then step right, around the corner to an anchor.

11. 150' 5.7 Easier climbing up the obvious corners leads to the Elephants' Trunk of Epinephrine

Descent: Rappel with two 60m ropes.

Directly above Texas Tower is a line of bolts leading up into a right-facing flake/corner system. This is the line of an old project, The Golden Desert, a stunning climb which was never completed.

⑫ Tri Tip 950' 5.11d **
Single rack to 3", triple 0.6"-1", double 1"-2", one 5", Rp's.

Three beautiful, long pitches of thin cracks and corners, and a couple of very serious sections. Start at the top of the fourth pitch of Yellow Rose of Texas.

5. 180' 5.11d. From the belay, step right to a left-facing flake. Up the flake to its top. Go up a smooth corner, then move left and climb the thin face until a move left leads to the base of a long right-leaning flake system. The last gear is at the top of the smooth corner, a 25' runout with some 10d/11a moves. Continue up the flake system until, at its top, a tricky sequence leads left underneath a small overhang to the anchor.

Variation: The runout can be avoided by climbing pitch 5 of

Yellow Rose of Texas then moving right to the flake system.

6. 130' 5.11c. Go up the corner system above to an overhang at its top. Move right and climb a right-slanting seam with poor protection (crux). The seam leads into a narrow ramp which is followed to an anchor.

7. 120' 5.11d From the belay, continue up the corner/ramp, then step right around the blunt arete. Climb a small chimney to a clean left-facing corner (crux, a 5" piece protects.) Move up, then left to small roof, then climb a right-facing corner to an anchor above.

Descent: Rappel with two 60m ropes.

⑬ The Shuffle 930' 5.13a/b **
Single rack to 3", triple to 0.6", Rp's.

And yet another great route up this superb wall. This route has a couple of hard, boulder problem cruxes with very enjoyable climbing in between. Start below the fourth pitch of Yellow Rose of Texas on the bushy terrace.

4. 200' 5.9+ Begin by climbing pitch four of Yellow Rose of Texas. At 35-40' break right where it is most obvious, and follow a nice corner (5.9+ with thin gear) to an anchor at the base of a massive, sweeping arete to the left of a huge, flaring corner.

5. 70' 5.13a Easy climbing leads up to the arete. Stay on the left side of the arete. Continue on positive holds past several bolts then with balancy moves towards the upper section of the arete. Finish by climbing around to the right side of the arete (pumpy) to gain a jug. A hard (V6-7) boulder problem off the jug is the crux. Climb up into a shallow corner with better holds to reach a two bolt anchor (8 b's).

5a 70' 5.10c An easier but somewhat bold alternative. From the belay, move right into the huge, flaring corner to the right of the arete. Enjoyable, easy flare climbing leads up the corner to reach the roof at its top. Undercling out left around the roof (crux) to reach the anchor.

6. 90' 5.11c Climb up the beautiful, clean left-facing corner above the anchor. The crack starts as tips and eventually widening to hands. The cracks lead to an anchor on a small ledge below an impressive thin crack.

7. 75' 5.13a/b Purple aliens or 00 c3's essential for this pitch, the gear is reasonably good but not easy to place. Bear hug up the tips crack above the anchor, then launch into a hard crux leading to a lurch left to a good hold. Finish up easier terrain to the anchor at the top of pitch 6 of Tri-Tip.

Variation: The Golden Desert 150' 5.12a
This is a wild alternate finish to The Shuffle, intimidating and tricky to protect in a few places. Start from the anchor at the top of pitch 5 of The Shuffle. Move left off the belay (b) to a steep, exposed flake system. Follow the flakes past a blocky section, then continue to a thin crack splitting the wall above. Make crux moves up the thin crack (tricky, thin protection) to reach better locks, then continue up and right to the anchor at the top of pitch 6 of Tri-Tip.

The next five routes climb the wall to the right of the big corner/gully system that borders the right edge of the wall containing Texas Tower. The best access is via the first pitches of Twixt Cradle and Stone, although it is also possible to use the approach described for Great Expectations.

Brian Bowman on the pitch 5 crux of The Shuffle. Page 68. Photo: Tom Moulin.

⓮ Twixt Cradle and Stone 2040' 5.10d

Double rack to 3", single 4".

This is a long, interesting route with some good climbing. It is usually climbed to the top of the eighth pitch, at which point the route can be rapped. The remaining pitches provide an enjoyable journey to the west summit of Black Velvet Peak.

Begin in the wash, below the left-facing corner/chimney 120' to the right of Epinephrine and just right of the start of Texas Tower Direct.

1. 90' 5.7 Climb the chimney (2 b's) to an anchor on a ledge. This is the variation start to Yellow Rose of Texas. Scramble up the gully above, tunneling under a big chockstone to get onto a big terrace. Walk along the terrace for 100' to a chimney/gully, the first real break in the wall above the terrace. Belay here.

2. 80' 5.7 Climb the chimney/gully to a bolted belay/rap station on the face to the right.

3. 100' 5.9 Step right and climb a delicate ramp to a bolt. Go up to a left-facing corner system which leads to a large ledge with a bolted rap/belay station.

4. 60' 5.7 Step right and climb a crack/ramp into the base of a chimney where there is a bolted belay station.

5. 140' 5.10a Climb cracks and face up the right-hand wall of the chimney and around the roof within the chimney (2 b's). Go left into the chimney. Chimney, stem, and face climb (3 b's). Hands, fists, and balancy stemming up the white flake (5.10a) leads to the semi-hanging bolted rap/belay anchor.

6. 140' 5.10d Climb the dwindling corner in the steep wall above. Higher up, the corner narrows to a thin finger crack in a steep slab. A sustained section of thin moves leads to a point level with a bolt on the left. Traverse left past the bolt to an anchor on a ledge.

7. 140' 5.9 Climb a ramp up and right to a left-facing corner. Climb the corner (b and tricky pro) to a resting stance at its top. Make polished face moves over a bulge (b) then climb a short,

steep face with positive holds (b). Continue up to a small ledge with a belay/rap station.

8. 140' 5.9 A nervy lead with mediocre protection and some fragile rock which requires careful handling. Step right and climb the wall trending slightly right to the right-hand side of the right-most roof, where a thin crack offers nut protection. Delicately turn the roof on the right (5.9) and continue (b) up the varnished face, climbing up and left to finish on a large ledge with a rap/belay bolted station.

It is possible to rap straight down the route from here using two ropes or one 80m rope.

Above is good quality, moderate, adventure climbing which leads up the north side of West Velvet Peak. There are no bolts on this 1000' portion of the route,

9. 200' 5.6/7 Enjoyable slab climbing leads up the ramp on the right.

10/11. 200' 5.0 Easy climbing and scrambling lead to the top of the ramp. Head left via ledges, past a small pine tree and on to the base of water-polished right-facing corner.

12. 180' 5.8 Climb the beautiful corner to a ledge.

13. 180' 5.6 Go up a ramp/crack on the right. About 60' up, traverse 20' right to another ramp which is followed to a ledge.

14. 160' 5.6 Make an exposed traverse right for 15'. Then go straight up over a few steep steps to a right-facing corner. Belay on a ledge above this corner (0.25" to 0.5" for the anchor.)

15. 180' 5.7 Climb straight up face for 20' to a chimney/crack system (with bushes/small trees.) Step right, out of the chimney, onto the exposed face/arête. Head straight up and belay on a large ledge in a small amphitheater of orange rock (with a "window" through the fin of the amphitheater wall).

16. 50' 5.8 Nice hand jamming up cracks to the left of the window lead to the summit of West Velvet Peak.

Descent: At this point, unrope and scramble about 500 feet to the west summit of Black Velvet Peak.

⓯ Plein Air 590' 5.11a

Double cams to 7", triple to 1.25".

A burly and sustained variation to the left of the big chimney of pitches 5 & 6 of the previous route. Start by climbing the first four pitches of Twixt Cradle and Stone.

5. 120' 5.10d From the belay at the base of the chimney, climb the impressive offwidth crack through the large roof and continue up jam cracks and a pod to a hanging, 2-bolt belay.

6. 160' 5.10b Continue up the crack system past a small roof. Thin cracks and varnished face climbing (3 b's) lead to a comfortable ledge with an anchor.

7. 140' 5.11a Go straight up from the belay, following a crack in the exposed arête, which leads into a right-facing, right-slanting, V-shaped crux corner with ultra-slick black varnish on its right-hand side. A delicate traverse leads to the right side of the white overhang, after which a stance with a 2-bolt belay/rap station is reached.

8. 130' 5.9 Go straight up double cracks which are steep, varnished, and incipient. Step right and follow parallel thin cracks to a roof, above which easier climbing leads up and left to a large ledge with a 2-bolt rap/belay station.

⓰ Velvet Revolver 950' 5.11b ★★

Tom Moulin, Rob Dezonia. November 2006.
Single rack to 4", doubles 0.4"- 0.75".

This is a very good route, taking a direct line up the impressive wall to the right of the chimneys of Twixt Cradle and Stone. The first pitch proper is a bold piece of climbing. From the belay above pitch 3 of Twixt Cradle and Stone, traverse 30' right into a gully and move up to a table-sized ledge at the base of the wall.

4. 130' 5.11b Stem up to a large undercling flake, layback up the flake and continue up a nice finger crack (crux) to its end. With your last protection in the top of the crack, traverse right 18' and move up (5.10b) into another crack and some much needed protection. Continue up this crack to an anchor.

5. 130' 5.10b Climb the crack systems above until a step left leads to an anchor on a 12" wide ledge where the black varnish ends.

6. 160' 5.11a Follow a right-facing lieback, then climb up to an impressive vertical crack. Follow the crack for 60', on better than expected holds, to reach a stance to the right of a shallow corner.

7. 100' 5.10d Step left into the corner. Climb the corner and another above to a patch of slick black varnish. Step left around the corner to the anchor on the big ledge at the top of pitch 8 of Twixt Cradle and Stone..

Descent: Rap Twixt Cradle and Stone.

⓱ Wax Cracks 610' 5.10a

Single rack to 4", double 1.75"- 2".

This route climbs a crack system (with some rock as slippery as a polished wax floor) up the left side of The Mushroom, a prominent, detached tower on the north face of West Velvet Peak. The top of The Mushroom lies about 200 feet to the right of the top

of pitch 6 of Twixt Cradle and Stone. Climb the first 3 pitches of Twixt Cradle and Stone .

4. 40' 5.4 Traverse right about 30 feet (easy class 5) into and across a gully, being careful to protect the second from swinging falls. Belay at a thick scrub oak tree which is a rap station on the descent.

5. 130' 5.9 A bolt protects some delicate moves (5.9) rightward, across the face into the crack system, which starts out steep, then moderates, then steepens again to some 5.9+ exit moves to reach an anchor on a bushy ledge. Continue 30' higher to a gear belay on a ledge at the very base of a steep inside corner.

6. 70' 5.9+ A bolt protects the first 10' (5.9+) of the corner. Continue up the steep, slippery crack to a ledge with a tree.

7. 100' 5.10a Climb through a gap in huge blocks, then continue straight up a beautiful flake that protrudes to the left. Step slightly right and go up through a tunnel behind a huge, well-wedged chockstone. Belay at a blocky area (near a threaded rap sling) between The Mushroom and the main wall.

Descent: Rappel the route with one 60m rope.

The next two routes are further west along the terrace from Twixt Cradle and Stone. They can either be accessed from that route, or perhaps more easily by following the approach for Great Expectations in order to reach the west end of the terrace, then traversing back to the east. Either way, towards the western of the terrace is a smooth, varnished wall, split by a hanging left-facing corner and capped by a big roof.

Black Mamba 450' 5.10c
Double rack to 7".
The left side of the smooth wall is defined by a big, right-facing, right-leaning arch of dark varnish.

1. 60' 5.6 Climb left and up along ledges to an anchor at the left edge of the base of the arch. This can be reached more directly at 5.8.

2. 100' 5.10c Climb the chimney and offwidth to an anchor.

3. 60' 5.9 Climb the squeeze chimney and offwidth to an anchor at a big foothold.

4. 75' 5.9+ Continue up the corner for 15' to a ledge. Move delicately left (2 b's) and go straight up a fragile, exposed arête (2 b's). Step left onto unstable-looking diving board then climb a steep face up and left for 30' to an anchor.

5. 65' 5.9 Go straight up a fragile crack to a large ledge with an anchor.

Variation 4a: 140' 5.9+ Follow pitch 4 to the top of the fragile, exposed arete. Where the normal route steps left onto the diving board, follow bolts along the lip of the arching roof. When the arch becomes horizontal, go straight up to the big ledge at the top of pitch 6. Contrived but exposed.

Descent: Rap with two ropes.

Velveteen Rabbit 270' 5.12a **
FFA: Josh Janes. Spring 2016.
Double rack of cams and wires to 1", optional 1.5".
A very good route on nice rock. Start below the left-facing corner in the smooth wall below the roof.

1. 70' 5.11c Climb the face (5 b's) stepping right to a belay ledge at the base of the long, leaning, left-facing corner.

2 110' 5.11b Climb the corner past a bolt, then continue on easier but runout ground. The upper corner has a long, technical section protected by wires and shallow cams, then at the top step right onto the arête and head up to an anchor on a sloping ledge.

3. 90' 5.12a Climb the face above (3 b's) then step left to a beautiful shallow crack in a black streak. Follow this to a stance below the massive roof. Bouldery climbing out the roof (2 b's) leads to an anchor just above the lip.

Descent: Rap with a single 70m rope.

Great Expectations 785' 5.9 ●
Jorge & Joanne Urioste, Mike Ward, Bill Bradley. September 1985. Single rack to 3".
This route follows the right skyline of Black Velvet Wall as seen from the approach. It actually climbs the angle between Black Velvet Wall and Western Spaces Wall. There are still some old 1/4 inch bolts on this route, but the anchors and key protection bolts have been replaced. The route is approached by continuing up the canyon from Epinephrine for 5 minutes to a steep canyon / gully in the left wall of the main canyon. Climb up the smooth slab at the base of this gully (fixed rope, or 5.7 past 5 bolts) to the deeper slot above. From here go up a class 3 chimney and gully in the left wall of the slot to the base of the wall. 1¼ hours. The route goes up a broad, white tower, a featured wall and finally the prominent right-facing corner at the top of the wall.

1. 165' 5.7 From the gully, traverse horizontally right on ledges to a bolt. Go straight up (2 b's) to an obvious flake system. Follow this past an anchor to the top of the white Tower.

2. 130' 5.7 Traverse 20' left to a bolt. Go up the face above (7 b's) to an anchor.

3. 140' 5.8 Continue up the face (5 b's) to an anchor.

4. 110' 5.7 Traverse 10' left to a crack. Climb this to its end, where the wall steepens. Continue (6 b's) to an anchor.

5. 130' 5.8 Move right into a shallow trough (b) and go up corners and chimneys (b) to an anchor in a cave.

6. 110' 5.9 Climb the face to the right of the cave (7 b's) staying to the right of the large right-facing corner mentioned in the introduction.

Variation: 5.10a From the cave exit to the left and climb up to the right-facing corner. Up this to the anchor.

Descent: Rappel with two 60m ropes.

WESTERN SPACES WALL

This remote wall is actually the north face of Black Velvet Peak. It is an impressive wall, with a lot of black varnish and some good climbing. These routes have seen very few ascents, and you can expect plenty of fragile edges and the occasional loose block. The wall faces almost due north and gets no sun, however, it is surprisingly sheltered from the wind.

Approach: A time consuming and strenuous approach, which includes some mandatory passages of hand-over-handing up rotten fixed ropes. This wall is approached by continuing up the canyon from Epinephrine for 5 minutes to a steep canyon/ gully in the left wall of the main canyon. Climb up the smooth slab (5.7 (5 b's), or fixed rope) into the base of this gully. Continue up the deeper slot canyon above, with a lot of 4th class, and using several fixed ropes to pass various blockages. Eventually, it is possible to gain slabs to the right of the gully and follow these to the base of the wall. 1.5 miles, 1000' elevation gain, 1½-2 hours.

The routes are described from left to right.

The first route starts on top of a large boulder which is the last blockage in the approach gully.

❶ Tranquility Base 560' 5.10c
Dave Wonderly, Warren Egbert. 1989.
Single rack to 4".
1. 110' 5.10c From the top of the boulder, face climb up to a bolt, then move left to a ledge. Continue (2 b's) to a roof. Move left around the roof and continue to an anchor.
2. 70' 5.7 Move right into a right-facing corner which is followed to a ledge at its top.
3. 90' 5.10c From the right side of the ledge, climb the wall (2 b's) to a ledge. Climb the wall above (b) to reach a crack which is followed to a belay just below where the crack branches.
4. 80' 5.10c Follow the right branch of the crack to reach the base of an arete. Continue up the left side of the arete (3 b's) and belay in a small alcove.
5. 120' 5.10a Continue up the left-leaning crack which leads up past a small tree to a big ledge.
6. 90' 5.9 From the left side of the ledge, climb up to reach a crack. Climb the crack to a belay where another crack comes in from the right. 4th class up the gully above to the top.

100 feet above the base of the cliff is a huge arch. The next route finds a line up the wall to the left of the arch, climbing an obvious, huge left-facing corner on its fourth pitch.

❷ Desert Solitude 560' 5.10c
Dave Wonderly, Warren Egbert. 1989.
Single rack to 4".
Start on a ledge which leads out left from below the left end of the arch. There is a belay bolt at the left end of this ledge.
1. 130' 5.10b Climb up to a right-facing corner. Follow the corner, then pull past a break and climb the wall (2 b's) to a small roof. Pull past the roof to a crack on the left which is followed to an anchor on a ledge.
2. 70' 5.10a From the left end of the ledge, go up to an arete and around to its left side. Continue (2 b's) to the top of the arete, then go up, then right into a right-facing corner. There is an anchor a short distance up the corner on the right.
3. 80' 5.10c Face climb up and right (2 b's) to a ledge at the base of the left-facing corner mentioned in the introduction. Climb the dwindling crack in the corner, past a tips lieback, to a belay ledge.
4. 70' 5.10c Climb the huge corner. At its top move right and climb a small crack past a tiny roof. Move right to the ledge.
5. 90' 5.10a Follow the left-leaning crack to an alcove.
6. 80' 5.9 Move right under the roof above and climb a 4" crack to a small ledge. Continue up to the big ledge above. Tranquility Base reaches the same ledge from the left.
7. 90' 5.9 Climb the right hand crack on the ledge, which arches left to join Tranquility Base at the belay where the two cracks meet. Scramble up the gully above to the top.

❸ Breathing Stone 590' 5.11d
Dave Wonderly, Dave Evans, Jennifer Richards. 1989.
Single rack to 4", doubles 0.6"- 1.25".
A spectacular route which breaks through the left side of the arch and continues up the steep walls above.
Start beside a small pillar below the center of the arch.
1. 70' 5.11a Climb the right side of the pillar to a bolt and continue up the varnished face above (4 b's) to a sloping shelf.

Traverse left along the shelf and move past a bolt to a notch in the left side of the roof. Pull the roof (11a) to an anchor.
2. 70' 5.9+ Climb the wall (pin+3 b's) to reach the left side of a big flake plastered to the wall. Continue up the flake to an anchor at its top.
3. 90' 5.11d Continue up the amazing wall (10 b's), pulling a small roof at the top (small cam and nut) to an anchor.
4. 70' 5.10b Continue up the crack above (b) to a hanging belay at its top.
5. 70' 5.9 Make a long traverse up and right, passing a couple of thin cracks before reaching a left-facing corner. Climb the corner to a belay ledge.
6. 80' 5.10b Climb the crack above, past a couple of roofs to a belay at the base of a big chimney.
7. 60' 5.8 Climb the chimney to a chockstone. Move right and climb the face, then move back left and re-enter the chimney at a second chockstone.
8. 80 5.5 Continue up the gully, then out right along a ramp to the top.

❹ Western Spaces 460' 5.11a
Don Wilson, Dave Wonderly, Warren Egbert. March 1989.
Single rack to 3", doubles 0.6"- 1.25".
This route takes an intricate line up the wall to the right of the arch. Start from a small ledge 20' above the bottom of the wall, reached by scrambling around from the right.
1. 110' 5.10a From the left end of the ledge, climb a shallow right-facing corner. At its top move left to a ledge and pull past a short awkward wall to a bolt. Continue to an anchor.
2. 130' 5.10c Climb up and right across the varnished wall (b) to reach a thin crack. Climb the crack, then make an airy traverse left and climb a thin crack to an anchor on the left.
3. 100' 5.9 Wander up the face and cracks above, eventually moving right to an anchor below an impressive thin crack in a shallow groove system.
4. 120' 5.11a Climb the thin crack (b) to an anchor.
Descent: Rappel with two ropes.

At the right end of the wall is a right-slanting finger crack in varnished rock, the line of Mr. Natural of the Desert.

❺ Black Sun 500' 5.10c
Warren Egbert, Dave Wonderly. 1989.
Double rack to 1", Single rack 1.25"- 4".
Start just to the left of Mr. Natural, beside some bushes.
1. 110' 5.10c Climb a right-facing corner and the face above (2 b's) to an anchor on a ledge.
2. 100' 5.10a Climb a thin crack on the right. Continue up the face above, then go over a roof and move right (b) to a belay at the base of a chimney. Large cams for the belay.
3. 90' 5.9 Climb the chimney to a chockstone. Climb the crack to its left and continue to a belay below a roof.
4. 100' 5.10c Climb over the roof and move up and right into a left-facing corner. Climb the corner to a belay just above a section of swiss cheese rock.
5. 100' 5.6 Continue up the corner to the top.

❻ Mr. Natural of the Desert 150' 5.10d *
Warren Egbert, Dave Wonderly. 1989.
A nice finger crack but it's necky to reach it. The route starts with a right-facing corner. At its top move right into the long right-leaning finger crack which is climbed to an anchor.

CORDUROY RIDGE

This is the name of the formation that splits the upper reaches of the south fork of Black Velvet Canyon. A route has been climbed on the left side of the ridge starting at the top of the smooth slab with a fixed rope, at the base of the ridge. This is the slab that must be climbed to approach the Western Spaces Wall. The next route is several hundred yards further up the main wash.

Sick for Toys 450' 5.10d **

Jorge and Joanne Urioste climbed the first two pitches in 1982 and climbed the currently described first pitch in 9/06. Brad Stewart and Danny Meyers climbed pitches 3 and 4 in 1988.
Single rack to 2", Rp's.

This route climbs a series of thin cracks up the large slab on the left hand side of the main wash about 600 yards west of Epinephrine. It is an enjoyable and well-protected route, and one of the few true slab climbs in Red Rocks.

About 100 feet above the wash is a pair of dark-colored overhangs that extend across the wall and taper towards the right. Underneath these is a smaller, white overhang shaped like a shallow inverted V. Near the right edge of this white overhang is a scrub oak. Begin directly below this scrub oak.

1. 150' 5.10d Difficult face climbing (3 b's) leads to the scrub oak. Above the scrub oak, head up and slightly left and climb through a series of overlaps (2 b's and mid-sized cams) to reach a crack system which is followed up and slightly right to a belay platform with 3 bolts.

1a. 90' 5.9 An easier alternative first pitch. Starts to the right of some overlaps at the base of the slab. Make a few tricky moves off the ground, then head right then up, before making a long traverse back left, below the overlaps. Climb over the roofs to an anchor on a ledge.

2. 120' 5.8 Follow a long crack up and right to an anchor.

3. 80' 5.10b Climb the face (2 b's) to a roof. Move around the left side of the roof to a ledge. Continue up the face (2 b's) then head right into a right-facing corner which is followed to an anchor.

4. 160' 5.10d Climb the right-arching corner above to a bolt. Continue to an overlap which is climbed on its left side. Follow the cracks above and when they end, make hard friction moves (crux) past a bolt, then continue more easily to an anchor. **Descent:** Rappel with two ropes.

The Bald and the Beautiful 90' 5.12b *

Opposite, and about 100 yards downstream from Sick for Toys is a very steep cliff about 200 feet above the canyon floor. The cliff is reached by awkward 5th class scrambling leading up and right from the wash to a terrace which is followed right again to the base of the wall. This route climbs a striking thin crack in a shallow corner system on the right side of the cliff.

BURLAP BUTTRESS

Burlap Buttress is the large formation which divides Black Velvet Canyon into a deep south fork and a short north fork. It actually consists of two buttresses, one facing south towards the Black Velvet Wall and the other facing eastwards towards the entrance to the canyon. The most popular climb by far is Arrow Place. K-Day is an obscure but classic hard route.

Descent: From the summit of the formation follow the long ridge to the west eventually going down into the south fork of Black Velvet Canyon. Descents into the north fork have also been reported, but the south fork is probably the safest bet. Both these walls get early morning sun in the winter months and can provide a haven of warmth when the rest of the canyon is cold and windy.

BURLAP BUTTRESS
Burlap South
Burlap East

Burlap – South

The next seven routes are on the wall directly across from the Black Velvet Wall. This wall faces south and is quite sheltered and sunny. A good alternative if the Velvet Wall is too cold.

Approach: From the parking area walk towards the canyon on a rough road. When the road swings south, continue straight, on a good trail. Eventually the trail splits, with one branch heading down into the wash on the right and the other heading up the hill on the left. Head down into the wash and follow it all the way into the canyon until underneath the Velvet Wall. From the wash scramble up the hillside on the right to the base of the wall. 1 mile, 600' elevation gain, 40 minutes.

❶ Brown 300' 5.11d
Single rack to 2".
This route starts at the top of a broken bushy ramp on the left side of the face. Climb up 60' to a ledge, then traverse right to an anchor at the base of a steep corner system.
1. 140' 5.11d Climb a right-facing corner, then continue up the face (crux) to a left-facing corner, which is climbed (friable) to a ledge at its top (8 b's).
2. 60' 5.9 The white seam above is un-climbed. Traverse right to a corner which is climbed to a big ledge. Anchor at the base of the big arete on the left.
3. 100' 5.10c The face to the right of the arete leads to an anchor on top (2 b's).
Descent: Rappel with two ropes.

❷ Kidney Pie 600' 5.8
Mark Moore & friend. Fall 1975.
This route climbs the prominent crack line which starts 50' left of the obvious huge white flake of Corn Flake.

❸ Kidney Stone 90' 5.11a
This is a sport route up the varnished face between Kidney Pie and Corn Flake (9 b's).

❹ Corn Flake 600' 5.9
Cal Folsom, Lars Holbek. Fall 1975.
Well to the left of the arch is a huge left-facing white flake. This route climbs the flake, then continues over a bulge into a long, varnished corner system, which leads to the top of the formation.

❺ Poultroonicus 250' 5.10a
Randal Grandstaff, Randy Marsh. Spring 1991.
Single rack to 2", Rp's.
The first ascent of this route was filmed for the movie "Moving over Stone". Start below the middle of the wall to the left of the arch.
1. 140' 5.10a Climb the face past several bolts to an anchor.
2. 110' 5.9+ Continue up the face to an anchor.

❻ Children of the Sun 460' 5.10b
Tom Cecil, Tony Barnes, John Rosholt. November 1994.
Start just left of the huge arch.
1. 150' 5.8+ Climb the black face to the left of the arch (8 bolts and 1 pin) to a rap anchor. Don't stop here, but instead traverse right to a ledge above the arch. Belay below an obvious crack.
Variation: Belay at the rap anchor then climb up and right across the face (3 b's) to join the crack of the regular route.
2. 150' 5.10b Climb the crack (3 b's) to an anchor at a ledge.
3. 80' 5.7 Climb up the face to reach a right-leaning chimney. Follow this to a ledge with a boulder.
4. 80' 5.9 Climb the left-facing corner above, then trend left across the face to a ledge.
Descent: There is an anchor at the left end of the ledge. Three double rope rappels to the ground from here.

❼ Arch Rival 180' 5.11d
Double rack to 2".
This route starts in the bottom right corner of the arch. Climb the arch, traversing left under the huge roof to an anchor at its left end. Pull over the roof into a steep corner. Climb the corner and exit right at the top to an anchor.

The next routes are on the northeast face of the Burlap Buttress. This wall gets morning sun, and often can be a little sheltered when the wind is whistling down the canyon.

Approach: From the parking area walk towards the canyon on a rough road. When the road swings south, continue straight, on a good trail. Eventually the trail splits, with one branch heading down into the wash on the right and the other heading up the hill on the left. Head down into the wash, then immediately cross the wash (cairn) to reach a trail which leads up to and along the crest of the broad ridge leading to the right hand side of the Burlap Buttress.

0.9 miles, 500' elevation gain, 35 Minutes.

Burlap – East

The Teabob 900' 5.8
Mark Moore & friend. Fall 1975.
An obvious feature of this buttress is a black south-facing wall that sits above an obvious triangular white slab. Start by climbing up a right-facing corner to reach the lower right corner of the slab. Climb the crack to the right of the slab until underneath the black wall. 80' of face climbing leads to a corner in the black wall. Follow this and continue via easier climbing to the top of the buttress.

❶ Ripcord 800' 5.8+
Mark Moore & friend. Fall 1975.
The east-facing wall in the center of the buttress has a prominent triangular roof on its left side. This route climbs the crack system to the left of the roof. Climb the crack past an obvious offwidth crux with steep face climbing above. Higher up, transfer into a crack system on the right, which leads more easily to the top.

❷ Yucca Butt 70' 5.11a
Optional 0.33" cam for the start and 3" cam between bolts 2 & 3.
This route climbs the arete to the left of the first pitch of Arrow Place. The bolts are well-spaced although the hardest moves are mostly beside the bolts, with easier climbing in between. Either stick clip the first bolt or place a couple of thin cams (0.33") in the crack just left of the start of Arrow Place and reach left for the clip. With the bolt safely clipped, make some hard moves straight past the bolt, then zig-zag up the arete to an exiting finish leading to the anchor of Arrow Place (4 b's). The sharp arete above can be top-roped from the anchors above pitch 2 of Arrow Place. (A short but fun 10c).

❸ Arrow Place 265' 5.9 **

Dick Tonkin, Jorge Urioste, Mike Ward. May 1979.
Single rack to 4", double 0.4", 0.5", triple 2".

The east-facing wall in the center of the buttress has a prominent triangular roof on its left side. This route climbs the first crack system to the right of the roof. An enjoyable route up a long, twisting corner. Start at the base of the corner system beside a yucca bush.

1. 70' 5.9 The initial moves are tricky and take a bit of work to protect well. Continue up the finger and handcrack, finishing with a wide stembox to reach an anchor on a ledge on the left.

2. 80' 5.8 Move right and climb the long, varnished hand crack in the corner above. When the angle eventually eases step out to an anchor on the left.

3. 105' 5.7 Move right to a chimney, up this, then either continue the crack above (5.8) or the face on the right (5.7) to easier ground. Head up and left to a tree.

Descent: Three rappels with a 70m rope or two shorter ropes.

❹ Three K 190' 5.11c *

Single rack to 3", optional 4". Tiny cam or ballnutz.

A nice, varied route which will become a lot better once it sees a bit of traffic. Start 40' to the right of Arrow Place, below a big left-facing corner.

1. 90' 5.10d Stem up the corner (2 b's) then transfer into the corner on the left. Up this to a rest. Continue up the corner (b) passing a scary-looking but well-wedged block to reach a semi-hanging belay.

2. 100' 5.11c Move past a bolt into a steep, shallow right-facing corner (Wild country Z2). Pumpy finger jams and laybacks lead up the corner (good slots for cams) to a bolt at its top. Continue up the thin crack in the spectacular varnished wall above (b) on better holds to an anchor over the top.

❺ Millepede 90' 5.10c

Single rack to 3", Double 0.6"-1", optional 4".

Follow pitch 1 of Three K to the rest, then move right and climb the pretty right-arching undercling to an anchor at its end.

❻ Wishbone 150' 5.9

Mark Moore, David Davis, Lars Holbek.
Single rack to 6".

To the right of Arrow Place, the wall swings around to face in a more northerly direction. This route starts in an unlikely looking right-facing corner of excellent black rock. Climb the corner then finish up an offwidth.

❼ Shooting Star 90' 5.11a

This is the first pitch of an unclimbed project. Start 40' to the right of Wishbone. Climb straight up the face, passing a small left-facing offset to reach a ledge and anchor (8 b's).

The second pitch moves up and traverses right into a desperate blank corner which is followed to an anchor. Around 13c, the moves have been done but the pitch has not been linked.

❽ K–Day 90' 5.12b **

Paul Van Betten, Jay Smith. 1990.
A few cams to 3".

An unsung classic. At the base of the right hand side of the wall is a huge boulder. This route starts above the boulder. Climb up (1.75" cam in a hidden pocket) to the first bolt at 25'. Move up then right to the base of a beautiful left-facing flake in a smooth wall. A desperate tips lieback leads up the flake to an anchor (5 b's).

Dustin Burd on K-Day. Page 77.

THE MONUMENT

Desert Gold   The Madcap Laughs   Seduction Line   Cornucopia   Lizard Locks

This is the large massif which forms the northern boundary of Black Velvet Canyon. It is more broken than is usual in Red Rocks, and although there are a few multi-pitch climbs in the middle of the east face, most of the routes here are single pitch climbs along the base. The Monument is rarely visited, but there are some excellent splitter cracks for the connoisseur.

Approach: The routes here are spaced a long way apart, which makes identification a bit tricky. The easiest way to identify the climbs on a first visit is to start with Desert Gold and work rightwards along the top of the red cliff band. From the parking area, walk towards the canyon on a rough road. When the road swings south, continue straight on a good trail. Follow the trail for three hundred yards, then cut north across the desert towards the Monument, aiming for a broad, shallow, and bushy gully which goes up the hillside, passing through a wide break in the red cliff band. There is a faint trail on the hillside to the left of this gully, which leads up to a small tower capped by a huge roof split by a crack, the line of Desert Gold. This is just to the left of the of the gully, and level with the top of the red cliff band. 0.7 miles, 450' elevation gain, 35 - 45 minutes.

Luke Olson on Desert Gold. Page 79. Photo: Tom Moulin.

The Monument - Desert Gold Area

C Monster 300' 5.8

This route climbs a nice left-facing corner, level with but several hundred yards to the left of the Desert Gold Area. Two pitches lead to an anchor out left, on top of a small pillar.

The next two routes climb nice cracks on the left wall of the gully that cuts up the hill just to the west of Desert Gold.

❶ Remembrance Day 50' 5.10d

Nick Nordblom, Wendell Broussard. Mid 1980s.

Climb a right-arching thin-hands crack. Rap from a bush.

❷ Cocaine Brain Strain 120' 5.10b

Mike Ward, Wendell Broussard. Mid 1980s.

This route climbs a big right-facing corner to the right of the previous route.

❸ Desert Gold 140' 5.13a***

The roof was climbed by Paul Van Betten and Richard Harrison in February 1984 (Desert Reality). The crack leading up to the roof was climbed by Paul Van Betten and Sal Mamusia in April 1987 (Desert Crack). Stefan Glowacz linked both sections in May 1987.
Single rack to 3", double 1.75", triple 2.5".

One of the best cracks in Red Rocks. Start at the base of a blocky left-facing corner that leads up to the huge roof.

1. 90' 5.8 Climb the crack in the face to the left of the broken left-facing corner under the huge roof. At the top, move right and up to a ledge under the upper part of the tower.

2. 50' 5.13a Climb the left edge of the corner on the left (b), then step back right into the corner and move up until it is possible to reach right into the base of the crack. The crack widens from fingers to thin hands (12c) and leads to the roof. The roof (11d) starts as perfect hands, widening slightly

towards the lip. Although there is an anchor over the lip, the best policy is to down-aid the roof and lower off the bolt above the initial crack.

The roof crack is often done as an end in itself. Instead of stepping out right to the thin crack, continue up the corner, then aid out right on two bolts to reach the roof.

❹ West Edge Lane 70' 5.11d *

A delicate and exciting climb up the sharp arete to the right of the first pitch of Desert Gold. Start by climbing the corner of Clipper for a few moves until it is possible to reach left to clip the first bolt. Once the bolt is clipped, step back down and start from the bottom of the arete (6 b's).

❺ Clipper 90' 5.11a *

Paul Van Betten, Mike Ward. February 1987.
Single rack to 2.5", a 4" cam.

The corner to the right of West Edge Lane provides enjoyable stemming and liebacking with a sporty crux. Climb the corner to an old bolt. Above the bolt, 15' of technical stemming leads to some protection in a wide slot (4" piece essential). Easier liebacking in a good crack leads up and left around an overhang to the anchor of Desert Gold.

❻ Violent Stems 90' 5.11d

Paul Van Betten. February 1987.
Single rack to 1.75", double 0.4"- 1".

Start just to the right of Clipper. Climb the tips crack in the back of the left-facing corner. After a flaky start, intricate stemming leads past a smooth section to better holds on the right arete. Continue up the easier upper corner to an anchor.

The Monument - Seduction Line Area

The next route climbs a very prominent varnished arete about 200 yards around the corner to the right of Desert Gold. The base of the arete is about 150 feet above the top of the red band and is reached by scrambling up a bushy gully, then moving up and left (5.5) to a platform at the base of the arete.

❼ The Madcap Laughs 140' 5.12c **
Double small cams and wires to 0.6", one 2" cam.

This is a superb short route, wildly exposed and with great climbing. Although it takes a bit of work to find and place in a few spots, the gear is good, and this route is a reasonable ground-up proposition. The route can be done as one long pitch, although the longer fall potential increases the risk of clipping the belay ledge if you blow the finish.

1. 100' 5.11d Climb up through a steep scoop (2 b's) to a ledge at its top. (#1 Bd stopper up and left in the bottom of a thin crack). Move awkwardly left to a small ledge at the base of the arete proper. Climb the long arete, staying right on the edge (3 b's). Above the last bolt, tricky small Tcu's in horizontal cracks provide the protection. After a final bulge (#2 Camalot), climb up to a good small ledge.

2. 40' 5.12c Climb the thin crack directly above the lower arete (good wires and small cams). A wild finish.

The next routes are reached by following the ledge on top of the red cliff band around the corner to the east. About 300 yards past Desert Gold you will pass underneath an impressive amphitheater with a couple of left-slanting seams

in smooth, white rock, which lead up to roofs. The next route climbs the left-hand of these two seams.

❽ Swallows Nest 70' 5.12a
Double 0.4"- 1", four 0.75", one 2.5".

A good crack climb with a burly crux at the top.
Use a fixed rope to reach an anchor on the loose ledge below the crack. Climb a short steep wall (b) to reach the crack. Jamming and liebacking leads to an anchor in a shallow alcove.

The right-hand of the two seams is a project in the mid-5.14 range.

❾ Papillon 280' 5.12c **
1 set of Bd wires, Wild country rocks #4,5 & 6. Cams to 1.75", triple blue tcu's, double 0.3 camalots & 1" cams.

This is a spectacular route up the tall, bulging wall between Swallows Nest and Seduction line. The first pitch is one of the more dramatic leads of its type in Red Rocks; long, pumpy and worrying, the only known ascents have been rehearsed. Start by scrambling up onto the loose ledge below the wall, belay on a big rock wedged in the chimney.

1. 100' 5.12b Climb up to a ledge at the base of a short left-facing corner capped by a roof. Climb the corner, then follow the tips undercling out left and layback up to a stem rest. Continue up the layback crack, then pull over a small roof to a shake (blue tcu, small stopper). Move left to a big pocket (nest of mediocre cams) and pull up to the thin crack above (good wires, pumpy to place, the author placed 5 wires here).

Hard moves lead up the face to a good horizontal, move up and then right to an anchor on a nice ledge. Phew!

2. 100' 5.12c Climb the face on the left (b) to reach a thin flake. Up the flake (blue tcu, #1 Camalot) to a ledge. Continue up the spectacular wall (7 b's) to crux moves over a roof and an anchor 20' higher.

3. 80' 5.11b Beautiful climbing up the varnished wall above (6 b's) leads to an anchor just below the top.

Just to the right of this section is an impressive right-facing corner with a tips crack.

⑩ Seduction Line 80' 5.12a *
Single rack to 2", triple 0.4"- 0.75".
Start on a loose ledge below the right-facing corner. Climb cracks to the left of the corner, moving back right into the corner at a bulge.Climb the sustained tips corner to an anchor at 80'.

⑪ Hand Bone 50' 5.10c *
Double cams 1.25" to 2.5".
This route climbs a beautiful, clean-cut hand crack in the back of a small left-facing corner, about 50 yards to the right of Seduction Line.

The epic first pitch of Papillon. Page 80.

As you walk east on the ledge above the red cliff band you pass underneath a large area of pink and white rock which contains the previous four routes. The next route climbs the first major crack to the right of this light colored rock.

⑫ The Down Staircase 600' 5.8
Randal Grandstaff, Mark Moore. Fall 1975.
Start in a short slot that appears to be blocked by an overhang. Climb a chimney and crack system to a large ledge (300'). Climb a steep left-leaning corner above this ledge, then easier climbing for a couple of pitches to the top.
Descent: Head west down the backside of The Monument, making a short rappel into a gully which leads down to the south.

⑬ Slotsafun 350' 5.9
Mark Moore & friend. Fall 1975.
This route climbs the second big crack system to the right of the large area of pink and white rock. This crack system starts as a huge corner which is blocked by an obvious roof 150' up. Start at the base of the corner. Climb an obvious squeeze chimney for 40', then continue up the face on the left for 60' until it is possible to re-enter the chimney and continue up to belay below the huge roof. Chimney up through the roof and emerge onto easier cracks.
Descent: Either continue up or traverse left to the huge ledge on The Down Staircase and make two double rope rappels to the ground from here.

⑭ The Blue Diamond Sanction 600' 5.8+
Mark Moore & Friend. Spring 1977.
About 100' to the right of Slotsafun is another area of white rock with a bushy gully to its right. Start to the right of the white rock and the gully. Climb up, heading for a left-leaning corner with a hand crack. Climb this, and when possible move out right and belay on the face. Climb an easy pitch, ending in the gully on the right, where a clean corner is capped by a 12' roof. Jam around the roof to a belay. Continue up to a ledge.
Descent: Make two double rope raps to the ground from here.

⑮ Cornucopia 650' 5.10a *
Mark Moore & Friend. Fall 1975.
Single rack to 6", Rp's.
This route climbs an impressive crack system on a steep brown wall about 100' to the right of the gully mentioned in the introduction of the Blue Diamond Sanction.
1. 150' 5.8 Climb up and right on ledges then straight up a crack to a belay below a left-facing flake/chimney.
2. 150' 5.10a Climb the chimney to a ledge, then continue up the steep cracks and face above to a belay ledge.
3. 150' 5.7 Continue up the crack and face to a belay ledge.
4. 50' 4th class Go up and left to the edge of the huge gully.
5. 150' 5.10a Face climb up a varnished wall to a crack in a corner. Follow this to a ledge on the left. Continue up a wide crack in a corner and belay on a ledge beside a tree.
300' of scrambling lead to the top.
Descent: Head down the backside of The Monument, making a short rappel into a gully which leads down to the south.

The following routes are towards the north end of the east face of The Monument, about 200 yards to the right of the white scar beside Blue Diamond Sanction and Cornucopia. They are centered around yet another scar of light colored rock. On the left side of the scar is a twin set of cracks that lead up to an ominous off-width flare.

⑯ The Squeezer 100' 5.10b
Andy Hansen, Jason Molina. Feb 21, 2012.
Single Rack to 3", double #5 Camalots.
Climb the left-hand crack then step right into the flare. Climb the flare and when it ends, face climb to a roof. Exit right to belay at the tree above Chinese Handcuffs.

The Monument - Right side

⑰ Chinese Handcuffs 90' 5.12a
Bill Price. 1980s.
Double 0.75"- 1.75", single 0.6", 2.5", 3".
This route climbs twin cracks in a corner at the back of the rock scar. Above the twin cracks move left and climb a vicious splitter tips crack (b) to a tree on the ledge above the climb.

⑱ Stemmer 90' 5.11b
Rp's, double 0.4"- 0.6", double 1.75", 2".
Start up the twin cracks of Chinese Handcuffs but instead of moving left, stem and lieback up the nice corner above. Above the corner move left to a tree.

⑲ Lizard Locks 60' 5.11b *
Rp's, 0.5"- 0.75", triple 1", double 1.25".
Towards the right end of the rock scar is an obvious splitter finger crack just left of an arete. Climb up over blocks and ledges to the base of the crack. Strenuous finger jamming leads up the crack. When it thins towards the top, the arete comes in useful.

⑳ All the Right Moves 60' 5.10d
Rp's, wires. Cams to 1".
This route climbs the right-facing corner to the right of Lizard Locks. Great climbing but a serious lead. Follow Lizard Locks to the base of the crack, then move around right into the corner. Make a few moves up the corner, then reach right (crux) and climb face holds for 15' until a scary step leads back into the corner. Continue to the anchor of Lizard Locks.
Variation: It is possible to climb straight up the corner (5.11b), excellent climbing but equally runout.

The last routes described in this chapter are found on an attractive triangular wall of varnished rock which is on the right hand side of the gully to the right of The Monument. The best approach is to walk through the desert below The Monument, and scramble up the first gully to its right. Walk all the way up the gully, taking the right branch until it is possible to scramble up and left onto a bushy ledge below the wall. 1 hour.

Huckleberries 385' 5.11d **
Single rack to 4", double small and mid-sized nuts, Rp's.
This route climbs a long, thin crack system on the right side of the face. Its starts just a few yards up and left of the approach gully, below a crack system that leads to a chocolate-colored, left-facing corner with a thin crack.
1. 120' 5.10a. Climb the crack to the base of the corner. Continue up the corner, making a few tricky moves on the left wall before continuing to an anchor above a big block towards the right side of the ledge below the upper wall.
2. 90' 5.11d Climb the thin crack just left of the anchor. From the top of a little scoop, move right to the base of a superb thin crack. Climb the sequential and sustained crack to a big hold on the right. Step up onto the hold then step back left and continue up the thin crack to an anchor on a small ledge.
3. 85' 5.10c Continue up the lovely thin crack above to its top, then move left to an anchor.
4. 90' 5.11a Climb up and right (b) on fragile blocks, pulling over a small bulge. Step left above the bulge and climb a thin crack for a few moves, then move right to the arete. Continue (3 b's) up the arete, past a delicate step, to reach an anchor on a small ledge.
Descent: Move left along the ledge and rap Mustang Cracks with a single 70m rope.

The Rube Goldberg 260' 5.12b *
Single rack to 1", triple small and mid-sized nuts, Rp's.
This route starts on the big ledge at an anchor just left of the anchor above pitch 1 of Huckleberries.
2. 60' 5.11a Climb the thin flake just right of the anchor, then continue up thin cracks until forced to make a thin traverse left to some small flakes. Continue to an anchor on a small ledge.
3. 110' 5.12b A complex and involved pitch with some bold climbing, tricky gear and a hard crux. Zig-zag up to a bolt. Move left, up, then back right to place some crucial gear above a small overlap directly above the bolt. With the gear placed, traverse 10' left to some small flakes. Make a sustained series of moves up then right to holds at the right side of a tiny overlap. The thin crack above provides a fierce crux, then easier climbing leads up the face to an anchor on a small ledge.
Descent: Rap with a single 70m rope.

Mustang Cracks 350' 5.10c *
Single rack to 4", Rp's.
A nice route on good rock which climbs the prominent crack and corner system in the center of the formation. Start directly below a tree which, from below, appears to be at the base of the crack system.
1. 90' 5.6 Scramble up blocky terrain to a short right-facing corner. After a couple of moves up the corner, climb the cracks on the right to the pine tree. Continue over a couple of short walls to a ledge at the base of the crack proper.
2. 90' 5.9 Climb the long crack, through a pod, to an anchor at the base of a prominent black corner.
3. 80' 5.10c Make some thin and reachy moves up the corner, then move out right and climb the face on good edges before moving back left to an anchor in the corner.
4. 90' 5.10c Continue up the lovely corner above, then step right to a two bolt anchor on a good ledge.
Descent: Rap with a single 70m rope. There is an anchor 20' to the right of the base of the pitch 2 crack, from here rap to the pine tree, then make a final rap to the starting ledge.

Mustang Corner 80' 5.12a *
Jerry Handren. Nov 8, 2016.
Single nuts to Bd #7, 3 sets to Bd #4, 2 sets Rp's, 1"cam.
The beautiful black corner that pitch 3 of Mustang Cracks avoids is a challenging lead with fantastic climbing. The gear is mostly good, but very small and sometimes fiddly. A few of the key pieces must be placed from precarious stances.

The Shiny Hiny 350' 5.11b
Single rack to 2", extra small and medium wires.
Start at the base of the crack of pitch 2 of Mustang Cracks.
2. 60' 5.10c Climb the first 20' of the crack, then traverse up and left to a thin, varnished right-facing flake. Make a bouldery move up the flake and continue more easily to an anchor on a small ledge.
3. 90' 5.11b Climb the nice thin-hand crack above the ledge until 10' below a bush, then move out right to a thin crack in the face. Climb the delicate and sequential crack (Bd #1 stopper at the crux) to the last decent hold then move left to the arete and make a couple of precarious layback moves up onto better holds. Continue up the arete to an anchor.
4. 110' 5.10c A gorgeous pitch at the grade. Climb the steep thin crack above the anchor for 20' then move right to the base of the long thin crack splitting the spectacular headwall. Climb the crack to an anchor on a small ledge.
Descent: Move right along the ledge and rap Mustang Cracks.

INDECISION PEAK

Labyrinth Wall

Dodgeball Buttress

Coffin Corner

Short Subject

Lucky Nuts Area

Introduction

Almost all the climbing in First Creek Canyon is on the huge north face of Indecision Peak. This chapter includes some of the longest routes in Red Rocks, on The First Creek Slabs/Labyrinth Wall section. Many of these routes were climbed quite recently, but others appear to be amongst the oldest technical climbs in Red Rocks. There is top quality cragging at the Lotta Balls Area, as well as quite a few good short routes on the cliffs at the entrance of the canyon. Further up the canyon Slippery Buttress has some of the nicest slab climbing in Red rocks.

Access

The First Creek parking area has the advantage of being outside the park loop road so these climbs are not subject to any time restrictions. As you drive south on Route 159 the parking area is on the right, 4.4 miles south of the loop road entrance. From the parking area a flat, braided trail leads into the canyon. As the canyon starts to narrow, these braids start to converge into two main trails, one down beside the creek and the second on the bench above the south side of the creek. This second trail is the most useful for climbers.

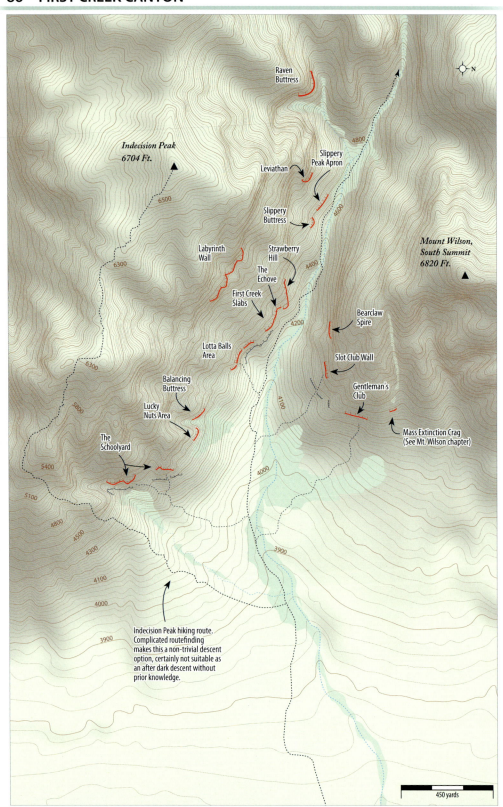

Raven
Buttress

Indecision Peak
6704 Ft.

6500

4800

Leviathan

Slippery
Peak Apron

6300

4600

Slippery
Buttress

Labyrinth
Wall

Strawberry
Hill

Mount Wilson,
South Summit
6820 Ft.

4400

The Echove

First Creek
Slabs

4200

Bearclaw
Spire

6300

Lotta Balls
Area

Slot Club Wall

5800

Balancing
Buttress

4100

Gentleman's
Club

Lucky
Nuts Area

Mass Extinction Crag
(See Mt. Wilson chapter)

The
Schoolyard

5400

4000

5100

4800

4500

4300

3900

4100

4000

Indecision Peak hiking route.
Complicated routefinding
makes this a non-trivial descent
option, certainly not suitable as
an after dark descent without
prior knowledge.

3900

450 yards

Glenda Huxter on The Undertone, pitch 2 . Page 109.

The Schoolyard

On the south side of the mouth of First Creek Canyon is an area of small cliff bands with a few worthwhile short routes. This area, The Schoolyard, was relatively popular as a cragging area in the early days of Red Rocks. It was briefly mentioned in Joanne Uriostes' 1984 guidebook, but the individual routes were never recorded and over time they fell into obscurity. Hopefully, with these more detailed route descriptions the area will receive more traffic in the future. The routes face east and northeast and only get morning sun, but the area is quite sheltered from winds.

Approach: Hike into the canyon on the main trail for around 1 mile to where the trail enters an area of pine trees. At this point a well-defined gully drops down towards the main wash from the south. Head up the broad ridge to the right (west) of this gully. As you pass around some huge boulders near the top of the ridge, bear left for routes near the Coffin Corner, or right for routes near the Schoolyard Bully. The first route described, Coffin Corner, is at the very back of the alcove where the approach gully originates. Scramble to the south across the top of a band of Chinle sandstone to a varnished buttress split by a long, elegant right-facing corner. 1.7 miles, 750' elevation gain, 50-60 minutes.

❶ Coffin Corner 140' 5.10a *
Joe Herbst, Tom Kaufman. 1970's.
Single rack to 4".
Climb the corner. One of the original routes and still the best in the area.
Descent: a long rappel from horns, or downclimb to the east and do a shorter rappel.

❷ Deja Vu 120' 5.7
Single rack to 4", triple 2"- 3".
Fifty yards to the right (west) of Coffin Corner is a smaller right-facing corner. Climb over the initial bulge to perfect hands in the corner. At the top of the corner, continue up delicate rock to a small ledge and rappel from a slung chockstone.

❸ Return of the Jedi 80' 5.9 *
Single rack to 4".
The face to the right of Deja Vu is split by a long, thin crack. Climb the crack to an anchor at its top. It is possible to lower off with a 60m rope.

❹ Improbable Prose 90' 5.9
Joseph Healy, Joanne Urioste, Larry DeAngelo. 2009.
Single rack to 1.75".
This route climbs the very thin crack system on the edge of the face, about 30 feet to the right of Return of the Jedi. A few awkward moves lead to a good ledge at 30'. Follow the crack up and right. When the crack ends, it is possible to traverse left to easier ground and the rap anchor on Return of the Jedi, but this would expose the second to a dangerous swing. Alternatively, make one more hard move straight up and belay in the varnish directly above the crack. A very short, easy, traversing second pitch then gives access to the rappel point.

On a north-east facing wall above the previous routes is a white face split by a very striking off-width, which is climbed by the next route.

❺ Honcho Imposter 465' 5.10c
Tony Thaler, DJ Norland, Carrie Bonneau, Josh Audrey. April 2009.
A full rack of wide gear.
The off-width is a good route of its type, unfortunately guarded by a couple of grubby approach pitches. Start 20 feet to the right of Return of the Jedi below a wide crack in a corner.
1. 120' 5.8 Climb the corner until a step right past some very loose rock leads to a wider crack/chimney. Continue up to a big ledge.
2. 80' 5.7 From the ledge, scramble around the big bush on the left and continue up enjoyable parallel cracks. Exit right onto another big ledge with boulders.
3. 150' 4th Class From the ledge, scramble around the corner to the right and up a couple bushy steps to the base of the obvious beautiful crack.
4. 115' 5.10c The crack begins as perfect hands then gradually widens until you can finally squeeze into it near the top.
Descent: Scramble and down climb the gully to the right until an 80' rappel from a chockstone leads back to the base of the crack. Scramble back down to the top of the approach pitches and do one 200' rappel back to the ground.

The next group of routes are to the right of a big gully which drops down from the eastern summit of Indecision Peak, to the right of the previous routes. Follow the approach ridge to where it starts to rise more steeply up to the cluster of huge boulders. Head across the gully on the right and scramble up through a break in a band of Chinle sandstone. Continue past a higher band of Chinle to the base of the rocks.

The first two routes are in a bushy alcove split by several crack systems. The most obvious line on the back wall of the alcove is a twin crack system splitting a white face, the line of Short Subject.

❻ Dunce's Corner 80' 5.7
Single rack to 4".
This is the corner at the back of the alcove, to the left of Short Subject.

❼ Short Subject 50' 5.7
Single rack to 3".
The twin crack system.

The next routes climb the obvious cracked buttress to the right of the bushy alcove. Schoolyard Bully is the widest, straightest crack in the center of the buttress. The face to the left of Schoolyard Bully is split by a system of three cracks that converge at the bottom.

❽ Multiple Choice 100' 5.8
Single rack to 3".
After the common start, climb the left crack.

❾ Sunday School 100' 5.7
Single rack to 3".
After the common start, climb the center crack.

❿ Pop Quiz 100' 5.9
After the common start, follow the right crack.

⓫ Schoolyard Bully 120' 5.7
A few 6"-8" are nice, but smaller gear can be found around the crack.
The obvious wide crack.

⓬ School of Rock 100' 5.5
Just to the right of Schoolyard Bully, a broken chimney wanders up the face. Climb this, being careful of loose rock.

Lucky Nuts Area

The next routes are on the left side of the canyon about 400 yards to the east of the Lotta Balls area. Look for a white, triangular buttress about 100' high, which is split from top to bottom by an obvious crack. There is a rap anchor on top of Lucky Nuts which requires a 70m rope, alternatively a tree further east can be used, if you have a shorter rope.

❶ Lucky Nuts 120' 5.9 *
Randal Grandstaff, Dave Anderson. April 1977.
Single rack to 4", double 2.5"- 3".
The obvious right-facing flare is an interesting and enjoyable climb, despite some soft rock. Well protected, but quite burly for the grade.

❷ Mudterm 120' 5.9 *
Joe Herbst and friend. 1976.
Single rack to 3", triple 0.75"- 1".
A good sustained finger crack. Start just right of Lucky Nuts. Climb over blocks to reach twin finger cracks. Follow these cracks, staying to the right of Lucky Nuts until 15' from the top, where a step left leads into the final crack of Lucky Nuts.

❸ Critical Cams 60' 5.10d
Richard Dicredico, Larry DeAngelo. 2004.
Double 5"- 7", single 3"- 5".
This route climbs the smooth offwidth to the right of Mudterm, finishing on top of a small pillar. Scramble down the gully on the right.

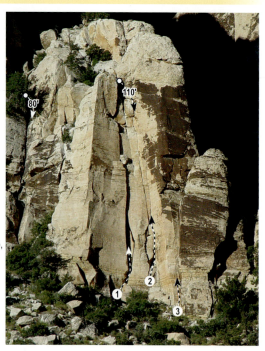

Balancing Buttress

The following routes are on an indistinct buttress between the Lucky Nuts and Lotta Balls areas. Most of these routes are quite bushy in places and have patches of flaky rock, however there are also a few good pitches here and there. The walls face north and, being slightly recessed from the main face, they receive very little sun.

Descent: Generally the descent goes down the steep gully to the right of the formation. Down lead from a platform at the top of the formation via a juggy offwidth. After making the down climb, locate a tree with rappel slings to the right. Make a short rappel and scramble down the gully trending left to another rappel tree. Two rappels lead to the ground.

To the right of the Lucky Nuts buttress is a big, bushy gully. The broken buttress to the right has a smooth, varnished wall at its base. The first obvious feature to the right of the varnished wall is a very prominent crack which leads past the left side of a bushy ledge 50' up. The next two routes start up the face to the right of this crack.

❶ Even Men Out 650' 5.7
George Wilson, Larry DeAngelo. 2010.
Single rack to 5".
Start below the face 20' to the right of the crack.
1. 100' 5.6 Trend leftwards up the face, passing left of the bushy ledge, then moving right above it to belay at the next ledge.
2. 200' 5.6 Continue up a chimney and a face. Belay on another bushy ledge.
3. 140' 5.7 Move the belay left about 20'. Start in a big left-facing corner and move up to the base of a water streak. Traverse left and climb the white face with sparse protection. Belay when the angle eases.
4. 60' Fourth class. Scramble up and right to the base of a chimney.
5. 120' 5.7 Step out to the right and climb a small corner past a nice lieback section. Belay on a platform at the top of the corner.

❷ Goods Are Odd 550' 5.8
George Wilson, Larry DeAngelo. 2010.
Single rack to 5", double to 1".
Start just right of the previous route.
1. 120' 5.5 Climb up and right across the face to a big crack system. Cross the crack to the face on the right and climb up to a belay on a small ledge.
2. 90' 5.6 Continue up, trending right to a belay on a huge boulder.
3. 3rd Class. Move the belay to the right around the corner to the base of a wall.
4. 90' 5.8 This is a really good pitch, but with sparse protection. Start up the wall below a seam and move through the roof. Belay on a nice ledge below a chimney.
5. 90' 5.8 Climb into and out of the chimney placing protection deep inside the chimney. Belay above the chimney.
6. 70' 5.4 Head up an offwidth, past a tree, and set a belay under a roof on a nice ledge.
7. 100' 5.7 Move up through the roof on soft rock but good holds. Continue up the nice, varnished face above aiming for an arete. Set up a belay at the base of the arete.

❸ Balancing Act 5.9

Josh Thompson, Larry DeAngelo. 2005.
Single rack to 3", extra small wires.

High on the right side of the buttress is a clean face split by a prominent crack. Below this face is an area of bushy corners and to their right is a big buttress split by a long corner.

1. 5.7 Climb the corner, passing a delicately balanced pillar with caution. Belay on top of the buttress.

2. 4th Class. Scramble past a few bushes to a belay beneath the obvious roof.

3. 5.9 Climb past the overhang to easier rock in the jam crack above.

4. 5.5 Continue up the crack and through a steep but easy v-slot splitting the top of the pillar.

5. 5.4 Move slightly left and follow the crest of the buttress as it levels off.

❹ Moody's Move 80' 5.8

George Wilson, Larry DeAngelo. 2010.
Single rack to 5", double 1"-3".

This route climbs a prominent hand crack in the right wall of the small gully where the descent from the previous routes hits the ground. Climb the hand crack into a short flare and continue up the crack system to belay on a small ledge. Either downclimb to the right or move up and left to the rappel tree. Rappel with a 60m rope.

Balancing Buttress

Dodgeball Buttress

The next three routes climb the buttress above and to the left of the Lotta Balls Wall. The most prominent feature here is the striking lightening bolt offwidth of Kick in the Balls, which splits a buttress a couple of hundred feet above the base of the cliff.

Descent: Rappel into the gully immediately west of the buttress. The first rappel (3 fixed nuts) is short and traverses to climber's right to a small tree that is easy to miss. Two or three rappels (they can be done with one 60m rope) bring you to easy ground. Scramble down for 50 or so yards until you can exit to skier's left (west), and downclimb easy rock until a traverse straight west on sloping ledges leads to the notch at the top of the Lotta Balls Wall. Continue down the Lotta Balls descent.

❶ Freaker's Ball 500' 5.8
Andrew Gomoll, Sandra Horna, Larry DeAngelo. 2008.
Single rack to 4".
This route starts up a prominent corner just to the right of the left edge of the buttress. From the start of Dodgeball, scramble up and left for 200' to a belay at the base of the corner.
1. 150' 5.8 Climb the main corner through an interesting, smooth, squeeze chimney. Shortly above the chimney, pull left out of the main corner into a left-facing, left-slanting corner which is followed to a small stance at its top.
2. 130' 5.7 Continue up the corner system on poor rock. Above a short offwidth, the crack ends beneath a towering fin of rock (possible escape onto Dodgeball on the right). Belay here.
3. 80' 5.8 A serious pitch with fragile, lichenous rock and long runouts. Climb the front face of the fin to a belay at its top.
4. 150' 5.2 Climb up and right to the top of the buttress.

❷ Dodgeball 700' 5.8 *
Michael King, John Liles, Larry DeAngelo. 2008.
Single rack to 4", double 0.6"-2.5".
In its lower half, this route climbs an aesthetic, curving left-facing corner with an alarmingly perched block halfway up. The second and third pitches are excellent. Start at an easy slab directly below this corner.
1. 70' 5.5 Climb a crack in the slab to a ledge with a large bush.
2. 150' 5.7 Climb the clean corner above, carefully passing the dangerously perched block. Above the block, continue up the corner on perfect hand jams, and belay at a semi-hanging stance when the crack ends. (0.6" to 1" for the anchor.)
3. 100' 5.8 Continue up the improbable face with surprisingly adequate protection (0.6" to 1") in intermittent cracks.
4. 50' 5.6 Follow easier cracks to a smooth, flared chimney. Climb the chimney, exiting right before the top. Continue up the water-polished rock to a belay alcove just right of a bush.
5. 160' 5.6 Climb back left into the crack and go up the smooth, left-arching chimney above the bush. When the arch ends, climb the long right-facing dihedral, which begins as a hand crack but soon widens to offwidth (save a large cam).
6. 80' 5.5 After a few fifth-class moves, the climbing quickly becomes easier, 4th class terrain leads to the top of the buttress.

The next route climbs the impressive splitter offwidth crack high on the buttress. It was originally approached from the top of Lotta Balls wall by scrambling up and left until it is possible to traverse left to the base of the crack. It could also be reached by moving right from halfway up Dodgeball.

❸ Kick in the Balls 280' 5.8
Josh Thompson, Marc Hemmes, Brian Kosta. Fall 1998.
Single rack to 7".
1. 160' 5.8 The crack starts as fingers and gradually widens to offwidth. Belay on an anchor to the left of the crack.
2. 120' 5.8 The crack continues to widen into a chimney which leads to the top.

Several rappels lead down the gully.

Scramble west to reach the Lotta Balls descent.

Lotta Balls Wall

This wall has very good rock and a nice spread of grades, with good routes from 5.5 to 5.11d. There are three sections in this area; the Lotta Balls Wall is the tall slender buttress, the Mysterious Amphitheater is just to its right, and right again are the lower-angled corners and cracks of the Romper Room area. The Lotta Balls section is shady during the winter, but by late spring it stays in the sun until well into the afternoon.

Approach: After about 35 minutes of hiking on the main trail the canyon begins to narrow and a black buttress can be seen at the base of the huge wall on the left. A rough trail slants up the steep hillside to the bottom of a tall black wall, the Lotta Balls Wall. For the routes to the right, in the Mysterious Amphitheater and the Romper Room area, scramble around to the right through some big blocks to reach a narrow terrace directly below the Mysterious Amphitheater. Continue along the terrace to reach the Romper Room Area. 1.9 miles, 570' of elevation gain, 50-60 minutes.

Descent: To descend from the top of the wall, go down a gully to the east of the formation. This starts with three short rappels and ends with some scrambling.

❶ Cougar Boy 440' 5.10c
G. Barnes, Sandra Horna, Josh Thompson. 2008.
Single rack to 3", Rp's.
This route climbs a crack system on the east wall of the buttress. Start at the base of the obvious corner/ramp in the left corner of the face.
1. 200' 5.7 Climb the ramp to a belay at an Oak tree.
2. 120' 5.10c Follow the obvious right-facing corner/overlap system up and right. About 30' up, face climb across a section of white rock to an obvious crack system. Follow these cracks up and left to trees. Climb up and right through the trees. Belay at a very good ledge directly below a varnished corner.
3. 50' 5.10b Stem up the varnished corner above, fiddling in nuts for gear. Belay on the obvious huge ledge, which is near the last pitch of Lotta Balls. Finish up Lotta Balls.

❷ Beerrun 180' 5.10c
J. Gleason, J. Thompson, J. Wilder. Feb. 2007.
Double rack to 5".
This route climbs the long, east-facing jam crack 10' left of the edge of the buttress. The route starts behind a bush and ends at a good ledge/cave with slung block anchor.

Mike Lorenzo on Mai Tai . Page 96.

Lotta Balls Wall

❸ Power to Waste 100' 5.8
Matt & Mark Hermann, Derek Wilmott, Mandy Kellner. 1995.
Wires and cams to 1".
This route climbs a corner in the left arete of the buttress to the left of Trihardral. Start on a sloping ledge with a bolt, level with the top of the huge boulder at the left edge of the wall. Climb a thin crack then trend left and up (b) into the corner. Climb the corner (4 b's) to an anchor under the large roof.

❹ Triharldral 480' 5.8
Joe Herbst, Betsy Herbst, Jorge Urioste, Joanne Urioste, Randal Grandstaff. December 1976.
On the far left side of the wall is a large, blocky right-facing corner which runs almost the full height of the cliff.
1. 140' 5.6 Climb a crack into the main corner, which is followed to a ledge.
2. 160' 5.8 Continue up the corner to a ledge.
3. 180' 5.6 Continue up the corner. When it ends, easy cracks and faces lead to the top.

❺ Lotta Balls 480' 5.8+ **
Betsy Herbst, Joe Herbst, R. Grandstaff, Tom Kaufman. March 1977.
Single rack to 3.5", double 0.75"- 2".
An excellent route with lots of enjoyable crack climbing and a short but thin face climbing crux. Start about 20' right of Trihardral below a series of stacked blocks which lead up to an attractive right-facing corner.
1. 100' 5.7 Climb up the blocks, then move up and right into the left-facing corner. Climb the corner, then follow the crack in its right wall, which turns into a flake and leads around right and up to an anchor.
2. 160' 5.8+ Delicate climbing up the lovely face above (2 b's) leads to the base of a long corner. Continue up the corner to an anchor on a beautiful ledge.
3. 180' 5.7 Continue up the stem box in the back of the corner, then step left around the arete about 10' below an overhang. Continue more easily up the crack system to a belay on a sloping ledge with good cam placements.
40' of easy climbing leads to the top.

❻ Lost Marbles 480' 5.9
Josh Thompson, John Wilder, Larry DeAngelo. 2004.
Single rack to 3", Rp's.
1. 150' 5.9 Start up Lotta Balls, but continue straight up the initial corner and the face above, eventually moving right to rejoin Lotta Balls at the second bolt on the crux pitch. Belay at the base of the long corner of Lotta Balls. **Variation:** a very runout 10d variation stays left and avoids the Lotta Balls bolt.
2. 110' 5.9 Step left and climb the steep, fragile face (5.9). Protection is essentially nonexistent for the first 40 feet. Above this point, the difficulties ease, and a wide crack leads to the second belay ledge of Lotta Balls.
3. 180' 5.7 Step left from the belay ledge onto the sweeping slab to the left of Lotta Balls. Aesthetic, moderate friction climbing without much protection leads up the middle of the slab and eventually joins the crack on the right. Continue more easily up the crack system to a sloping ledge with good cam placements. 40' of easy climbing leads to the top.

❼ Bruja's Brew 490' 5.9+
Todd Swain, Debbie Brenchley. December 1991.
Single rack to 3".
This route climbs straight up the wall to the right of Lotta Balls. Start just to the right of Lotta Balls below a left-facing corner

leading up to a roof.
1. 130' 5.9+ Climb the corner to the roof, then move right to the arete. Climb straight up the face (b), then trend up and right to a ledge. Go up a crack for 10' then move out right and up to the left edge of a small roof. Climb the white, left-facing corner to a stance with an anchor.
2. 140' 5.6 Climb the varnished face above to a belay about 30' below the roof.
3. 120' 5.6 Climb up towards the right end of the roof, then follow a long ramp leftwards through the roof onto the white face above. Belay at a crack.
4. 100' 5.5 Easy to the top.

❽ Voodoo Doll 280' 5.9
Julia Snihur, Larry Hamilton, Larry DeAngelo.
Single rack to 3", Rp's.
Start immediately to the left of Black Magic.
1. 130' 5.9 Climb straight up the right-facing corner, continuing past some awkward flakes to easier face climbing. Up and slightly right, an old bolt protects a face move into a fingertip crack in a darkly varnished face. When the crack ends, a few easier moves take you straight up to the first belay station on Bruja's Brew.
2. 150' 5.9 Go straight up 10 feet. At this point Bruja's Brew continues upward over unprotected scoops; instead move right a short distance to a very thin crack. Climb this, then trend to the right, eventually reaching the second anchor of Black Magic. Continue up Black Magic to the top.

❾ Black Magic 500' 5.8 ***
Jorge Urioste, Joanne Urioste. April 1978.
Single rack to 3".
This fine route climbs the right edge of the wall. It has great climbing and spectacular situations for the grade. Start 40' down and right of Lotta Balls, on top of a huge boulder below a steep corner.
1. 140' 5.8 Climb onto a flake to the left of the corner, then continue up a short left-facing corner to a bolt. Step left, then move up to a second bolt. Move right and climb a long, shallow corner and the face above (b) to a bolt and thread anchor.
2. 150' 5.6 Climb the varnished face above to an anchor about 25' below the roof.
3. 100' 5.8 Step right and climb up a crack into a short left-facing corner under the roof. Move out right (b) and climb a steep wall to lower-angled rock, then trend left to a crack. Belay beside a bush.
4. 100' 5.4 Easy to the top.

❿ Borderline 280' 5.8
Larry DeAngelo, John Wilder. Mid 2000's.
Single rack to 3", Rp's.
Just to the right of Black Magic is a broken face and crack system which ascends the right edge of the Lotta Balls Wall. This route is two pitches long and joins up with Black Magic at the top of the 2nd pitch.
1. 150' 5.8 Begin on the ground under the boulder right of Black Magic. Make one reachy move to gain the face to the right of the corner. Follow this broken face up and through a roof, eventually arriving at a stance, with a good gear belay.
2. 130' 5.8 Continue up the cracks above, moving through a thin section with good pro, then stepping right to the arete. Move through a small bulge, then trend up and left to Black Magic's second belay. Finish up Black Magic .

Mysterious Amphitheater

Around to the right of Black Magic is a small amphitheater of superb gray rock sitting above a nice ledge. This is called the Mysterious Amphitheater. This is a very shady section of wall, getting almost no sun, except in the morning in late spring.

The left edge of the amphitheater is bounded by a large corner leading to a huge smooth roof 20' up. About 50' to the right is a long, smooth-walled corner, facing right, the line of Gin Ricky.

**❶ Straight Shot 60' 5.11d **
Paul Van Betten, Nick Nordblom. 1983.
Wires, Tcu's 0.4"- 0.75", double cams 0.75"- 1.5".
Start 20' around to the left of Gin Ricky below a steep, smooth corner. Athletic stemming with good protection leads to a rest below a roof. Traverse right around the roof and finish with a strenuous lieback to reach an anchor.

❷ Gin Ricky 180' 5.10c *
Nick Nordblom, Randy Marsh. 1983.
Double cams to 4", including double 0.5",0.6".
The long corner crack is an excellent climb, sustained with a variety of sizes.

❸ Rob Roy 170' 5.10b **
Richard Harrison, Paul Crawford, Paul Van Betten, P. Obenheim. 1983.
Single rack to 2", Rp's. Bring a 3" cam for a bolt-free ascent.
Another superb climb, it has been led without clipping the bolts

and is only marginally bolder in this style. To the right of Gin Ricky is an attractive left-facing corner, starting 25' above the ledge. The base of the corner is guarded by smooth overlaps. Starting below the corner, climb up and left to a bolt. From the bolt, move up then traverse right into the corner (crux). Continue up the long corner (2 b's) to the anchor.

❹ Mai Tai 120' 5.10d **
Richard Harrison, Paul Crawford, Paul Van Betten, P. Obenheim. 1983.
Single rack to 2.5", double 0.4"- 1.25", Rp's.
The corner to the right of Rob Roy is a classic trad testpiece, bold and beautiful. Climb a shallow corner to a bolt, then move up into the main corner. Continue up the corner (b) to another bolt near the top, then traverse right to an anchor on Friendship Route. The protection is mostly good, although sometimes spaced.

❺ Friendship Route 160' 5.9
Joe Herbst & friends. Fall 1976.
Single rack to 7", double 3"- 4".
This route climbs the large, low-angled left-facing corner which forms the right boundary of The Mysterious Amphitheater.
1. 110' 5.7 Climb the corner to an anchor, low-angled but with an awkward wide section.
2. 50' 5.9 Stem up the steep black corner above (b) to a big ledge. Traverse left along the ledge to the anchor of Rob Roy.

Romper Room Area

To the right of Mysterious Amphitheater is an area of lower-angled corners and cracks. This is the Romper Room Wall. It has a very good collection of routes in the lower grades. About 60' to the right of Friendship Route, the ledge underneath the cliff is blocked by a huge block.

❶ Guise and Gals 75' 5.4 *
Kimi Harrison, Leslie Appling. April 1992.
Single rack to 3.5".
Climb a waterworn groove behind the block, then move left into a left-facing corner. Climb the corner to an anchor on the left.

❷ Girls and Buoys 75' 5.5
Kimi Harrison, Leslie Appling. April 1992.
Single rack to 3".
Start on the right side of the huge boulder. Climb a short corner to the left of the main corner, moving right into the main corner after 25'. Continue to a ledge at 40'. To the left are two corners. Climb either corner to an anchor.

❸ Kindergarten Cop 130' 5.7+ **
Donette Swain, Todd Swain. September 1994.
Single rack to 4", Tcu's to 0.75". Tricams work well in the pockets.
Start 25' to the right of the huge boulder, on top of another rock which sits below a roof. Climb through a break in the roof onto a long, black and white wall which leads (4 b's) to an anchor.

❹ Magic Mirror 130' 5.5
Donette Swain, Todd Swain. September 1994
Single rack to 5", double 2.5"- 3.5".
Climb a corner with a varnished left wall, to the right of the boulder. The corner leads to the anchor of Kindergarten Cop.

To the right of Magic Mirror is a very obvious flat, varnished wall bounded on the left by a chimney. The next route climbs the next major corner system to the left of this chimney.

❺ Buzz,Buzz 75' 5.4
Kimi Harrison, Leslie Appling. April 1992.
Single rack to 3.5", double 2.5"- 3.5".
Start below a chimney at the base of the corner system. Climb the chimney and the corner above to reach an anchor.

❻ Doobie Dance 90' 5.6 **
Single rack to 3", extra set of wires.
The flat, varnished wall is split by two crack lines. Doobie Dance follows the crack on the left to an anchor. An impressive line, made reasonable by great edges and locks.

❼ Romper Room 90' 5.7 ***
Single rack to 3", double 0.6"- 1".
An excellent route up the steep flakes to the right of Doobie Dance. Very enjoyable despite some hollow rock.

❽ Hall of Mirrors 550' 5.10c
Ryan Prentiss, Chris Hagen. 2010.
Double cams to 3", 4"- 6" optional.
This route climbs the prominent left-slanting crack which splits the long face above Doobie Dance and Romper Room.
1. 150' 5.9 Follow Doobie Dance to its anchor. Continue up the brittle left-leaning crack above, through 2 roofs to a belay in a small nook.
2. 140' 5.8 Continue up the crack to a bush.
3. 180' 5.10c Continue up the long crack, past various wide and thin sections until eventually some thin face climbing leads to a ledge.
4. 80' 5.9 Continue up and to the left to a crack and a ledge at the top of the route.

❾ Algae on Parade 550' 5.7 *
John Martinet, Jeff Gordon. 1978.
Single rack to 4".
This route starts up the corner to the right of the flat, varnished wall, then continues up beautiful moderate cracks to its left.
1. 150' 5.7 Climb the left-facing corner/crack, pulling a small overhang onto a ledge with an anchor and a large bush. Scramble up to the next large bush on a higher ledge.
2. 110' 5.4 Climb the low-angle crack system to the left of the main corner to reach a belay stance in a left-facing corner.
3. 110' 5.6 Head up the easy crack/face on the left to a ledge.
4. 180' 5.7 A right-facing corner then easier cracks to the top.
Descent: A short scramble around to the west leads to the First Creek Slabs descent gully.

First Creek Slabs

The First Creek Slabs are the huge sweep of lower-angled rock on the south side of First Creek Canyon, just upstream from the Lotta Balls Wall and Romper Room areas. The routes in this section all end on the ramp/gully below the massive, fluted, upper wall; Labyrinth Wall.

The First Creek Slabs have a nice collection of moderate routes. Although the cracks are sometimes choked with vegetation, the ribs and faces between the crack lines provide some airy and enjoyable routes. Furthermore, the scale, the lack of fixed anchors and the complex descent makes these routes feel like quite committing adventures for the grade.

Descent: The upper edge of the First Creek Slabs is a wide brushy ledge system separating the slabs from the steeper upper tier of cliffs. The basic descent for these routes begins by gaining this ramp and following it down to the east. At a lowpoint in the ramp there is a big pine tree. Look for a slabby gully dropping down to the north. The descent of this gully involves a mixture of scrambling and rappelling, the exact amount of each depending on whether you have one or two ropes. Eventually, at the bottom of the gully, exit skier's right to a tree. There is a bolted anchor 10' below the tree. Two single rope rappels lead to the bushy terrace to the left of Rising Moons. A short scramble leads to the base from here. Allow 1 to 1.5 hrs for this descent.

A couple of hundred feet up canyon from the Romper Room area, a slender pillar leans against the wall above a terrace 100' up the cliff. The first routes described are in the alcove to the left of the pillar. This is the alcove where the standard descent from the top of First Creek Slabs ends up.

❶ Smiley Face 200' 5.7
Single rack to 3".
This route goes straight up the back of the alcove.

❷ Smooth Sailing 200' 5.8
Single rack to 3".
This route follows the water-polished crack on the right (western) side of the alcove.

❸ Falling Stars 200' 5.7
Single rack to 6".
This route follows the left (eastern) side of the pillar to join Rising Moons at the top of its second pitch.

The corner formed by the right side of the pillar is climbed by the second pitch of the next route.

❹ Rising Moons 380' 5.5 **
Jono McKinney & friends. 1990.
Single rack to 6".
Start at the base of a right-arching chimney in the lower wall, directly below the pillar.
1. 150' 5.3 Climb the lovely chimney to the terrace and scramble up to a ledge at the base of the corner to the right of the pillar.
2. 140' 5.5 Climb the corner, and the face to its right, to an anchor at the top of the pillar.
3. 90' 5.5 Climb the wide crack above to a ledge.
Descent: It is possible to rappel directly down the route, but these raps are notorious for stuck/snagged ropes. A more

rope-friendly alternative descent is; from the ledge above the top pitch, to traverse east a short distance to a pine tree in the gully; two raps to the ground from here with a single 60m rope.

The Temp Files 1000' 5.9
Jed Botsford, Dave Page. Mid 2000's.
Start just to the right of the initial chimney of the previous route. Climb through a roof at a thin crack and continue to a large terrace. The next pitch climbs the crest of the pillar to the left of Rising Moons. Above, the climb follows the left-arching crack system on the east side of the upper rib.

❺ Sunset Slab 1000' 5.7 *
Homer Morgan, Howard Booth, Dan Allison, Joe Herbst. Late 1960s.
Approach as for Rising Moons, then scramble west to a gully about 30 yards to the right. Third class climbing goes up dark pocketed rock to a large ledge.
1. Start up the corner and move right just above a tiny pine tree, about twenty or thirty feet up. Belay a short distance up the right-trending ramp. This is a short pitch to allow enough rope to comfortably reach a good ledge.
2. Climb slightly left up the featured slab to a good ledge on the left edge of the buttress.
3. Face climb straight up on excellent rock. Move left slightly to a crack that leads past a darkly varnished headwall. A good belay stance is just above and left of the headwall.
4. Continue up the easy, low-angled crack for another long pitch and set up a belay where you can get some good placements in varnished rock.
Variation: It is possible to climb straight up the face to the right of pitches 2-4. Also 5.7 but a little more sustained and runout
5. A shorter pitch leads up to a flat ledge near some bushes.
6. Though it appears that you could scramble left into a broken brushy area, the preferred route jogs to the right and climbs up a long clean fin in the reddish rock. The long pitch ends when you can find anchor possibilities on the varnished slab.
7. 5.7 Climb up about 50 feet to a hand crack in a small dihedral on the right side of the fin. Follow this crack to the top.
Descent: From the ledges at the top of the route, go up and right (west) in a brushy gully for fifty or so yards until a scramble left gains the large ramp system that separates the lower slabs from the huge upper tier of cliffs looming above.

❻ Big Sky 1000' 5.7
Matt Clarke, Larry DeAngelo. Mid 2000's.
Start about 60 yards to the right (west) of Rising Moons, below a tight right-facing corner.
1. Climb the arete of the corner past an overhang with a large jutting fin of rock.
2. Continue to a right-leaning trough which is followed to a big ledge on the edge of a gully.
3. Continue up the gully then move right to a crack which is followed to a hanging belay.
4. Continue to the top of the crack, move right and climb a water runnel to another hanging belay.
5. Continue up a fragile, runout slab to trees. A dirty scramble leads to the base of a prominent crack in the headwall above.
6. Climb the crack. At the top of the crack, there is a third class ramp on the right. Do not follow this. Instead, follow easy 5th class cracks on the rib just to the left. A short bit of class 3 scrambling gets you to the big ledges at the top of the slabs.

The descent starts from a huge pine tree at a lowpoint of the terrace below the upper wall

Algae on Parade

Benny Benson on The Undertone,
pitch 1. Page 109. Photo: Matt Kuehl.

❼ Lady Luck 1000' 5.7 *

M. Miller, Catherine Conner, Jodie Bostrom, Larry DeAngelo. 2008. Single rack to 3", double to 1".

An enjoyable, moderate route, one of the best routes on the First Creek Slabs. Start about 60' right of Big Sky (The right-facing corner with the jutting overhang)

1. 120' 5.4 Start up a seam, then trend right up the middle of the face to a big ledge.

2. 150' 5.3 Climb the middle of the face to trees and bushes.

3. 200'+ 5.3 Climb up and left up the enjoyable face to a huge ledge below a beautiful, varnished corner.

4. 110' 5.6 Climb the enjoyable, varnished corner and exit right to a small belay stance level with the big overhangs.

5. 180' 5.3 Don't continue up the crack, instead make a few improbable, but easy, steps left to a finger crack directly above the overhang. Climb the crack and face to a belay.

6. 200' 5.3 Straight up the nice, varnished face until a belay appears about 50' below the start of the finishing hand crack.

7. 90' 5.7 Climb the face to reach a clean hand crack in a small, right-facing dihedral. Climb the corner to the top. (Same last pitch as Sunset Slab.)

❽ Romanian Rib, left side 1000' 5.7

Raluca and Karsten Duncan, Larry DeAngelo. 2006.

This is a slightly more difficult variation to Romainian Rib. Start on the featured face just to the left of the series of stair-stepping roofs that mark the beginning of the standard route.

1. Climb straight up the face. Pass a small bulge and belay at a stance just up and to the left.

2. Follow the easy crack above to the left side of a large overhang. Pass this on the left. Easy face-climbing back right avoids the second overhang just above. Belay in the crack twenty feet above the second overhang.

3. Continue up the aesthetic crack to a point where an easy traverse can be made to the right. Go up the crack, passing the obvious bulge, and belay in the varnished area on the left. Continue to the top via the standard route.

❾ Romanian Rib 1000' 5.7

This is the next rib to the right (west) of the Big Sky rib. A few old pitons and a vintage 1970 carabiner found lying on a ledge indicate that this may have been one of Red Rock's earliest routes. Start in a low-angle crack system just to the right of a series of roofs that stair-step up and to the right. Follow the crack and face for 3 or 4 pitches, eventually climbing past a varnished, wave-like bulge that extends to the left. Belay above this bulge in a varnished area on the left. An easy pitch leads to ledges near the top of a small buttress. Then finish the buttress and climb easy slabs above to a belay at a tree. The next pitch goes up and left, moving onto the small buttress to join big Sky just below the jam crack on its pitch 6. Follow the crack and the rib on the left for another pitch or two to the top. Descend via the standard First Creek Slab route.

The Labyrinth Wall

This is the massive fluted wall above the lower slabs. A complete ascent of the lower slabs and any of the routes on the Labyrinth Wall involves over 2000' of climbing and makes for a very long day, especially since the descent from Indecision Peak is long and complex. To reach these routes climb any of the routes on the First Creek Slabs to reach the ramp below the upper wall. Celtic Cracks starts almost directly above the big tree at the top of the Slabs descent gully.

Descent: It is possible to rappel Contrail with two ropes. There is also a scrambling descent down the gully system behind the wall. Scramble down the opposite side of the formation into a gully using a few easy 5th class moves. The gully requires one single-rope rappel from slings on a tree and lots of 4th class scrambling. Once you reach the bottom of the gully, continue east and head down the second obvious gully to your left (north). Scramble down generally trending left. This will lead to a narrow gully with a huge block wedged in it. Squeeze under the block and slide down an unlikely but easy offwidth with a large pine tree and a ledge system. From here traverse west (left) along a ledge system until you are at large dead tree, very close to the wall, with rocks stacked around its base. If you start 5th classing up, you have gone too far. Just before this dead tree carefully scramble down to a medium size pine tree on the left side of the gully with yellow rap slings (be careful here). A two rope rappel leads down to the ramp system between the upper wall and the lower slabs. (There might be other possibilities for a few single rope raps that would be worth exploring). Traverse the ramp system to the left (west) to reach the base of the route. Descent from this point uses the standard First Creek Slabs descent, described on page 98.

❿ Celtic Cracks 1235' 5.10d

Karsten Duncan, Andrew Gomoll. March 17, 2007. Double cams to 8".

This is a big route up a striking line, slightly spoiled by a lot of fragile rock. The route is left of the obvious, large left-facing corner of Guinness Book. Start behind the big pine tree that marks the standard descent from the top of First Creek Slabs.

1. 170' 5.9 To the right of a right-facing chimney/offwidth, climb an hourglass-shaped flake up to the mossy crack that starts 30' up. Follow this crack to a small ledge with a bush anchor.

2. 120' 5.8 Move up and left from the belay and climb to a long ledge. Traverse on the ledge to the right through bushes to reach the base of a large dihedral with the spectacular sweeping Shamrock Roof above. Belay in cracks.

3. 80' 5.10a Climb up the corner, using the crack and features on the face. Pass one small ledge and belay at the second stance on another small ledge.

4. 90' 5.10d The Shamrock Roof. Climb up the corner and out the spectacular sweeping roof. Move out a few feet left from the roof to a small stance and good cracks to belay.

5. 200' 5.9 Climb straight up past a bush in a dihedral. Just past the bush, move up and right on steep holds turning the outside corner onto a featured face (5.9). Continue climbing up and right on the face until you meet up with a crack that widens into a chimney (5.6). Belay in a notch.

6. 195' 5.8+ R Chimney, offwidth, stem, and face climb, up to a stance for the belay.

7. 175' 5.7+ R Stem and face climb up, protecting the chimney/offwidth crack to a nice large ledge (a bush can be seen about 25' above through the crack)

8. 205' 5.7+ Continue up the chimney/offwidth until it tops out as a hand and finger crack.

⓫ Jet Stream2 1255' 5.10c
Dan Briley, Todd Kincaid. October 1998.
Rp's and a full rack of cams to 7".

This route follows a line of cracks and corners to the left of The Guinness Book, going through a prominent rectangular slot two thirds of the way up. Start behind the big pine tree that marks the standard descent from the top of First Creek Slabs.

1. 200' 5.9 Start up pitch 1 of Celtic Cracks. When the crack eases off and widens, angle up and right across easy runout slabs to a small pine tree on a ledge at the base of an attractive dihedral.

2. 100' 5.10c Climb the dihedral passing a camouflaged, microwave-sized loose block to a weakness and small ledge on the right.

3. 175' 5.9 Go right, into the chimney on the other side of the pillar forming the dihedral. Climb the chimney to a bushy ledge.

4. 180' 5.8 From the bottom right side of this ledge, traverse 15' right to a crack. Follow this crack (which is part of The Guinness Book and becomes the right side of the huge channel) up past a couple trees and belay at a comfortable stance when the crack widens.

5. 200' 5.10c A scary lead with very sparse protection. Leave the crack to the left and face climb the prow next to the crack for 40' before angling left to the base of a shallow, right-facing dihedral that begins at a headwall. Climb the dihedral for 40' then step left onto the arete. Climb the arete (5.9 and no protection for 50') to a ledge that forms the bottom of a large rectangular slot in the center of the back wall of the huge recess in the upper wall.

6. 200' 5.9 From the left end of the ledge, climb left around the edge of the recess into the crack around the corner. Follow the crack and belay on a comfortable but small ledge on the right at the end of the rope.

7. 200' 5.7 Follow easy discontinuous cracks and slabs up and right to the top at the center of the huge channel.

Descent: Either use the standard descent or rappel Contrail.

⓬ Contrail 1250' 5.10d, A1
This route starts at the top of pitch 2 of Jet Stream2, it is basically a more direct version of that route. The long, left-facing corner system on pitches 2 and 3 is excellent.

3. 175' 5.10d Continue up the stellar dihedral to the top of the pillar.

4. 200' 5.8 Traverse down and right to reach the crack system of The Guinness Book. Follow this crack past a couple trees and belay at a comfortable stance when the crack widens.

5. 210' 5.9 Jet Stream2 climbs up the prow and then moves left to a shallow dihedral. Instead of following the prow left of the crack, climb more to the middle of the face angling left to the head wall left of the shallow dihedral. Climb the steep face wandering left then back right to the belay at the large rectangular slot (11b's).

6. 100' 5.10c A1 Climb the corner forming the left side of the slot. It starts as fingers and widens to an offwidth at the roof. Cross under the roof (A1) to exit the right side. Belay on the large, wedged blocks that form the roof.

7. 100' 5.10b Climb the steep, less mossy crack to a ledge.

8. 200' 5.7 Continue up the crack the top.

Descent: Rappel the route with one exception, the first rappel goes to the small ledge at the top of pitch 6 of Jet Stream2. This seams to have been done to avoid going over the roof of the rectangular slot.

⓭ The Worried Wives' Club 1200' 5.10d
Jed Botsford, Larry DeAngelo. May 2007.
Double Tcu's and a 7" cam.

This route climbs 4 pitches up the long crack and chimney system directly above the pillar at the top of pitch 3 of Contrail.

One of the more prominent features of the upper wall is a huge continuous chimney system in the right corner of a massive recess, the line of The Guinness Book. The chimney system starts to the right of the big tree that marks the standard descent from the top of First Creek Slabs.

⓮ The Guinness Book 1200' 5.9
Jay Smith and party. Mid 1980's.

The great east-facing dihedral system was Jay Smith's first big route in Red Rocks. The climbing is fairly straightforward and follows the huge corner/chimney system for its entire length.

⓯ The Minotaur 1000' 5.10a
Karsten Duncan, Andrew Gomoll. Nov 10, 2007.
Double rack to 3", Single 3"- 5".

The Minotaur is a relatively moderate climb in a spectacular position, nevertheless it has some sections of mediocre rock and is a committing and serious undertaking.

1. 180' 5.10a/b Start up a right-angling crack that turns vertical. Continue up the thin crack and face and make a delicate traverse right 10' to gain the upper thin crack. Belay at a bush.

2. 205' 5.9 Climb up 15' and traverse left into the right facing dihedral. Climb the dihedral to a ledge.

3. 50' 3rd Class Scramble back and up 3rd class terrain to the right.

4. 165' 5.9 Climb up a right-facing corner passing a short 6" offwidth section and up a groove. Where the groove dead-ends into a steep, blank wall traverse left and climb up onto a short step and belay.

5. 40' 3rd Class Step left and through a short corridor to another wall.

6. 215' 5.9 Climb the handcrack up 40', traverse right to another crack and take it up and through a roof. Belay where the crack bends left and makes a small ledge.

7. 185' 5.7 From the belay first traverse right on the face for 15'. Place gear and move up and generally trend left on face holds and almost no protection to a ledge with stacked blocks around the left corner.

8. Move up and then left from the belay and follow a large crack on poor rock. Continue up a white rock chimney to another ledge.

⓰ Tiers of the Setting Sun 1300' 5.11a
Andrew Gomoll, Karsten Duncan. Sept 2006.
Double cams to 6", Big Bro's optional.

Start from the long ledge system above the lower slabs. The route starts to the right of the prominent left-facing corner/crack of the Guinness Book. The first ascent team climbed Sunset Slab to reach this point. From the top of Sunset Slab scramble/ bushwhack up 100 feet to the base of the headwall above. The first pitch begins up and right of a striking hand and finger crack. Climb about 30 feet to a broken, hueced crack with a bush, and continues on cracks heading up the large multi-tiered face. All belays are natural.

1. 180' 5.9 Take the crack to a ledge with a large bush. Continue up the chimney to a right-facing corner, pull a 5.9 roof, and belay on a sloping ledge.

2. 180' 5.9 Ascend the 5.9 offwidth, using the crack and edges

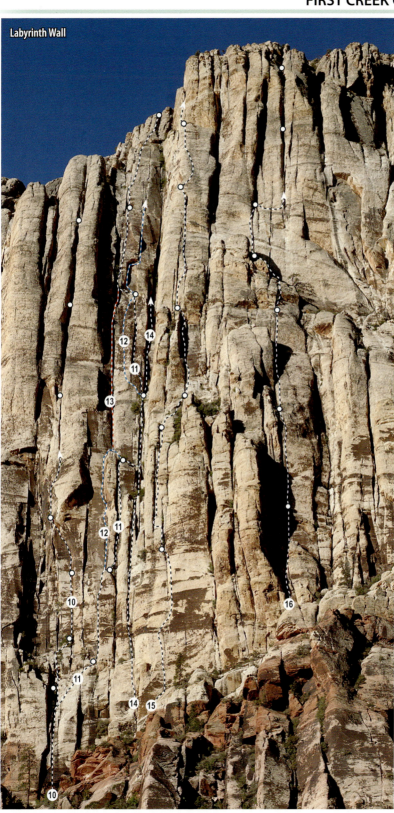

Labyrinth Wall

on the face, to a good stance. This pitch is R unless you bring big gear. Belay in a sheltered alcove under a large block on the left.

3. 180' 5.9+ Continue up and right to an easy squeeze and a 5.6 ramp. Continue up the ramp to a stance below a spectacular, dead vertical 5.9+ hand and fist crack with lots of lichen. Follow the crack up and onto a ramp to the best belay stance you can find.

4. 180' 5.9 Continue up the ramp and onto some 5.7R face on poor rock, past a bush, through a 10' section of 5.8 crack to a large ledge with a tree. Climb some awkward 5.9 moves to get to another ledge 25' higher on the left. The final headwall will stretch above.

5. 180' 5.11a Climb the mossy hand crack that splits the spectacular headwall. Belay at a sizeable bush.

6. 200' 5.10d From the belay go down and right on 5.6 R face moves and traverse right 50' (no pro!) to gain a 5.7 crack. Continue up the crack, which becomes harder (10d) and less protected. The crack turns to stemming, then offwidth and ledges out at the base of another wide crack.

7. 200' 5.9+ Climb the 5.9+ chimney to some 5.7R face climbing to reach a ledge.

8. 100' 5.5 Scramble to the top.

The Echove

On their east, the First Creek Slabs feature a sequence of ribs that run from the ground all the way up to the major ledge system below the upper tier of cliffs. Just to the west of these ribs, about 200 yards upstream from Rising Moons, the cliff face retreats into a small alcove with several good routes. Stand in the right spot and you can hear some excellent echos from the face of Mount Wilson across the canyon.

❶ **The Panda Pillar 5.8**
Ryan Mcphee, Larry DeAngelo. Mid 2000's.
Standard rack down to Blue Alien.
On the left side of the recess, climb the crack system up the front of the black and white pillar. Rappel with one rope.

❷ **Comeback Corner 5.9**
Jed Botsford, Tim Fearns, Matt Clarke, LarryDeAngelo. Mid 2000's.
Standard rack with small cams, including Blue Alien size.
Start at the lower left side of the Echove, immediately next to the pillar. Climb straight up to ledges even with top of the first pitch on Hot Flash. Go left here and make a few friction moves to reach a niche on the far left side of the recess. Climb the hidden left-facing corner until it ends, then face climb (easy) to a belay ledge beneath a bulge with a clean crack. The next pitch passes the bulge and continues up to the huge left-facing corner that pierces the main overhang. Climb this and belay near a bush just above. Easy friction and face climbing then goes up and right to a good ledge at the base of the obvious, tall, pink corner. A long pitch up the corner ends at a small belay stance. Then climb the face to the left of the corner, passing a large shrub. Above the shrub, a crack leads a few hundred feet to the upper headwall (or alternatively traverse right to join Hot Flash by the mossy red dihedral). Until someone does a direct finish, go up a short way then traverse right for a hundred feet to a belay beneath a small overhang. Climb the crack and face past the overhang to the summit. This last pitch is the same as on Hot Flash.

❸ **Hot Flash 1280' 5.8 ***
Larry De Angelo, Bill Hotz, Jorge & Joanne Urioste. October 2006.
Single rack to 4".
This route climbs a tall face of waterwashed slabs several hundred yards to the right of the Lotta Balls Wall. There is a ramp at the top of the First Creek Slabs, which separates the Slabs from the Upper Cliffs. The high point of this ramp coincides with the high point of the Slabs, which is distinguished by two towers, which cap the Slabs. This route ascends the buttress beneath the east tower, and tops out just west of this tower's summit block. Begin by walking into First Creek. Go about 10 minutes beyond Lotta Balls Wall, and locate the drainage (with gray water-polished rock) between the two aforementioned towers. Class 3 for half a rope length up this drainage to a ledge below a leaning, right-facing corner/flake.
1. 100' 5.8 Climb the smaller flake (5.8) located about 10 feet right of this right-facing corner. Cracks now leads up and left to a large ledge with scrub oak.
2. 140' 5.8 Step a few feet right from the belay and climb a blank, 10' face to a crack, which protects well. Go up the crack 20', then climb right for 10' across a blank face, to another crack. Climb this through the lower of two overhangs to a standing belay.
3. 80' 5.8 Diagonal left across the blank face (no pro, 5.6), until

a crack is reached. Head straight up through an overhanging corner (5.8), and exit right. Go right on the white, low-angle wall above and belay in some wide cracks.
4. 180' 5.6 Climb straight up from the belay, then diagonal left for 40' on varnished plates (5.6 with no pro), to reach a crack. Climb straight up and belay on one of a couple of good ledges.
5. 100' 5.7 Go right 10' and ascend a steep face with a splitter crack in varnished, pink rock. Belay before the angle steepens, by heading right 10' to a belay stance.
6. 180' 5.8 Head back left 10' and climb the steepening crack to its end below the prominent roof. Face climb left to cracks (5.8), which lead through the overhang. Belay on a variety of stances in the rock that has suddenly become fragile.
7. 60' Class 4 Go up for 60' to a belay on the large ledge.
8. 180' 5.5 The large inside corner is mossy, so climb the arete on the right (5.5) to a belay stance.
9. 100' 5.5 Continue up the arete to a stance below the steepening crack.
10. 100' 5.7 Ascend the crack through a rotten looking 5.7 bulge (not too bad) and continue upward to a belay stance on the west shoulder of the east tower.
11. 60' class 4 Scramble 60 feet into the gully.
Descent: Use the standard First Creek Slabs descent, described on page 98.

❹ **Tin Pan Alley 1100' 5.9**
Joseph Healy, Larry De Angelo. Mid 2000's.
Single rack , 7" cam useful.
This route follows the big gully/corner system that marks the western edge of the Echove. Start at the same flake as Hot Flash, but move right as soon as possible into a water-worn crack system leading to the big overhang. The gully above is lower angle, but features smooth, water-polished rock. Continue for several pitches, using judicious route-finding to choose when to transfer to a parallel crack system. When the gully opens up into an alcove with an expansive slab, the easiest route is probably the relaxed crack near the slab's left edge, but not the corner system itself. Eventually, the crack runs out and you are forced to the very left side. Carefully choose a belay spot where you can get good gear. Instead of the unprotected slab above and to the right, follow a faint, but protectable, crack system on the wall to the left.

❺ **Karsten's Pyramid 1300' 5.9**
Karsten Duncan, A. Gomoll, John Wilder, L. De Angelo. Mid 2000's.
This route follows the long rib just to the right of the Echove and culminates on the second, western, tower above the First Creek Slabs. This rib is fairly blank, and belay options are slightly restricted. The FA team climbed long pitches with 70-meter ropes and found stances without much effort. With shorter ropes you might need to plan ahead. Scramble up to the base of the Echove, then up into the chimney/gully separating the Strawberry Hill buttress from the main wall. Go up the gully for a pitch and a half then exit left onto the main wall, gaining a clean, thin crack system (2 or 3 pitches). When the crack system finally starts to wander to the right off of the rib, move left and climb a long easy slab pitch with minimal protection. This pitch reaches a right-facing corner system in the center of the rib. Follow this crack system for several hundred feet to the summit. Use the standard First Creek Slabs descent, described on page 98.

Strawberry Hill

To the west of the Echove, a rounded buttress rises to the right. It is separated from the main wall by an inhospitable-looking gully. The top half of the buttress is made of pink rock.

Descent: Cross from the summit to the main wall. The easiest way to do this is from the large ledge 20 feet below the summit on the east side. Walk west on the ledges to a large dead pine tree. A long (2-rope) rappel from this tree leads to a small stance. Two or three more rappels and a little scrambling lead to the base.

❻ Margaritaville 5.7
Paul & Steven Van Betten, Rex Parker, Larry DeAngelo. Mid 2000's.
On the very left edge of the Strawberry Hill buttress is a small, clean corner. Scramble (4th class) up to the base of the corner and belay. Climb the corner and the overhang above. Continue up to a belay on the prow of the buttress. An easier pitch leads up to a large ledge with some healthy bushes. This ledge can also be reached by following easier wide cracks about 15' to the right of the corner. The next pitch goes up the black left-facing corner above the big ledge. The climbing is easy, but protection opportunities (small cams) are limited. A few hundred feet of easy climbing leads to the summit. Walk right to the rappel tree.

❼ Berry Nice 700' 5.6
Joanne and George Urioste, Bill Hotz, Larry DeAngelo. Mid 2000's.
At the lower, easternmost toe of the Strawberry Hill buttress is an area of varnished rock with a few right-slanting cracks. Begin in a crack on the right, heading up toward some left-facing corners. About 100' up, there is a good belay ledge on the right. Continue up the crack above for another 100' to a belay ledge beneath an expansive slab. Climb the slab on mostly easy rock with mostly decent protection for a long pitch to a good ledge on the left. Three or four hundred feet of 4th and easy 5th class climbing up the pink rock leads to the summit. Walk right (west) to the descent tree.

❽ Strawberry Hill 5.5
David Lucander, Larry DeAngelo. Mid 2000's.
The center of the Strawberry Hill buttress has a right-facing corner system that goes up for a few hundred feet. Start in steep, varnished rock at the base of this corner. A long pitch leads to a big ledge. Move left to a small, left-facing corner just above a bush. After a tricky boulder move to get started, the climbing eases up the large right-facing corner above. Three more pitches of pleasant face-climbing lead to the top. Walk right (west) to the descent tree.

The following routes are on the wall on the upper right side of the buttress. From the top of the approach hill, follow cairns up and right on a 3rd class slab. A switchback to the left leads to a ramp at the base of the wall. The routes start from various points along this ramp.

❾ Fine Whine 5.9 *
Paul Van Betten, Larry DeAngelo. Mid 2000's.
Tucked in on the right side of the Strawberry Hill buttress is a right-facing corner system in clean, beautiful rock. Start at the bottom left side of the approach ramp at the base of the corner. Follow the cracks above as they lead to an easy chimney and a huge brushy ledge system. (This ledge system leads right

(west) to a spot where a single rope rappel can be made back to the base.) The third pitch goes up easy rock, following a crack with two bushes in it, to a belay ledge by a pleasant chimney. Climb the crack directly above the chimney until you can move left, traversing across the top of an improbable varnish patch, the straight up to the summit. Walk right (west) to the descent tree.

❿ Rolling Thunder 5.9
Paul Van Betten, Steven Van Betten, Larry DeAngelo. Mid 2000's.
Start about 20 yards to the right of Fine Whine, where a thin crack system rises above a short chimney slot. This is close to the point where the approach first reaches the ramp.
1. Climb the chimney and belay on a small ledge just above.
2. The next pitch follows the thin crack above, passing an overhang, and ends on a large brushy ledge system. Climb another 40' and set up a belay on a small pillar below a dark, right-facing corner.
3. 200' 5.9 Climb the corner, which is not as easy as it looks.

⓫ Squeeze Of Lime 400' 5.7
Larry DeAngelo, George Wilson. 2010.
Start about 60' further up the ramp from Rolling Thunder. Look for a broken, blocky corner.
1. 80' 5.5 Make a face move or two up to the broken corner, continue around a few boulders and go up a slab to the huge belay ledge.
2. 90' 5.7 Above the ledge are twin chimney systems. Make some easy, well-protected moves up to the left chimney, getting into the squeeze chimney is a bit awkward. Top the chimney and set a belay another 20' higher.
3. 150' 5.6 Climb up the face, trending slightly right to an easy hand crack. Climb to the top of the hand crack, and continue up the face to a belay.
4. 80' 5.4 Climb an easy pitch to a ledge. Belay at a bush.
Descent: Scramble and bushwhack down and left (east). A pocketed chimney leads down to the main rappel route.

Under Raps 350' 5.10c
Larry DeAngelo, George Wilson. 2000's.
Single rack to 4", double to 1.75".
This route more or less climbs up the rappel route. Follow the approach ramp up and right to the base of a waterwashed, grey crack near its top.
1. 80' Follow the crack for 30', then step right into a left-facing corner. Up this to a huge belay ledge. A dirty, awkward pitch.
2. 100' Above the ledge is a right-facing corner capped by a roof. Start up the corner, then exit onto its left arete and pull over a bulge (crux) then continue on better holds to the anchor.
3. 80' Climb the thin cracks above, then traverse left on good holds to the base of a corner and belay.
4. 100' Climb the corner and continue up the thinly-protected face above until easier climbing leads up and left to the top.

Country Quencher 550' 5.7
Larry DeAngelo, George Wilson, Jose Tejada. 2000's.
Single rack to 3", double 4".
Start below a chimney at the very top of the approach ramp.
1. 80' Make an awkward move to gain a chimney, climb the corner/face to another chimney. Belay on the huge ledge.
2. 100' Start in the right chimney (the left is Squeeze of Lime). At the top of the chimney, move right and climb up on jugs.

Belay on a ledge with small cams.

3. 140' Go up the ramp to the right and gain a hand crack. Climb the crack to a huge ledge and belay from a tree. This is a good pitch.

4. 130' Go up and right to a boulder and climb the corner to another ledge. Belay on a ledge.

5. 90' This pitch is mostly 4th class. Belay on a huge ledge from a tree.

Descent: Scramble and bushwhack down and left (east). A pocketed chimney leads down to the main rappel route.

Guitar Man 200' 5.10b *

Steven Van Betten, Paul Van Betten, Larry DeAngelo. Mid 2000's.
Immediately above the big pine tree which is the first rappel point for the main descent, there is a steep headwall split by a right-leaning varnished crack. When the angle eases, the climbing gets easy, but it is a long way to a belay ledge. A long rappel (a little under 60 meters) can be made from a pine tree above a brushy ledge just left of the route.

Slippery Buttress

Slippery Peak is the attractive pinnacle whose cliffs frame the left side of the upper part of First Creek Canyon when viewed from the approach trail. Below and slightly east of the peak are some red slabs, called the Slippery Peak Apron. At their left side the slabs end in a small amphitheater, to the left again is a 350' high, varnished buttress split by a long right-facing, right-leaning corner. This is Slippery Buttress. The slab to the right of the corner provides three good slab climbs on high quality varnished rock...a rare treat in Red Rocks.

Approach: These routes are accessed by hiking a long way up the canyon. When the buttress comes in to view, cut left up a short, steep hill. There is a trail through the bushes which reaches the cliff just to the left of the base of the long right-leaning corner. 2.2 miles, 1000' elevation gain, 1½ hours.

❶ Slip of the Arrow 450' 5.7
Single rack to 2", double 0.75"-1.25" cams.

Quite a nice route which is slightly spoiled by the fact that the descent feels more challenging than the climb. Start in a small opening at the point where the approach reaches the cliff, about 30' to the left of the base of the long right-leaning corner.

1. 190' 5.7 Climb a hand and finger crack to a ledge on the right at 70'. Step up to a bolt in a smooth scoop on the left. A few delicate moves up the left edge of the scoop (crux) lead to better holds. Continue up the easy face to a long finger crack. Continue up the finger crack and belay. There is no ledge, but the crack opens up to give very good placements for an anchor in numerous spots.

2. 190' 5.6 A little higher the crack deepens into a right-facing corner and leads to some small roofs. Move onto the left arete of the corner and climb up until it is possible to step back right to rejoin the crack. Follow the crack for another 40' to its end. Step left to some right-facing corners which lead up to a big blocky ledge on the left.

3. 60' 5.7 Climb the arete above (unprotected) until the climbing gets easy. Traverse left on a small footledge and belay. Be careful to protect the second on the opening moves.

Descent: Keep traversing left to reach easy slabs which lead down to the east edge of the buttress. Follow the edge of the buttress back down to the base.

The next three routes climb the lovely varnished slab to the right of the big right-facing corner that splits the buttress.

❷ Slippermen 90' 5.10a
A few small wires and cams.

A slightly unbalanced route with a tricky, thin move past the first bolt followed by much easier climbing.

Start 40' to the right of the big right-facing corner, below a shallow right-facing scoop with a bolt. Make hard moves past the bolt then continue (b) past a flake (gear) and continue (2 b's) up the face to an anchor above a block/ledge in the main corner. It is possible to continue past a bolt in the slab above to join the upper part of the next route.

The next route starts about 10' down and left of the arete that forms the right edge of the slab.

❸ Tongue and Groove 320' 5.10d *
Small wires and tiny cams for pitch 1, Single rack to 3", double 0.75" - 1.25" for pitch 2.

This route has some sections of really nice slab climbing, with reasonable protection for this type of route. It is probably a good idea to stick clip the first bolt since the hardest moves on the route are below it.

1. 160' 5.10d Climb straight up to the first bolt (crux), then move past the second into a thin crack (good wires). Above the crack, continue up the face (6 b's) passing a slight bulge to a bolt close to the big corner on the left. Make delicate moves up and right to a small flake (Tiny cams) then continue up the pretty slab (b) to an anchor in the main corner.

2. 160' 5.10a Continue up the main corner, easily at first. A steep, smooth section has good finger locks but slants awkwardly, it leads to better holds and an easier upper crack which is followed to an anchor on a good ledge.

Descent: Move 15' right to another anchor. Two raps lead straight down from here.

❹ The Undertone 310' 5.10d **
Single rack to 3", double cams to 1".

An enjoyable, varied route up the right arete of the formation.

1. 120' 5.10b Climb the right arete (3 b's) to a thin crack (gear) and make easier but runout moves to the next bolt. Move left to a bolt in a bulge. Pull over and either climb straight up a thin seam (harder with better gear) or step right to another seam and climb that (easier but poorer gear). Either method leads to the anchor.

2. 190' 5.10d Climb the long right-facing groove above (2 b's) to a bolt at a small bulge. Pull over the bulge, then move right (b) and pull around a roof into a right-facing corner. Battle up the awkward, slanting corner, which gradually eases and leads to a chain anchor.

Descent: Two raps lead straight down (i.e. to the right of the route) from here.

Slippery Peak Apron

Slippery Peak is the attractive pinnacle whose cliffs frame the left side of the upper part of First Creek Canyon when viewed from the approach trail. Below and slightly east of the peak are some red slabs, called the Slippery Peak Apron.

Approach: These routes are accessed by hiking a long way up the canyon. The slabs almost come down to the wash and are very obvious. 2.3 miles, 1000' elevation gain, 1½ hours.

Real Domestic Chickens 360' 5.10c *
Rick Dennison, Mark Fredrick, Dan Cox. Spring 1994.
Rp's, double cams to 1".

This route climbs straight up the center of a very smooth section of white and light tan rock in the center of the slabs. A very good pure slab climb, one of only a few in Red Rocks. Start at the right end of a left-slanting, almost horizontal, crack below a long overlap 60' up the cliff.

1. 140' 5.10c Climb up to a bolt at 20' then climb up and right around the right end of the long overlap. Continue up the face finishing with a long runout to the anchors (6 b's).

2. 80' 5.9 Climb up the slab (2 b's) to an anchor on a ledge.

2. 130' 5.9 Continue up the slab (2 b's) then make a long

runout up a shallow, right-facing corner which arches right at the top to a bolt. Pull over the overhang to an anchor.

Descent: Rap the route with two ropes.

The Red and the Black 450' 5.7
John Martinet, Jeff Gordon, Scott Gordon. 1978.
Single rack to 4".

This route climbs up the center of the slabby wall. The rock is poor and the protection and belays marginal. Start 80 yards left of a huge left-facing corner, at the base of a crack system.

1. 140' 5.7 Follow the crack past a bolt to a prominent bush.

2. 130' 5.6 Continue up to belay under a small roof

3. 180' 5.5 The angle starts to ease and a long pitch leads up, over an overlap, to a tree at the top of the wall.

Descent: Traverse left to a slung tree above Real Domestic Chickens. Double rope rappel to top anchor of Real Domestic Chickens. 2 more double rope rappels to the ground.

Advance Romance 450' 5.6
John Martinet, Scott Gordon. 1978.

This route climbs the large left-facing corner that borders the right edge of the wall. Three pitches.

Leviathan 700' 5.9
Karsten Duncan, Larry DeAngelo. 2009.
Gear to 6".

Above the right side of Slippery Peak Apron is a big, pyramidal buttress with a huge pillar on its crest. This route climbs the big corner system on the right side of the pillar. To reach the base of the route, scramble around the right side of Slippery Peak Apron to reach a ledge system which is followed back up to the east to the bottom of the big corner on the right side of the pillar.

1. Go up the corner system.

2. When it becomes obvious that the corner itself will be blocked by a large roof, move right on face holds and climb to a good ledge.

3. Go up short squeeze chimney to easier climbing leading into the belly of a deep chimney.

4. Climb the huge chimney leading to the top of the tower. This chimney is twenty or more feet deep, and flares from very tight out to full-body bridging. There is not much protection, but you can choose the precise width you like the best.

5. From the top of the tower, follow a slanting crack up and right to a ledge with a bush below a big gully/corner.

6. Climb the easy gully to the summit ridge.

Descent: Climb down the easy gully to a rappel station at the top of the slanting crack. Rappel straight down the blank face to the right of the chimney. Three long rappels bring you back to the start.

Stout-Hearted Men 800' 5.9
Larry DeAngelo, Bill Thiry. 2003.

This route climbs the crest of Raven Buttress, a large and remote formation which splits the south branch of the canyon into two forks. Hike up the canyon to just beyond the Slippery Peak Apron. Go up the south branch to the base of Raven Buttress. Scramble up to a ledge with some large pine trees just right of the crest. Easy climbing leads to a ledge below a right-facing corner. Climb the corner past a 5.9 roof and continue up the obvious crack system for a few pitches to the top of a tower. Straightforward climbing leads up and left across a headwall to a crack which leads back right through a break in the overhangs. A short 4th class pitch leads to the large Crows Nest ledge and the route finishes with a couple of hundred feet of third class.

Descent: It is possible to follow the ledge system down to the west from Crows Nest Ledge, to reach the approach gully. Alternatively, from the top of the buttress hike east along the ridge to the summit of Indecision Peak and follow the complicated hiking route back down to the east from there.

Bearclaw Spire

❶ Dirtbaggers Compensation 1040' 5.10a
Shawn Petro, Dave Pollari. February 1993.
Single rack to 4".

This route climbs Bearclaw Spire, a prominent tower on the south face of Mt. Wilson. It is roughly opposite the Lotta Balls area. It has a pointed white summit, a red middle section glossed with black varnish (and several vertical cracks that look like bear claw scratches), and a steep lower cliff band guarding the base. Approach the route by hiking the main trail into First Creek Canyon. From below the Lotta Balls Wall, cross the creek and hike up towards the Slot Club Wall. Scramble up the steep gully immediately to the left of the Slot Club Wall, to reach a bushy terrace below the striking crack system of The Maw. Follow the terrace west for another couple hundred feet to the base of a varnished, right-facing corner. 200 vertical feet above this point is a huge ponderosa pine tree on a major ledge system.

1. 100' 5.9 Climb the varnished corner, past 1 bolt, to a belay alcove in the chimney (1 belay bolt).
2. 100' 5.10a Climb the flare and corner to the ponderosa.
3. 50' Class 3 Go slightly left through brush, then right and up to a ledge below a beautiful left-facing corner (the corner is located below a blank area on the steep face above).
4. 100' 5.9 Climb the corner to a large ledge with a 2-bolt station.
5. 50' 4th class Go right on the ledge for 50 feet past a blank section in the face above, to a black face with 1 belay bolt.
6. 130' 5.9 Go straight up the face past 3 bolts (5.9), then trend slightly left to a 2-bolt belay stance.
7. 150' 5.8 Continue up the black, varnished face on intermittent cracks to a belay/rap station with 1 bolt and fixed nuts.
8. 160' 5.7 Climb up and slightly right on the run-out, fragile face to a belay/rap station with several good fixed nuts.
9. 100' 5.0 Climb up and slightly right on the white, rounded rock to a large ledge below the summit. There is a very unsafe rap station here with a slung chockstone.
10. 100' 5.0 Take the ramp up and right, then cut left, following corners to the summit.
Descent: Rap with two ropes or go down the gully to the east.

❷ The Maw 400' 5.10d
This long lost route was originally climbed by the Urioste's in the late 1970's. They used some protection bolts, but on getting to the top of the climb they found a fixed anchor. In view of this, Jorge removed the bolts, but it was never clear if the route had been climbed or not. It received a bolt-free ascent in 2012.
Double rack to 6". A single 9" piece.

Almost directly above the Slot Club Wall is a tall tower split from top to bottom by an impressive crack system. Approach by scrambling around the left side of the Slot Club Wall to the terrace below the tower. A short scramble or a bolted face leads up to the base of the crack.

1. 100' 5.10a This route climbs the long twin cracks to an anchor where they converge at the base of the huge corner.
2. 80' 5.10d Continue up the wide corner/crack and belay at a bolt in the alcove below the huge slot roof.
3. 50' 5.10d Battle out the offwidth roof and around the lip to an anchor. A real groaner that suites the pigeon chested.
Descent: Rappel with two ropes to the anchor above pitch 1.

Slot Club Wall

This is the lowest band of rock directly opposite the Lotta Balls Wall, sitting several hundred feet above the creek bed. It is a very sunny wall of white and brown rock, split by some obvious wide cracks. The cliff gets sun for most of the day in the winter, in the summer it gets shade by mid-to-late afternoon.

Approach: Follow the main trail into the canyon and once opposite the Lotta Balls area, leave the creek bed and hike up the steep slope on the right. The most obvious features of the cliff are a pair of left-facing offwidth flakes with a hand crack in between. 1.8 miles, 850' elevation gain, 1 hour.

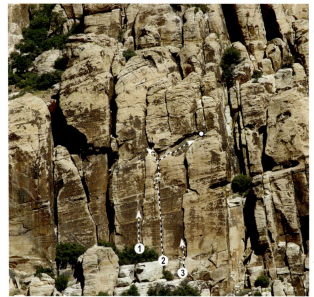

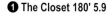

❶ The Closet 180' 5.9
A long, sustained pitch up the left hand of the two wide flake cracks. Descend by scrambling over to the west and going down a steep gully.

❷ Pinball Crack 100' 5.9+
Single rack to 3", double 1.25"- 3".
This route climbs the hand crack between the two flakes. Starting from a sloping ledge, climb the excellent hand crack to a ledge below a small, black, cracked bulge. Either move left and finish on the flare at the top of The Closet or follow a thin horizontal crack around to the right to finish on Slot Club.

❸ Slot Club 100' 5.10a *
Single rack to 3.5", double 3.5"- 7".
A good route which climbs the right hand of the two flakes, on nice, varnished rock. The crux is an awkward move around a nose at 50', but the route finishes with a poorly-protected 5.9 flare. The route ends on a sloping ledge with fixed anchors.

Robert Fielding on pitch 5 of Gift of the Wind Gods. Page 124.

Mount Wilson - East Face

Introduction

The huge east Face of Mount Wilson is described as a separate entity in this book, rather than including the routes in the sections for the adjacent canyons, First Creek to the south and Oak Creek to the north. Mount Wilson contains many of the longest routes in Red Rocks, which also include very long approaches and descents. Many of these routes have the feel and scale of alpine routes and should be considered serious undertakings.

Access

Generally the routes are approached from one of various points along Route 159, or the Oak Creek Trailhead parking area, which is accessed off the loop road. The best option depends on which route you are doing and what descent you choose to follow.

Descent options

Some of the routes on Mt. Wilson allow for the option of a rappel descent, in which case just rappel your route and reverse the approach. For routes that go to the summit there are two descent options, which one makes most sense depends on a variety of factors.

First Creek Descent: From the summit descend the easy ridge westwards to reach the limestone in 20-30 minutes. From here, scramble down easy slabs and gullies to the south to reach the upper part of First Creek Canyon. The descent of First Creek is easy to follow but a little bushy towards the top, and involves endless boulder hopping until the bottom of the canyon is reached. Tiring and tedious, but safe. This descent is very straightforward and easy to follow and is seldom ice or snow covered. 3 hrs.

Oak Creek Descent: When done correctly this descent is faster and less tiring than the First Creek descent. However it is also harder to find, in particular descending to the north too early usually results in an epic. Also, these north-facing slopes and gullies tend to hold snow and ice and are best avoided in colder weather.
From the summit, descend the easy ridge westwards towards the limestone. When close to the limestone, drop off to the north following gentle slopes down to reach a

grove of ponderosa pine trees nestled in a slot. The ponderosa grove is just to the east of an obvious curving sandstone ridge which swoops down to the north, this is the last sandstone ridge before the limestone. From the ponderosa stand, go down and north into a small drainage. Go down the drainage for a few minutes to reach an open area with a red tower that has a rock balanced on top. Traverse around the right (north) side of that tower then back left onto steep, waterworn, multicolored slabs. Weave down these slabs into the start of the South fork of Oak creek. The upper section has some cliff bands which can mostly be avoided. Two sections that can't be avoided have anchors and/or fixed rope to hand over hand down. Once the main canyon is reached, boulder hopping leads to the hiking trail at the entrance to the canyon. 2.5 hrs.

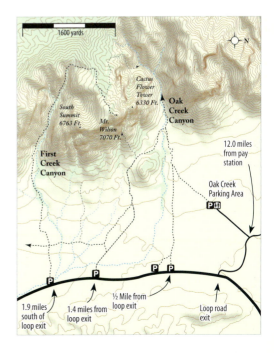

The Gentleman's Club

Below the Aztec Sandstone rocks on the southeastern corner of the east face of Mount Wilson is a long band of pink Chinle sandstone. Most of the Chinle sandstone in Red Rocks is rather loose, and this crag is no exception. The rock is soft, sandy and, in places, dangerously blocky. Despite these negatives, the cliff is split by a collection of moderate cracks, many of which are quite pure and smooth-walled, something that is quite rare in Red rocks. The routes were mostly the work of

Andrew Gomoll and Karsten Duncan in the fall of 2007. The cliff faces southeast and receives sun until early afternoon. It sits in a small hollow and is quite sheltered from wind.

Approach: Start at the First Creek trailhead. Hike along the main First Creek Trail for 20 minutes, to a large grove of trees beside the creek. Cross the creek and head up a broad, shallow gully to the cliff. 1.6 miles, 750' elevation gain, 40 minutes.

❶ Ladies Drink Free 40' 5.8
Single rack to 3".
Climb a nice hand crack to a tricky finish. The route ends at a prominent tree.

❷ Play it again Sams 35' 5.9+
Single rack to 6".
Climb the offwidth to the right of the previous route. At the top, traverse left to the tree.

The next route start under a smaller tree about 40' to the right of the previous routes.

❸ The Chicken Ranch 30' 5.6
Single rack to 3".
Climb the widening corner/crack below the tree.

To the right of the previous route is a pair of short, splitter hand cracks in good, varnished rock.

❹ Spearmint Rhino 30' 5.8
Single rack to 3".
Climb the crack on the left.

❺ Rick's Tally Ho 30' 5.8
Single rack to 3".
Climb the crack on the right.

About 20' to the right is a grubby chimney.

❻ Happy Ending 30' 5.9+
Single rack to 1.75".
Climb the thin crack just to the left of the chimney.

❼ Back Alley 35' 5.5
Single rack to 4".
Climb the chimney.

❽ Silicone Sag 30' 5.7 (Tr.)
The loose and dirty chimney to the right of the previous route.

About 30' to the right is a straight-in fist crack.

❾ Male Revue 30' 5.9
Single rack to 4".
Climb the fist crack to a tree.

❿ Coyote Ugly 30' 5.8+
Single rack to 4".
Climb the hand crack to the right. Belay at the same tree.

⓫ Lap Dance 30' 5.8
Single rack to 3".
Start 30' to the right of the previous route. Climb a hand crack which eventually widens to offwidth and finishes in a flare.

⓬ Web Cam Delight 30' 5.8
Single rack to 3".
Start 8' to the right of Lap Dance. Climb the widening crack.

⓭ Champagne Room 35' 5.9
Single rack to 6".
Start up the wide, right-leaning crack a few feet to the right of the previous route. After a mantle onto a ledge the route finishes up a finger crack.

⓮ Adult Superstore 35' 5.9+
Single rack to 4".
Close to the right end of the cliffband is a deep gash with twin cracks in the back. Climb the cracks, exiting through a tunnel to a tree belay at the top.

Mass Extinction Crag

This is the huge overhanging block at the base of the southernmost of the deep gullies on the east face of Mount Wilson, i.e. the gully to the left of the Blue Diamond Ridge approach gully. It is somewhat unique in that it contains a collection of wildly overhanging routes with natural protection. The climbs face northeast and get shade from mid-morning on.

Approach: Start at the First Creek trailhead. Hike along the main First Creek Trail for 20 minutes, to a large grove of trees beside the creek. Cross the creek and head towards a broad ridge which leads up towards a deep gully in the east face of Mount Wilson. The block is perched on the steep hillside just to the south (left) of the entrance to the gully and just to the right of a long band of Chinle Sandstone.
1.7 miles, 800' elevation gain, 40 minutes.

The routes are described from left to right starting on the left arete of the block.

Fossil Record 50' 5.11c *
Single rack to 1.75".
Start around to the left of the left arete. Pull onto a short ramp, then reach up to a flake which leads left (b) to a little groove in the arete. Follow the groove to its top then continue up thin cracks to the top.

Dying Breed 50' 5.12b ***
Jerry Handren. Fall 2006. After rehearsal.
Two sets small wires, Rp's. Optional small cams.
A wild lead, bold and very strenuous to protect. A quick rappel to check out the placements is probably a good idea. Start 12' right of the arete. Boulder up the lower wall, avoiding the temptation to sneak off left into Fossil Record. The gear is small, difficult to place and not very good until about 20' up where a short crack takes good wires. Blast up the beautiful, varnished wall above to reach the anchor.

● Supreme Species 50' 5.12c *
Stick clip the first bolt and climb straight up the black streak in the middle of the wall (4 b's).

Decline of Man 50' 5.12b **
Jerry Handren. Fall 2006. After rehearsal.
Single rack to 1.75", double to 1".
A very strenuous lead, well-protected with work, but not without some big air potential. Start just left of the right arete. Pull onto the wall, then move left to reach a line of cracks which is followed to the top.

Impact Event 50' 5.11d *
Josh Horniak. Fall 2006. After rehearsal.
Single rack to 2.5", double 0.75"- 1.5".
Start as for Decline of Man, but move right and follow a line of big holds and good cracks up the right edge of the wall. Pumpy.

Fossil Record. Page 115.

The south side of the east face of Mount Wilson is a complex collection of gullies, buttresses and ridges. Just below the south end of the summit ridge is a large wall with obvious slanting crack lines. This is called the Basin Wall. Starting about halfway up the gully that leads up to the Basin Wall, a long ridge, Blue Diamond Ridge, leads up and right to the summit ridge. The ridge tends to blend into the rock walls behind it when viewed from Route 159. However, at certain times of day it catches the sun and appears as an obvious and elegant line. To the left of, and at a slightly lower level than Basin Wall is a tall, narrow wall of attractive tan rock, The Outlaw Wall. You can approach these walls using one of two gullies. Both are long and tiring, though the south gully is probably the better option since it involves easier scrambling.

The South gully: Approach as for the Mass Extinction Crag. Continue up the broad gully above Mass Extinction for a couple of hundred feet. Cut right (north) out of the gully just before a deep, dark, chimney. Traverse out right under a cliff band which bars entrance to the right branch of the gully. 4th and easy 5th class climbing up the right side of the cliff band leads into the upper gully. Continue through a large dark passage and up to a saddle on the right. To get to the Outlaw Wall scramble up and left from the saddle. To get to Basin Wall and Blue Diamond Ridge; Drop down (northwest) into the gully to the north. The start of Blue Diamond Ridge is a short distance below. To get to Basin Wall, traverse straight across then scramble up through bushes to the base of the wall.
2.15 miles, 2000' elevation gain, 3 hrs.

The North Gully: Start at the First Creek Canyon pull out. Follow the First Creek trail for 500 yards to an unmarked trail on the right. Follow the trail on the right, across a wash, and continue for a couple of hundred yards to an old road. Follow the road west towards Mount Wilson. Follow the road until almost directly below the huge steep gully which curves up towards the Basin Wall. Head up the hill into the gully. A long scramble leads up the gully to the bottom of Blue Diamond Ridge, about 1200' above the canyon floor.

❶ Highwaymen 595' 5.11c
Double cams to 3", one 4". Extra 1" cams optional.
This route climbs an impressive corner and crack system on the right side of the Outlaw Wall. This is a steep and impressive route with some good climbing on the first and last pitches but also some scrappy rock in the middle of the route. On the right side of the wall is a long system of corners and cracks.
1. 170' 5.11b Climb up the lower corner (b) and make some thin stemming moves (b) to reach a classic layback which leads to the anchor.
2. 125' 5.11b Continue up the steep but straightforward corner to where it splits. Move right into a steep, sandy fist crack which is followed to a roof (b). Follow the crack right and over the roof (crux) to an anchor below a deep varnished corner.
3. 180' 5.11c Start up the right wall of the corner then cross left onto the left wall (crux, 2 b's). Continue up the corner (loose) then face climb (3 b's) to an anchor below a left-curving seam.
4. 120' 5.11b Continue up the seam (5 b's) and when it peters out continue up discontinuous cracks and seams to an anchor.
Descent: Rappel with two ropes. The route is steep enough that the first climber down needs to use directionals to reach the anchor in a few places, especially when rapping pitch 2.

❷ Trial & Terror 1700' 5.9+
Karsten Duncan, Andrew Gomoll. March 22, 2008.
Double cams to 3", with a few bigger pieces optional.
This route climbs Basin Wall, the large cliff directly below the south end of the summit ridge of Mt. Wilson. Trial & Terror goes up a right-leaning crack system to above a prominent roof then follows weaknesses back left and up to the top. The route has no fixed gear, patches of flaky rock and a few healthy runouts. The scarcity of belays led the first ascent team to do some simu-climbing on the first few pitches.
1. 230' 5.9 Begin at the far left (south) side of the wall on a small tongue of white rock just left of an offwidth corner. Climb up past a bush and through some interesting and sparsely protected climbing. Continue up the crack until reaching a stance in the corner.
2. 230' 5.9 Continue up the corner crack, climbing past a small roof on the left. Just past this roof make an improbable traverse up left out of the angling dihedral on face moves. Continue up an easy featured slab above (5.6) until you reach a small stance.
3. 220' 5.9 Move straight up from the belay over several ledges to get to another long right-angling crack system. Continue up this crack until you reach a small white rock ledge.
4. 150' 5.9R Continue up the crack system on this crux pitch. The dihedral above the belay arches right and becomes a long, small roof. Continue up and right under the roof on face moves protecting in the roof above when possible. Exit the dihedral/roof onto a small ledge. Belay here.
5. 160' 4th Class Traverse right for 60' to a good ledge. Move as far as possible to the right (north) on the ledge system and belay in a small corner.
6. 195' 5.8+R From the belay face climb back left. Keep moving left past one crack to another thin crack. Move up this crack as it widens to a hand crack. When possible traverse left on face holds protecting where possible for 60ft. Move up 15ft on a short, steeper section and belay on black plates.
7. 130-200' 5.6 Move up and left finding the easiest path over a short steep section and up easy climbing above.
8. 400-500' 4th Class Climb toward the base of a bushy gully. Continue up the gully and arête on the right to the summit.

❸ Blue Diamond Ridge 2000' 5.9
Paul Van Betten, Andrew Fulton. March 1997.
Single rack to 4".
Blue Diamond Ridge is a long, serious route with a distinctly alpine feel. The route starts by traversing right out of the gully to an obvious crack. Climb the crack (5.9) to a ledge. Continue up the loose face (5.8) to bushy, broken terrain. Move together up this to the base of the next step. Climb parallel cracks (5.9) to a tree belay. Diagonal right across the face and up a left-facing corner to a belay ledge; (5.8). Go straight up a face and over a 5.9 roof with poor pro and loose blocks; continue to reach a slanting belay ledge. Now go up a large trough (5.8) to a giant boulder and move together up the face above, past trees to a belay on top of blocks. Turn an overhang on the right, (5.9), then go straight up a 5.8 crack to a belay at a tree. Continue straight up a crack to a belay ledge. The arete above, called The Equalizer, is a wild and serious pitch. Above the arete, a pitch of 5.7 leads up and left across the face to a belay at a tree. Now bear left across the face and crack (fixed wire), climb around a dangerous block, and keep climbing up and left to reach a tree, which marks the end of the route.

MOUNT WILSON – SOUTH SUMMIT

Basin Wall

Outlaw
Wall

South Gully
Approach

North Gully
Approach

The next two routes climb long crack systems on the wall to the right of Blue Diamond Ridge. They are both long and involved routes with a lot of climbing and a long, bushy approach.

Approach: Start at the First Creek Canyon pull out. Follow the First Creek trail for 500 yards to an unmarked trail on the right. Follow the trail on the right, across a wash, and continue for a couple of hundred yards to an old road. Follow the road west towards Mount Wilson. Follow the road to its end, then continue up and right across the hillside to gain the crest of a ridge to the left of a bushy gully which slants up and left (south). Climb the ridge to a saddle at its top, then cross over to the right, across the top of the gully. Go over a small cliff band with a fixed rope, then scramble up and right on third class terrain and get into a gully which leads up to the base of the wall. From where the gully ends, a short, easy descent leads down and to the left (south) to the base of Lady Wilson's Cleavage.
2.3 miles, 2000' elevation gain, 2 - 3 hrs.

❶ Double D 1500' 5.10d
Rack to 5", Rp's.

This is a true adventure climb. It had been climbed at least a couple of times in mistake for Lady Wilson's Cleavage before its official first ascent in 2007. Halfway up the final approach gully is a very prominent slot/gully system splitting the buttress to the left, the route starts up a nice 4" crack in the face to the right of the slot.

1-4 . 400' 5.7 Begin up a pleasant crack on good rock. Continue up past a bush and generally in or around the crack for 400ft. As the crack peters out, trend left onto a sloping ledge.

5. 200' 5.8+ Continue up thin cracks and face to the left of a wide dihedral. A serious pitch with tricky protection and long runouts.

6. 5.8 Move up until the buttress comes to a point and belay on a nice ledge around the corner on the right.

7. 5.8 Move back left to the crack and continue up it for a short way until reaching easier ground. Watch rope drag on this pitch.

8. 5.9 Climb the arete above past large blocks and pass a roof on its left side. Belay on top of buttress.

9. 5.6 Move down and left into the gully and up the gully into the thicket of brush.

10. 4th class Scramble through the brush to the main face (same face as Lady Wilson) and the obvious large chimney.

11. 190' 5.10c Climb a short offwidth on the left wall of the chimney to reach a ledge. Move back right to get back to the chimney above. Continue up the dirty chimney until a crack angling rightwards out of the chimney can be taken. Continue up this crack system to a good belay stance in a small corner.

12. 190' 5.10d Move up the corner then exit out on face holds and sketchy-to-no protection to traverse up and back left to the main crack and belay from a tree in the crack.

13. 5.8 Climb the squeeze chimney up and into the upper wide mouth gully above.

From here follow the rotten gully to the summit with a few 4th class moves and a section of fixed rope.

❷ Lady Wilson's Cleavage 1115' 5.9 *
Joe Herbst, Jorge Urioste, Joanne Urioste. March 1977.
Single rack to 7", double 2"-7".

This route follows a continuous chimney/crack for 1000'. A long approach and descent, and sustained, awkward climbing up wide cracks makes this route a big undertaking. The route climbs a long crack which splits the wall below and slightly to the south of the south summit of Mount Wilson.

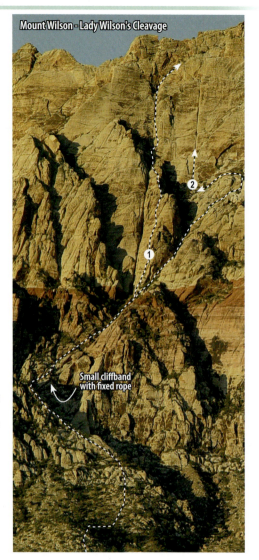

Mount Wilson - Lady Wilson's Cleavage

Small cliffband with fixed rope

1. 120' 5.9 Climb the crack past a wide section. Continue up the corner to a good ledge.

2. 80' 5.8 Continue up the crack to a belay in a sandy bottomed cave.

3. 140' 5.9 Continue up the crack to a belay at small trees.

4. 150' 5.8 Climb up a flared slot through an overhang, and up to a belay at some trees.

5. 165' 5.9 Continue up the chimney above, past a couple of constrictions, then up a thin corner which leads to an easier wide crack. Belay in a niche.

6. 120' 5.7 Continue up the crack above, then follow a gully up and right to a belay under a steep chimney.

7. 40' 5.9 Delicate climbing up the left wall of the chimney leads to a step back right into the gully.

8. 150' 4th class Continue up the gully belaying where it turns into a steep, smooth chimney.

9. 150' 5.9. Climb the impressive chimney and continue to a belay beside a large pine tree.

Easy scrambling leads to the top.

The following routes all start in Willy's Couloir. Willy's Couloir is the left branch of the prominent gully that runs up to the west underneath the Aeolian Wall.

Approach: Hike up the old Oak Creek road until behind the Wilson Pimple. Leave the road just past the height of land between Mount Wilson and the Wilson Pimple, at an area of red soil. Follow a faint trail up a steep hillside onto a broad ridge and continue up the ridge to the red cliff band. Traverse left underneath it to a steep gully (White Rot Gully) which is the only break in the wall. This gully is 150' to the right of the fall line of the main Aeolian Wall gully. Scramble up the gully, passing underneath a huge chockstone, and continue a short distance further until it is possible to go over the ridge on the left and scramble down into the main gully. Continue down the main gully past a steep section, until it is possible to head south across slabby ribs and bushy ledges into the obvious deep gully slanting up to the south.
2.25 miles, 1500' elevation gain, 1¾ hrs.

On the way down it is best to go all the way to the bottom of the Aeolian Wall gully and do two rappels straight down, thus avoiding White Rot Gully.

The first three routes climb the wall of dark rock which forms the left side of Willy's Couloir, about 15 minutes from its bottom. All three routes rappel from an anchor at the top of Slick Willy to the anchor at the top of pitch two of Free Willy. From there, a 150' rappel leads back to the couloir.

Otters are People Too 280' 5.8
John Rosholt, John Cross. 1996.
This route climbs the steep, right-slanting ramp around to the left of Slick Willy.
1. 140' 5.8 Climb the ramp, past a short section of offwidth.
2. 140' 5.7 Continue up the ramp to the top.

Slick Willy 270' 5.11b, A0 ***
John Rosholt & Friend. 1996.
4 sets 1"- 1.75", double 2",3",0.75".
A short bolt ladder leads to a long, smooth corner/crack, one of the nicest in all of Red Rocks. Burly and very sustained. Start at a tree below and to the right of a long right-facing corner.
1. 160' 5.11b Traverse left across a slab to a short bolt ladder which leads up into the corner. Varied crack climbing leads up the corner to an anchor.
2. 110' 5.11a A long pumpy lieback leads to a rest before a final steep corner. Anchor on top.

Free Willy 220' 5.11c *
John Rosholt, John Cross, Jack Herrick. 1996.
Single rack to 3", triple 1.75", double 1.25".
Another excellent crack climb.
Start up the gully to the right of Slick Willy, on a ledge below a clean-cut corner crack.
1. 70' 5.11a Climb the nice, thin hands corner crack and the finger crack above. When the crack ends, technical face moves lead to a sloping ledge.
2. 70' 5.11c Climb up and left into a burly lieback crack which arches right to become an undercling. Continue to an anchor on top of the flake.
3. 80' 5.11a Climb the thin flake above the anchor, then traverse left into the final corner of Free Willy, which is followed to the top.

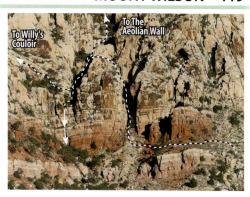

❸ Sentimental Journey 2000' 5.9
John Williamson, Keith Hogan. 1970. A year later, unaware of the first ascent, Joe Herbst soloed a more direct version of the route.
One of Red Rock's oldest routes and a big step into the unknown at the time it was climbed. The route climbs the big gully below the right edge of Sherwood Forest. From Sherwood Forest the route continues up the central of three crack systems in the wall to the right of the upper continuation of the gully.

At the entrance to Willy's Couloir, on the right, a white triangular buttress leans against the wall.

❹ Pink Tornado Right 1000' 5.10c
Don Gieseck, Geoff Conley. 1975.
To the right of the white triangular buttress are twin cracks. Climb either crack; the left is 5.9 the right is 5.8. Both cracks lead to the base of the crack on the right hand side of a pink pillar, the Pink Tornado. Climb the crack, which contains a 5.10 offwidth, to the top of the Pink Tornado. 5.7 climbing up the walls above is followed by a long stretch of easier climbing to reach Sherwood Forest.

❺ Pink Tornado Left 1050' 5.9
Don Gieseck, Geoff Conley. 1975.
Single rack to 4".
Start in the recess on the right hand side of the 200 foot high triangular white slab.
1. 200' 5.9+ Climb steep, hard flakes that are treacherous because of their sandy texture. The rock improves as one climbs higher. Midway through the pitch is a step-across move to bridge the gully. Continue to the top of the slab and belay in the wide chimney between the slab and the main wall.
2. 160' 5.9 Step across the chimney onto the main wall and go straight up via cracks in the pink, varnished face, to a hanging 2-bolt belay beneath an overhang.
3. 110' 5.8 Follow crack straight up through overhang to a 2-bolt station which can be by-passed. Step right and climb to a belay ledge beneath a left-facing corner.
4. 150' 5.7 Go straight up the left-facing corner.
5. 110' 5.7 Continue up the corner to a large ledge with bolted rap/belay anchors.
6. 50' Class 3-4. Step across the void, to the slab just north of the current belay ledge, go up the slab, and continue across the brushy gully, which bars access to the main wall of Wilson. Belay at the base of a left-facing corner system, which contains some red rock.
7. 160' 5.9 Climb this corner system to a belay stance.

Mount Wilson - East Face

Horseshoe Wall

Sherwood Forest

Willy's Couloir

Resolution Arete

8. 160' 5.7 Continue a short distance up corner system, exiting left, past a 2-bolt rap anchor. Broken ledges lead upward to a bushy belay ledge.

The next few hundred feet consist of class 3-4 scrambling up brushy ledges and open slabs (passing a prominent, dead, sliver-colored ponderosa pine tree) to reach Sherwood Forest Ledge. Routes on the upper wall can be done to complete the ascent of Mount Wilson. If rappelling is preferred, one may rap from the top of pitch 5 (with two 60 meter ropes, and following a rap line slightly south of the climbing line followed by pitches 3-5), or traverse south along Sherwood Forest ledge to rappel Dogma (which can be done with a 70m rope.)

❻ Dogma 2000 ft. 5.11c *
Brian McCray, Mike Lewis. 1999.
Single rack to 1.5", tcu's 0.4"- 0.6".
This route takes a wandering line through the walls to the right of Willy's Couloir to reach Sherwood Forest. It then blasts straight up the left side of the Horseshoe Wall above, staying just left of an obvious water streak. Although the start and finish of this route are a little undistinguished, the middle third, up the huge vertical face above Sherwood Forest, is an incredible stretch of wall climbing, a bit like a steeper Black Velvet Wall. Most of the hard climbing is bolted.

Start about 100' higher than Slick Willy, on the right side of the couloir. Look for a fin of rock between two chimneys in the right wall of the couloir. There is a cairn at the base.

1. 70' 5.4 Climb the fin between the chimneys to an anchor on the left.

2. 200' 5.9 Follow two left-leaning ledges to below a steeper wall. A few thin moves lead up the wall to a tree. Continue up past a ledge and a right-facing corner to another tree.

3. 200' 4th class. Climb up and right on a fin of rock to easy terrain which is followed to the right towards a huge recess in red rock. Before reaching the recess, zig-zag up to a bushy ledge below an obvious right-facing chimney which starts beside a bulge 40' up.

3. 140' 5.11a Start up a tricky, thin crack to reach the chimney. After a short steep struggle up the chimney, step right and continue up the face to an anchor on a ledge below a smooth slab.

4. 100' 5.8 Climb up and right into a slabby corner, which is followed to a ledge at its top.

5. 200' 5.6 Climb up the unprotected face, then trend left and pull over a bulge and climb up beside a corner to a rap anchor. Continue up and left to a tree on a ledge.

6. 300' 3rd class. Follow a ramp up and right, then cut back left and head up slabby ribs up and left until it is possible to move right across a slab to reach Sherwood Forest. The route continues up the left side of the Horseshoe Wall above, starting close to a huge tree.

7. 110' 5.11c Start up a steep corner for 50', then move right onto the steep wall. Climb up and right, pumpy with well spaced bolts, to an anchor.

8. 100' 5.11a Continue up, past a sporty start, onto a superb wall which leads to an anchor.

9. 100' 5.10c Continue up the wall to an anchor.

10. 100' 5.10c Continue up the wall to an anchor

11. 100' 5.11a Make thin moves past a thin, slanting crack, then move right and up a sustained slabby face to reach a tree on the huge ledge below the upper wall.

The upper pitches start a short distance to the left along the ledge. The rock on these pitches is a little soft and sandy.

12. 100' 5.11a After a bouldery start move left and climb a steep crack which leads onto an easier face and an anchor.

13. 100' 5.8 Climb straight up to an anchor.

14. 100' 5.8 Climb straight up to an anchor.

15. 100' 5.8 Climb to an anchor on the summit ridge.

Descent: The route can be rappelled with a single 70m rope.

The next two routes climb the right hand side of the Horseshoe Wall, starting from Sherwood Forest. They can be approached by scrambling to the top of Willy's Couloir then heading out right across slabs to reach Sherwood Forest. This is neither easy nor pleasant, much less so now because of a recent rockfall. A much better alternative is to start up one of the two Pink Tornado routes. This natural combination creates one of the longest routes in Red Rocks.

❼ Scotty 900' 5.10
Scott Gilbert, Geoff Conley. 1978.
On the right side of the Sherwood Forest Ledge is a group of tall trees. Start 100' to the left of the left most tree and follow an obvious right-leaning crack system for one pitch to reach a huge corner system. This is to the left of the huge drainage to the left of Resolution Arete. Follow the corner for 700' to the base of The Mushroom, a small buttress protruding from the summit plateau. The final pitches climb the left side of The Mushroom.

❽ Gwondonna Land Boogie 1450' 5.10a
Phil Broscovak and Geoffrey Conley. January 1981.
Single rack to 4", double 1"- 1.5".
Begin on Sherwood Forest Ledge just north of a group of ponderosa pine trees which lie directly below "The Mushroom", the little pointy formation on the Mount Wilson summit plateau. There is a shallow arch at a level a bit higher than the pine trees. Begin in the crack which heads up and slightly left to connect with the right portion of this arch.

1. 120' 5.9 The start of the crack is hard to protect and awkward to jam. Face climbing a few feet right can be more appealing than climbing the crack itself (5.9). Belay at or just above the small roof formed by the above-mentioned arch. The belay is hanging and a bit challenging to build, but can be made adequate for the subsequent runout.

2. 200' 5.8 Climb the obvious closed crack for 40 feet before the first pro placement (5.8). The rock steepens and cracks lead straight up and slightly right over improbable terrain, to a good ledge with tiny tree. This pitch can be split if one desires, but the belay will be hanging and awkward.

3. 160' 5.10a Climb the shallow left-facing corner for 50 feet until it curves left and ends. Head left across the steep face, following a line of bolts, some of which are 20 feet apart on steep, thin, fragile, remote terrain. End at a good ledge with a 2 bolt belay and rap rings. Here, one may rappel straight down "Scotty" to escape (using two 50 meter ropes).

4. 150' 5.8 Go left 15 feet on ledges. Go straight up, pass a pro bolt, and follow cracks and corners. At the top of the pitch, traverse left for 15 feet to a good belay stance with some bushes. The anchors consist of 2 bolts and rap rings.

5. 160' 5.7 This pitch leads up and left to the first tree on the large ledge with trees.

6. 200' Walk left on a narrow ledge and belay in the chimney.

7. 160' 5.9 Chimney and stem to the top of a pillar.

8&9. 300' 5.9 The obvious right-facing corner leads to the top.

Descent: Walk down Oak Creek Canyon or rappel Dogma.

Aeolian Wall

The northeast corner of Mount Wilson is a 2000' high wall bounded on the left by the obvious turreted ridgeline followed by Resolution Arete, and on the right by a steep gully. The routes here are amongst the longest in Red Rocks and, with the long approach and descent, they are more like alpine climbing than cragging.

Approach: Hike up the old Oak Creek road until behind the Wilson Pimple. Leaving the road at an area of red soil, follow a faint trail up a steep hillside onto the broad ridge to the right of the broad drainage that is the lower continuation of the Aeolian Wall gully. Continue up the ridge to the red cliff band and traverse left, staying high underneath it, to a steep the gully which is the only break in the wall. This gully is 150' to the right of the fall line of the main Aeolian Wall gully. Scramble up the gully, passing underneath a huge chockstone, and continue a short distance further until it is possible to go over the ridge on the left and scramble down into the main gully. The gully cuts steeply up to the west, underneath the Aeolian Wall. 2.25 miles, 1900' elevation gain, 2 hrs.

On the way down it is best to go all the way to the bottom of the Aeolian Wall gully and do two rappels straight down, thus avoiding White Rot Gully.

❶ Resolution Arete 2500' 5.11d (or 5.10c, C1) **
Phil Broscovak, Geoff Conley. January 1981. FFA Paul Van Betten, Richard Harrison 1984.
Single rack to 5", double 1"- 1.25".
Resolution Arete climbs the long, turreted arete which forms the left edge of the Aeolian wall. Despite a few scrappy sections, this is a classic alpine endeavor requiring good route-finding skills and efficient climbing. The route starts on the right hand side of a buttress at the base of the arete. Look for a ledge system which leads out left to a large ponderosa pine. Start about 50' to the left of the pine tree in an alcove above a chimney.
1. 100' 5.9 Face climb across left for 30' to a crack in a right-facing corner. Climb the corner, setting up an anchor on good cams beside an old bolt.
2. 150' 5.8 Continue up the crack to the top of a red pillar.
3. 100' 5.9 From the right side of the pillar, face climb into a right-facing corner system. Climb the corner, past a delicate section with dicey protection. Continue to a belay in the base of a chimney.
4. 150' 5.8 Climb the chimney and continue up to set a belay on the highest ledge, 20' above the top of a red band.
5. 160' 5.8 Go up the face for 50', then trend right towards the lower of two pine trees.
6 & 7. 250' 4th class. Climb over broken rock towards the Aeolian Wall, then go left into the notch behind a huge triangular buttress. From the notch go round to the south side of the ridge and go up 75' to the base of a corner with jammed blocks.
8. 140' 5.9+ Climb the corner, easily at first, then past a beautiful section of 5.9+ stemming to a belay in an alcove.
9. 100' 5.9 Climb over blocky rock, trending left. Belay 20' below a large roof.
10. 100' 5.11d (5.9+, A1) Climb up to the roof, then under-cling/lieback around right (crux). Once around the corner, 5.9+ face leads up to a belay at the base of a thin, smooth

left-facing corner.
11. 80' 5.10d Climb the corner until it is possible to step left to easier climbing. Belay on a large sloping ledge with a bolt.
12. 150' 5.8 Head right to the top of the sloping ledge, then climb an awkward left-leaning corner to a belay just below a notch.
13. 150' 5.8 Follow the broken ridge past a 5.8 step to the base of a long left-slanting crack.
14. 100' 5.9+ A beautiful pitch up the diagonal crack leads to a belay at the base of a chimney.
15. 160'. 5.7 Climb the chimney, then follow the easy blocky ridge to the base of a blocky pillar.
16. 80' 4th class Enter a hole near the right side of the pillar and belay at the base of a chimney.
17. 150' 5.9 Climb the chimney, then exit left and follow a broken ridge up and left past a 5.9 move. Follow ledges left to the base of a crack which is followed to a ledge with a small tree. Watch for rope drag on this long, winding pitch.
18. 120' Walk left on an exposed ledge.
19. 120' 5.8 At the left end of the ledge is a 20' wide chimney. Climb the left side of the chimney to a belay about 40' below a rotten white roof on the left wall of the chimney.
20. 80' 5.7 Climb carefully around the roof and belay on a large ledge with a ponderosa pine.
21- 24. 600' 4th class Past the tree, descend 10' then follow easy rock for 600' to the summit

❷ Inti Watana 1500' 5.10c **
Jorge Urioste, Mike Clifford. July 1997.
Single rack to 3".
This route climbs the north face of a prominent tower on Resolution Arete. About 100' to the right of the pine tree at the start of Resolution Arete is a steep gully in the left wall of the approach gully. Follow the gully up to a giant chockstone, which is passed on the left through a hole. Once through the hole the route climbs the face to the right of the gully. A line of bolts indicates the first pitch.
1. 90' 5.9+ Climb the face (7 b's) to an anchor in an alcove.
2. 100' 5.10c Climb the face (10 b's) to an anchor.
3. 110' 5.8 Climb up and right, then back left to an anchor (12 b's).
4. 120' 5.9 Go straight up the face, following intermittent thin cracks (3 b's) to an anchor in a recess.
5. 95' 5.7 Step right and climb a hand crack up and right to a platform. Step right to a crack which is followed to an anchor.
6. 110' Trend right up the face (4 b's) to an anchor.
7. 125' 5.9 Step right into a thin crack which leads to an s-crack, an overhang, and a hanging belay at an anchor.
8. 105' 5.9+ Climb the face (4 b's) to a recessed ledge.
9. 50' 5.9 Go over a large bulge (5 b's) to an anchor.
10. 110' 5.9 Step left and climb the face (12 b's) to an anchor.
11. 60' 5.9 Climb the face (5 b's) to an anchor.
12. 70' 5.10c Face climb up (7 b's), then step left over a loose bulge and up to an anchor.
Descent: The route can be rappelled with a single 80m rope or two shorter ropes. It finishes above the 15th pitch of Resolution Arete, which can be followed to the top.

Mount Wilson - Aeolian Wall

❸ Aeolian Wall Original Route 1800' 5.9, A3

Joe Herbst, Larry Hamilton. March 1975.
Single rack to 7", doubles to 3". Good selection of pins.

The original route on the wall follows a steep corner to reach the left most of two left-slanting chimneys in the upper part of the wall. The route starts from a ledge system above the approach gully. From a short distance above Resolution Arete, climb up a mossy crack (5.9) on the left-hand side of a water-streaked slab to a small shrub. Move left on easier terrain then up to the large ledge system below the wall. Continue back right up ramps to the base of a huge left facing corner system.

1. 120' 5.9 Climb flakes in the corner, loose rock, to an anchor.

2. 150' 5.9 A2 From the anchor, move right to the chimney climbing past a star-drive bolt. Free and aid the chimney and follow a nice crack leading onto the right face. Belay at a stance with hand sized gear about 20' below a bolt.

3. 190' 5.9 A3 Continue up the corner past a bolt into a knife-blade seam. At the roof move right on 4 original bolts and then continue out the roof on knifeblades (A3 exciting and airy). Pull the lip, clip another ancient bolt and continue up 5.9/A1 cracks to a claustrophobic chimney with fixed bong in the back.

4. 110' 5.8 Continue out the chimney and up cracks to a good bivi spot.

5. 195' 5.8 Follow a chimney that goes up and angles left into a slab. Climb the slab past a bolt to a cool cave-like ledge. (Another good bivi spot).

6-7. 220-260' 5.8 Continue up the sparsely-protected chimney above to reach a ledge.

7. 190' 5.8 From the ledge climb a small step through bushes and up a 4-6" crack. When convenient, traverse right into the next gully system over.

8-9. 100-250' 5.9 Move up the gully system through a series of ledges and chimneys to reach a saddle (near Resolution Arete). Belay from trees/bushes.

10-13. 3rd class Turn right (west) and climb up, generally keeping on the left side of the rock towers near the top to reach the summit ridge.

❹ Woodrow 1800' 5.10a ❶

Richard Harrison, John Long. Spring 1981.
Single rack to 4".

This route climbs an obvious water streak to reach the right hand of two left-slanting chimney systems on the upper wall. Start below the center of a 400' high buttress leaning against the lower part of the wall.

1. 200' 5.7 Follow cracks (5.7) up the center of the buttress.

2. 200' 5.7 Continue to the top of the lower buttress.

3. 120' 5.10a From a tree at the top of the buttress, poorly protected face climbing (2 b's) leads up just to the left of a water streak, finishing at an anchor.

4. 150'. 5.10a Continue up the face (b) to the base of the left-slanting chimney mentioned in the introduction.

5. 150' 4th class. Climb the chimney to the base of a lieback.

6. 150' 5.9 Climb the lieback crack.

7. 150' 5.8 Continue up a 4" crack.

8. 200'. 5.8 Continue up a corner, then make a 5.8 traverse to the left across a face to reach a ledge with a tall pine tree. The Original Route reaches this ledge at its left end. Finish up the Original Route, climbing a 5.9 pitch then easier loose terrain to the top.

❺ Woman of Mountain Dreams 2110' 5.11a

Joanne Urioste, Mike Moreo, Jorge Urioste, Dave Krulesky. May 1997.
FFA Aitor Uson, Joanne Urioste. May 1998.
Single rack to 3".

This route follows a spectacular direct line to the summit of Mount Wilson. While there is some good rock lower on the route, the final few pitches are quite loose and require careful climbing.

The route is approached by continuing up the Aeolian Wall approach gully to a col at its top. Drop down the opposite side of the col to another gully. Scramble up red rock in the bed of the gully for 100' then head left to a large ponderosa pine which marks the start of the route. The first 3 pitches climb the crack formed by the right edge of the 400' high buttress which leans against the lower part of the wall.

1. 150' 5.8 Head up left-leaning wide cracks and grooves to an anchor just above the pink rock.

2. 160' 5.8 Continue up the crack / gully to an anchor.

3. 120' 5.9+ Continue up the crack system to the top of the buttress. There is an anchor on the highest ledge.

4. 140' 5.11a Thin, slabby face climbing (11 b's) up the right hand water streak (just right of Woodrow) to an anchor.

5. 160' 5.10a Continue up the face (5 b's) to a shallow, arching, right-facing corner. Step left and go up the face (b) to an anchor in a scoop at the base of the huge left-slanting chimney of Woodrow.

6. 80' 4th class Go up 20' then head left across a slab to a large ledge with a tree.

7. 100' 5.10a From the tree continue up the face (2 b's), following the right hand crack to an anchor on a small sloping ledge.

8. 100' 5.9 Continue up the face for 75', following thin cracks (6 b's), then head left to an anchor.

9. 160' 5.9 Climb a crack for 10', move right 5', then go up a steep face and crack to an anchor on a sloping ledge.

10. 100' 5.9 Step left and climb a crack for 30', then step left and climb a dirty and loose crack which leads to an anchor on a bushy ledge.

11. 160' 5.8 Go right, around the arete onto a face. Climb the face, past a ledge. 15' below a lichenous overhang, step out left onto a face (poor pro). Go up 20' then step back right into the crack system, which is followed to a pine tree.

12. 120' 5.9 Go left up a ramp for 40', then face climb up to loose, blocky corners leading straight up to an anchor on a good ledge.

13. 140' 5.10a Make an airy traverse right to a bolt. Continue up the thin crack above, and when the wall blanks out, go 10' left to another crack which leads (loose) to an anchor.

14. 120' 5.8 A loose corner leads to a pine tree.

15 &16 300' 4th class. From the tree at the top of the last pitch, go left up a ramp for 20', then go over a 10' step to a stout tree. Continue up the 3rd class ridge above then go over another 10' step directly to the summit block.

❻ Gift of the Wind Gods 1500' 5.10d *

Mike Clifford, Joanne Urioste, Patrick Putman. June 1996.
Single rack to 2", two 3"- 4" pieces. Extra wires.

This route climbs the left edge of the impressive, smooth wall on the right hand side of the Aeolian Wall. A sustained, airy, and enjoyable route. The route starts up the first pitch of The Woman of Mountain Dreams.

1. 150' 5.8 Head up left-leaning wide cracks and grooves to an anchor just above the pink rock.

2. 130' 5.10a Traverse out right for 15', then climb up past two bolts. Traverse right again for 15' to a thin crack which is climbed (b) to an anchor below a shrub.

3. 160' 5.8 Climb the crack above. Halfway up, step into the right hand crack then continue straight up to an anchor.

4. 150' 5.10d Step left into a thin crack which is followed, passing a bulge (5 b's) to an anchor.

5. 95' 5.8 Go straight up a crack then step left to an anchor.

6. 85' 5.9+ Go straight up an intermittent crack (4 b's), then make a technical series of face moves up and right to an anchor at a good stance in an area of smooth rock called The Maroon Spot.

7. 160' 5.10d Traverse horizontally right to two bolts. There is an off route bolt 20' higher. Technical moves lead up and right (9 b's) up the face. Eventually step right, into a cleft which leads to an anchor in a niche at the base of a large right-facing corner.

8. 100' 5.9 Climb the corner past a squeeze chimney, an offwidth, and an overhang (2 b's) to an anchor.

9. 150' 5.7 Follow the easiest line up the corner system above to belay at a small pine tree.

10. 50' 4th class Scramble to a ledge.

The route finishes on easy ground several hundred feet below the summit. Walk to the right for 10 minutes. After crossing a defined drainage, head up a gully with 3 large pine trees at mid height. This gully leads up, past a few tricky sections, to the summit plateau.

❼ Pagan Sacrifice 1600' 5.11c (or 5.10, A2)
Robert Warren, Steve Johnson. April 1997.

This route follows Gift of the Wind Gods for 6 pitches to the point where a long traverse to the right leads to the final corner. Instead of traversing right after the top of pitch 6, Pagan Sacrifice climbs a vertical crack system just right of center of the prominent buttress in the upper part of the wall, called Wind God Tower.

7. 5.11c or A2 Climb up the left side of The Maroon Spot, then traverse right (2 b's) to an anchor.

8. 5.9 Climb a crack, traverse left (2 b's), then wander back right on a runout face to an belay stance.

9. 190' 5.8 Climb a crack, then jog right(bushes) and climb cracks to a ledge.

Go right on the ledge to a tree, head up (5.4) bearing right. Continue up broken loose rock to the top.

Cactus Connection 360' 5.11b
Blake Herrington, Chris Weidner. April 4, 2012.
Single rack to 5", double 0.75"- 3".

Cactus Connection is located on the far right side of the Aeolian Wall, about 100' below the notch between Cactus Flower Tower and Mt. Wilson. It is the right most route on Mt. Wilson and is probably most useful as a spectacular finish to any of the routes that go to the summit of Cactus Flower Tower. From the summit of Cactus Flower Tower scramble and downclimb to the notch between Cactus Flower Tower and Mt. Wilson. The final move involves a leap across a chasm (belay recommended). Rappel 70 feet to the east off a small tree to a flat area beneath the northeast face of Mt. Wilson.

1. 100' 5.6 Traverse left through talus and trees aiming for the base of two parallel and splitter thin cracks. Climb a short, steep section to a small ledge with a tree and a wide, left-facing corner.

2. 130' 5.11b Ascend the offwidth corner for about 30 feet until

it is possible to face climb left toward a bush and the base of a thin, right-leaning crack. Jam the finger crack to a stance, then leave the widening crack for a perfect hand crack eight feet to the left. Follow this to a stance in a chimney/pod and belay.

3. 130' 5.10a Climb the right-facing corner and the crack on the right to a ledge beneath a brown, right-leaning corner. Step left around an arête and follow a curving crack and blocky ledges to the second of two pine trees and belay. Small gear useful. Scramble up for around 600' to the summit of Mt. Wilson, climbing several short and exposed fifth-class sections along the way. (45 minutes).

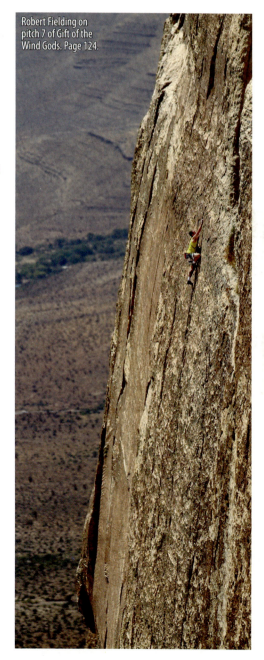

Robert Fielding on pitch 7 of Gift of the Wind Gods. Page 124.

The burly roof of Boondoggle. Page 169.

Introduction

The northern flank of this huge drainage basks in the sun all day long, making it the premier destination in Red Rocks for climbing long routes during colder weather. As is normal in Red Rocks, the sunny faces are often composed of softer, light colored rock, and less traveled routes can be a little sandy and fragile in places. However, the passage of many pairs of hands and feet on routes such as Solar Slab and Levitation 29 has cleaned the rock up considerably, leaving behind some of the most enjoyable climbing in Red Rocks.

The positioning of the Eagle Wall above Solar Slab allows for some tremendous link ups. Beulah's Book to Solar Slab to Rainbow Buttress, for example, provides a day of alpine proportions, with great climbing and amazing scenery throughout. Black Orpheus to Eagle Dance provides a similar day at the 5.10 level.

Despite its popularity, Oak Creek Canyon still has a lot of potential for new routes on its shady southern side. Many 500' walls composed of solid, dark rock offer obvious possibilities for climbers interested in doing a bit of exploring.

Access

Oak Creek Canyon is most easily reached from the Oak Creek Trailhead. Drive around the loop road for 12 miles and take a right on a gravel road which leads to the parking area, after a little less than a mile. A trail leads into the canyon from the parking area.

For the routes on Cactus Flower Tower, and also in order to get an early start for some of the longer routes in the main Canyon, climbers sometimes opt to use one of two trails, which both begin outside the park loop road and thus allow for early starts, an important factor on a short winter day. The first option is a small pullout on the right, half a mile south of the Scenic Dive exit on Route 159. From here, a trail leads straight into the canyon, staying to the right (north) of the main wash. The second option is to park in a pullout in front of a gate, 1.4 miles south of the exit from the Scenic Drive. This is the entrance to the old Oak Creek Campground. From here, an old road leads all the way behind the Wilson Pimple, a small hill in front of Mount Wilson, and down into the lower reaches of the Canyon. These options will add one or two miles to your day respectively.

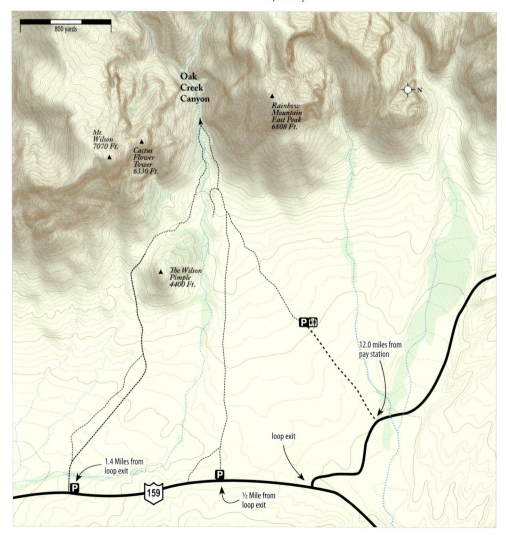

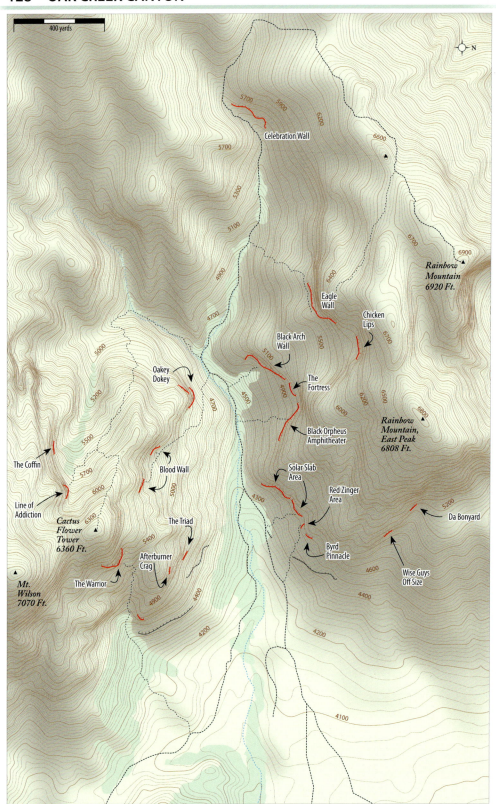

400 yards

N

Celebration Wall

5700
5900
6200
6600
5700
5300
5100
4900
4700

Rainbow
Mountain
6920 Ft.

6400

Eagle
Wall

6700

Chicken
Lips

Black Arch
Wall

5500

6700

Oakey
Dokey

5000
5200
5100
4000
4500
4700
4100

The
Fortress

6200
6000
6500

Rainbow
Mountain,
East Peak
6808 Ft.

6800

Black Orpheus
Amphitheater

The Coffin

5500
5700
6000

Blood Wall

5000

Solar Slab
Area

Da Bonyard

5200

Line of
Addiction

Cactus
Flower
Tower
6360 Ft.

6300

The Triad

5400

Red Zinger
Area

4300

Byrd
Pinnacle

Wise Guys
Off-Size

4600

Afterburner
Crag

Mt.
Wilson
7070 Ft.

The Warrior

4900
4400
4200

4400

4200

4100

Cactus Flower Tower

Cactus Flower Tower is the name given to the prominent sub-peak to the north of Mount Wilson. It forms the southern flank of Oak Creek Canyon. It is separated from Mount Wilson by the deep gully below the Aeolian Wall. Amazingly for such a prominent feature, the first recorded rock climb to its summit was climbed as late as 1996. The routes that go to the summit are some of Red Rocks' most classic adventure climbs, especially because any of the descent options are quite long and involved.

Approach: The following routes are most easily approached by parking 1.4 miles south of the loop exit, at the entrance to the old Oak Creek Campground, and hiking down the old Oak Creek Road. Follow the road past the Wilson Pimple, until directly below the northeast face of Cactus Flower Tower. Head up a bushy open gully to the base of the tower. 1¼ hrs.

Descent: From the summit, the normal descent heads down the west ridge, with several easy fifth class sections of down climbing. From a point almost opposite the obvious buttress of Line of Addiction, scramble down to the gully to the south. Go down the bushy gully a short distance then cut out right (north) to a huge, slabby ledge system which leads back to the ridge. Continue down the broad lower ridge, with several short sections of down climbing and some tricky route finding (cairns). Eventually reach a broad, slabby drainage which leads down to the south fork of the main canyon.

If you know where to find the final anchor of The Warrior, it is possible to rap that route and reverse the approach gully. There are rap slings on several trees on the right side (looking down) of the approach gully which allow the fifth class sections to be bypassed by half-rope rappels.

Both options are a nightmare to descend in the dark.

This small cliff faces northeast. As you go up the gully towards the base of Cactus Flower Tower, a small red cliff band is passed on the right. Ramen Pride Cliff is above this cliff, just to the right of the approach gully.

Ramen Pride 130' 5.11b
Paul Van Betten, Sal Mamusia. 1983.
Start below an attractive left-facing corner. Climb over some blocks to reach a ledge at the base of the corner proper. From the left end of the ledge, go up a crack which arches back into the main corner. Intricate stemming leads up the corner to an anchor below a roof.

Zippy 80' 5.8
Paul Van Betten, Sal Mamusia. 1983.
Start 20' to the right of Ramen Pride. Climb a nice looking splitter crack, which arches right at the top, to an anchor in a left-facing corner.

Stemtation 40' 5.9
Paul Van Betten, Sal Mamusia. 1983.
Start 30' to the right of Zippy. Climb a wide crack in a left-facing corner to a pine tree on a ledge.

From the top of the approach gully, the next two routes described are up and to the left along the base of the wall.

❶ League of Notions 400' 5.10b
Mark Moore, Randal Grandstaff. Fall 1976.
Single rack to 7", double 1"-2" and big cams.
The wall at the base of tower is seamed with several long, attractive crack systems. This route starts up the left most crack system, which begins as a large right-facing corner.
1. 5.10b Climb the attractive right-facing corner.
2. From the belay, climb down and right on small holds, traversing into the chimney at the back of the corner on the right. Climb the chimney, which narrows to offwidth. Belay on a good stance above the offwidth.
3. Continue up the chimney, which narrows again and forms a huge flake. Exposed liebacking and jamming leads up this to easier climbing.
Descent: Rappel the route with two ropes.

❷ Homunculus 400' 5.10
Mark Moore, Dave Anderson. Spring 1977.
This route starts about a rope length to the right of the previous route, very close to the top of the approach gully. The general line of the route is the huge right-facing slot on the right side of the lower wall.
Start to the right of the fall line of the slot, below a large left-facing corner with an offwidth.
1. Climb the offwidth to the right end of a large bushy ledge.
2. From the left end of the ledge, climb out left onto the face, then head up and left to a horn. From the horn go up and right to reach a crack, which leads into the base of the huge slot.
3. Climb the chimney in the back of the slot.
4. Continue up the chimney in the back of the slot. Belay below the steep corner/crack on the left.
5. Jam up the corner to a bolted anchor below an overhang.
Descent: Rappel the route with two ropes.

❸ Cactus Flower Tower - East Ridge 1500' 5.8
A worthy alpine style excursion. Start in the gully at the base of Gift of the Wind Gods (see Mt. Wilson, page 124). Go up then right onto the ridge which forms the right side of the gully. Follow the ridge to the summit. 8 Pitches.
Descent: As for Cinnamon Hedgehog.

❹ Cinnamon Hedgehog 1050' 5.10a

Andrew Fulton and Partner. 1996.
Double rack to 3".

This route climbs the upper east face of Cactus Flower Tower. It is a major undertaking with serious climbing, a long and very involved approach, and an equally long descent. Use the same approach as routes 1&2, but at the base of the tower, head up and right into the gully that skirts the north side of the tower. The gully has a lot of fourth and easy fifth class climbing. From high in the gully, at a point where it narrows and steepens, the approach breaks out left. Leave the gully, and traverse out left around a slabby rib, to below a mossy slab. Climb the mossy slab, exiting left, then continue up an airy rib to a dead tree in an alcove below a chimney in a right-facing corner. Climb the corner, and another above it to a ledge with a prominent large tree (100', 5.7). Rappel off the left end of the ledge and hike and scramble up around to below the east face. Start on white rock at the base of the face. 2.5 miles, 1600' elevation, 3 hrs.

1. 200' 5.9 Climb up and right (2 b's) then slightly left to a crack which leads to an anchor.

2. 200' 5.8 Follow the crack to its end, then climb up and right (2 b's) to a left-leaning crack, which is followed to an anchor.

3. 200' 5.8 Continue up the crack for 50', then exit right onto a slab and follow thin seams and cracks up into the white rock to reach an anchor.

4. 150' 5.10a A tricky pitch with good gear. Climb the white face (b), trending slightly left to a good ledge. The anchor takes #00, #0 and #3.5 friends.

5. 100' 5.3 Continue up a low-angled boulder, cross a gully and climb a slab to a three-foot wide varnished ledge. Walk north on the ledge, and jump over to reach a pine tree.

6. 200' 5.6 Go up and right on a large ramp for 30' to reach a crack. Continue up the crack to a slab.

Continue up a blocky, tree-filled gully, tunneling through a chimney to reach the summit of the tower.

❺ Blood on the Tracks 1000' 5.9+

Blake Herrington, Chris Weidner. April 4, 2012.
Single rack to 6", double to 4".

This route climbs the double cracks in the rounded arete between Cinnamon Hedgehog and The Warrior. It has sustained crack climbing for nearly 1000' and is another long, adventurous route. There are patches of flaky and dirty rock, but also some good climbing. Approach as for Cinnamon Hedgehog. After climbing the 5.7 chimney, down climb 30 feet until beneath two right-facing corners. Begin in the left of the two corners in scooped, white rock.

1. 180' 5.9 Climb up the wide right-facing corner to a small stance below a large bush. The rock is mossy on the first half of this pitch.

2. 200' 5.9+ Continue up the corner through a chamber-like chimney and over a juggy roof. Belay at a stance where a two-foot wide ledge leads rightward.

3. 215' 5.8 Walk right on the ledge to just before the right-hand crack system. Face climb up and right on creaky flakes to join the crack about 30 feet above the ledge (alternatively, walk the ledge all the way to the crack and climb it). Continue up the crack and belay when the rope runs out.

4. 150' 5.9+ Follow the crack to a large ledge 20 feet higher. Climb an intermittent seam straight up over a bulge of dark rock, then follow it up and slightly right. Protection is tricky but adequate. When the rock turns slabby, head right and belay in

the wide corner beneath a gully.

5. 165' 5.9+ Face climb up and right into the left-facing, flaring chimney with some loose rock. Climb it to its top and belay in a flat alcove.

6. 80' 5.8 Face climb up and left into a shallow right-facing corner and follow this to a wide, flat area and belay.

7. 130' 5.7 Gain a ledge just above with the help of a large pine tree. Walk the ledge right to a wide, juggy left-leaning crack and climb it to a large ledge on the right with two bolts – the top anchor of The Warrior. Rap from here, or continue scrambling up a gully that leads up and left past some pine trees to the summit of Cactus Flower Tower.

❻ The Warrior 1050' 5.11a **

Single set to 8", Four sets 2.5"- 3". (Six #3 camalots would not go unused on pitch 3, and kneepads are nice.)

This route climbs the mighty corner system on the northeast arete of Cactus Flower Tower, one of the finest natural lines in the area. It goes up a series of unusually smooth corner/ cracks which provide sustained and physical climbing. The nature of the climbing, along with the arduous approach, and long descent, makes for one of the more adventurous outings in Red Rocks.

Follow the approach to Cinnamon Hedgehog, but after gaining the ledge at the top of the moss-covered, slabby groove, traverse right on the ledge until below the right-hand of the two possible starts to the huge right-facing corner system. 2¼ hrs.

1. 160' 5.9 Climb the impressive curving chimney to an anchor at a small ledge on the left arete.

2. 100' 5.10b Climb the delicate stemming corner above until a better crack leads to a ledge. Continue up into a chimney at the base of the huge slanting corner. Climb the chimney for 30' and set up a belay on a nice ledge.

3. 120' 5.10d Climb the perfect hand and fist crack in the back of the tight corner above. At the top, move right to an anchor on a small ledge. A magnificent pitch.

4. 170' 5.10b Layback up the corner above. Turn a roof and continue more easily to a huge alcove. To protect the next section, it is possible to climb up into the roof of the alcove to place a high piece before stepping back down. Climb through an overhang to reach a sustained offwidth which is followed to an anchor on the right.

5. 170' 5.11a Continue up the corner. Above a small overhang, a short section of technical stemming provides the crux of the route, and leads to a good finger crack. Continue up the corner until the crack fizzles out. Step right and face climb (5.8 R) to a bolt. Continue up and right (2 b's), then pull over a roof to an anchor a few feet higher.

6. 180' 5.9 R Step right from the anchor and climb a thin seam for 40'. Move left and climb another seam for 25' then move right and rejoin the original seam. Continue up the seam and the wall above to an anchor. Not technically hard, but an airy and bold lead.

7. 150' 5.8 Follow a thin seam up and right for 30', then go straight up, following another thin seam through a patch of nice varnish. Continue over some steeper bulges on big varnished holds. Continue to an anchor on the shoulder of the northeast arete of Cactus Flower Tower, beside a small dead tree. Easier climbing leads to the top of the tower.

Descent: It is possible to rap the entire route. Alternatively use the Cactus Flower Tower descent into the south fork of Oak Creek Canyon.

Aeolian
Wall

CACTUS FLOWER
TOWER

Ramen Pride Cliff

Afterburner Cliff

The routes on this wall are well worth the approach, quite a statement since getting there involves a really nasty scramble through thick bushes and steep, awkward gullies. The cliff is a little hard to identify, it is worth taking the time to figure out the wall and the approach from the opposite side of the canyon before starting. The wall is mostly shady, but gets some sun in the morning.

Approach: Directly across the canyon from the base of Solar Slab, at the bottom of the wall, is a 200' high white buttress split by some obvious smooth-walled offwidth and chimney lines. This is The Triad area. The Afterburner cliff sits at the top of the gully which cuts up the steep, broken walls to the east (left) of The Triad. The cliff is a flat wall, with a band of light tan rock at the base, dark rock in the middle, and white rock on top. The approach is up the gully to the left of The Triad, until it is possible to move out right onto ledges and short walls, which lead to the base of the wall. Two large pines sit on either side of the ledge underneath the wall. 1.5 miles, 650', 1¼ hrs.

❶ Finger Fandango 150' 5.11a
Paul Van Betten, Jay Smith, Paul Obenheim. 1984.
Climb a right-facing corner on the left side of the wall (pin),

then continue up a tips crack to an anchor on a ledge.

❷ Afterburner 150' 5.12a
Paul Van Betten, Sal Mamusia. 1984.
The thin finger crack to the right of the previous route (pin) leads to the same anchor.

❸ Eliminator Crack 130' 5.11d ★★★
Single rack to 2.5", double to 1", Rp's.
Paul Van Betten, Randy Marsh. 1983.
The superb finger crack that splits the center of the wall. One of the best of its type in Red Rocks. Climb the crack, angling right at the top to an anchor.

❹ Deguello 90' 5.10a
Sal Mamusia, Danny Meyers, Paul Van Betten, Brad Stewart. 1984.
This route climbs the right-slanting hand crack on the right side of the wall to reach a ramp. Scramble off to the right.

34 Ford with Flames 80' 5.10d
Mike Ward, Bob Yoho. 1985.
This long lost route is just to the left of Vagabondage, on The Triad. It climbs a light colored slab with four bolts.

The Triad

Directly across the canyon from the base of Solar Slab, at the bottom of the craggy hillside, is a 200' high, white buttress split by some obvious smooth-walled offwidth and chimney lines. This is The Triad. The name refers to the trio of obvious cracks splitting the north face of the buttress. The wall is mostly shady, but gets some sun in the morning.

Descent: It is possible to rap from the lowest of several trees at the top of Beauty with a single 70m rope.

The first route is on a small east-facing wall around to the left of the main face.

❶ Vagabondage 80' 5.11a
Mike Ward, Danny Meyers. Late 1980's.
Climb a long, left-leaning finger crack which splits a nice white and tan wall. It ends at a small tree.

The rest of the routes are on the north face of the buttress.

❷ The Ugly Sister 180' 5.8
Single rack to 4", double 5".
This route climbs the obvious right-facing corner on the left side of the main wall. Climb blocky cracks to the base of the upper corner. Beware the large, loose block at the base of the upper corner. Stem past the block and continue up the corner to a large ledge on the left. Easy to the top.

❸ Beauty 180' 5.10c *
Joe Herbst, John Byrd.
Single rack to 8". The largest Big Bro's work on the crux.

This route climbs the obvious offwidth splitting the wall to the right of The Ugly Sister. Insecure and runout, it is one of the harder routes of the Herbst era. Start up a hand and fist crack in a black corner which leads to the base of the offwidth. An ancient bolt protects the initial bulge, then 40' of sustained, insecure climbing leads to the easier upper chimney and a tree belay.

❹ Truth 180' 5.8
Joe Herbst and friend.
Single rack to 4".
The central line. A steep start, up a fist crack in a right-facing corner, leads to blocks at the base of a lovely, clean-walled chimney. Finish up the chimney, fairly easy but very airy and completely unprotected, not for the faint of heart.

❺ Wisdom 180' 5.7
Joe Herbst and Friend. 1970's.
The right-hand line. A blocky start leads to a deep squeeze chimney which ends in a big alcove. Finish up the squeeze chimney at the top of the alcove.

❻ The Forgotten 170' 5.10b
Single rack to 3", four 2.5".
This route climbs the perfect hand crack a few feet to the right of Wisdom. Either start up Wisdom and move right, or start up the left-slanting lower continuation of the crack. Continue, following the crack over an arching roof and up the wall above to the upper alcove of Wisdom. Either finish up Wisdom or the unprotected wall (5.7) to the right of the upper alcove.

The following two routes climb the cracks on either side of a tower a couple of hundred feet above The Triad and just to the east of Crack McMuffin. They are most easily approached by climbing up the steep gully about 100 yards to the right of The Triad.

Tuxedo Junction 300' 5.9

Karsten Duncan. A. Anagnostou, Gigette Miller, Larry DeAngelo. 2006.
The crack to the left of the pillar. The route can be approached by airy third class just to the right of the Triad.
1. 150' 5.9 Work up into the main left-facing corner, which is climbed to a ledge shared with Stairway to the Stars.
2. 150' 5.7 Climb out of the notch, then up the face to the left of the offwidth.
Descent: Rappel to the west with two ropes.

Stairway to the Stars 400' 5.9 *

Anthony Anagnostou, Larry DeAngelo. 2006.
Single rack to 6".
The main corner pitches of this route are excellent. From the top of the approach gully, scramble up and left for a couple of hundred feet, up to easy fifth class, to get into the base of the huge right-facing corner to the right of the tower.
1. 150' 5.9 Climb a squeeze chimney to reach a beautiful, thin-hands crack which leads to a big ledge.
2. 150' 5.7 Step left and climb up another varnished corner with an offwidth crack (5.7). When the corner is blocked by a sandy overhang, make an inobvious step left and finish on solid rock with good holds.
Descent: Down climb then rappel to the west with a single 70m rope to reach a point high in the approach gully. Descend-ing the approach gully is tricky and very unpleasant, instead traverse west on easy slabs and reverse the Crack McMuffin approach.

Up and right of The Triad, at the top of the south wall of the canyon, is a long wall of darkly varnished rock split by several enticing looking crack systems. This is the Blood Wall. The Blood Wall sits above a large bowl. Below the left side of this bowl is a 300' high black wall whose base is about 500' above the creek bed. The following route climbs the crack in the center of this wall, finishing at a large pine tree.

Crack McMuffin 300' 5.7+

Stephanie Petrilak, Mike Gilbert, Joanne Urioste. September 1979.
Quite a steep and sustained route for the grade. This route is reached by scrambling up slabs to the base of the wall. From a point in the wash well to the west of the route, scramble up to reach a bushy ramp leading back to the east. Follow the ramp as it rises back to the east, then scramble up and right across a fourth class slab to the tree ledge at the base of the route.
1. 20' 5.7 Climb a short wall to a pine tree on a ledge.
2. 80' 5.7 Climb the steep crack.
3. 120' 5.7+ Continue up the crack.
4. 80' 5.6 Continue up the crack to a large pine tree at the top.
Descent: Just east of the wall, two 80' rappels lead into a gully which leads back to the base of the route. Some may want to rappel parts of the lower slabs as well. This requires an extra rope. It is also possible to descend to the west along slabs and ledges and connect with the Blood Wall approach route, this option doesn't require any raps but has a few short fifth class steps and some tricky route finding.

Colbin Smith on The Main Vein. Page 136.

The Blood Wall

This is the beautiful, varnished wall high on the south side of the canyon, opposite Black Orpheus. The wall faces due north; it gets very little sun for most of the year, but in the late spring, as the sun gets high in the sky, it gets sun both early and late. The wall is very exposed to any wind that may be blowing.

Approach: The approach is fairly involved, with lots of 4th class and a few 5th class steps; it should be done with proper approach shoes. Look for a towering, varnished arete on the left side of the big cliff containing Oakey Dokey (TC Arete). Scramble up into a shallow, gray, waterwashed gully below the arete. This leads to a big pine tree about 200' above the wash. The first obstacle is the steep left sidewall of a gully. This is crossed about 100' above the large tree, on a blocky ramp with a small tree/bush. Continue left up easy slabs and ledges then follow an open gully to a ramp underneath the upper wall. Follow the ramp up and east to a saddle with great views. The right end of The Blood Wall is directly above. To get to the left end of the cliff, drop down into a bushy bowl then zig-zag along the slabs below the wall until easy chimneys lead to a lovely flat corridor behind a small buttress in front of the main face. 2.2 miles, 1300' elevation gain, 1¼ hrs.

Descent: Most of the routes on this wall use rappel descents. To descend from the summit, scramble down to the west to get into a big, slabby bowl which drains out into the south branch of the canyon a couple of hundred yards west of the main fork in the canyon.

The wall is split into two distinct sections separated by an area of more broken rock. The left-hand section is described first. It is an attractive wall of dark varnish split by three very prominent wide crack systems.

❶ Transfusion 360' 5.10b

Bob Goodwin, Merlin Larsen. Spring 2006.
Single rack to 7", double 3"-6".
This is the left-most of the three obvious wide cracks on the left side of the Blood Wall. To approach this route, stay low going around the small buttress in front of the wall. Scramble up and left, across a large dead tree in a chasm, then head up to the base of the crack.
1. 180' 5.9 Chimney to a stance below a chockstone.
2. 180' 5.10b Climb around the chockstone and continue up through a steep fist section.
Descent: Rappel with two ropes.

Between the big crack systems of Transfusion and Seppuku is a tall, slightly convex face of immaculate varnish.

❷ Glass Half Empty 55' 5.12b

Start at the left end of the corridor. Boulder up to a small roof at 15' then pull into a very shallow left-curving groove. Continuously technical moves lead up the groove to better holds then the anchor (5 b's).

❸ Venipuncture 95' 5.12b ***

Single rack to 1".
Although it's not quite up to the standard of its amazing neighbor to the right, this is still a brilliant route. Start up The Main Vein then traverse left and climb a long, intricate wall to a horizontal (5 b's). Move up to a good rest in a big hole. Pull left

out of the hole and move up (b) to a thin crack. Climb the crack and thin face above (b) to the anchor.

❹ The Main Vein 100' 5.12c ***

Single rack to 1.25", 2 sets Rp's.
One of the better single pitch routes in the entire region; beautiful rock, superb, well-protected climbing and a stunning line. Start 40' left of Seppuku below the left of two flakes. Climb the flake then an intricate wall (3 b's) to a small flake on the left (small gear) up this to a horizontal. Continue to two side by side scoops (2 b's) then step left to a good rest in a big hole. Pull right out of the hole to the base of an amazing thin crack which slices up the shield of varnish above. The crack has a distinct crux but feels pretty sustained all the way to the anchor.

❺ Hemodynamics 95' 5.13a *

Single rack to 1".
This route has a short but very hard crux. Possibly high in the grade, but height-dependant.
Start below the right hand of two flakes to the left of Seppuku. Climb the flake and continue up the shallow scoop to reach good holds (8 b's). Move right to the base of a long, thin left-leaning crack. Climb the crack past a short crux, to an anchor at the top.

❻ Seppuku 450' 5.11a *

Karsten Duncan, Andrew Gomoll. September 12, 2006.
Single rack to 7", doubles 4"- 7".
This route climbs the central of the three cracks, the crack to the right of Transfusion. It appears as a wide crack, splitting a varnished face, with a characteristic left kink about 120' up.
1. 130' 5.11a Climb a large, flaring chimney which gradually narrows and is capped by a small roof. Continue up the crack above the roof as it deepens into a chimney. When the crack arches left, step left and climb the face to rejoin the crack where it turns vertical. Belay here on nuts and small cams.
2. 120' 5.9 Climb a nice, tight dihedral with lots of features. When the crack splits, take the left branch, which angles up and left across a featured face. Belay just below a rotten roof, or traverse to the right, and down a bit, to a large block with rap slings.
3. 200' 5.9 Traverse about 60' to the right into a large chimney system. After 40' the chimney turns into a hand crack and the angle eases off. Continue up featured, but lower quality rock, and belay at a large boulder.
Descent: Three raps with two 60m ropes.

❼ OW Negative 800' 5.10c *

Larry DeAngelo, Karsten Duncan. August 5, 2007.
Double to 7", triple 3"- 4".
Start at the base of the right-hand of the three crack systems.
1. 100' 5.7 Move up the varied chimney to where the chimney opens up and a wedged boulder makes a nice stance.
2. 120' 5.10c Move back, deep into the gaping chasm and then climb up the chimney placing a large cam as high as possible near the lip. Drop back down and out of the chimney. Do several awkward moves through the rotten roof. Continue up excellent rock for another 60' of 5.9 offwidth to just below a wide spot in the crack.
3. 190' 5.9 Chimney up the edge of the cave opening. When it

The Blood Wall – Left side.

The Blood Wall - Right side.

squeezes down, climb the beautiful offwidth crack to just below a small roof.

4. 200' 5.8 Continue up and left, taking a hand crack above (shared with Seppuku). Continue up the crack to a big ledge with a slung boulder. It is possible to do three double-rope rappels down Seppuku from here.

5. 80' 5.9 Walk back from the face to another small white rock wall with a right-angling crack on the face. Climb the angling crack and continue up it as it turns vertical. Belay on ledge.

6. 100' 4th class Continue up and right to the top.

The following routes are on the tall buttress on the right side of the wall which is split by several attractive crack and corner systems. From the saddle, drop into the bushy bowl and scramble up to the highest ledges at the base of the wall.

Descent: Take a gully, skier's left from the summit. Down climbing leads to rappels from trees, at least two of these rappels require two ropes, finishing to the climbers' right of the steep amphitheater at the base of the wall.

At the base of the wall is an amphitheater of smooth, steep rock capped by roofs. The first route climbs a corner system that is just to the left of this feature.

❽ Impulse 700' 5.10b *

Bob Goodwin, Rob Dezonia. Nov 2006.
Rp's, Single rack to 3", double wires, small cams.

This route has a couple of nice sections up the elegant right-facing corners that border the left edge of this buttress. The corner is as clean as it appears from the ground, but there is a bit of flaky rock in a few places. Start below the left-hand of two corner systems at the left side of the amphitheater.

1. 170' 5.9 Start at a dead pine leaning against the wall. Climb around this, into a right-facing corner (the left most and easier-looking of two corners). Continue through a blank section, which requires a bit of runout, to the top of the corner. Move left and climb a short crack system to a big ledge.

2. 175' 5.10a From the right side of the ledge, climb the steep left-leaning corner into a thin crack. Follow the crack into the obvious right-facing corner above. Belay on a sloping ledge after a clean 5.8 section.

3. 185' 5.10b Continue up the clean corner above (crux, Rp's). The climbing eases higher up, then take a steep thin crack up and right to a ledge.

4. 170' 5.8 Climb the corner/gully through some brush to the summit.

Variation: Climb a 5.10 flake up toward an obvious crack in the summit block. Climb a thin-hand crack through a roof and an overhanging slot to the summit. **(180', 5.11d).**

❾ Blood Sweat and Beers 470' 5.12b

Single rack to 3", extra wires and small cams.

This route climbs a very prominent corner and crack system in the center of the buttress which is guarded by a steep amphitheater at its base. The first pitch is excellent but the upper pitches are a bit flaky and not very enjoyable. An obvious left hand finish is unclimbed but may provide a more enjoyable alternative to the last pitch. Start below a thin corner/ramp on a high ledge below the right side of the amphitheater.

1. 120' 5.12b Climb the thin corner for 30', then move right and climb the steep wall (5 b's) to reach a slanting crack/rail which is followed up and left to an anchor on a small ledge below some roofs. It is possible to lower off with a 70m rope.

2. 60' 5.11d Make a hard pull over the roof above the belay and continue up easier cracks to a stance.

3. 70' 5.9 Continue up the cracks above and belay a short distance below some greenery.

4. 150' 5.10c. A very serious pitch with flaky rock and poor gear. Traverse up and right into a big corner system. Climb the big corner to a bulge at its top, then follow the arch up and right to a ledge with some bushes.

Descent: Using tree anchors, three raps with two ropes lead down the big corner system below the right end of the ledge.

❿ Bloodbath 700' 5.9

Johnny Ray, Larry DeAngelo. 2007.
Single rack to 3".

This route follows the prominent left-facing corner and crack system on the right edge of the Blood Wall. Four pitches up the crack lead to easier, broken rock near the summit. The crux is a steep section on the second pitch.

⓫ Bush League 700' 5.9

Ted Fisher, Matt Unger, Doug Hemken, K. Duncan, L. DeAngelo. 2007.
Single rack to 3", optional big cam for the easy offwidth.

Start immediately to the right of the obvious left-facing corner of Bloodbath. There is some good climbing on this route, but it is somewhat offset by occasional battles with hostile shrubbery. A long, sustained pitch leads to a belay alcove beneath a polished wall. The second pitch goes past the polished headwall, through a bush or two, then up a slickly-varnished, left-leaning crack. The third pitch follows the world's friendliest offwidth (5.0) to more broken ground. Fourth class leads to the top.

The Fork Buttress

On the south side of the Canyon, above the point where it splits into north and south branches, is an impressive north-facing buttress. An obvious feature of the buttress is a pair of huge left-facing arches. Oakey Dokey climbs the face to the left of the arch on the left, joining it at the top.

Approach: The approach involves some 4th class and a few 5th class steps; it should be done with proper approach shoes. Start a short distance below the main fork in Oak Creek Canyon. Follow slabby ramps back to the east, then scramble up to the base of the wall.

1.8 miles, 750' elevation gain, 1 hour.

Descent: From the summit it is easy to scramble west down the broad ridge (cairns) to get into a big, slabby bowl which drains out into the south branch of the canyon a couple of hundred yards west of the main fork in the canyon.

❶ TC Arete 600' 5.11d

This route climbs the huge arete to the left of Oakey Dokey. Not much is known about this route, but its a good-looking line that crosses some nice, varnished rock.

Follow bolts on the first pitch to a small roof, pull the roof on the left, and follow shallow cracks and face climbing to the summit.

The Fork Buttress.

❷ Oakey Dokey 500' 5.10b
Bob Harrington, Alan Bartlett, Bill St. Jean. 1978.
Single rack to 4", Rp's.
Start about 100' to the left of the left most of the two arches.
1 & 2. 5.9 Go up and right to the base of a left-facing corner capped by a roof. Lieback up the corner, then exit the corner before the roof, going up and right to a ledge. Belay towards the right end of the ledge.
3. 5.10b Climb to a ledge at the base of a left-facing flake.
4. 5.9 Face climb to the left of the flake and continue up into a large left-facing corner.
5. Easy climbing leads to the top.

The following routes climb the upper face to the right of the right most of the two big arches. To reach these routes it is probably easiest to scramble up the left (south) branch of Oak Creek to a point just before a big slabby drainage which comes in from the south. Climb up to a brushy ramp which can be followed back east to the wide ledge area at the base of the wall.

❸ Cheap Drills 300' 5.8
This route climbs a crack system in the wall to the right of the right edge of the big arch. From the slabby ledges at the base of the wall, scramble all the way left on exposed 4th class terrain to a bolt anchor close to the arete of the arch.
1. 150' 5.8 Climb straight up, following thin cracks. Eventually, bear right and climb up to another bolted anchor.

2. 150' 5.8 Go up and slightly left until you can move back right on a rounded rib in the white rock. This leads to a hand crack and the summit. There is a third bolted station next to the hand crack on the top of the formation.

Tres Bon 300' 5.7
Bruno Girard and Larry DeAngelo. 2010.
Start at the same point as Cheap Drills.
1. 150' 5.7 Follow thin cracks that slant up and to the right. Set up a gear belay beneath a small bulge.
2. 150' 5.7 Go straight up via thin cracks and face climbing to reach the left-hand of the two parallel cracks in the upper wall. Follow this to the top.

Summerset 300' 5.7
Steven Van Betten, Paul Van Betten, Larry DeAngelo. 2010.
Midway between Tres Bon and Les Miserables, there is a faint, ramp-like weakness running up and right on the varnished face. It leads to the right-hand of the two parallel cracks in the upper white wall. Follow this to a gear belay. The second pitch continues straight to a crack on the white face. When this crack peters out, move left to join the crack on Tres Bon.

Les Miserables 300' 5.9
Bruno Girard, Larry DeAngelo. 2010.
This route climbs a dirty crack system which leads up into a big gully at the top of the wall.

There are numerous walls in the network of gullies on the northwest side of Mt. Wilson and Cactus Flower Tower. The next two routes are near the top of the gully that leads up to the saddle between Mt. Wilson and Cactus Flower Tower.

Approach: Go up Oak Creek, taking the south fork when the canyon splits. A short distance up the south fork, a large slabby drainage opens up on the left. Scramble up this drainage, then when it is blocked by a 15' high waterwashed wall, scramble

up onto the broad, slabby buttress on the left. Continue up this buttress (cairns) zig-zagging through short walls and gullies. As height is gained, the buttress narrows into a better defined ridge. Before this point, a big slabby shelf leads across the right side of the ridge. The shelf reaches the bushy gully on the right a short distance below a very prominent steep buttress on the right side of the gully. Line of Addiction climbs this buttress, The Coffin climbs the flat, varnished wall to its right.
2.6 miles, 1800' elevation gain, 2 hrs.

The Coffin 570' 5.11c

Brian Bowman, Dave Melchior, Damon Smolko. 2001.
FFA Tom Moulin, Brian Bowman. Spring 2006.
Single rack to #5 Camalot, Rp's.

This route follows a single crack system splitting a tall tombstone of rock for its entire length.

1. 100' 5.10b Climb a moss covered slab for 40' to where the wall steepens. Continue up a crack for 50', with flaky rock, then step right to a pine tree.

2. 100' 5.9 Climb the loose and dirty crack, setting up an anchor in a pod.

3. 110' 5.11c Continue up the steep crack, past a fixed piton (crux) into "The Coffin".

4. 70' 5.10b Stem up the Coffin, turn the lip on the right, and go up a black, varnished face for 25' to a sandy flare. Set up a hanging belay just above the flare.

5. 220' Face climb up a seam to a fixed pin, continue face climbing to a ledge, then traverse right past loose blocks to a mossy and loose crack which is climbed to the top.

Descent: Rap from the top on a fixed line, to a ledge. Rap off the end of the fixed line with two 70m ropes to reach the Coffin. Another rap leads to the pine tree above pitch 1, then another to the ground.

❹ Line of Addiction 800' 5.11d *

Single rack to 6", double 4", Rp's, offset green/yellow alien is crucial.

This route follows an elegant right-facing corner system on the crest of the buttress. To its right is an even more prominent left-facing corner which starts above a smooth, varnished face.

1. 100' 5.9+ Climb a left-facing crack to a ledge, traverse left, and climb a thin crack to an anchor.

2. 100' 5.10b Lieback the righthand corner (7 b's) to an anchor.

3. 85' 5.11a From the belay, step over left into the 4" crack in the big right-facing corner. Climb the corner to anchors.

4. 120' 5.10c Climb up and left onto the arete (b) then traverse right to a small ledge in the corner. Climb the corner to an anchor. Continue up the corner to where the crack pinches off, then face climb to another anchor.

5. 50' 5.8 Climb up and left (b) to an anchor on a nice ledge.

6. 100' 5.11d Climb up on poor rock to a left-facing corner just left of the arete. Climb the corner (crucial green/yellow offset alien) then traverse right to the arete. Climb the arete into a beautiful overhanging corner. Up this (6 b's) to anchors.

7. 85' 5.6 Climb to a nice, long ledge with a large pine tree.

8. 100' 5.9 Walk past the tree and climb the first crack for 10', then traverse left across the face for 10' to a right-facing corner. Climb the corner until it is possible to traverse left into a chimney. Climb the chimney until you can walk out the other side to a big pine tree. 150' of scrambling lead to the top.

Descent: Rappel with two ropes. It is possible to rap from the top of the crux pitch with a single 70m rope.

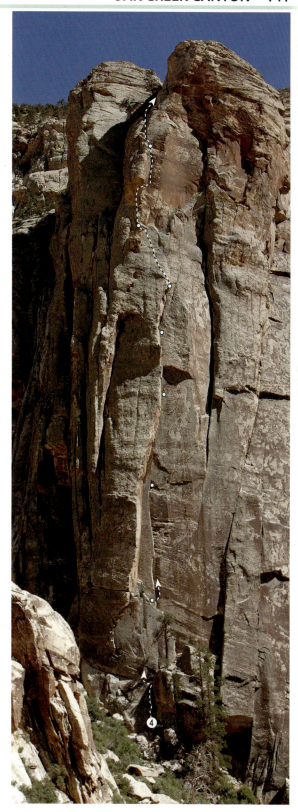

RAINBOW MOUNTAIN - SOUTH FACE

The rest of the routes described in Oak Creek Canyon
are on the enormous south face of Rainbow Mountain.
All these routes lie above the main canyon and its
north branch. This entire wall gets a lot of sun exposure, making it one of the best areas in Red Rocks for
multi-pitch climbing in cold weather.

Eagle Wall

The Fortress

Upper Solar Slab

The Painted Bowl

Celebration Wall

Black Arch Wall

Lower Solar Slab

Sunspot Ridge

Da
Boneyard

Wise Guys
Off Size

The
Friar

Red Zinger
Area

Byrd
Pinnacle

Celebration Wall

The Celebration Wall lies just below the limestone, at the very top of the north fork of Oak Creek Canyon. It faces southeast and gets afternoon shade. The wall is distinguished by a black slab on the left side, and several long, left-slanting cracks in white rock on the right hand side. Although there are many routes in Red Rocks that offer similar climbing in much more accessible locations, the enjoyable approach and descent, the gorgeous surroundings, and the spectacular views give this wall a unique appeal.

Approach: From the Oak Creek Trailhead take the trail into the canyon, which is followed to the main fork in about 40 minutes. Scramble over huge boulders into the north fork and follow the rugged creek bed up water-washed slabs and over boulders. Close to the top of the canyon, there is an area of beautiful water-washed slabs and bristlecone pines which lie below the black slab on the left hand side of the Celebration Wall. 2.5 miles, 1600' elevation gain, 2 hours.

❶ Coltrane 785' 5.9 * ❶
Jorge Urioste, Joanne Urioste. April 1979.
Single rack to 2.5".
This route climbs the center of the black slab.
Start below the left hand of two breaks in the band of over-hangs that run along the base of the slab. This point is reached by continuing up the canyon until above a large slabby waterfall, then making a traverse right, across dicey slabs to the ledge at the base of the wall. Follow this rightwards until below the left hand break.
1. 140' 5.9 Steep climbing on beautiful dark rock (3 b's) leads onto an easier slab. Up this (2 b's) then traverse left until it is possible to go up and right (b) to a belay platform at the base of a shallow right-facing corner.
2. 165' 5.7 Climb straight up the wide open slab (4 b's) to an anchor.
3. 165' 5.8 Climb straight up for 80' to a bolt, then go diagonally right (2 b's) to an anchor.
4. 165' 5.8 There is a white pillar on the right. Climb to the top of the pillar (b) then downclimb 20' on the opposite side. Traverse right 15', then climb straight up (3 b's) to an anchor on a large ledge.
5. 150' 4th Class Scramble up to a huge terrace where the route ends.
Descent: Follow the terrace to the left, around the corner to where the cliff dwindles. Continue traversing west into a shallow, slabby gully which leads back into the upper reaches of Oak Creek Canyon. 20 minutes back to the base.

❷ The Easter Egg 300' 5.6
Jorge Urioste, Joanne Urioste. April 1979.
On the right hand side of the slab, almost at the edge of the black rock, a tower leans against the wall. Start on top of a bushy triangle of broken and white rock. Climb up and left, following thin cracks, to reach a ramp that forms the left side of the tower. Scramble up this to the top of the formation.
Descent: Scramble back down to the base of the ramp and rappel from here to the ground with two ropes.

There are two long, diagonal, crack systems that cut across the white rock on the right hand side of the Celebration Wall. Underhanging Overhang is the crack on the left and Catwalk is the crack on the right. Both these routes face south and get sun well into the afternoon.

❸ Underhanging Overhang 1200' 5.7+
Joe Frani, Margo Young. February 1975.
Start in the wash below the left hand crack.
1. Climb steep but easy rock to a wide ledge at the base of the left hand crack.
2. Climb the crack to an awkward belay.
3. Continue up the crack. Where it branches, take the left hand line to a large ledge on the right.
4. Walk over to the large left-facing dihedral on the right. Go up a crack to a small belay.
5. Continue up the crack, over a small overhang and up to a sloping ledge where the wall steepens.
6. Go up a black face, then step left into a white crack which is followed to a ledge.
7. From the right hand side of the ledge, go through an over-hang, past a loose block, then follow the cleft through the roof.
8. 150' 5.6+ Continue up the crack in the black face, and when the angle eases, climb up and right to a ledge.
9. 60' 5.3 Easy climbing leads to a tree and the top.
Descent: A short hike to the west leads to a slabby gully which leads down into the upper reaches of Oak Creek Canyon.

❹ Catwalk 1200' 5.6+ *
Margo Young, Joe Frani. February 1975.
Single rack to 3".
This route climbs the right hand of the two crack systems. Start below an obvious slabby break that leads up and right to the base of the right hand crack system. 400' of 4th and easy 5th class climbing up the slabby break lead to a ledge at the base of the crack, this is about 80' below a large overhang. Some climbers may want to pitch sections of this approach depending upon the level of experience.
1. 80' 5.4 Follow the crack, with scarce protection, to a ledge just below the roof.
2. 130' 5.6 Continue up the crack past the left side of the roof and continue to a belay in a pothole just to the left of the right most of several obvious black streaks.
3. 165' 5.6 Continue up the crack to a right-facing corner with some bushes. Belay on a spacious ledge on top of the tower that forms the corner.
4. 150' 5.5 Continue up the crack into a huge right-facing corner. Up the corner to a ledge below a smooth, light-brown face with a chimney on its left side.
5. 80' 5.6 Climb the chimney, exiting left at its top. Continue to a belay on the highest of three ledges.
The last two pitches are common with Underhanging Over-hang
6. 150' 5.6+ Continue up the crack in the black face and when the angle eases climb up and right to a ledge.
7. 60' 5.3 Easy climbing leads to a trees and the top.
Descent: A short hike to the west leads to a slabby gully which leads down into the upper reaches of Oak Creek Canyon.

Eagle Wall

This huge, steep buttress sits high above the upper reaches of the north fork of Oak Creek Canyon. It faces due south, and because of its location, high above the canyon floor, it receives sun all day. The routes here are best during cooler weather, however, this can create a few problems. Shorter days combined with the long approach and descent leave little room for error if a party is to avoid benightment. During colder weather, even when the climb is warm, there can be lots of black ice in the drainage, making the descent more time consuming and dangerous. And lastly, the wall is very exposed, and as result, high winds are an issue that can sometimes rule out the possibility of a rappel descent. Nevertheless, racing up this wall on a crisp winter day makes for an unforgettable outing. Pitch after pitch of spectacular climbing is followed by the beautiful terrain on the summit, then the amazing views of the high country of Red Rocks on the descent hike.

Approach: From the Oak Creek trailhead take the trail into the canyon, which is followed to the main fork in about 40 minutes. Scramble over huge boulders into the north fork and follow the rugged creek bed up water-washed slabs and over boulders. After about 30 minutes of scrambling, there are two huge pine trees in the canyon. They sit a little west of the Eagle Wall and mark the start of a slabby ramp which leads back to the east, towards the base of the wall; the ramp ends at a small saddle just west of the black pillar at the start of Eagle Dance. Dances with Beagles starts up and left from this point. All the other routes are reached by scrambling down the other side of the saddle to a bushy ramp which leads along the base of the wall. About 2.6 miles, 1700' elevation gain, 1.5 - 2 hrs. total time. Other options on the photo below.

Descent: Anyone climbing this wall should make the effort to go to the top at least once. However, if time is short, some of the routes allow for a rappel descent, which can provide a faster alternative. To walk off from the top of the wall, scramble north to low-angled terrain below Rainbow Mountain. Follow ledges and ramps leading west below Rainbow Mountain. These ramps head towards an obvious red tower, called George Washington Tower, which sits on the ridge to the west of Rainbow Mountain. Skirt the tower on its northern (right) side, scrambling across slabs and blocks to reach the ridge to the west of the tower. Once on the ridge, descend down slabby gullies on the south side. These gullies eventually lead into the upper reaches of Oak Creek Canyon. It takes about 1-1.5 hrs. to get back to the trees at the base of the approach ramp.

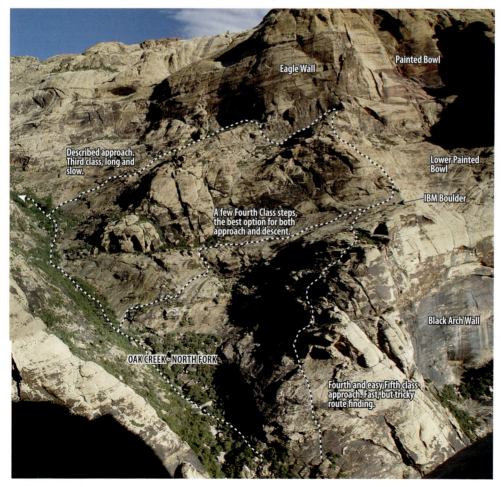

Mountain Skills guide Jay Foley on pitch 5 of Mountain Beast. Page 148.

❶ Dances with Beagles 430' 5.11d *

Jeff Rhodes, Todd Swain. Spring 1993.
Single rack to 1.25".

This route is on the left hand side of the wall. Start about 300' left of Eagle Dance, at a point about 40' to the left of a 50' high pillar. This is just to the right of a huge, varnished left-facing corner.

1. 140' 5.8 Climb an easy varnished corner to a steep seam. Follow the seam (2 b's), which jogs up and left. When the seam ends, head up and right to a ledge.

2. 130' 5.11b Follow a flake above the belay to a thin left-slanting seam in smooth rock. Climb the seam and pull over the roof above (b). Move up and right (b) to a thin crack which is followed to an anchor.

3. 160' 5.11d Climb the steep face (17 b's) to an anchor.

Descent: Rappel with two ropes.

❷ Eagle Dance 1060' 5.10c, A0 ***

Jorge Urioste, Joanne Urioste. March 1980.
Single rack to 2".

The Eagle Wall is named after a large patch of varnish in the middle of the wall, which bears a resemblance to an eagle flying west. Eagle Dance climbs through the eagle's neck. Eagle Dance is a superb classic on excellent rock. The route can be rappelled from any point below the 10th pitch. Although not quite a sport route, it is heavily bolted. It is rare to find such an amenable route in such spectacular surroundings.

At the base of the wall is a large, detached pillar of dark rock. The approach ramp ends on a little col just west of this feature. Start 50' to the right of the pillar, at the base of a shallow, varnished corner which leans slightly to the left.

1. 90' 5.9 Climb the corner to a small ledge.

2. 120' 5.7 Continue up the crack for 30', when the crack system splits, follow the thin, left-slanting, left branch to the base of a short ramp which leads back right to an anchor.

Pitches 1 & 2 can be combined if the second climbs up 10'.

3. 160' 5.10a It is a good idea to use long slings on the first few bolts of this pitch to reduce rope drag higher up. Move right then up (2 b's). Step right, into a seam which is followed up and left (4 b's) to an optional anchor. Continue up the seam (4 b's) to an anchor on top of a huge detached block.

4. 90' 5.10c Climb straight up the spectacular white face (14 b's), passing through the eagles' neck to reach an anchor at a black band.

5. 120' 5.10a Continue up the face (9 b's) to an anchor at a sloping ledge.

6. 50' 5.10a Pull up past a bolt to a right-leaning ramp. Follow the ramp for a few feet, then climb up loose flakes into a right-facing corner. Follow the corner (2 b's), exiting left to an anchor below the huge bulge.

7. 60' 5.8, A0 Follow a thin crack leftwards to reach a bolt ladder leading through the bulge. Aid out the bolt ladder (8 b's) to an anchor.

8. 40' 5.10b Climb the awkward, tight corner above (4 b's) to an anchor.

9. 100' 5.10c The crux pitch. Sustained and awkward climbing up a long, holdless corner (7 b's) leads to an anchor on a large ledge. There are no fixed anchors above this point.

10. 130' 5.9 Follow the lower-angled crack up and left (4 b's) to a large platform.

11. 100' 4th Class Scramble to the top.

Descent: To rappel the route, start from the top of the 9th

pitch. From above the bulge, skip the anchor under the bulge and continue down to the anchor on the sloping ledge above the 5th pitch.

If you go to the top, follow the descent described in the introduction to the Eagle Wall.

❸ Levitation 29 1060' 5.11c ***

Jorge Urioste, Joanne Urioste, Bill Bradley. April 1981. FFA (1st 7 pitches only) Lynn Hill, John Long, Joanne Urioste. May 1981.
Single rack to 1.75".

This route climbs straight up the wall through the tail of the Eagle. The beautiful direct line and continuous steepness more than make up for the occasional patches of sandy and flaky rock on this well-established classic.

Start about 200' to the right of a huge black pillar that leans against the base of the wall, below some thin, varnished cracks that lead up to a roof about 150' above the ground.

1. 80' 5.10b Nice climbing up varnished cracks and short corners (4 b's) leads to an anchor.

2. 80' 5.11a Climb up and right, following big holds up a series of flakes into the roof. After a short, athletic crux, a few moves lead out left to an anchor (8 b's).

3. 120' 5.8 Climb up a crack for 75', then move up and right (2 b's) to an anchor.

4. 140' 5.10b Climb up to and over a small roof, then continue up the face and crack (7 b's) to an anchor at the base of a gently overhanging wall.

5. 90' 5.11c A brilliant pitch. Pumpy climbing leads up the crack and corner system above to a hanging belay (13 b's).

6. 60' 5.10d Continue up the steep crack system (5 b's) which slants up and left to an anchor.

7. 85' 5.11a A wild, sustained pitch on soft, white rock. Make a series of delicate face moves up into a scoop. Once in the scoop, move right to a steep, rounded crack which is followed to an anchor (13 b's).

8. 90' 5.9 Climb up a left-facing flake (b) to second bolt at its top. Traverse 20' right to a left-slanting crack. Continue up the crack and face above (5 b's) traversing left after the last bolt to an anchor on a slab.

9. 90' 5.9 Climb up and left on fragile rock to gain a right-facing corner. Awkward rounded rock leads up the corner to an anchor at the top (7 b's).

10. 60' 5.5 Climb up and right to the top.

Descent: The route can be rapped, starting from the top of the 9th pitch; a 70m rope works (barely) but 80m is better. If you go to the top, follow the descent described in the introduction to the Eagle Wall.

❹ Mountain Beast 960' 5.10d *

Joanne Urioste, Mike Moreo. February 1997.
Single rack to 3".

This route starts up Ringtail, then after three pitches branches out left. A good climb with a couple excellent pitches.

Start at the top of the approach ramp, about 30' to the left of the drop-off into the Lower Painted Bowl.

1. 120' 5.9 Climb a left-leaning crack system in the left arete of a small buttress to reach easy rock. Go into a left-leaning corner, which leads to an anchor at a sloping ledge.

2. 60' 5.10d Step right and go straight up (4 b's) until it is necessary to traverse left across a thin, varnished slab (2 b's) to an anchor at the base of a corner.

3. 120' 5.10a Make a few awkward moves (2 b's) to reach an easier crack which is followed to a sloping ledge.

Eagle Wall

4. 80' 5.8 Climb the short corner above, then move left and climb cracks in the arete to the left (b), passing a scary bulge to reach an anchor.

5. 140' 5.10b Step right and continue up the amazing vertical wall (9 b's) on good holds. At the top of the pitch, angle right to an anchor at the base of a shallow left-facing corner.

6. 140' 5.10a Climb the shallow corner to a ledge, then face climb past two bolts into a beautiful thin crack splitting the varnished wall. Follow the thin crack to easier ground, then continue past two more bolts to an anchor beside a tiny pine tree. This is the best place to start a rappel descent.

7. 150' 5.7 Step right and climb an obvious corner system (this is the upper part of pitch 7 of the original version of Rainbow Buttress), past a bush then on to a large ledge with a big pine tree.

8. 150' 5.8 Climb up the slabby face (8 b's) to an anchor at the top of the wall.

Descent: Follow the descent described in the introduction to the Eagle Wall.

❺ Ringtail 460' 5.10d *
Jorge Urioste, Joanne Urioste. January 1981.
Single rack to 3".

This route climbs the left side of the 500' high black tower that marks the right edge of the Eagle Wall. Start 30' to the left of the top of the approach ramp.

1. 120' 5.9 Climb a left-leaning crack system in the left arete of a small buttress to reach easy rock. Go into a left-leaning corner, which leads to an anchor at a sloping ledge.

2. 60' 5.10d Step right and go straight up (4 b's) until it is necessary to traverse left across a thin varnished slab (2 b's) to an anchor at the base of a corner.

3. 120' 5.10a Make a few awkward moves (2 b's) to reach an easier crack which is followed to a sloping ledge.

4. 90' 5.9 Go straight up the huge corner system to an anchor.

5. 70' 5.9 Climb a thin crack in the back of a flare to the top of the tower.

Descent: Rappel with two ropes.

❻ Rainbow Buttress 880' 5.8+ ***
Joe Herbst, Joe Frani. 1975.
Single rack to 5".

Rainbow Buttress is a great old-style classic. There are no fixed anchors or protection on the route, the approach and descent are long and tiring, and the climbing is up a series of stout crack pitches. Overall the route feels remote, serious and very rewarding.
Start at the very top of the approach ramp.

1. 100' 5.6 Easy climbing leads up a small buttress then right, into a short, dark corner. Up the corner to a huge ledge.

2. 60' 5.8 Climb the strenuous left-leaning corner above to a big ledge.

3. 130' 5.7 An awkward struggle leads up the steep offwidth into a flare, after which a move right leads onto the face. Continue up the easier corner to a ledge below some bushes.

4. 90' 5.7 Continue up the corner to the top of the Black Tower.

5. 90' 5.6 Step off the tower to a crack. Move right into a right-facing corner which is climbed for a short distance until it is possible to make an easy but poorly-protected traverse out right for 40' to reach a huge left-facing corner. Belay in the corner on large cams. (3"-4" needed).

6. 160' 5.8+ Climb the long, sustained corner to a big ledge. A burly pitch.

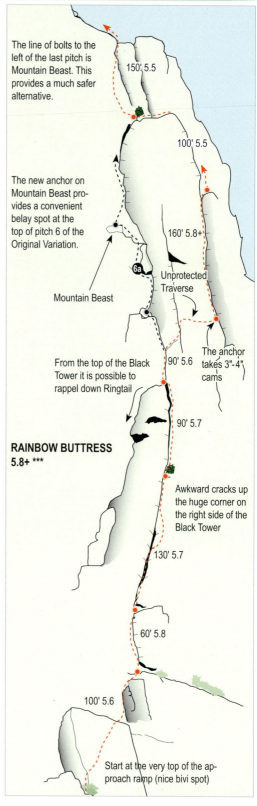

The line of bolts to the left of the last pitch is Mountain Beast. This provides a much safer alternative.

150' 5.5

100' 5.5

The new anchor on Mountain Beast provides a convenient belay spot at the top of pitch 6 of the Original Variation.

160' 5.8+

Mountain Beast

Unprotected Traverse

From the top of the Black Tower it is possible to rappel down Ringtail

The anchor takes 3"-4" cams

90' 5.6

90' 5.7

RAINBOW BUTTRESS
5.8+ *

Awkward cracks up the huge corner on the right side of the Black Tower

130' 5.7

60' 5.8

100' 5.6

Start at the very top of the approach ramp (nice bivi spot)

7. 100' 5.5 An easy chimney leads to a huge, sloping ledge with a pine tree.

8. 150' 5.5 From the right end of the ledge climb up sandy rock intersecting a crack on the right. Continue up the wide crack to the top. A fragile and poorly protected pitch.

6a Variation: This variation was climbed on the original ascent of the route. It starts from the top of the black tower

5a. 90' 5.8 From the top of the tower step across to the main wall and climb straight up cracks and face holds eventually stepping left to a ledge with a bush.

6a. 70' 5.7 Go up the corner/crack above to a roof, which forces a traverse left on face holds to reach a ledge. Don't belay here but instead climb up another 20' to a higher ledge and belay here.

7a. 190' 5.7 Follow a ramp up and left to a crack system. Follow the crack and the face to its right, eventually reaching the huge sloping ledge with the large pine tree. Finish up pitch 8 of the regular route.

Descent: Follow the descent described in the introduction.

❼ Kaleidoscope Cracks 980' 5.8
Jorge Urioste, Joanne Urioste. April 1977.

This route climbs the first pitch of Rainbow Buttress, then moves right and climbs a separate crack system before rejoining Rainbow Buttress just below the top.
Start at the top of the approach ramp.

1. 100' 5.6 Easy climbing leads up a small buttress then right, into a short corner. Up the corner to a huge ledge.

2. 100' 3rd class Walk to the right on the huge ledge to a tree.

3. 70' 5.7 From the pine tree, climb 20' to a bolt then traverse up and left, go around a small overhang then up to a ledge.

4. 80' 5.7+ Climb a black right-facing corner. When the corner splits, stay left and continue to a ledge. Climb a short, dark wall to a higher ledge and belay.

5. 70' 5.7 Climb the face, traversing right and around the corner to a bolt. Continue up and right to cracks leading into a wide chimney.

6. 80' 5.8 Continue up the chimney past an overhang and up the left hand cracks to a ledge with a tree.

7. 80' 5.5 Follow the crack for 50' then move right to a chimney.

8&9 250' 5.7 Continue up the chimney, eventually exiting left onto the huge sloping ledge with the pine tree, below the top pitch of Rainbow Buttress.

11. 150' 5.5 From the right end of the ledge, climb up sandy rock intersecting a crack on the right. Continue up the wide crack to the top. A fragile and poorly protected pitch.

Descent: Follow the descent described in the introduction to the Eagle Wall.

The following two routes are on the impressive wall on the right side of the Painted Bowl. The Painted Bowl is the area of swirling pink, red and white rock to the right of the Eagle Wall. The Lower Painted Bowl is the name given to the huge basin of bare rock above the Black Arch Wall, and below and to the right of the Eagle Wall. The most efficient approach to these routes is to climb Solar Slab. From the top of Solar Slab continue scrambling up the slabs for 800' to reach a saddle in the gully behind the very top of the buttress. There are gullies going down on either side of the saddle. To reach the following two routes go down the gully to the west, exiting onto a ledge system at the base of the wall. The routes start from this ledge.

Strawberry Sweat 640' 5.9
Joanne Urioste, Jorge Urioste. April 1980.

This route climbs the crack in the attractive prow of light colored rock 500' to the right of Rainbow Buttress.
Start in the chimney to the right of the crack.

1. 130' 5.4 Climb the chimney to a ledge on the left. Continue up an easy crack to a belay above a tree.

2. 150' 5.9 Continue up the crack until an easy traverse leads left across the face to the straight-in crack on the prow. Up the crack to a small stance (4 b's).

3. 160' 5.7 Continue up the crack.

4. 120' 5.7 Continue up the crack, which gradually narrows. Stay on the crest of the buttress and belay at a bolt and pin.

5. 80' 5.7 Go straight up to the top (b) towards a large tree.
3rd Class to the top. The route finishes very close to the top of Rainbow Buttress etc.

Chicken Lips 830' 5.10b *
Jorge Urioste, Joanne Urioste. April 1980.
Single rack to 5", double 1.75"- 3".

This is an enjoyable and varied climb, well worth the effort needed to reach it. In the center of the wall above the Painted Bowl is a flat wall with swirls of pink and red and varnished rock, and some huge overhangs on its upper left side. Chicken Lips climbs the long corner system to the right of this wall. If you are using the Solar Slab approach, the first pitch lies a short distance up and right from where the gully exits onto the ledge system. Look for a line of bolts on a slabby, white face.

1. 100' 5.10b Technical climbing up a thin seam (7 b's) leads to a good ledge at the base of a corner.

2. 100' 5.10a Continue up the corner. Where it splits, climb steeply up the right branch, then head back left and belay at the base of a pretty, varnished corner.

3. 130' 5.8 Climb the hand crack in the corner for 60', then exit onto the left arete. Continue up the arete (3 b's) to an anchor.

4. 150' 5.10a Continue with enjoyable face climbing up the rounded arete (7 b's), eventually moving right to an easy crack which leads up to a huge ledge with a tree.

5. 120' 5.9 A burly lieback up the corner at the back of the ledge leads into the base of a huge chimney system.

6&7 250' 5.8 Enjoyable chimneying leads to the top.

Descent: From the top of the climb, head east a short distance then scramble south down short walls and ledges, aiming in the general direction of the saddle at the top of the approach gully. Eventually a steep wall bars access to the gully. On top of this wall is a ledge with a pine tree. About 50' to the right (west) of the tree is a hidden anchor at the top of a water streak. A long rappel leads down to the saddle from this anchor. Scramble back down the gully to the base of the route. This descent is a bit complicated and exposed, but amazingly fast. From the base of the route, scramble down and a bit left to some bushes at the top of a chimney. Rappel 70' down the chimney. Continue down to a tree and make another rappel onto 3rd class slabs in the Lower Painted Bowl. A long scramble leads down the slabs on the west side of the Lower Painted Bowl. Aim for a solitary squarish boulder on the west shoulder of the bowl, the "IBM" boulder. From here, a long ramp system leads down and west. At the point where the ramp turns into a vegetated terrace, go down a steep gully then, zig-zag down some steep slab and ledges. Eventually, from the lowest ledge, a 20' slither down a smooth slab leads to the creek. 1½ hrs from summit to creek.

Black Arch Wall

This is the huge amphitheater of varnished rock whose west end is just to the east of the fork in the main canyon. Although there are patches of soft rock, this wall has some large areas of glassy-smooth varnish which makes for some interesting climbing. This is a very sunny and sheltered location useful for a cold, windy day. It holds the sun until the early afternoon.

Approach: Walk up the canyon until below the left end of the wall. This point is about one hundred yards before the fork in the canyon. A gully comes down from the bowl below the left end of the wall all the way to the creek bed. Unfortunately some large boulders at the base of the gully make identifica-

tion difficult. It is worth taking the time to find the gully because it is relatively bush free, whereas the slopes on either side are covered in dense scrub oak and manzanita.
1.9 miles, 800' elevation gain, 1 hr.

Descent: Above the right side of the wall is an area of bushes and a pine tree. Just below the pine tree is another, smaller pine tree with rappel slings, and below that is a bolted anchor. Three raps to the ground from here. A single 70m rope works. The top of the wall is at the bottom of The lower Painted Bowl and it is possible to walk off to the west using the standard Painted Bowl descent as described in the Solar slab section.

Black Arch Wall - Left side.

❶ Black Baby 330' 5.7
Tom Cecil, Mark Miller, Tony Barnes and John Rosholt. 1984/85.
This is a moderate route which climbs a crack system on the sunny buttress that forms the left side of the amphitheater. Start down and left of the back-left corner of the amphitheater, below a low-angled, black ramp which leads to a big sentry box.
1. 210' 5.7 Climb the ramp and continue up the crack system, through the sentry box, and on to a big ledge with some bushes.
Scramble up and left onto a higher ledge and belay below the varnished crack splitting the face above.
2. 120' 5.6 Climb up past the left side of a small overlap and continue up the crack to where it splits. Climb either branch and the easy rock above to the top.

❷ Black Crack 320' 5.9
Tom Cecil, Mark Miller, Tony Barnes and John Rosholt. 1984/85.
This route climbs the big corner system in the back-left corner of the amphitheater. There are two big cracks in the back of the corner, start below the crack on the right.
1. 150' 5.9 Start up the big crack, then step left to a thinner crack which is climbed to a bushy ledge. Climb the corner on the left to a slabby bowl below some steeper rock.
1a. 150' 5.8 Climb the crack on the left, staying to the left of the regular first pitch all the way to the slabby bowl.
2. 170' 5.9 Climb up and left to reach the highest of three right-slanting ramps. Follow the ramp to the base of the big right-facing corner above. Follow the huge corner, past several bushes, to the top of the wall.

At the western end of the wall are two big right-leaning arches.

❸ Black Betty 400' 5.10b †
Tom Cecil, Mark Miller, Tony Barnes and John Rosholt. 1984/85.
Start at a small flake plastered to the low-angled black slab below the left end of the upper of the two arches..
1. 150' 5.10b Climb up the slab (b) to the left end of the upper of the two arches. Follow a blind crack up and left (awkward and a little bold) to a finger crack. Continue up the cracks above to an anchor at the right end of a ledge below a bowl of steep rock.
2. 150' 5.10b Move right and climb a steep crack then move up and left into another crack system. Follow the crack to easier climbing and a ledge.
3. 100' 5.7 Continue up the crack system to some bushes below a roof. Move left and escape up a chimney.

❹ Arch of Blackness 250' 5.10c †
Tom Cecil, Mark Miller, Tony Barnes and John Rosholt. 1984/85.
This route climbs the upper of the two big right-leaning arches. Start up Black Betty then move right into the arch. Follow the arch to the anchor above pitch 2 of Black Widow.

❺ Black Widow 300' 5.12c *
Tom Cecil, Mark Miller, Tony Barnes and John Rosholt. 1984/85.
FFA (Complete Line): Joshua Janes & Darren Snipes. March, 2012.
Single rack to 3".
At the top of the approach gully, a large scoop of black rock has been carved out of the cliff. This route climbs the intermittent crack system that comes out the top of this scoop. Start below a thin seam in the left arete of the scoop.
1. 135' 5.11b Climb up the low-angle crack to a ledge beneath the steep, black wall above. Climb up and right (2 b's) into a water groove/crack system. Follow this (4 b's) past a thin face climbing crux and continue to a bolted anchor at a small hole.
2. 120' 5.10d Face climb directly above the anchor with spaced protection to a body-length, horizontal roof. A bolt at the lip protects a pull over the roof, then continue up the face above to another bolted anchor at a tiny ledge.
3. 120' 5.12c Face climb directly above the anchor on fragile rock to the arch. Steep, bouldery climbing leads out the arch to better holds and a chance for a shake. A few more tricky moves get you out from underneath the arch and up onto the exposed upper headwall. Follow a steep crack system for 90' to a belay stance on white rock.
4. 125' 5.7 Climb up the low-angle slab (unprotected), or slightly left along a nice finger crack, and then work back right to a final vertical, varnished crack. Climb one of several cracks up this to a belay stance 100' from the IBM Boulder.

❻ Howl's Moving Castle 400' 5.11c
Single rack to 4", double to 1", 4 or 5 x 0.4"- 0.5".
This route climbs the big left-leaning arch (the higher of two) in the center of Black Arch Wall. Start by scrambling up onto a bushy ledge below the right end of the arch.
1.75' 5.10b Climb straight up from the bushy ledge towards the left end of another bushy ledge below a chimney at the bottom of the main corner. Climb the unprotected chimney to a roof at its top (good gear). Exit left and go over the roof then step left to a bolted belay on top of a large flake.
2. 80' 5.11a From the belay, step right and climb the slippery, leaning corner. Liebacks and eventually fist jams lead to a good stem rest below a tips section. Lieback through the thin section (11a) then reach a large flake and make a thin mantle (b) followed by easier climbing up and left to a bolted anchor at a comfortable stance below an impressive crack slicing through the roof of the arch.
3. 90' 5.11c Powerful moves on good holds lead out the crack and around the lip. Continue up the crack system to a good belay ledge out right.
4. 75' 5.10d Continue up the crack system on soft, white rock but with good protection. Belay just above the top of the wall at a comfortable stance.

❼ Black Ops 260' 5.12a
Joshua Janes, K. McCullough, C. Galitsky. Winter, 2012.
Single rack to 3", double to 1".
About 100 yards left of Plate of Fate is a long, shallow, white right-facing corner. Another 20' further left is a low roof. Begin below an oven-sized inset in this roof.
1. 180' 5.10a Climb easy rock to the inset in the roof. Pull the roof and continue up the varnished face, following a seam (spaced but good protection) to a small ledge. Move right onto softer rock and continue for another 75' to a belay under the arch.
2. 80' 5.12a A wild pitch. Climb up and right off the belay and pinch and sidepull a unique tufa-like flake up the 45 degree headwall. At an incut (crucial 0.5"- 0.75" gear) fingertip traverse right to a few powerful moves up to huge incut jugs and more pro. Eventually, pull onto the low-angle face and continue to a belay just below the lip of the Painted Bowl.

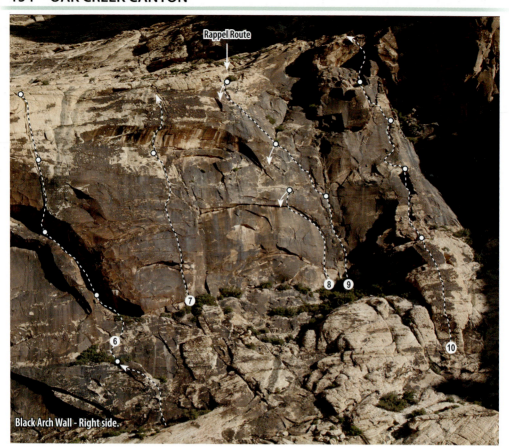

Black Arch Wall - Right side.

❽ The Secret World of Arrietty 140' 5.11c *

FFA: Joshua Janes & Josh Thompson. Spring 2012.
Single rack to 4", double to 1".

The Secret World of Arrietty climbs the arch-feature immediately left of the Plate of Fate, pulling through the big roof at it's widest point. No hard moves, but sustained and spectacular. Start immediately left of the Plate of Fate. Climb the left edge of the plate and pull up (b) onto better rock above. Continue up a vague seam/corner to a large, wedged flake. Continue to a strange hole in the wall above the arch (crucial 0.75 Camalot placement). Pull past this, up and over, to a precarious rest. Step back down below the arch, and begin a wild traverse left using underclings, hand jams, and occasional jugs, before a final, burly reach left to a large, flat hold at the lip of the arch (b). Mantle onto this and continue up the face, making a thin move or two to reach the final station on the Plate of Fate rap route. It is not possible to lower to the ground from here with a single 70m rope.

❾ The Plate Of Fate 310' 5.9+

Jorge Urioste, Bill Hotz. 2000's.
Small rack to 2".

This route lies on the slabby wall to the right of The Black Arch, about midway between the right edge of the arch and the prominent buttress that defines the upper portion of Black Orpheus. Begin about 30 feet to the right of the rappel route from the Painted Bowl, at a white detached flake, with a bolt about 20 feet above the ground.

1. 120' 5.8 Climb to the bolt, then step right to a crack system, which is followed up, past another bolt, to a bolted anchor.
2. 90' 5.8+ Go left a few feet, then up 20 feet. Go left to a bolt and continue left and up to a shrubby belay ledge.
3. 100' 5.9+ Climb diagonally up and left, passing 2 bolts that protect delicate face moves, heading for the bolted anchor near some small trees.

❿ There and Back Again 400' 5.8 *

Jim Boone, Ellen Dempsey. February 1980.

This route climbs lower-angled rock on the right hand side of the wall. On the right hand side of the wall is a white recess. Start about 150' to the left of the recess, where a huge slabby block leans against the cliff.

1. 165' 5.5 Climb the center of the slabby block to its top.
2. 90' 5.7 Continue up via face climbing, cracks, and corners to the top of a tower.
3. 80' 5.8 Traverse left, then climb up and right in a shallow groove to the base of a corner. Up the corner to a ledge at the top of another tower.
4. 80' 5.8 From the left end of the ledge, go up a thin crack in a short steep face to the base of an easy corner. Go up the corner then left to a ledge.
5. 110' 5.8 Climb up an overhanging corner then diagonal left to a belay.
6. 80' 4th class Scramble up and left into the bottom of the Painted Bowl.

The Fortress, pitch 4. Page 156.

The Fortress

This is the name given to the huge, steep pillar that separates the Black Arch Wall on the left from the Black Orpheus amphitheater on the right. The pillar faces straight south and gets sun for most of the day before going into the shade in the mid to late afternoon depending on the time of year. A good choice for a sunny winter day, although the pillar is very exposed to winds.

Approach: These routes can be reached either by following the approach to The Black Orpheus and scrambling up and left to reach the start, or following the approach to the base of There and Back Again and scrambling up and around to the right. The first three routes start at a single bolt about 40' below a varnished right-facing corner which forms the right side of a vague, low-angled, black pillar at the base of the wall.

❶ Tuscarora 440' 5.12c *
Tom Cecil, John Barnes, John Rosholt. 1995.
Single set to 2", double to 0.5".
This route climbs the lower half of The Fortress, following a series of cracks close to the crest of the buttress. Exposed, well-protected climbing with a short, but difficult crux that is very hard for the fat-fingered. Start from the bolt belay below the corner.
1. 160' 5.7 Climb up and left, then back right into the corner. Follow the corner and belay at an anchor in a scoop.
2. 100' 5.10b Climb up and left (b), then back right into a blocky corner. Climb the corner, then at its top move right (b) into a thin crack which leads to a belay directly under the big roof.
3. 100' 5.11b Climb a slot through the left side of the roof (11b) then continue past several bolts to a ledge.
4. 80' 5.12c Climb past 5 bolts (11b) to a stance with an incomplete anchor. Continue up a thin crack (crux) and past 3 more bolts to the anchor.
Descent: Rappel with a single 70m, or two shorter ropes.

❷ Marijuana 660' 5.11d *
Single rack to 5", double 0.5" - 1".
A nice varied climb. Start above pitch two of Tuscarora.
3. 50' 5.5 Traverse right to the base of a corner system.
4. 50' 5.11b Climb up into the pretty left-facing corner above. Follow the corner (2 b's) to an anchor on the ledge on the right.
5. 110' 5.11d Climb a small corner to the right of the main corner system. This leads to the base of a long, smooth right-leaning ramp. Follow the ramp (4 b's) to an anchor at its top.
6&7. 180' 5.10a Corners to the top.
Descent: Tricky diagonal raps with two ropes. It is possible to rap with a single 70m if you leave some biners on the crux ramp. From the top of the buttress, scramble down to the west into the Lower Painted Bowl and rap Black Arch Wall.

❸ The Fortress of Xanadu 630' 5.13d ***
FFA Tom Moulin, Brian Bowman, Chad Umbel. December 2, 2007. After a year of effort Moulin finally pulled the crux of this monumental route, to create the hardest climb in Red Rocks.
Single rack to 3", double Wild Country #Z2, double #0.1 Camalot.
The route starts as for Tuscarora.
1. 100' 5.8 Climb most of the first pitch of Tuscarora, then move right to a small ledge with an anchor, in the middle of a slabby wall.
2. 120' 5.13a Move right, across the slab (b), to a small groove. Climb the groove then move out right and make very bouldery moves over a small roof (V7ish) onto a wall of beautiful white varnish. Climb the wall (7 b's and some small cams (0.4",0.5") to a big ledge below an obvious corner system.
3. 110' 5.11b This first part of this pitch follows pitch 3 of Marijuana. Climb the steep cracks above the anchor then move left into a big left-facing corner. Tricky stemming up the corner (2 b's) leads to a good ledge with an anchor at 60'. Move left and climb the crack through a steep bulge (5.11b) into a chimney. Continue up the chimney to an anchor on a good ledge 40' below a huge roof.
4. 80' 5.13d Continue up the corner to the roof. Pull into the roof then move out right to a rail which is followed out right to crux moves around the lip (5 b's). Continue up the slabby wall to an amazing small ledge with huge overhangs all around.
5. 70' 5.12d Climb the thin crack above, over a bulge (12d) to a small slab sandwiched between overhangs. Follow the slab out right. Move up, then continue right to a huge ledge. Some thought is required to protect the second on this pitch. Not the least of the problems is a razor sharp edge on the lip of the crux bulge.
6. 150' 5.10b Move right around the corner into the final crack of Marijuana. Up this to the top of the formation. If you choose to climb this pitch bring cams to 6".
Descent: From the top of pitch 5 it is possible to make a short rap to the anchor at the top of the ramp of Marijuana (top of pitch 5). From here a long diagonal rappel leads to the anchor half way up pitch 3. A couple of straightforward raps to the ground from here.

❹ The Bandit 280' 5.11b
Russ Ricketts, Adam Wilbur. 2001.
This route climbs a big left-leaning arch/corner to the left of Black Orpheus.
1. 100' 5.11a Lieback up the corner (5.10b) into a short corner which is followed to a belay.
2. 180' 5.11b Continue up and left under the arch to some old anchors.
Descent: Rappel straight down with two ropes.

Black Orpheus Area

❺ Black Orpheus 1370' 5.10a **
Joanne Urioste, Jorge Urioste. April 1979.
Single rack to 3", double 1.25"- 1.75".

Black Orpheus climbs the huge southwest-facing wall on the west side of Solar Slab. This is a long and very enjoyable route which can be climbed quite quickly. There are long sections of easier climbing with only a couple of sections of 5.9 and a short 10a crux.

The base of the wall is guarded by 500' of third class scrambling. Follow the trail into the canyon. The trail drops into the wash a few hundred yards past Solar Slab. The canyon soon narrows, with a steep buttress coming down all the way to the wash from the right. Leave the wash about 300 yards after the canyon narrows; a cairn on a boulder marks the spot. Head up the slabs, aiming for an attractive left-facing corner system which is the most obvious feature of the lower buttress. Start at the base of the corner system.

1. 110' 5.8 Climb the corner to an anchor.

2. 140' 5.8+ Continue up the corner to a ledge. Above the ledge a steep, awkward lieback leads to an anchor on a ledge.

3. 110' 5.7 Move left (b) then back right and continue to a large ledge.

The feature you are now aiming for is the huge right-facing corner system which starts 500' above, in the top left hand corner of the large area of low-angled rock above the initial corner.

4-7. 500' 5.5 Move 75' up and left on large ledges. Climb up a steep wall, past a loose block, and continue to a ledge. Continue up the slabs above, eventually moving right to the start of a long, left-slanting ramp. Follow the ramp to its end below a steep wall. An exposed but easy traverse leads across the slab on the left. Belay below a small, triangular roof, on a ledge just right of the main dihedral.

8. 160' 5.9 Make a very exposed traverse left into the corner and move up past a bolt to reach a good crack. Enjoyable jamming and chimneying lead up to the top of the corner, where an awkward exit leads to a ledge on the right.

9. 110' 5.10a A short distance above the belay, a powerful pull (crux) up a thin crack in a short, steep wall (2 b's) leads into a corner. Climb excellent twin cracks in the corner and belay on the higher of two ledges above.

10. 120' 5.6 Lieback up the huge corner (b) then, as the angle eases, traverse out right on sloping ledges to an anchor.

11. 120' 5.6 From the anchor face climb right then up (3 b's), eventually intersecting the top of the corner. Climb through the corner and follow the crack above to the top of the buttress.

Descent: See descent for Solar Slab, page 160.

Bossa Nova 360' 5.11b
Merlin Larsen, Jim Munson. 1996.

This route follows a line up the buttress to the right of the lower pitches of Black Orpheus. Start 30' to the right of Black Orpheus.

1. 150' 5.11b Climb a big flake into a chimney in the back of a corner. Go up and left to a finger crack in a corner, up this to belay on a sloping ledge.

2. 110' 5.10b Walk right around a fin. Pull onto a sloping shelf, then go up a right-facing flake. Mantel over an overhang and face climb up to a belay at a blocky corner.

3. 100' 5.9 Go up and right for 15', then move back left through an overhang. Climb a plated face to a big ledge.

Descent: Either finish up Black Orpheus or find the top of the its' initial corner and rap with two ropes.

The following routes are found in the alcove to the right of the lower pitches of Black Orpheus. They all end towards the right hand side of the lower angled section in the middle of the wall. To descend, traverse right to reach the notch on Sunspot Ridge. Descend 20' on the opposite side and make a single rope rappel from a small bush to the top of pitch 2 of Solar Slab. Continue down Solar Slab.

Death in the Afternoon 400' 5.9
John Campbell, John Wilder, Larry DeAngelo. Mid 2000's.
Climb the first pitch of The Great Gritsby, then bear left into a corner/chimney system. At the top of this crack system is an overhang. Go left, following a diagonal crack to easier ground.

The Great Gritsby 400' 5.10a
Tom Randal, Larry DeAngelo. Mid 2000's.
Single rack to 7".
Scramble up to a dark corner on the left side of the wall, at the back of the alcove. Climb the corner to a large ledge. The second pitch leads up the crack system directly above. Pitch three continues straight up the offwidth on soft rock, traversing to the right hand crack system when it becomes easy. The fourth pitch is a relaxed scramble to the unroping spot.

Farewell to Arms 270' 5.9
This route starts at the base of the Six Pack.

1. 150' 5.7 Climb up and left on rounded varnished plates.

2. 120' 5.9 Climb a clean left-facing corner to a good ledge.

❻ Six Pack 450' 5.10a
Mike Ward, John Hegyes, Steve Bullock, Dave Melchoir. and two others. February 2006.
This route climbs the crack system on the right side of the alcove, about 300' to the right of Black Orpheus. Not recommended due to a lot of poor rock.

1. 200' 5.10a Climb rotten rock (5.8/9) to a 10a crux that is hard to protect. After the crux, head left to a right-facing corner system that ends atop a pillar on a broad ledge.

2. 5.8 Step left and climb up 20', then traverse right 20' to a prominent left-facing corner system which is followed to a belay alcove.

3&4 5.5 Continue up the crack system to easier ground.

Offset Corners 110' 5.11b * ❶
Single rack to 2.5".
An obscure but beautiful pitch.

This route sits by itself on the face of a huge block overlooking the canyon. The block is about 200' above the canyon floor and is visible on the right, about 150 yards after the approach trail drops into the canyon after passing below Solar Slab. Look for a square wall with two attractive left-facing corners, one above the other. After you first spot the wall, keep going up the wash until a break can be seen leading back right to the base of the block. Scramble up and right along the break, past a couple of 5th class steps, to the base of the wall.

Climb the initial corner, and where it ends make a few hard moves up and right to a rest at the base of the upper corner. Climb the upper corner to a strenuous finish (5 b's). There are no anchors on top.

Scramble to the top of the block and downclimb an easy chimney on the backside, which soon leads back to the base of the wall.

SOLAR SLAB AREA

Solar Slab is the enormous sweep of white rock which dominates the north side of the entrance to Oak Creek Canyon. For the purpose of this book, the area is divided into three different sections, see the overview photo on page 142 & 143. **Sunspot Ridge** is the buttress at the left end of the wall, and Solar Slab itself is split into **Lower Solar Slab** and **Upper Solar Slab**. The entire area faces south/southeast and is very warm and sunny, providing reasonable climbing conditions during cold weather. In mid-winter it goes in the shade by late afternoon. The climbing here is very enjoyable, with good rock, a short approach, and a pleasant non-serious atmosphere. However, it is worth remembering that this is a really big chunk of rock (1500'). Furthermore, if you decide not to use the rappel options, and choose instead to go to the top of the formation, the descent is complicated and long, and adds greatly to the overall seriousness of the routes. The climbs here are not only great routes in themselves, but can also be used to approach the climbs on the Eagle Wall and the Painted Bowl. For example, by combining Beulah's Book, Solar Slab and Rainbow Buttress you get close to 3000' of climbing on what is to be one of the best days out at the grade anywhere.

Approach: From the Oak Creek Trailhead, follow the trail into the canyon. As you enter the canyon proper there is a red cliff band on the right. Shortly after the red cliff band ends, the trail passes an area of large boulders and trees in front of a second, smaller red cliff band. Just after, a trail in red soil branches out right and heads up the towards the base of the Solar Slab Gully. 1.5 miles, 550' elevation gain, 50-60 minutes.

Descent Routes:

(1) All the routes here have the option of a rappel descent. The starting points for these rappels are described in the individual route descriptions.

The following descents start from a huge shoulder close to the top of the buttress, reached by several hundred feet of third class from the top of the routes.

(2) Look for cairns on the left (west) side of the shoulder, and follow these around to the west to reach the top of a ramp. Follow the ramp down to the west to an anchor at its very end. Two rappels with two ropes (or three with 70m one rope) lead straight down into the slabs of the Lower Painted Bowl. A long scramble leads southwest towards the right (west) side of the Lower Painted Bowl. Aim for a large boulder on the right (west) shoulder of the bowl, the "IBM" boulder. From here, a long ramp system leads down and west. At the point where the ramp turns into a vegetated terrace, go down a steep gully, then zig-zag down some steep slabs and ledges. Eventually, from the lowest ledge, a 20' slither down a smooth slab leads to the creek.

(3) With one 60m rope. Follow option (2) to the rappel anchor at the base of the ramp. Instead of rappelling straight down, do a diagonal rappel to a slabby ledge on the right (facing out). From the far end of the ledge, a rappel down a chimney leads to a pine tree. Another rappel leads into the slabs of the Lower Painted Bowl. Follow option (2) from here.

To continue up a route on the Eagle Wall after climbing Solar Slab, descend into the Lower Painted Bowl, then climb the ridge that borders the west edge of the bowl. 4th class.

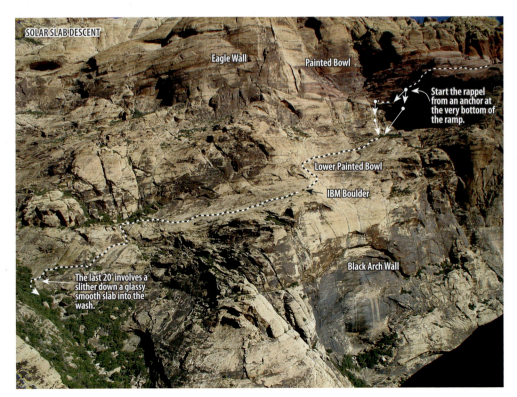

SOLAR SLAB DESCENT

Eagle Wall

Painted Bowl

Start the rappel from an anchor at the very bottom of the ramp.

Lower Painted Bowl

IBM Boulder

Black Arch Wall

The last 20' involves a slither down a glassy smooth slab into the wash.

Matt Kuehl on the nice hand crack of pitch 5 of Solar Slab. Page 166.

Sunspot Ridge

This is the long ridge separating Solar Slab from the huge wall containing Black Orpheus. While the upper part of the ridge is broad and low-angled, the lower part of the ridge forms a steeper varnished buttress which comes down almost to the creek bed. The lower buttress is easily recognized by some clean, varnished corners separated by overlaps.

❶ Sunspot Ridge 5.8

John Hegyes, John Wilder, George Urioste, L. DeAngelo. Mid 2000's.

On the left side of the lower buttress is a gully system. Some bushwhacking leads to a belay alcove at its base. Climb a pitch up the crack on the left wall of the gully and belay in a cave-like tunnel. Move up and right, passing a small bulge. Continue right and up the varnished face, protected by tricky wired nut placements. Eventually move left and belay on a good ledge. Climb up for about thirty feet to a small triangular ceiling, then traverse right until you reach a left-slanting crack. Follow this crack to the Lower Shoulder. This shoulder can also be reached by climbing Solar Flare, or by complicated scrambling and easy climbing from the west.

From the large shoulder platform, scramble up on an easy pitch of mostly 4th class climbing, staying slightly left, to a good belay niche near a bush. The next pitch involves face-climbing straight up the knobby ridge crest above. Another face-climbing pitch continues up the ridge, with limited protection, to some good ledges. Two more fourth class pitches lead up the ridge, passing a gendarme or two. These pitches end at The Notch, a spacious and airy perch where the ridge merges into the main wall. The improbable headwall above turns out to be beautiful 5.0 climbing on varnished plates. Another pitch up one of the cracks above (both are about 5.7) leads to the ledges at the top Solar Slab's fifth or sixth pitch. Either continue to the top and descend via the Painted Bowl, or rappel Solar Slab via the bolted rap stations.

❷ Solar Flare 490' 5.10c *

This is a good quality line which climbs the obvious varnished corners in the lower buttress. The rock is mostly solid, and the climbing is mostly moderate. Start below a big right-facing corner leading to a roof 110' up.

1. 100' 5.7 A pleasant crack leads up 100' to a small stance beneath an overhang.

2. 70' 5.10c Traverse right to a break in the roof and move up past a bolt (5.10) to easier climbing and a bolted belay station.

3. 100' 5.7 Easy climbing up the corner above takes you to another bolted belay station.

4. 100' 5.9 Continue up, passing a protection bolt (5.9) on the bulge above, to reach another bolted station.

5. 120' 5.6 Moderate climbing goes up the cracks and face to the Lower Shoulder. There is an optional bolted belay/rap station a short distance below the shoulder.

Descent: Rap with two ropes.

❸ Corona 100' 5.10a

About 30' to the right of Solar Flare is a clean, left-facing corner. When the corner gets too smooth, make a delicate step left. There is a bolted anchor a short distance above the overhang. It is possible to move left below the overhang and join the easy crack leading to the second belay on Solar Flare.

❹ Sunshine Boys 500' 5.9

FRA: George Urioste, Larry DeAngelo. Mid 2000's.

To the right of Corona is a moderate-looking, straight-in crack. Climb this (5.9) to a good ledge that leads right to the gully. Avoid the gully by climbing straight up on an easy knobby face and crack. Belay in a small alcove beneath a shrub. The third pitch steps left to an obvious chimney. When the climbing becomes easy, step left onto the Lower Shoulder. The easiest descent is to rappel Solar Flare.

❺ Dubious Flirtations 150' 5.10b/c *

This route is located in a small alcove just left of Sunburn and just to the right of the buttress containing the previous routes. In the alcove there is a small, varnished face split by a razor thin crack rising from the right side of a very clean, rectangular ceiling. The route starts in the corner leading up to this crack. Move up to a short-but-wide left-facing corner on face holds and blocks. Continue up the wide corner (5" cam) through the small roof and onto the finger crack spitting the face. Climb the finger crack until it seals up. Move out right on face holds to a chimney system and stance. Belay takes 1"-3" cams.

At this point, you can move right and up (careful for loose rock!) to a rappel from a pine tree next to the second belay on Sunburn, or continue upward on that route.

❻ Sunburn 1500' 5.7

Anthony Anagnostou, Karsten Duncan, John Campbell, Larry DeAngelo. Mid 2000's.

About 100 yards to the left of Beulah's Book is an indistinct buttress leading up to the left side of a huge roof. The buttress is bordered on its left side by a brushy, unappealing gully. Start at the very toe of this buttress.

1. Pleasant face climbing leads up to a right-slanting crack. Belay at its top.

2. Step right and climb over a slight bulge, then face climb straight up, staying near the junction of the white and dark rock. Belay on a ledge to the left.

3. Step right and continue up a small dihedral. Belay at a small stance with shrubbery and a chimney above.

4. Move up the dihedral, past a bush and into a featured squeeze chimney. Climb this chimney to a wide, clean gully and continue up to a stance above a large chockstone.

5. Climb out of the gully onto the arete and face on the left side of the slot, then up and out onto a slab. Move up to reach a ledge approximately even with the large Solar Slab Terrace.

6. Continue straight up the rounded buttress above on pleasant slab climbing. A very long pitch (60m+?) leads to a good belay ledge at a pine tree. (Alternatively, divide the pitch in two by belaying at a varnished scoop.)

7. Climb up and slightly right on even more pleasant slabs until reaching a large brushy ledge.

At this point you can scramble right (class 3) for 100 feet, passing the top of Going Nuts, and join Solar Slab two pitches above the terrace. Alternatively, and more direct, continue straight up over broken rock and join Sunspot Ridge at The Notch. Continue to the top by one of these routes, and descend as for Solar Slab.

Lower Solar Slab

The lower 500' of Solar Slab consists of a steep wall, bordered on the right by a gully system, Solar Slab Gully. An obvious feature of left side of this lower wall is a huge right-facing corner that starts 150' up, the line of Beulah's Book.

❼ The Pamphlet 165' 5.8

Immediately left of Beulah's Book is a much smaller dihedral. Climb this until just below a roof, then move right and face climb on easier rock to a large belay ledge.

❽ Beulah's Book 550' 5.9 *

Randal Grandstaff, Dave Anderson. 1979.
Single rack to 4", double 0.6"- 1.5".
The big corner on the second pitch is excellent.
Start below a small corner to the right of the base of a long left-slanting flake/chimney which leads into the big corner.
1. 165' 5.7 Climb the corner to a jammed block, then continue up the rib to the left of the main chimney (b). Higher up, step back right into the chimney and continue to an anchor at the base of the huge corner.
2. 160' 5.9 Chimney up the imposing slot (b) then continue up the corner as it turns into a smooth lieback. Above the lieback the corner ends at a roof, exit left to an anchor.
Variation: Climb the left arete of the imposing slot (3 b's).
3. 140' 5.6 Climb up and right on white rock with little protection. After pulling over a steep section, easier climbing leads up and right to the anchor.
4. 50' 5.0 Scramble to the top.
Descent: Rappel and downclimb Solar Slab Gully with one rope. If you can find the anchors it is possible to rap Johnny Vegas with two ropes.

❾ Sandstone Overcast 535' 5.12b/c

Larry DeAngelo, J. Wilder. Mid 2000's. A few points on aid on pitch 3.
FFA Mike Lorenzo. Dec 3, 2008.
Single rack to 3", double 0.4"- 0.6", a set of Ballnutz.
1. 185' 5.8 Start in a right-facing corner 60' left of Johnny Vegas. Head up this, (b) and continue to the first belay of Johnny Vegas. Climb the 20' corner above and belay on the ledge at its top.
2. 150' 5.8 In the middle of the ledge is a crack system heading straight up. Follow this until it starts to arch to the left, then step right and go straight up the face, aiming for where the roof above is at its smallest. Belay just above the roof at a stance.
Variation: When the crack arches left, instead of stepping right, follow the thinning crack until a thin move (10a) is made to the roof. Over the roof (5.6) and finish up Beulah's Book.
3. 50' 5.12b/c Climb easy ground to the base of the corner on the left side of the huge overhang above. Climb the corner and set up an anchor just over the lip to reduce rope drag.
4. 150' 5.4 Step to the right and head up and past the bolted station at the top of pitch 3 of Johnny Vegas.
Variation: To avoid the aid, traverse left under the roof and belay, then continue to the top. 5.9.

❿ Johnny Vegas 480' 5.7 ***

Tom Cecil, Dave Cox, Harrison Schull, Todd Hewitt. November 1994.
Single rack to 3".
A superb climb at the grade, this route climbs up the center of the wall between Beulah's Book and Solar Slab Gully. It is a little bold in places but the rock is excellent.

The route starts about 80' left of the bottom of Solar Slab gully. Scramble up and left over a couple of smooth white blocks to a nice, flat ledge behind a pillar.
1. 150' 5.6 Above the starting ledge is a steep corner. Climb cracks in the left wall of the corner. When the cracks end, angle up and left to an anchor at the base of a short, steep right-facing corner.
2. 150' 5.7 Climb the corner, then move out right to a crack in a bulge. Initially the crack is very steep, but the holds are good. As the angle starts to ease, the holds thin out and the pitch ends with a stretch of wide open wall climbing with good but spaced wires for protection.
3. 130' 5.6 Move up to the arete on the right. Straightforward climbing (5.5) leads up the arete with no protection until you are level with the roof on the left. Follow a short corner out left, above the roof, and pull onto the slab above, moving left to an anchor.
Variation: 5.9 Climb the corner to the left of the belay to a bolt. Move right past the bolt to join the regular route a few feet below the roof.
4. 50' 5.0 Scramble to the top.
Descent: Rappel and downclimb Solar Slab Gully with one rope, or rappel the route with two ropes.

⓫ Frieda's Flake 340' 5.9

Just to the left of Solar Slab Gully and to the right of Johnny Vegas is a huge, 250' tall white flake that is leaning up against the wall. This route climbs the chimney formed by the right side of the flake. Approach as for Johnny Vegas, but climb up a small gully to the base of the chimney (50', 4th class)
1. 170' 5.9 Head up the chimney system through two distinct cruxes before exiting left onto the face and then up about 30' to a belay stance.
2. 170' 5.7 Head up the corner for about 15' before exiting right onto the face. Continue up the face (just right of pitch 3 of Johnny Vegas) until meeting up with Johnny Vegas high on its third pitch. Finish via easy climbing on Johnny Vegas.

⓬ Sideline 500' 5.9

John Wilder, Gigette Miller, Larry DeAngelo. Mid 2000's.
Start on the very left side of the Solar Slab Gully.
1. Follow the crack and chimney system for a long pitch to a belay alcove beneath a brushy obstacle.
2. Move left to a right-slanting crack. Go up (5.9), then traverse right to a slanting ramp/chimney. There is a good belay ledge at its top.
3. Just to the left of the ledge is a smooth chimney, formed by a huge, precariously-balanced block. Cross left to the left end of the block where a clean, thin crack (5.9) leads straight up the steep face above. Follow the crack as it bends right to a good ledge.
4. Easy climbing follows a ramp system to the right until it is possible to face climb up on softish white rock, eventually reaching the large terrace.

⓭ Solar Slab Gully 500' 5.3 *

Single rack to 4", double 1.25"- 3".
Solar Slab Gully goes up the system of gullies and chimneys to the right of the lower wall. It is one of the easiest multi-pitch climbs in Red Rocks and as a bonus is fixed with solid belay/rappel anchors. It is an enjoyable climb in its own right and

also provides quick access to the routes on the upper Solar Slab. Start on the right side of the gully beside a small tree.

1. 150' 5.1 Climb a wide crack past an anchor at 80' to an anchor on a ledge with a tree.

2. 80' 4th class Scramble up and left to a ledge at the base of a wide chimney split by a rib.

3. 150' 5.1 Climb the crack on the right side of the rib. Continue up an easy slab, then move up the left wall of the gully to reach an anchor at the base of a smooth-walled gully.

4. 120' 5.3 Go up the gully, stemming past a steep section (crux.) Continue up the gully to an anchor on the right.

🄮 Horndogger Select 450' 5.8
Dave Pollari, Shawn Pereto. February 1993.
Single rack to 4", double 1.75"- 2.5", extra wires.

This route has a couple of nice sections, but also a lot of fragile rock. The lower part of the route climbs the front side of a big buttress, to the right of a deep left-facing corner about 150' to the right of Solar Slab Gully.

Start below an obvious face crack leading up to the right end of a large overhang 80' up.

1. 150' 5.8 Climb the crack up into the corner formed by the right edge of the overhang. Move right around the overhang and continue up on good holds to a steep white wall. Climb up and slightly left following short cracks to a horizontal band. Traverse right for 12' to belay at the base of a shallow scoop.

2. 160' 5.8 Continue up the line of huecos in the back of the scoop to reach a steeper white wall. Move out left, traversing a thin crack which leads left then up to easier ground. Continue to a belay on a huge ledge.

Move the belay across the huge ledge to the top of the gully The next pitch climbs a finger and hand crack about 20' to the left of an obvious left-facing flake.

3. 140' 5.8 Climb the crack. When it thins at the top, a few delicate moves on rounded rock lead to lower angled terrain. Continue to the huge terrace below the upper Solar Slab.

🄯 The Friar 300' 5.9+
Joe Herbst, Tom Kaufman, Steve Allen. April 1977.
Single rack to 3".

200' to the right of Solar Slab Gully is a detached pinnacle sitting on top of a 300' high buttress. This is the Friar. Start below an attractive, varnished corner on the front of the buttress.

1. 100' 5.7 Climb 10' up to a ledge at the base of a long right-facing corner. Nice climbing leads up the corner to a ledge.

2. 90' 5.7 Move into the crack on the right, which is followed to a ledge.

Variation: Climb straight up from the belay staying to the left of the normal route. (5.7 with poor pro)

3. 80' 5.6 Scramble up some ledges, then head up thin cracks in a face (poor pro) to below the summit block. Traverse around to the left, past an anchor to the backside of the block.

4. 40' 5.9+ This pitch has been the scene of a couple of bad accidents...be careful with the protection. A couple of good nuts can be placed to protect moves up and right to a ledge with a bolt. Continue around the corner to the right then up left to an anchor on top.

Descent: Rappel with one rope.

Upper Solar Slab

19

21

20

16   17   18   19

20

22

Top of Solar
Slab Gully

Routes 8 to 12

14

varnished plates (to have enough rope for the last pitch).

5. 200' 5.6 Proceed straight up the glorious face on relatively easy climbing until you can set up a belay after about 59 meters. At this point you can either join Solar Slab for the 3rd class pitch and cruise to the top, or rappel the main slab.

㉑ Sunflower 750' 5.9 *

John Martinet, Randal Grandstaff. Spring 1979.
Single rack to 3".

This is an excellent route which climbs straight up the center of the upper Solar Slab. The crux pitch was first done with only two bolts.

The first pitch climbs the corner just to the right of the first pitch of Solar Slab.

Start on the terrace, slightly to the left of the top of Solar Slab Gully below an obvious crack which starts 50' up the wall.

1. 140' 5.7 Climb up and right into an obvious black corner. Climb the corner past an awkward wide section to a ledge and anchor shared with Solar Slab.

2. 120' 5.9 From the anchor climb a right-slanting crack to a good ledge.

3. 165' 5.8 Climb the right-facing corner above and its continuation thin crack. From the end of the crack, go up and left (b) 20' to a hidden bolt anchor.

4. 165' 5.9 A long pitch leads straight up the slab (5 b's) to the base of an obvious crack which deepens into a right-facing corner. Belay in a pod.

5. 165' 5.6. Continue up the nice corner until about 20' below a roof. Climb up and left across the face until it is possible to step down and left to the anchor at the top of Solar Slab.

Descent: Rappel Solar Slab with two ropes.

㉒ Sundog 730' 5.9+ *

Ed Prochaska, Joanne Urioste. 1997.
Single rack to 3", optional 5" cam for final crack.

This is an enjoyable and varied route up a series of features on the right edge of the upper Solar Slab. Start on the huge terrace below the upper slab and about 200' up and right of the top of Solar Slab Gully.

1. 190' 5.6 Climb a scarcely-protected face to reach an area of low-angled slabs below the upper face. Scramble up the slabs and look for a single belay bolt in the slab just before it steepens. This bolt is below the left end of a prominent patch of varnish

Variation: This pitch can be avoided by third class terrain on the right.

5. 180' 5.7 Climb intermittent cracks (b) up the face to a ledge at the base of a dark left-facing corner. Climb the face immediately left of the wide crack in the corner to an anchor.

6. 140' 5.8 Continue up the face past a couple of steep sections (4 b's) to reach a thin crack which is followed past a couple of fixed nuts to an anchor.

7. 120' 5.9+ Above the anchor, pull over a bulge on a fragile horn to reach a small ledge. Continue over a steep section and up a delicate face (5 b's) to a thin crack which is followed to an anchor.

8. 140' 5.9 Climb the awkward right-arching corner to reach a wide crack which leads straight up through the top of the arch. An anchor appears on the left, just as the angle eases.

Variation: From below the offwidth, traverse right until it is possible to head up and left across a poorly protected face (5.9) with tiny cams for protection.

Descent: Rappel the upper slab with two ropes. From the terrace, go down Solar Slab Gully.

Red Zinger Area

This is the west-facing wall on the right side of the first major gully to the right of the Solar Slab, just to the east of the Friar. A good collection of routes on excellent, splitter rock. This is a very sheltered wall which faces due west. It gets sun from late-morning to late afternoon..

Approach: From the Oak Creek Trailhead, follow the trail into the canyon. As you enter the canyon proper there is a red cliff band on the right. Follow the trail until below the west end of the red cliff band. Leave the trail and head straight up the hillside, passing just to the left of the red cliff band. The buttress directly above is split by an obvious offwidth leading up to a roof. Red Zinger is around the corner to the left of the sharp arete to the left of the offwidth. It climbs a large left-facing corner capped by a huge roof.

1.4 miles, 550' elevation gain, 40-50 minutes.

About 20' to the left of Red Zinger, a smooth, bolted corner leads to an anchor at 30', the line of Feather.

Trim 30' 5.12b

Three 0.75", two 1", one 1.25", 1.75".

The ferocious splitter finger crack to the left of Feather leads to the anchor of that route. Good locks but no feet.

● Feather 30' 5.13a *

A desperate and intricate stream of moves up the glassy corner (4 b's). Good training for the smooth corners which provide the cruxes of many of Red Rocks' hardest long routes.

Lemon Bomb 170' 5.11d

Jerry Handren, Dave Sorric. 2004.
Single rack to 4", Rp's.

Start as for Red Zinger. A bit of a battle.

1. 90' 5.9 Lieback up the wide flake to the left of the main corner. Continue up the cracks above to an anchor on a ledge.

2. 80' 5.11d Continue up the tips crack into an awkward flare. Above the flare an easier fist crack leads to a ledge on the right with an anchor.

Descent: Rappel with one rope.

Red Zinger 180' 5.10d ***

Joe Herbst. 1970s.
Single rack to 3", double 1.25"- 1.75".

A superb corner/crack.

Start on a bushy ledge at the base of the corner.

1. 90' 5.10c Climb the corner past a punchy crux at 2/3rds height to a ledge and anchor.

2. 90' 5.10d A burly lieback leads to an optional anchor under the huge roof. Traverse left under the roof to a fist crack which leads to a ledge on the right with an anchor.

Descent: Rappel with one rope.

Boondoggle 90' 5.12a

A few pieces to 7". The first ascent used a Wild Country #6.

The burly off width roof that blocks the top of the corner on the second pitch of Red Zinger.

Deciphering the cryptic crux of Feather. Page 169.

Byrd Pinnacle

The following routes are on a buttress of brown, varnished rock called the Byrd Pinnacle. It is located at the base of the cliff, to the right of the offwidth mentioned in the approach description to the Red Zinger Area.

❶ Whoosh 300' 5.8
Joe Herbst, Matt McMackin. 1970's.
Three pitches up the crack system to the left of Byrd Pinnacle.

V-Formation 110' 5.8
Single rack to 4".
Climb the corner on the left side of Byrd Pinnacle.

❷ Byrd Pinnacle: Left 100' 5.7+ *
Joe Herbst, John Byrd, Matt McMackin, Nanouk Borche. Spring 1973.
Single rack to 3", double 1"- 1.75".
This route climbs a nice, splitter hand crack on the left hand side of the buttress. Start below twin cracks in excellent varnished rock. Climb either crack to gain a right-arching hand crack, up this and easier cracks above to an anchor on top of the pinnacle.

❸ Xyphoid Fever 100' 5.10c
Joe Herbst. Fall 1977.
Single rack to 2.5", 5" cam.
This route climbs a burly 5" crack over a roof to the anchor at the top of the buttress. **Variation:** The clean left-facing corner to the left of the roof makes this pitch a pleasant 5.9.

❹ The A Crack 110' 5.9
Joe Herbst, John Byrd. Spring 1973.
This route climbs an obvious corner on the right hand side of the buttress. Climb the corner past a roof to the top of the buttress.

The following routes are on the crags scattered along the base of the east face of Rainbow Mountain.

The Growler 60' 5.9+
Matt Kuehl, Ryan Strong. 2013.
Double 2"- 4".
This route climbs a right-facing corner directly below the following routes. The crack starts as hands and gradually widens into a flaring fist crack which leads to a tree anchor.

The next three routes are on a southeast-facing wall about halfway up the hillside towards the height of land between Oak Creek and Juniper canyons. Look for a very obvious left-leaning offwidth in varnished rock, which starts above some bushy ledges, the line of Wise Guys Off Size.

❺ Tickled Pink 50' 5.11b
Just below and to the left of the obvious crack of Wise Guys Offsize is a smooth wall with a very impressive offwidth in its center. At the left end of this wall is a very steep corner with a thin-hand crack in the back. The corner is reached by a long pitch up bushy cracks and ledges.

❻ Beelzebub 60' 5.11b **
Tr: Richard Harrison. Early 1980's. Lead: Matt Kuehl. Nov 20, 2012.
This route climbs the steep offwidth. A very pure crack climb of its type with few face holds, one of the nicest in Red Rocks.

❼ Wise Guys Off Size 150' 5.10c
Mark Moore, Joe Herbst. Fall 1973.
The classic offwidth. The base of the climb is reached by a pitch of bushy scrambling.

La Muerte 250' 5.10
Joe Herbst, Mark Moore. March 1973.
This three pitch route climbs a long offwidth crack which splits

Skyline 2000' 5.8
John Williamson, Keith Hogan. January 1971.
This route, which is one of Red Rock's oldest climbs, finds a way up the blocky southeast ridge of the east summit of Rainbow Mountain.

a white face with a large patch of varnished rock in the middle. The wall is a little up the hill from the previous routes and faces slightly down the hill to the southeast.

Little Brown 60' 5.8
Double 2"- 3".
About 70 yards down the hill to the left of Da Bonyard is a nice hand crack in the back of a tight, varnished corner. Climb the corner to an anchor at the top.

Da Boneyard 220' 5.10b *
Pat Dezonia, Rob Dezonia, Jerry Handren. Nov 2006.
Singles to 2.5", doubles 3"- 5", triple 5"- 12".
This is the name given to the awe-inspiring offwidth splitting a tall, varnished tower located about 200 yards south of the height of land between Oak Creek and Juniper canyons. One huge pitch, a little flaky but classic nevertheless.

The Unsung 100' 5.13a/b *
Small cams and wires.
This route climbs the beautiful thin crack in the arete to the right of Da Bonyard. It has excellent climbing, but is a really stout trad challenge with bouldery, technical climbing and protection that is difficult to place. Start at the base of Da Bonyard.
1. 55' 5.9 Climb the wide crack in the corner to the right of Da Bonyard. A few pieces to 8". Belay in a big alcove.
2. 45' 5.13a/b Move left into the thin crack. Bouldery moves and hard-to-place protection lead to better locks, a few feet higher move up and right to an anchor.

Rockingstone Groove 130' 5.9+
7" cam, double 0.75"- 5".
This route climbs twin cracks in the back of the huge, pink left-facing corner 50 yards up the hill from Da Boneyard. Climb the corner to an anchor on a sloping ledge.

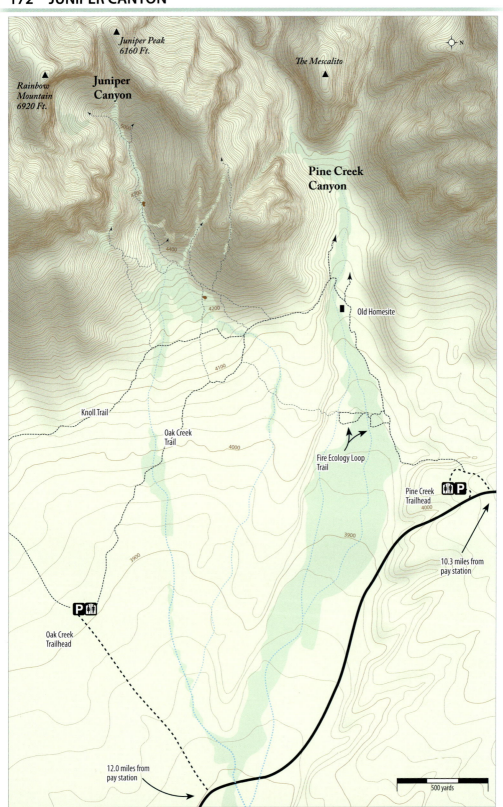

Juniper Peak
6160 Ft.

The Mescalito

Rainbow
Mountain
6920 Ft.

**Juniper
Canyon**

N

**Pine Creek
Canyon**

Old Homesite

Knoll Trail

Oak Creek
Trail

Fire Ecology Loop
Trail

Pine Creek
Trailhead

P

10.3 miles from
pay station

Oak Creek
Trailhead

P

12.0 miles from
pay station

500 yards

Introduction

This small canyon has more than its fair share of good rock and high quality climbs. Many of the routes face to the north and east and are best during warmer weather. However, Rose Tower and the Jackrabbit Buttress both have south faces that are very warm and sheltered.

Access

Juniper Canyon can be approached from either the Oak Creek or the Pine Creek Trailheads. The Pine Creek Parking area is on the right, 10.3 miles around the loop road from the fee station. To reach the Oak Creek Trailhead, drive around the loop road for 12 miles and take a right on a gravel road which leads to the parking area after a little less than a mile.

Approach

This canyon is usually approached from the Pine Creek parking lot. Follow the Pine Creek Trail to just past the old home site then take a left on the Oak Creek trail. This heads up and around to the south, along the base of the escarpment. Follow this trail for about 10 minutes to where an unmarked trail splits off on the right. This unmarked trail is a little braided, but eventually leads into the entrance to Juniper Canyon proper.

The approaches described in this chapter all start with the Pine Creek Trail approach described above. However, there are quite a few alternatives and short-cuts which should be obvious from the map. One such option is to come in from the Oak Creek Canyon Trailhead, following the Oak Creek Trail. This exits from the north side of the parking area and heads towards the mouth of the Canyon. Another is to follow the Fire Ecology Loop in Pine Creek, When the trail hits the second drainage there is a climber's trail on the far side which leads up through the sidewall of the main drainage and across the desert to join the Oak Creek Trail.

Near the mouth of the canyon there is a maze of climber's trails which can make navigation a bit confusing. Only the most commonly used trails are shown on the map.

Simon Peck on Pro Life. Page 196.

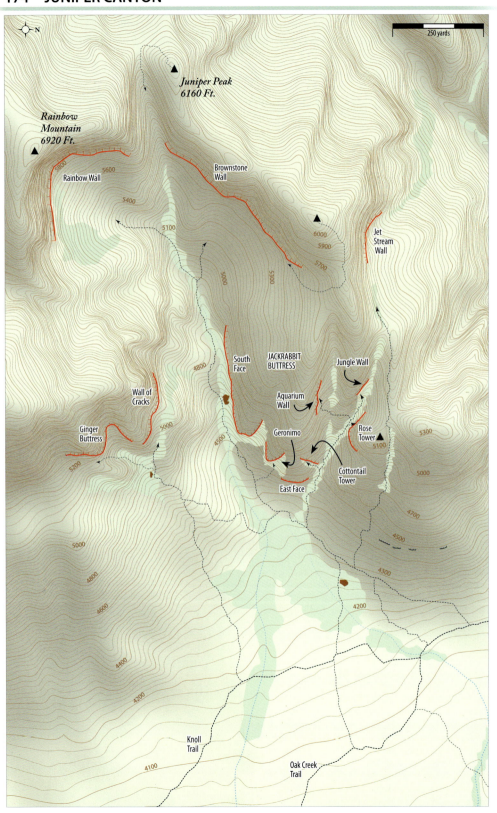

N

250 yards

Rainbow Mountain 6920 Ft.

Juniper Peak 6160 Ft.

Rainbow Wall

Brownstone Wall

5800

5600

5400

5100

6000

5900

5700

Jet Stream Wall

South Face

JACKRABBIT BUTTRESS

Jungle Wall

Aquarium Wall

Wall of Cracks

Ginger Buttress

Geronimo

Rose Tower

Cottontail Tower

East Face

5000

4800

4500

5200

5300

5100

5000

4700

4500

4300

4200

5000

4800

4600

4400

4200

4100

Knoll Trail

Oak Creek Trail

Pitch 5, the crux of Desert Solitaire. Page 186.

Ginger Buttress

The right side of the east face of the East Peak of Rainbow Mountain has an obvious black water streak starting from a small bowl 400' up the face. To the right of this is an attractive triangular tower, about 700' high, which forms the lower part of the right edge of the east face. This is Ginger Buttress.

Approach: These routes are normally approached from Pine Creek Canyon. Follow the approach for Juniper Canyon. Once on the trail continue until close to the main Juniper Canyon wash. At this point a trail branches off to the left while the main trail heads up the hill to the right of the wash. Follow the trail on the left, through bushes, to the slope on the south side of the wash. A rough trail leads up this slope, eventually heading up and right along a huge ramp to the base of the route Crimson Chrysalis. At the base of the ramp, just above a large red boulder, leave the main trail and follow a side trail up into a broad, shallow gully leading up and left for a couple of hundred yards to the base of Ginger Buttress. To reach the next six routes, continue up and left along the base of the wall following the gully, which becomes deeper and better defined. 1-1.5 hrs.

Snake Buttress 2000' 5.9
John Williamson, Chris Saal. April 1973.
From the height of land between Oak Creek and Juniper Canyons, this route finds a way up through a long series of cracks and chimneys to the east summit of Rainbow Mountain.

❶ Fist or Flips 120' 5.10c *
Paul Van Betten, Mike Ward. 1984.
Double 1.75"- 4", triple 3".
This route climbs a beautiful hand and fist crack which splits the east face of a small, varnished tower located a couple of hundred feet up the gully which slants up and left from the base of Power Failure. Scramble up the gully then exit to a big ledge below the route. From the right side of the ledge, a thin hand crack leads to the base of the crack proper. Follow the crack up the face to an anchor on the right edge of the tower.

❷ Power Failure 450' 5.10b **
J & J Urioste, B. Hotz, T. Krolak, S. Pratt, G. Fike, K. Campbell. 1998.
Single rack to 2.5".
A fine route with nice rock and enjoyable climbing. Start below and slightly to the right of the water streak, at a small clearing.
1. **130' 5.8+** Climb past a bolt to a bushy ledge at 30'. Step left to a flake on the ledge and climb up (6 b's) finishing with a traverse right to an anchor.
2. **160' 5.10b** Follow a thin crack to its end. Go right to a left-facing corner. Up this to an anchor (6 b's).
3. **160' 5.10a** Climb the thin left-leaning crack above. Higher up the crack deepens into a left-facing corner and leads to an anchor in the bowl at the top of the water streak.

❸ Somewhere Over the Rainbow 1100' 5.11d
Roxanna Brock, Gary Fike. 2001.
Single rack to 7", double 1.25", 2.5", 3".
This route climbs the wall above the bowl where Power Failure ends. From the bowl scramble up and right to a large ledge. Follow the ledge leftwards to its left end.
1. **140' 5.11a** Climb a thin seam in a black, varnished wall to a flake. Continue up the crack above to an anchor in a pod.
2. **100' 5.7** Exit the pod to a right-facing corner. Climb the corner, then continue up and left on ledgy terrain to an anchor.

3. **130' 5.11b** Climb up and left to a thin, varnished crack. Climb the crack (11b) into a right-facing corner with a wide crack which is climbed to an anchor on the right.
4. **120' 5.8** Move left into the offwidth, then when it ends step out to the face to its left. Climb the face to a crack. When the crack ends, move up to a ledge. Run it out up the face above (4" cam in hole) and continue to an anchor.
5. **110' 5.10c** From the anchor climb up and right to a ledge below a right-facing corner. Climb the corner to a chockstone, move right, and continue up the crack to an anchor.
6. **50' 5.11d** Climb a wide crack to reach the roof. Follow the hand crack leftwards and pull the roof to an anchor. Most will want to rappel from here.

❹ All You Can Eat 430' 5.10d *
Kal Conley, Geoff Conley, Anthony Anagnostou.
Single Rack to 4", Double 6"-8".
This route follows a line to the right of Power Failure. Start by climbing past a bolt (5.5) onto the ledge at the base of the wall. Start 40' along this ledge to the right of Power Failure.
1. **85' 5.10c** Climb a small crack just to the left of a thin finger crack with a couple of bolts. Traverse right to the second bolt and follow the crack as it curves up and right to an anchor on top of a pillar. **Variation: 11d** Climb directly past the first bolt.
1a. **90' 5.11b** About 25' to the right of the regular start is an offwidth corner/left-facing crack. Climb the offwidth to a hand crack. From here the crack constricts and is tips liebacking. Lieback up under the block and surmount the block. Traverse left on a left-slanting finger crack and up onto the pillar.
2. **90' 5.10a** Climb the left-facing corner above, passing a rap anchor, (3 b's) to a belay anchor below a small roof.
3. **80' 5.10c** Traverse left past the roof, then climb up and right (5 b's) to an anchor.
4. **90' 5.10d** Climb up and left over a bulge, then up and right to an anchor (6 b's).
5. **75' 5.9** Go up, then traverse right over a bulge and climb a large flared chimney to an anchor.
Descent: Rappel with one 60m rope.

❺ Unimpeachable Groping 700' 5.10b **
Mike Clifford, Jorge Urioste. April 1999.
15 quickdraws, a few nuts are optional but not really necessary.
This multi-pitch sport route climbs straight up the east face of Ginger Buttress. With exposed and exciting wall climbing and a beautiful location, this route deserves to become popular. Start beside a pine tree with a wedged block, about halfway up the gully at the base of the east side of the buttress.
1. **105' 5.10a** Climb the tree until it is possible to clip the first bolt. Continue to a bolt anchor.
2. **110' 5.10b** Continue to a bolt anchor.
3. **40' 5.10a** Continue to a large ledge.
4. **120' 5.10b** Continue over a roof then up to the anchor.
5. **80' 5.10b** Continue up the steep face.
6. **80' 5.10b** Continue up the steep face to a good ledge on the shoulder of the wall.
7. **160' 5.8** Continue to the top of the pillar.
Descent: Either rap the route from the top of pitch 6 with an 80m rope, or from the top, scramble down to the saddle to the west and rap south into the bowl above the water streak. Scramble down to the top of the water streak, locate the skiers right of two anchors and make 4 raps with a 70m rope.

Ginger Buttress - Left side

Rappel route
for a single
70m rope

100 yards

1

2

3

4

4a

5

❻ Ginger Cracks 930' 5.9 *

Mark Moore, Lars Holbek. 1977.
Single rack to 3", double 0.5"- 1.25".

This route sees little traffic but is a worthwhile and varied climb. Definitely worth a try if you can't get on Crimson Chrysalis. On the very prow of Ginger Buttress is an obvious right-curving chimney; this route follows cracks on the face to the right. Start at the toe of the buttress, where an obvious crack leads to a tree ledge at 40'.

1. 100' 5.7 Climb the 6" crack to a ledge with a tree. Climb the right hand of the two flakes above. After 30' move left and climb the flake/chimney to an anchor at its top.

2. 150' 5.8 Move right into a thin flake/crack. Follow this crack, past a slot capped by an overhang (5.8). Continue up the thin cracks above (b) to an anchor on a good ledge.

3. 90' 5.7 Continue up the right-facing corner and the crack above to an anchor.

4. 140' 5.9 Step right and climb the long crack past a steep section (2 b's) to a small ledge below an overhang.

5. 180' 5.8 Pull over the bulge and continue up the crack to ledges. Continue to a higher ledge and belay from a tree.

6. 160' 4th class Continue up the bushy gully to an alcove below an impressive wide crack. Traverse left on a slabby ledge, then climb a corner to a nice ledge with an anchor.

7. 120' 5.6 Move right and climb the left-facing corner to the left of the main corner. Move right into the main corner and climb this to the col behind the top of the buttress.

Descent: One rap leads down to the south. Scramble down into the bowl above the water streak. Locate an anchor at the very bottom of the bowl and do four raps with a single 70m

Ginger Buttress - Right side

rope down the water streak left of Power Failure.

6a Blade Runner 350' 5.10b
A few 1"- 3" cams.
This route climbs the striking arete to the right of the final corner of Ginger Cracks. Climb Ginger Cracks to the belay above pitch 5. For a route of a more consistent grade it is also possible to climb the first 6 pitches of Unimpeachable Groping, before traversing right to the belay at the base of the route.
6. 110' 5.8 Move right and climb the face just left of the arête to the first bolt. Avoid a huge, overhanging block on the arête by moving left to a short hand crack splitting a large patch of black varnish. Go up this a short distance before returning to the arête (b). Continue directly up the exposed edge (4 b's) to a belay platform.
7. 130' 5.10b Climb directly up the spectacular arête (9 b's) to a belay on a block.
8. 110' 5.9 Continue up the arête (5 b's) to reach a low-angle hand crack. Follow this to a bolt then traverse left on an obvious ledge to a bolted anchor.
Descent: Two single rope raps lead straight down to the east to reach the notch at the top of Ginger Cracks.

7 Spice 320' 5.10c
Double rack to 2".
About 30 feet right of Ginger Cracks is a corner system with a bush about 70 feet up.
1. 60' 5.7 Climb the corner system to the ledge with the bush.
2. 170' 5.9 Tricky gear in places. Climb the long corner system above to a bolted anchor at a small footledge.
3. 90' 5.10c Climb the seam above the anchor then move left (b) and follow another seam into a left-facing corner. At a roof where the corner switches to become right-facing, step right (b) and follow an easier thin crack up and right to an anchor.

8 Sugar 325' 5.10d *
Single rack to 2".
Immediately right of Spice, a small buttress forms a low angle apron. Start on the right side of the apron.
1. 85' 5.7+ Climb up and right (3 b's) to a thin seam which leads to the anchor.
2. 80' 5.10a Climb a seam to a bolt then move up and right into a nice corner which is followed (5 b's) to a big, sloping ledge.
3. 150' 5.10d A great pitch which is spicy in places. Move up and right onto the narrow face between a seam on the left and the arete on the right. Climb the face then trend left to a bolt in an overlap below a shallow corner. Move up and left to an easier thin crack which leads to the anchor of Spice (9 b's)
Descent: With a 60m rope, start with one rap down Spice, then three raps down Sugar

9 Cayenne Corners 690' 5.10d *
Jimmy Pinjuv, Andrew Fulton, Steve Porcella, Gary Sutherland. 2000.
Single rack to 4", double 1-3".
This route climbs a series of corners and cracks up the next buttress to the right of the Ginger Cracks buttress. Start in a small recess at the base of Waterstreak Chimney.
1. 165' 5.9 Climb a left-facing corner in varnished rock, passing a bolt at the base of the corner. Continue up the corner and crack, eventually stepping left to a 2 bolt anchor in white rock.
2. 185' 5.10d Step back right into the crack system and climb up to square cut roof above a right-facing corner. Traverse right under the roof, pulling up and around into the right-facing

corner. Continue up crack to two bolt anchor on the left.
3. 110' 5.9 Move left and climb the mossy crack left of a shallow dihedral. Follow the crack until it is easy to escape right across slabs to the base of a pillar. Climb the left side of the pillar and belay on top from a fixed pin and bolt anchor.
4. 140' 5.10b/c Climb the obvious splitter crack up to the roof, traverse right under the roof and climb around its right edge. Continue up a crack, past some foliage and mossy face climbing to a two bolt anchor on the left, below a small roof.
5. 90' 5.9 Climb past a fixed pin, traverse left around the roof, and climb a widening crack past some foliage to face climbing and a fixed pin/bolt anchor on the left.
Descent: Rappel with two ropes.

To the right of Ginger Buttress is a large amphitheater. Guarding the entrance to the amphitheater is a water-streaked wall above a bushy ledge.

10 Waterstreak Chimney 230' 5.8
Gary Sutherland, Jimmy Pinjuv. 1997.
Single rack to 3.5".
The chimney on the left side of the streaked wall.
1. 70' 5.8 Follow a ramp up and left to the base of the chimney.
2. 160' 5.8 Climb the long chimney.
Descent: Traverse right to the anchors of After Hours and rappel that route with two ropes.

11 After Hours 245' 5.10b
Gary Sutherland, Jimmy Pinjuv. 1997.
Rp's, small cams, wires.
A serious route which climbs the face to the right of the right hand of the two most obvious water streaks.
1. 70' 5.7 Wander up the face to the bushy ledge.
2. 175' 5.10b The face to the right of the water streak starts with thin and badly protected climbing, which gradually eases towards the top. **Descent:** Rappel with two ropes.

The next two routes climb crack systems on the east facing wall at the left end of the Wall of Cracks. It is possible that both routes are the same, since they are both based on the left hand of the two crack systems.

12 Sweet Honey Pumpkin Love 335' 5.10c †
Jimmy Pinjuv, Gary Sutherland. 1997.
Single rack to 4", double 4"- 7".
Start on a bushy ledge up on the left side of the wall.
1. 110' 5.9 From the ledge, traverse left into a left-facing corner. Up this, then move right to a bushy belay ledge, runout.
2. 85' 5.10c Move left into a slot. Climb the crack which widens from hands to chimney. Belay above the chimney.
3. 140' 5.9 Follow the hand crack above to a tree.

13 Its A Boy! Its a Girl 495' 5.10d
Jorge Urioste, Mike Clifford, Jules George, Bill Hotz. Fall 1997.
Single rack to 6".
Start on the face below crescent-shaped, right-facing corners.
1. 165' 5.8 Climb the black face to a large ledge.
2. 165' 5.10d Climb the short face leading to a right-facing corner. Climb the corner to a chockstone (optional two bolt belay) and continue up on the outside of the chockstone on a steep finger crack. Above, a crux offwidth leads to an anchor.
3. 165' 5.10b Stem through the overhang above the anchor and continue up a crack system to an anchor.
Descent: Rappel the route with two ropes.

The Wall of Cracks

On the north side of the east peak of Rainbow Mountain, rise a series of towers and cracks above an obvious ramp. The towers get higher to the west, culminating in a 1200' high pillar capped with red rock, called The Cloud Tower.

Approach: These routes are normally approached from Pine Creek Canyon. Follow the approach for Juniper Canyon. Once on the trail continue until close to the Juniper Canyon wash. At this point a trail branches off to the left while the main trail heads up the hill to the right of the wash. Follow the trail on the left, through bushes, to the slope on the south side of the wash. A trail leads up this slope, eventually heading up and right along a huge ramp to the col at the base of the Cloud Tower. The routes start at various points along this ramp. 1.8 miles, 1200' elevation gain, 1-1½ hours.

❶ Nerve Ending 490' 5.10a
Geoff & Cal Conley, Joanne Urioste, Cara Liberatore. November 2007.
Single rack to 3".
The left edge of The Wall of Cracks is bounded by a buttress. Begin about 20 feet left of the base of this buttress, on steep, golden rock with 2 bolts.
1. 160' 5.9 Pull through the first 30 feet with long reaches on positive holds, then go straight up the center of a steep, blank-looking black face. Bypass the rap station, and climb the large corner to a station on a vegetated ledge on the left.
2. 80' 5.10a Face climb up, then left (4 b's) to a wide crack. Stem high in crack to avoid the rotten face, clip the bolt, then step right to a thin crack which leads to a hanging belay.
3. 160' 5.10a Go straight up the steep, somewhat fragile face (8 b's, plus a rap anchor mid-way). At the top of the pitch, trend slightly right, then go straight up to a ledge.
4. 90' 5.7 Go straight up fragile rock (b) to a large ledge.
Descent: Rap the route with a single 60m rope.

❷ The Pachyderm 580' 5.9 ❶
Jorge Urioste, Joanne Urioste. April 1980.
Single rack to 4".
This route climbs two disconnected crack systems on the north face of the second pillar from the left.
Start at the base of a chimney slightly to the left of center.
1. 100' 5.8 Climb the chimney and belay in a recess.
2. 100' 5.9 From the left side of the recess climb straight up steep rock (2 b's) to a narrow ledge.
3.150' 5.6 Traverse right on the ledge to a chimney. Climb the chimney to a platform.
4. 190' 5.8 Continue up the chimney to the top.
Descent: Rappel down the gully to the west.

❸ Laceration Spur 1500' 5.9
Jeff Raymond, Larry DeAngelo. Mid 2000's.
Single rack to 3.5" and 7" cam.
This is a very long, alpine style endeavour.
Start out climbing the first continuous crack system to the left of Test Tube to a large, brushy ledge area on the right. Climb the gully above, fourth class at first. Higher, the gully is split by a protruding buttress; face climb the buttress, with limited protection, to another large brushy ledge. At the right (western) end of the ledge there is a clean corner behind a pine tree. Go up the corner to a belay by a bush. Jog right for a few feet, then climb back left into a left-leaning cleft. Follow the path of least resistance (with some hard climbing) until reaching the flat top of a flake/pinnacle feature in the red rock. Cross left to the opposite end of the ledge and make a face move to reach

a clean offwidth crack (probably best to belay at the base of this crack). Climb the crack and continue generally straight up for a few hundred feet until reaching an apparent impasse in a small cave. Exit to the left on very soft rock. The difficulties soon ease and the summit ridge is reached.
Descent: The FA party continued up to the eastern summit of Rainbow Mountain, then worked west to the normal Oak Creek descent route. This took almost six hours.

Midway up the ramp is a slender pillar about 300' high, which is climbed by the route Spare Rib.

❹ Test Tube 295' 5.9 *
Jorge Urioste, Joanne Urioste. May 1980.
Single rack to 4", doubles of 1.25"- 2.5".
A good crack climb on excellent rock. Test Tube climbs the deep, smooth-walled chimney to the left of Spare Rib.
1. 135' 5.9 A hand and fist crack leads into a huge alcove.
2. 80' 5.7 Climb the deep chimney above to a platform.
3. 80' 5.7 Climb the chimney to the platform where Spare Rib finishes.
Descent: Four single rope rappels down Spare Rib.

❺ Spare Rib 290' 5.8 *
Jorge Urioste, Joanne Urioste. May 1980.
Single rack to 2".
This is an enjoyable but slightly sporty route with very exposed climbing and a few moderate runouts.
Start below the obvious rib.
1. 80' 5.8 Climb a thin crack (b) on the left side of the pillar to a ledge and anchor.
2. 70' 5.8 Climb the thin crack on the left and the face above (4 b's) to an anchor.
3. 70' 5.6 Continue up the face (4 b's) to an anchor.
4. 70' 5.4 Continue up (b) to a platform with a tree above.
Descent: Four single rope rappels starting from the tree.

❻ Tiger Crack 160' 5.12c **
Dan McQuade, Merlin Larsen. 2001.
Single rack to 7", double 1"& 4", triple 2".
The amazing lightning bolt crack which splits the overhanging wall to the left of the first pitches of Clod Tower.
1. 80' 5.7 Climb a crack to the base of the steep wall.
2. 80' 5.12c The pitch has a hard start up a thin lieback flake (3 b's) then widens from fingers to offwidth. Anchor on top.

❼ The Clod Tower 1200' 5.10b/c *
Mark Moore, Lars Holbek. 1977.
This seldom traveled route climbs the chimney/gully system to the left of Cloud Tower. The black corner/crack at the start of the route is one of the best pitches of its grade in Red Rocks. Start in the bay to the left of the Cloud Tower, below the leftmost of two obvious crack systems. Scrambling leads to a steep, clean crack in the back of a huge black corner (5.10c). Go up this crack, which becomes less steep and narrower. Continue up another flare of lighter colored rock until forced right into the main corner system. Continue up this for three pitches. Higher up, a thin crack leads to a hand crack through a bulge. Scramble up the wide gully to its top.
Descent: The first ascent party descended eastwards down the steep open gully behind the Wall of Cracks. This involves down climbing and rappels. It is also possible to get to the summit of Cloud Tower from the top of the gully and rappel Crimson Chrysalis.

❽ Hook Climb and Whimper 350' 5.10a
Bruce Lella, Mike Carr. March 1989.
Single rack to 2.5", double 1"- 2".

This route climbs four pitches to the left of Crimson Chrysalis before moving right to join that route at its fourth belay. Start 30' to the left of Crimson Chrysalis.

1. 120' 5.8 Climb the face and thin cracks to an anchor.
2. 90' 5.9 Climb a crack and corner system above the belay to a ledge and anchor.
3. 60' 5.10a Go up and right to a ledge (3 b's). From the ledge angle left (5.9 R) then up past a bolt to an anchor.
4. 80' 5.8 Continue up the face (b) then trend right past a bolt, (5.8 R), joining Crimson Chrysalis at the fourth anchor.
Descent: Rap Crimson Chrysalis with two ropes.

Above the top end of the approach ramp, a slender pillar soars up to a red-capped summit. This pillar is climbed by the following route which has become a world-renowned classic.

❾ Crimson Chrysalis 960' 5.8+ *
Jorge Urioste, Joanne Urioste. October 1979.
Single rack to 3".

For the first 500' the route goes up the wide crack system that splits the lower part of the pillar. Eventually the crack dwindles, and face climbing leads up to the summit. Despite looking very intimidating from below, the climbing is amazingly reasonable; the wide sections lower down are generally avoided by using face holds beside the crack, and higher up the impressive looking faces are covered in good holds. Protection is generally good although some of the easier face climbing can be a little runout. Not only is this a world class route, it also attracts world class crowds. This is especially a problem since the descent is to rappel straight down the route. The best policy is to avoid this climb on busy weekends during the spring and fall months. Start 30' west of the col at the top of the approach ramp, below the impressive crack system.

1. 140' 5.7 Climb the crack and the face to its right (6 b's).
2. 90' 5.8 Continue to an anchor in a recess (5 b's).
3. 100' 5.8+ Climb the chimney (b) then move out right and climb steeply past two bolts to easier-angled rock. Continue to a ledge.
4. 140' 5.8 Up a chimney (b) into a long, thin crack which leads past two steep sections to a nice ledge.
5. 110' 5.8 Up the finger and hand crack to a ledge. Continue up the dwindling crack (b) to an anchor.
6. 100' 5.8+ Move up and left, making bouldery moves past a steep section (2 b's) to reach a ledge. Continue up and right (3 b's) to an anchor.
7. 130' 5.7 Continue (9 b's) to an anchor in the red band.
8. 75' 5.7 Climb up over a bulge, then go 10' up and right to the base of a ramp which is followed up and left to its end. Continue left (3 b's) to an anchor.
9. 75' 5.8 Climb through a small roof, move right, then up the face to an anchor on top of the tower (4 b's).
Descent: Rappel the route with two ropes.

❿ Cloud Tower 800' 5.11d *
Paul Van Betten, Richard Harrison, Nick Nordblom. Spring 1983.
Double cams from 0.4" to 3.5", single 4", triple 0.4",0.5"; five 2".

With everything from tips to offwidth, on superb splitter rock, this is one of Red Rock's finest crack climbs. The pitches tend to be long and sustained, and are very well-protected, except for the pitch 6 offwidth. Start 150' to the west of the saddle at the top of the approach ramp. Look for a smooth-walled V-groove/chimney with a couple of small trees low down, that turns into a long left-facing corner.

1. 120' 5.8 Climb the chimney and pull through a steep section into the left-facing corner. Up this to a ledge.
2. 120' 5.8 Continue up the corner to a bushy terrace.
3. 150' 5.10a Continue past some steep, blocky ledges into a nice thin-hands crack. Follow this to its end, then face climb leftwards and belay beside a bolt.
4. 100' 5.11d Move up into the slanting corner. Negotiate this sustained, technical and strenuous tips corner, then belay at the base of a slot.
5.140' 5.10c 10' above the anchor, pull over a small roof into a beautiful hand crack which gradually widens. Belay on a small ledge on the left at the point where the crack becomes a chimney.
6. 60' 5.10c Climb easily up the chimney until it bottlenecks. Move out to a ledge on the right. Lieback (5.10c) up the final wide crack with gear 15' below, to reach the top of a tower. Belay on 2"-2.5" cams here or use these for protection and down climb the crack on the back side of the tower to a good ledge 15' down, this has the advantage of allowing the belayer to see the leader on the final pitch. The final offwidth can be avoided by squeezing through the back of the recess below the final wide crack to reach the ledge directly.
7. 110' 5.11c Climb the superb hand crack for 80' to a good rest (11a). Continue stemming and liebacking up the overhanging corner above, with a strenuous pull (11c) over the final bulge to an anchor.
Descent: The rappel route goes down to the west of the climb. The first rappel is 160' and leads to a sloping ledge. A short rappel from a bolt anchor at the right end of the ledge leads down to a tree. From here a few rappels off bushes and small trees leads to the terrace above the second pitch. Go east along the terrace and rappel down the first two pitches to the base of the route.

⓫ Cloud Tower Direct Finish 360' 5.12d
Start at the anchor above the 7th pitch of Cloud Tower.
8. 80' 5.12d Continue up the corner (5 b's), with desperate stemming past a short, steep section, to reach an anchor below an offwidth.
9. 100' 5.10c Climb the offwidth and continue to a small notch behind the summit block of Crimson Chrysalis. Either scramble up to the top of the block and rappel Crimson Chrysalis or...
10. 40' 5.8 Climb a chimney in the buttress above the notch. Belay above a chockstone.
11. 140' 5.10a Climb the hand crack on the left to the top.
Descent: The first ascent party down climbed and rappelled to the west.

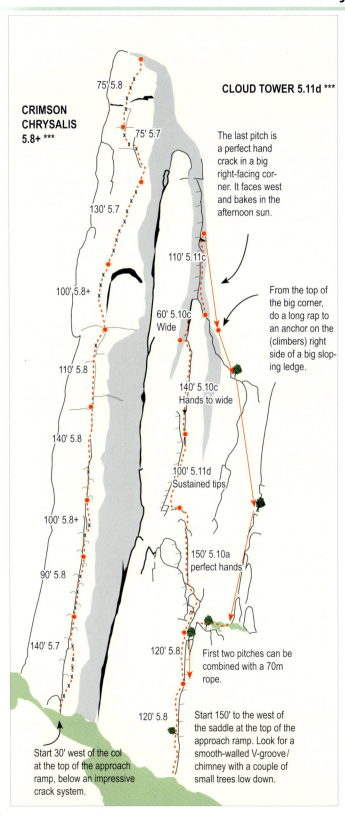

CLOUD TOWER 5.11d ***

CRIMSON CHRYSALIS 5.8+ ***

75' 5.8

75' 5.7

130' 5.7

100' 5.8+

110' 5.8

140' 5.8

100' 5.8+

90' 5.8

140' 5.7

The last pitch is a perfect hand crack in a big right-facing corner. It faces west and bakes in the afternoon sun.

110' 5.11c

60' 5.10c Wide

140' 5.10c Hands to wide

From the top of the big corner, do a long rap to an anchor on the (climbers) right side of a big sloping ledge.

100' 5.11d Sustained tips

150' 5.10a perfect hands

120' 5.8

First two pitches can be combined with a 70m rope.

120' 5.8

Start 150' to the west of the saddle at the top of the approach ramp. Look for a smooth-walled V-groove/chimney with a couple of small trees low down.

Start 30' west of the col at the top of the approach ramp, below an impressive crack system.

Upstream from the Cloud Tower area, the south side of Juniper Canyon is dominated by an obvious buttress of light-colored rock separating the downstream walls from the wide bowl beneath the Rainbow Wall. The buttress is split by an obvious crack/corner system that is climbed by following route.

Thagomizer 500' 5.10c

Karsten Duncan, Lucas Krajnik, Johnny Ray, Larry DeAngelo. 2008.
Double rack to 6".

The easiest way to approach this route is to hike up the main Juniper Canyon trail to a point where the trail leaves the main wash and goes up a steep, red, dirt slope on the left. From the top of the dirt slope, a brushy gully leads up through the band of cliffs on the left. Follow this to its top and scramble right (west) to the base of the main corner.

1. Climb straight up the varnished corner, passing a difficult section at a bulge. Belay on a ledge above.

2. Continue up the crack just left of the main corner. Pass a small overhang and continue past a bush to a good ledge with a small tree beneath a prominent chimney.

3. Squeeze up the chimney to an overhang at its top, then belay on a ledge about 20' higher.

4. At this point the crack system has diverged from the main corner and reached an impasse beneath an unprotectable varnished headwall. The route continues up the impressive corner to the right. Pitch 4 starts with a traverse right and up to gain the main corner at the lip of a giant overhang. A committing move leads to a rest in the corner above. Difficult climbing continues for another 40' until the angle begins to relent. Easier climbing then leads to a large ledge on the very crest of the buttress.

Descent: Walk west on the ledge system until reaching the first drainage. Go down and right (east) to a rappel from a large pine tree on the right edge of the drainage. Two double-rope rappels led to the canyon floor.

Rainbow Wall

This imposing wall, towering over the upper reaches of Juniper Canyon, is one of the more impressive chunks of rock in Red Rocks. There are very few face holds here, instead the routes tend to follow long corner systems with smooth rock. Routes such as Original Route, Desert Solitaire and Dreefee are amongst the best big wall free climbs in the country, offering great climbing on mostly excellent rock, but almost all the other routes are serious undertakings with stretches of dangerously soft and/or blocky rock in their upper sections. The Wall is in the form of a huge corner which faces northeast, and as a result receives very little sun, which, along with its high elevation, makes it a perfect warm weather venue. This is also one of the few walls in Red Rocks that is still popular with aid climbers, the Original Route being by far the aid route of choice.

Approach: These routes are normally approached from Pine Creek Canyon. Follow the approach for Juniper Canyon. Once on the trail, continue until close to the main Juniper Canyon wash. At this point the main trail heads up the hill to the right of the wash and when the canyon narrows, drops into the wash. Continue up the rough wash and when things get a little bushy, the trail leaves the wash and heads up a dirt slope on the left. Eventually, it reaches a pretty bowl filled with large trees at the base of the upper canyon. A short thrash up the upper canyon leads to a point where there is a waterfall on the left wall. This is the drainage for the enormous bowl underneath the Rainbow Wall. Hand over hand up a fixed rope beside the waterfall (or climb to the left, low fifth class) and scramble up the endless slabs of the bowl to reach the base of the wall.
2.1 miles, 1900' elevation gain, 1½-3 hrs.

Descent: The most efficient descent is to rappel The Original Route. Look for a tree with rappel rings directly above the huge corner in the center of the wall. It is also reasonable to walk down Oak Creek Canyon, 2- 3 hrs.

The routes are described from left to right.

❶ Sergeant Slaughter 1070' 5.12b *
Richard Harrison, Paul Van Betten. Winter 1984.
FFA Brian McCray, Roxanna Brock. May 1998.
Double cams from 0.4"- 4" singles from 4"- 7".
This route climbs a corner system on the front of the pillar that forms the left boundary of the wall. A burly, sustained route with great climbing on the lower pitches. Higher up the quality of both the rock and the climbing deteriorates considerably. Start below a crack in the apron below the pillar.
1. 100' 5.7 Climb the crack to a ledge.
2. 130' 5.12b Start up a left-facing corner. Move right and follow a right-facing corner around a roof and up a long, burly lieback, which gradually widens from tips to offwidth.
3. 80' 5.11a Climb a thin, loose crack (2 pins) into a tight flare. Climb the flare and continue to an anchor.
4. 60' 5.11d Battle up another flare to an anchor.
5. 110' 5.11b Tricky route finding on this pitch. Climb up to a bolt and make a hard move right, into a right-facing corner. Follow the corner, then traverse up and right (b) to the anchors.
6. 80' 5.10b Climb the white face up and right to a big ledge. Loose and runout.
7. 110' 5.11a From the left side of the ledge, climb a squeeze chimney to a blocky ledge. Follow thin seams up a right-facing corner, then move right to the belay ledge.

8. 80' 5.10a Another loose, dangerous pitch. Make crux moves off the belay (2 b's) and continue up the loose face to a ledge.
9. 90' 5.11a Go up and left (b) into a right-leaning, right-facing corner. Up this (poor gear) then pull over its top to a huge tree.
10. 80' 5.8 Climb a right-leaning, right-facing corner to its top. Climb up and a little left on loose rock to a belay ledge.
11. 40' 5.8 Climb the face to the top of the wall.

What Dreams May Come 1100' 5.13c *
Micro to #3 camalot. Triples from micro to 0.5". An offset 1.5" cam is helpful for pitch 3.
This is a challenging line which largely follows a right-facing corner system immediately to the right of Sergeant Slaughter. The difficult climbing is on small pin scars and pods which are likely to punish the sausage-fingered. There are many bolts, but all the pitches require supplemental gear. The climbing is reminiscent of the Original Route; steep, smooth-walled corners, but much harder.
1. 120' 5.7 Climb Sergeant Slaughter all the way to its first belay, then move right on a ledge to a bolted anchor below a wide crack.
2. 60' 5.11a Jam and chimney up the flared crack, past a technical overlap (2 b's), to a belay on top of a small pillar. A technical pitch that requires decent crack climbing skills.
3. 150' 5.12b A big pitch with a number of difficult sections separated by good rests. Use a short, offset seam (2 b's) to reach a large right-facing corner. Several boulder problems lead to a well-earned, no-hands rest (5 b's). Clip a pin and move up to an unnerving undercling right past a small roof (offset cam). Climb up the arete on good holds (2 b's) to a short corner (2 b's) and a right-facing flake. Belay at a foot ledge.
4. 40' 5.13c Climb the blank corner above (micro cams), making increasingly difficult moves as the crack thins. At the top of the corner a climactic sequence (3 b's) gains the belay ledge.
5. 100' 5.10d Clip a bolt and step right to a crack. Follow it to honey-combed rock and mantle onto a ledge on the left.
6. 90' 5.13a The right-facing corner above leans hard to the right, making for a difficult section when the crack thins and the feet disappear. Begin with easy moves up to a stance (3 b's). After the third bolt, make a powerful move to begin a series of difficult laybacks up the corner. A final section of 12a climbing on friable rock (3 b's) guards an anchor on the left.
7. 80' 5.10c Climb a dirty, unprotected face to a wide crack that ends on a big ledge. The wide crack protects with small gear. Follow the last few pitches of Sergeant Slaughter to the top and descend the Original Route.

❷ The Big Paycheck 1400' 5.10c, A3
Kevin Daniels, Tony Sartin, Dave Evans. March 1998.
This is a long, committing aid route which climbs the huge right-arching corner to the right of the pillar at the left end of the wall. Start below a crack in the apron below the pillar.
1. 100' 5.7 Climb the crack to a ledge. This is the first pitch of Sergeant Slaughter.
2. 40' Third class. Traverse right to a thin crack leading up into the huge corner.
Variation: 5.10b It is possible to reach this point by climbing up the runout face directly below.
3. 150' A2 Follow the thin crack into the corner to an anchor.
4. 100' 5.10 A3 Continue up the corner, then move out right to the anchor.

The brilliant third pitch of Dreefee. Page 186.

5. 150' A3, 5.10 Continue following the roof out right to an anchor.
6. 100' Continue up the upper corner.
7. 150' A3 Continue up the crack system to a bivi ledge on the right.
8. 110' A2 Unprotected face climbing leads up and left to another crack system, which is followed to a single bolt belay.
9. 150' 5.9, A2 Free climb up and right, then aid to an anchor.
10. 150' 5.9, A2 Follow a long groove up and right to a ledge.
11. 200' 5.9 Climb to the right of a tower to reach the notch behind it. Continue up a chimney to the top.

❸ Emerald City 1390' 5.12d
Randal Grandstaff, John Thacker. Spring 1983. FFA Roxanna Brock, Brian McCray. 1998.
Double set of cams to 5", single 7".
This route climbs a long crack system almost in the middle of the wall to the left of Original Route. Start about 100 yards to the right of The Big Paycheck, beside a big, dead tree stump.
1. 100' 5.10b Climb up and left across a slab to reach a crack which is climbed to an anchor.
2.110 5.12d Move up and right and continue with ultra-thin stemming up a holdless corner (b); continue to a ledge with a tree.
3. 110' 5.10a Follow the crack on the left to an anchor.
4. 150' 5.10c Climb a crack to a roof. Pull the roof and go up and right, past a large block to an anchor.
5. 120' 5.12a Climb a lichenous slab to reach a chimney. Squeeze up the chimney to a belay.
6. 130' 5.10b An intricate and serious pitch with loose rock and poor protection. Head left out of the chimney onto the face. Climb the face to a loose pillar. Gain the top of the pillar, then climb a left-facing crack to its top. Hand traverse left on a rubble covered ledge, then move up to an excellent bivi ledge.
7. 110' 5.11b Climb a crack which slants up and right to a belay. The old aid line climbs the crack that goes straight up from the belay.
8. 40' 5.6 Traverse left and belay on a ledge below an arching corner.

9. 120' 5.10c Climb the right-arching corner (loose) then the crack above up to an anchor.

10. 180' 5.11b Climb a right-leaning crack, then face climb up and left and belay on a ledge.

11. 60' Fourth class. Climb to a belay below a big offwidth.

12. 100' 5.9 Climb the offwidth to a big ledge.

13. 100' 5.6 Climb a short offwidth, then head up easier rock to the top.

❹ Dreefee 1200' 5.13d ***
Bart Groendyke, Todd Alston. May 1992. FFA Unknown.
Triple to 0.75", double .75"-1.5", single to 4" , Bd wires with extra 4, 5, 6.
Red slider nut. Green WC zero. HB brass offsets.

This route climbs a beautiful series of shallow corners up the crest of a huge pillar close to the leftmost of two prominent water streaks to the right of Emerald City. It is one of the hardest and best long routes in Red Rocks with immaculate rock and gorgeous features almost the entire way. Start down and right of the water streak at a couple of trees at a highpoint at the base of the wall.

1. 150' 5.7 Follow shallow grooves to a ramp which leads left into a corner. Climb the corner for 15' to an anchor.

2. 100' 5.12a Climb grooves (b) into a short stembox. Make a hard move out of the top of the stembox (microcams) to a rest, then continue up a tricky small corner to a hanging belay at an anchor above a small footledge on the right arete.

3. 90' 5.13b A brilliant pitch, sustained and technical the entire way. Climb over the small roof above the anchor into a left-facing corner. Make crux moves past a bolt, then continue up the sustained and tricky corner to a rest on a small ledge. Follow the right-slanting corner above (a little bold) to a good foothold, then negotiate an abstract sequence (b) to good holds above a small roof. The anchor is a few feet higher.

4. 65' 5.13b Tricky stemming right off the anchor (b) leads to a good slot (4" cam). Desperate palming and friction (b) leads up the right-slanting offsets above to a good fingerlock. An easier (12b and a little bold) but still punchy thin crack then leads to better holds. Pull over a slight bulge to an anchor at the base of a left-facing corner.

5. 90' 5.13c Climb the left-facing corner (b) and the face to its left, then, when the corner switches, layback into its right-facing continuation. Hard moves lead up the corner (2 b's) to a semi-rest in a shallow scoop at its top. Traverse down and right (3 b's) on good holds to an anchor on a welcome ledge.

6. 40' 5.13c Delicate layback moves lead up the pretty arch on the right, then pull over a bulge into an open black corner. Bouldery moves lead up the corner to a hard exit on sloping holds, and an anchor just above (5 b's).

7. 120' 5.13d Follow a shallow ramp up and right onto a glassy, varnished wall. Move right on edges and make a desperate move to stand up (V9?). Move back left and continue (still tricky) to a good hold. Continue with great climbing up the varnished wall (optional #9 Bd stopper & 000 Bd C3) to an anchor at a small ledge (12 b's).

Variation: 5.13c/d It is possible to skip a bolt and avoid the crux move on the left.

8. 150' 5.12a Traverse left 20' and make bouldery moves through an overlap onto sustained and slopey 5.10 climbing leading to an anchor. (11 b's, cams to 1.25", extra micro cams).

9. 100' 5.10c Go up a left-facing corner to big ledges, then up another left-facing corner with small roof (2 b's) to an anchor.

Descent: It is possible to finish by moving left into Emerald

City. Otherwise, rappel with two ropes from the top of pitch 8.

❺ Battle Royale 1200 5.9, A2
Richard Harrison, Nick Nordblom, Wendell Broussard. Spring 1983.
In the middle of the wall to the left of Original Route are two prominent black water streaks. This route starts up the right hand water streak. Dirty and sandy low down, and loose and blocky higher up.

Start below the water streak, in the crack to the left of a small pillar with a tree at its top.

1. 5.7, A2 Climb the crack then continue up a seam which leads to a big flake. Above the flake, traverse to a belay below a left-facing corner.

2. A2 Continue up the left-facing corner. Pass a roof to get into another left-facing corner which is followed to a ledge.

3. A1 Climb the right-facing corner above to reach a long left-facing corner which is followed to a chimney. Climb the chimney to a blocky ledge.

4. A2 Climb the right-facing corner and pass the roof above to get into a left-facing corner. Up this and the right-facing corner above to a tree. Continue to belay on a higher ledge.

5. A2 Start at the left end of the ledge. Climb a loose right-facing corner, then pendulum right into another corner. Climb the corner, then make another pendulum right into a left-facing corner. Continue up this corner, over a roof, to a belay.

6. A2 Climb a loose right-facing corner to its top, then climb up and left to a ledge below a chimney. The first ascent party bivied here.

7. 60' 5.7 Climb the chimney to a ledge.

8. 80' 5.8, A1 Climb a crack to reach another chimney. Belay at its top.

9. 100' 5.8 Move right and climb a fragile runout face to a ledge to the right of a huge, blocky corner.

10. 120' 5.9, A2 Climb the corner past some trees to a ledge.

11. 120' 5.9, A2 Climb a rotten crack which leads to the top of a pillar.

12. 150' A2 Pendulum into a right-facing corner on the right. Climb this and follow a ramp up and right to a belay at a single bolt at the top of a pillar. Another rotten pitch.

13. 120' 5.9 Gingerly weave around the blocks above to reach a ledge. Go left along the ledge and follow a crack to a pine tree at the top of the wall.

❻ Desert Solitaire 1200' 5.13b **
Nick Nordblom. Spring 1983. FFA Unknown.
Double cams to 3". Single 4". Brass wires, slider nuts, extra tips cams.
If going to the top, bring extra .75"-2" cams and many slings.
The long, sinuous line of corners to the left of The Original Route is another great climb with lots of technical corner work. After pitch 8 the quality of the climbing deteriorates considerably, but the route can be rappelled with two ropes.

The route starts in the great bivy ledge 50' up the cliff and about 150' to the left of the huge corner of Original Route.

1. 200' 5.10c Exit the bivy ledge on the right and wander up easy rock to a small bulge. Pull over the bulge into shallow, opposing corners (b). Step left to a thin left-facing corner and belay at an anchor below a short, tight corner.

2. 140' 5.11d Climb the awkward corner (2 pins) to its top then continue more easily to a pin at the base of a right-facing corner on the right. Layback up the corner and continue to a ledge at the base of a long, elegant corner.

3. 70' 5.12b The corner starts easily enough with fun stemming. At the top of the corner a short but desperate sequence

Pitch 6 of Dreefee. Page 186.

on tiny holds (b) leads to better holds and an anchor on a small ledge on the right.

4. 100' 5.12a A superb pitch. Layback up a short slot (b) to a rest and continue up the beautiful corner (4 b's), sustained and technical stemming, to an anchor below another classic corner.

5. 65' 5.13b Lurking above is one of the harder corners in Red Rocks, the pitch starts with complex, insecure stemming which leads straight into a very powerful layback on miserable sloping holds and finally the first real hold at 40'. Move up then right across a bulge to better holds which lead more easily to the anchor (7 b's).

6. 90' 5.12a/b Climb a shallow corner, then make some technical moves (b) up into the hand/fist-crack flake above. Belay on the far right end of the ledge at bolts.

7. 100' 5.12a Climb slightly right to gain a line of 6 bolts traversing straight left along a hand-traverse flake. The traverse ends on a 1 ft ledge below a flaky face with 3 bolts and an anchor above. An attentive belay is necessary to prevent hitting the ledge in the event of a fall.

8. 170' 5.11d Make unprotected moves up a right-facing, hollow flake to gain a nice corner. The corner widens to chimney-sized, then narrows back to tips. Belay at bolts on a pillar left of the crack. The fun has now ended.

9. 50' 5.9 Float up the loose chimney to a spacious bushy ledge with bolts on each end.

10. 180' 5.10c Climb a horrible pitch that wanders between two loose cracks on the left wall of the large right-facing corner. Belay at a sloping, grassy ledge atop the left wall from a single bolt and a 2 inch crack.

11. 150' 5.9 Move straight up the horrible gully and pull over a ledge (b) using stacked blocks poised to fall on your belayer. Once on a large ledge, walk left about 50 ft to a short crack leading to a small tree atop the wall.

❼ The Original Route 1160 5.12a ***
Joe Herbst, Larry Hamilton. April 1973. FFA Leo Henson. 1994. Single rack to 3", Rp's.

This route climbs the huge corner in the center of the wall. It is one of the gems of Red Rocks, with clean rock, attractive features and superb climbing. Overall, this is a much more amenable route than the pitch grades would suggest since most of the cruxes are short and well-protected.

Start by scrambling onto a perfect flat ledge directly below the huge corner.

1. 70' 5.6 Zig-zag up short cracks and steep ledges to an anchor on a small ledge below a steep crack.

2. 70' 5.12a Climb the crack into a smooth, black corner. Stem up the corner (2 b's), then move left and climb the slabby wall to an anchor.

Variation: 5.11c It is possible to reach this anchor by following a long arching line to the left of the first two pitches (6 b's).

3. 80' 5.11d Lieback up the sharp-edged crack above the anchor, and continue up the corner (4 b's) until forced onto the wall to the right. Climb the wall past a bolt (this bolt seems to come and go, if it's gone this section feels quite necky) then move back left into the corner. Climb the corner to a sloping ledge.

4. 70' 5.11a Continue up the corner to an anchor.

5. 80' 5.11b Continue up the corner past a booming block (b), then lieback around a roof and up to an anchor.

6. 50' 5.10c Continue up the corner.

7. 70' 5.10a Continue up the corner. At the top of the corner,

exit right to an anchor on a bushy ledge.

8. 200' 5.7 A long pitch leads up and right, passing through a couple of chimneys then over some ledges and short, steep steps to a bushy ledge below a left-facing corner. Climb the corner to an awkward exit right in a slanting chimney. This leads to a belay below another left-facing corner.

9. 60' 5.7 The corner is 5.9 and a bit sketchy. An easier option is to traverse right around the base of the corner onto a slab. Climb the slab (5.5) to reach an anchor on a beautiful flat ledge.

10. 80' 5.8 Traverse left (b) from the ledge, then climb back up and right to an anchor at a small ledge at the bottom of a beautiful, red corner system.

11. 70' 5.11d Climb the corner (2 b's) past a bouldery move and continue more easily to an anchor at a small ledge.

12. 60' 5.12a Continue up the corner (3 b's) to an anchor on the left. (This pitch was featured on the cover of the third edition of Swains' guidebook)

13. 80' 5.11b Step left (b) and climb up to the left end of a roof. Continue up the corner on the left to an anchor.

Variation: The original version of this pitch steps back right into the corner and climbs up to the roof before traversing back left (5 b's). At 12b this pitch is a good bit harder than anything else on the route.

14. 90' 5.10b Continue up the rounded groove to a pine tree at the top of the wall.

The route can be rapped with a single 60m rope.

❽ Rainbow Country 1050' 5.12d *
Dan McQuade, Eric Camillo. December 1996.

This is a direct variation to The Original Route. It has some good 5.11 climbing and a short but intimidating crux which has rebuffed more than a few attempts.

Start this route by climbing the first six pitches of The Original Route.

7. 100' 5.11b Start up the seventh pitch of The Original Route, but instead of moving right onto the big ledge system, continue up and left into a long corner system which is climbed past one set of anchors to a belay at the second.

8. 90' 5.11b Climb up into a chimney; climb the chimney and make an airy exit. Continue past a small roof to an anchor.

9. 75' 5.12d Climb up into a right-facing corner which is followed (6 b's) past a roof (medium nut) to an anchor.

10. 60' 5.12a Traverse right (2 b's) and head up to the anchors below pitch 11 of the Original Route.

The huge wall to the right of The Original Route faces east and gets sun until early afternoon, making it less useful for warm weather climbing than the rest of the wall.

❾ Saurons Eye 1000' 5.10d, A4
Brian McCray. February 1999.

This is a serious and committing aid route which climbs the huge arching corners to the right of Original Route. Start at a small pinnacle at the bottom left corner of the huge arch.

1. 150' 5.7, A3 Follow discontinuous cracks up and right to a thin seam which is followed to an anchor.

2. 100' A1 Climb the left-facing corner above into a right-facing corner. Climb this corner, then pendulum left and go up a right-facing corner to an anchor.

3. 160' A2+ Follow a seam into a right-facing corner. Traverse left on hooks and climb a face (3 b's) to a knifeblade crack which is followed to an anchor. (400' to the ground from here).

Rainbow Wall - Left side

4. 170' A4 Follow the crack under the huge arch and follow 5 b's out the huge roof to an anchor just above the lip. The roof has a sharp lip therefore the second should aid clean this pitch. (440' to the ground from here).

5. 190' 5.10d A wide band of soft white rock cuts all the way across the wall above the roof. A long, worrying pitch leads through this band to a big pine tree.

6. 180' 5.7, A1 Follow a line of cracks up and right to reach a loose groove which is followed to an anchor.

7. 180' 5.7 Climb the groove above to a large ledge.

Descent: Traverse the ledges rightwards to reach an anchor below the final corner of Brown Recluse. There is a rappel route which goes straight down from here, to the left of Brown Recluse.

There is an unfinished project which attempts to follow the left-facing corner systems leading up to the right edge of the arch.

Kor Route †

Layton Kor climbed a route on this part of the wall during a brief return to climbing in the mid-1980s unfortunately the details of the exact line are not available.

⑩ Brown Recluse 900' 5.12b

Roxanna Brock, Brian McCray. June 1998.
Single rack to 3", double 0.4"- 0.75", Rp's.

This route starts up nice, varnished corners on the right side of the wall, but finishes with five pitches of soft white rock, with some unnervingly fragile climbing.

Start by scrambling up to a ledge with a bolt, below the obvious big corner system on the right side of the wall. This is about 150 yards to the right of the huge red arch.

1. 90' 5.10a Climb the bolted face to the left of a right-facing corner (9 b's) to an anchor below a short, steep wall.

2. 100' 5.11b Make awkward moves up the wall (4 b's) to reach the start of a crack system which is followed to an anchor.

3. 120' 5.11b Climb the big left-facing corner (8 b's) to an anchor on the left. A great pitch, the best on the route by far.

4. 150' 5.10b Continue up the corner a short distance then traverse out left and climb a long, slabby face (3 b's) with long runouts and fragile rock. This leads to an anchor on a ledge on the left.

5. 120' 5.10d Traverse out left and climb a thin seam (4 b's) in very sandy rock (worrying) to an anchor.

6. 180' 5.11a Continue up a long left-leaning crack / corner system to an anchor on ledges below a big left-facing corner.

7. 120' 5.12b Continue up into the big corner which is followed easily at first until it arches steeply to the right. Hard moves up the arch (4 b's) lead to an anchor on the right. This pitch used to be 11c until a key flake came off with the author attached.

8. 100' 5.8 Continue up the upper corner to an anchor.

9. 75' 5.5 An easy pitch leads to the top. Traverse right on ledges to reach an anchor above the crack line.

Descent: Three raps down the route lead to the base of the big corner. From here the rap route goes straight down, staying to climbers left of the route. The first ascentionist did this rappel with a single 70m rope but some of the raps barely make it, a single 80m rope would be more comfortable.

⑪ Bird Hunter Buttress 1200' 5.9

Jorge Urioste, Joanne Urioste. 1982.
Single rack to 4".

This route climbs the blocky buttress that forms the right edge of the Rainbow Wall. A lot of fragile rock limits the appeal, but the length and spectacular scenery give the route a distinct alpine feel.

Start by scrambling up and right across slabs and ledges to reach a large pine tree at the base of the right edge of the wall.

1. 130' 5.7 From the tree head up and left and climb the leftmost of a couple of cracks. Pull a bulge and continue (3 b's) to an anchor.

2. 50' 5.7 Move left and climb a crack to an anchor.

3. 110' 5.7 Continue up the crack (b) to an anchor.

4. 80' 5.8 Continue up the wide crack to an anchor on a sloping ledge just below the top of a tower.

5. 90' 5.9 Continue up the face above (3 b's), step left to a crack and continue (2 b's) to an anchor.

6. 70' 5.9 Continue up the face (3 b's) to an anchor on top of a small pillar.

7. 30' 5.8 Climb a wide crack (b) to the top of a higher pillar.

8. 120' 5.9 Up and right, moving around an arete to reach a crack which leads straight up to an anchor on a ledge (7 b's).

9. 120' 5.9 Climb a right-facing corner (7 b's) to a ledge below a pine tree.

Scramble up and left along ledges for 60' to a higher pine tree.

10. 90' 5.7 Climb a chimney (b) to an anchor.

11. 90' 5.8 Chimney out left and climb the corner (2 b's) to a big ledge.

12. 90' 5.4 Climb a face (b) to a belay beside a bolt in blocky overhangs.

The route finishes with several hundred feet of scrambling. Grovel left and continue up the ridge for a couple of hundred feet to a step. 300' of scrambling with a few 5th class sections lead up this step to the summit of the Rainbow Wall.

Descent: There are several descent options. From the summit, Rainbow Wall Original route can be rapped with a single 60m rope. There is also the option of the long walk down Oak Creek Canyon, probably the best bet if there is much wind. It is possible to rap the route from the top of pitch 12 with two 60m ropes. It is also possible to rappel down Brown Recluse. At the top of the pitch 12, traverse from the bolt around the corner to the left onto a large ledge. It is possible to see an anchor in a gully below the ledge; the rappel descent starts here. The Brown Recluse rap is doable with a 70m rope, but an 80m is more comfortable.

⑫ Paiute Pillar 1500' 5.9

Vince Poirier, Andrew Fulton. 1998.
Single rack to 4", double finger to hand sizes.

This route starts below and right of Bird Hunter Buttress at the bottom of the long buttress on the right edge of the Rainbow Wall. The route climbs up cracks and faces for 900' until it crosses Bird Hunter Buttress, and finishes to its left. The route is quite loose, dirty and runout in places and probably rates as a quite serious undertaking.

Climb the fixed ropes at the base of the Rainbow Wall bowl then immediately traverse right on slabs. The route starts on top of a pedestal below a band of dark red rock split by an obvious crack.

1. 180' 5.9 Climb up the prominent splitter crack in the middle of the red cliff band.

Rainbow Wall - Right side

2. 200' 4th Class Angle up and right to reach a large ledge.

3. 110' 5.9 Head straight up the face to the ledge with a tree.

4. 200' 5.9 Traverse up and right to a small, varnished arete. After pulling onto the arete move slightly back left toward the crack that splits the licheny face. Belay at a ledge.

5. 170' 5.9 Climb the runout face to a gear belay at the base of a prominent right-facing corner.

6. 100' 5.8 Climb up the face to the left of the right-facing corner (3 b's). Belay at a ledge with a bush.

7. 175' 5.7 Either climb up the pillar above or the (better) mossy 5.8 right-facing corner to the right, part of Bird Hunter Buttress. Poor, old bolts protect but the crack takes small cams.

8. 200' 5.9 Head up the face right then up over a roof to belay on a ledge. Alternatively, climb the fun and grovelly 5.7 squeeze chimney on Bird Hunter Buttress. One bolt. Belay at a prominent ledge.

9. 180' 5.8 Move slightly right passing one bolt then through a roof.

10. 80' 4th Class Go up and left to the top.

Descent: The first ascent party down climbed and rappelled to the north west to reach Gunsight Notch. Alternatively, finish up Bird Hunter Buttress to the top of Rainbow Wall.

Brownstone Wall

The Brownstone Wall is the long east-facing wall at the head of Juniper Canyon. It is bordered on the left by a distinctive V-shaped notch, called the Gunsight. The right side of the wall forms the summit of Juniper Peak. There is a generous supply of nicely-varnished corner systems here, making it well worth the long walk.

Approach: Follow the approach for Juniper Canyon. Once on the trail continue until close to the main Juniper Canyon wash. At this point the main trail heads up the hill to the right of the wash and, when the canyon narrows, drops into the wash.

Continue up the rough wash, and dirt slopes to the left, eventually reaching a pretty bowl filled with large trees at the base of the upper canyon. From the top right side of the bowl, head up to a talus slope and scramble up slabs to the base of the wall. 2.2 miles, 1200' elevation gain, 1¼ hrs.

Descent: For all the routes finishing on top of the wall traverse the summit ridge to the south and scramble down into the Gunsight Notch. The gully to the east of the notch leads down past a few sections of easy fifth class, to the base of the wall, and the upper reaches of Juniper Canyon.

Brownstone Wall - Left side

A prominent feature of the left hand end of the wall is a deep right-facing corner starting a couple of hundred feet up, the line of Black Dagger.

❶ Peanut Brittle 700' 5.7
Joanne Urioste, Jorge Urioste. February 1978.
Single rack to 4".
This route climbs cracks in the pillar to the left of Black Dagger, joining that route for the final two pitches.
Start at a large pine tree.
1. 100' 4th Class Scramble up the easy face to the left of a wide crack. Continue up to a belay behind a large block.
2. 150' 5.5 10' Above the belay, step right around a corner then climb steep cracks to a small ledge.
3. 80' 5.5 Move up and step right to a crack. Follow the crack, past an overhang, to a small ledge.
4. 150' 5.7 Climb a steep chimney above the belay then continue up a short crack which peters out in a low-angled face. Climb the face (sparse protection) to twin cracks which are followed to an overhang. Turn this and belay immediately above on a good ledge.
5. 80' 5.5 Continue straight up a crack, passing some varnish patches, to the top of a pillar and a junction with Black Dagger.
6. 100' 5.6 Climb the face to a smooth, pink right-facing corner; up this to a ledge below a roof.
7. 120' 5.5 Climb the face to the roof, pull over this, and follow a right-facing corner to the top.

❷ Black Dagger 680' 5.8 **
Joe Herbst, Rick Wheeler. 1977.
Single rack to 3", optional 6" cam.
This is one of the few classic climbs of its grade in Red Rocks where it would be unusual to share the route with other climbers. Interesting, varied climbing in a beautiful location.
Start directly below the huge right-facing corner which starts 200' up the wall.
1. 100' 5.4 Easy climbing leads to a ledge on top of a block, 15' below an obvious white roof.
2. 140'. 5.7 The initial part of this pitch is a bold. Traverse left and climb the face to the left end of the white overhang. Step right onto the lip of the overhang (fragile rock) and traverse right to a crack. Follow this to a good ledge at the base of the huge corner.
3. 120' 5.8 The superb, heavily varnished corner. The crux is a thin stemming move low in the corner, but higher up there is some sustained liebacking and jamming on very glassy rock. Belay at the base of an attractive, smooth-walled chimney.
4. 80' 4th class Climb the chimney, exiting via a tunnel on the left to reach an exposed ledge on top of a pillar.
5. 100' 5.6 Climb the face to a smooth, pink right-facing corner. Up this to a ledge below a roof.
6. 120' 5.5 Climb the face to the roof, pull over this, and follow a right-facing corner to the top.

The impressive smooth wall to the right of Black Dagger is split by two obvious crack systems.

❸ Cat Scratch Fever 650' 5.8
Joanne Urioste, Jorge Urioste, John Rosholt. March 1977.
Single rack to 4".
This route climbs the leftmost of the two crack systems. Start about 100' to the right of Black Dagger, below a crack leading to a roof.

1. 150' 5.7 Climb the crack and face to an anchor just below the roof.
2. 175' 5.8 Traverse to the right end of the roof to reach a crack. Follow this crack, and before it finishes move left to another crack; up this to a nice stance in a horizontal break.
3. 130' 5.6 Continue up the crack to a belay.
4. 50' 5.5 Step right and follow the right hand crack to a ledge under a roof.
5. 150' 5.6 Pull over the roof and follow the above crack into a chimney. Belay in the chimney. Easier climbing leads left into pitch 6 of Black Dagger, up this to the top.

❹ Me, Myself and I 620' 5.7
Randal Grandstaff. 1970's.
This route follows the right hand of the two crack systems. This crack is offwidth for much of its length, although there are plenty of face holds on the edges. Start 150' to the right of Cat Scratch Fever, directly below the obvious crack system.
1. 75' 5.4 Follow a trough in the white rock, up and right to a belay.
2. 80' 5.7 Continue up cracks to reach pink rock. Traverse left for 40' to the base of the crack.
3. 140' 5.5 Continue up the crack
4. 160' 5.5 Continue up the crack
5. 165' 5.7 The crack widens to a chimney and leads to the top.

The left side of Brownstone Wall is split by two steep gullies. The base of the gully on the right is blocked by some blocky bulges with crack systems on either side. The next route starts up the crack system on the right then climbs the nice corner system in the right wall of the gully.

❺ Stone the Crows 500' 5.10b
Start by scrambling up to the highest of several ledges below and right of the crack system.
1. 140' 5.8 Follow a white ramp up and left to merge with the crack system. Follow the crack system past a blocky bulge to the base of the cleft. Traverse out right on an easy slab to an anchor on a sloping ledge to the right of the corner system in the right wall of the cleft.
2. 100' 5.10b Follow the corner to a ledge below a smooth section. Stem past a bolt then make a punchy layback to a rest on a small ledge. Continue up the corner, exiting right on a hand crack to an anchor on a big, sloping ledge.
3. 160' 5.10a Move to the right end of the ledge (bolt) step down and move right onto a wide open wall. Climb the beautiful, varnished face (steady, but a little bold, with small, fiddly gear) heading slightly right then left to a good horizontal crack. Climb to a bolt 15' higher then make a tricky technical step up to better holds. Finish up a thin crack to an anchor on a big sloping ledge. **Descent:** 3 raps with two ropes.

**❺ₐ 160' 5.10d ** ** Climb the beautiful varnished arete above the anchor (5 b's). From the last bolt move up and right to a horizontal crack and continue up the steep face (5 b's) to the big, sloping ledge.

❺♭ 160' 5.10d (Tr.) From the fifth bolt on 5a, move left to some footholds at the base of a nice corner. Climb the corner to a ledge, then continue up the lovely upper corner to the an anchor at the left end of the big, sloping ledge of the regular route.

A huge, deep cleft splits the Brownstone Wall. To the left of this cleft, a 500' high pillar called The Hourglass leans against the cliff. The next route climbs a very impressive left-facing corner system up the wall to the left of this pillar.

❻ Bad Guys Approaching 500' 5.10c
Paul Van Betten, Robert Finlay. 1989.
Single rack to 2.5", triples 2.5"- 4".
The route starts up the first major crack system to the left of The Hourglass, about 100' to the left of Times Up.
1. 5.10a Climb the left-leaning crack.
2. 5.10c, A0 Traverse into the corner on the right and follow it until a pendulum leads around the arete to the right onto an easier face. Up the face to a belay.
3. 5.8 Continue up cracks in the face to a big ledge, move right, and belay at the base of a huge left-facing corner.
4. 5.10c Climb the hand and fist crack in the corner to an anchor. A fifth pitch with dirty, rotten rock and little protection ends at an anchor in poor rock. Best to rap from the previous anchor and avoid this pitch.

❼ Time's Up 480' 5.12a **
Jorge Urioste, Mike Ward, Joanne Urioste, Bill Bradley. April 1984.
Single rack to 3".
This route climbs the beautiful, varnished corner on the left side of the Hourglass. An unusual route with sport climbing protection but all the features found on a classic crack climb. Start slightly to the left of the fall line of the corner on a flat spot in the slabs.
1. 110' 5.8 Climb the slab up and right into a left-facing black corner. Follow the corner to an anchor on a small ledge.
2. 70' 5.10a Continue up the corner (b), at the top move up and right to an anchor on a blocky ledge.
3. 60' 5.11a The crack starts with a wide lieback to reach a rest. Above the rest the crack narrows to tips, and technical stemming leads to a ledge on the right (8 b's).
4. 90' 5.12a A magnificent pitch. Wide liebacking on glassy rock leads to a bomb-bay chimney and an awkward pull into the deep corner above. Stem up this corner past a very thin section to reach a bolted anchor (13 b's).
5. 90' 5.10b Leave the hanging belay awkwardly and continue up the corner to a roof. Move around this to the right and angle back left above the lip to reach a ledge and anchor (9 b's).
6. 50' 5.9 Continue up the thin corner/crack to the top.
Descent: Rappel the route with a single 60m rope.

❽ The Nightcrawler 445' 5.10c ***
Jorge Urioste, Joanne Urioste. April 1978.
Single rack to 4".
This route climbs the corner system on the right side of the Hourglass. The clean-cut corners on the third and fourth pitches are the best of their grade in Red Rocks, with sustained and well-protected climbing on superb rock. The route can be done without using any of the protection bolts (bring Rp's and a couple of extra tiny cams). It's reasonably well-protected but the extra effort involved on pitch 3 bumps the grade up to solid 10d and perhaps makes for an even more memorable route. Start by scrambling up to a ledge below a long left-trending thin crack that leads up to the right of the fall line of the corner.
1. 150' 5.7 Climb the crack past a steep section, then traverse left to an anchor at the base of the corner.
2. 120' 5.9 Start up a chimney then continue to a slanting roof. Traverse steeply right around this to a ledge.

3. 100' 5.10c The corner starts with a wide crack. Strenuous stemming leads past this section, then higher up some liebacking leads to a nice ledge (7 b's).
4. 65' 5.10c Sustained liebacking and jamming leads up the final corner to the top (2 b's).
Descent: Rappel the route with two ropes. The first two raps should be kept short since the rope can easily jam in the crack.

❾ Hourglass Diversion 600' 5.9
Joanne Urioste, Jorge Urioste, John Rosholt. March 1978.
This route starts up the first two pitches of Nightcrawler, then follows a ramp out to the right and finishes up a long, thin crack. Start at the second anchor of Nightcrawler.
1. 90' 5.4 Follow a ramp up and right to the bottom of a steep thin crack.
2. 80' 5.9 Climb the crack to a belay.
3. 165' 5.8 Continue up the crack to the top.

❿ Kentucky's Finest 325' 5.11b *
Single rack to 3", extra 0.75"-1.5".
This route climbs directly up the face to reach the final cracks of Hourglass Diversion to make for a good, direct line. Start at the same point as Nightcrawler.
1. 120' 5.10b Start up the initial ramp of Nightcrawler then step right to a bolt. Continue past another bolt to a thin crack which leads (b) to an anchor.
2. 115' 5.11b Climb a short face to a bolt in a varnished headwall. Make crux moves past a second bolt into a thin crack which is followed to a small shelf. Step left and climb up to an anchor at the base of a big, open corner.
3. 90' 5.10b Steep laybacks and finger jams lead up the sharp-edged crack in the back of the corner. Continue past a short slot to a ledge (junction with Hourglass Diversion) with an anchor on the right.
Descent: It is possible to rap with a 70m rope with a bit of downclimbing, but two ropes are better.

⓫ High Anxiety 650 5.10c
Joanne Urioste, Jorge Urioste. May 1978.
This route follows the long, black corner system to the right of the Hourglass. Start below and to the right of the corner.
1. 165' 5.6 Climb up and left across to belay in a scoop.
⓫ª Variation: 190' 5.10a Start 40' to the left of the regular route. Climb the long crack and corner system to the belay.
2. 160' 5.7+ Climb up the face (2 b's), using discontinuous cracks to reach a ledge at the base of the huge left-facing corner.
3. 80' 5.8+ Climb the flake to the left of the corner then up to a ledge (2 b's).
4. 80' 5.10b Climb the corner to a ledge.
5. 150' 5.8 Climb the corner a short distance, then move left to another corner. Up this to a ledge.
6. 165' 5.7+ Continue up broken corners and lower-angled rock to the top.

⓬ Pro Choice 480' 5.11a *
Single rack to 3", double wires and cams to 1".
The Brownstone Wall is split by a huge gully system. Begin about half a rope length to the left of this gully.
1. 120' 5.7 Climb 120 feet of the first pitch of High Anxiety. Belay on a sloping ledge about 30 feet below the rap slings atop the first pitch of High Anxiety. The belay is below and left of a small overhang, which tops a small left-facing corner.

Brownstone Wall - Central

2. 100' 5.10b Two bolts protect the overhang moves (5.9). The steep face straight above can be adequately protected (a few small brass stoppers useful). As the wall steepens even more, step right, then left, to surmount the finger crack in the solid, brown headwall. Continue to an anchor.

3. 120' 5.9 Step right and ascend the steep face (5.9) for 120 feet to a bolted belay ledge.

4. 140' 5.11a Step left and climb to a small right-facing corner, which curves right to form a "crescent". A bolt protects the crux moves (5.11a). A beautiful, varnished left-facing corner (5.8) leads to a belay stance with rappel anchors.

Descent: Rappel with two ropes.

The next three routes climb the beautiful varnish to the right of the last pitch of Pro Choice. They can be reached by climbing either Pro Choice or Senior Dimensions.

⓭ Pro Life 140' 5.12b *
Double rack to 1".
This route climbs the beautiful arete to the right of the last pitch of Pro Choice. Follow the last pitch of Pro Choice to the base of the final corner. Move right and climb up the arete, tricky, hard-to-read climbing on perfect rock (4 b's). Move left past the last bolt to reach a long, thin crack which quickly eases and leads to the anchor.

⓮ Immaculate Conception 125' 11a/b *
Single rack to 1.5", double to 1".
Start on the big ledge above pitch 3 of Senior Dimensions. Climb the finger crack to the left of pitch 4 corner of Senior Dimensions. Continue onto the blunt arete above. The crux is low on the arete, above which continue on better holds to the big ledge and anchor at the top of Pro Life.

⓯ Corruption of the Jesuit 105' 5.11c/d **
Single rack to 1.25", Rp's, optional 2" piece.
A superb route with technical climbing on great rock. Start from the anchor above pitch 4 of Senior Dimensions. Climb straight up a thin crack above the anchor, then move up and left (2 b's) to reach a series of blind right-facing flakes. Climb the flakes, initially with tricky protection, then continue up the face, eventually moving left to reach a ledge on the arete, the anchor of Pro Life is a few feet left along this ledge.

⓰ Senior Dimensions 5.10c
Single rack to 2".
High on the right side of the face to the right of Pro Choice is a beautiful, scooped wall of varnish. This route starts with three rather flaky pitches before it finishes with a superb pitch up the scooped wall. Perhaps the best combination of pitches in this vicinity is to climb the first three pitches of Pro Choice then finish up the last two pitches of Senior Dimensions; this combination is worth two stars. Start below the rounded white arete on the right edge of the buttress. There is a right-curving, right-facing corner which starts about 80 feet up. Begin on white, low-angle rock directly below this corner.

1. 80' 5.8+ Climb a thin crack in the white slab, then traverse right about 10 feet to the base of a steep, black, varnished face (bolt). Climb to the right of the bolt, first straight up, then a bit left to reach a large ledge with a tree and fixed anchors.

2. 80' 5.10c Climb the right-facing corner for about 50 feet, to a bolt. Step left onto the face where balancy moves lead left to a 2nd bolt. Bypass the large overhang on its left, then step back right to a belay stance with fixed anchors.

3. 120' 5.8+ Climb straight up the face (4 b's) to a large ledge with fixed anchors.

4. 50' 5.9+ Climb the left-facing corner above the anchor. Move onto its right edge and continue to an anchor.

5. 130' 5.10b Traverse 20 feet right to a bolt, where gorgeous, sustained edging on black varnish leads straight up the face (5 b's) to a large ledge with fixed anchors.

Descent: Rappel with two ropes.

Brownstone Wall - Right Side

The center of the Brownstone Wall is split by a huge, steep gully/cleft. The section of wall to the right of the cleft has two mushroom-like summits. The route Armatron climbs a fairly direct line up to the right hand of the two summits. A few bolts low on the first pitch are a useful landmark. This wall is a little more broken than the section to the south and contains a nice selection of routes which usually have at least a pitch or two of really nice rock. The wall faces east and a little south, so is usually in the sun until early afternoon.

Approach: As for Brownstone Wall, but continue up and right on the open slabs to the base of the wall. 1½ hrs.

Descent: For routes that go to the summit, there is a very quick descent which drops off the north side of the peak and follows a trail down the gully to the north of the formation (15 to 30 minutes back to the base).

The routes are described from right to left, starting with the low-angled pink slab at the far right side of the wall.

❶ Birthday Cake 350' 5.6
Climb the low-angled crack which splits the pink slab, then continues up more broken rock to the summit of Juniper Peak.

❷ Requiem for a Tadpole 670' 5.9+
Single rack to 3", double 1.75"- 3", optional 6".
From the base of Armatron, walk up and right to the highest point on the slab. Step up past a ledge in the gully, then scramble up a few yards to a stance.

1. 125' 5.7 Climb varnished huecos to a crack which is followed to a belay.

2. 125' 5.7 Continue up the crack to a belay above a bushy ledge, below a prominent hand crack in red rock.

3. 125' 5.7 Climb the crack, exit left then up into a corner. A delicate sandy step with little protection leads to blocks and an anchor in a notch in the arete.

4. 165' 5.9+ Move left into a big, black chimney. Climb the chimney for 70', then step right onto the brown slab. Climb the face just left of the arete (sporty) to reach Humerus Ledge.

❷ₐ Variation: 150' 5.8: From the belay climb straight up the arete (7 b's) to Humerus Ledge. This is much more in keeping with the rest of the route.

5. 130' 5.6 From Humerus Ledge mantel the big block and continue up the arete (2 b's) to the subsidiary summit. Scrambling leads to the main summit.

Adam Floyd on the classic pitch 4 of Times Up. Page 194.

Brownstone Wall - Right side

From the summit, it is possible to rap straight down the routes.

Humorous Ledge

Single rack to 2", Extra wires.

5 single rope raps

❸ **Armatron 455' 5.9 ****

The route was named by, Geoff Conley, Jimmy Newberry, Jorge Urioste, Jeffrey Johnson, Joanne Urioste. June 03.
Single rack to 2", Extra wires.

This route starts from some open slabs at the base of the wall. A large red boulder sits on the slab directly in front of the route. A nice, open climb on great rock.

1. 100' 5.8 Climb up and slightly left (5 b's) on black plated rock to reach an anchor.

2. 125' 5.9 Climb a thin crack straight up for 30'. When the wall steepens, go right (b), passing a large horn, to a thin crack.

Climb the crack to reach a left-slanting ramp of white rock. Step out right (b) and climb up the face for 40' to an anchor below a small overlap.

3. 150' 5.6 Go straight up an awesome varnished face to an anchor.

4. 80' 5.6 Climb slightly left up the face above, then step right, to an anchor.

The route originally finished here, two ropes are needed for the rap. However a finish has been done, the Humerus Finish.

5. 120' 5.7 Continue up the arete (3 b's) to Humerus Ledge. Finish up pitch 5 of Requiem for a Tadpole.

❹ Sweet Thin 730' 5.9
Single rack to 6", double 1.5"- 4".
This route starts up Armatron then climbs a series of short pitches to its left to reach Humerus Ledge.
1. 100' 5.8 Armatron, pitch 1.
2. 125' 5.9 Follow pitch 2 of Armatron to the left-facing corner. Armatron moves right here; Sweet Thin continues up the corner to an anchor.
3. 80' 5.6 Continue up the widening crack to an anchor.
❸ₐ Variation: 5.8 Go up and left to the beautiful black face of Mayday Malfactor (5 b's) which is climbed to a ledge.
4. 95' 5.7 Continue up the wide crack then step left onto blocky terrain below a big bush. Traverse left past an anchor of Mayday Malefactor to another anchor a few yards up a ramp, just short of a big bushy gully.
5. 110' 5.9 Head up the ramp, then climb a hollow, razor-edged flake (6 b's) to its top. Step right past a left-arching thin-hands crack into a hand crack which is followed to an anchor.
6. 90' 5.9 Climb the prominent black crack above the anchor. The crack ends on Humerus Ledge.
7. 130' 5.8 Move the belay left to below a wide corner/crack. Climb the wide crack, moving left around a roof, then continue up a finger crack and finish with runout face climbing to the subsidiary summit.

❺ Mayday Malefactor 705' 5.10c
Single rack to 3", double 0.5"- 1", extra wires.
Start from the left side of the Armatron slab in a dish to the right of a water streak.
1. 160' 5.7 Climb plates, discontinuous cracks, and shallow corners to a bulge on the right side of the huge, white hanging face. A short hand crack through the bulge leads to a stance.
2. 175' 5.9 Continue up the crack, then step right (2 b's) and climb the face to a section of smooth, varnished rock. Continue up the face (3 b's, it's nice to have a brown tricam to supplement the bolts) to reach an anchor on a ledge. Sweet Thin crosses the same ledge.
3. 140' 5.10c Step up and right (3 b's), then climb a shallow right-facing corner past a small bush. Continue to a lone bolt where a crux move leads to an anchor.
❺ₐ Variation: 5.10c Not as good as the main route. From the anchor climb straight up (3 b's.) Go around a big bush and up a left-facing corner to a ledge with a bush. Pull up into a widening crack, then traverse up and right to the anchor.
4. 100' 5.7 Runout. Climb up and left on easy face climbing to reach Humerus Ledge.
5. 130' 5.9+ Walk up and right around the base of the sub-summit block. Climb the thin, varnished crack to the left of the last pitch of Requiem for a Tadpole. When the crack ends, runout face climbing leads to the top.

The Sandcastle Formation is the big pyramidal face capped with varnish-plated pink rock, to left of the Armatron Buttress.

❻ Sand Castle 405' 5.10c
Single rack to 3.5", two sets wires , Double 0.4"- 0.75".
This route climbs a line between the two obvious chimney/cracks which split the face.
1. 190' 5.10c Climb a finger crack above some bushes to a slab. Go left and climb up a left-facing corner to below a roof, pull right (10a, runout) onto a varnished rib. At the top of the rib, pull over a roof then traverse left and belay in the base of a left-facing corner.

2. 215' 5.9+ Climb the corner and continue on good huecos until a step past a bulge leads to a nice, plated face. Climb the face to a platform with a bush and yucca.
Descent: Walk left on the ledge to a pine tree. Rappel Ten Minute Shift from here in five single-rope rappels.

❼ Hueco Thanks 450' 5.7
Anthony Anagnostou, Joanne Urioste. May 2006.
Single rack to 3", double wires.
This route climbs the leftmost of the two prominent chimney/cracks on the Sandcastle.
1. 170' 5.7 Climb the face to reach the chimney. Belay at a good stance beside a bush.
2. 120' 5.7 Chimney up past an overhang (crux) and continue up the crack to a belay beneath an alcove.
3. 160' 5.7 Stem up the steep alcove and follow the crack on good holds to the top. (1.5"- 2" for the anchor)
Descent: Walk left to the pine tree of Ten Minute Shift. Five-single rope rappels to the ground from here.

❽ Ten Minute Shift 345' 5.11b
Single rack to 3".
This route starts directly below a big left-facing corner a few pitches up on the left side of the Sandcastle formation.
1. 80' 5.10b Step up past a bouldery start with a perched block to a ledge with a left-leaning ramp. Step up and right, and climb the wall (7 b's) to another ledge with a huge perched block and an anchor.
2. 80' 5.11b Go up to a bolt, then step left to gain a handrail that goes up right. Go straight up (10 b's) to a burly undercling and roof exit and an anchor above. (Finger size nut or cam above the last bolt).
3. 50' 5.10a Climb the varnished flare/chimney (thin cams), or more easily the face to its right. Continue up easier terrain out left then up to an anchor.
4. 65' 5.9+ Climb the big corner to a slick, huecoed face and a flaring crack, then an anchor.
5. 70' 5.8 Continue up the corner to an anchor consisting of a bolt and a slung tree.
Descent: Five single-rope raps.

❾ Three Choclateers 750' 5.10b
Karsten Duncan, Anthony Anagnostou. May 2006.
Double set to 3.5", one 5", Rp's.
Start as for Ten Minute Shift.
1. 180' 5.9+ Pull one stiff move, then climb a left-leaning ramp. Climb up on dishes (scary) to another weakness which leads up and left to the main chimney. Climb the chimney to a ledge with a wide crack and a bush.
2. 180' 5.9+ Continue up the crack to a blocky ledge at 150'. Continue to a stance 30' higher.
3. 100' 5.4 Continue in the same line to a huge, bushy break. From here it is possible to rappel by traversing right to the tree of Ten Minute Shift. To continue, move up to the base of the upper wall where a huge rock creates a 40' gully with a varnished ramp in it leading up and left. Scramble up this ramp and belay at its top.
4. 120' 5.10a Climb up then step right to the tree on the face, and then move around it to the crack slanting up and right through a steep section. Step right until almost on an arete, and then go straight up to a belay at a bush on a flat ledge.
5. 170' 5.6 Continue up the crack system to gain the top .
Descent: Walk north to the summit of Juniper Peak.

JACKRABBIT BUTTRESS

This is the large buttress of white rock that forms the right side of Juniper Canyon. It consists of several different sections: The South Face, The East Face, and the Northeast Face, as well as the Jungle Wall.

Descent: To descend from the top of Jackrabbit Buttress, walk straight back towards the Brownstone Wall then head south down slabs into the upper reaches of Juniper Canyon. This is surprisingly easy and fast.

Jackrabbit Buttress - South Face

The south face of Jackrabbit Buttress has a useful collection of moderate routes in a very sunny and warm location. The face gets sun until mid-afternoon in the winter, and is quite low-lying and sheltered, making this a good cold weather venue for routes in the 5.7 to 5.9 range. Most of these routes are relatively recent and the rock is still quite soft and flaky in places, but as is usual in Red rocks they will clean up quickly as they get more traffic.

The gully at the base of the wall is densely vegetated which can make route identification a little difficult on a first visit. Its a good idea to stay on the main Juniper Canyon trail which generally goes up the left (south) side of the wash and has a good view of the face. Once you have identified your route it's easy to drop back into the wash and head up to the base.

Approach: Follow the approach for Juniper Canyon (page 173) until close to the main Juniper Canyon wash. At this point the main trail heads up the hill to the right of the wash. A short way up the hill a trail branches off to the right, leading to the base of the route **Geronimo**. Continue following the main trail. After a couple of hundred yards, the canyon starts to narrow and the trail drops into the wash. For **Myster Z,** don't drop into the wash, but instead head up the gully to the right of the buttress. For the rest of the routes, drop into the wash and continue up to a huge, black boulder on the right. The boulder is a useful landmark, the route Rose Hips starts up a big chimney just to its right. 1.5 miles, 600' elevtion gain, 30- 40 minutes.

The routes on the south face are described from left to right.

❶ Blind Spot 200' 5.9
Johnny Ray, Larry DeAngelo. May 2008.
Single rack to 7", double or triple 4"-7".
At the far left end of the face is a deep recess. This route climbs the crack system in the front face of the buttress forming the left side of the recess, starting in the small corridor formed by a small tower in front of the main cliff.
Follow the chimney to where it turns into an offwidth at an overhang about twenty feet up. Squeeze past the bulge (crux) and continue up the crack to the top of the buttress.
Descent: From the top of the route you can traverse back (left) to a clump of bushes with a long rope extending over the edge. A double rope rap leads back to the base.

❷ The Black Pearl 170' 5.9 *
Larry DeAngelo, Karsten Duncan. March 31, 2008.
Single rack to 6", double 1.75"- 4".
A nice, varied crack climb up the long, varnished corner/crack in the left wall of the dark recess. Descend as for Blind Spot.

To the right of the recess containing Black Pearl is another deep recess with a big chimney at the back. An obvious landmark is the huge chockstone 100' up the chimney.

❸ Saddle Up 590' 5.9
Doug Foust, Andrew Yasso. March 2013.
Single rack to 4", doubles 0.5" to 2",optional 6" for the first pitch.
Bushwack into the alcove and scramble up some third class to the base of the chimney.
1. 110' 5.7+ Climb the chimney and belay on the top of the

Benny Benson on Jungle Wall. Page 209. Photo: Matt Kuehl.

Jackrabbit Buttress - South Face

huge chockstone.

2. 120' 5.9 Move right off the chockstone to reach a nice, steep hand crack. Climb the crack, passing a white flake on the left and belaying just above.

3. 160' 5.7 Continue up the hand crack as the angle eases. Go past an awkward varnished alcove to a nice ledge 15' above.

4. 200' 5.4 Follow the left-trending crack until it ends, then angle right to the top.

❹ Smooth Operator 850' 5.9

Joanne & Jorge Urioste, Kevin Campbell. 6/7/2008.
Single rack to 4".

This route starts up a corner about 200' left of the huge boulder. To reach the start of the climb, either go uphill along the base of the cliff from the boulder, or go halfway up the steep dirt portion of the Juniper Canyon approach trail before cutting back toward the base of the cliff. Both methods are bushy.

1. 120' 5.8 Climb the chimney and corner to a sloping belay stance below a bulge.

2. 110' 5.9 An exposed diagonal traverse leads up and left through the bulge, with lots of air below, but good pro. When you're back in balance, a sloping traverse leads left about 30 feet. Now go straight up a steep jamcrack to a roomy ledge.

3. 190' 5.8 Poorly protected face climbing for 30' leads to a chimney, which is followed by moderate moves up the continuing crack system to a ledge where the crack system splits.

4. 70' 5.9 After an exposed move right, jam a steep crack for 20 feet. About thirty feet of exposed, varnished face lead right and up to the base of a prominent, black left-facing corner, where a hanging belay is established.

5. 160' 5.8 Climb straight up the face and corner, then up easier terrain to a belay ledge.

6. 200' 5.1 Easy climbing leads to the unroping spot.

❺ Degunker 700' 5.8

Karsten Duncan, Doug Hemken, Larry DeAngelo. June, 2008.
The route starts in the obvious chimney about twenty feet left of Ernest Stemmingway. A nice pitch goes up the pleasantly varnished and featured chimney to a belay position in a small alcove. The second pitch continues up the steep crack on somewhat softer and less pleasant rock. Pitch three frictions up to a left-slanting ramp. The route finishes on easier slabs.

❻ Earnest Stemming Way 640' 5.8+

Joanne Urioste, Jeffrey Johnson. March 9, 2008.
Single rack to 5", Rp's, extra wires.

This route climbs the prominent chimney system about 100 feet left of the gigantic black boulder in the creek bed.

1. 190' 5.8+ Climb the steep rib of varnished plaques on the left, just outside the cavernous chimney. This leads to the corner above the wide chimney. Follow this corner until a flat area allows the climber to walk inward about 30 feet into the deep chimney, which is climbed to a hanging belay.

2. 170' 5.8+ Go straight up via chimney and corner to the steep offwidth (#4 or #5 camalot), which can be bypassed by climbing on the face to its left. Continue up the corner system to a sloping belay.

3. 100' 5.7 The crack system soon splits into a major left branch and one that continues straight up. The FA party went straight up and belayed below a grainy, steep offwidth.

4. 180' 5.8+ Struggle up the sandy offwidth (#4.5 camalot nice here), traversing left, across the face, at its top to reach a belay. Easier climbing leads to the unroping area.

❼ Rabbit Stew 480' 5.9

Joanne Urioste, Bill Hotz, Jorge Urioste. 2/16/2007.
This route follows the crack system 20 feet left of Rose Hips.

1. 120' 5.8 This crack system does not reach the ground, so climb the steep, exposed face below and to the right of it. A straight-in crack goes up, then left, to reach the base of the main crack system. Now follow the main crack system to a belay ledge below a long chimney (intricate pro).

2. 120' 5.9 Climb the sparsely protected chimney (#4 camalot) to where it narrows and steepens. Bridge over this airy obstacle (#3 or #4 camalot) and continue 30 feet to a belay.

3. 120' 5.8 Follow the crack system which leads up, then slightly right, over very steep terrain. Belay on a stance when the rock becomes slabby. (Very airy and sustained).

4. 120' 5.8 Easy, runout face climbing leads diagonally right to reach a corner that jogs back left. It steepens (5.8), then one traverses left to a comfortable belay stance.

5. 100' 5.9 Climb the steeper face above (b's) to an anchor.

Descent: Rappel straight down in four rappels, the third going over a huge roof.

❽ Rose Hips 1000' 5.7

Chris Dabroski, John Hoffman. 1999.
Begin in the prominent right-facing corner system behind the gigantic black boulder in the creek bed. Start at the base of a left-slanting chimney.

1. 200' 5.7 Climb the face to the left of the chimney for 120', then head up a right-leaning crack; belay beside the crack.

2. 110' 5.6 Continue up the crack until level with a ledge on the right. Follow the wide flake on the left then when above the level of the roof to the right, step back right into the left-facing corner and set up a belay.

Variation: 5.9 Instead of climbing the wide flake, step right and go up a layback crack to the roof, step left around the roof to join the regular route just before the belay.

3. 100' 5.6 Continue up the crack and belay near it's top.

4. 185' 5.6 Traverse right for 35' (5.6 no gear) to a large corner/crack which is followed by a belay.

5. 50' 5.4 Continue up the crack to a large ledge. Easier climbing leads to the top of the buttress.

❾ Myster Z 1100' 5.7 *

Jimmy Newberry, Phil Broscovak. 2003
Single rack to 3" with extra long draws.
Go up the gully to the right of the buttress for a couple of hundred feet until it is possible to scramble up 15' into a small cave with a tree.

1. 160' 5.6 Climb a wide crack which doglegs left past a roof, Belay on a small ledge inside the chimney.

2. 145' 5.6 Continue up the slot to its top, then face climb left to a crack which leads to a ledge below a "zebra stripped" slab.

3. 190' 3rd class A pitch of easy climbing leads up and over left to a small tree at the base of a nice, black finger crack.

4. 170' 5.6 Follow the finger crack, which angles up and right and ends at a chimney beside a large block atop a detached pillar.

5. 170' 5.7 Behind this pillar is a large bush in a flare. Stem past the bush and continue up a nice crack. Follow the crack to below an overhanging chimney, then make a very exposed traverse right and climb a nice 5.7 black crack to a belay in a horizontal.

Four hundred feet of easier climbing leads to the very top of Jackrabbit Buttress.

Jackrabbit Buttress - East Face

Geronimo, with its enjoyable moderate climbing and sunny location is the feature route of this sector. Apart from Geronimo, these routes see very little action.

Approach: Follow the approach for Juniper Canyon until close to the main Juniper Canyon wash. At this point the main trail heads up the hill to the right of the wash. A short way up the hill a trail branches off to the right, leading to the base of the route **Geronimo**. A short gully cuts up into the southeast corner of Jackrabbit Buttress. Geronimo, climbs the buttress to the left of this gully.

❶ **Crazy Horse 450' 5.8 †**
Allen Currano, Jeremy Collins. November 2001. Single rack to 3".
This route starts 100 yards left (west) around the corner and up the hill from Geronimo. It starts with a dark right-facing corner, eventually passing through a roof and stopping at a black varnished face (300'). Climb this black face to meet up with the final pitch of Geronimo.
Descent: As for Geronimo.

❷ **Senior Discount 60' 5.10b**
Double to 4", triple 3".
This route climbs the prominent clean-cut fist crack in a right-facing corner just to the right of the start of Crazy horse. Approach the bushy belay ledge at the base of the crack proper from left via easy 5th class climbing. A 100' rap leads back to the base.

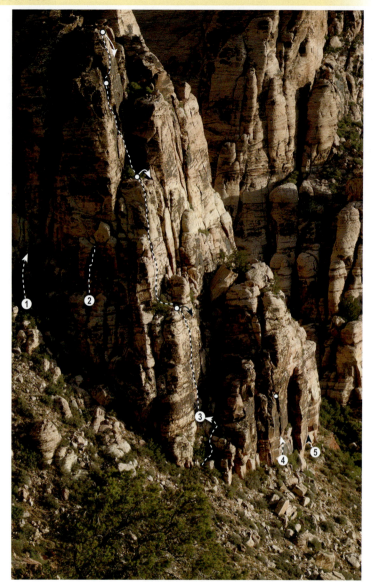

❸ **Geronimo 560' 5.6 ***
Bill Cramer, Michelle Cramer. May 1992. Single rack to 3", doubles 0.75"- 2".
This route faces south east and gets a lot of sun. It is an enjoyable route with steep, exposed climbing on big holds. Start below a dogleg crack a short way up on the left wall of the approach gully.
1. 165' 5.6 Climb the crack to a large ledge.
2. 180' 5.6 Towards the left hand side of the ledge, climb a thin crack to a ledge (optional belay). From here, either climb the arete (5.5) or easy rock around the corner to the left. Both variations end on a large terrace.
3. 160' 5.6 Climb the face above the terrace towards a corner on the arete. Follow this to a small stance on the arete. 3"

cams provide a good anchor.
4. 90' 5.6 Move up and right onto a shelf and finish up the spectacular arete on good holds.
Descent: From the top, a long two rope rap reaches the terrace above pitch 2. On the right side of this ledge, is another rap station. Another long rap leads to the large ledge at the top of P1. The final rap anchor is the large boulder near the edge of the ledge.

Nauterjugg 90' 5.11d
Single rack to 1.25", Rp's.
Climb the initial fist crack of Juggernaut, then move left and climb past a peg to a short, smooth wall. A desperate pull up the wall (b) leads to the base of a thin flake which leads to the anchor of Juggernaut.

❹ Juggernaut 90' 5.10d
Paul Van Betten, Paul Obenheim. 1983.
Double rack to 1.25", 3" cam for the start.
This route climbs a thin crack in a slender, left-leaning left-facing corner of nice, varnished rock. It is about a rope length to the right of the bottom of the gully that leads up to Geronimo.

❺ The Monday Funnies 300' 5.9
Mark Moore. Late 70s.
This route climbs an unusual crack on the lower east face of Jackrabbit Buttress. It is most easily approached by traversing left from the bottom of the Olive Oil gully. Start in the middle of the east face in a large keyhole-shaped cave.
1. Climb a chimney on the left wall for 12', then pull over a roof. Climb into a hole, then tunnel out to a long, narrow ledge.
2. Climb a thin corner for 25', then more easily to a short, strenuous fist crack in a corner. Climb to the left on weirdly eroded rock until it is possible to move back right into the main corner, which becomes a steep hand crack. Belay at its top.
3. Go up and left. **Descent:** The route ends on easy ledges about a third of the way up the buttress. Follow the ledges north and drop into a bushy gully which leads down to the bottom of the Olive Oil approach gully.

Jackrabbit Buttress - Cottontail Tower

The following routes, on the northeast face of Jackrabbit Buttress, are all accessed from the Olive Oil Gully. They are very shady, receiving only a sliver of morning sun. The routes are reached by scrambling up the first side gully on the left as you go up the Olive Oil Gully. This is only about 75 yards above the entrance.

Cottontail 180' 5.8
Jake Burkey and Friend. 1997.
This two pitch route climbs the chimney on the left side of a small tower; it starts at the top of the approach gully.

Don't Touch That In Front of Grandma 90' 5.7
Jason Martin and Jay Hack. April 2002.
Climb the loose face just to the right of the first pitch of the previous route. To descend, rappel off jammed slings..

Stuffed Animals on Prozac 190' 5.8
This route climbs a white face to the right of the tower, to reach a varnished right-facing corner/crack.
1. 100' 5.8 Climb the face (b's) into a crack which is followed to a big ledge below the corner .
2. 90' 5.7 Continue up the corner to the top. Rappel the route with two ropes.

Jackrabbit Buttress - Aquarium Wall

Higher up the main gully, almost directly opposite Olive Oil, is an attractive varnished wall split by several long crack systems. This is called the Aquarium Wall. This is a very shady wall which gets almost no sun except for midsummer mornings.

Approach: Follow the approach for Juniper Canyon described on page 173. Once on the Juniper Canyon trail, continue for a few minutes until a trail branches off right heading towards the second of two gullies. There is a earlier trail, that heads up to the first gully; this is the descent trail from Rose Tower. Follow the trail up into the second gully. The route Olive Oil is a useful reference point. Its start is located about 250 yards up, on the right side of the gully in a small cleared-out area beneath a deep, left-facing left-leaning chimney/corner. From the base of Olive Oil, cross to the other side of the main gully and go though a gap in the sidewall of the main gully to reach a narrow gully to the south, directly under the Aquarium Wall. Head up through a tunnel and continue beside the gully wall until a bushy ledge leads around to the left. Follow this ledge, heading down to a small clear area. Rope up here. A short section of climbing (5.5) followed by scrambling leads to a nice clean terrace at the base of the main wall. 45 minutes.

Descent: The routes end on top of a small tower. A short rap to the west leads to a long ridge which is followed (amazing views) to the Brownstone Wall. From here a trail marked with cairns wanders down the open slabs into the upper reaches of Juniper Canyon.

While most of the routes on the Aquarium Wall start on a terrace a couple of hundred feet above the approach gully, approached using the above description, the next route starts in the approach gully and climbs a chimney system in the lower wall to reach the left end of the same terrace.

❶ Luna 740' 5.9+
Single rack to 3".
This route climbs a series of variations based on Aquarium. Start at the base of a narrow chimney with a clean, sloping ramp-like bottom.
1. 130' 5.2 Climb the obvious chimney and huecoed crack system to its right, to a small pine tree. A straightforward pitch but with little protection.
2. 100' 5.7 Go straight up, past a 5.7 squeeze move, to the large ledge which extends across the base of the Aquarium Wall.
To descend from here, rappel from a bolted rap anchor for 100' to the small pine tree. Then rappel 130' to the gully (the last 30' can be down climbed if you use a single 60 meter rope).
Once on the large ledge, walk right for 100' to a varnished, smooth portion of the ledge about 30' right of a large chimney.
3. 60' 5.6 Climb 20' up featured 5.6 rock. Then diagonal up and left for 15'. Now go straight up for about 20' to a ledge atop a detached pedestal.
4. 120' 5.9 This is the same as pitch 2 of Aquarium. Climb straight up the crack system through the steep, varnished face. About 60' up, the crack leans right. Here, it's easier to step right a few moves across the face to another crack. This crack leads up to a bolted rap/belay semi-hanging stance. From here, it's a 130' rap to the large ledge below.
5. 130' 5.8+ Climb straight up the crack above. Just before it begins to close into a hairline crack, step left and climb the beautiful, black varnished face (2 b's) to a belay ledge with bolted belay/rap anchors.

6. 100' 5.7 Climb straight up (merging with Moondog and Aquarium) and follow the crack system to the right of the obvious tree. Establish a gear belay.

7. 100' 5.9+ Bust out left over the overhang, onto the superb varnished face above. Go straight up the steep black face (b's and gear), to a bolted rap/belay station on a ledge.

Descent: Rappel the route with two ropes.

The following routes start on the terrace below the main wall.

❷ The Octopus Cave 200' 5.9
Greg Barnes, Bruce Bindner. April 2008.
Single rack to 4", double 1"- 4".
This route climbs the big chimney system to the left of Aquarium. Left of Aquarium there's a nice black ledge. Scramble to the left (a 3rd class down-step) to the base of the chimney.

1. 100' 5.9 A wild pitch up into the huge, deep chimney left of Aquarium. Climb the leftmost crack for 30', transfer to the middle crack (hands), up that for 20', then transfer right past a thin crack (overhung stemming) to pass the chockstone. Take the brown offwidth on the left (crux) until you can chimney through the hole to the outside.

2. 100' 5.8+ Start up the right crack for 50', then transfer left to the nice thin crack which ends in the steep black face.

Descent: Rap 190' from nuts to the black ledge at the start.

❸ Aquarium 1000' 5.9 *
Single rack to 4", double 1"- 3", optional 7".
A good route with varied and interesting climbing. Above the left end of the ledge underneath the face is a big right-facing corner/chimney system. About 30' up the chimney a long crack branches out right and heads up the varnished face. Start about 40' to the right of the chimney below the right side of a big flake.

1. 60' 5.9 Follow a flake up and left to a ledge which is followed left to a right-facing corner. Belay on 1-2" cams.

2. 115' 5.9 The crux of the route is at the start of this pitch and is unprotected, although a huge (7") cam may work. Stem past a wide section on delicate holds, then continue up the corner until moves right lead past a crack into another corner, which is followed to a belay.

3. 110' 5.7 Continue in the crack above, then traverse right and climb a hand crack to a ledge.

4. 90' 5.6 Face climb up and left, passing the left end of an arch, to reach a right-leaning corner which leads to a belay.

5. 100' 5.8 Continue up the right-leaning corner, past a section of offwidth, to reach a belay.

6. 80' 5.7 Continue up the corner, then traverse left on horizontal cracks passing the final anchor of Luna. Continue left then climb the varnished face to the left of a corner to reach a belay.

7. 190' 5.7 Climb the long, fragile white face above. At the top of the pitch, a green Camalot in a horizontal protects 5.7 face moves to reach the belay at the base of a corner.

8. 170' 5.6 Climb the corner, then go through a notch and continue to the top of a tower; the end of the route.

❹ Rathcke's Run-out 150' 5.8
A serious pitch with some long runouts and good climbing. Start up Aquarium, then, from the top of the flake, branch right and climb up the varnished face (several 1" to 1.5" cams in horizontal cracks) to the bolted anchor of Aquarium/Luna.

❺ Moondog 830' 5.9
Joanne Urioste, Karsten Duncan. Fall 2007.
Single rack to 4".
This route climbs the left-hand of a pair of thin cracks which go straight up the center of the varnished face to the right of Aquarium. Start below a wide chimney located right of the plumb line from the bottom of the crack, and just to the right of the first pitch flake of Aquarium.

1. 140' 5.8 Climb the chimney to its top. Traverse left 10 feet to a belay stance. Beware of loose rock in the chimney.

2. 170' 5.7 Climb the crack in the solid, varnished face straight up to a belay ledge.

3. 170' 5.7 Head up, then left 20 feet (almost to the tree). Now go straight up crack systems and belay on a small ledge.

4. 150' 5.9 Climb the ten-foot crux finger crack through a steep headwall directly above. Continue straight up the white face to a belay ledge.

5. 200' 5.7 Wander up face and cracks to the top of the buttress, mostly on white rock.

To reach the next two routes, after squeezing through the vertical tunnel on the Aquarium Wall approach, continue up the canyon for another hundred yards. Cross left to the wall at an obvious ledge. Traverse left along the ledge until below a clean-cut dihedral which is climbed by Guppies on Ritalin.

❻ Minnows on Mescaline 700' 5.8
Andrew Gomoll, Larry DeAngelo. Nov 2007.
Single rack to 6".
This route starts in the varnished crack immediately to the left of the clean-cut corner of Guppies on Ritalin. Climb the varnished crack to the major chimney. The direct start is hard (5.10?) but there are easier variations on the adjacent face. Three pitches up the chimney system lead to an exit on the right. The fourth pitch continues straight up the rounded buttress above, passing a few delicate moves to a belay stance near an obvious diagonal crack. Go right along the diagonal, then up to a small stance on the side of a chimney. A long pitch up the chimney leads to the top.

❼ Guppies on Ritalin 700' 5.8
John Wilder, Karsten Duncan, Larry DeAngelo. 2007.
On the right (western) side of the Aquarium Wall, there is a very clean corner that leads toward an unpromising slab. Delightful climbing ascends the corner to a stance where the crack widens to hand size. Pitch 2 follows the crack to its end, then frictions up and left to another crack, eventually belaying beneath a steeper section. Three more pitches go up the crack system to the top.

The next route is on the opposite side of the approach gully from the previous two routes. Approach through the corridor into the main gully below the Aquarium Wall. Instead of crossing the gully go up its right side, hugging the steep sidewall. A short distance up there is an impressive left-leaning offwidth slicing up the steep wall.

Heinous Penis 80' 5.12a
A full rack of big cams and big bro's.
The gruesome off-width is a real struggle. Climb the lower crack to a bulge where it slants left. Follow the crack to easier ground and an anchor. The edge of the crack is very sharp and therefore careful rope management is important.

Jackrabbit Buttress - Aquarium Wall

Jungle Wall

This is the beautiful varnished wall on the left, towards the top of the Olive Oil Gully.

This wall faces north and is very shady, only getting a sliver of morning sun in the late spring. It is also very sheltered, making it a reasonable venue even in colder weather.

Approach: The Jungle Wall is reached by a bushy thrash up the gully from the base of Olive Oil. Stay on the Olive Oil side of the gully until just past a huge left-facing corner, the line of Jaws II. Cross over, below a huge boulder, to the opposite side of the gully to reach the base of the wall. 40-50 minutes.

The routes are described from left to right.

❶ Pukey Mon Ridge 1500' 5.9
Matt Clarke, L. DeAngelo. Spring 2007.
Climb the prominent corner to the left of the Jungle Wall. From the bush at its top, squeeze through a tight, vertical tunnel to gain the upper ridge. Continue to the Brownstone Wall.

❷ Left Edge 140' 5.10d
Al Peary, Jim Gregg. Spring 1988.
Start below the rounded arete on the left side of the wall. The pitch starts with a long reach over a varnished bulge, then continues up the easier arete to an anchor (8 b's).

❸ Jungle Wall 150' 5.11b ***
Jim Gregg, Al Peary. Spring 1989.
A brilliant wall climb up the gorgeous varnished sweep to the right of The Left Edge (12 b's). The route starts up a series of pockets to a bolt at 20'. After the start, the route climbs up then right on good holds to a thin ledge. Above the ledge, a sustained and slightly committing headwall leads to the anchor.

❹ Bear Necessities 180' 5.8
Single rack to 6", doubles 1" to 3".
Start at the base of the cliff, just right of Jungle Wall. Climb the left-facing corner/flake to a ledge at 30'. Climb the thin cracks above which deepen into a big, right-facing flake/corner. Enjoyable jamming and stemming leads up the corner until it is possible to step right to the anchor of Jungle Gym.

❺ Jungle Gym 120' 5.10d *
Al Peary, Jim Gregg. Spring 1990.
Single rack to 0.75".
A long enjoyable climb, straight up the wall to the right of the big crack. The route starts up a thin crack, then moves right to the first bolt. The section between the second and third bolts is protected by small cams of dubious quality.

❻ Black Rose 170' 5.11b ***
Jim Gregg, Al Peary. Spring 1988.
Single rack to 1.75", Rp's.
This route climbs the long black streak in the middle of the wall. A superb, sustained and varied route. Start on top of a block at the base of the black streak. Sustained, intricate climbing leads up the black streak (5 b's). From the fifth bolt move right and climb a long, curving crack. When the crack ends, climb the wall past a steep bulge (4 b's) and the tricky slab above. Move left into an easier groove which is followed to the anchor.

❼ Jorge Of The Jungle 120' 5.10c
Jorge Jordan. Fall 2017.
Single rack to 3", doubles to 0.75", Rp's.
To the right of Black Rose is another block/pillar at the base of the cliff. Climb the steep, wide crack on the right side of the pillar to the ledge at its top. From the left side of the ledge, climb straight up on juggy horizontals to an attractive thin crack system in nicely varnished rock. At the top of the thin crack, step right and climb an easier, wider crack to an anchor.

❽ Canopy Crack 120' 5.10a/b
Jorge Jordan. Fall 2017.
Single rack to 4", doubles to 2".
This route climbs the big crack and corner system that makes up the right hand of the two major cracks on the wall. Start to the right of the pillar of the previous route. Climb twin cracks to a ledge below a big right-facing corner. Climb the wide crack in the corner, climbing around the roof at the top of the corner (crux). Continue up easier cracks to an anchor.

❾ Mowgli 140' 5.10c
Al Peary, Jim Gregg. Fall 1988.
Another long wall of nice varnish. This route climbs straight up the face just to the right of Canopy Crack, the right most of the two crack systems on the wall (11 b's).

❿ Bush Pig 130' 5.9+ *
Alex Finger. 2017.
Single rack to 3", double to 0.5".
This route climbs the wall to the right of Mowgli. Start down and left of a big arch, below a right-facing corner of nicely varnished rock. Follow a thin seam for 20' to a narrow ledge. Traverse left into the corner. Climb the corner then go slightly left. Pull over a bulge then stem up to a nice stance below a bulge at 75'. Traverse slightly left on the varnished ledge, then continue on good holds, following the crack for protection. Higher up, the rock gets smoother and a long stretch of excellent wall climbing leads to an anchor.

Suzi Urioste on Pitch 5 of Olive Oil.
Page 210. Photo: Joanne Urioste.

Rose Tower

Rose Tower is the attractive pink dome halfway between Pine Creek and Juniper Canyons. From the north it appears small and insignificant. However, when viewed from the south it presents a high face split with attractive corner and crack systems. These routes are very sunny and sheltered from winds.

Approach: Follow the approach for Juniper Canyon described on page 173. Once on the Juniper Canyon trail, continue for a few minutes until a trail branches off right heading towards the second of two gullies. There is an earlier trail, that heads up to the first gully; this is the descent trail from Rose Tower. Follow the trail up into the second gully. The route Olive Oil is a useful reference point. Its start is located about 250 yard up, on the right side of the gully in a small, cleared-out area beneath a deep, left-facing, left-leaning chimney/corner.
1.5 miles, 800' elevation gain, 40 minutes.

Descent: Follow the ridge westwards towards a saddle, just before reaching it a short, steep step must be down climbed. From the saddle drop into the gully to the north and follow a good trail in the gully, down to the east.

❶ Rose Tower - Original Route 700' 5.7
Joe Herbst, Larry Hamilton. February 1976.
Single rack to 4".
This route is seldom climbed nowadays since Olive Oil now provides a much nicer way up this face.
Climb a few hundred feet of class 3, 4 and 5 to a large platform approximately halfway up the wall. At this point the FA team worked their way left into the right most crack on the face. The direct approach to the crack involves some very loose rock (and looks to be harder than 5.7!). There is an old bolt off to the right that may have been used for pro. Their route continued straight up the crack and eventually finished in the huge corner that later became the last pitch of Olive Oil.

❷ Olive Oil 665' 5.7 ***
Jorge Urioste, Joanne Urioste, John Williamson. February 1978.
Single rack to 4", double 1"- 2". A 70m rope is useful but not necessary.
Excellent, varied climbing and a sunny location make this a very popular route during the colder months. Some of the easier climbing on this route is quite runout.
Start below the chimney/corner.
1. 90' 5.7 Climb the slabby rib to the left of the chimney with sparse protection. A delicate step past a slight bulge at 40' is the crux. Belay in a sandy alcove.
2. 120' 5.7 Climb up the steep black corner above, then move right into a beautiful splitter hand and finger crack to the right of the main corner. Follow this crack to a small belay spot.
3. 100' 5.6 Continue up the crack, over a slight bulge, then up the face until it makes sense to step into the corner on the left. Climb the corner to a nice ledge on the left arete.
4. 160' 5.7 Traverse back right and follow a delicate, right-slanting seam to better holds. Continue up the runout but easy face, trending right into a deep left-facing corner. Follow this to a huge platform below the impressive final corner.
5. 195' 5.7 Starting about 20' to the left of the final corner, pull over a short, steep wall, then trend right into the main corner. Protection is sparse at first but gradually improves higher in the corner. Just as the rope runs out set up an anchor using 0.6"- 0.75" cams.
4th class climbing up the ramp on the right leads to the top.

❸ One-Armed Bandit 490' 5.7
Larry Hamilton, Tom Kaufman. March 1976.
Single rack to 3", optional 7".
An enjoyable but serious route with poor protection in places, as well as some fragile rock. 100 yards up the gully from Olive Oil is a brown left-facing corner. Just to its left is a short, steep right-facing corner formed by the right side of a small buttress/pillar. The route starts in the corner formed by the left side of this pillar, another fifty yards higher up the gully.
1. 70' 5.7 Climb a left-facing corner to a bushy ledge, traverse right along the ledge and belay.
2. 100' 5.7 Climb onto the top of the pillar, then go right, then back left up a little ramp until it is possible to trend up and right across the face and belay above the big left-facing corner mentioned in the introduction. (Climbing this corner direct from the ground is an excellent 5.10a variation).
3. 80' 5.7 Climb the crack above to a belay in the base of a loose chimney.
4. 140' 5.7 Continue up the chimney, and when it opens up climb the right-facing corner above and the face to its right to reach a belay.
5. 110' 5.7 Climb the right-facing corner above to a large ledge. Scramble up and right finishing at the top of Olive Oil.

Jaws II 250' 5.10b *
Wendell Broussard, Richard Harrison.
Single rack to 7", double 3"- 5".
This route climbs the huge, left-facing offwidth corner about 50 yards higher up the gully from One-Armed Bandit.
Scramble up to belay at a large bush in the corner system.
1. 50' 5.6 Climb the corner past a short pod, and follow the slabby corner to the base of the massive chimney. Belay off a chockstone.
2. 180' 5.10b Continue up the huge chimney, eventually belaying in an alcove.
3. 205' 5.6 Face climb up to a left-facing corner with a bush. Climb the corner to its top then traverse right on a ledge to reach the summit.

Just to the left of Jaws II there are two obvious crack systems:

The Deep 5.9
Start up the initial dihedral of Jaws II.
1. After about twenty feet (and before you get to the main corner) follow a crack up and left on the face. A long pitch ends in a lower-angled area beneath a large converging chimney.
2. Start up the chimney. Before the chimney converges, climb straight back into the depths of the rock. After about 30 feet the fissure opens up into the base of a huge pit; belay here.
3. The last pitch makes a few face moves up a weakness at the back left side of the pit, then goes up easy class 4 slabs to the top.

Finding Nemo 5.9
Just to the left of Jaws II there is a chimney leading up and left. Climb the chimney in three pitches.

At the top of the descent gully for the Rose Tower formation there two obvious cracks in the varnished wall. The right (upper) one is about 5.7, while the lower (left) one is 5.8.

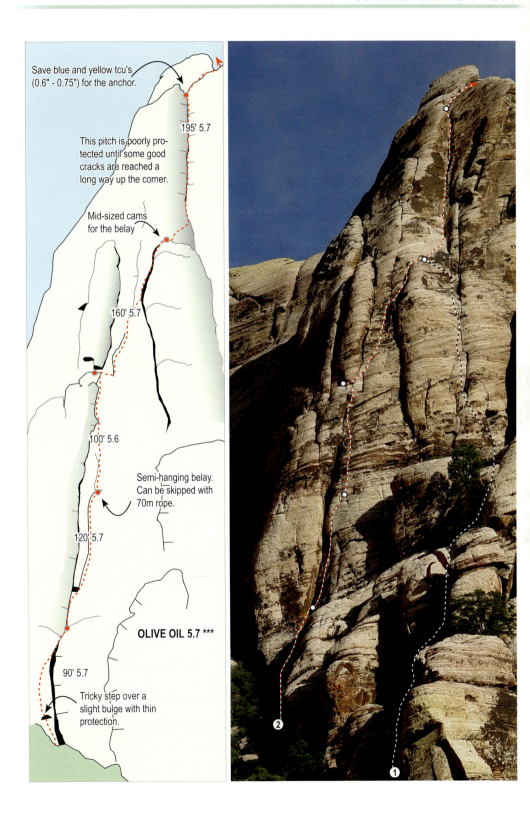

Save blue and yellow tcu's (0.6" - 0.75") for the anchor.

195' 5.7

This pitch is poorly protected until some good cracks are reached a long way up the corner.

Mid-sized cams for the belay

160' 5.7

100' 5.6

Semi-hanging belay. Can be skipped with 70m rope.

120' 5.7

OLIVE OIL 5.7 *

90' 5.7

Tricky step over a slight bulge with thin protection.

Adam Floyd on the crux of Mushroom People. Page 254.

JUNIPER PEAK

Jet Stream Wall

MAGIC MOUNTAIN

Paiute W

MESCALITO

ROSE TOWER

Dark Shadows Wall

Dependant Variable Area

Cat in the Hat

Spectrum Area

Brass Wall Beer & Ic Gully

Introduction

Pine Creek is a beautiful drainage, with year-round running water, lush vegetation, and spectacular scenery. The areas around the entrance of the canyon are some of the most accessible in Red Rocks. Deeper in the canyon there are quite a few remote and impressive walls with a more intimidating atmosphere. The quantity of rock is enormous, and, despite being one of the most popular areas in Red Rocks, there are still numerous unclimbed walls throughout the canyon. With such a large and varied selection of climbs, it is not surprising that Pine Creek is very popular. However, most of the traffic is concentrated on a handful of trade routes such as Cat in the Hat, Dark Shadows and Birdland. Fortunately, worthwhile alternatives can be found near these climbs if the lines at the base get too long. Since Pine Creek Canyon has a lot of walls facing a lot of different directions, it is usually possible to find some reasonable climbing conditions on all but the most extreme days. In particular, on very cold days in the winter, the Brass Wall is one of the better venues in Red Rocks for short trad routes.

Access

The Pine Creek Parking area is on the right, 10.3 miles around the loop road from the fee station. Late exit fees apply; if you have any doubt about a timely return then get a late exit pass.

Andy Reger on the crux slab of Cat in the Hat. Page 234. Photo: Matt Kuehl

BRIDGE MOUNTAIN

Fear & Loathing

Eagles Nest

Stick Gully

Flight Path Area

Gemstone Gully

The Abutment

Straight Shooter

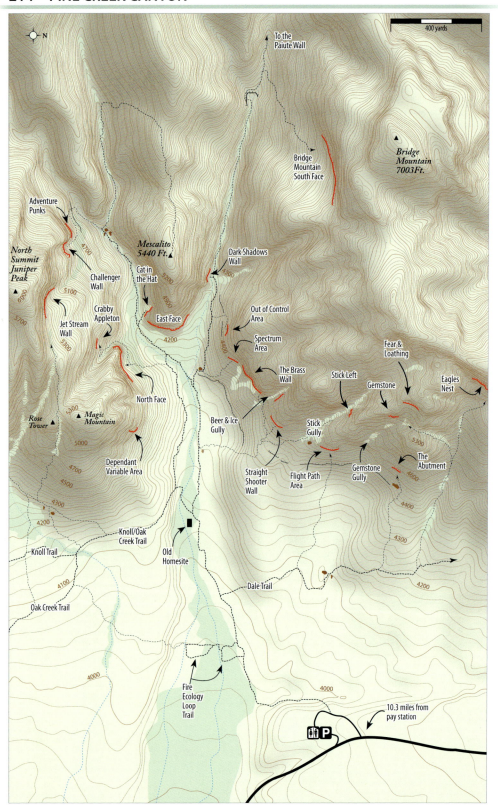

N

400 yards

To the
Paiute Wall

Bridge
Mountain
South Face

▲ Bridge
*Mountain
7003Ft.*

Adventure
Punks

*North
Summit
Juniper
Peak*
▲ *6000*

*Mescalito
5440 Ft.*▲

Dark Shadows
Wall

Challenger
Wall

Cat in
the Hat

5100
5700

Crabby
Appleton

Out of Control
Area

Jet Stream
Wall

East Face

Spectrum
Area

Fear &
Loathing

5300

4200

North Face

The Brass
Wall

Stick Left

Gemstone

Eagles
Nest

*Rose
Tower* ▲

▲ *Magic
Mountain*

Beer & Ice
Gully

Stick
Gully

5300

5000

Dependant
Variable Area

Straight
Shooter
Wall

Flight Path
Area

Gemstone
Gully

The
Abutment

4600

4700

4500

4400

Knoll/Oak
Creek Trail

4300

4300

Knoll Trail

4200

Old
Homesite

4200

Oak Creek Trail

Dale Trail

4100

Fire
Ecology
Loop
Trail

4000

4000

10.3 miles from
pay station

🚻 P

Dependent Variable Area

At the base of Magic Mountain, at the very entrance to the canyon, and facing east, is an obvious pink corner about 80' high. This is the climb Dependent Variable.

Approach: Follow the main canyon trail to just beyond the home site, take a left on the Oak Creek trail and follow it up the hill to a flat area. Leave the trail and hike west up to the base of the corner. 1.2 miles, 500' elevation gain, 35 minutes.

❶ Dog Police 160' 5.10c *
Paul Van Betten, Sal Mamusia. 1983.
Single rack to 3", double 0.75"- 1", triple 0.6".
An excellent splitter crack in smooth rock. The route follows a thin crack-line which snakes up the gray wall on the right, at the top of the gully that slants up and left from the base of Dependent Variable.
From the top of the gully, climb 20' up a huecoed crack on the right to a bushy ledge at the base of the initial crack.
1. 110' 5.10c The crack starts as a left-slanting hand crack then thins to a tight finger crack and zig-zags up to a small ledge.
2. 50' 5.10a Continue up the crack line, past a small tree, and into a short corner which leads to the anchor.
Descent: A 200' rappel reaches the base of the huecoed crack which leads up to the starting ledge.

❷ Without a Paddle 80' 5.11d *
Mike Tupper. 1988.
This is a great route up the clean-cut arete left of Dependent Variable . There is some fragile rock, and the bolts are spaced, but the climbing and situations are spectacular (8 b's).

The next two routes start on top of the huge detached flake at the base of the pink corner.

❸ Dependent Variable 70' 5.12b
Mike Tupper. 1988.
Rp's, cams 0.4"- 1.75".
Despite being a great looking line, this is a poor route with contrived climbing and flaky rock. Climb the pink corner to a couple of bolts close together. Make a hard step out right and face climb on holds immediately left of Cold Blue Steel, moving back left into the main corner above a bolt. Continue more easily to an anchor (4 b's).

❹ Cold Blue Steel 75' 5.10b
Greg Mayer. 1988.
Rp's, cams 0.4"- 1.75".
This route climbs the first 10' of Dependent Variable, a bit sketchy, then moves right and climbs a shallow scoop in the wall 10' right of the main corner (5 b's). After clipping the 5th bolt, step down and traverse left to the anchor of Dependent Variable.

❺ Canoe Crack 120' 5.10b
Single rack to 5", triples 2.5"- 6".
This route climbs through a bulge of rotten rock to gain the steep hand and fist crack in the wall around to the right of Cold Blue Steel.

Magic Mountain - North Face

This 800' wall is split into an attractive series of pillars. There are several excellent long routes, including the classic Community Pillar, as well as a handful of single pitch routes on good rock along the base. These routes are rarely climbed. Most of the wall faces north and is very shady, although a few routes on the western facets of the pillars, such as Edge of the Sun, face west and get some afternoon sun.

Approach

Follow the main canyon trail to just beyond the home site. Take a left on the Oak Creek trail for a few hundred yards. When the main trail starts cutting eastwards up the hill, follow an unmarked trail on the right, which continues west up the canyon. Follow this trail, which leads all the way along the base of the hillside underneath the wall. Leave the trail at a convenient spot and hike up the hillside to your chosen route. 1.4 miles, 500' elevation gain, 35 - 45 minutes.

❶ Honeycomb Chimney 900' 5.9 *
Jim Trogdon, John Campbell, Larry DeAngelo. Mid-2000's.
Single rack to 6".
This surprisingly good route goes up the left edge of the Community Pillar. Halfway up is a dark chimney. This is the Honeycomb Chimney and is the main landmark of this route. Start at the far left side of the broad base of the buttress.
1. A short pitch leads through some fragile rock and a chimney to a good belay ledge beneath a dark offwidth crack.
2. 200' 5.7 Start up the wide crack, but exit right onto easy face climbing up solid, varnished potholes. Move back to the crack and pull over a small bulge (5.7) to an easy chimney.
3. Class 3 climbing leads up the broken gully to the base of a huge, dark chimney.
4. 5.7 High quality climbing on the varnished honeycomb takes you to the top of the chimney.
5. 5.8 Climb up and slightly left to the constricted slot above you. A bit of fiddling with large cams in pockets gives some amount of protection for the squeeze moves (5.8) through the slot. Continue up and left on easy rock, belaying just above a small tunnel.
6. Class 4 scrambling leads left and a little down for about 100 feet across a broken ledge system.
7. 5.9 Climb the spectacular corner to a large ledge. At this point you can descend by walking right (west) and joining the standard Community Pillar descent where it rappels from the pine tree.
8. 5.7 Scramble up for 50 feet (class 3) over loose rock to the base of a small but clean corner. Go straight up the crack (5.7) and through the chimney in the giant split boulder to a belay on the summit ridge.

❷ Birthday Party 700' 5.10a
Larry DeAngelo, Jeffrey Raymond, John Wilder, Brandon Arens, Casey Bevando. July 2005.
A single rack to 4", double 2"-3".
About 150 feet left of Community Pillar is an obvious crack system. About 30 feet further left is a short chimney leading to a left-facing, varnished corner.
1. 50' 5.10a Climb past the roof (5.10a), with good protection, and continue up the corner to a comfortable ledge.
2. 60' 5.9 Follow the crack to a good ledge at the base of the

large chimney.
3. 100' 5.7 On the left hand side of the monster chimney you is a smaller chimney. Head up this and then step right, following a crack to a dihedral. This leads to a stance at the top of the corner.
4. 190' 5.9 Head up the slab and crack above, eventually stepping right over a loose boulder, and then following the crack until it ends. From here a short traverse to the left (optional hanging belay) gains a second crack. Follow this crack until it ends at a huge ledge.
5. 190' 5.8 R From here, head up the obvious slot above, following the chimney until you reach its end. From here, head left and up the slabs, aiming for a tree at the top. Belay here. This pitch is loose and runout; it can be avoided by traversing left from the belay to finish up Honeymoon Chimney.

The next route climbs the wide crack system that splits the tallest pillar on the wall, which from below appears to lead to the high point of Magic Mountain.

❸ Community Pillar 790' 5.8+ **
Joe Herbst, Tom Kaufman. March 1976.
Single rack to 4", doubles 4"- 7".
A great line and some unique situations make this an appealing climb. There are some very runout sections, but at least the climbing feels fairly secure, as long as you are comfortable with wide cracks.
Start at the base of a crack system in a 10' wide chimney blocked by a huge chockstone
1. 160' 5.8 Tunnel behind the chockstone or skirt it on the left, (optional belay) then ascend the wide crack in the clean left-facing corner above to a large, comfortable platform.
2. 150' 5.6 Continue up the easy crack system to the base of a steeper chimney. Climb the chimney and tunnel behind another chockstone. Belay on top of the chockstone.
3. 130' 5.8+ Climb the long off-width and chimney on the right; at its top yet another tunnel leads to a comfortable ledge. Carry big gear or be prepared for some long runouts.
Variation: 5.9 From the ledge climb the corner on the left then continue straight up an excellent hand and fist crack to the regular belay.
4. 100' 5.7 Climb the crack on the left to a belay in a huge cave.
5. 90' 5.8 Either climb the rotten chimney in the back of the cave or the offwidth on the outside. Belay in another cave.
6. 160' 4th Class Exit out a window in the left side of the cave and scramble up easy slabs and cracks to the top.
Descent. Scramble south across slabs to a pine tree. Rappel down the gully below the tree (loose.) From here are several options, all of which require care. It is possible to scramble north to a huge tree and make a short rappel to a bushy ledge just above the top of Chocolate Flakes and use the new rappel anchor on this route. The main gully just to the west also has a rappel route, though the anchors at the top may need some backup. Also, It is possible to rap the gully to the east of the Magic Triangle in 5 single rope rappels. Another descent scrambles down the back side of the wall eventually leading to a rappel into the Crabby Appleton gully; this is tricky and requires careful route finding.

The next four routes are located in the amphitheater of dark, brown rock to the right of the upper half of Community Pillar. They all share the first two pitches of Cartwright Corner, which starts up the deep gully to the right Community Pillar.

❹ Cartwright Corner 625' 5.10b
R. Harrison, Nick Nordblom, Paul Van Betten, Wendell Broussard. 1985. Single rack to 7".

Start by scrambling up the deep gully to the right of Community Pillar to a mossy, shallow alcove.

1. 100' 5.8 Lieback up the thin crack on the right side of the alcove, continuing over a bulge to belay on a ledge with a tree. Move the belay out of the main gully to a ledge 20' up and to the left, below a deep corner.

2. 165' 5.9 Climb the corner and continue up the steep flake on the left until it is possible to move right to another crack. Up this to belay beside a tree.

Move the belay up 30' to a large ledge below the upper amphitheater of dark rock. Cartwright Corner continues up the huge corner off the left end of this ledge system.

3. 120' 5.10b Climb the corner (b) to an anchor below a wide crack.

4. 40' 5.10a Run it out up the wide crack, then head into a huge chasm. There is a rap anchor here, alternatively continue to the back of the chasm where the route joins Community Pillar. Finish up the last pitch of Community Pillar.

5. 200' 4th class Easy to the top.

Descent: Descend as for Community Pillar. Using the rap anchors of Chocolate Flakes is the best option since this allows you to leave gear, extra rope etc. on the big ledge below the upper pitches. A series of single rope raps from fixed anchors leads back down the initial gully to the ground.

❺ Saucerful of Secrets 230' 5.11d ★★
Single rack to 3".

This is an incredibly spectacular and exposed route up the huge arete between the final pitches of Cartwright Corner and Chocolate Flakes. Start on the large ledge below the upper amphitheater.

1. 50' 5.7 Climb up onto the highest ledge below the arete.

2. 140' 5.11d Climb past a fragile roof (b) and continue up the steep crack on the right side of the arete. Eventually, the crack snakes around onto the left side of the arete and ends at a good shake. Continue up the arete (8 b's), staying close to the edge but switching sides from time to time, to reach an anchor on a small ledge at the base of a steep corner.

3. 40' 5.10c Climb the corner to an anchor at the top (4 b's).

Descent: Either rap with two ropes or climb down to the anchor above Chocolate Flakes and rap that route with one rope.

❻ Chocolate Flakes 160' 5.10d ★
Robert Finlay, Tom Ebanoff. 1985.
FFA Paul Van Betten, Nick Nordblom. 1985.
Single rack to 2", double 0.75"- 1.25".

Start on the big ledge below the corner of Cartwright Corner. Good climbing up an elegant series of corners and flakes.

1. 80' 5.10d Climb the corner system to a bolted anchor.

2. 80' 5.10a A steep lieback leads to an easier corner. Up this to anchor just below the top

Descent: Two single rope raps lead back to the starting ledge. A series of single rope raps from fixed anchors leads back down the approach gully to the ground.

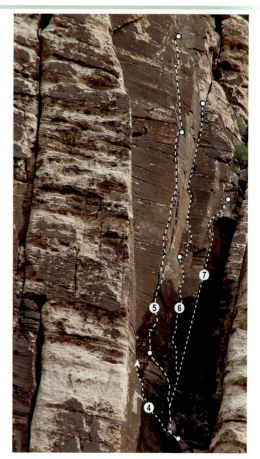

❼ Dark and Long 140' 5.11d ★★
Bob Goodwin, Jerry Handren. January 2006.
Single rack to 3", triple 0.75"- 1.75".

A clean-cut corner/crack on perfect rock. Climb the first 15' of Chocolate Flakes, then follow the right branch of the crack system. The crack deepens into a right-facing corner which is climbed (pumpy and a little bold) to below a roof. It is possible, but not easy, to arrange some gear at the roof before making a move left around the arete to easier ground. To keep rope drag reasonable, belay on 1.25"- 1.75" cams in a horizontal crack 10' above the roof. There is a rap anchor at the top of the gully to the right.

The buttress to the right of Community pillar is split by a series of huge roofs at half height. At the base of the cliff underneath the roofs a couple of huge blocks lean against the wall.

❽ Dukes of Hazard 150' 5.9
Randal Grandstaff, Shelby Shelton. 1983.
This route climbs the left arete of the block on the left; it starts a few feet up the Cartwright Corner approach gully.

❾ In the Red 90' 5.11d
Selection of tiny cams to 1", one 2", skyhook.
A very serious route which climbs the west-facing wall to the left of Small Purchase. Climb the face to slopers. Move left then right below an overhang. Finish up the overhang to an anchor.

Luke Olson on the big arete of
Saucerful of Secrets. Page 218.

The next two routes are on the rightmost block, whose right side forms a right-facing corner with a sharp left arete.

⑩ Five & Dime 90' 5.10d

6 bolts, 0.6" cam.
The sharp arete. Either climb up the right side of the arete beside the bolts (11a) or on the left side (easier but with a potentially awkward fall).

⑪ Small Purchase 90' 5.10a **

Joe Herbst. 1970s.
Single rack to 2.5", double 0.6"- 1".
The corner. A good introduction to the grade.

The next formation to the right is topped by a triangle of excellent black rock.

⑫ The Magic Triangle 750' 5.9

Joe Herbst, Randal Grandstaff. 1977.
Single rack to 6".
Start about 50' to the right of the gully separating the Magic Triangle from the formation to its left, below an obvious blocky crack system with some white rock.
1. 100' 5.8 Climb the crack
2. 100' 5.8 Climb the crack to the obvious white traverse ledge
3. 150' 5.8 Traverse across the ledge, past a 5.8 section, to the base of a crack that is to the right of center of the upper wall.
4. 100' 5.8 Climb the crack to a belay in a horizontal break.
5. 100' 5.9 Go left to where it is possible to pull the roof (5.9), then up a crack to a belay near the right edge of the wall.
6. 100' 5.9 This pitch is scary and intricate. Move right, then go

up until a thin traverse leads left to a thin crack; up this (5.9) and finally right to a belay spot.
7. 100' 5.6 Straight to the top.

Descent: Five single-rope rappels down the gully to the left of the formation.

⑬ Masquerade 5.10c

John Wilder, Kevin Campbell, George Urioste, Larry DeAngelo.
Single rack; the F.A. party had #6 Friend and used it a couple of times.
This is a good route. Much of the climbing looks difficult, but turns out to be surprisingly moderate. The short crux, on the other hand, is harder than it looks. In fact, the upper part of this route (p 4-5) is easier and better protected than the standard Magic Triangle route.
1. Start about 40 feet to the left (east) of Midnight Oil. Easy rock leads to a belay ledge on the right about 60 or 80 feet up.
2. Make a few tricky moves (5.10) right off the ledge, then continue up the crack above. After a flared slot, belay on small but good ledges.
3. Climb the steep corner on the right and belay on the large midway ledge of the formation.
4. Go up and left on white rock, then move back right to the varnished crack. The climbing becomes easy when the rock gets dark. Belay in the obvious alcove.
5. Continue up the wide crack. What looks like it is going to be a horrendous offwidth turns out to be moderate face climbing.
Descent: From the final belay ledge, descend by rappelling the gully below. Four rappels (with a 60 meter rope) and a little scrambling take you to the ground.

⓮ Midnight Oil 165' 5.11a
Richard Harrison, Paul Crawford, Randy Marsh. 1983.
This route generally follows the line of a large left-facing corner in the lower wall of the Magic Triangle. An impressive splitter offwidth just to the right of the start is an obvious landmark. Start at the base of the corner, on a ledge.
Climb a hand crack in the lower corner then go out onto the left wall following a seam (crux) and up past a mantel then back into the main corner. Up this past a bolt to a rap anchor on top.

⓯ Bro's Before Holes 70' 5.10c
Rob & Pat Dezonia, Jerry Handren. Nov 2006.
Three each 3 & 4 Big Bro's, Two #6 Camalots.
This route climbs the impressive offwidth just to the right of Midnight Oil. Burly and sustained.

Advanced Placement 250' 5.9
Joe Lee, Bill Lee, Larry DeAngelo. Spring 2008.
Single rack up to 6". Double 2"-6".
This route starts up the wide, right-facing crack that is the right side of the big flake whose left side forms Bro's Before Holes.
1. 140' 5.9 Climb the corner, passing a wide, hollowed-out section, then a short fist crack at the base of the arching wide crack above. Climb the crack, which eventually dead-ends at a steep, loose section. Bypass this by face-climbing left, then up before traversing back right into the main crack system. Continue up a short, steep fist crack leading to an easier squeeze chimney and a ledge.
2. 110' 5.7 Climb right and up to a deep, dark chimney with excellent face holds. Climb this and belay in an amphitheater.
Descent: A fourth class pitch then goes straight left on friction and ledges, passes a large bush, and descends a short ramp to the rappel station at the top of Midnight Oil. A 50-meter rappel leads to the ground from here.

The next six routes are at the right end of the wall, defined on the right by the long, sharp arete of Edge of the Sun. On the left hand side of this section, a buttress leans against the wall going the full height of the cliff. This feature is called The Bottle, and two routes climb the cracks on either side, providing a healthy dose of offwidth for the enthusiast.

⓰ Bottle Bill 350' 5.9
Joe Herbst, Tom Kaufman. March 1977.
Single rack to 2.5", doubles 2.5"- 5".
Start in the gully to the left of The Bottle. Scramble up behind a large, detached block to the starting ledge.
1. 5.9 Up a straight in hand crack in a smooth face, then follow a ramp leftwards then up to belay in an alcove.
2. Jam the left side of the recess (there is an offwidth on the right), then move right and belay in a hole.
3. Continue up to the ceiling and a semi-hanging belay around on the left.
4. Go over the bulge and up the corner to a large, flat ledge.
5. Climb straight over the series of overhangs above.
Descent: Rappel Edge of the Sun with two ropes.

⓱ Clone Babies 160' 5.10d
Paul Crawford, Richard Harrison. 1983.
At the base of the cliff, to the right of the Magic Triangle there are some large blocks below the wall. This route climbs a steep, twin crack system behind the block. The crack starts hard but eases after 50'. Continue up and left on big huecos to an anchor on top of a pillar.

There are several routes on the huge block at the base of the cliff, including a short, bolted 12c arete and some 5.9 offwidths.

⓲ Five Pack 390' 5.10b *
Joe Herbst, Tom Kaufman, Steve Allen, Scott Woodruff, Larry Hamilton. April 1977.
Single rack to 5", double 2"- 4".
This route climbs the crack on the right side of The Bottle. Start below a 20' high left-facing chimney filled with chockstones.
1. 80' 5.8 Climb the chimney to a big ledge (or scramble around from the right to reach the same point). Continue up the wide crack above to a ledge.
2.140' 5.8 Climb the big chimney above ,which gradually narrows into a nice hand crack. Follow the hand crack to a semi-hanging belay at the base of a left-facing corner below a roof.
3. 80' 5.9 Climb the corner for a few feet, then move out left, skirting the left side of the roof before traversing back right into a big right-facing corner. Follow the corner for 30' and belay in a pod.
4. 90' 5.10b Jam up the corner to where it starts to slant steeply to the right. Traverse right on a tiny ledge, then move up on huecos (5.7 moves 20' out) to regain the corner at a small ledge below the final crack. Finish up the crack (crux).
Descent: Use the Edge of the Sun rappel route.

⓳ Texas Longneck 5.8
George Urioste, Larry DeAngelo. Mid-2000's.
Single rack to 4".
Start in a small left-facing dihedral about 40 feet to the right of Five Pack.
1. Climb the dihedral and belay on top of a pillar. Move the belay down and right to a good ledge for the next pitch.
2. Climb the corner to some good ledges.
3. Climb up, then right on face holds until you reach a crack that leads back to the left.
4. Continue up the right-facing corner. Exit from the main dihedral system by climbing left on easy friction (this is at the point where Five Pack crosses from left to right into the main dihedral). Belay in a varnished crack at the base of a small knobby corner.
5. Go straight up the corner past a bulge to a large white ledge.
6. The FA party threaded a path through the overhangs above, but this involved difficult, reachy climbing (maybe 5.10) on unreliable rock with limited protection. A better option looked like climbing up 20 feet, then traversing left to easier terrain and the top.
Descent: Use the Edge of the Sun rappel route.

⓴ Edge of the Sun 350' 5.10d **
Dave Wonderly, Warren Egbert. 1988.
Single rack to 2", Rp's.
Both the first and second pitches have sections of runout climbing on fragile rock. Nevertheless, the situations are spectacular and the third pitch is superb.
Start just right of the arete.
1. 130' 5.10a Climb the wall to meet the arete; move around to the left side and up to the anchor.
2. 130' 5.10a Great but scary climbing on fragile knobs leads up the left side of the arete to a hanging belay.
3. 120' 5.10d Follow bolts out left to a thin crux on the final headwall (7 b's).
Descent: Rappel the route with two ropes. The first rappel

goes down to the anchor below the top pitch. From there, two rappels straight down, i.e. to the west of the arete, lead into the Crabby Appleton gully.

㉑ Lunar Escape 350' 5.11a
Dave Wonderly, Warren Egbert. 1988.
This route takes a winding line up the steep wall to the right of Edge of the Sun. Start 50' to the right of the arete.

1. 100' 5.10a Climb the black face to an anchor.
2. 110' 5.10c Traverse right then up the face (7 b's) to an anchor.
3. 110' 5.11a Climb straight up past a couple of bolts then move right into a left-leaning corner. Climb the corner to a steep scoop in the final headwall, which is climbed to a rounded finish.
Descent: Rappel Edge of the Sun with two ropes.

Crabby Appleton Area

To the right of Edge of the Sun, a steep gully slants up to the east, separating Magic Mountain from the main mass of Juniper Peak. Half way up this gully, on the right, is an obvious diamond of black rock. The next routes climb this formation.

Approach: Follow the main trail into the canyon and where the canyon splits follow the south fork. Walk up the wash to a point below the obvious approach gully. A bushy thrash leads up the hill to the base of the gully. Follow the gully, with several awkward 5th class sections, until a ledge leads out of the gully to the base of the wall. 1.6 miles, 800' elevation gain, 1-1½ hrs.

Descent: From the top of the wall, scramble west down slabs until it is possible to turn back to the east, following a steep ramp which slants down underneath the wall.

❶ Crabby Appleton 550' 5.9+
Richard Harrison, Wendell Broussard, Paul Van Betten. 1982.
This is a moderate route with a short and well-protected crux at the top. Start on the ledge which you first reach after exiting the approach gully. Follow a left-facing corner/ramp onto a higher ledge and belay
1. 100' 5.3 Traverse right for 80' to a crack. Climb the crack to a ledge.
2. 120' 5.7 Climb the crack then move right into another crack which is followed to a belay with a bolt in a scoop.
3. 120' 5.8 Leave the scoop on the left, regain the crack, and follow it past an overlap to an anchor below a big left-facing corner.
4. 100, 5.5 Climb a short distance up the corner, then move out right and climb the varnished face to a terrace underneath a headwall.
Variation: 5.9 Go to the top of the corner before moving right. It is possible to traverse left into the approach gully from this ledge.
5. 130' 5.9+ Go right along the terrace for 20' to a vertical crack. Climb the crack over the bulge and continue to the top of the wall.

❷ Tom Terrific 370' 5.10a
Richard Harrison, Wendell Broussard. 1985.
Single rack to 4".
This route starts well to the right of Crabby Appleton, at the base of the descent ramp.
1. 100' 5.10a Climb over a bulge and continue up the face to a belay with a bolt in a scoop.
2. 110' 5.7 Continue straight up the face and belay on large cams at the left end of an arch.
3. 160' 5.9+ Step left around the arch, then climb straight up the face to the top of the wall.

❸ Creepshow 300' 5.10d †
Robert Finlay, Richard Harrison. 1985.
The bolts on this route were added when another party re-climbed the same line thinking that they were doing the first ascent.
1. 150' 5.10b Climb a crack, past a hueco to an anchor.
2. 150' 5.10d Continue up the face (4 b's) to the top.

JUNIPER PEAK - NORTH FACE

This huge wall towers above the upper reaches of the south fork of Pine Creek Canyon. It sits above a large terrace, which is nearly 1000' above the canyon floor at its eastern end, but slants down to meet the south branch of the south fork at its western end.

There are three different climbing areas; the **Jet Stream Wall** is the most easterly of the three. It is the very smooth wall above and slightly to the west of Crabby Appleton. A huge right-curving arch in the center of the wall is an obvious feature when viewed from the road a few hundred yards before reaching the Pine Creek parking lot. **The Challenger Wall** sits in an amphitheater towards the western end of the wall. The **Adventure Punks Wall** is just around the corner to the west of the Challenger Wall, at the western end of the terrace, just above the floor of the canyon. Despite being nearly 800' high, this wall is one of the least obvious in Red Rocks, only becoming visible when you are directly below it. Adventure Punks is the huge left-curving corner.

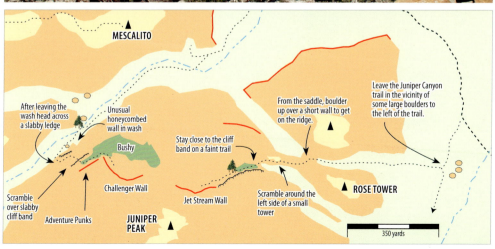

Jet Stream Wall

The rock on this wall is superb. It faces north and is very exposed to any winds that are blowing. Climbing here can be very comfortable even with temperatures in the high 90s in Las Vegas. The wall is generally quite shady, but in the late spring it gets sun until mid-day or so.

Approach: Considering the high and remote location, this wall has a very reasonable approach. Go up the Olive Oil descent gully; this is the first gully to the north of Rose Tower. From the saddle at the top of the gully, get onto the ridge on the left (south) and follow it to a tower. Follow ledges around the left side of the tower and continue to the saddle at the top of a gully on the left (this is the top of the Olive Oil gully). Cross the top of the gully and pick up a trail which heads west staying fairly close to the base of the wall. This leads across to the base of the Jet Stream Wall. A steep but surprisingly straightforward approach with some amazing views.
1.8 miles, 1500' elevation gain, 1 hr. 10 minutes total.

❶ Jet Stream 560' 5.13a *
Camalots, 0.5, 0.75, 1; Tcu's, Four #00, three #0, single #1, #2. Hb's 1 set, double #4, #5. 1 set stoppers.
Bulletproof rock, a gorgeous line and superb climbing–up there with the best routes in Red Rocks. Protection is good throughout, although it takes a bit of work to get it in on pitches 3 & 4. The most obvious feature of the Jet Stream Wall is a huge right-curving arch in the center. Start from a sloping shelf a couple of feet above the ground, about 100 yards up the hill to the left of this feature and directly below a very elegant left-facing corner starting 300' up the cliff.
1.80' 5.10a Scramble up past a bush, then step left and follow slabby corners to a ledge with a tree. Climb the right-facing corner above to a nice, flat ledge on the left.
2. 100' 5.13a Bouldery moves (4 b's) lead to the base of a thin crack, up this for a few moves then step left and climb the easy face, trending left (b) to a rap anchor. Traverse left to another anchor at the base of a smooth left-facing corner.
3. 100' 5.12a Stem up the corner (3 b's). After 45' move onto the right arete and after a few moves go right then up to a bolt. Climb past the bolt then easier to a nice ledge at the base of the impressive corner mentioned in the introduction.
4. 100' 5.12b Abstract stemming leads up the corner to an anchor on the right. The gear is small but good.
5. 100' 5.11a Continue up the corner to a rap anchor; go left and up to an anchor at the base of an imposing corner which slices through the final headwall.
6. 80' 5.12a Burly climbing out a roof (2 b's) leads to a tips lieback, then a rest below the final roof. Pull right, then go over the roof (2 b's) to an anchor on the slab above.
Descent: Rappel straight down with a single 70m rope.

❷ Airhead 270' 5.12a **
Josh Janes, Cole Nelson. 2016.
Single rack to 3". For the main pitch, double to 1", wires. Slings are useful to reduce rope drag.
The meat of this route is the nicely varnished arete to the right of the second and third pitches of Jet Stream. This provides a superb long pitch on great rock.
1.100' 5.10d Follow the first pitch of Jet Stream to where it pulls out left to the anchor. Undercling right underneath the large roof (crucial, blind #3 Camalot around the right end of the first roof) then pull up through the tiered roofs (2 b's) to an anchor at the base of the smooth wall.

1.170' 5.12a Step up from the belay (b) to a thin seam. Climb the seam (good wires) and the arête to the right (b) to easier climbing. Continue (gear placements) to a good rest before committing to the steeper wall above. Increasingly difficult climbing (5 b's) leads to an intricate crux at a fixed draw. Continue (gear placements) onto a steep, blunt arete which leads (3 b's) to the ledge at the top of pitch three of Atmospheres.
Descent: Rap with two ropes.

❸ Atmospheres 470' 5.13a **
Wires, four #1,#2 BD stoppers. Wild Country z2, Tcu's #00- #2. Camalots, 0.75, 1.
A beautiful, varied and very hard climb which sees few ascents. Protection is reasonably good, but requires care on the crux pitch. Start at the base of Jet Stream.
1. 90' 5.10b Follow Jet Stream for 60', then move right and climb a fist crack up to a flat ledge at the base of a tight left-facing corner.
2. 100' 5.12c The crack in the back of the corner starts as fingers and gradually narrows to tips. An insecure struggle (b) leads to the top of the corner, then reach out left to holds on the lip of the roof above the corner. Continue over the roof, then move up and head right to a ledge.
3. 140' 5.13a A brilliant pitch. Climb the long, thin crack (b) for 50' to a rest below a slight bulge. (Nest of crucial #2 Bd stoppers a few feet above). A desperate crux leads into a long offset (3 b's). After 100' move left over a large flake (.75" cam) and up to a bolt. Traverse left to a comfortable ledge.
4. 140' 5.12d Intricate, bouldery face climbing leads to better holds at 30', then enjoyable easier climbing (10d) up a slight arete in the varnished wall leads to an anchor (9 b's).

❹ 20% 460' 5.11d *
Single rack to 3", double 1"-2". Rp's.
This route is based on the left of the two big corner systems in the middle of the cliff. Start on a terrace with a lone pine tree directly below this corner system.
1. 100' 5.10c Start 15' left of the tree. Scramble to a high, hard-to-see first bolt and make a big reach/jump to a flat jug. Climb the slabby wall above (5 b's), past a high crux, finishing with moves left to a good ledge.
2. 130' 5.11d Move right and climb the low-angled corner to where it starts slanting steeply to the right. Step left and make hard moves up the face to the left of the corner to regain the crack system (5 b's). Continue up the arching flake and corner system, past another crux (large brass offset) then follow a right-leaning ramp to a belay.
3. 90' 5.11a Move back down the ramp to regain the crack system and follow it to a bolt at a thin flake. Continue up a shallow corner (2 b's) before some committing climbing leads up and right across a varnished face to an anchor below a prominent bomb-bay chimney.
4. 140' 5.10d A wild pitch at the grade. Start up the cleft above on poor rock. After a key #1 camalot placement, move right and make strenuous and strange moves to get up into the chimney. Continue on really nice varnish until the chimney closes into a hand and finger crack in a right-facing corner. Follow this to an anchor at the top of the wall.
Descent: The first rap goes to an anchor to the left of the bomb-bay chimney. From here, either rap straight down the route with an 80m rope or with a 60m rope swing left and use the anchor at the base of the tight corner of Atmospheres.

❺ Cold Front 450' 5.12b *

Single rack to 3", double 0.75" to 3".

This route climbs the right of the two huge corner systems in the center of the wall. Begin down and left of the corner on the large, flat, polished rock terrace near a large pine tree and scramble up and right for 90' to a ledge.

1. 50' 5.8 Climb a lichen-covered slab to a short finger crack just right of the gully system beneath the central corner. From the finger crack, bushwhack leftwards across the top of the gully to a belay out left at a good stance with an anchor.

2. 120' 5.10c Climb the amazing corner. An awkward start leads to great climbing punctuated with several rests. Belay at a cramped stance below the steeper wall above.

3. 50' 5.12b The boulder problem (V4) crux. Follow face holds up a steepening wall to a good rest beneath a roof. Move left to underclings, then pull up over the roof (crux) and step around the corner to the left and belay on a foot ledge (6 b's).

4. 90' 5.9 This pitch is bold towards the top. Climb up a series of hollow flakes, eventually working left to a semi-hanging belay beneath an attractive corner. Extend the belay to a stance 10' below this anchor for a more comfortable position.

5. 140' 5.11a Above is a beautiful, varnished corner. Climb through the first crux (b) immediately above the belay, and continue up the corner to a tricky but well-protected corner switch to the right. Exposed moves (b) up the arete separating the corners lead to yet another pretty corner. This is followed past a final tricky section (b) using a flake on the right face. Continue to a ledge system at the top of the wall (3 b's).

Descent: Traverse left to the anchor at the top of 2% and rap that route with a 70m rope.

❻ Drifting 510' 5.11d ***

Single rack to 3", Rp's.

A good introduction to the area, this is a magnificent climb up the huge, open face on the right side of the Jet Stream wall. Never desperate, but sustained. Start beside a pine tree in the middle of the wall. Scramble up 20' to a bush on a ledge and follow the ledge up and right to an anchor below a small roof.

1. 70' 5.11d A stout warm-up. Climb straight up the wall then move right under a bulge to an anchor on the right (7 b's).

2. 140' 5.11c Move left and climb the tips lieback (3 b's) to good holds. Move left (b) and climb up 15' to good protection at the base of a thin crack. Follow the crack for 30', then go left and up to a seam which is followed to a bolt on the left. Move left and slightly down past the bolt to the base of a flake which leads to an anchor on a small ledge.

3. 100' 5.11b Climb up to the base of a left-slanting corner. Climb the right arete of the corner (3 b's) moving back left across the top of the corner to a flake. Climb the flake to an anchor above the huge roofs.

4. 100' 5.11a Climb up and right into a very steep left-slanting corner; at its top pull right and climb over the roof (b). Airy and moderately runout climbing (4 b's) up the easier wall above leads to a hanging belay.

5. 100' 5.11c A great pitch. Continue up the outrageously exposed wall (6 b's) to an anchor on top.

Descent: Rappel straight down with a 70m rope. The last two rappels are to the left of the route. Knot the ends, some of the rappels are long.

❼ Tooth or Consequences 800' 5.11c

Single rack to 2.5".

This route climbs the prominent buttress leading to a sharp, red tower (The Tooth) at the upper right edge of the Jet Stream Wall. An enjoyable long route with an alpine feel. Start well down and right of the fall line of the tower and scramble up slabs to the base of a right-facing scoop/roof just left of a lone pine tree. Bolts lead up the left side of the roof.

1. 110' 5.10b Make a few thin and reachy moves around the left side of the roof, then trend right following lower-angle crack systems to the base

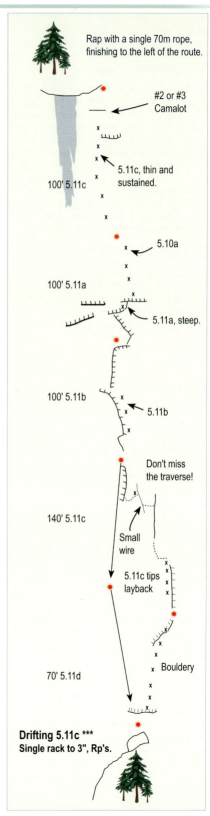

Rap with a single 70m rope, finishing to the left of the route.

#2 or #3 Camalot

5.11c, thin and sustained.

100' 5.11c

5.10a

100' 5.11a

5.11a, steep.

100' 5.11b

5.11b

Don't miss the traverse!

140' 5.11c

Small wire

5.11c tips layback

Bouldery

70' 5.11d

Drifting 5.11c ***
Single rack to 3", Rp's.

of a small roof in the varnished wall.
Move up into a pod and belay at a
fixed anchor.

2. 110' 5.8 Follow the crack through
soft, red rock onto a varnished face.
Good climbing on excellent rock
leads to a big, rocky ledge. Belay at
a fixed station just below the broad,
vegetated ledge above.
Move the belay up to the base of
the arête.

3. 110' 5.8 Climb the left side of the
arete, and continue up cracks (poor
rock) to an anchor below a heavily
varnished wall.

4. 110' 5.10a Broken cracks lead to
the base of a varnished face. Follow
thin edges and dimples up the varnished slab to an anchor in a scoop
below a mini-roof. A good pitch with
delicate climbing on great rock.

5. 110' 5.8 Move left off the
belay and climb up to the base of a
vegetated corner system. Continue
up the low-angle corners and shrubbery to a ledge system with several
anchors. Use the leftmost anchor,
the right is for the rappel route.

6. 100' 5.10a Begin up good edges
on a short wall left of the belay.
Once on the ledge above, move
right around a boulder and back
left to the base of a finger crack in
a white dihedral. Climb up into the
crack, clip a bolt on the steep, white
wall and pull around the left side
of the arete onto a featured face.
Follow this face to a stance with an
anchor.

7. 100' 5.10b/c Another very good
pitch. Climb the steep face, then
trend back right to the arête. Watch
for a loose block out on the arête
towards the end. Finish at an
anchor on a sloping ledge below the
northwest side of the "tooth".

8. 110' 5.11c (or 5.9 A0) The 5.11
climbing on this pitch can be easily
aided (A0). Pedal up a thin, varnished slab to a stance at the base
of the arete. A short, bouldery crux
turns the arete. Fun face climbing
leads to a fixed belay on the summit. An attentive belay is needed for
the crux moves - it's well-protected
but extra slack in the system could
put a falling leader back on the slab.
Descent: Rappel straight down with
a single 70m rope.

Tom Moulin on pitch 2
of Jet Stream. Page 225.

Challenger Wall

The Challenger Wall is seldom visited despite being glaringly obvious from all around the scenic loop road. The unique feature here is the texture of the rock. Face holds are few and far between; instead the wall bristles with long, clean-cut crack and corner systems which provide tough routes of outstanding character; in some ways quite atypical of Red Rocks.

This wall faces north, getting very little sun at any time of the year, making it a good choice for warmer weather. The topography of the surroundings seems to somehow amplify any winds that may be blowing. On certain days this can be a serious problem and under such conditions it is probably better to climb elsewhere.

Approach: Follow the main trail into the canyon. Where the canyon splits take the south fork. There are many trails here, but the easiest option is to follow a good trail above the right bank of the creek. Follow this trail around to the south side of the Mescalito where it drops back into the creek. (30 min.) Continue up the beautiful canyon until it forks again; take the south (left) fork. After 10 minutes of rough boulder hopping, you will be at the point where the bushy terrace underneath the wall intersects the creek bed (30 min). A faint trail cuts into the bushes, leading up above slabs and over some cliff bands to the base of the wall. The huge wall directly above the point where the trail meets the cliff is the Adventure Punks area. Adventure Punks is the curving, 500' high, left-facing corner. For the Challenger area continue east along the base of the cliff for 10 minutes (very bushy), scrambling up into a large amphitheater of dark, red rock split by many clean-cut crack and corner systems. 1.9 miles, 1000' elevation gain, 1¼ hrs. Routes are described from right to left.

❶ X15 540' 5.11b *
Jay Smith, Paul Van Betten. 1986.
Double Rack to 4". Triple 1"- 2.5", Rp's, double medium stoppers.
X15 follows the gigantic east-facing corner that borders the right edge of the Challenger amphitheater, one of the most striking lines in Red Rocks. The climbing is varied and demanding, culminating in a dramatic 11a friction traverse to escape out of the top of the corner.
Start on a good ledge 10' above the ground. There are good cams in a crack just left of the main corner.
1. 180' 5.10d Climb an easy chimney, passing a couple of chockstones of soft, white rock. Above this, continue up a steep and sustained thin crack with some flaky rock. This eventually eases to a hand crack. Belay on a huge ledge.
2. 150' 5.10b Continue up the beautiful, red corner above on surprising holds. Belay on #1+2 Camalots on the highest ledge, below an ominous offwidth.
3. 100' 5.10d A short struggle up the offwidth leads to a rest before a punchy thin crack crux, then an easier hand crack leads to a beautiful small ledge where the main corner splits. Belay here on #.5,.75,1 Camalots.
4. 110' 5.11b A bold pitch. Move up into the corner on the left. A thin move (smallest Rp can be placed above your head) leads to a good Tcu crack. Up this to the roof, step down and traverse left with very thin friction moves to reach the left end of the roof (.75 Camalot) Move right past a bolt to a ledge, and continue up an easy corner for 30' to a ledge on the left with a bolted anchor.
Descent: Rappel to the anchor at the top of Enterprise. 3 more raps lead to the ground. A single 70m or two ropes.

❷ Exocet 530' 5.11a
This route climbs a pretty corner and flake system to the left of the second and third pitches of X15. It starts on the big ledge above the first pitch of X15, which can be reached by traversing out right from the first belay of Enterprise and climbing a dirty corner. A much better start is the first pitch of X15.
1. 180 5.10d X15 Pitch 1.
2. 120' 5.10d Climb the small left-facing corner at the left end of the belay ledge. Continue up the steep lieback flake above, stepping right to belay on a small ledge.
3. 120' 5.10d Continue up the flake. Where it ends, make a few face moves to the beautiful small ledge below the last pitch of X15.
4. 110' 5.11a Finish up the last pitch of X15.
Descent: Rappel to the anchor at the top of Enterprise. 3 more raps lead to the ground.

❸ Enterprise 395' 5.11a *
Jay Smith, Randal Grandstaff. 1986.
Rp's, extra medium wires, double cams to 2", single #3- #4 Camalot.
An elegant series of left-leaning corners. Mostly good rock, but watch out for the occasional loose block. Start at the base of a left-facing corner, about 15' left of the obvious chimney of X15.
1. 165' 5.10a Climb the corner taking the left option each time it branches. Belay on a small ledge 25' below a large roof using #2 Camalots.
2. 70' 5.10b Up the crack to the roof (#3.5 Camalot), step down and make a delicate traverse left on fragile rock. Make an awkward step around the left end of the roof and continue for 20' to a ledge on the right, beside a fixed nut and sling.
3. 110' 5.10b Climb easy flakes on the left to a ledge. Continue

up the main crack, with an awkward move out of the top of a small slot. Belay on a ledge a few feet higher.
4. 50' 5.11a Climb the crack left of the main corner and where it curves left, move across right into the main corner. Immediately move out right and climb a ramp to the anchor.
Variation: 45' 5.12a Climb straight up the corner on the right. Excellent. *2 each #00,01 Tcu's.*

❹ Voyager 405' 5.11b **
Jay Smith, Paul Van Betten. 1986.
Double cams #00 Tcu- #4 Camalot. Rp's.
This route climbs the left-slanting corner/flake to the left of the upper pitches of Enterprise, one of the longest, cleanest and most aesthetic crack pitches in Red Rocks.
1.165' 5.10a Enterprise pitch 1.
2.100' 5.10b Follow the second pitch of Enterprise but instead of stopping at the belay ledge continue to the higher ledge. Move left down this to an anchor at the base of the crack.
3.140' 5.11b Climb the crack, moving out left at the top and continuing up the runout face to a bolted anchor.
Descent: A long rappel into the huge corner of Steep Space. One more rappel to the ground.

❺ Invasion of Privacy 180' 5.11c ❗
Single rack to 1.5", Rp's.
A serious old-school face climb with long runouts and creeky rock. Check out the original rap anchor at the top of the second pitch, which consists of a thread around the point where the two suitcase sized blocks, perching on the ledge, lean against each other. Two bolts now provide a slightly safer alternative. Start below a thin flake in the smooth wall to the left of the first pitch of Enterprise.
1. 140' 5.11c Climb the flake past a bolt (crux) and continue past dubious gear in a small flake, making 5.10 moves to the next bolt. Continue up the face (3 b's) making another long runout to the sixth bolt, in a small roof. Traverse left and move up to an anchor on a ledge.
2. 40' 5.10d Up the wall (2 b's) then make a long runout (5.9) to the death block ledge.
Descent: 1 long rap with two ropes.

❻ Starfighter 120' 5.11a
Robert Finlay, Paul Van Betten. 1986.
This route starts 20' to the right of Steep Space. Climb a flake up into a ramp on the steep wall. Up this, then over the bulge at the top (crux). Continue on the ramp above, moving left at its top into the corner of Steep Space.
Descent: Rap 130' to the ground.

❼ Steep Space 600' 5.10d
Paul Van Betten, Paul Crawford, Paul Obenheim. 1986.
This route climbs the huge corner at the back of the Challenger amphitheater, climbing through the cave-like feature on the right and up a line of flakes and corners in the wall above. It's a safe bet that the rap anchors will need to be replaced.
1. 130' 5.9 Climb the corner to a bushy ledge.
2. 120' 5.10d Continue up the corner, then move up into the huge, roofed chimney on the right. Climb through the roof and continue to a belay ledge.
3. 130' 5.10c Continue up thin cracks above to an anchor.
4. 100' 5.10c Follow cracks on the right to an anchor below a roof.
Descent: Rappel with two ropes.

Challenger Wall - Left side

❽ Astral Winds 130' 5.11b
Paul Van Betten, Sal Mamusia. 1986.
Starting just left of Steep Space, climb up to reach a left-trending line which is followed to the belay of Jupiter 2.

❾ Jupiter 2 510' 5.11c ✱✱
Paul Van Betten, Sal Mamusia. (Pitches 1&2). Paul Van Betten, Nick Nordblom, Paul Crawford. 1986.
Single rack to 3", double 1"-2.5", Rp's.
The crux of this route is a beautiful 30' high corner at the top of the second pitch. The rest of the route offers varied and enjoyable 5.10 climbing. Start 60' to the left of Steep Space, below a deep V-groove which starts 30' up the cliff.
1. 130' 5.9+ Zig-zag up shallow grooves to the deep V-groove. Up this, taking the right branch where the corner splits. At the top, move right to a nice ledge.
2. 100' 5.11c A crack in a shallow right-facing corner leads to a stance below a clean-cut left-facing corner. Up this (crux) to a good ledge.
3. 100' 5.10d Move up and right (Rp's), then back left to a bolt. Move left past this onto a slab, mantel, then make a bold move (5.9+) right into a thin crack. Up this to a huge block, go around the left side and up to a nice ledge on top.
4. 90' 5.8 Move left to a bushy groove, up this for 40', then traverse over to a groove on the right. Up this to a ledge.
5. 80' 5.10d Excellent climbing up the steep corner/crack on the right leads to an easier wide crack. Up this for 25', then traverse left past blocks to a great ledge around the corner to the left.
5a. 75' 5.11d Climb the pretty corner to the left of the normal finish.
Descent: Six single rope rappels, starting with two down Jupiter 2, then four down Challenger.

❿ Challenger 560' 5.10d ✱✱
Jay Smith, Randal Grandstaff. 1986.
Single rack to 2.5",double 0.5, 0.75, 1 Camalots. Rp's.
An excellent varied climb.
The route starts 15' to the left of Jupiter 2, below a wide slot capped by a large roof.
1. 90' 5.10d Climb up to the roof. Undercling out right and pull around the lip, burly. Continue to an anchor.
2. 90' 5.10d. Climb the crack on the right and pull up into a nice right-facing corner with a tips crack. This crack gradually widens to hands.
3. 75' 5.10b. Move into the crack on the right. This becomes a right-facing corner which leads to the left end of a long roof.

Move left around the roof and up to an anchor.
4. 70' 5.10c Head up the right-facing corner, then move right past a loose flake to an anchor on Jupiter 2. The last two pitches of Jupiter 2 provide a really nice finish to this route.
Descent: 4 single rope rappels.

⓫ Space Cowboy 250' 5.10b
Paul Van Betten, Ron Olevsky. 1986.
Single rack to 3.5". Rp's.
Start as for Challenger .
1. 90' 5.10b Climb the first 15' of Challenger, then move left and climb into a deep V-groove, up this taking the right branch when the corner splits. This leads to the anchor of Challenger.
2. 90' 5.10a Climb the left-facing corner above. Move onto a block on the left, then back into the corner on the right. Up this into a smooth, black corner. Thin moves with thin protection lead up the corner until a traverse right leads the anchor of Challenger.
3. 70' 5.10a Steep moves lead into the right-facing corner above. Up this to a ledge on the left.
Descent: 3 single rope raps.

⓬ Mission Control 160' 5.11d
Mike Tupper, Paul Van Betten, Paul Crawford. 1986.
Single rack to 3", Rp's.
This route climbs the left-facing corner which starts above a tree just to the left of Space Cowboy.
Climb up into the corner. Climb the corner (b) and at its top continue straight up into a thin crack, (b) up this to an anchor.

⓭ Right Stuff 210' 5.11b ✱
Jay Smith, Paul Van Betten. 1986.
Single rack to 3", Rp's.
The first pitch of this route winds around a lot; careful rope management is required to keep the rope drag reasonable.
1. 120' 5.11b Climb a deep corner to a small ledge. Move left and up into underclings which are followed leftwards to a stance on a big flake. Move up, then traverse left into a right-facing corner. Up this (crux) to a ledge.
2. 90' 5.10a Climb the big corner past the roof to an anchor.

⓮ Explorer 100' 5.10d
Paul Van Betten, Jay Smith. 1986.
Single rack to 3", double to 0.75".
This route climbs the roof to the left of the previous route. Start 20' left of the deep corner at the start of the Right Stuff. Climb a thin corner to the roof (5.10b). Burly moves out the roof (5.10d) lead to an easier crack. Anchor 25' higher.

Adventure Punks Area

This is the wall above the western end of the terrace below the north face of Juniper Peak. The most obvious feature of the wall is the huge left-curving corner of Adventure Punks.
Approach: Use the Challenger Wall approach.

Adventure Punks 550' 5.10d ✱✱
Richard Harrison, Sal Mamusia, Paul Van Betten. 1983. The story was that when Mamusia was following the last pitch, he fell and pulled Harrison onto the anchor. A pin that was half of the anchor pulled and Harrison and Mamusia shock loaded the other half of the anchor, a ¼ inch bolt. When I asked him about it years later Harrison said he didn't remember it being that bad, but sure enough on a subsequent ascent the last pitch ended at an old ¼ inch bolt with a tattered old sling and loose peg hanging from it.

Single rack to 4". For last pitch double 4"- 7".
This is a great route up one of the bigger lines in Red Rocks. The rock is excellent and the climbing interesting and sustained. The route now has new anchors.
The most obvious feature of the wall is the huge left-curving corner which starts about 150' up the cliff. The steep, brown slab below the corner is split by a long, attractive left-facing flake. Start on a sloping ledge 15' above the base of the cliff, directly below the flake.
1. 120' 5.10b Climb up and left on slabby rock, then make a scary traverse right (5.9 with no protection) to the base of the flake. Excellent liebacking leads up the long flake system to

an anchor.

2. 110' 5.10b Climb up an awkward left-facing corner (pin) into the base of the main corner. Twin cracks and shallow corners in the back of the main corner lead to an anchor.

3. 80' 5.10a Continue up the beautiful, varnished corner to an anchor.

4. 90' 5.10b Move across right into the deep corner. Climb up this for 25', then step left and make awkward moves up a rounded groove to reach a superb finger crack. Follow this till it ends, then face climb up for a few moves before traversing right to an anchor in an alcove.

Variation: 5.9 Instead of stepping left, continue up the main corner to the same anchor, also excellent.

5. 120' 5.10d Continue up the wide crack in the back of the awkwardly slanting corner until it is possible to move onto the face on the left, which leads to a ledge and anchor.

Descent: Rap straight down the route with a single 80m or two shorter ropes.

MESCALITO

This is the 1000' high, red-capped pyramid that splits Pine Creek Canyon into north and south forks. Most of the routes on this formation involve climbing up 3 or 4 pitches then rappelling. However, I would recommend a trip to the summit at least once, to enjoy the amazing scenery and interesting descent. Good candidates for this excursion would be Cat in the Hat or Dark Shadows.

Descent: Mescalito is a real summit with no easy way off. For experienced climbers familiar with the route, Cat in the Hat provides a very efficient descent which starts with a rappel down the summit chimney, then continues over a small tower and scrambles down very exposed third and fourth class slabs to the anchor above pitch six. Rappels lead to the base from here. This can be done with a single 70m rope if you are prepared to do a little easy downclimbing.

There is a descent into the south fork of Pine Creek which does not involve rappelling, but is long and complicated. It starts by heading down into the saddle to the west of the Mescalito. From the saddle the route continues up the steep, broad ridge above, slightly to the north of the ridge line. After several hundred feet the ridge narrows and becomes almost horizontal. At this point an unusual windblown pine tree to the left of the ridge is a useful landmark. Go down a short, steep gully on the left just before the tree. At the bottom of the gully, contour west on ledges which lead to a long, broad ledge system which leads gradually down to the west. The ledge system eventually ends a couple of hundred feet above the wash. At this point it is necessary to scramble down a small cliff band

Johnny Switchblade 120' 5.10a
Nick Nordblom, Paul Van Betten and a cast of thousands. March 1986.
This route climbs the sparsely bolted rib to the left of the first pitch of Adventure Punks.

Cocaine Tiger 140' 5.11d
Crawford, Van Betten, Harrison, Charles Cole, Rusty Reno. 1986. Rp's, Single rack to 2.5".
Climb the hand crack to the right of Rooster Ranch to a roof. Pull the roof on the left side (3 b's) and up to an anchor.

Rooster Ranch 280' 5.10c
Paul Obenheim. 1986.
This is a two pitch route protected mostly by bolts. It starts up the varnished rib to the left of the previous two routes.

(cairns) to reach a tree at the top of a steep, dirt gully which leads down to the wash. Most of the route is marked with cairns, but it is still hard to follow and will take several hours.

There is a route into the north fork of Pine Creek which no-one seems to find on the first (or even second) try. From the summit, traverse west along the ridge until an easy scramble (cairns) leads down and north towards a terrace. (Dark Shadows ends on the same terrace). Follow cairns leading west, over a notch and into a large bowl that drains north. Continue following cairns across the bowl, then back to the far west side, aiming for the furthest west gully. Scramble down this gully for about 100' to a fixed anchor. A double rope rap leads to a gully. Walk down about 300' to a rap anchor on a tree. 140' rap ends in the north fork of Pine Creek about 5 minutes upstream from the start of Dark Shadows.
Pick your poison!

For those who want a bit more after climbing the Mescalito, it is possible to follow the ridge west all the way to the limestone crest. This involves a great deal of fourth class as well as a couple of fifth class pitches and makes for a great day out with a distinctly alpine feel. The best descent from the limestone is to scramble down to the south to get into the drainage immediately to the south of the Mescalito. The descent of this drainage is easy to follow and reasonably fast, but includes a coupe of short sections of fifth class downclimbing and/or a short rappel or two.

Mescalito - South Face

The south side of the Mescalito is an impressive wall that so far only has one full length route, up its right edge. The first two routes climb cracks on a buttress that leans against the base of the wall at its eastern end. These routes sit a couple of hundred feet above the canyon floor and are reached by scrambling up a right-slanting ramp, finishing with some 5.6 climbing up a chimney to reach a ledge below the routes.

Approach: Follow the main trail into the canyon, and where the canyon splits take the south fork. There are many trails here, but the easiest option is to follow a good trail on a flat area above the right bank of the creek. Follow this trail around to the west side of the south east buttress. Drop back down into the wash and continue upstream a short distance to the base of a very impressive wall. 45 minutes.

Andy Reger on pitch 5 of Cat in the Hat.
Page 234. Photo: Matt Kuehl

OB Button 185' 5.10b *
Paul Obenheim. 1982.
Single rack to 4", triple 1.25"-3".
This route climbs a thin-hands crack in the face to the left of OB Fist.
1. 110' 5.10b Up the crack then over a roof, where the crack thins. Continue to a ledge.
2. 75' 5.9 Climb the face above to an anchor.

OB Fist 110' 5.9
Nick Nordblom, Paul Van Betten. 1982.
Single rack to 6", double 2.4"- 4".
The most obvious feature of this section is a left-facing corner with a fist crack capped by a roof. Climb the crack, over the roof to a ledge.

Crack Rock 735' 5.12a *
Tom Moulin, Brian Bowman. December 2006.
Single rack to 4", triple 0.5"- 0.75", 2". Rp's.
This route climbs a very impressive thin crack splitting a headwall high on the right hand side of the south face, almost directly above the previous two climbs. This crack provides a bold and strenuous pitch in a wildly exposed position. Intimidating.

The route is best approached from the base of Cat in the Hat, by scrambling up and left for 100 yards onto a large, flat platform on the left edge of the broad gully. From here continue up and left, and belay below an obvious left-facing corner.
1. 150' 5.9 As the wall ramps up, gain the left-facing, flaring corner. 20' below a roof in the corner, step left to flakes and a shallow right-facing corner. At the top of the corner, step left to another right-facing corner with a small ledge.
2. 225' 5.10c Follow the right-facing corner, then sparsely protected face climbing leads up and right to a slab with a mango sized undercling. Go directly up through the slab, pulling around a small roof and heading up and left on easier terrain to a ledge 30' below the headwall. Intricate and very poorly-protected.
3. 140' 5.12a Start up the headwall, moving right then back left to the crack (crucial, blind #3 Camalot placement on the left). Continue up the crack to a belay in a small alcove where the angle eases.
4. 120' 5.9 Continue up the crack to a large bush.
Descent: The descent is from a series of trees and bushes to the east of the climb. Scramble up the gully to a large, flat buttress on the right. Rappel the bushy gully behind the buttress to a large pine tree. From here three 70m rappels lead back to the base of the route.

Mescalito - South East Buttress

This is the left skyline of the Mescalito when viewed from the parking lot. This feature is climbed by Cat in the Hat, one of the most popular multi-pitch moderates in Red Rocks. These routes are very sunny and warm.

Approach: Follow the main trail into the canyon and where the canyon splits take the south fork. There are many trails here, but the easiest option is to follow a good trail on a bench above the creek bed and below the East face of the Mescalito. Follow this trail around to the west side of the southeast buttress where a trail leads up the talus slope to a clearing at the base of an obvious left-slanting crack.
1.5 miles, 500' elevation gain, 40 minutes.

❶ The Grinch 500' 5.9
Larry DeAngelo, Karsten Duncan. Mid-2000's.
Start up the hill to the left of Cat in the Hat.
1. Climb the varnished wall to a belay near the top of Cat in the Hat's first pitch.
2. Climb a jam crack on the face to the left. Above is a cavernous overhang: skirting its left edge is dicey (5.9).
3. Climb a short, sandy chimney, then step right onto a varnished face and go up the crack above.
4. Continue up moderate varnished rock to the shoulder where pitch 5 of Cat in the Hat ends.

❷ Cat in the Hat 1090' 5.7 **
Bruce Eisner, Joanne Urioste. April 1976.
Single rack to 4", Double cams 0.6"- 3".
This is one of the most amenable multi-pitch routes in Red Rocks. Big ledges, fixed anchors, excellent rock and a sunny location give it a non-intimidating feel. It is commonly done by rappelling from the top of the 5th pitch. Continuing to the top of the Mescalito makes for a great adventure, but greatly increases the overall seriousness of the route.
Start below an obvious left-slanting crack.

1. 150'. 5.5 Climb the left-slanting crack for 75' then move up to the right to an optional belay at 90'. Continue the left-slanting fist crack above to a ledge. Continue the wide crack above to a belay on a big sloping ledge. Anchor out right. Wander up slabs to the base of a short, steep wall.
2. 50' 5.5 Boulder up a short, black wall to gain a ledge. From the left end of the ledge, pull over a small overhang into a left-facing corner. Up this to a ledge with a tree.
3. 120' 5.6 From the ledge 15' above the tree, climb a thin crack in the black face to the left of a small corner. Traverse left under a small, white roof to reach a finger crack. Up this to a ledge. Belay on slings around a block.
4. 50' 5.3 Step down and traverse right to a ledge at the base of a varnished wall split by a nice crack.
5. 110' 5.7 Climb the crack; when it ends go up and right making tricky moves past a bolt (crux). Continue with a serious runout to the anchor.
Most parties rappel the route from here with either a single 70m or two ropes.
6. 500' 4th class From the belay scramble up for 400' to the top of the lower buttress. From here cross the notch and climb to a tree at the base of the big chimney splitting the final band of red rock.
7. 120' 5.7 Climb the chimney, passing some steep, loose blocks. There is an anchor at the top of the chimney.
A short scramble leads to the summit.

❸ Bed of Nails 200' 5.9
B. Bindner and E. Holland. 1980's.
Big Bro's and cams to 12".
The big chimney to the right of the first pitch of Cat in the Hat.

❹ Rabbit's Arete 80' 5.10d
This route climbs the bolted, brown arete above the block belay at the top of pitch 3 of Cat in the Hat. Exposed and technical.

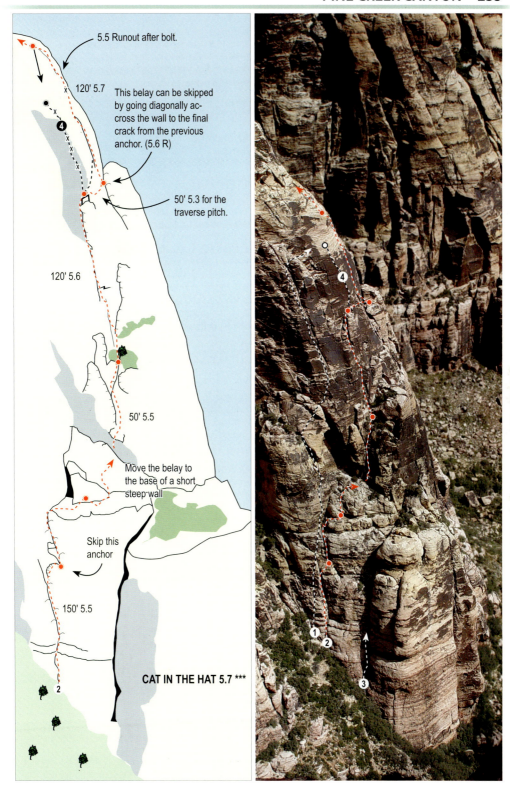

5.5 Runout after bolt.

120' 5.7

This belay can be skipped by going diagonally across the wall to the final crack from the previous anchor. (5.6 R)

50' 5.3 for the traverse pitch.

120' 5.6

50' 5.5

Move the belay to the base of a short steep wall

Skip this anchor

150' 5.5

CAT IN THE HAT 5.7 *

Mescalito - East Face

This is the heavily varnished wall that faces the Pine Creek pull out. It gets morning sun and afternoon shade.

Approach: Follow the main trail into the canyon and, where the canyon splits, take the south fork. After about 100 yards follow a trail up the bank to the right of the creek. This leads to a flat area at the base of the wall, from which all the routes are easily reached. 1.4 miles 500' elevation gain, 35 minutes.

The first group of routes described here are on the series of deep cracks and corners on the left side of the face. These routes finish at various points on Cat in the Hat, which provides a convenient descent route.

❶ The Wasp 340' 5.9+
Joe Herbst, Randal Grandstaff. December 1976.
Single rack to 4".
This route climbs the deep corner/crack which splits the lower portion of the South East Buttress.
1. 180' 5.9 Climb the huge corner, passing a big hole, to an anchor on the right wall.
2. 160' 5.9+ Continue up the corner for 20' to a roof. Undercling and layback around the roof, and continue up the nice, varnished crack to a belay on a ledge at the top of the corner.

❷ Black Widow Hollow 370' 5.9 *
Joe Herbst, Mark Moore. November 1976.
Single rack to 4" double wires.
This route climbs the next deep corner to the right of The Wasp. The long, smooth-walled chimney on the second pitch is a good warm up for Epinephrine, it is better-protected but harder than the chimneys on that route.
Start at the base of the obvious wide chimney.
1. 70' 5.7 Climb the blocky chimney to a belay beside a tree.
2. 210' 5.9 Climb the long, sustained chimney to a belay on a good ledge at its top. This pitch can be split by belaying in a big alcove 20' below the top of the chimney.
3. 100' 5.8 Climb the nice, varnished crack which splits the wall above. When the crack ends, move right into a V-groove which leads onto easy ground a short distance above the tree at the top of the second pitch of Cat in the Hat.
Descent: Rappel Cat in the Hat with one rope.

The next routes start on a terrace above a small cliff to the right of Black Widow Hollow.

❸ Pauline's Pentacle 275' 5.10a
Randal Grandstaff, Randy Marsh, Pauline Schroeder. 1982.
This route climbs the face to the left of Cookie Monster.
1. 110' 5.10a Start on the right edge of the face. Climb up through some large huecos and continue up and slightly left to an anchor.
2. 165' 5.9 Climb up a varnished corner on the left edge of the wall, and continue up the face above to an anchor.
Descent: Rappel with two ropes.

❹ The Cookie Monster 340' 5.7 *
Joe Herbst, Betsy Herbst. 1970s.
Single rack to 4".
This route climbs the big corner to the right of Black Widow Hollow. An enjoyable, well-protected moderate.
Starts below the huge corner at the left end of the terrace.
1. 140' 5.6 Climb the corner to a belay ledge.

2. 120' 5.7 Continue to a belay in an alcove.
3. 80' 5.7 Continue up the crack to the top.
Descent: Traverse left to reach easy ground a short distance above the tree at the top of the second pitch of Cat in the Hat.

To the right of Cookie Monster is an impressive prow split by a crack system. This is the line of The Walker Spur.

❺ The Walker Spur 350' 5.10b *
John Long, Lynn Hill, Richard Harrison. Spring 1981.
Single rack to 3", double; #1 Tcu, 0.5, 0.75, 1 Camalots.
This is an excellent route up an impressive line. Start just to the right of the prow.
1. 100' 5.10b Climb the easy face to a ledge below a bulge. Pull over the bulge (b) to a ledge. A crux move past a pin leads to a thin crack. Up this to an anchor at a small ledge at the bottom of the deep V-groove.
2. 150' 5.9 Continue with great climbing up the left arete of the V-Groove (5.9 R), then pull right over a bulge into a perfect hand crack. Up this to a belay at the base of a wide slot. Bolt and medium wires for the anchor.
3. 100' 5.7 Climb past the slot and the crack above to a ledge. Climb the left-slanting crack above to a big ledge. Traverse left on this to a rap anchor on Cat in the Hat.

❻ Pine Nuts 235' 5.10a
Chris Gill, Paul Ross, Todd Swain. December 1998.
Double cams 0.5"- 1.25".
This route climbs the face between the Walker Spur and When a Stranger Calls. Start 20' to the right of the prow.
1. 105' 5.10a Climb the highly featured face to the roof (2 b's). At a flake, make a burly pull over the lip with mediocre wires for protection. Continue to a bolted anchor.
2. 130' 5.8 The varnished face to an anchor on the left arete.

❼ When a Stranger Calls 350' 5.9
Randal Grandstaff, Steve Anderson. Spring 1981.
Single rack to 4", double 2"- 3".
This route climbs the first major crack system to the right of the prow climbed by The Walker Spur. The first pitch is excellent and is usually done as an end in itself.
1. 170' 5.9 The crux of the route is the runout face leading to the base of the crack. Once the crack is reached, easier climbing on good holds leads to a big pod. Move out right to a rappel anchor consisting of a nest of slings.
2&3 The route continues up the same crack system for 2 pitches to below triangular roof, exit left to a terrace and follow it left to reach Cat in the Hat.

❽ Crunchy Cat 150' 5.8
Single rack to 3", extra wires.
Start at the base of the initial crack of C11 H17NO3.
Trend out left onto the face, over a small roof (crux) and up the face to a ledge and rappel anchor shared with When a Stranger Calls. Runout and fragile.

❾ C11 H17NO3 535' 5.7
Bob Logerquist, John Williamson. April 1971.
Single rack to 6".
This route follows an obvious corner system up the east face of the Mescalito. Start at two parallel cracks 75' left of a huge left-facing corner, and about 30' right of When a Stranger Calls.
1. 170' 5.7 Follow either crack up into a chimney. Climb the

Mescalito East Face - Left side

Cat in the Hat, pitch 5

chimney to a ledge with bushes, then hand traverse left and belay in the corner.

2. 200' 5.6 Continue up the large right-facing corner. Move right under the roof and up to a belay in the chimney/cave.

3. 165' 5.6 From the cave go up the low-angled right-facing corner. After a white bulge, exit left, via cracks and plates, and up to the anchor on top of Cat in the Hat.

⑩ Mescalito Regular Route 1100' 5.7
Jeff Lansing, Peter Wist. 1968.

The first recorded technical route in Red Rocks. It starts by climbing the corner to the left of the huge block in the middle of the east face, and continues for about 150' to the top of a flake before traversing right into a huge flake/corner system. Follow this crack to its end, then move left and join Cat in the Hat a couple of hundred feet below the final chimney. Finish up Cat in the Hat.

In the center of the east face of the Mescalito a huge block leans against the base of the cliff. The next two routes climb the slab of beautiful, brown varnish to its right.

Left of Disco 130' 5.10c
Single rack to 2".

The route on the left. Follow an arete past a high first bolt. Pass a small roof and crack system and continue past a few more bolts to the shared anchors (6 b's).

⑪ This Ain't No Disco 140' 5.10a *
Randal Grandstaff, Randy Marsh. 1982.
Single rack to 3.5".

The right route up the slabby wall to an anchor (4 b's).

⑫ Welcome to Red Rocks 150' 5.12b *
Sal Mamusia, Paul Van Betten. 1986.
Cams to 1.5", Rp's, double #1- #3 stoppers.

An excellent stemming test piece.

This route climbs a very smooth 60' high corner which starts about 90' above the ground. The route starts just to the left of Pauligk Pillar.

1. 90' 5.7 Climb a left-leaning ramp to a belay (single bolt and gear) at the base of the corner.

2. 60' 5.12b Climb the corner to a bolt. A long sequence of wild moves using the left arete leads to a good hold in the corner. Easier moves lead to the top of the corner, then traverse 15' right to an anchor.

Variation: 5.11b It is possible to avoid the crux section (and the good climbing) by traversing out right on a horizontal and traversing back in higher up.

⑬ Pauligk Pillar 270' 5.7 *
Mr & Mrs. Roland Pauligk, Randal Grandstaff. 1981.
Double rack to 3". Optional 6".

This route provides some interesting corner work.

About 200' to the right of the huge block leaning against the middle of the face is a deep right-facing corner which after 270' ends on a ledge with a tree. This is the line of Pauligk Pillar.

1. 160' 5.7 Climb the corner past a mid-anchor. Continue on nice, varnished rock to a higher anchor.

2. 110' 5.7 Continue up the corner, face climbing past a couple of wide sections, to just below the top. Move out left and climb the face to the tree.

Rappel with a single 70m rope.

⑭ Y2K 515' 5.10a *
Todd Swain, Paul Ross. November 1998.
Single rack to 2", Rp's, extra small & medium wires.

Y2K climbs up the front of the narrow buttress to the right of Pauligk Pillar for two pitches, then traverses right to finish up the deep corner on the right. The climbing is mostly 5.7/8 except for a short pull over the roof on the first pitch and the last 20' of the final corner.

Start on top of a boulder at the base of an obvious, red right-facing corner capped by a roof.

1. 160' 5.10a Face climb past 6 bolts leading over the roof to a varnished face. Up this, following a thin crack and face (b) to an anchor on the left.

2. 165' 5.8 Continue up the left edge of the face then move back right up a white flake. Continue up the wall (3 b's) to a ledge and anchor.

3. 60' 5.4 Move up to a ledge then make a long traverse right (b) into a varnished corner.

4. 130' 5.9 The real crux. Climb the corner, which starts easily but rears up to vertical at the top. Thin stemming with small nuts for protection leads up this section to a ledge on the left. Follow easy rock up and left to an anchor.

Descent: 3 double rope rappels. The first rappel is a notorious rope snagger, pull as far to the left as possible.

⑮ Too Many Tantrums 220' 5.7
Francis Baker, Rex Parker. 2006.
Single rack to 3".

This route climbs the crack system 10' left of Splitting Hares.

1. 80' 5.7 Climb up to a cleft at the base of the corner system.

2. 140' 5.7 Continue up the corner, traversing right on horizontals just below the final roof of Splitting Hares, to reach the anchor of The Next Century. This pitch can be split on a good ledge at the end of the corner.

Descent: Rappel Next Century with two ropes.

⑯ Splitting Hares 225' 5.9
Ignazio Delgado, Francis Baker. September 2006.
Single rack to 3", double cams to 2".

Start just left of The Next Century in a corner capped by a white roof.

1. 85' 5.7 Climb the corner and continue up the varnished face to a ledge down and left of the anchors of The Next Century.

2. 140' 5.9. Continue up the long flake system above, eventually pulling a roof and moving right to the anchor of Next Century.

Descent: Rappel with two ropes.

⑰ The Next Century 200' 5.10d **
Todd Swain, Paul Ross. November 1998.
Single rack to 3", double 0.6"- 1".

Down and to the right of Y2K is another varnished pillar which marks the right edge of the East Face of the Mescalito. The second pitch is superb.

Start at the base of the pillar, to the right of a low overhang.

1. 80' 5.9 Climb the crack on the right to a ledge and continue up the thin corner to the right of the arete. Where the corner ends, move left around the arete and climb the face to an anchor.

2.120' 5.10d The thin slab above the anchor (2 b's) is the crux of the pitch. Above this continue up the face and arete (2 b's) to an anchor hidden over the top.

Descent: Rappel with two ropes.

Ride the Tiger

Skip this
anchor

16
15
16
15
12   13   14
15   16   17

Mescalito East Face - Right side

Mescalito - North East Corner

The northeast corner of Mescalito contains a huge corner with a cone of bushy and low-angled outcrops at its base. These routes get a little morning sun, but are generally shady.

Approach: Use the approach to Dark Shadows for Deep Space and the routes to its right. For the routes to the left of Deep Space use the East Face approach and contour around right to the base of the left side of the cone.

❶ Ride the Tiger 600' 5.9
Nick Nordblom, Randal Grandstaff. 1982.
Climb the chimney on the left side of the cone for 200'. Belay beside some bushes below a big flake crack in the wall above the approach chimney.
1. 150' 5.7 Lieback the long flake system and belay at its top.
2. 150' 5.9 Move left around the arete and climb the face to the top of the buttress.
Descent: Rappel bushes down the left side of the buttress.

❷ Bloodline 300' 5.11a *
Single rack to 3", double .75" to 1", four 0.6".
This route follows a line up the buttress to the left of the third and fourth pitches of Deep Space. The fourth pitch is excellent.
1&2 300' 5.4 Climb the easy chimney to the top of the cone.
3. 180' 5.10c Climb the varnished wall to the left of the chimneys of Deep Space (10 b's) eventually reaching a ledge at the base of a big right-facing corner.
4. 100' 5.11a Climb the long finger crack splitting the face to the right of the big corner, finishing at an anchor above a roof.

❸ Deep Space 1200' 5.9
Joe Herbst and Larry Hamilton. May 1975.
Single rack to 5".
The route starts in the chimney on the right side of the cone, just left of the Dark Shadows Wall.
1&2 300' 5.4 Climb the easy chimney to the top of the cone.
3. 5.8 Climb the chimney and the varnished wall to its right.
4. 5.6 Continue up the crack system on easy rock to the base of an impressive slot.
5. 5.9 Airy and runout stemming leads up the wide chimney to a jam crack on the right wall, pass a small roof and belay.
6. 5.9 Climb the steep face, bearing right at a bulge then left to a belay below an offwidth crack (5.9). An old piton, predating the first ascent, used to exist on this pitch.
7. 5.8 The offwidth crack leads to a good ledge.
8. Easier climbing leads up and slightly left.
9. Go up, then right and eventually back left (5.7) to a hanging belay at the base of a jam crack.

10. Climb the crack to a belay in red rock.
Easier climbing continues for a couple of hundred feet to the summit of Mescalito.

❹ Centerfold 1100' 5.9+
Scott Woodruff, Larry Hamilton and Joe Herbst. April 1977.
Single rack to 3.5".
Centerfold is the long crack system a hundred feet right of Deep Space. The route starts and finishes in this long crack system, after venturing out onto the varnished wall to its right. Approach up the chimneys as for Deep Space.
1. 5.8 Face climbing leads up a short ways to an obvious ledge at the base of the crack system proper.
2. 5.9 Climb the right-most of two chimney-cracks above to an overhang. Traverse down and left, around a corner. Difficult climbing up a thin crack leads to another good belay.
3. 5.8 Follow the vertical gully above, moving right at its top to a comfortable ledge with a bush.
4. 5.7 Climb up a few feet and make an obvious, long traverse to a narrow ledge on the face to the right.
5. 5.8 Go up through the varnished section above, then angle up left to a narrow, exposed ledge with an ancient bolt anchor.
6. 5.9+ Climb down from the left side of the belay until it is possible to traverse a few moves and regain the main crack system. Follow this over a difficult bulge and belay.
7. An easy, obvious rope length to a dirty belay.
8. 5.7 A strenuous, though moderate, chimney and crack pitch.
9. Climb the smooth, left-hand chimney, simple but unprotected. This leads to ledges marking the end of the Centerfold crack. Hike and scramble west on ledges until it was possible to walk to the summit.

❺ The Flakes of Wrath 455' 5.10d R †
Nick Nordblom, Kevin Lowell. 1990.
This route climbs the wall to the right of Centerfold. Start 40' down and right of Centerfold.
1. 100' 5.8 Climb the runout varnished face to a nut and pin anchor.
2. 75' 5.8+ Continue up the steep black face to an anchor above a large varnish plate.
3. 150' 5.10b Climb a line of thin cracks on the left, passing some big varnished plates, then move right to an anchor at the base of a corner.
4. 130' 5.10d R Climb the corner and continue with a long dangerous runout up thin seams in the face above to an anchor on the shoulder of the wall.

Mescalito - Dark Shadows Wall

On the north side of Mescalito, a high wall rises straight out of the creek bed. This is Dark Shadows Wall, one of the gems of Red Rocks, which houses a concentration of great routes on beautiful, varnished rock. This wall gets almost no sun, but is quite sheltered from wind.

Approach: Follow the main trail into the canyon all the way to where the red cliff band on the right intersects the trail. The trail cuts back east above the cliff band, goes around a pair of huge boulders, then continues west along the hillside well above the creek bed, until it angles down to the base of the wall. 1.5 miles, 500' elevation gain. A casual 40 minute stroll.

❶ Negro Blanco 1100' 5.11a *
Lynn Hill, John Long, Richard Harrison. Spring 1981.
Single rack to 7".
The left side of the Dark Shadows wall is defined by a right-facing flake/chimney that runs almost the full height of the wall before dwindling into the face. This is a classic line, but the penalty clause is the first pitch, which is both hard and very bold. Lynn Hill took a forty footer here on the first ascent. Start to the right of the base of the chimney below a left-facing corner/crack.
1. 170' 5.11a Climb the corner/crack to a ledge below the

Negro Blanco

Dark
Shadows
Wall

chimney. Stay to the right, climbing a short corner for a few moves before moving left into the chimney. Place pro high in the chimney, step back down then lieback up the outside edge to a rest at the top of the slot. Move up and transfer into the corner on the left (crux). Continue to a ledge.

2. 50' 5.8 Climb up the wide crack to a comfortable belay (b) on top of a white flake.

3. 150' 5.8 Climb up the flake, and where it ends, face climb for 15' to a belay stance.

4. 100' 5.8 Go back left to a corner, climb it to its end, then face climb straight up to a ledge.

5. 100' 5.9 Face climb up to an obvious crack. Belay part way up this.

6. 150' 5.6 Continue up the crack which becomes a right-leaning ramp and eventually joins Heart of Darkness at the top of pitch 8.

❷ Lethal Weapon 90' 5.12b/c
Mike Tupper, Greg Mayer. Fall 1989.
Single rack to 3".
Follow Negro Blanco to the ledge above the initial corner. Continue up the corner on the right (b) to the roof. Make a very bouldery traverse (b) to a rest at the right end of the roof. Thin moves up the shallow corner above (b) lead to the anchor.

❸ Parental Guidance 170' 5.12a ★★
Mike Tupper, Greg Mayer. Fall 1989.
Single rack to 1.25".
The first pitch of this route is superb. Start just to the right of Negro Blanco, below a bolt above a small roof 15' up.

1. 80' 5.10d Unprotected moves (5.10b) gain the bolt. Face climb up (3 b's) then move right lo a ledge. Gain the amazing lieback flake above and follow it (b) to its end, where a move left leads to the anchor shared with Lethal Weapon.

2. 90' 5.12a After a hard boulder problem, zig-zag up the face to the right of the flare (4 b's.) Continue up the thin crack above the flare. Finally, thin face moves lead past two spaced bolts to the anchor.

❹ Short Circuit 60' 5.11b ★
Mike Ward, Nick Nordblom. 1989.
#00 - #1 Tcu's, #1 Camalot.
Start a few feet to the right of the previous route, on a boulder below a shallow right-leaning corner. Bouldery moves lead past a scary pin (#1 Camalot) and two bolts to the base of a short corner. Up this (2 b's) to the anchor.

❺ Risky Business 380' 5.10c ★★★
Mike Tupper, Greg Mayer. Summer 1985.
Single rack to 2.5", Rp's.
This is a tremendous route straight up the center of the Dark Shadows Wall. Generally, the protection is reasonable, although all the pitches have sections of quite pushy climbing. Start below the right end of an obvious arch about 70' up. There are two lines of bolts on the slab, Risky Business follows the bolts to the left. Getting onto the wall can sometimes be a problem when the water is high. If necessary, it is possible to traverse left along an easy horizontal all the way from the boulder above the small waterfall.

1. 90' 5.10b Climb a left-facing flake then continue (2 b's) to a step right (runout 5.9) to a right-facing flake leading to a small ledge 15' below the arch. Traverse left and move up to an anchor below a corner.

2. 100' 5.10b A runout leads up into the corner (b) then climb

the thin crack above to a second bolt. Move right and up to a horizontal crack. Continue up the face to an anchor.

3. 120' 5.10c Move left to a bolt. Delicate moves lead up to a horizontal, then traverse right to a crack. Follow the intermittent crack, past a steep section, then make an unprotected traverse up and left (5.8) to the base of a shallow right-facing corner. Up this (pin) to an anchor. A sustained and heady lead.

4. 70' 5.10a Climb the wall (4 b's) to a rap anchor on a ledge.

Descent: Rap with two ropes or a single 70m.

❻ Excellent Adventure 350' 5.11a ★★★
Mike Tupper, Greg Mayer. Fall 1989.
Single rack to 1.75", Rp's, extra wires.
Another great route which takes a parallel line to the right of Risky Business. The last pitch is an amazing piece of climbing, but very intimidating for both leader and second.

1. 150' 5.10c Climb the slab right of Risky Business (b) to the right end of arch. Follow the arch to the left until it is possible to pull over the lip. Continue left to a flake system. Follow this to a good ledge on top of the flake.

2. 110' 5.11a Go left to a bolt, then step up to clip a second bolt. Step down and make a technical series of moves to reach the better holds on the vague arete to the left. Continue up the arete (2 b's) eventually stepping left to an anchor about 10' below the edge of the huge roof.

3. 90' 5.11a The crux. Move up then traverse right (4 b's) above the lip of the overhang. A scary sequence of thin moves leads up to a bolt. Continue up the wall on flakes and shallow corners to reach the right end of a ledge. Step left to the anchor of Risky Business.

Descent: Rap Risky Business with two ropes or a single 70m.

❼ Sandstone Sandwich 150' 5.10c ★★
Bob Conz, George Smith, Jim Lybarger. July 1990.
0.5, 0.75 camalots.
A superb wall climb which leads to the first anchor of Excellent Adventure, and is actually a nicer way to start that route. Start up Excellent Adventure (2 b's) then move up and right to a horizontal crack (1',1.5" cams). Follow bolts trending leftwards up the wall (5 b's) to finish on the final few moves of the first pitch of Excellent Adventure.

❽ Heart of Darkness 1100' 5.11c
Richard Harrison, John Long, Lynn Hill. Spring 1981.
Single rack to 4", double 1.5"- 2.5".
This route climbs through the huge roof above the pitch 4 traverse of Dark Shadows, and continues to the top of Mescalito up a crack system on the buttress to the left of the final pitches of Dark Shadows.

1-4 340' 5.7 Climb the first 4 pitches of Dark Shadows. Belay on an anchor below the huge roof.

5. 150' 5.11c Move leftwards across the roof (peg and b) with a very bouldery move to reach good holds at the base of the wide crack springing from the lip. Continue up the easy crack to a blocky alcove. A short distance higher, just below a huge platform, head left for 25' on a ledge, to an anchor below a splitter crack.

6. 100' 5.8 Climb the crack to the end, then face climb up and slightly left to a ledge with an anchor.

7. 80' 5.9 A bulge (5.9) and steep, discontinuous cracks (5.9) lead straight to a roof that extends across the top of the wall. Traverse right a short distance and belay beneath the right-most of two cracks in the roof.

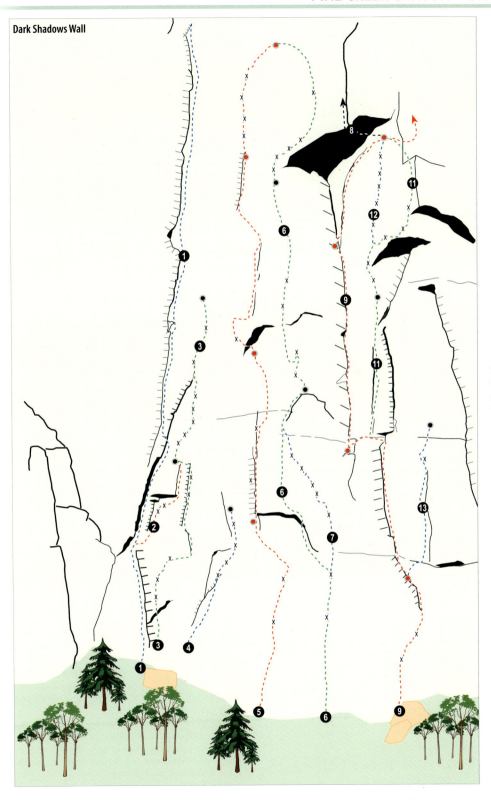

Dark Shadows Wall

8. 40' 5.8 Go over the roof then up a 2" crack to a huge ledge.
9. 100' 5.7 Follow the crack system up and slightly right.
10. 100'. 5.9 Pull over a bulge and face climb up.
11. 250' 4th Class easier climbing leads to the top.

❾ Dark Shadows 1040' 5.8 ***
John Martinet, Nick Nordblom. Fall 1979.
Single rack to 3".

The huge corner that gives this wall its name is an impressive sight from below. The route is described all the way to the top of Mescalito but the vast majority of ascents end on top of the fourth pitch. These pitches provide some of the best quality 5.7/8 climbing that you will ever do. The remainder of the climb is not quite as good quality as these first four pitches. Nevertheless, the complete ascent, when combined with the complicated descent of Mescalito, makes for an outstanding adventurous outing, but not one to be taken lightly. This fact is highlighted by the number of bivi sites on the upper pitches. Start on a boulder which rests against the cliff creating a small waterfall.
1. 70'. 5.5 Climb up and right (2 b's) to reach the base of a flake which slants back left to a hole with an anchor.
2. 75'. 5.6 Climb the beautiful, clean-cut right-facing corner above. At its top traverse left around the corner then step down to a perfect ledge.
3. 120' 5.8 Climb the huge corner to a small ledge on the left. The crux is at the bottom, after which perfect holds appear whenever things start to get difficult.
4. 75' 5.8 Climb the right-curving crack in the right wall to a ledge with an anchor.
Variation: 5.7 From the belay the original route climbed the wide crack in the back of the main corner before traversing out right to the same anchor.
Descent: With one 60m rope rappel straight down to the anchor of Chasing Shadows/Edge Dressing. Then to the second anchor of Dark Shadows. Two more raps to the ground from here.
To continue to the top; instead of stopping at the anchor continue around the corner to the right to another bolt anchor.
5. 120' 5.7 Follow a seam past a bolt to a roof. Continue up a widening left-trending crack to an anchor on the large platform at the top of a huge pillar.
6. 120' 5.7 Step across the void and climb the right side of a chimney with hueco's on the left wall. Go up 30' to a bolt on the left, then another 30' to an old piton anchor. Just above is a pod, above which the chimney turns into a dirty gully. Traverse left 20' then climb up 20' to an anchor on a ledge at the base of a crack.
7. 120' 5.7 Climb the crack to a small ledge below a roof.
8. 60' 5.7 Go up the right side of the roof, through a crack to a bushy ledge. Continue to a higher ledge below broken twin cracks.
9. 110' 5.7 Climb the twin cracks to a varnished ledge with one bolt.
10. 170' 5.8 Go up a right-facing corner to a huecoed roof then continue to the huge tree ledge a rope length or so below the summit of the Mescalito.

❿ Lost Shadows 340' 5.9
This appears to be a very old route which somehow got lost over the years.
1&2 130' 5.6 Climb the first two pitches of Dark Shadows but instead of traversing left to the normal belay, set up an anchor

at the top of the corner.
3. 70' 5.7 Continue up the wide corner/crack above, then move left to the anchor of Chasing Shadows.
4. 115' 5.9 Move back right and climb up to the large roof. Traverse right (b), then continue up the arete to reach the anchor above pitch four of Dark Shadows.

⓫ Chasing Shadows 315' 5.8+ *
Randy Marsh, Pier Locatelli. Summer 1990.
Single rack to 4".
An excellent route which can save the day if there is a traffic jam on Dark Shadows. The final pitch involves a straightforward but very exposed traverse above a large roof.
1&2 145' 5.6 The first two pitches of Dark Shadows.
3. 70' 5.8+ Climb the steep crack on the right, past some wide pods and a final bulge, to an anchor.
4.100' 5.8 Climb up the arete until above the roof on the right (2 b's). Traverse right (3 b's), then climb up the exposed arete (easier but runout) finally stepping left to the anchor of Edge Dressing.
Descent: As for Dark Shadows.

⓬ Edge Dressing 305' 5.10b *
Randy Marsh, Pier Locatelli. Summer 1993.
Single rack to 4".
1,2&3 215' 5.8+ Climb the first 3 pitches of Chasing Shadows.
4. 95' 5.10b Follow the line of bolts straight up from the anchor. The crux is a thin section passing the last two bolts before the Dark Shadows anchor.
Descent: As for Dark Shadows.

⓭ Slot Machine 150' 5.10b **
Bob Conz, Sal Mamusia. July 1990.
Single rack to 1.75", rp's, extra small wires.
A very good tips crack. Protection is decent, but awkward to place. Climb the first pitch of Dark Shadows to the hole. From here move right to the base of the crack. Up the crack, and when it fizzles, face climb (b) to a ledge and anchor.
Descent: 2 single rope rappels.

Peyote Power 1050' 5.9 *
Single rack to 4", extra set of wires.
A long route with some good climbing. The route is set up to be rappelled, so the scary last pitch is easily avoided.
This route climbs a tall face around to the right of the Dark Shadows Wall. Go about 100 yards up canyon from the base of Dark Shadows, then scramble up 10' to get on a wide ledge which slants up and left. Follow the ledge for about 100' to a point below a roof about 30' above the ledge.
1. 180' 5.7 Climb thin seams (5.7) with little protection, passing just to the right of the roof to reach a ledge with an anchor. Climb the short corner on the left, then move up into a right-slanting crack which is followed to an anchor.
2. 200' 5.7 Climb up 15' to a ledge. Follow the ledge rightwards and climb up the flake at its right end. Continue up a nice, thin crack above, then move right into a long left-facing flake which is followed to an anchor on the left.
3. 200' 5.9 Climb the short, steep wall just right of the anchor. Move left then back right up a flake. A short distance up the flake, launch out left onto an amazing wall of varnished rock. Wander up the wall past a short but punchy crux and continue to an anchor where the angle eases.
4. 170' 5.7 Climb straight up the face above (b) to an anchor just right of a chimney.

Mountain Skills guide Jay Foley on pitch 3 of Risky Business. Page 243.

5. 150' 5.7 Climb out right from the belay to avoid some steeper rock, then slant up left, eventually moving past a bolt to reach the crack/groove that is the continuation of the chimney. Continue up the crack/groove, past a roof to an anchor at the base of a rounded, white rib.

6. 150' 5.9 Climb up the left side of the rib, traversing into the white corner on the left. Up this for a short distance then move out right and climb the face (3 b's) to the top. Fragile rock and long runouts make this a worrying lead.
Descent: Rappel with two ropes.

The Paiute Wall

The Paiute Wall sits at the top of the north fork of Pine Creek Canyon. It is a remote wall with a complicated approach and descent. The wall was mentioned in Joanne Urioste's 1984 guidebook, after a recon mission by the Uriostes in the early 1980's. It took Joanne another 25 years to return and make the first ascent! Facing directly east, the wall gets sun until late morning, however its altitude makes it cold during the winter months.

Approach: There are 2 ways to access the Paiute wall.
(1) Hike up the north fork of Pine Creek Canyon. This is a long hike with lots of boulder hopping, bushwhacking and the occasional fifth class step. Near the top, the drainage is blocked by a cliff. Just before entering the big bowl below the blockage, scramble up a slabby buttress on the left, zig-zagging around obstacles (4th and easy 5th class) to reach a ledge system which leads back right to the base of the wall. 3 hrs.
If you use this approach, the descent is to go down the north shoulder of the wall, following the Bridge Mountain trail. Once you reach the saddle before the final 3rd class scramble up Bridge Mountain, descend slabs back south into Pine Creek.
(2) The Alternative approach is to hike in along the Bridge Mountain Trail from the crest of Rocky Gap road. The upper portion of Rocky Gap Road has become very rough in recent years and requires a high clearance vehicle. Follow the Bridge Mountain Trail to the saddle below the final 3rd class scramble up Bridge Mountain. 3-4 hrs.
To reach the base of the wall, descend the slabs from the saddle. Look for a ledge leading across an amphitheater of rock on the northern shoulder of the wall. Walk this ledge until oak brush forces you to climb down and around it. It may be desirable to rope up and climb a 200' horizontal pitch here, as the climbing is very exposed, but easy. After this traverse scramble up the obvious slabs to reach the base of the wall. The route tops out very close to the Bridge Mountain trail, which can be followed back to the trailhead.

❶ Original Route 510' 5.10b/c
Joanne Urioste, Josh Thompson. March 2009.
Double rack to 4".
This route climbs the obvious crack and corner system on the right edge of the main east face of the wall.
1. 190' 5.9 Start up a right-facing corner. Climb over a varnished flake and layback the finger crack above. Continue through a couple of squeeze chimneys and a bit of face climbing. Belay at a good stance about 8-10' above a small pine growing out of the rock. Save 2" to 3" cams for the belay.
2. 130' 5.9 Climb a very short distance up, then traverse left to reach a polished slab and a left-facing corner. Follow the corner up, with good gear and holds in a crack on the right. Belay at a sloping stance directly below the obvious steep, black cracks of the third pitch. The belay takes 1" pieces.
3. 190' 5.10b Start climbing the left of the two cracks above,

aiming for a chimney about 30' up. Climb the chimney for 15'. Pull out of the chimney and climb the hand and fist crack. Near the top of the pitch, and the wall, you will pull into an exit chimney. Climb to a tree at it's top and belay. Medium size cams for the belay.

From the Bridge Mountain Trail

North Fork of Pine Creek Canyon

BRIDGE MOUNTAIN - SOUTH FACE

The rest of the routes described in Pine Creek Canyon are on the south and east facets of Bridge Mountain. These sunny walls provide the biggest concentration of cold weather traditional climbs in Red Rocks.

① Pisces Wall 1500' 5.10d, A3
Andrew Fulton, Dan Briley. Spring 1997.
From near the top of the north fork of Pine creek Canyon, follow a bushy ramp back east to the base of the wall. 3hrs. The entire route can be rapped with two ropes.
This route is on the south face of the main summit of Bridge Mountain. The face is covered in unusual eyebrow features and also sports an enormous red eye in the middle. This is a long, mixed aid and free route on a high and remote face, it remains unrepeated and is obviously a big undertaking.

A Rope a Rubber Chicken and a Vibrator 350' 5.10a
This route is on the right, a long way up the north fork.
1. 5.6 Climb huecos to the right of a right-facing corner.
2. 5.10a Climb a right-facing corner, past a roof to a big ledge.
3. 5.6 Climb a crack, past a bush to the top.

Red Throbber Spire 470' 5.9+
Brian Kay, Dave Polari. 1993.
This is the name given to a tall, curving tower directly across canyon from the Dark Shadows Wall. The tower is a good 1000' above the canyon floor and requires a long and involved approach. Follow the approach to Out of Control, but follow a bushy gully which leads up and slightly west towards the base of the tower.
1. 165' 5.9+ Climb a runout corner to a ledge.

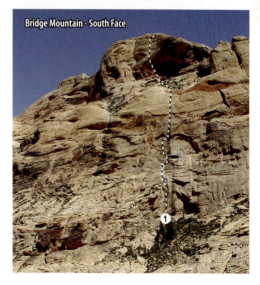

Bridge Mountain - South Face

2. 50' 5.8 Move the belay around a boulder on the ledge.
3. 140' 5.8 Another runout pitch. Climb up the face (b) to a small notch.
4. 120' 5.7 Continue up the arete to the summit.
Descent: Rappel to a notch, then down into a bowl. To return to the creek it is possible to do three raps down the gully directly below the tower; alternatively reverse the approach gully.

Out of Control Area

The following routes sit above a terrace a hundred feet or so above the base of the wall. They are directly across the canyon from the Northeast Corner of Mescalito. This is a very sunny and sheltered location. It holds the sun a bit later than the Brass Wall, making it a useful venue for a cold afternoon.

Approach: Follow the main trail into the canyon all the way to where the red cliff band on the right intersects the trail. The trail cuts back east above the cliff band, goes around a pair of huge boulders, then continues west along the hillside, well above the creek bed, until it starts to angle down to the base of the Dark Shadows Wall. At this point look for an open gully on the right where the lower cliff band starts to dwindle in size. Go up the gully to where a few feet of scrambling gain a large terrace. Follow the terrace to the right.

1.4 miles, 800' elevation gain, 45 minutes.

Pitch 2

6

Pitch 1 is hidden in a huge chasm.

1

2   3   4

?

5

❶ American Ninja 100' 5.10c *
Paul Van Betten, Robert Finlay. 1986.
Single rack to 1.5", Rp's.
Above the middle of the terrace is an obvious, clean-cut, red corner with a thin crack. Scramble up 50' to belay at the base of the corner. Climb the corner. Rap anchor on top. Thin moves and thin protection, but good climbing.

Indirect Proof 80' 5.10b
Greg Horvath, Noel Scruggs. 2009.
Single rack to 3", Rp's.
Start 10' right of American Ninja. A tricky, hard-to-protect layback leads up the left-facing corner. Exit right and continue up the easier (5.6) but unprotected face just right of the arete to reach the anchor of American Ninja.

Towards the right end of the terrace is a large left-facing corner. The white face to the left of the corner is split by the beautiful, long crack of Out of Control.

❷ Control Freak 100' 5.10c
Start 20' left of Out of Control. Climb a finger crack which arches left into a big crack system. Follow the crack to a big ledge. Traverse left to an anchor.

❸ Out of Control 130' 5.10c ***
Randal Grandstaff, Dave Anderson. 1986.
Single rack to 4", triple cams 0.75"- 2.5".
The crack. This is an excellent pure crack climb, starting with fingers then gradually widening to thin-hands before a short wide slot, and finally a burly roof with a rap anchor just above. A second pitch has been done.

❹ Remote Control 130' 5.9 *
Dave Anderson, Randal Grandstaff. 1978.
Single rack to 4", double 2"- 3" cams.
The huge left-facing corner to the right of Out of Control. A bit blocky in places.

The next route starts at the base of the big corner to the right of a the huge pillar that is below the right end of the terrace where the previous routes start. There is a mystery route up the steep, varnished face on the west side of this pillar.

❺ Nowhere Man 100' 5.8
Joanne Urioste and Karl Wilcox. 1990's.
Single rack to 4".
This route climbs an obvious deep cleft starting in a cave on the right side of the pillar. Climb up into the cave and exit by climbing left to right and squeezing out to the outer corner. Continue up the corner above to an anchor.

❻ The Hidden Persuaders 560' 5.9
Larry DeAngelo, George Wilson. 2011.
Single rack to 7".
This route starts about 100' above the base of the escarpment in a big chasm. From the bottom of Birdland scramble up and west until you come to a tunnel. At the back of the tunnel, boulder up and head west again until you get to a large chasm with a black, varnished wall. Boulder up to the start.
1. 100' 5.9 A necky pitch which requires careful rope management. Start on a boulder and make a move or two up to a horizontal in the left edge of the Chasm. Move up to a higher horizontal then climb up and right across the face (crux) to the crack/corner at the apex of the chasm. Up this to a belay ledge.
Move the belay left to below a big right-facing corner.
2. 100' 5.8 Climb the corner and traverse right about 50' and set up a belay.
3. 160' 5.7 Climb the hand crack and when it ends, go up the face for 40' then zig-zag left then right and set a belay below the varnish.
4. 200' 5.5 Climb the beautiful face until the angle eases into a large ramp. Set a belay near the top of the ramp.
Descent: Head east toward a small notch, passing some old pitons along the way. Rappel off slung boulders (The original Big Horn descent) until you can join the Birdland rappels.

Spectrum Area

The next seven routes described are on the 800' high buttress to the left of the Brass Wall. The most obvious feature is a huge, right-curving arch in the lower right hand corner, the line of Spectrum.

Approach: Follow the main trail into the canyon, all the way to where the red cliff band on the right intersects the trail. The trail cuts back east above the cliff band, and goes around a pair of huge boulders. At this point go up the steep hillside, trending right through bushes to the base of the huge arch.
1.3 miles, 600' elevation gain, 30 minutes.

❶ Rawlpindi 580' 5.7
Single rack to 4".
Start half a rope length to the left of Birdland, in the steep gully which is also a possible start for The Big Horn.
1. 160' 5.7 Climb fun rock up the steep gully, staying left at the overhang. Belay on a good stance.
2. 160' 5.7 Continue up steep gully/crack system to a small tree on the right. Beneath the tree, traverse right for 15 feet, and belay on a comfortable ledge.
3. 160' 5.7 Climb the steep, featured face above (2 b's), heading slightly right to an anchor.
4. 100' 5.7 Step right and head straight up blocky cracks, then face, to a bolted rap anchor.
Descent: With two ropes, rappel the top 2 pitches then continue down Birdland for two more raps.

❷ The Big Horn 700' 5.8+ *
Joe & Betsy Herbst, Matt McMackin, Randal Grandstaff. Late 70's.
Single rack to 4" , optional to 6", extra 0.75"- 1.75".
This route starts with the first two pitches of Birdland.
3. 50' 5.3 Move up and left into the huge chimney system bordering the left edge of the buttress.
4. 120' 5.8+ A crack splits the center of the varnished face to the left of the chimney. Climb the crack to a bolted anchor and rap slings. It is best to rap from here, although the route does continue for a couple more pitches to the top of the wall.

❸ Psycho Date 100' 5.10d
Brad Stewart, Danny Meyers. 1986.
Single rack to 1.75".

This route climbs the varnished face to the left of the second pitch of Birdland. Climb straight up the face (2 b's) to an anchor.

Valore 300' 5.8
Karl and Heidi Wilcox. 1999.
Single rack to 3", double to 0.75".

Valore starts just to the right and below the start of Birdland, in a grotto behind a huge boulder.
1. 120' 5.7 A loose and scary pitch. Climb out of the grotto, traverse somewhat right on a ledge, and then move up the right-hand side of the face (adequate protection available) some 30 feet to a protection bolt. From the first bolt, continue up to a second bolt another 30 feet up, then bear slightly left to a short crack that ends the pitch at a good-sized ledge and solid belay/rap bolts. This pitch, although only 5.7, requires some care in placing pro. It's also hard to see the bolts from the ground.
2. 150' 5.8 Climb the obvious and rather steep crack system directly above the belay. This pitch protects well. The crux is a technical bulge which rates at easy 5.8. Pitch two ends at a bolted belay/rap station just to the right of an off-width crack and just above a large ledge.
Descent: Rappel the route using two ropes.

❹ Birdland 560' 5.7+ ***
Mark Limage, Chris Burton. 2001.
Single rack to 3".

This route connects the lower pitches of The Big Horn with the final pitches of Spectrum to create a superb, sustained route at the grade. As an added bonus, it also provides a convenient rappel descent for Spectrum. Start below the leftmost of two obvious, long cracks which split the varnished buttress to the left of the huge arch of Spectrum. This is a few yards above a huge boulder which leans against the base of the cliff, forming a tunnel.
1. 110' 5.6 Climb the left crack to an anchor on a tree ledge.
2. 110' 5.7 Climb straight up from the anchor, then follow the crack in the wall to the right of the main chimney to reach a ledge. Continue up the steep corner above. At the top move up and right under a block to reach an anchor at the right end of a big ledge
3. 85' 5.7+ Climb up and right for 10' into a short left-leaning corner. At the top of the corner traverse left past a bolt until it is possible to move up into a steep crack which is followed to a small ledge. Head up and right to an anchor.
4. 95' 5.6 Head up 20' to a horizontal crack, move right then follow thin, discontinuous cracks and seams up and right across the face to an anchor.
5. 95' 5.7+ Move up and right to a thin, varnished crack which is followed over a bulge, then up a varnished slab to an anchor on a tiny ledge.
6. 75' 5.7 Climb up, passing just right of a small roof. Continue up and right to an anchor in a small right-facing corner. A fragile and runout pitch, not recommended.
Descent: Rappel with a 70m rope.

❺ Spectrum 640' 5.11a *
Jay Smith, Randal Grandstaff. 1989.
Single rack to 3", double 1.5"- 2.5".

Although the crux roof is a great piece of climbing, the rest of the route is at a much lower grade. Perhaps the best way to climb Spectrum is to use a point of aid to get off the ground on the variation first pitch then three points of aid on the roof and a mediocre 5.11a becomes a tremendous 5.9.
Start at the base of the huge arch.
1. 60' 5.9 Climb the corner to an anchor 15' below the roof.
2. 90' 5.10b R Climb across the face below the roof, stepping down to a bolt anchor. Continue traversing more easily for 30' to an anchor at the base of a black corner.
Variation: 5.10d. This variation leads straight up to the anchor in the middle of the traverse. Start 15' right of the regular route. Climb a crack through the undercut base, then climb the easier face up and right to the anchor.
3. 100'. 5.7 Climb the black corner to a point 15' below a roof. Move left and climb up the face, then across left to a ledge at the base of another corner.
4. 110' 5.9 Climb the corner, over a bulge (5.9). Continue in the upper corner until it is possible to move out right to belay at the base of a short crack.
5. 90' 5.7 R Traverse up and right across the wall (good but spaced small wires), staying low until it is possible to move up into a crack which turns into a large flake. Belay on #2,#3 Camalots at the top of the flake.
6. 40' 5.11a Move left and make powerful moves through the first roof. Traverse left under the second roof and belay in a good crack just around the corner.
7. 150' 5.8 Continue up the crack for 100' until it is possible to traverse left on a horizontal and step down to the belay below the steep finger crack of Birdland
8. 60' 5.7+ Climb the Birdland crack to an anchor.
Descent: Rappel Birdland with a 70m rope.

❻ Brass Balls 400' 5.10d
Don Borroughs, Gary Fike. December 1997. The upper part of this route was climbed by Steve Bullock and Mark Gallen in 1994.
Single rack to 6".

This route climbs the large corner/gully to the right of the buttress containing Spectrum and Birdland. The base of the gully is blocked by a huge pinnacle. The route starts up the crack on the left side of the pinnacle. Start on a bushy ledge 30' above the base of the cliff, below a smooth bulge which blocks access to the crack.
1. 80' 5.10d Pull over the bulge (3 b's) and follow the crack to an anchor where it deepens into a chimney.
2. 100' 5.9 Climb the right edge of the chimney to the top of the pinnacle. Step across the gap and continue up the big right-facing corner until a traverse right under an overhang leads to an anchor in a small alcove.
3. 80' 5.7 Continue up the corner above, then traverse under an overhang to an anchor. **Variation:** Climb the hand and fist crack to the right of the regular route. If you do this variation traverse right 15' below the top of the second pitch and set up a belay at the base of the crack.
4. 70' 5.9 Climb the awkward corner on the left, and the easy chimney above, to an anchor beside a tree.
5. 70' 5.9+ Climb the slot above, past a roof and continue to an anchor
Descent: Rappel with at least a 60m rope.

Spectrum Area

The Brass Wall

When looking at Bridge Mountain from the Pine Creek parking lot, there are large areas of very dark varnish at the base of the south face. The area around these varnished walls is called the Brass Wall. This is a very sunny and warm location which consequently is very popular during colder weather.

Approach: Follow the main trail into the canyon to where a ridge comes down from the right end of the red cliff band. A trail winds up the left side of this ridge. Once above the cliff band go left, then head up the slope to the base of the wall. 1.25 miles, 600' elevation gain, 30- 40 minutes.

Brass Wall - Left side.

The following route is at the left end of the Brass Wall, about 40' to the left of the arete of Ripcord.

❶ Freefall 160' 5.11c
Jay Smith, Nick Nordblom. 1989.
Climb up into a right-facing corner capped by a small roof. Climb the corner, pull the roof, and continue up the long, steep wall above, trending left to an anchor (8 b's).

❷ Ripcord 410' 5.12a *
Jay Smith, Nick Nordblom. 1989.
Double cams to 3".
This route starts up the arete where the black varnish ends, then moves left to climb a long corner and crack system on the overhanging wall to the left. This is a very exposed and exciting climb and the final corner is superb.
Start below the varnished arete.
1. 90' 5.12a A bouldery sequence of moves leads past a bolt onto a featured arete. After a few moves, easy climbing on large huecos (2 b's) leads up the arete to an anchor.
2.110' 5.10d Move left and make a runout past a bolt (10a) into a corner. Up this (5.8) with poor pro. As the corner steepens the protection gets better but the climbing gets harder. At the top exit right to a ledge and anchor.
3.110' 5.11d A long, strenuous pitch. Follow bolts up the face to the left of the crack, with crux moves to gain a small roof. Move right and follow the pumpy crack (bolts, pins & fixed wires) to a ledge and anchor.
4. 100' 5.11b Continue up the left-facing corner, climbing over a small roof (5.11b). Necky climbing up the final corner (5.10c), with a #00 Tcu for protection, leads to a small ledge with an anchor.
Descent: Rap down the route with a single 70m rope. This involves some tricky diagonal rappels. A more direct rap line goes down to the anchor of Freefall.

❸ Freebull 90' 5.11b
Randal Grandstaff. 1980's.
Start below a left-facing corner just to the right of Ripcord. Climb the corner, moving left at the top to the anchor of Ripcord.

❹ Cut Away 100' 5.10d
Jay Smith, Nick Nordblom. 1989.
Single rack to 3".
Start below a bolt with a sling, on the lip of an overhang 25' to the right of Ripcord. Make a powerful pull over the roof, then continue more easily until a very thin move up a shallow right-facing offset (b) leads to better holds. Continue up and right to an anchor shared with the next three routes.

❺ Sea of Holes 435' 5.10b R
Nick Nordblom, Jay Smith. Fall 1980.
Single rack to 3.5", double 4", Rp's.
Despite a fair bit of fragile rock, this route is worth doing. It takes a spectacular line though the overhangs and up the steep walls above Black Hole.
1. 110 5.8 As for Black Hole.
2. 160' 5.10b Traverse up and left to the left end of the roof. Over the roof at a crack. Continue up the arete to a belay.
3. 160' 5.10a Continue up the wall; near the top trend rightwards to an anchor in a gully.
Descent: 3 double rope rappels down the gully.

❻ Black Hole 170' 5.10c
Jay Smith, Nick Nordblom. 1980.
Single rack to 4", double 2.5"-3.5", extra Tcu's for pitch 2.
This route climbs a deep left-facing corner 15' to the right of the Cut Away.
1. 100' 5.8 Climb the corner to an anchor at its top.
2. 70' 5.10c Continue over a bulge with sketchy protection to a rest in a short stembox. Follow the left arching crack and pull over a small bulge at its end. Move left and finish up the arete before stepping back right to the tree and nut anchor.

❼ Drop Zone 100' 5.10c/d
Jay Smith, Jo Bentley, Mark Hesse. 1989.
This route climbs the face to the right of Black Hole (b) to the communal anchor.

❽ Frap 60' 5.10b R
Jay Smith, Nick Nordblom. 1989.
The huge left-facing corner, capped by large roofs, to the right of Black Hole appears to be unclimbed in its entirety. This route climbs the loose initial corner to an anchor at 60'.

❾ Sky Dive 110' 5.11c **
Jay Smith, Jo Bentley. 1989.
Double cams to 0.6", wires, Rp's. One each 3" and 1".
This route climbs the attractive corner system in the buttress to the right of Frap. A very good route despite some flakey rock, the climbing is very sustained and a little bold in places.
Pull over a small roof (b) into a left-facing V-groove. Climb the V-groove and layback up to a bolt. Climb past the bolt to a rest ledge at the base of an open, varnished corner. Climb the corner (b) and exit left to the base of a right-facing offset. Climb the offset (2 b's, crux) then move right past the next bolt to big jugs on the arete. Easy climbing leads to an anchor 15' higher.

To the right of Sky Dive, the cliff swings around to face in a slightly more easterly direction. While the left hand part of the Brass Wall consists of a series of left-facing corners, the right hand part of the wall is flat. The first routes described here are on a short face, covered in huecos, which leads to a tree ledge at 40'. This face is to the left of some large boulders sitting at the base of the cliff.

❿ Arachnoworld 40' 5.4
Start below the left side of the tree ledge. Climb a short left-facing corner and a right-slanting crack above to the ledge.

⓫ Zen and the Art of Web Spinning 40' 5.4
Start a few feet left of a left-facing corner. Climb up to a shallow left-facing corner. Up this and through the huecos above to the tree ledge.

At the left end of this part of the Brass Wall is an obvious cutaway roof just above the ground.

⓬ Sniveler 60' 5.5 R
Start on a boulder below the roof. Step off the boulder onto an arete. Continue up the face and crack (runout and fragile) to a big ledge. Traverse right to the anchor of Topless Twins.

⓭ Heavy Spider Karma 60' 5.6
Start 20' to the right of Sniveler. Climb the crack to the ledge. Traverse right to the anchor of Topless Twins.
Variation: 5.5 R leave the crack early and climb diagonally up to the anchor.

⑭ Raptor 660' 5.10c

Nick Nordblom, Randy Marsh. 1990.
Single rack to 3", Rp's, double 0.75"-1" cams.

This route climbs a steep crack system directly above the Topless Twins area, to a point about 700' up, where a leftward traverse leads to the descent gully.

1. 60' 5.6 Climb Heavy Spider Karma to the platform.

2. 110' 5.8 From the middle of the upper part of this platform, step across the chasm onto the main wall. Fragile face leads slightly left to thin cracks. After going up about 40' traverse right for 20' (unprotected, steep, fragile 5.7) to a good crack system, which is followed to a belay stance in a left-facing corner before the wall steepens. A serious pitch.

3. 160' 5.10c Climb straight up the left-facing corner to a bolt where the face steepens. A thin seam with crisp edges offers delicate pulls through this first crux (5.10b). The crack becomes less difficult as it leans slightly left, then it pinches off at a steep, white slab with a bolt on its right (5.10a). Continue up the now-open thin crack to a steep, varnished, third crux where the crack pinches again, and holds on the right wall are key (5.10c). Belay on a stance 20' below a right-facing corner.

4. 150' 5.8 Climb the overhang via giant knobs to base of the right-facing corner. At top of corner traverse left and up, across the face for about 40' to another crack system. Climb this to a good ledge.

5. 180' 5.9+ The varnished left-facing corner above is closed at first. After about 12', a small/tiny brass nut can be placed. After one more move, a bomber 1" cam can be placed. Climb straight up this corner (the first 30 feet are 5.9+). After half a ropelength, the angle becomes less steep, but some cavernous gullies cut in from the left and must be negotiated. Belay on a good ledge.

Descent: Climb up and left through blocky terrain, then make a 100' horizontal traverse left on a class 4 ledge, heading for the brush in the first gully. Cross the brush patch into the second gully (Sea of Holes Gully) where a threaded rap anchor is found. Rappel 200', then make an exposed class 4 traverse to skier's right (west) for 20' to a good bolt/wired nut anchor. Three raps with bolted anchors lead straight down to the ground from here.

⑮ Topless Twins 70' 5.9 *

Randal Grandstaff, Wendell Broussard. 1980.
Single rack to 3".

10' to the right of Heavy Spider Karma, a series of short corners leads into twin varnished cracks. Climb the corners and continue up, mostly using the right hand crack. At the top traverse left to the anchor.

⑯ Mushroom People 100' 5.10d **

Dave Diegleman, Randal Grandstaff, Greg Child. 1979.
Single rack to 2.5". Rp's.

This route climbs an attractive thin crack which angles left across the smooth wall to the right of Topless Twins, and left of a big tree ledge 70' up. The first 15' are awkward and unprotected (5.9). Continue to a very thin section which provides a short crux. Above, the crack widens and enjoyable hand jamming leads to the anchor.

⑰ Bush Pilots 70' 5.10a

Randy Marsh, Paul Van Betten. 1984.
Single rack to 2", double 0.75"- 1".

Start below the left end of the tree ledge, below an overhang 12' above the ground. Make an awkward traverse right under the first roof, then climb up to another overhang. Move left around this, then up to the tree ledge.

Brass Wall - Right side.

⑱ Fungus Folks 60' 5.11b
Randal Grandstaff. 1982.
Single rack to 1.25", Rp's.
This route climbs the thin seam which starts 20' up the black slab below the middle of the tree ledge. Solo up and left to the base of the seam (5.10a). Good small wires protect a vicious pull on a thin jam, then easier climbing leads to the ledge.

The next two routes start on the tree ledge, most easily reached by climbing the first pitch of Varnishing Point.

⑲ No Laughing Matter 110' 5.10a *
Greg Child, Randal Grandstaff. 1979.
Single rack to 3".
Despite some scary, fragile flakes, this is a well-protected and enjoyable climb. Start below the obvious crack in the middle of the ledge. Climb the crack, which jogs left then back right into a blocky corner. Follow the corner to an anchor.
Descent: One 60 m rope just makes it down to the tree ledge.

⑳ Serious Business 100' 5.11a
Paul Van Betten, Randy Marsh. 1982.
Single rack to 2", Rp's.
Start near the right end of the ledge. Lieback over a small roof. Continue up the face to the base of a thin seam. Up this to the anchor of No Laughing Matter.

㉑ Alternative Facts 100' 5.11c *
Xavier Wasiak. 2017.
Double to 2". Triple to 0.75". 5 bolts, but it has been led on gear.
This route climbs the big corner above the No Laughing Matter/ Serious Business anchor.

㉒ Varnishing Point 160' 5.8+ **
Joe Herbst, Larry Hamilton. 1976.
Single rack to 4".
This route climbs the crack formed by the left side of the huge flake at the right end of the Brass Wall. A very enjoyable route with good rock and good protection. Start below the right end of the tree ledge.
1. 60' 5.4 Climb the huecoed crack to the tree ledge.

2. 100' 5.8+ From the right end of the ledge, continue up the left of two corners, with a burly lieback around a small roof. Easier climbing leads to the base of the huge flake.
Descent: One rappel with two ropes from the anchor on the backside of the summit block.

The next four routes end on a ledge with an anchor, on the right side of the flake just below the top. One rappel with two ropes to the ground from here. There are quite a few variations on this face but only the main lines are described.

㉓ Go Greyhound 120' 5.11a *
Paul Crawford. 1983.
Single rack to 2".
This route is bold but has excellent climbing. Start below a 25' high flake about 25' right of Varnishing Point. Climb the left side of the flake. Step left to a thin flake. Up this, then continue up the bigger flake above to its end (b). Thin moves up the wall lead to a sloping horizontal, a runout mantel (10b) and another bolt. Move right 8' and follow a line of big holds to the top.

㉔ One Stop in Tonopah 150' 5.10c
Paul Crawford. 1983.
Start in the same place as the previous route. Climb the right side of the white flake. Move up and right past a bolt to ledges. Above, bold moves up the varnished wall lead to a hueco. Continue up and left (b) eventually joining Go Greyhound for the last few moves.

㉕ Simpatico 130' 5.10a
Jay Smith, Jo Bentley, Jenni Stone. 1980.
Single rack to 3", double 0.33" - 1".
This route climbs the short right-facing corner 10' left of the right edge of the huge flake. Climb up to a ledge at 15', then continue up the corner to a roof. Pull over this to better holds and continue up the arete (5.8 R) to the anchor.

㉖ The Bus Stops Here 130' 5.8 R
Paul Crawford. 1983.
Single rack to 7".
The awkward wide crack on the right side of the huge flake.

Beer and Ice Gully

The right hand side of the Brass Wall is defined by a huge gully which cuts steeply up into the cliffs. This cleft is known as The Beer & Ice Gully. In its upper portion the gully becomes a bushy but steep corner system.

Approach: Follow the main trail into the canyon to the point where a ridge comes down from the right end of the small red cliff band. Starting from a patch of red soil, a trail winds up the left side of this ridge. Once level with the top of the red cliff, a trail goes up the hillside, then starts to cut left through bushes towards the base of the gully. The routes are described from bottom to the top of the gully, starting on the right hand side about 200' up the gully. 35 minutes.

The first three routes are on the overhanging right wall of an alcove in the right wall of the gully. They all finish on a large tree limb which leans across the top of the alcove.

Too Pumped to Pose 60' 5.12b (Tr.)
Paul Van Betten. 1987.
This route climbs a line of features on the right edge of the wall.

Posby 60' 5.12b (Tr.)
Paul Van Betten. 1987.
A line of huecos just right of the next route.

Twenty Nine Posers 60' 5.11d **
Paul Van Betten, Bob Yoho. 1987.
Cams 0.5"- 1.25".
This is a superb, strenuous test piece. Steep. Start below the flake on the left side of the face. Gain the flake and follow it to its end. Continue on huecos (2 b's) to the tree. Blind #1.5 Friend placement just below the top.

The next routes are 100' higher up the gully, reached by a bushy scramble. The most obvious feature is the very steep left-leaning corner climbed by This Bud's For You.

Moisture Brau 120' 5.11a
Paul Van Betten, Bob Conz. 1988.
Single rack to 5".
Start below a left-slanting crack to the right of This Bud's For You. Climb the crack to intersect with This Bud's For You. Pull up into a hand and fist crack. Follow it to its top, then traverse left to finish up the final corner of This Bud's For You.

This Bud's For You 80' 5.11c ***

Paul Van Betten, Bob Conz. 1988.
Single rack to 3", double 0.6"- 2".

Wonderful climbing on superb rock. This route is a stout traditional classic. Start below the right end of the slanting corner. Climb up a vertical left-facing corner to reach the left-leaning corner. Contort up the corner and at its top move up into another corner. This leads to an anchor.

Corona Crack 100' 5.11d

P. Van Betten, Sal Mamusia, Bob Conz. 1988.
Double cams 0.33"- 3", Rp's. Extra small wires.

The short but technical crux at the start is poorly-protected. Start below a curving, flaring finger crack uphill from the previous routes. Climb the crack to a ledge. Move right to the anchor of This Buds For You.

Stout Roof 50' 5.11b

Mike Ward, Paul Van Betten, Bob Yoho. 1987.
Single rack to 3.5".

Climb a crack through a roof to the left of Corona Crack.

Chilly Ones 200' 5.10d R/X

Paul Van Betten, Sal Mamusia. 1988.
Double 2"- 5".

Start directly across the gully from This Bud's For You. Climb over a white bulge and continue up the runout face (3 b's) to reach a crack which widens from tips to offwidth.

Terminal Velocity 550' 5.13a *

Mike Tupper, Greg Mayer. 1989.
Single rack to 3", Rp's, double 0.22"- 0.4" or Lowe ballnuts.

This route climbs the impressive wall on the right at the top of the gully. Start at the top of the lower gully.

1.160' 5.9 Scramble up the gully for 20', then move onto the left wall. Climb the face and crack above to a belay.

2. 60' 5.11d Move up to a steep, thin flake which is liebacked (3 b's) to its top. Move left and up a shallow corner (b) to a belay.

3. 70' 5.11c Traverse 15' straight right, over the lip of a small roof. Continue up the right-slanting corner to an anchor. (5

4. 6ʊ 5.13a Climb the corner above (5.12a); at a bolt move left and climb a vertical, no feet, tips crack to an anchor.

5. 65' 5.11d Stem a corner (2 b's) to a finger crack in a corner. Up this then left to an anchor.

Descent: 4 rappels with two ropes lead straight down to the start of the route, the last two being to the right of the route.

Adam Floyd on This Buds for You. Page 256.

Straight Shooter Wall

These routes are on the sunny buttress to the right of the Beer & Ice gully.

Approach: Follow the main trail into the canyon to the point where a ridge comes down from the right end of the small red cliff band. Starting from a patch of red soil, a trail winds up the left side of this ridge. Once level with the top of the red cliff, a trail goes up the hillside. The route Straight Shooter is directly up the hillside at this point, on a small buttress at the base of the cliff. This is a smooth wall which is darkly varnished in its lower half and patchy orange on top.
1.2 miles, 600' elevation gain, 25 minutes.

The next route starts 150' or so to the left of this wall, just to the right of the entrance to the Beer and Ice Gully.

Orange Clonus 550' 5.10d *
Tom Kaufman, Joe Herbst. April 1977.
Double cams, 1"- 3.5", triple 2.5".
The heart of this route is an excellent splitter crack on the left hand side of an obvious, smooth buttress, a couple of hundred feet up the cliff, and almost directly above Straight Shooter. Start just to the right of the entrance to Beer and Ice Gully at the base of a smooth, left-facing, black corner with some bolts.
1. 100' 5.10d Technical moves lead up to better holds at 25'. Continue up the upper corner to a ledge (5 b's).
Variation: 5.9+ Climb a corner to the left, finishing on the same ledge. The original start.
2. 100' 5.6 R Climb a fragile crack and face on the left side of the face above. Belay at the base of a steep chimney.
3. 100' 5.5 Climb the steep chimney above the belay. After 20' the chimney becomes a ramp which slants up and right to a huge ledge.
4. 50' 5.6 Move right into a gully. Up this to a huge ledge. Walk across right to below a right-leaning corner system in white rock that leads to a ledge below the obvious splitter crack.
5. 60' 5.8+ Climb the corner to the ledge.
6. 70' 5.10d Climb a finger crack into the base of a flare. Chimney and stem up the flare to a thin hands corner. Up this to a small ledge on the left just below an overhang. Belay on 2.5"-3" cams.
7. 70' 5.10a Continue up the hand and fist crack which ends on a big ledge.
Descent: Follow the ledge back to the big corner/gully. Down climbing and three rappels with one rope lead down this gully to the Beer and Ice Gully.

The next six routes are on the same piece of rock as the route Straight Shooter. Straight Shooter is the splitter finger crack on the right side of the smooth, black slab mentioned in the introduction to this area.

❶ Forget Me Knot 100' 5.11b *
Mike Tupper, 1985. The final crack of this route was climbed as a finish to Straight Shooter by P. Van Betten and S.Mamusia. 1984.
Single rack to 1.5", Rp's. Tiny cams and/or loweballs.
The route has been led without either of the bolts. Start 20' to the left of Straight Shooter, below a thin seam. Climb the scary seam (10b) to a bolt on the right. Move past the bolt (5.10d) to a bolt below a thin right-leaning crack. After a hard start, easier climbing leads up the crack to an anchor on the left.

❷ SlabbaDabbaDo 45' 5.11b
Mike Tupper. Winter 1985.
Climb the very smooth black face (3 b's). At the top move right to the Straight Shooter anchor.

❸ Straight Shooter 45' 5.9+ **
Joe Herbst. 1975.
Single rack to 1.75".
The splitter thin crack. A classic little test piece with good protection and a short, punchy crux.

❹ Sidewinder 45' 5.11d *
Rick Dennison, Daryl Ellis. April 1991.
The thin face to the right of Straight Shooter. Climb up and left past the first bolt to reach technical climbing up a series of shallow right-facing flakes (6 b's). The loss of a big undercling and the rounding of several other holds has made this route much harder and more sustained.

❺ The Lazy Fireman 5.11a
C. Robbins, R. Marsh. Spring 1991.
One large nut.
This route climbs the short, steep wall to the right of the Straight Shooter slab to an anchor. (4 b's) There is a big detour to the left between the third and fourth bolts.

The next two routes climb the twin cracks that split the buttress around to the right of the previous route. At the top, traverse left to the anchor of The Lazy Fireman.

Crispy Critters 45' 5.7
Single rack to 2".
This is the left hand of the two cracks.

Captain Crunch 45' 5.7
Single rack to 4.5".
The rightmost of the two cracks.

Stick Gully

From the Pine Creek parking area, this is the most obvious of the gullies cutting into the face of Bridge Mountain.

Approach: Follow the main trail into the canyon to the point where a red dirt ridge comes down from the right end of the small red cliff band. Starting from a patch of red soil, a trail winds up the left side of this ridge. Once level with the top of the red cliff, head across right, scrambling up into the bushy gully. The first route is on a large boulder on the right at the very entrance of the gully.

Lick the Plug 30' 5.12c
This route climbs the white and tan arete on the downhill side of the huge boulder. The hard start is the crux, but there are some tricky moves higher up as well (3 b's).

The next routes are on the right about 300 yards up the gully. Two cracks go through a bulge about 30' up, forming an alcove at their base. 50 mins.

Stickball 100' 5.9.
Todd Swain, Donette Swain. March 1999.
Single rack to 3".
Start on a boulder below a varnished arete to the right of the alcove. Climb a small right-facing corner, then follow a weakness to the anchor. Fragile rock and slightly sketchy protection.

Stick Right 90' 5.9
Richard Harrison, Van Betten, Sal Mamusia, Nick Nordblom. 1982.
Single rack to 5".
Climb the right hand crack.

Stick Left 100' 5.10c *
Harrison, Paul Van Betten, Sal Mamusia, Nick Nordblom. 1982.
Single rack to 4", double 2.5"- 3.5".
Start 20' to the left of Stick Right, below a steep right-facing corner. Up the corner and the crack above to the anchor.

The Elephant Penis 265' 5.10a *
Harrison, Paul Van Betten, Sal Mamusia, Nick Nordblom. 1983.
Single rack to 6", two 1.75", four to five 2", two 3".
At the entrance to Stick Gully, on its left side, is an 800 foot buttress called The Pearl Buttress. At the base of the left side of this buttress, is an alcove with a spectacular black corner.
1. 80' 5.9 Climb the chimney and cracks on the right side of the alcove, to a ledge with a bolted rap/belay station.
Step left and scramble through brushy gully to a higher ledge with a large pine tree.
2. 115' 5.10a Hand jam a straight-in crack for 40 feet to the base of the spectacular corner. One may belay here if gear is needed for the upper corner. Jam and stem up this corner; a bit of slick offwidth is found at the top. There is a bolted rap/belay station on a small ledge at the top of the corner.
3. 70' 5.9 Chimney up the flare a few moves and place the #5 Camalot. Then continue straight up the left corner system, being careful with the fragile rock. Reach a belay ledge with a bolted station on the right.
Descent: Rap the route with a 70 meter rope.

Nature is Fun 370' 5.9+
Richard Harrison, Paul Van Betten, Sal Mamusia, Nick Nordblom. 1983.
Double rack to 4".
On the face opposite the Stick climbs is a beautiful flake/chimney above a white face. This route starts up an offwidth on the left side of the gully, to the right of the white face. The base of the crack is reached by tunneling under some large boulders.
1. 120' 5.9 Climb a varnished hand crack in white rock to a belay above a slot.
2. 100' 5.9 Traverse left across the face to a right-leaning hand crack which is followed to a belay below the chimney.
3. 150' 5.9 Climb the chimney to a bulge. Move right and follow a large crack to the top.

Flight Path Area

These climbs are on a short wall at the base of the broken buttress between Stick Gully and the Gemstone gully. Although the rock is a little flaky, this is a warm and sheltered little cliff, useful as a cold weather alternative to the Brass Wall.

Approach: Follow the main Pine Creek trail into the canyon. Turn right at the Dale Trail which is followed for five hundred yards to a cairn at a sharp bend in the trail. From this point a climbers trail cuts off left towards Bridge Mountain. Follow this trail (cairns) through a small red cliff band to the base of the cliff. The trail reaches the cliff to the right of a right-facing corner that ends on a ledge with a pine tree. 1.4 miles, 700' elevation gain, 50 minutes.

❶ Commuted Sentence 80' 5.9+
Todd Swain, Jake Burkey. January 1999.
Single rack to 5".
Climb the corner .

The next three routes are on the varnished face to the right.

❷ Doin' the Good Drive 80' 5.9
Tom Beck, Steve House. December 1998.
Single rack to 3".
Start about 30' to the right of Commuted Sentence. Climb the obvious finger crack to a ledge. Continue up over two bulges to a lower-angled black face. Traverse right to the anchor.

❸ Car Talk 80' 5.9
Todd Swain, Jake Burkey. January 1999.
Single rack to 5".
Climb the initial crack of the previous route, then veer right at a triangular ceiling. Continue straight up to the anchor.

❹ A Simple Expediency 80' 5.8 +
Tom Beck, Steve House. December 1998.
Single rack to 3".
Start at the base of the finger crack of Doin' the Good Drive. Go up and right to a vertical crack on the right side of the face. Follow the crack past two bulges and a thin section to easier face climbing and the anchor.

The next routes are located about 60' to the right.

❺ They Call the Wind #!&% 110' 5.8
Todd Swain, Teresa Krolak. February 1999.
Single rack to 2".
This route climbs the right edge of the pillar, starting on a ledge at the base of the corner on the right. Move up and left to the arete and climb its right side to finish in a thin crack (5 b's).

The next 5 routes all share an anchor.

6 Sex in the Scrub Oak 80' 5.7
Single rack to 3".
This route climbs the huge right-facing corner of pink rock to the right of the white pillar. Climb the corner to an alcove and an anchor.

7 Ignore the Man Behind the Screen 100' 5.6
Single rack to 3".
Climb the first few feet of the previous route, then step right and climb up the crack just to the right of the corner, which is followed to the communal anchor.

8 Belief in Proportion to the Evidence 100' 5.10a
Tom Beck, Teresa Krolak, Jules George. Spring 1999.
Optional nut between third and fourth bolts.
Start 10' right of the previous route. Climb past 5 bolts, staying left after the top bolt.

9 Common Bond of Circumstance 100' 5.9+
Steve Haase, Tom Beck. Spring 1999.
The line of bolts to the right of the previous route joining that route for last few feet (6 b's).

10 Radio Free Kansas 100' 5.7+
Teresa Krolak, Tom Beck. January 1999.
Single rack to 1.75".
Start on the right side of the face, beside a block and below a left-leaning crack. Climb the crack and the face above (3 b's).

The next two routes are 100 yards to the right of the Flight Path area, and about 80 yards to the left of the bottom of the Gemstone gully. Look for a prominent right-facing flake/corner to the left of a pretty, scooped face.

Flight Path 355' 5.10b
Tom Beck, Steve Haase. Spring 1999.
Single rack to 3".
Start just to the right of the flake/corner, in a small corner.
1. 120' 5.8+ Climb the corner and crack above, then move left and up to an anchor (3 b's).
2. 85' 5.8 Up the soft white rock (b) above to an anchor.
3. 150' 5.10b Climb out of an alcove then move up and right to 2 bolts at a bulge. Follow cracks to the summit.
Descent: Rappel using two ropes.

Pattizabzent 285' 5.10b
Tom Beck, Clarissa Hageman, Mark Rosenthal. 2000.
Double rack to 3", triple .4"- 1".
To the right of the Flight Path buttress is a large corner with several bushes. Start on a ledge 20' up at the base of the corner.
1. 100' 5.9 Climb twin cracks out of a right-facing corner to white rock and a hanging belay at an anchor.
2. 85' 5.10b Move left and climb a splitter crack (5.9) to its end. Move left into the main corner and climb it (4 b's) to the anchor.
Variation: 5.9+ Climb straight up (b) using thin cracks, then traverse left to the anchor.
3. 100' 5.10a Continue up the corner to an anchor.
Descent: Rappel using two ropes.

Gemstone Gully Area

Right of Stick Gully, there is an open gully blocked by cliff bands at the bottom, and with an impressive wall of dark rock at its top, this is the Gemstone Gully. Since the base of the gully is blocked by several cliff bands which require 5th class climbing, the easiest approach is to use another gully further to the northeast.

Approach: Follow the main trail into the canyon for 500 yds. then turn right on the Dale Trail which is followed for about a mile and a half, past Skull Rock and up the slopes above. As the trail contours north along the hillside, it crosses an obvious huge drainage which leads up into the east side of Bridge Mountain towards the Eagles Nest. Go up into the obvious wide drainage. Halfway up, look for a gully which cuts left behind a large formation of white rock. Follow this gully to a saddle at its top, then down the other side into the upper part of the Gemstone gully. To descend from these routes it is possible to downclimb and rappel the lower gully with two ropes. The first route is on the west side of the gully, opposite and below the saddle. It follows a beautiful left-leaning crack on a dark face. 2 miles, 1500' elevation gain, 2hrs.

Gemstone 280' 5.10b **
Nick Nordblom, Jenni Stone. 1985.
Single rack to 4", triple 0.75"- 2.5".
1. 140' 5.10b Climb the superb thin-hands crack to a nut and block anchor.
2. 140' 5.10a R Climb a wide section into a subsidiary crack which curves up and left. Follow this to a white right-facing flake. Continue up and right and up the face to the top.
Descent: Rappels down the gully to the right.

Fear and Loathing 400' 5.10d **
Richard Harrison, Nick Nordblom. 1982.
Double rack to 4", triple 1.75"- 3".
This route climbs the right hand of the two impressive lines in the dark, red cliff at the top of the Gemstone gully. From the saddle, drop down and then go up the Gemstone gully to the terrace below the wall. Scramble up to the base and pass through a short tunnel. The climb begins from the left side of the tunnel. Pitches 2 & 3 have some of the best crack climbing of their grades in Red Rocks.
1. 75' 5.7 Climb the face to the base of the main corner.
2. 110' 5.10d Climb the huge corner to a ledge.
3. 215' 5.10b Continue up the widening corner/crack. Belay on top of a block.
Descent: Head back east aiming for a large pinon pine. A short rappel off the tree leads into the chimney to the east. Scramble north down the chimney then rappel off a large scrub oak. After this rappel scramble down onto a large ledge. On the east side of the ledge, rappel from a large block aiming for another large Pinon Pine. From this pine it's possible to scramble back onto the terrace at the base of the wall.

The next route starts a couple of hundred feet above the base of the cliff, almost directly above the midpoint between Cantilever Corner and The Abutment. This point is most easily reached by traversing left under the lower cliffs from The Abutment. From here scramble through the lower cliff bands and follow a bushy ramp up and right for 100 yards.

Tri-Burro Bridge 530' 5.10b
Todd Swain, Jake Burkey, Reina Downing. February 1999.
Single rack to 5".
The heart of this route is a huge, west-facing corner high above the base of the wall.
Start at the base of a crack which doglegs to the left. This is to the right of a brown and white face with huecos.
1. 130' 5.6 Climb the crack to a pine tree.
2. 100' 4th Class Thrash through bushes to the base of a chimney formed by the right side of a huge block. Climb the chimney to an anchor on top of the block.
3. 80' 5.8 Climb a shallow right-facing corner to a roof. Move left around this into a left-facing corner. Up this to a ledge.
4. 90' 5.8 Climb the obvious left-facing corner just above a cave; at the top the corner turns offwidth. Climb a varnished finger crack above, exiting left to an anchor.
5. 130' 5.10b Go up and left (b) to the base of a corner/crack. Up this (b) to an anchor.
Descent: Rappel with two ropes.

Spanning the Gap 220' 5.9
Todd Swain, Donette Swain. May 1999.
Single rack to 2.5".
Around to the right of the base of the Gemstone gully is a square, black face. Start in the middle of the face below a varnished left-facing corner.
1. 130' 5.9 Pull over a bulge and climb the corner to a ledge. Climb a short face to a roof, then up loose rock (2 b's) to a ledge. Continue up and right to belay in a left-facing corner.
2. 90' 5.8 Go up and right around a white bulge, then back left to an anchor just below the top of the wall.
Descent: Rappel with two ropes.

Cantilever Corner 75' 5.8+
Single rack to 4".
The right side of the wall is bounded by a deep left-facing corner. Start on top of a pedestal at the base of the corner. Climb the corner to an anchor.

The Abutment

This small but attractive wall is at the right end of the lower cliff bands, just to the left of the large open gully used to approach Gemstone and The Eagles Nest.

Approach: Follow the main trail into the canyon for 500 yards, then turn right on the Dale Trail which is followed for about a mile and a half. Go past Skull Rock and up the slopes above to the point closest to an obvious huge boulder a couple of hundred feet below the base of the cliff. Leave the trail and head up past the boulder to the wall. 1 hr.

❶ Pier-Less 60' 5.10c
Single rack to 5".
Start on a ledge at the base of the corner to the left of the varnished buttress. Climb the leftmost crack in the steep wall to the left of the corner.

❷ Crazy Girls 55' 5.10a
Dave Wonderly, Warren Egbert. 1988.
Single rack to 1", Rp's.
This route is sporty but high quality. Start 20' to the right of the big corner. Climb the varnished face (3 b's).

❸ Coffee Generation 60' 5.11a
Paul Crawford, Richard Harrison, Wendell Broussard. 1984.
Double rack to 1", Rp's.
A necky lead up the right side of the varnished face. Start at a small left-facing corner 20' to the right of the previous route. Climb up to a ledge. Pull over a bulge at a thin seam, then climb the face up and slightly right (b) to the top.

❹ Bridge of Sighs 50' 5.9
Single rack to 5".
Start just left of a pine tree. This route climbs the crack that borders the right side of the varnished face.

❺ Robin Trowel 60' 5.7
Single rack from 2"- 5".
The right-curving corner/crack behind the pine tree.

The Eagles Nest

This is the name given to the east face of the East Peak of Bridge Mountain. It is the obvious large, red face that sits on top of a long, bush-covered slope overlooking the loop road.

Approach: Follow the main trail into the canyon for 500 yds. then turn right on the Dale Trail which is followed for about a mile and a half, past Skull Rock and up the slopes above. As the trail contours north along the hillside, it crosses an obvious huge drainage which leads up into the east side of Bridge Mountain towards the Eagles Nest. Scramble up this drainage cutting out right at the top to reach the base of the wall. 1.9 miles, 1700' elevation gain, 2 hrs.

Descent: A complicated scramble down the ridge to the north of the wall (cairns). 2-3 hours back to the road.

❶ Bromancing The Stone 1200', 5.10d
Chris Weidner, Jon Glassberg. January 8, 2015.
Single rack to 7", double 1.5"- 3".
A long, adventurous outing up the huge crack system on the left side of the wall.
1. 120' 5.6 Begin in a bushy right-leaning crack below a tree about 50' up (alternatively, traverse a sandy face from the left (5.8) to avoid the initial vegetation). Climb up past a chimney and more bushes to a two-bolt anchor.
2. 85' 5.8 Climb a varnished flare to a bushy ledge 50' above the belay then bushwhack 30' left to a belay beneath a crack splitting the face.
3. 65' 5.9 Head up the crack and face to a beautiful flare that ends at a two-bolt anchor.
4. 85' 5.10c Climb up the gaping chimney, which narrows to a squeeze then a tricky bulge and finally a varnished finger and hand crack. Belay (wide cams) beneath a wide crack in a roof.
5. 165' 5.9 Navigate the roof with helpful face holds then squirm upward. When the chimney peters out, step right over a pillar of white rock to a small stance at a varnished hand crack. Continue another 50' (easy) to a large, flat area beneath another chimney.
6. 130' 5.10a Battle the steep slot to reach easier crack climbing leading to the top of the buttress.
7. 120' 5.2 Walk and scramble up and right for about 100' then downclimb a short corner to flat ground.
8. 120' 5.9 Ascend the bushy weakness trending left, then squeeze up a varnished chimney to belay at a chockstone in a tight alcove beneath a roof.
9. 75' 5.10d Climb delicately out the wide roof crack using fragile face holds and jams, then go up a crack to a slab. Traverse right across the slab and into a cave to belay.
10. 85' 5.10a Squeeze up the smooth, splitter chimney on the left to a bushy ledge at its top.
11. 165' 5.5 Step left around a yucca to an easy crack and rounded arete. Climb past a final, short chimney on the left to the top of the ridge.

Waterfall Wall 450' 5.10
There is a large water streak in the middle of the wall. This route starts up an obvious white crack to its left.
1. 150' 5.10a Climb the crack.
2. 150' 5.10 Continue up the face to an anchor.
3. 150' 5.10 Continue up the face to an anchor.

Where Eagles Dare 450' 5.10b
Bob Conz, Sal Mamusia. 1987.
Start in a big chimney to the right of Waterfall route.
1. 150' 5.10b Climb the chimney to a cave.
2. 150' 5.10a Pull onto the face and follow bolts to an anchor.
3. 150' 5.10a Continue up then left (b's) to the anchor of Waterfall Wall.

Scrambling and a short rappel leads down the ridge.

BRIDGE MOUNTAIN

NORTH PEAK

Buffalo Wall

Hidden Wall

Frigid Air
Buttress

The Refrigerator Wall

The
Necromancer

Sunnyside Crags

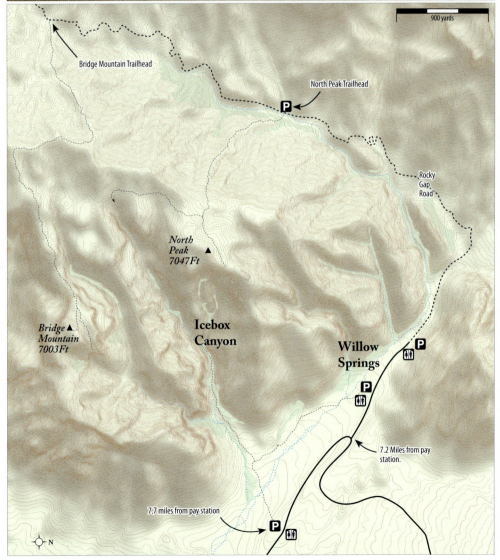

900 yards

Bridge Mountain Trailhead

North Peak Trailhead

Rocky
Gap
Road

North
Peak
7047Ft ▲

Bridge ▲
Mountain
7003Ft

**Icebox
Canyon**

**Willow
Springs**

7.2 Miles from pay
station.

7.7 miles from pay station

N

Introduction

This lower reaches of this canyon have some very accessible short and mid-length traditional routes. There are many large, mysterious walls in the various branches of the upper canyon which are guarded by some of the most complex topography and longest, most involved, approaches in Red Rocks. By Red Rocks' standards this is quite a narrow and steep-walled canyon; so that during the winter even south-facing walls see very little sun. In fact, cold air often sinks down from higher elevations and lurks around in the lower reaches of the canyon. On days like this, the canyon truly lives up to its name. Although there aren't that many routes in Icebox Canyon, a high proportion are of good quality, thanks to large areas of darkly varnished rock. The main canyon trail is popular with hikers. But the climbs don't see much action, making this a good option to avoid the crowds on busy weekends and holidays.

Access

All the routes in the lower canyon are accessed from the Icebox Canyon parking area which is 7.7 miles along the loop road from the pay station. A good trail leads straight into the canyon from the parking area. Some of the walls high in the canyon are often reached by driving up the Rocky Gap Road from Willow Springs. This is an unmaintained road which leads up behind Red Rocks before eventually dropping down into Lovell Canyon. Unfortunately it has become really rough in recent years. Reaching the North Peak parking area requires 4wd and reasonable clearance, beyond this point the road gets very difficult, requiring a high clearance vehicle and a bit of experience. The North Peak parking spot is 3.1 miles past the Willow Creek Turnoff. Look for a short loop on the west side of the road just after the point where the road drops into the wash.

Pitch 4 of Buffalo Soldiers. Page 281.

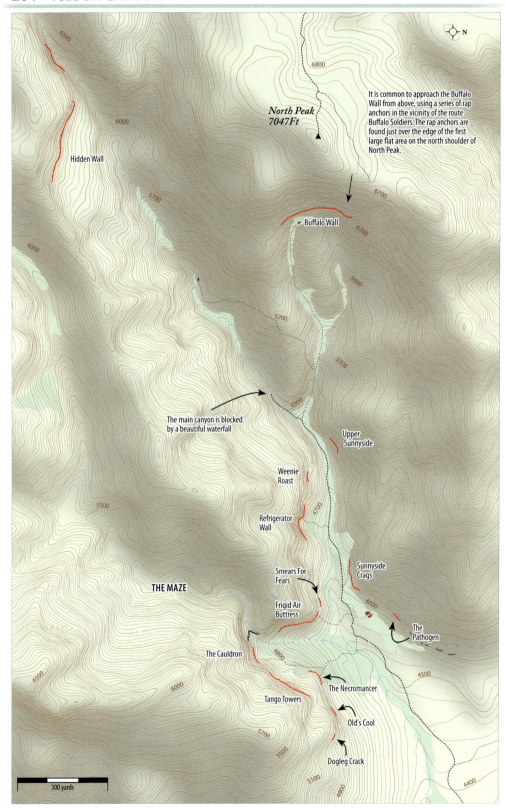

N

North Peak
7047Ft

It is common to approach the Buffalo Wall from above, using a series of rap anchors in the vicinity of the route Buffalo Soldiers. The rap anchors are found just over the edge of the first large flat area on the north shoulder of North Peak.

Buffalo Wall

Hidden Wall

The main canyon is blocked by a beautiful waterfall

Upper Sunnyside

Weenie Roast

Refrigerator Wall

THE MAZE

Smears For Fears

Sunnyside Crags

Frigid Air Buttress

The Pathogen

The Cauldron

The Necromancer

Tango Towers

Old's Cool

Dogleg Crack

300 yards

Tom Moulin on pitch 3 of
Crystal Dawn. Page 278.

At the entrance to the canyon, on the left side, is a triangle of dark rock called The Necromancer. The first three routes are on the walls to the east of The Necromancer.

The first route is about 200 yards to the east and slightly higher than The Necromancer, almost at the very entrance to the canyon. It climbs a prominent S-shaped crack on a large free-standing pillar of varnished rock. It is approached by bush-whacking straight up the hill from the creek bed.

The Dogleg Crack 200' 5.8
Bill Bradley, Joe Herbst. Spring 1979.
Single rack to 5".
The route starts with a poorly-protected offwidth. It then continues up the narrowing crack to a large ledge at the base of a corner on the right side of the pillar. Climb the face on the left to the top of the pillar. It's a good idea to split the pitch at the large ledge to keep rope drag manageable.
Descent: Walk off down the gully on the left (east) side of the pillar back to the base of the climb. There is an optional short rappel at the start of this descent.

The next two routes are around one hundred yards to the right of Dogleg Crack, about halfway between that route and The Necromancer. The routes climb crack systems on a tall face just to the left of a big roof 80' above the base of the cliff, they start from a ledge system 20' up, reached by scrambling up easy rocks to its left end.

❶ Bold's Cool 180' 5.10a
Jay Smith, Paul Van Betten. Nov 8, 2008.
Start from the left side of the ledge system. Climb up and left to a thin crack. Climb the crack then continue up and right to the left end of a roof system that runs up and right across the face. Climb the left-facing corner above and when it fizzles out, continue up the face, past a horizontal crack, to the top of a small buttress.

Descent: Rap off the right side of the formation to a ledge system. Traverse right along the ledges to a tree. A single rope rap from the tree leads to the base.

❷ Old's Cool 95' 5.10c
Paul Van Betten, Jay Smith. Nov 8, 2008.
Start from a big block on the ledge system. Step left to a thin right-leaning crack in varnished rock. Follow the crack to its top, then traverse right to a left-facing corner. Climb the corner to the roof system that runs up and right across the face. Climb a thin crack on the right, then pull directly through the roof and continue up the face until it is possible to move up and right to belay at a bush on a ledge system.
Descent: Traverse right along the ledges to a tree. A single rope rap from the tree leads to the base.

The Necromancer

The following routes are in the vicinity of The Necromancer, a triangle of black rock which sits very low on the south side the canyon, close to the entrance. There is some very good face-climbing on these slabby walls, sometimes a little runout but on excellent, varnished rock.
The wall faces north-northwest. It gets no sun mid-winter, but is low-angled enough that it gets a lot of sun during the afternoon in the warmer months.

Approach: Follow the main canyon trail for 15 minutes until you are almost past the obvious triangle of black rock on the left. Scramble steeply down to the creek bed and head up and left, following a faint trail which leads up and left across the bushy hillside to the base of the wall. 0.75 miles, 300' elevation gain, 25 minutes.

Descent: For the routes that finish on top of the formation, down-climbing and short rappels lead down the gully to its left.

❶ Atras 240' 5.8 *
Joe Herbst, Bill Bradley. Spring 1979.
Single rack to 5", double 3"- 4".
Atras climbs a large right-facing corner just to the left of the gully on the left side of The Necromancer. Start by scrambling up 100 feet into the base of the gully then move left and belay

below the corner.
1. 120' 5.8 Climb the wide crack in the corner. At the top, go through blocks and bushes to a belay below a roof .
Variation: The crack around to the left is 5.6.
2. 120' 5.8 This pitch climbs the ugly chimney on the left, pulling around an improbable roof and finishing up a squeeze.
Variation: The chimney on the right is 5.7.
Descent: From the top, scramble down to the right (west) and descend The Necromancer descent gully.

❷ Back in Time 115' 5.10a *
This route climbs the beautiful, varnished face to the right of Atras. Start by scrambling up the gully to a belay on the highest comfortable ledge. Some of the climbing is slightly runout but it is possible to supplement the bolts with a few wires and cams. Climb a dirty corner then step left onto the face. Climb the face to an anchor as the angle eases (7 b's).
Rap with a single 70m rope.

❸ Hop Route 260' 5.7+
Dave Hop, Joe Herbst, Betsy Herbst. March 1975.
Single rack to 3".
A buttress leans against the bottom of the left side of The Nec-romancer, forming a large right-facing corner on its right side.

Start 15' to the right of the base of the corner.

1. 100' 5.7 Climb a hand crack up the face and follow it as it curves left into the main corner. Continue up the corner to a ledge on the left.

Variation: 5.7+ It is possible to climb straight up the bottom of the initial corner (6" cam). Loose.

2. 160' 5.6 Move left along the ledge and climb a long crack, close to the left edge of the formation, to the top.

❹ Black Magic Panties 110' 5.10a *

Nick Nordblom, Jenni Stone, Danny Rider. 1988.
Single rack to 3", Rp's.

A sparsely-protected route with very good climbing. This route climbs straight up the black face to the right of the previous route. Start about 10' to the right of the hand crack of Hop Route. Wander up the sparsely-protected face to a bolt at 100'. Move left (b) and climb a crack through the roof to a ledge. Belay here. To descend either traverse right to the anchor of Sensuous Mortician, or left to Hop Route.

❺ Sensuous Mortician 120' 5.9 **

Nick Nordblom, John Martinet. Spring 1979.
Single rack to 3", extra small and medium wires.

Enjoyable wall climbing up the center of the black slab at the base of the Necromancer. Start below a huge, white block 10' above the ground in the center of the slab. Climb the thin crack past the right side of the block. At the top of the crack, move right and climb up the face to a bulge. Make crux moves over the bulge to reach an anchor.

❻ Fold Out 290' 5.8 **

Tom Kaufman, Joe Herbst. March 1976.
Single rack to 3".

A nice, varied climb. Start beside the right edge of The Necromancer below an obvious crack.

1. 130' 5.7 Climb the crack, passing a thin section to reach an anchor.

2. 160' 5.8 Move up and left to a water streak and negotiate a section of thin face climbing (b) to reach a crack which leads to the top of the formation.

Tango Towers

The following routes are above The Necromancer, on a series of towers called the Tango Towers.

Approach: The easiest way to approach these routes is by climbing a route to the top of The Necromancer. An alternative is a very bushy scramble around to the right of The Necromancer, which leads to some steep, dirty slabs. The particular line taken up these slabs depends on your chosen route. Be prepared for plenty of fifth-class climbing. 1 hr.

❶ Crawford's Corner 310' 5.10d *
Paul Crawford, Jay Smith. 1987.
Single rack to 5", double 1.25"- 3", triple 1.75"- 2.5".
This route climbs a beautiful corner above The Necromancer. A long approach, and a scrappy approach pitch are rewarded by a superb corner/crack. From the top of The Necromancer, scramble up and right to the base of a huge left-facing corner formed by a big tower. This is the line of Rojo Tower.
1. 150' 5.8 A dirty pitch leads up the slabs, flakes and corners to the left of the main corner. Belay below a flake at the base of the long, elegant corner system to the left of the huge corner of Rojo.
2. 160' 5.10d Climb to the top of the flake then continue up a perfect crack in the corner. At the top, the corner leans to the right, and steep liebacking leads to an anchor on a good ledge.
Descent: Two raps with two ropes.

❷ Rojo Tower 200' 5.11a †
Jay Smith, Sal Mamusia, Mike Ward. 1988.
This route climbs the big left-facing corner to the right of Crawford's Corner. Finishing on top of a big tower.

Well to the right of Crawford's Corner, but at the same level, is an obvious tower split by a big crack system.

❸ Tuff Guys Don't Dance 260' 5.11c
Jay Smith, Sal Mamusia, Mike Ward. 1988.
Single rack to 2.5", Rp's.
Reaching the base of this route is a bit of an adventure in itself.
1. 130' 5.11c Climb past a bolt to get onto a ledge. Continue up the crack system above. Towards the top a burly traverse left leads into the crux corner, at the top of which is an anchor.
2. 130' 5.10d Gain the crack on the right (b). Follow the crack over a roof and up a left-facing corner to a pod. Exit right out of the pod and continue over right until easier climbing leads to an anchor at the top of the tower.

❹ Desecrater Monks 180' 5.12a
Paul Van Betten, Robert Finlay. 1984.
This route climbs the next tower to the right of the previous route. It is reached by scrambling further up and right. Climb past a bolt (11c) to reach a long, thin crack which is followed to an anchor.

Tango Towers

Jay Foley on Back in Time.
Page 266.

The Cauldron Wall

The following routes are about 100 yards up and to the left of the waterfall at the back of the short, left branch of the canyon. They are on a tall, recessed wall hemmed in by huge corner systems on either side. The routes have a tendency to collect dirt, but the rock is very nice, and when clean the routes offer some good climbing. The walls face straight north and get almost no sun at any time of year.

Approach: Follow the trail towards The Necromancer. Near the base, look for a trail which branches off to the right. The trail mostly hugs the base of the rocks, contouring around to the right for a couple of hundred yards to the base of the wall. 0.9 miles, 500' elevation gain, 35 minutes.

The routes are described from right to left.

The right side of the wall is defined by a gigantic left-facing corner. The first three routes start by scrambling (5.4) up some easy rock to reach the left side of a tree ledge 30' up.

❶ Waterboys 420' 5.10a/b *
Single rack to 5", double to 2".
This route climbs the huge left-facing corner. The first couple of pitches are a little scruffy, but the third is a classic.

1. 80' 5.9 Start from the right side of the ledge and follow a series of right-leaning corners to an anchor in the main corner.
2. 80' 5.9 Climb up into twin corners left of the main corner. A few delicate moves (5.9) lead to better holds. Continue to a dirty alcove in the main corner then step left and layback a sharp flake to an anchor above a small pedestal.
3. 160' 5.10a/b A long pitch up the beautiful corner leads to an anchor on a small ledge.
The good climbing is over at this point but a further pitch was done continuing up the corner then moving out left across the face to join The Regatta below the last pitch.

❷ The Regatta 600' 5.11d *
Single rack to 6", double to 3".
This route has an excellent first pitch and an exciting finish up a steep, exposed headwall. Start in the middle of the ledge below a shallow left-facing groove.

1. 105' 5.11b Climb the shallow groove (no pro, 10a) to a pin at 25'. Continue up the corner, stepping up past a roof at its top (3 b's) then making a delicate move left into a slanting crack.

The Cauldron Wall

Climb the crack and the face above (2 b's) to a shelf. Move right along the shelf and climb a shallow corner (2 b's) to an anchor on a small ledge. Single rack to 1".

2. 105' 5.11d Boulder up the blank face above (2 b's, reachy) to better holds, then continue up the left-facing corner to a ledge on the right.

3. 100' 5.10a Step right off the belay and face climb up to a thin crack system. Climb the thin crack into a deep right-facing corner with a nice hand and finger crack. Climb the corner and the face above to a good ledge. Single rack to 6", double 1.75"- 3".

4. 100' 5.11a Climb the delicate slab above (3 b's) then continue up the easy, dirty face to an anchor in the top-left corner of the slab.

5. 110' 5.11a Climb the crack above the anchor (b) then, after a bulge, move into the crack on the right. Follow this onto an exposed headwall and continue to an anchor above a short chimney. Single rack to 5", double to 3".

Descent: Rap the route with a single 70m rope.

❸ Big Hat, No Cattle 300' 5.11c *
Single rack to 1.25", double to 0.6".

This route climbs the spectacular arete to the left of The Regatta. Start on top of the raised ledge, at its left end.

1. 200' 5.11c A huge pitch with sustained climbing which is slightly bold in places. From the ledge, step left to a mossy crack. Follow the crack through a patch of orange rock then climb up and left past a flake onto the arete. Follow the arete to an anchor (9 b's).

2. 100' 5.11a Continue up the arete to an anchor (3 b's).

Descent: With a 70m rope. Rap the top pitch then continue with two raps down The Regatta.

The next two routes start from a ledge almost 100' up the cliff. Start about 20 feet to the right of the big right-facing corner that defines the left side of the wall. Scramble up and right on bushy terrain to the starting ledge. The first route starts from an anchor on the right side of the ledge.

❹ Achilles 100' 5.10c
Climb straight up from the anchor (3 b's), passing a small roof and continuing to a ledge. Continue up the big flake above to an anchor.

❺ How'Ard 120' 5.9
Single rack to 2".

This route climbs the left side of the slab. Climb 8' up a left-facing corner that forms a pillar. Traverse left, making an exposed move to clip the first bolt (5.8). A few more bolts leads to intermittent right-leaning cracks with a mixture of bolts and gear. Following the path of least resistance to an anchor.

Descent: A 70m rope will reach the top of the initial pillar, from here, 8-12' of 5.6 down climbing reaches the ledge.

The next route climbs an attractive right-leaning crack system in the left sidewall of the huge corner that defines the left side of the wall.

❻ Double Sculls 200' 5.11d
Single rack to 5", double to 2". triple 0.6"-1".

1. 160' 5.11a Start up the crack system staying to the left of the detached block/crack, the rock is better than it looks. Continue climbing the crack as it curves far right to a belay.

2. 40' 5.11d Start up the tricky thin crack system (two green c3's) that eventually leads into a powerful lieback, continue up the overhanging/burly crack system to a good stem rest, then continue a short distance to the anchors.

Frigid Air Buttress

The following routes are on the 900' prow of rock which juts out into the canyon separating a dark amphitheater on the left from the main canyon on the right. These routes face northeast and get morning sun.

Approach: Follow the main canyon trail for 15 minutes, then scramble steeply down into the wash below the big prow. To reach Burlesque and the other routes on the left side of the prow, scramble up the steep wash that comes down from the dark amphitheater. The other routes are reached by a short but bushy hike out of the main wash. 0.75 miles, 200' elevation gain, 20 -25 minutes.

Descent: The routes that top out on Frigid Air Buttress all descend down Burlesque.

The first route climbs a crack line up the buttress just to the right of the waterfall at the back of the dark amphitheater.

❶ Burlesque 480' 5.9
Joe Herbst, Tom Kaufman. May 1979.
Single rack to 7", double 5"- 7".

Start to the right of the waterfall, below a chimney to the right of a mossy slab. 150' of third class leads up the chimney to a bushy ledge.

1. 80' 5.7 Climb up and right on a left-facing flake to a tree on a higher ledge.

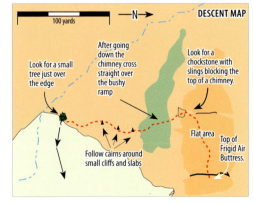

2. 160' 5.8+ Climb up to a hand crack in a large left-facing corner, which is followed to a ledge. Traverse left on the ledge to the base of a large flake.

3. 160' 5.9 A great pitch up a beautiful varnished offwidth and squeeze chimney. Climb the left side of the flake (b) into a tight squeeze chimney. Up this then the corner above to a ledge.

4. 80' 5.6 Easy rock leads to a tree at the top.

Descent: Rappel with two ropes.

❷ Come Again 520' 5.10c
Tom Kaufman, Joe Herbst. May 1979.

This route climbs a crack system roughly halfway between Frigid Air Buttress and the waterfall at the back of the dark amphitheater. Start a rope length to the right of Burlesque at the base of a smooth-walled flare about 50' high.

1. Climb the flare to the top and continue left to a good ledge.
2. From the right side of the ledge, climb a crack in a left-facing corner to a small ledge. Continue up the corner (5.10c) to easier ground.
3. Go up a short wall, then slightly left up a chimney. A long traverse leads right and over a large block to a left-facing corner.
4. Go up the corner and slightly left to a bushy ledge on the upper face.
5. Head up and left to a large chimney which is followed to the top.
Descent: Rappel Burlesque with two ropes.

The following two routes climb a steep, smooth buttress to the left of the main prow of Frigid Air Buttress. An obvious feature is the prominent, left-arching corner of Hot Point which starts in dark, varnished rock and ends in white rock.

❸ Chill Out 165' 5.10c
Jay Smith, Nick Nordblom. 1988.
Single rack to 2", double 0.4"- 1", double set Rp's.

This route wanders up the face to the left of Hot Point to join that route at the anchor at the top of the second pitch.

❹ Hot Point 250' 5.11d
Jay Smith, Nick Nordblom. 1988.
Double rack to 3", one 4" cam, Two sets Rp's.

A serious route with poor protection and several sections of rotten rock. Start by scrambling up and right to the highest ledge below the right side of the buttress.

1. 130' 5.10c Climb up a series of short flakes and corners, then traverse left to the base of the big left-arching corner. Up this to a ledge on the left with a bolt and fixed nut.
2. 65' 5.11d Continue up the corner (b) and follow the rotten arch left (serious) to an anchor in a hole.
3. 80' 5.11c Move back right and climb up past a horizontal, then up the face (b) to an overhang. Continue up the crack above the overhang to an anchor on a ledge.
Descent: Rappel with two ropes.

❺ Middle Earth 600' 5.9
Ryan McPhee, Bill Thiry, John Wilder, Larry DeAngelo. Mid 2000's.
Single rack to 7".

This is an interesting route with some good climbing. So named because of a long, fully enclosed tunnel on the fifth pitch. About a hundred yards to the left of the Frigid Air Buttress, a rounded whitish apron leans against the lower wall. Scramble up ledges on its left side for a few hundred feet to a rope-up point where the rock steepens.

1. On the right, climb a convoluted offwidth crack formed by the left edge of a huge flake (5.9). The easier chimney above is unprotected. The flake rounds off to a good belay ledge (which is also the ledge beneath the 5.9 hand crack halfway up the Frigid Air Buttress route).
2. Avoid the Frigid Air Buttress crack, and instead climb the left-leaning jam crack in the clean, varnished wall on the left.
3. A short pitch up and left to a big ledge.
4. Move to the back right corner of the ledge and climb a varnished corner, then go left and belay among broken rocks

in the main gully system.
5. Climb to the back of the gully, then go up a dark, tight, fully enclosed vertical chimney/tunnel.
6. Easy climbing leads to the top
Descent: Scramble left to the standard rappel route (2 ropes) down Burlesque.

❻ Frigid Air Buttress 940' 5.9+ **
Joe Herbst, Larry Hamilton. March 1976.
Single rack to 4", double 2.5", 3".

This is an excellent, varied crack climb which follows a line slightly to the left of the prow of the buttress. Start to the left of the toe of the buttress, on a ledge below a right-facing flake.

1. 180' 5.7 Climb the flake to an anchor at its top. Climb up a thin, varnished crack above (5.7) for 20', then move left around the arete and cross an easy slab to a dirty gully. Climb the slab to the left of the gully and belay at a tree.
2. 160' 5.8 Climb a short, steep wall to a bushy ledge, then go right to a large corner. Climb the corner to a ledge at its top. Move up and left along a fragile flake to reach another big ledge.
3. 100' 5.4 Climb the lovely chimney above the back of the ledge to a belay on the highest ledge below a long, widening crack.
4. 120' 5.9 The crack starts as a 5.8 hand crack, above a sloping ledge, the crack continues as a 5.9 fist crack and leads to a large ledge.
5. 120' 5.9 Climb the short chimney above to its capping roof and make an awkward swing out left to reach a ledge. Climb up the chimney above to where it bottlenecks. Wide stemming up the outside edge passes the bottleneck. Continue up and left to a large ledge. Belay beneath a pine tree in a corner at the back of the ledge.
6. 110' 5.4 Climb the corner and the easy face above, then scramble over to the base of the final steep wall.
7. 150' 5.9+ Climb the pretty finger crack which splits the headwall and continue up easy rock to the top.
Descent: The descent from Frigid Air Buttress is a little hard to find. From the top of the last pitch, cross over a slot that cuts from north to south and climb up the rock on the other side (5.2) to reach a flat area. Walk across to the left and into the top of another gully. A few yards down, the gully is blocked by large chockstones. There is a rappel anchor, but it is very easy to go under one of the chockstones and downclimb the chimney to a bushy, flat area. This bushy ramp slants down to the west towards the Maze. Instead of going down the ramp, go straight across it and continue heading south (cairns), meandering around short cliff bands and eventually reaching a bare rock ridge above the south end of the main face. A tree just over the edge of the cliff marks the start of the Burlesque rappels. 4 rappels with two ropes.

❼ Blue Bunny 140' 5.7
Single rack to 1.75".

This route climbs the face to the right of the first pitch of Frigid Air Buttress. Runout face climbing (6 b's) leads to an anchor.

❽ Linda's Route 1000' 5.9+
Linda Marks, Joe Herbst, Nanouk Borche, Matt McMackin. 1978.

This follows an easier line to the right of Frigid Air Buttress, finishing up the last pitch of that route.

Frigid Air Buttress

❾ Lebanese Jojo 160' 5.9+

S. Mamusia, B. Conz, F. Lybarger, M. Ward, P. Van Betten. 1990.
Single rack to 3", extra small wires. Double ropes help.

On the right side of Frigid Air Buttress, at the base of the cliff, is a buttress of darkly varnished rock. The base of this buttress is blocked by a steep, yellow wall and roof. To the left of the overhangs, climb a corner to a tree. Traverse right above the lip of the roof to a shallow groove. Up this (b) then move right to a thin crack. Zig-zag up the cracks above to an anchor.

To the right of the buttress of Lebanese Jojo is a deep right-facing corner.

❿ Grumblefish 100' 5.10a

Single rack to 4".

Start below the deep right-facing corner. Climb past two bolts to reach the crack in the corner. Continue up the awkward, slanting corner, eventually stepping right to the anchor of Smears For Fears.

Right of Grumblefish is a steep, varnished slab which houses two classic face climbs, both with a high fear factor.

⓫ Smears for Fears 110' 5.11d **
Mike Ward, Sal Mamusia, Robert Finlay. 1989.
1 set of wires, #3, #4 Camalot.

Start on a nice, flat ledge below the left side of the slab. Climb up into a short, smooth corner. Thin moves lead to its top, then continue more easily up the face past some horizontal cracks. Move left and continue up the wall until it is necessary to reach right and clip the fifth bolt. A very thin sequence leads past the bolt onto a steep, black slab. Teeter up the slab with the bolt quickly receding below your heels. Eventually, easier climbing leads to the anchor (5 b's).

⓬ Rojo 110' 5.11d *
Paul Van Betten, Sal Mamusia. 1989.
Single rack to 2", double 0.4"-0.6", Rp's.

Start just to the right of Smears for Fears. Climb an easy right-slanting crack which leads into a right-facing corner. Great stemming up the corner (b) leads to a hard move at its top (b). Continue up a hair-raising sequence of thin moves to a bolt in the final slab. Continue to the anchor.

⓭ Romeo Charlie 130' 5.10a
Sal Mamusia, Mike Ward, Robert Finlay. 1989.

Start about 80' to the right of Rojo. Climb a right-slanting crack to reach a rounded arete. Continue up the rounded arete and the face to its right, pulling over a final bulge onto a mossy slab which leads to the anchor.

Smears For Fears Area

Bridge Mountain, Northeast Arete 740' 5.6 **
Sal Mamusia, Richard Harrison. 1982.
Single rack to 2.5".

The Northeast Arete of Bridge Mountain towers above the south side of Icebox Canyon and makes for a very appealing alpine style objective. It can be approached by climbing a route on Frigid Air Buttress then negotiating an area of corridors and fins called the Maze. This is best done by staying high on the right side of the drainage. A final obstacle is a steep cliff band at the base of the arete. This is best avoided by traversing up and left to the east arete of Bridge Mountain, then traversing back right above the cliff band to the base of the arete. An alternative approach is to come in from the Rocky Gap Road, following the trail to Bridge Mountain. After scrambling through the arch and up the other side you will see a slot canyon with trees below the final summit dome. Head down from the left side of the trees, following a drainage system down to a ledge system above steeper terrain. Walk a short distance south on this ledge to a cairn at the start of the route. Although not a difficult climb, this is a remote and serious undertaking with beautiful scenery and a real summit. Start on a ledge at the base of the arete.

1. 130' 5.6 Climb a crack in the arete past a small roof 30' up. Belay on a sloping ledge.
2. 140' 5.6 Climb up and right to a crack which is followed past a small tree. Stay to the left and belay at the base of a

chimney.
3. 160' 5.5 Climb the chimney to a ledge then move right and up another chimney and up to a large ledge.
4. 160' 5.3 Continue up the crack to a ledge below a roof.
5. 150' 4th Class Avoid the roof on the left and continue easily to the top.
Descent: The descent goes down a ramp on the west side of the summit dome, which slopes down to the northwest. Once below the summit dome, a steep scramble to the west down a long crack, leads through the lower rocks to the base of the upper part of Bridge Mountain. From here an easy trail leads over the limestone ridge and down to the Rocky Gap Road.

Hidden Wall

This wall sits on the south side of the upper reaches of the south branch of Icebox Canyon.

Canyon Approach: Follow the approach to Buffalo Wall, but about a third of the way up the gully follow a side gully on the left. When this ends, continue traversing left to reach the main drainage that leads up below the Hidden Wall. A serious approach with loose rock and plenty of fifth class climbing.

Rocky Gap Approach: This wall can also be approached from the top, using the Rocky Gap Road approach to the Buffalo Wall. Follow the Buffalo Wall approach to the rim of the sandstone. Head south to the top of the main canyon. There is currently a tree with blue slings above the entrance slabs marking the head of the correct canyon. Scramble down the canyon, staying generally left. Eventually move to the right side of the gully and head out onto a ledge that separates the lower slabs from the steep upper wall. Follow this ledge system around the pedestal that divides the lower part of the wall. Once around the pedestal, scramble up to where the pedestal meets the wall.

Blitzkrieg 1035' 5.11b
Sal Mamusia, Richard Harrison. 1982.
Double rack to 4", triple 1"- 2". Rp's.
This route climbs beside some water streaks on the left side of the wall. It is a remote, serious route which is very dirty in places.
1. 215' 5.10c Start up a left-facing corner system. Continue up the obvious crack and corner system aiming for the first big bush-covered ledge and belay.
2. 190' 5.10c Climb off the left side of the ledge towards a slightly lower-angled, bushy area. Avoid most of the bushes by climbing on the right. Step back left through the biggest bush. The crack above the biggest bush is filled with loose blocks, these can be avoided by traversing out left on a ledgy area then back right into the corner. Once back in the corner climb up until a foot rail appears on the right. Follow this out and around the corner to a ledge. Continue up another 40' to a huge, bushy ledge.
3. 150' 5.8 Move the belay to the other side of the ledge. On the ledge, stop under the only crack that doesn't pinch down into nothing, its 3/4 of the way across the big ledge.
4. 130' 5.10d Climb the crack. About half way up is a slab section. The left side is full of vegetation, so step over right to the corner (crucial #3 Camalot placement). Stem up the wide channel to a roof which is passed on the right. Continue to a big, flat ledge.

5. 150' 5.11b Start by traversing out left on the ledge, balancy and exposed. Climb the corner/flake system above to a sloping ledge. Climb off the right side, over a bulge, to the face above. Climb past a tree and up the corner and slab above on the black water streak in the center of the wall. From a stance, climb through a bulge and small holds to a crucial in-situ thread. From here the goal is to get into the obvious chimney/ flare on the right. Early ascents traversed right from the thread, a more recent party climbed higher, fixed a cam and tensioned right into the chimney. Climb the chimney/ flare up to a big, bushy ledge.
6. 200' 5.6 Head up and right, then back left, then right again following the path of least resistance to the top of the wall.
Descent: A short walk along the crest of the formation leads back to the top of the canyon.

Roraima 700' 5.11d
Tom Moulin, Xavier Wasiak. 2002.
Single rack to 7".
This route is at the very top of the south branch of the Canyon. It is on the south side of the canyon and faces northwest. It climbs a prominent corner system.
1. 80' 5.11c A scary pitch with marginal gear. Face climb and undercling up and right to a ledge. Move the belay left along the ledge.
2. 130' 5.9 Climb the large corner to a tree ledge. Move the belay for the next pitch.
3. 150' 5.11d Climb a beautiful corner to a rounded crack in white rock. Climb the crack, past a pod to a ledge. Move the belay.
4. 100' 5.8 Climb up and right following a large crack in a slab, pulling over a final roof to the top.
The first ascent team scrambled up and left to a ridge which was followed back to the limestone.

Refrigerator Wall

This is the tall wall on the south side of the canyon, about a third of a mile west of Frigid Air Buttress. The climbs here face north and, since the canyon is very steep and narrow at this point, they receive very little sun at any time of year. The wall is very sheltered from the wind most of the time.

Approach: Follow the main trail all the way into the canyon. Shortly after passing Sunnyside Crags on the right, the trail drops into the main wash. A few yards up the wash a cairn on a boulder (sometimes it's there, sometimes it isn't) marks the start of a bushy trail which leads up to the base of the wall in the vicinity of Breakaway. To reach the first routes described, follow the base of the wall up to the left to a flat area with a couple of large pine trees at the base of a huge recess. 1 mile, 400' elevation gain, 30 minutes.

❶ Greased Lightning 145' 5.10b *
Nick Nordblom, Randy Marsh. 1989.
Single rack to 2", double to 1", Rp's.
On the left side of the recess is a rounded arete split by an incipient crack system. This provides a nice pitch with some very good rock and generally decent protection. Start up the ramp of Swing Shift, then move left and climb the discontinuous crack system to a ledge and anchor.

❷ Swing Shift 700' 5.10c
Mark Moore, Joe Herbst. Spring 1977.
Single rack to 3", Rp's, extra wires.
This route climbs a long system of cracks and corners on the left wall of the recess. Start on the left side of the recess in a short right-facing corner on a low-angled slab.
1. 60' 5.6 Climb up to a ledge with a few small trees.
2. 120' 5.9 From the left side of the ledge, climb a long, impressive thin crack to a belay in an alcove.
3. 50' 5.9 Move left past loose blocks into a short, loose corner. Up this until a hand traverse leads left (b) around the corner. Continue up and left to a belay bolt.
4. 80' 5.10b Unprotected face climbing (5.8) leads up and right into a steep, difficult corner. At the top of the corner mantel onto a smooth, white ledge and belay.
5. 100' 5.10c Climb up to a smooth corner with a tips crack. Climb the corner (crux) and belay in a recess below a chimney.
6. 175' 5.9 Climb the chimney for 110' to a ledge. Follow the ledge leftwards to its end and climb up to good anchors.
7. 100' 5.5 Easy climbing leads past two trees, then up an easy corner to a blocky ledge.
Descent: The first ascent party rappelled, mostly using trees to the right of the route, only sharing the anchors above the crux pitch and the first pitch.

The right side of the recess is a very impressive slabby wall of beautiful, dark rock.

❸ Pork Soda 90' 5.9
Killis Howard, Jason Griffith. 2010.
Single rack to 6".
Start in a bushy alcove down and left of Grape Nuts, below a thin-hands crack. Climb the corner/ramp to a ledge. Move right and rap from the anchor of Grape Nuts.

❹ Grape Nuts 100' 5.10c
Rick Dennison, Randy Faulk, Alex Malfatto. August 1991.
This route climbs a black rib on the left side of the slabby wall to the anchor of Amazing Grace (6 b's).

❺ Amazing Grace 110' 5.9+ *
Danny Meyers. 1985.
Single rack to 3".
Continuous and good quality. Start behind the leftmost of the pine trees. Face climb past three well-spaced bolts, moving right past the third to reach a left-facing flake. Continue up the flake, which deepens into a corner and leads to an anchor.

❻ Kisses Don't Lie 250' 5.12a/b ***
Greg Mayer. October 1994.
Single rack to 2.5".
This is a beautiful climb, one of the best of its type in Red Rocks. Unfortunately, several of the bolts on the first pitch are very hard to clip. On the first ascent Greg Mayer got around this problem by leaving long slings on several key bolts.

1. 140' 5.12a/b Technical and sustained climbing up the slight rib in the center of the slabby wall leads to a ledge (11 b's).

2. 110' 5.11d Pull through a small overhang above the anchor and continue up the wall (2 b's) into a short corner. Continue to a bolt at the top of the corner. Down climb then move right, making a hard move up to the base of a right-facing flake. Up this to a roof (3 b's) then step right and pull over the roof to an anchor.

The right side of the slab is bordered by a large left-facing corner. The next route climbs the face to the left of this corner.

❼ Earth Juice 150' 5.11a * ❶

Kurt Reider, Chris Robbins, Augie Klein. 1979.
Single rack to 1.5".

Thin face climbing with some scary runouts. Start at the base of a blocky ramp leading up into the corner.

1. 70' 5.10b Scramble up the ramp, then head up the smooth face (3 b's) to a short crack. Follow the crack to a bolt then move left to an anchor.

2. 80' 5.11a Climb up a steep corner to a bolt. Traverse right then move up a flake to a ledge (b). Make bold moves up a shallow, right-facing corner (crucial small wires) then traverse left, finishing on the same ledge as Kisses Don't Lie.

Descent: Rappel with two ropes.

❽ Naysayer 60' 5.12b

Single rack to 4", double 0.4" and 1"-3".

This route climbs the sharply overhanging wall and arete that forms the right side of the deep right-facing corner to the right of Earth Juice. Start by scrambling up to a belay below the arete. Move past a bolt onto the arete and climb it for 30' until it is possible to swing left into the sharply overhanging crack. Climb the crack, pulling over the final roof to an anchor. Pumpy.

One of the most prominent features of the Refrigerator Wall is a prominent black streak which streams down a very impressive wall starting 150' feet up the cliff.

❾ Breakaway 240' 5.10d **

Danny Meyers, Mike Ward. Summer 1991.
#0.75, #1 Camalot, Blue Tcu.

This route climbs the impressive black streak. Follow the approach trail to the base of the cliff, then go up and left a short distance before cutting back right on a ledge system. Start on the highest ledge below a black slab.

1. 100' 5.7 Nice climbing up the straightforward slab (3 b's) is followed by a long runout (5.5) up and left to a small ledge below the black streak.

2. 140' 5.10d After a sporty 5.8 section to get started, the route blasts straight up the incredible wall on great but amazingly thin holds. Quite pumpy for the grade, but gradually easing towards the top. At the top of the wall, move onto the left arete, where a final 5.7 runout leads to an anchor.

Descent: Rappel to the anchor above the first pitch of La Cierta Edad. Another rappel leads to the ground.

❿ La Cierta Edad 560' 5.10b *

Jorge Urioste, Joanne Urioste. March 1981.
Single rack to 5", double 1.75" - 3".

This route climbs a series of steep cracks, corners and chimneys on the left edge of the huge corner of Unfinished Symphony. Start as for Breakaway on the highest ledge below the black slab.

1. 110' 5.8 Climb the slab (3 b's). From the third bolt, move up

and right (b). Pull over a slight swell and continue to an anchor at the top-right corner of the slab, below a wide chimney.

2. 100' 5.9+ Climb the chimney (b) and continue up the crack system to an anchor.

3. 80' 5.10a Continue up the crack to an awkward hanging belay at an anchor.

4. 130' 5.10b After a hard start, the crack gets easier and leads to a good ledge on the right. Continue up the crack, taking the leftmost branch to a belay on a blocky ledge with a small tree.

5. 70' 5.8 Climb a nice, varnished corner on the left, then exit right to an anchor on a small ledge.

Descent: A long rappel leads to a good ledge. Walk west along this ledge to an anchor in the huge corner of Unfinished Symphony. Continue down Unfinished Symphony. It is also possible to rap straight down the route with two 60m ropes.

⓫ Unfinished Symphony 550' 5.11d **

Ross Hardwick, Joe Herbst, Andre Lagenbach. Fall 1978.
Single rack to 7", double 7".

This route climbs the huge, offwidth corner on the right side of the Refrigerator Wall. For most of the route, face holds beside the crack make the climbing very reasonable and enjoyable. The mighty final corner, however, offers no such relief and provides a gut-wrenching struggle. Follow the approach trail to the base of the cliff, then go up and right to a flat area at the base of the huge corner.

1. 80' 5.9 Climb over awkward sandy blocks on the left, then move right below an overhang and continue over a bulge and up to a ledge.

2. 100' 5.8 Climb the corner to a ledge and continue up to a large, sloping ledge in an alcove at the base of a huge corner.

3. 100' 5.10a Climb the corner into a wide pod. Awkward climbing out the wide crack in the top of the pod leads to an anchor a short distance higher.

4. 70' 5.8 Enjoyable climbing up the varnished offwidth above leads to the base of the final corner.

5. 120' 5.11d The final corner is smooth-walled and leans sharply to the right. Climb the corner (3 b's). After 60' the climbing eases and steep stemming leads to an anchor under a block. The old bolts are easily backed up.

Descent: Rappel with two ropes.

⓬ Music to My Fears 300' 5.10c

Robert Finlay, Brad Ball. 1984.

This route climbs the face to the right of Unfinished Symphony. From the base of Unfinished Symphony, scramble up and right onto an obvious block of light-colored rock.

1. 80' 5.9 Climb the thin crack above to reach some huge blocks. Belay on top of these.

2. 150' 5.10c Climb the long crack system on the left. At the top of the crack system move left to belay on a ledge close to Unfinished Symphony.

Descent: Traverse into Unfinished Symphony and rap.

Weenie Juice 140' 5.10a *

R. Harrison, Van Betten, W. Broussard, S. Mamusia, L. Cronin. 1983.
Single rack to 7", triple 5"- 7".

This route sits by itself on the left side of the canyon, about 300 yards upstream from where the trail drops into the wash. Look for a right-facing arch on an attractive, slabby wall of gray rock. The route starts from a bushy ledge about 150' above the wash, reached by a steep bushwhack to a platform then 50' of scrambling. Excellent climbing up the awkward, arching crack leads to an anchor.

Buffalo Wall

This 1000' high wall sits at the head of the north branch of Icebox Canyon, forming a huge bowl which faces east. The Buffalo Wall is so named because, from a distance, the entire formation looks like a buffalo with its head to the south, the summit forming the hump.

This is a steep and intimidating mass of rock with few obvious lines, guarded by a burly approach. It was the last of the major formations in Red Rocks to free climbed. The aid routes are perhaps the best big wall adventures that Red Rocks has to offer, being hard, steep and remote, but on generally good rock. The recent free routes are two of Red Rocks' finest and most challenging big wall free climbs.

The right side of the wall is surprisingly sheltered and warm, getting the sun until early afternoon in the winter. The routes on the left side of the wall face more to the north and lose the sun by mid-morning.

Canyon Approach: Follow the main trail into the canyon. After dropping into the wash just beyond Sunnyside Crags, continue boulder-hopping up canyon for 15 minutes until a large drainage branches off on the right. Follow this drainage past several fourth and fifth class sections to the base of the wall. A brutal march with big packs. 1.5 miles, 1900' elevation gain, 2-3 hours.

Rocky Gap Approach: From the North Peak Trailhead, cross the wash area following a trail that heads up onto a long, curving ridge that goes all the way from the wash, finally reaching the crest about four hundred yards south of the summit of the Buffalo Wall. 1.3 miles, 1500' elevation gain, 1.5 hrs.

Rappelling: Both Buffalo Soldiers and Crystal Dawn are set up for rappelling. These routes were first free climbed by fixing ropes from the top, and working the route from a base camp in one of several superb bivi spots close to the summit.

For rapping the wall, Buffalo Soldiers is the route of choice. The raps begin on the first big, flat area on the north ridge of the peak. The rap anchor is a little tricky to find, being hidden over the edge, but is basically directly above the bottom end of the escape ramp at the top of the route.

The routes are described from left to right.

❶ **Crystal Dawn 1040' 5.13c** ***
Single rack to 5", optional double set to 2" for pitch1.
This route finds a cunning line through the huge, overhanging amphitheater in the lower-left side of the Buffalo Wall. It navigates a maze of bulging walls and overhangs, often following a tenuous line of holds, surrounded by acres of blank rock. After five pitches it joins The Buffalo Wall, Original Route and finishes up the final three pitches of that route.
The superb rock, varied climbing and an amazing, intricate line make this one of the finest long, hard routes in the country. Shorter climbers have reported finding the pitch 2 roof very hard, to the point that for some this is the crux of the route. The most obvious feature in the lower part of the amphitheater is a long, right-facing corner which leads up to huge black overhangs.
1. 215' 5.12a Climb a small overlap which gains a crack in a small, varnished corner. Continue up the right-facing dihedral above to an overhang (bolt). Face climb on good edges right

of the corner/crack. The finish of the pitch takes a step left onto a slab then traverses right under an overhang to mantle onto a nice, varnished slab. Move easily up into the corner.
2. 70' 5.13a Move out left along the base of the slab to reach the arete. Move awkwardly up the arete (0.6" cam) to a rest. Traverse out left across the wall, moving up to a roof. A hard boulder problem (v7) leads over the roof to an anchor (7 b's).
3. 60' 5.13c Continue up the bulging wall, past a bouldery crux, to a rest below a big roof. Another hard sequence leads over the roof to a small stance (7 b's).
4. 100' 5.12c Follow the amazing line of crimps up and right, until it is possible to climb straight up on easier ground to a nice ledge (8 b's, Small to medium cams optional).
5. 90' 5.12d Continue up the immaculate slab, moving right around the final overlap and up to a ledge (8 b's). Intricate, sustained and tenuous; a true test for a tired body and mind.
6. 160' 5.10d Make committing moves off the belay then step slightly right to an aluminium hanger with a quarter inch rivet. Face climb to reach a big left-facing flake/crack. Climb the flake and exit right to an anchor.
7. 150' 5.11b Follow the long ladder of uninspiring rivets (at least they're close together), climbing an amazing patina face to a big balcony.
8. 220' 5.9 Continue up the big, white right-facing corner system to the top.

❷ **Buffalo Wall 1200' 5.11, A3**
Paul Van Betten, Sal Mamusia, Richard Harrison. April 1991.
Hooks, pitons, double rack to 7".
The original route on the wall climbs a line through the chest of the buffalo to the summit. It starts up a series of left-leaning arches slightly to the right of center.
1. 165' 5.10, A1 Climb a loose face to reach a left-leaning arch. Belay at the high point of the arch.
2. 120' 5.10 Pull over the arch to another arch above. Follow this to an anchor at its top.
3. 165' 5.11, A2 Pull into the next arch above and follow the wide crack under the arch leftwards, the free climbing crux of the route. Aid over the arch (A2) and continue up the wall (bolts) to an anchor.
4. 100' A2 Continue up the face to reach a good ledge. (Nice bivi.)
5. 100' A2 Move left into a thin flake. Up this, then follow more bolts to the right end of a big ledge.
6. 165' 5.9 A3 Climb past a bolt to a wide crack in a left-facing corner. At the top of the corner aid (A3) to an anchor.
7. 100' A3 From the anchor head up the right side of a patch of white rock. Lots of hooking. This leads to a good ledge, (possible bivi.)
8. 165' 5.10 From the ledge continue up a series of cracks to a ledge on the right.
9. 60' 5.9 Continue up cracks to the top of the wall.

❸ **Tatanka 900' 5.10, A2**
Richard Harrison, Paul Van Betten, Sal Mamusia. April 1993.
Double rack to 4", Rp's, pitons, hooks.
This route follows a fairly direct line through the stomach of the buffalo. The route starts up a series of left-facing arches to the right of Buffalo Wall Route.
1. 5.7 Scramble up and right on a ramp and belay below a huge arch.

Tom Moulin on pitch 5 of
Crystal Dawn. Page 278.

Rappel Route

2. A2 Aid up the arch, pull over its roof, and continue up to an anchor.

3. A3 Head right to a ledge, climb the left-facing corner above, then follow bolts to an anchor.

4. A3 Go up a left-facing corner and continue up the wall above, staying on the right side of an area of white rock, (hooks.)

5. 5.10 Face climb (2 b's) to a good bivi ledge.

6. A2 From the ledge, aid up to a long bolt ladder which leads up a very steep headwall.

7. 5.10, A3 Follow a right-arching corner (5.10) and continue to a ledge with a tree. Hook moves lead up the wall above to a higher ledge with an anchor.

8. 5.10 Face climb up and right to a right-facing corner which is followed to the top, a short distance from a large tree.

❹ Buffalo Soldiers 700' 5.12c **

Paul Van Betten, Sal Mamusia. 1998. FFA. Brian Bowman, Chad Umbel, December 2009. After Rehearsal.
Double rack to 6", single 8". Lots of wires to hook over old studs.
This route climbs a series of elegant corners on the sunny right wing of the Buffalo Wall. This is a sustained and challenging climb with several serious pitches with mediocre protection, and one long and very bold 11b runout on the second pitch. The route is peppered with old 1/4 inch studs, and, apart from the runout on pitch 2, the route may well become a lot less serious if these old aid bolts ever get replaced.
Start on a series of big, sloping ledges at the base of the long corner system.

1.100' 5.11d Climb the corner system to an anchor.

2.170' 5.12a/b Continue up the lovely varnished corner past some hard moves with tricky, thin protection. Near the top of the corner, exit out left and follow a line of ancient bolts up and left up the face to the base of a smooth, varnished corner (It is possible to avoid the runout above by making a few aid moves on old rivets in this corner). Arrange some tiny, thin gear, then move right and make awkward, committing moves up the rounded arete (11b/c 20' from gear) until the climbing eases and it is possible to step back left into the corner. Continue up the corner to a small ledge and anchor at its top.

3. 100' 5.11a Move up and left to a long offwidth. Follow the offwidth to an anchor on some big, sloping ledges on the right at its top.

4. 110' 5.12c Move right then back left on blocky terrain to the base of a big left-facing corner. Climb the corner to a stem rest, above which the corner slants to the left. Follow the corner then make hard moves (ancient 1/4" bolt) out of the corner onto its slabby right arete (crux). Continue to a higher corner and at its top grovel into a wide horizontal break. Follow the break awkwardly out right to a big ledge at the base of a beautiful, white corner.

5. 90' 5.12a Layback up the corner, then the crack to its left, past a tricky series of layback moves until it is possible to step back right to a rest under a roof. Layback around the roof and continue up the corner to a belay at the bottom of a big right-slanting terrace at its top. Scramble up the terrace to the top of the wall.

Brian Bowman on pitch 5 of Buffalo Soldiers. Page 281. Photo: Tom Moulin

Chad Umbel on the runout of Buffalo Soldiers pitch 2. Page 281. Photo: Tom Moulin

Upper Sunnyside Crag

This crag has several good trad routes on solid, varnished rock. It is a sheltered and very sunny wall.

Approach: Follow the main trail into Icebox Canyon. The trail soon passes beneath the main Sunnyside Crag, then drops into the streambed. These routes are on a south-facing wall about 200 yards upstream from where the main canyon trail drops into the wash. Look for a sunny cliff on the right. An obvious landmark is a wide, varnished alcove formed by a huge roof.

❶ Broussard Buttress 250' 5.6
Sal Mamusia, Paul Van Betten, Richard Harrison. 1983.
Single rack to 3", Rp's, extra wires.
This route climbs the cracks and seams on the left side of the wall. More serious than the grade would suggest.

❷ Hot Time 260' 5.9+
Joe Herbst, Tom Kaufman. April 1977.
Single rack to 3".
Start below the right-facing corner which forms the left side of the alcove.
1. **100' 5.8** The thin 5.8 corner leads to the left edge of the first roof. Undercling and lieback around the roof and continue up the crack, then head right to a large belay ledge below the right

side of the upper roof.
2. **160' 5.9+** Climb straight through the slotted roof. Continue to a large ledge.
Descent: From the right end of the ledge, either rappel to the gully below, or to the anchor of Good Time Charlie.

❸ Gourmet Meil 100' 5.11c
Joe Herbst, George Meil. 1977.
Start to the right of Hot Time. Climb through the right side of the lower roof then straight up to the large belay ledge.

❹ Good Time Charlie 130' 5.8
Single rack to 3".
This is the left-hand crack system on the darkly-varnished wall immediately to the right of the alcove. Start in a small dihedral around to the right of Gourmet Meil. Climb the crack until it peters out, then go up and right, joining Drat Crack for the final few feet to the belay.

❺ Drat Crack 130' 5.8
Single rack to 4".
Climb the crack to the right of the previous route to a thread anchor.

Sunnyside Crags

These small, varnished buttresses are on the right side of the canyon, just as it starts to narrow. The walls face due south. However, the canyon is narrow and deep enough at this point that they get very little sun in the winter. Conversely, as the sun gets high in the sky in late spring, the cliff bakes till late afternoon. Nevertheless, a short approach and a lot of excellent rock make this a very worthwhile cragging venue.

Approach: Follow the trail into the canyon, the Sunnyside Crags are the steep, varnished buttresses on the right, just as the canyon narrows. 0.8 miles, 300' ascent, 15 minutes.

Sunnyside Crags - Left side.

The most obvious feature on the left side of the Sunnyside Crags is a rectangular buttress about 70' high. The front side of the buttress is a beautiful, varnished wall split by an incipient crack, the line of Spring Break.

❶ Crossfire 110' 5.11b
Jay Smith, Nick Nordblom. 1989.
Single rack to 2.5", double 0.4"- 1", extra wires.
Start 40' to the left of Spring Break, below a steep left-facing corner that starts 50' up the cliff. Climb a crack which slants up and left to the left end of a small roof. Pull over the roof and continue up (b) until it is possible to move right, into the base of the left-facing corner. Climb the corner and continue up the short face above to an anchor.

❷ Hideous Taco 50' 5.12c
Paul Van Betten, Sal Mamusia. 1980's.
Single rack to 1".
Good climbing with a short, reachy crux at the second bolt. Climb a thin crack just to the right of Crossfire. Move right and up the slanting offset (2 b's) to an easier crack. Follow this to an anchor under a roof.

❸ Tarantula 70' 5.12a *
Paul Van Betten, Sal Mamusia. Spring 1986.
Single rack to 2.5", double 0.4"- 1.75", Rp's.
An exciting route up the left edge of the Spring Break Buttress. Protection is better than it appears from below, although the route is still bold in places.

Climb the initial crack of Spring Break, then move left on the first horizontal, making a hard move up onto the arete. Continue up the arete, moving right at the top to finish at the communal anchor.

❹ Spring Break 65' 5.11d ***
Paul Van Betten, Sal Mamusia. Spring 1986.
Single rack to 2.5", double 0.4"- 1.5", Rp's.
The incipient crack splitting the center of the varnished wall. This is a tremendous lead with superb, strenuous climbing and decent but hard to place protection.

❺ Gotham City 65' 5.12a ***
Paul Van Betten, Sal Mamusia. Spring 1986.
Single rack to 3", double 0.4"- 1". Rp's.
Another great route up a series of short seams to the right of Spring Break. With difficult moves and spaced, thin protection this route is the hardest of the trio.

❻ Mister Masters 85' 5.9+ *
Paul Van Betten, Danny Meyers. 1987.
Single rack to 3".
Climb the very steep crack in the right wall of the Spring Break Buttress. After pulling over a bulge at 40', climb the smooth face up and left to the arete. Step left around the arete and move up to a horizontal crack, traverse left 15' to the anchors of Spring Break etc.

Sunnyside Crags - Right side.

On the left hand side of the crag, just to the right of the Spring Break Buttress, is a recess capped by large roofs. Right of the corner at the back of the recess is a sharp right-facing flake.

7 Hot Dog 50' 5.10d (Tr.)
Paul Van Betten, Jay Smith, Paul Crawford. 1987.
Using a toprope from the half way anchor on Water Dog, lieback up the sharp edge of the flake.

8 Pit Bull 50' 5.10c
Paul Van Betten, Jay Smith, Paul Crawford. 1987.
Single rack to 2.5".
Climb either the corner formed by the flake, or the crack just to its right, to reach an overhang. Pull through the overhang to the lower anchor on Water Dog.

9 Water Dog 80' 5.10c *
Paul Van Betten, Jay Smith, Paul Crawford. 1987.
Single rack to 2.5".
A very nice crack climb. Start 10' right of Pit Bull. Climb up to thin, switching corners which are followed to a roof. Pull over the roof to a thread anchor.
Variation: 5.11d From the anchor, move left (b) and pull up through loose roofs to an anchor on the slab above.

10 Mercedes 100' 5.11a *
Jay Smith. 1988.
1.25" cam, wires.
This route climbs the steep, varnished wall on the right side of the recess. Start just right of Water Dog. Climb to a bolt at 25'. Continue to a small roof (.75 camalot), pull the roof on its right, then move left and climb the wall (3 b's), pulling past the last bolt to a good horizontal. Move right and continue up an easy varnished wall for 30' to an anchor.

11 Tie Me Tightly 80' 5.10c
Nick Nordblom, Jenni Stone. 1988.
Single rack to 3".
Start up the first 15' of Mercedes, then move right to an attractive flake. Lieback up the flake, then exit right and up to the anchor of the next route.

12 Bad Day at Black Rocks 80' 5.10b
Randy Marsh, Greg Child. 1989.
Single rack to 2.5".
This route climbs the rounded rib on the right edge of the recess (2 b's) to an anchor.

On the right hand side of the crag, there are two deep, right-facing corner systems that run the full height of the wall. The corner on the right, Cold September Corner, has a large overhang just to the left of its base and another cave 30' to the right. The deep corner about 75' to the left of Cold September Corner is Shady Ladies. The next four routes all share an anchor. A 60m rope works for the rappel.

13 Van Allen Belt 90' 5.7
Single rack to 4".
Start about 20' to the left of Shady Ladies, below a smooth corner. Climb the initial corner (protection at 20') and the crack above to a roof at 40'. Move left under the roof onto the arete. Continue up the crack and face above to an anchor on a ledge.

14 Magallenic Cloud 90' 5.9+
Single rack to 4".
Climb the first 15' of Shady Ladies, then follow a crack up and left to the arete, joining Van Allen Belt for a few moves to the roof. Move right across a bulge into a left-facing corner. Climb the corner to the anchor of Van Allen Belt.

Tom Moulin on The Pathogen.
Page 285. Photo: Luke Olson.

⓯ Shady Ladies 100' 5.7 *
Jineen Griffith, Barbara Euser. May 1978.
Single rack to 3".
Enjoyable climbing leads up the huge corner for 90', before a traverse left leads to the anchor of Van Allen Belt. The climb continues for three more pitches up a bushy corner.

⓰ Mr Freeze's Face 110' 5.10c
Single rack to 2", Rp's.
This route wanders up the varnished face to the right of Shady Ladies (b). At the top traverse left along a horizontal to the anchor of Shady Ladies

⓱ Hot August Night 90' 5.11a
Tony Bubb, Alex Thayer. March 2006.
Single rack to 3".
This route starts just to the left of Cold September Corner. Pull up through the huge roof and continue up the thin crack system in the rounded arete. At the top, make crux moves past a small roof then, traverse right to the anchor.

⓲ Cold September Corner 80' 5.8 *
Joe Herbst, Stephanie Petrilak, Bill Bradley. Fall 1978.
Single rack to 3.5".
Climb the right hand of the two huge corners to an anchor under a roof.

⓳ Meteor 150' 5.11b/c *
L. Hutchinson, P. Van Betten. 1988. Pitch 2, J. Smith, Van Betten. 1988.
Single rack to 2.5", double 1.5"- 2".
A very good route with awkward, strenuous climbing. Start at the back of the cave 30' to the right of Cold September Corner.
1. 60' 5.11b/c Follow the roof crack out left to a calf burning "rest" at the lip. Another awkward section leads to the anchor.
2. 90' 5.10d Climb the short corner above the anchor (10d), then move right into a bigger corner. Follow the corner, then move out right, making a runout to the final roof. Pull over the roof to an anchor on the slab above.

At the right end of Sunnyside Crags is a pillar with a large roof 30' up. This is the pillar just to the right of Meteor.

⓴ Whiplash 150' 5.11d **
Van Betten, Smith. October 1987. Pitch 2, Crawford, Van Betten. 1988.
Single rack to 3".
The first pitch is wildly steep and fun.
Start in the bushes at the bottom of the pillar.
1. 60' 5.11d Climb a tricky thin crack (10c) to the roofs. Swing out left (b) and pull through the bulge to a steep crack. Jam up the crack to an anchor on a small ledge.
2. 90' 5.9 Cracks up the face to an anchor below a roof.

㉑ Backlash 50' 5.11c
Paul Van Betten, Jay Smith. October 1987.
Single rack to 3".
Climb the initial crack of Whiplash, then follow the crack on the right through the roofs to an anchor.

㉒ Whipper 60' 5.10b
Jay Smith, Paul Crawford, Jim Bridwell. 1988.
Single rack to 3".
This route climbs a crack through a roof about 50' to the right of the previous two routes.

The next route climbs a big roof about 100 yards to the right of a big, split boulder which is about 50 yards to the right of the last routes on the right edge of Sunnyside Crags. Look for a rectangular, varnished slab leading up to a 30' roof about 100' above the lowest cliff bands. Scramble through the lower cliff band to a ledge at the base of the varnished slab.

The Pathogen 125' 5.13c **
1. 90' 5.7 Climb thin cracks up the slab to an anchor under the roof.
2. 35' 5.13c Climb out through the roof to a rest position just beyond an anchor at the lip. Acrobatic and intricate (6 b's).

Lost & Found Crag

Wheat Thick

Nadia's Nine Area

N'Plus Ultra

Bighorn Buttress

Pillar Talk

Hidden Falls

Introduction

Willow Springs is the most popular area in Red Rocks for short traditional routes. There is a good selection of crags, most of which are only a few minutes from the road. The most popular wall is Ragged Edges cliff which can be busy, but crowds are seldom a problem on any of the other walls. Most of the climbing faces east and northeast and loses the sun by the early afternoon. With the right choices of wall and time of day, climbing can be reasonable here at any time of the year.

Access

From the pay station drive around the loop road for 7.2 miles, then turn right on a paved road which turns to dirt after around half a mile. There are two main parking areas along this road; the first is on the left after 600 yards, called the Lost Creek parking area. The second is on both sides of the road where the pavement turns to dirt, called the Willow Springs picnic area.

Dave Allfrey on pitch 2 of Bighorn Buttress. Page 296.

Lost Creek Canyon

The Graduate

The Case Face

Mossy Ledges Area

Ragged Edges

Childrens Crag

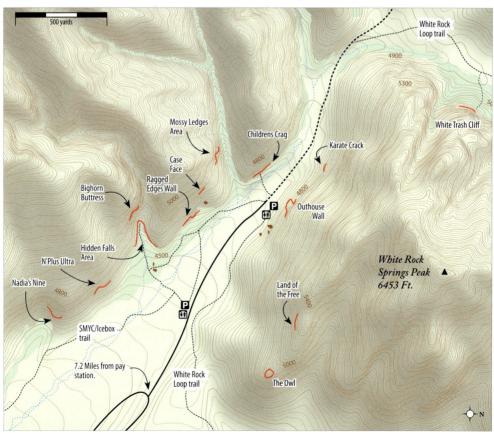

500 yards

White Rock Loop trail

4900

5300

White Trash Cliff

Mossy Ledges Area

Childrens Crag

Karate Crack

Case Face

4800

Ragged Edges Wall

Bighorn Buttress

5000

Outhouse Wall

4800

P

White Rock Springs Peak 6453 Ft.

Hidden Falls Area

N'Plus Ultra

4500

Nadia's Nine

4800

Land of the Free

5400

P

SMYC/Icebox trail

7.2 Miles from pay station.

5000

White Rock Loop trail

The Owl

N

Nadia's Nine Area

Midway between Icebox Canyon and Lost Creek there is a section of the escarpment which faces south. Nadia's Nine climbs a prominent right-facing corner on a small, varnished buttress on this south-facing section.

Approach: Start at the Lost Creek Parking area. Follow the Lost Creek trail for 100 yards then take a left on a trail marked SMYC/Icebox Canyon. Follow this trail for 500 yards to a small saddle. At this point the next four routes are visible on the right. A vague trail leads up and left to Nadia's Nine from the saddle. 0.4 miles, 100' elevation gain, 10 minutes.

❶ Nadia's Nine 180' 5.10a **
Joe Herbst, Mark Moore. Spring 1977.
Single rack to 5".
Interesting crack climbing on excellent rock. The route starts beside a pine tree below a black corner. This is the only pine tree in the immediate vicinity, and is a short distance left of a small cave.
1. 80' 5.10a Climb thin cracks up the tight, black corner to a bushy ledge.
2. 100' 5.8 Continue up the wide corner crack to the top.
Descent: Rappel straight down the route.

❷ Fun and Games 180' 5.8
Joe Herbst & friends. 1970's.
Single rack to 5".
This route climbs the large left-facing corner around to the right of Nadia's Nine.
Start at the base of the corner system in a loose alcove.

1. 90' 5.8 Stem up on loose rock to the crack above the alcove. Continue up the corner to a bushy ledge.
2. 90' 5.8 Continue up the huge corner to the top.
Descent: Rappels from small trees.

The next two routes are on a varnished wall around to the right of Fun and Games. Use the same approach as the previous routes, but cut up and right up a gully to the base of the wall. The rappel tree is a little bit set back from the top of the routes, so it is probably a good idea to bring a long sling or cordalette to back up the existing slings and extend the anchor for easier rope pulling.

❸ Dark Star 80' 5.11d
Paul Van Betten, Bob Conz. September 1988.
Single rack to 2.5". Rp's.
Start below a varnished seam on the left side of the wall. A bouldery start (3 b's) leads to better holds on a bulge. Easier climbing leads to the top of the buttress.

❹ Wheat Thick 80' 5.11b *
Paul Van Betten, Sal Mamusia. October 1988.
Single rack to 2.5", Rp's, optional 4".
A strenuous route. Start below an arete on the right side of the wall. Make a few moves up the arete, then move left into a left-facing flake. Climb the flake and pull up the wall above to reach a horizontal. Move up and right to where easier climbing leads to the top of the buttress (4 b's).

Lost and Found Crag

This area is located above and slightly to the south N'Plus Ultra. There are two cliffs separated by a narrow chimney/gully.

Approach: Start at the Lost Creek Parking area. Follow the Lost Creek trail for 100 yards then take a left on a trail marked SMYC/Icebox Canyon. Follow this trail for 300 yards to where the soil turns red. At this point, go up and right towards the N'Plus Ultra descent. Use the N'Plus Ultra descent to get onto the terrace above that route, then scramble up and left (A few 4th and 5th class steps) to the cliff. 0.3 miles, 230' elevation gain, 15 minutes.

The left-hand cliff is split by a couple of crack systems and has a big roof on its right side. The first route climbs a crack on the left side of the wall. The easiest descent is to climber's left.

❶ Rope Souled Ho 80' 5.4
Dustin Hoover, rope solo. November 10, 2013.
Single rack to 3", optional 4" and 5".
Climb the face to reach a low-angled crack which finishes just to the left of a big block sitting on top of the cliff.

❷ Communist Plan 80' 5.7
Dustin Hoover, rope solo. November 10, 2013.
Single rack to 3".
This route climbs the big crack which passes through the alcove in the left side of the big roof.

❸ Don't Mind Dyin' 80' 5.10a
Dustin Hoover, rope solo. November 10, 2013.
Single rack to 3".
This route climbs through the right edge of the roof to reach a hanging corner. Climb the rib at the right end of the wall to the roof. Pull through the roof (serious, with very poor protection) to reach the hanging corner. Climb the corner to the top.

The following routes climb the right-hand of the two cliffs, a flat, varnished wall split down the middle by a prominent crack.
Descent: Scramble down on either side of the wall.

❹ Forever Malevolent 80' 5.4
Dustin Hoover, rope solo. November 10, 2013.
Single rack to 1".
Start at the left edge of the varnish, just to the right of a rib of white rock. Climb straight up to the terrace at the top of the cliff. Easy but poorly protected.

❺ Lost And Found 80' 5.5
Dustin Hoover, Rope solo. November 10, 2013.
Single rack to 3".
The obvious central crack. Well-protected.

❻ Chrome Fleece 80' 5.5
Dustin Hoover, Jim Mercer. November 17, 2013.
Single rack to 1", include Ball nuts and offset cams.
Start 20' right of Lost and Found. Climb up and slightly left across the patchy varnish to finish just right of the central crack.

The next route climbs a separate wall up and to the right of the previous routes. Start below an obvious seam.

❼ Slobber Knob Job 60' 5.6
Dustin Hoover, Jim Mercer. November 17, 2013.
Single rack to 3".
This route has solid rock and is surprisingly well-protected with small gear. Follow the obvious seam until near its end then trend right to the top of the formation.
A few finger/hand sizes for belay.

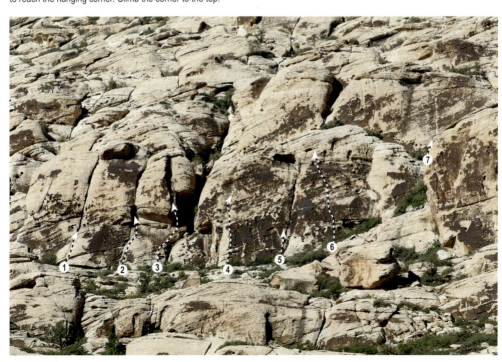

N'Plus Ultra Area

The next group of routes are best reached by following the Lost Creek Trail for 100 yards, then taking a left on the SMYC/ Icebox Trail. Follow this trail for 300 yards to where it goes up a small staircase onto red soil; at this point it is possible to scramble up and right to reach the climbs. N'Plus Ultra climbs an obvious wide crack splitting a huge roof. 10 minutes.

N'Plus Ultra Area

Start by scrambling up to a ledge at the base of a wide right-facing corner crack below and left of the huge roof.

❶ The Abdominizer 120' 5.11b
Paul Van Betten, Richard Harrison, Shelby Shelton. April 1990. Single rack to 3", double 4"- 5".
Follow N'Plus Ultra to the roof, then climb through the roof to its left (2 b's).

❷ N'Plus Ultra 30' 5.10b *
Joe Herbst (Tr.) 1975. First Lead, Randal Grandstaff. 1976. Double 3"- 5".
This route climbs a 4" crack through a huge roof that sits above the lower tier of cliffs, about 150' to the left of Pillar Talk. Start by climbing the wide easy gully below the left side of the roof, and belay on a ledge below the impressive roof crack. The roof starts with a couple of fist jams before some big jugs lead around the lip.
Descent: Go south and scramble down the gully to the left of the formation

The next three routes are based around a big right-facing corner around to the right of the start of the approach scramble to N'Plus Ultra.

❸ Gimp's Arete 100' 5.8
Single rack to 3".
This route climbs the left arete of the big corner. Start 10' left of the corner. Climb past some cracks onto the arete and continue (b) to an anchor.

❹ New Hips Corner 80' 5.5
Single rack to 3".
Climb the big corner to a ledge, then move right to the anchor of the next route.

❺ Geezer's Face 80' 5.8
Single rack to 3".
Start 10' right of New Hips corner. Climb a corner past a large tree, then step left onto the arete and continue up the varnished face (b) to an anchor.

The next two routes climb the face to the right.

Double Pin-etration 75' 5.8
Single rack to 3".
Follow a thin, varnished seam past two pins then follow a crack to the anchor.

🔴 Frankenberry 75' 5.5
A very nice moderate sport route. Start just right of the previous route and follow big holds through the varnished rock to the shared anchor (6 b's).

The next two routes climbs crack systems in the center of the big, varnished buttress to the right of the previous routes and left of the big pillar of Pillar Talk.

❻ Lucky Charms 80' 5.7
Single rack to 4".
Start below the leftmost of two big crack systems. Climb the varnished crack to a rotten overhang, then traverse 15' left on white rock up through the slot in the bulge to reach a ledge. Either rap off a bush or traverse left to a rap anchor further along the ledge.

❼ Senior Moment 160' 5.5
Single rack to 4".
This route climbs the right of the two cracks to the top of the buttress. To descend traverse right and use the tree anchor at the top of Sleeper.

❽ Little Black Book 170' 5.4
Single rack to 4".
This route climbs the corner to the left of Pillar Talk. Start under a roof problem off the ground (crux) to get into a giant open book. Climb the left wall, going up and left into another crack which leads through a bulge to the top.

❾ Pillar Talk 180' 5.7 *
John Landaker, Jim Whitesell, Mark Moore, Joe Herbst. 1973.
Single rack to 3", double 3"- 5".
This route climbs a prominent white pillar split by a hand and fist crack on its right side.
1. 150' 5.7 Climb the wide crack to below a roof. Make a bold hand traverse left to the arete. Continue up the easier face to a belay.
2. 50' 5.4 Easier face climbing leads to the top of the pillar.
Variation: 5.10a Instead of hand traversing left continue through the roof on the wide crack.
Descent: Rappel Sleeper with two ropes or a single 70m.

❿ Big Iron 150' 5.11c
Paul Van Betten, Bob Conz. Summer 1990.
The bolted face on the right side of the pillar. The start 10' up the chimney on the right, before moving left to the first bolt.

⓫ Sleeper 110' 5.9
Wendell Broussard, Rocky Paravia. 1981.
Single rack to 4".
Start below a crack in the face to the right of the chimney on the right side of the pillar. Climb past a small tree and up flakes to a bulge at 50' where the crack starts. Pull over the bulge and continue up the crack to a pine tree on top.
Descent: Rappel with two ropes or a single 70m.

⓬ Fruit Loops 50' 5.6
This route climbs the face just right of a big, rotten, right-facing corner. Start in a bomb-bay crack and continue up through giant huecos and ledges to an anchor.

The next route starts on the terrace above the lower wall, almost directly above Lucky Charms and Senior Moment. It is hidden from view, climbing a beautifully varnished and heavily pocketed wall which forms the right side of a deep chimney.

⓭ Chocolate Tranquility Fountain 90' 5.7 *
C. Long and D.McNair. 2010.
Single rack to 3", a few extra tiny cams.
A nice, well-protected route on very good rock. From a rectangular block, climb up into the chimney on light-colored rock to reach a finger crack running up through pockets on the right hand wall. Enjoyable climbing on interesting features leads to a flake where the crack ends (crux.) Continue past a thin horizontal seam, as the angle eases and holds get bigger toward the top.
Descent: A short scramble down to the south leads back to the terrace at the base of the route. From the terrace rappel Sleeper with a single 70m rope.

⓮ Above and Beyond 90' 5.9 *
Start 10' right of the previous route at the entrance to the chimney. Climb a short, right-slanting finger crack and continue up big huecos to finish up another crack system.

Hidden Falls Area

Hidden Falls is the area around the waterfall at the back of Lost Creek Canyon, to the west of the Lost Creek parking area. This is one of the more consistent waterfalls in Red Rocks, with water flowing for much of the year.

Approach: Park at the Lost Creek parking area. A trail leads all the way to the waterfall. 500 yards, 5 minutes.

On the way into the canyon the trail passes two huge boulders on the right. Both these routes are currently off limits due to nearby petroglyphs.

❶ Scooped 25' 5.12d (Tr.)
This route climbs the very impressive scoop in the west face of the boulder closest to the road. Delicate yet powerful. There is a bolt on top for toproping.

❷ Pooped 25' 5.12b (Tr.)
This route is on the boulder to the west of the scoop. It climbs the sharp arete facing the scoop. There is a bolt on top for toproping.

The first routes are on the left hand side of the entrance to the canyon, a short distance above the main Hidden Falls trail. They are on a very steep, varnished buttress with an impressive left arete. This section is very shady, getting only a little sun in the morning during the warmer months, and almost none during the winter.

Descent: From the top of the buttress there are two descents. To walk off, scramble over the top of the buttress and down the gully on the west side of the buttress. There is also a rappel anchor above Left Out. This is most safely reached by a short rappel from the tree well back from the edge.

❸ Pointless 30' 5.10b (Tr.)
A short ex-sport route at the left end of the wall. The bolts were recently removed from this route.

❹ Stupid 70' 5.8 (Tr.)
Start from the ledge at the top of the previous route and continue up the face above finishing at the anchor of Killer Clowns.

❺ Killer Clowns 90' 5.10c
P. Van Betten, S. Mamusia, R. Harrison, K. Biernacki. September 1989.
Single rack to 3", double 2". Has been led without the bolt.
Start at the base of the cliff to the left of the arete. Climb an easy chimney to an alcove at 20'. Move right and jam through the bomb-bay slot into a thin crack. Continue up the thin crack to a bolt. Move up and left to easy ground which leads to an anchor just below the top of the buttress.

❻ Left Out 90'. 5.10d ***
Joe Herbst. 1975.
Single rack to 3", double 2"-3", 0.75".
The impressive crack beside the left arete of the buttress is an excellent route. High in the grade with strenuous and sustained climbing. Climb up and left on a steep ramp to reach the arete. Good holds lead up the arete to the start of the crack. Follow the crack to where it ends just below the top. Face climb left then up to finish the route. There is an anchor on the right at the top.

❼ Outrageous Fortune 90' 5.13c **

Jared McMillen. 2004. Originally 13b, This route subsequently became a lot harder when several of the crux holds lost their edges.

The smooth wall between Left Out and Black Track. The crux is a desperate boulder problem on tiny edges (9 b's).

❽ Black Track 100' 5.9 **

Joe Herbst. 1973.
Single rack to 4".

The crack in the center of the buttress. Enjoyable hand jamming (5.9) leads to an anchor at 70'. Continue up the offwidth to the top. **Variation: 11c** Climb the steep face above and left of the anchor (2 b's).

The next two routes are on the face to the right of Black Track and end at the mid route anchor of that route.

❾ Stupid Foot 60' 5.11a (Tr.)

Climb the face immediately right of Black Track.

❿ Sole Slasher 60' 5.10a

Mark Robinson, Eric Keto, Al Rubin. March 12, 1989.
Nice climbing up the wall to the right of Black Track (4 b's).

⓫ Camel Toe 60' 5.10a

This route climbs the right side of the face (3 b's), staying just left of a big crack.

⓬ Buffalo Balls 40' 5.11d

Bob Yoho (Tr.) 1989. Don Borroughs, Alan Busby. May 1992.
This route climbs the short, overhanging wall to the right of the previous routes. This route is a little contrived, since it is possible to reduce the grade by using the crack on the left. If you go straight up the wall, it's quite bouldery past the second bolt (4 b's).

Immediately left of the waterfall at the back of the canyon is a huge roof. To the left of the roof is a black slab and left again is a steep prow of brown rock.

⓭ Brave Like a Flash 110' 5.11a

Single rack to 2.5". Optional 4" for the initial crack.
Van Betten, Mamusia, Harrison, Kevin Biernacki. 1989.
Start below the prow. Climb a wide crack to a bush at the base of a small corner in the prow. Lieback up the steep corner and continue up the fragile face above to the top (4 b's).

There are bolts in the steep face to the right of the arete.

⓮ Coronet 80' 5.12c

This route starts at the left end of the huge roof. Boulder up a very steep bulge (3 b's) to a stance at the base of a black corner. Climb the arete to the right of the corner (4 b's) to an anchor on a ledge.

Hidden Falls - Left side.

Matt Kuehl on Left Out. Page 291.

The following routes are all to the right of the waterfall on the sunny wall that lines the right side of the canyon. Some of the routes have rappel descents, but for most it is necessary to walk east along the top and descend around the right side of the wall, a bit of a journey. This section of wall faces southeast and is very warm and sheltered. A good option for a cold morning.

For all these routes it is best to walk all the way in to the waterfall then cut back right on a trail that has been cut through the dense undergrowth below the wall.

⓯ The Threat 80' 5.11a
Joe Herbst, Randal Grandstaff. Summer 1973.
Single rack to 5".
This route climbs the crack just to the right of the waterfall. It is best climbed when the waterfall is dry. Start to the right of the crack. Climb up to a bolt, then move left (crux) into the crack. Climb the crack, past another bolt at the top.

⓰ Flight Line 80' 5.12c
Paul Van Betten, Richard Harrison. Summer 1990.
Start 10' to the right of The Threat. Climb up flakes to a steep, smooth bulge. Pull over the bulge (2 b's) then up a short slab to the top.

⓱ Mind Bomb 60' 5.11d
Paul Van Betten, Richard Harrison. Summer 1990.
Single rack to 1".
Start on top of a boulder below an undercut arete about 40' to the right of The Threat. Climb the arete (3 b's).

⓲ Tholian Web 50' 5.10b
John Martinet. 1970's.
Boulder up the left-leaning seam in the short, steep wall 25' to the right of Mind Bomb. The difficulties ease at 25'.

⓳ Bowling Balls and BB Brains 50' 5.10c
Wendell Broussard. 1980's.
The next seam to the right of Tholian Web.

⓴ Little Big Horn 90' 5.9+ **
Jay Smith, Randy Marsh. 1981.
Single rack to 2.5".
Steep and enjoyable. Start about 150' to the right of the waterfall, below a varnished left-facing corner. Climb to the corner and follow it steeply to an exit right onto a varnished slab. Up this to the top. Rap from a big horn up and left of the finish.

About 100' to the right of Little Big Horn is a narrow buttress with a body-length roof 15' up.

㉑ Unknown
Climb the smooth, shallow groove in the left edge of the steep buttress (3 b's) then go up the easier face, heading up and right to the tree above Grippity Gravity.

㉒ Grippity Gravity 120' 5.10b
John Martinet, Randal Grandstaff. 1976.
Single rack to 2".
This route climbs the crack that goes through the big roof. Climb the crack over the 10' roof into an easy corner crack. Up this to a tree anchor.

㉓ Unknown
Start on top of the same boulders as Grippity Gravity. Climb a crack on the right then move left into a slanting, left-facing corner. Climb the corner (b) then continue up the rounded arete above (2 b's) until it is possible to move right to the anchor of Sportin' a Woody.

Rap from big horn

Hidden Falls - Right side.

㉔ Sportin' a Woody 90' 5.11d
Paul Van Betten, Sal Mamusia, Bob Conz. February 1990.
Single rack to 1.75". Rp's.
A bouldery crux in the lower corner leads to a necky finish. Start on top of the same boulders as for Grippity Gravity. Climb an easy crack until it is possible to move right into a steep left-facing corner (b). Climb the corner, with a hard move to reach a good hold on the left (b). Move up to the top of the corner, then exit right and climb the slab above (b) to an anchor at the top. **Variation:** The crux can be avoided on the left (5.11a).

The next two routes are on the tall wall which is the highest part of the cliff on the right side of the canyon.

㉕ Captain Hook 150' 5.11c
Paul Van Betten, Jay Smith. Fall 1988.
Single rack to 1.25", Rp's.
Start on the left side of the wall. Climb past two spaced bolts to reach a long left-slanting seam. Follow the seam, past uninspiring gear (bold), to its top, then move right and climb the wall (2 b's). Head into a left-leaning crack then break out right and go up the wall an anchor at the top.

Captain Curmudgeon 150' 5.11a
Nick Nordblom, Jenni Stone, Paul Van Betten. Spring 1986.
Single rack to 1.25", Rp's.
Start in the middle of the wall. Climb up to the middle of a roof at 25', pull the roof, and continue up a line of fragile flakes to the top (3 b's).

Captain Crunch 150' 5.10c
Nick Nordblom, Jenni Stone, Paul Van Betten. Fall 1988.
Single rack to 1.5", Rp's.
A fragile, badly-protected and dangerous route which climbs

the right edge of the wall. Climb up to the right edge of the roof, pull the roof, then head up and left to a bolt. Finish up and right to the top.

㉖ Cochise 120' 5.8
Jim Whitesell, Debra Devies, Mark Moore. Summer 1973.
Single rack to 3", double 3.5"-7".
The long left-slanting offwidth on the right side of the wall. Awkward and sustained.

㉗ Tuckered Starfish 100' 5.10c
Paul Van Betten, Don Borroughs. June 1992.
Single rack to 1.75".
This route climbs the prow of the slender buttress to the right of the previous routes (4 b's).

Rock Rastler 100' 5.12c
Paul Van Betten. 1985.
On the right side of the wall, a dirty hand crack leads to an offwidth roof, then a hard, unprotected exit.

Heatwave 80' 5.10a
Paul Van Betten, Pauline Van Betten. 1988.
Single rack to 1", Rp's.
This route climbs a runout, slabby face at the far right end of the wall. Climb the center of the slabby face (3 b's) to the top.

Hot Climb 30' 5.10c
Nick Nordblom, Wendell Broussard. 1989.
Single rack to 1.5", Rp's.
Climb a short black wall at the top of the gully to the right of Heatwave.

Hidden Falls - Right side.

Lost Creek Canyon

Lost Creek Canyon is the deep canyon above Hidden Falls. It is very steep-walled and narrow, cutting steeply up to the west then to the south, eventually leading very close to the top of the Buffalo Wall.

Approach: 4th class up the slabby gully to the right of the buttress containing Left Out and Black Track. The first two routes are above the Left Out Buttress. They are at the top of the approach gully, in a corridor to the left of a large dead pine tree. 25 minutes.

Possum Logic 80' 5.9+
Nick Nordblom, Shelby Shelton. 1988.
Single rack to 1.5", Rp's.
The runout face just left of the tree (4 b's).

The Pocket Philosopher 80' 5.10a
Nick Nordblom, Danny Rider. 1988.
The face 50' to the right of Possum Logic (2 b's).

❶ Bighorn Buttress 390' 5.11a **
Nick Nordblom, Jenni Stone. Spring 1987.
Single rack to 3", Rp's. Double ropes are nice for the crux pitch.
This is a beautiful route with great rock and interesting climbing. It is a little bold in places.
Bighorn Buttress is the tall, slender buttress about 200 yards up and left from the top of the waterfall, and about 100 yards to the right of the top of the approach gully.
1. 150' 5.10b Climb a short left-facing corner, then a face of nice, brown rock to reach a thin crack. Climb the crack to a horizontal. Move right and climb up the face to a bolt below a bulge. Pull boldly over the bulge into a thin seam, which is followed to a belay on a small ledge.
2. 80' 5.11a Climb a little higher in the crack, then move right to the arete (b), step around the arete (b) then move right and make a committing sequence of moves to better holds. A 10d variation climbs straight up from the second bolt and traverses right to reach the same point. Either way, continue right into a right-facing corner. Climb this to a belay. Careful rope management is required to keep the rope drag reasonable on this pitch.
3. 80' 5.10a Move out right and climb up two short left-facing corners. Above the corners, continue on tricky smooth rock (b) to an anchor.
4. 80' 5.10b Go up and right (b), pulling over a small roof into a steep right-facing corner which is climbed to the top.
Descent: Rappel straight down with two ropes. The last anchor is not on the route.

❷ Beau Geste 200' 5.9+
Nick Nordblom, John Martinet. Late 1970's.
This route climbs the dirty right-facing corner down and right of Bighorn Buttress in three pitches. It conveniently provides the final rappel anchor for that route.

Grey Matter 100' 5.7
Kevin Bunderson.
Starting on the next buttress to the right of Bighorn Buttress, this poorly protected route climbs a slabby, yellow face to an anchor below a big roof.

Crack of Infinity 500' 5.8+
Joe Herbst & friends. 1970's.
Single rack to 6", double large sizes.
This route climbs the buttress that forms the left side of the entrance to upper Lost Creek Canyon. The route begins just to the left of the second waterfall.
1. 5.8+ Climb up a nice, left-facing black corner to its top, then traverse left to a belay beside a small tree with a bolt.
2. Traverse left to a crack and a tight chimney and continue up for a long way to a tree.
3. Easier climbing leads to a belay at the base of a huge chimney.
4 & 5 Continue up the chimney on strangely eroded rock for two more pitches.
Descent: Rappel with two ropes.

Fiddler Crack 280' 5.10b
Paul Van Betten, Sal Mamusia. 1983.
The next route climbs an attractive finger and hand crack which splits an east facing wall on the right side of the canyon, about 150 yards up and right of the waterfall. The crack is climbed in two pitches. Descend by a long walk off to the right.

Ragged Edges Area

Low on the hillside to the southwest of the road, between the two parking areas is a prominent, rectangular buttress of darkly-varnished rock. It is split down the middle by an obvious crack system, the line of the route Ragged Edges. This area also includes routes on the wall to the left of the main buttress. The rock is generally very good and the area is quite popular thanks to an excellent collection of short traditional routes. The wall faces northeast. It gets shade from early afternoon during the summer, and gets very little sun at all in the winter.

Approach: From the Picnic Area parking a good trail leads south to a bushy area very close to the wall. From here several short trails lead through the bushes to the base of Ragged Edges. 500 yards, 150' elevation gain, 5-10 minutes.

Descent: For the routes on the Ragged Edges buttress proper, walk off to climber's right. Most of the routes on the wall to the left of the buttress use rappel descents. The tree at the top of Tonto is used for routes that don't have an anchor on top.

The routes are described from left to right, starting at the left end of the long wall to the left of the main buttress.

❶ Crooked Crack 120' 5.6
Single rack to 2".
This is a good climb on nice rock. Start below an attractive hand crack which zig-zags up the middle of a smooth, low-angled wall about 300' to the left of the Ragged Edges buttress. A 70m rope makes it down with a little downclimbing.

To the right of the wall containing Crooked Crack is a pillar with cracks on either side. There is a small tree at the base.

❷ Diplomatic Immunity 70' 5.5
Single rack to 5".
The wide crack to the left of the pillar. Once above the pillar, rappel from a small tree.

❸ Revoked 70' 5.5
Single rack to 4".
The hand crack to the right of the pillar.

❹ Lethal Weapon 60' 5.8+
Single rack to 2", Rp's.
To the right of the previous routes is a low, varnished wall. Start below a right-facing corner in the middle of the wall. Climb the corner, at its top pull left onto the face and continue up to a bushy ledge.

❺ Midnight 60' 5.7+
Single rack to 2", Rp's.
Climb the face 5' to the right of Lethal Weapon (b) to an anchor on the ledge at its top.

The most obvious feature of the wall to the left of the Ragged Edges buttress is a cavernous right-curving chimney in grey rock, the route Kemosabe climbs the left arete of this chimney.

❻ Go Ahead and Jump 130' 5.6 *
Single rack to 3".
Start about 50' below and left of the chimney at a small clearing at the base of the cliff, just to the right of a white block which buts up against the base of the wall. Climb a finger and hand crack, with rounded rock on the opening moves. Higher up, the crack leads into a chimney which is followed to a tree on the left with rappel rings. Either rappel from here (50') or continue through a squeeze chimney to the top and rappel down Tonto.

❼ Ok Ok Ok 60' 5.6 *
Single rack to 4".
Climb the long crack with a couple of wide looking sections, about 40' to the left of the curving chimney and 15' to the right of the previous route. The crack ends on top of a small pillar; traverse left and rappel from the tree midway up Go Ahead and Jump.

❽ Dense Dunce 60' 5.8
Single rack to 2.5".
Start 20' to the right of Ok Ok Ok. Climb some large huecos in rounded grey rock. The crux moves at 20' are unprotected. Continue up and left to a right-facing flake which leads to the top of the small pillar. Traverse left and rappel from the tree midway up Go Ahead and Jump.

⑨ Kemosabe 100' 5.10a *
Sal Mamusia and a cast of thousands.
Single rack to 2", double 0.4"- 1", Rp's.
Start at the base of the curving chimney. Climb the left arete of the chimney to reach a thin crack. Follow the crack then continue up a delicate face (b) to the top.

⑩ Tonto 100' 5.5 **
Joe Herbst, Betsy Herbst. 1972.
Single rack to 2.5".
Start 10' to the right of the arch, below a long, straight crack. Climb the crack until 25' below the roof. Move around to the right and climb a left-facing corner. At the top move left to the rappel tree. It is possible to go straight up the initial crack, 5.7.

⑪ The Lone Ranger 100' 5.9
Climb the varnished face to the right of Tonto, over a small roof then angling left to finish up Tonto.

⑫ Theme Book 120' 5.9
Joe Herbst. May 1973.
Single rack to 7".
The wide crack to the left of the Ragged Edges buttress. Climb the initial smooth offwidth to a ledge at 30'. Continue up the huge recess above on weirdly eroded rock and finish up the final narrowing crack. Traverse left to the tree of Tonto.

Ragged Edges - Right

Descend to the right

⑬ Vision Quest 50' 5.12d
Paul Van Betten, Sal Mamusia. October 1988.
Single rack to 2".
This route climbs the sharply overhanging wall on the left side of the Ragged Edges buttress. Start as for Theme Book. This route has lost some holds and it is unclear if it has been climbed since.
1. 50' 5.12d Climb up a short corner, then move right to the first bolt. Three more bolts lead to an anchor.
2. 120' 5.10d Continue up the left-slanting crack to the top.

⑭ Bodiddly 180' 5.10d *
Richard Harrison, Robert Finlay. 1985.
Single rack to 3", double 0.6"- 1.25", Rp's.
This route is a little bold in places. It climbs the wall just to the right of the left arete of the buttress. Start below the arete. Climb up the lower arete, then the wall to its right (3 b's) to reach a flake in a steep bulge. A strenuous pull past the flake leads to easier rock and the top.
Variation: Bodacious. 5.11a. The original version of the route. Above the second bolt move left 10', then up past a bolt to rejoin the original route.

⑮ Plan F 180' 5.11a **
Sal Mamusia, R. Harrison, Paul Van Betten, Nick Nordblom. April 1983.
Single rack to 3", Rp's.
An excellent but tough route. The crux moves are technical, a little bold and don't ease up as quickly as you might like.
Start at the base of Ragged Edges. Climb up and left into a nice, splitter finger crack which is followed to an anchor (5.9+). From below the anchor, move left to a beautiful, varnished wall. After a sustained crux section (2 b's), easier climbing leads to the top.

⑯ Ragged Edges 190' 5.8 ***
Joe Herbst, Jeff Lansing. 1970s.
Single rack to 6", double 2"- 4".
The long crack that splits the middle of the buttress is a great classic. It is probably best led in one huge pitch, but the first pitch as described is popular in its own right.
1. 50' 5.7 A nice hand crack leads to an anchor on the left.
2. 140' 5.8 Continue up the gradually widening crack, past a section of fist jamming. Higher up, when it widens even more, stemming, and face climbing around the crack lead to the top.

⑰ Chicken Eruptus 200' 5.10b *
Harrison, Broussard, Paul Van Betten, Sal Mamusia. Spring 1983.
Single rack to 3".
A superb face climb up the wall to the right of Ragged Edges. Start just right of Ragged Edges. The route has been led without the bolts and as such is quite a bold lead, bring a very thin cord for a thumbnail spike beside the first bolt. Climb up and right along a ramp for 40'. Climb straight up to a horizontal, then move up and right (b) to a good hold (pin). Climb straight up the wall above (b) to a good horizontal. Move left and climb an easier crack and the face above to the top.

The following routes all end on a terrace 2/3 of the way up the cliff. It is possible to descend by walking along to the right end of this ledge.

⑱ Akido Gun Boy 90' 5.11d **
P. Van Betten, R. Harrison, S. Mamusia, D. Meyers. 1991.
Rp's, Cams 0.3"- 2".
This is a bold and continuous wall climb on great rock. Start 40' to the right of Ragged Edges, below a bolt in a yellow bulge. Climb past the bolt into a brown scoop. Continue up the scoop to a rest (good but tiny cam) and a committing step up to a bolt. At the top of the scoop, exit right around a bulge to a good hold. Continue up the very thin wall above (2 b's) to reach a good horizontal/ledge.

⑲ Sheep Trail 90' 5.10a *
John Bachar, Mike Lechlinski, Richard Harrison. Spring 1983.
Single rack to 3".
A good climb, but bold and strenuous for the grade. Start 40' to the right of Ragged Edges. Climb up and right on a series of rounded horizontal cracks to reach a crack in a steep bulge.

The Graduate Cliff

This is the short, steep wall directly above Ragged Edges.

Approach: Walk around the right side of the Ragged Edges wall then move back left once above the cliff. Scramble up a shallow gully to the base of the wall. 15 minutes.

❶ Walk to School 60' 5.7
Jon Martinet, Randal Grandstaff, Scott Gordon. 1975.
Single rack to 3".
Start about 40' to the left of The Graduate and just to the right of some large, white blocks at the entrance to a corridor. Climb a crack to a ledge at 50'. Traverse right on the ledge to the anchor of The Graduate.
Variation: It is possible to continue up the crack to the top.

❷ The Graduate 70' 5.10a *
Randal Grandstaff, Jon Martinet, Scott Gordon. 1975.
Single rack to 4", double 2"- 3".
This route climbs the steep right-facing corner which is the most obvious feature of the cliff. Lieback and jam up the hand crack to the roof which caps the corner. Traverse left around the arete, go up and back right above the roof to an anchor.

❸ Acid Jacks 60' 5.12a *
Richard Harrison, Kevin Biernacki. Summer 1989.
Rp's, Cams 0.4"- 0.75",1.75".
Great climbing up wall to the right of The Graduate, finishing at the same anchor (4 b's).

Pull up past the crack to a rest. Continue up the face until it is possible to move right into a thin crack. Up this to a good horizontal/ledge.

⑳ Dense Pack 90' 5.10c *
Nick Nordblom, Robert Finlay. Spring 1984.
Single rack to 2.5", Rp's.
This route climbs a very steep right-facing corner which starts above a ledge 20' above the ground. The route starts by traversing left along the ledge to the base of the corner. Climb the corner, exiting left at the top. Climb the face to the ledge.
Variation: Twelve Pack 5.10d From the top of the corner, undercling right, then climb the face (b) to the ledge.

The next routes are above the Dense Pack approach ledge.

㉑ Why Left 35' 5.12b
Sal Mamusia, Paul Van Betten, Luis Saca. August 1992.
Start just left of a black streak. Climb the wall past two bolts, then move left and climb the wall to an anchor (4 b's).

㉒ Why Right 35' 5.12b
Paul Van Betten, Sal Mamusia, Luis Saca. August 1992.
Start up Why Left, then after the second bolt continue straight up to an anchor (4 b's).

㉓ Sheep Dip 50' 5.11a
Richard Harrison, Robert Finlay. 1986.
Single rack to 4".
This is a bold route. Start on the traverse ledge of Dense Pack, below a black streak leading to a white, left-facing corner. Climb the black streak to a horizontal (crux, unprotected) and continue up the corner to reach the terrace.

❹ Circle Jerks 60' 5.11d
Paul Van Betten, Richard Harrison, Kevin Biernacki. Summer 1989.
Climb the wall 25' to the right of Acid Jacks (6 b's).

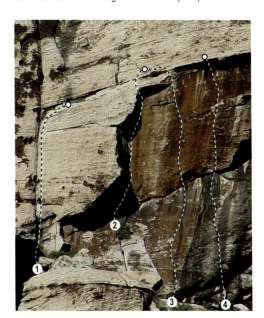

Acid Jacks. Page 299.

Case Face

This face is slightly above and about 150 yards to the right of the top of the Ragged Edges Wall. It is a slabby wall with white rock at the bottom and dark rock on top. An obvious feature is a left-slanting crack, the line of Hard Case. The cliff faces North-East and gets sun until mid/late morning.

Approach: Scramble around the right side of the Ragged Edges wall then up and right across the hillside for 150 yards to the base of the wall. 15 minutes.

The first routes are on a dark wall to the left of the Case Face.

❶ Territorial Imperative 80' 5.10c
Kurt Reider, Randal Grandstaff. 1980.
Single rack to 2", Rp's.
This is a good climb on excellent rock, but a serious lead. Start in the alcove around to the left of the Case Face. Climb a black water streak up the huecoed wall.

❷ DIC 100' 5.10b
A few small pieces to 1" for the initial corner.
Start 10' right of Territorial Imperative. Climb an easy left-facing corner (optional small gear) for 25' then step left to a pocket and climb the attractive varnished wall to an anchor (4 b's).

❸ Just in Case 40' 5.5
Donette & Todd Swain, George Reid, Catriona Reid. October 1994.
Start beside a pine tree on the left side of the Case Face. Climb to a bolt. Step left, then climb the easy but unprotected face to a belay on top of a flake. To descend, traverse left across a slab to a corner which is down-climbed to the base.

❹ Space Case 40' 5.7
Randy Marsh, Pauline Schroeder. 1983.
Start 10' right of Just in Case. Climb up the face (b) to gain a left-slanting crack. Climb the crack to its top, then either head up and right to the roof and traverse across the face to a communal anchor, or use the Just in Case descent.

❺ Head Case 80' 5.8 *
Todd Swain, Donette Swain. October 1994.
An enjoyable face climb. Start on top of a boulder in the middle of the wall. Delicate face climbing on knobs and edges (4 b's) leads to the communal anchor.

❻ Hard Case 85' 5.9 *
Joe Herbst, Matt McMackin. 1975.
Single rack to 4".
Climb the obvious left-leaning hand crack, through an awkward roof 20' up. Continue up the crack and when it ends, face climb up and left to the communal anchor.

❼ Easy Case 90' 5.4
Reina Downing & Denise Childress. 2002.
Single rack to 3".
Right of Hard Case is a chimney/crack, follow this feature onto the upper face. Continue up the face to the roof. Traverse left under the roof to the anchors on Hard Case.

Mossy Ledges Area

A couple of hundred yards to the north of the Ragged Edges Cliff and almost directly west of the main Willow Springs picnic area, a narrow, bushy canyon cuts west into the escarpment. The following routes are on a series of buttresses on the left side of this canyon, close to the entrance.

Approach: Park in the picnic area parking. Follow the trail towards Children's Crag, then cut left and head into the canyon. Go west up the canyon. The routes are reached by scrambling up to the base of the cliffs from directly below in the wash.

The first four routes start in a big alcove behind two large pine trees on a ledge about 200' above the wash. The routes face north. The routes are on superb rock, but sometimes get a little dirty and overgrown.

Descent 1: Scramble down a gully to the left of the formation until you reach a slab. Heading skiers left leads back to the pine tree via a short 4th class step, skiers right will take you to the Case Face.

Descent 2: There is a rappel tree immediately above C.U. Up Top which allows for a rap descent with a single 70m rope.

CU on Top 100' 5.5
Fran Baker, Ignacio Delgado. 2007.
Single rack to 4".
Start from the upper pine tree. Climb past a bush then go up and left on low-angle grey rock. Work left to a ledge below a big, right-facing corner. Climb the corner and the face to its right to the top.

❶ Rapper's Disappointment 100' 5.9

Fran Baker, Ignacio Delgado. 2007.
Single rack to 2", double to 1".

This route starts up CU on Top, then climbs the corner to the right of its final corner. Climb past a bush then go up and left on grey rock to a smooth, black right-facing corner. Follow the finger crack in the corner to top.

❷ Soylent Green Jeans 120' 5.10a ★★

Paul Van Betten, Pauline Van Betten. 1985.
Single rack to 4", double 0.4"- 1", Rp's.

This route climbs the large right-facing corner just to the right of the upper of the two pine trees. Climb the corner past a small tree to a yellow triangular roof. Go over the roof into a lower-angled corner and belay at its top on 2"- 4" cams .

Mossy Ledges Wall.

❸ Sterling Moss 180' 5.10b *
Harrison, Grandstaff, Broussard, Nordblom, Mamusia. Spring 1982.
Single rack to 4", double 0.4"- 1", Rp's.
A good but bold route. Start 40' right of the upper tree. Climb the face (b) to a bolt. Climb up and right to a left-facing flake, then move right and climb a low-angled corner which leads to the right side of the triangular roof of Soylent Green Jeans. Pull through the right side of the roof (crux) into the final corner of Soylent Green Jeans, which is followed to the belay at the top.

❹ Roberto Duran 120' 5.7
Single rack to 2", double cams to 1".
Climb discontinuous, thin cracks in the right wall of the broken corner system immediately to the right of Sterling Moss. A fingertip lieback halfway up is the crux.

The next group of routes are directly above the alcove containing Soylent Green Jeans etc. on a north-east facing wall on the right side of a big gully.

Pussy Nuts 100' 5.7
Dustin Hoover, Chris Brunner. September 2011.
Single rack to 3". Small cams.
The route goes up a nice wall with a roof about 50 yards or more up and left of Cheatstone Crack.

The Boldness 60' 5.9
Dustin Hoover, Chris Brunner. September 2011.
Start about 20' left of Cheatstone Crack. Climb a crack system up the buttress, finishing with face climbing.

❺ Cheatstone Crack 80' 5.9-
Karsten Duncan, Rex Parker, Larry DeAngelo. 2008.
Single rack to 3".
A jam crack, similar in character to Ragged Edges. The cheatstone itself is a boulder about the size of a utility shed. A few stems off this boulder simplify the opening moves. Good hand jams lead up the steep, pocketed face to a small alcove with a wide crack. Stem to the top and walk off to the left.

Hookers and Blow 60' 5.11a
D. Hoover, Jim Mercer, Dale King, Chris Brunner. September 9, 2012.
Start in the corridor 20' right of cheatstone crack. Make bouldery moves up the varnished face of the cheatstone boulder until it is possible to transition onto the main face above the initial overhang. Continue up the wall to the top.

To the right of the alcove of Sterling Moss and Soylent Green Jeans is a broad buttress with a huge, hanging block on its right side. A smaller, mini-buttress lies against the face below and right of the hanging block. To reach the first three routes, scramble up to ledges beneath the big corner on the left side of the hanging block.

❻ Hundred-Foot Stick Clip 150' 5.9 (Tr.)
Climb the slab to the left of the big corner of The Barking Dog. Climb over a short headwall that guards the base of the slab, then wander up the lower-angled rock above to an anchor.

❼ Secret Ingredient 140' 5.7
Fran Baker, Larry DeAngelo. 2008.
Single rack to 2", double cams to 1".
Start just left of The Barking Dog at a short flake just to the right of the dark headwall. Climb the steep flake. Continue up, staying just right of a blunt arete, to the left end of a large roof. Pass the roof on the left then step left to the anchor.

❽ The Barking Dog 120' 5.9
Single rack to 4".
This route climbs the big, left-facing corner system formed by the left side of the huge, hanging block. Easy climbing goes up the left-facing corner leading to a big overhang. Once past this obstacle, continue to the top of the buttress.

❾ Coronary Bypass 220' 5.5
Single rack to 4".
Start at the same point as The Barking Dog. Climb up and right to a belay stance beneath the right edge of the huge, hanging block. Climb past a small overhang and continue up the varnished face to the big ledge. A bolted rap station is on the right side of this ledge.

To reach the next routes, scramble up to ledges in a small alcove to the right of the mini-buttress that leans against the base of the cliff below the huge, hanging block.

❿ Chocolate Sunday 140' 5.8 *
Fran Baker, Ignacio Delgado. 2008.
Single rack to 2", extra small cams.
This route climbs the nicely varnished face on the right side of the buttress. Start to the right of the mini-buttress below the hanging block, below a varnished face. Climb the varnished face to the roof. Traverse left and pull over the roof then climb up and right on the varnished face to the top.

⓫ Pincushion 400' 5.8
Single rack to 3".
This route climbs the corner system on the right side of the hanging block buttress. Start just right of Chocolate Sunday.
1. 140' 5.7 Climb a white crack, passing the right edge of a roof, to reach a right-facing corner. Climb the corner past a roof with an offwidth crack. Continue up the wide crack to a large ledge.
2. 120' 5.8 From the right end of the large ledge, climb the corner system and belay in a small alcove with some fixed pins.
3. 140' 5.8 The next pitch continues up the crack, past a small roof, a short offwidth, and a few more fixed pitons. Eventually climb a featured chimney to the top.
Descent: As for Numic Warrior

⓬ Numic Warrior 400' 5.9
Rex Parker, Karsten Duncan, Larry DeAngelo. 2008.
Single rack to 4".
Start just to the right of the small buttress of Pincushion, above a large pine tree. Climb up to a small right-facing dihedral then move right and up to a thin crack on the face. Follow the crack until it ends. Move right to a small, dirty, mossy and polished corner and belay on a good ledge above. The next pitch starts with easy face climbing to a ledge in an alcove thirty feet up. Climb the right-slanting crack (5.9) on the left side of this alcove. A short, easy pitch up the cracks above leads to the top. (An alternative start may be possible thirty feet to the right, where a thin crack leads to a rusty old bolt.)
Descent: Walk left (east) to a wide, broken area. On the eastern edge of the broken area, a rappel from a pine tree leads down a featured slab to the ledges above Soylent Green Jeans. There is a rappel tree here also, but it is easier to scramble (skier's right) down a short 4th class section, coming out at the big pine tree beneath Soylent Green Jeans.

Children's Crag

This crag is on the left side of Willow Springs just beyond the point where the pavement ends. It sits very low in the canyon, facing northeast. There are some petroglyphs at the base of the cliff to the right of the prominent water streak and as a result climbing is off limits in this section.

Approach: Park at the picnic area parking. A short trail leads to the base of the cliff, in the vicinity of the rock art. 3 minutes.
Descent: The routes end on a terrace which can be followed right (north) to an easy down climb around the right side of the cliff. 5 Minutes.

Mandy Williams on Peaches. Page 305.

Traverse ledge to descend

❶ Zebedee 70' 5.9
Start 40' to the left of Peaches. Climb a crack through the steep wall at the base of the cliff. After the start, the crack gets wider and easier and leads to a tree.

Buckety Goodness 65' 5.11b
Paul Van Betten. 1987.
Single rack to 3", double 0.4"- 1".
This route climbs the flake plastered to the left wall of Peaches. Start up Peaches then move left and climb the flake. When it ends move right and follow a line of jugs up the steep wall to an anchor on the left arete.

❷ Peaches 130' 5.8 **
Joe Herbst. 1970s.
Single rack to 3", double 0.6"- 1.25".
This popular and very enjoyable route climbs the pink right-facing corner on the left side of the crag. Start about 50' to the left of the prominent black water streak. Climb the pink corner and the nice hand crack to its right to reach the roof which blocks the top of the corner. Go up and right under the roof (punchy) to reach a short chimney which leads to a tree belay on a long terrace.
Variation: 5.9 Climb the awkward wide crack through the final roof. (3.5"- 6")
Variation: 5.5 After the first 20' move right and climb the face to the right of the main corner.
Descent: Either rappel from the tree with two ropes (or a single 80m) or traverse along the ledge to the right.

The following routes are on the attractive white slab on the right end of the wall. They provide very good friction climbs.
Descent: Walk off to the right, or rappel from a tree above Ice Climb with one 70m or two shorter ropes.

❸ 22 Minutes Till Closing 110' 5.7
Todd Lane. May 2006.
Single rack to 3". Two 5" cams are handy for the anchor.
Start as for Tarzan's Arm, but instead of following the right-leaning crack, head straight up to an obvious corner. Climb the corner, past a short offwidth crux, to the top.

❹ Tarzan's Arm 100' 5.8+
Start 50' left of the Sumo Greatness tree. Climb a right-leaning crack towards a large bulge. Traverse right under the bulge and gain the wide crack to its right which is followed to the top.

❺ Mitten's Revenge 100' 5.8
Mike McGlynn. May 2006.
Single rack to 5", optional extra 5".
Start at the base of a right-leaning corner 20' left of the right-leaning corner of Sumo Greatness. Climb the groove system to a bulge. Pull over the bulge (crux) and move right into a chimney/groove. Up this, then when it ends, continue up the thin seam above (2 b's) to reach an anchor just over the top.

❻ Sumo Greatness 90' 5.9+ *
Richard Harrison, Sal Mamusia, Paul Van Betten, Nick Nordblom. 1982.
Single rack to 1.25".
Start just left of a pine tree, in the bushes below a right-leaning corner on the left edge of the slab. Climb the corner to its top, then move up and right to a bolt. Thin, sustained face and friction climbing leads to another bolt 15' higher. A final runout leads past a swell to an anchor in the slab above.

❼ Ice Climb 110' 5.10b **
John Long, Lynn Hill, Randal Grandstaff, Doug Robinson. 1981.
Single rack to 3".
Although the hardest moves are well-protected, the final slab involves thin moves 12' above a poor Camalot.
Start to the right of the pine tree, below a wide, rounded crack through a bulge. Climb the face around to the left of the crack to reach a ledge. Zig-zag up the face above to a bolt. Make a hard move past the bolt to a seam which is followed (pin) to a sloping niche in the middle of the slab (poor #2 or 3 Camalot). Step left and run it out up the final slab (5.9) to the top.

❽ Dean's List 110' 5.11b *
Wendell Broussard, R. Harrison, Paul Van Betten, Druce Finlay. 1990.
1.25" cam
The climbing on this route is really precarious, thankfully it is much more closely bolted than the other two routes. The rock is excellent, but can get a little sandy towards the top. A quick rappel to clean off the final slab is often a good idea on this route. Start on top of some boulders below the right edge of the slab. Move up and right under the initial roofs to a ledge. Go right then up to a flake (.75 Camalot), then traverse up and right to the first bolt. Continue straight up (2 b's) to the top.

❾ Stemming Corner 80' 5.6
This route climbs a corner crack about 40' to the right of the white slab. Start beside some green graffiti and stem up twin cracks in the corner, past a small tree to the descent ledge.

The following two routes climb cracks through a large roof, a couple of hundred feet up and right from the right end of Children's Crag. They are reached by a steep, bushy scramble up the short walls and ledges below the left side of the roof.

Cocaine Pizza 60' 5.11a
Paul Van Betten, Richard Harrison. 1982.

This route climbs onto a block and follows the left hand crack through the roof.

Sinsemilla Salad 60' 5.11a
Paul Van Betten, Sal Mamusia. 1982.
This route climbs through the right side of the roof.

Mother's Crag

Mother's Crag has a couple of very moderate routes that are useful as introductory gear leads. The cliff lies about 200 yards further up the road from Children's Crag on the west side of the canyon.

The cliff faces north-east and gets sun until mid-to-late morning. The most prominent feature of the cliff is the large, low-angled, left-facing corner of Motorcycle Mama.

Approach: Drive west up Rocky Gap Road and park in one of several spots past a BLM interpretive sign. A short, bushy scramble leads directly up to the cliff. It's best to aim for Dream Girl then cut left to the rest of the routes. 3 minutes.

Descent: There is a tree on top of Motorcycle Mama, a single rap with a 60m rope reaches the ground from here.

The routes are described from right to left.

❶ Mike's Route 90' 5.7+
Mike Trono. 2011.
Single rack to 3".
Start 10' left of the base of the corner of Motorcycle Mamma. Climb the straight up the intermittent crack system finishing at the rappel tree.

❷ Motorcycle Mama 90' 5.5
Jonathan O'Brien, Mike Trono. 2011.
Single rack to 3", optional 5". Either tiny cams or Rp's.
Motorcycle Mama is the large left-facing corner on the left side of the crag. An enjoyable, well-protected moderate. Follow the corner using jams, liebacks, and face climbing.

❸ Yo Mama 80' 5.6
Matt Carpenter. May 2014.
An unprotected route up the center of the buttress to the right of Motorcycle Mama.

❹ Crag Hag 90' 5.7+
Jonathan O'Brien. 2011.
Climb the blocky, broken corner between Motorcycle Mama and Dream Girl.

❺ Dream Girl 120' 5.4
Jonathan O'Brien, Mike Trono. 2011.
Single rack to 3". double 1.25" - 3".
Dream Girl starts well to the right of Motorcycle Mama on a nice platform below a small right-facing corner. Jam and lieback up to a roof, traverse left under the roof (crux) to reach a vertical hand crack that leads to the top of the cliff.

White Trash Cliff

A very steep and impressive cliff which is slightly spoiled by some poor rock at present. The routes are long, pumpy and challenging mixed climbs.

The cliff faces almost due north and sits very low on the north side of White Rock Springs Peak, getting almost no sun at any time of year. There is a lot on rock in this general vicinity and obvious potential for more routes.

Approach: Park at the north-west end of Willow Springs, just before the road crosses a large wash, beyond which the road starts to go up more steeply towards Rocky Gap. Walk up the road a short distance then turn right on the White Rock Springs Loop trail. Follow the trail for around 400 yards. The north side of White Rock Springs peak is a steep, rock covered escarpment split by many steep gullies. The third major gully has some tall, very steep walls on its east side. White Trash Cliff is the red and white wall at the bottom of the escarpment to the left of this gully. The approach from the loop trail is quite bushy, its best to aim for the left end of the wall, then cut right along the base of the cliff to the routes. 0.9 miles, 25 minutes.

The routes are described from right to left, starting just to the left of a gully/chimney at the right end of the wall.

❶ Punch the Clock 70' 5.11a
Single rack to 4".
At the right end of the wall is a crack which starts about 20' above the ground. Face climb (2 b's) to reach the crack, then follow it as it deepens into a left-facing corner. There is an anchor on the right just below the top.

❷ Workin' Man 90' 5.12a
Single rack to 4".
An impressive route following a strong line. This is the long, steep crack to 25' to the left of Punch the Clock. Follow the crack past a few bolts to an anchor just below the top.

❸ Blue Collar Crack 100' 5.12b
Single rack to 4".
This route follows the steep, left-slanting crack 30' to the left of Workin' Man. Another long, impressive pitch on very steep rock. Follow the crack past a few bolts to an anchor in a small niche just below the top.

To the left of Blue Collar Crack is a thinner, right-slanting seam which deepens into a crack and joins Blue Collar Crack just below the anchor. This is a partially cleaned project. Left again is a long, bolted face which is still a project.

The rest of the routes in Willow Springs are on the right (east) side of the road as you drive up the canyon.

Karate Crack 50' 5.9+ **
Brad Stewart, Danny Meyers. 1984.
Double 1"- 3", wires.

An excellent crack which is located about 500 yards north of the outhouse. Head up the dirt road, looking for an interpretive sign on the left about 500 yards beyond the outhouse. Directly opposite the interpretive sign is an obvious cave below a tree a couple of hundred feet up the hillside. Karate Crack climbs the crack system in the white face to the right of the tree. It starts as twin finger cracks which lead into a left-leaning hand crack.

Crack Ninja 50' 5.12b
Josh Janes. 2018.
Single rack to 1.5", double 2".

This route starts on the ledge above Karate Crack. From the top of Karate Crack move around to the left to a small alcove. This route climbs the thin left-slanting flake and corner in the right wall of the alcove to an anchor.

Decepta Roof 100' 5.12a
Paul Van Betten, Mike Ward. 1984.

This route climbs a large roof about 150' to the right of Karate Crack. Start below the middle of the roof, to the right of some obvious, smooth, varnish patches on the face below the roof. Climb a left-facing flake to the roof and battle over the roof to the finish.

Kilimanjaro 80' 5.11b
Pete Absolon. 1980's.

A left-facing corner 100 yards to the right of the previous route. Climb a right-arching crack, past an obvious block, into the corner. Up the corner to the top.

Outhouse Wall

These routes are on the sunny wall on the right side of Willow Springs Canyon. At the point where the pavement ends there is an outhouse on the right. These routes are on the buttress above the outhouse. These routes face southwest and get sun from mid-morning to late afternoon.

Approach: From the outhouse hike straight up the hill for 50 yards to a recess formed by a huge block on the right.

Descent: Walk to the north from the top. It is possible to rappel from the tree above Spiderline with one 70m rope or two shorter ropes.

❶ Tricks are for Kids 100' 5.10a
Paul Van Betten, rope solo. 1982.
Single rack to 2.5".

Start at the top of the recess. Lieback up a flake to a ledge at 20'. Make a very high step into the slanting corner above. Continue with some tricky stemming up the corner to a bulge. An awkward move up and right leads into a good crack which is followed to the top.

❷ Spiderline 120' 5.7 *
Single rack to 1.25", 3"- 4" for the initial crack.
A nice, varied climb. The upper wall is excellent and surpris-

ingly well-protected.

Start at the base of the recess, below a wide crack in the left wall. Climb the crack to a ledge. Continue up the wall above the ledge, climbing the left edge of the varnish and pulling through a small bulge to reach the top. Belay from the tree 10' back from the edge.

❸ Roasting Affair 120' 5.10a
Wendell Broussard, Richard Harrison. 1983.
Single rack to 1.25", 3"- 4" for the initial crack.
This is a short but serious route.
Climb the initial crack of Spiderline to the ledge. From the left end of the ledge, step up onto the wall, then move left and climb up to a bolt. A sequence of thin moves lead to the base of a rounded crack which leads to the top.

The next two routes start from a platform about 50' above the ground, at the left edge of the upper face climbed by Spiderline and Roasting Affair. They can be reached by walking around the left side of the lower cliff band then scrambling back up and right along the ledge system. The face below the platform is a useful top-roping venue. The face can be climbed pretty much anywhere at a 5.7/8 level.

❹ Sin City 60' 5.11b
Paul Van Betten, Sal Mamusia. 1983.
Rp's, small wires.
Start from the far right end of the ledge. Climb up then right over a bulge with a solitary thin nut for pro. Continue up the face above to the top.

❺ Jam Session 30' 5.11a
Paul Van Betten, Sal Mamusia. 1984.
Double 1"- 2.5".
At the very back of the ledge is an overhanging splitter crack just right of a corner.

Crag Rat Roof 60' 5.10c
Paul Van Betten, Sal Mamusia. Early 1980's.
Single rack to 6".
This route climbs a prominent left-facing corner capped by a roof. It is reached by scrambling 100 yards up and right from the Outhouse Wall. Climb the initial corner to the roof. Pull around the roof into a flare and continue to the top.

The Owl is the small pinnacle at the lower (south) end on the long ridge that forms the right flank of Willow Springs.

❶ The Division Bell 80' 5.12b/c
Sustained, pumpy and technical with a few clips that require care. Start to the left of the chimney of The Owl. Climb up onto a big boulder beside the wall. Step onto the wall and climb the face to an anchor at the top (8 b's).

❷ The Owl 150' 5.10c
Joe Herbst, Matt McMackin, Nanouk Borche. Early 1970's.
Single rack to 4".
Start at the base of a chimney in the southwest side of the formation. Climb the chimney, squeezing past a tight slot at 40'. Continue up a hand crack, and when it widens, traverse right and up to a belay ledge. An easy chimney on the north side of the pinnacle leads to the top.

The Leper 110' 5.10d
Neil Cannon and friend. 1986.
Single rack to 3".
Start 40' to the right of the chimney of the regular route. Climb up to an undercling / roof which is followed rightwards until runout climbing leads to the top.

The following two routes climb excellent, varnished rock on a small buttress several hundred yards up and left along the ridge from the Owl. The routes have a common start to a high first bolt, bring a #.75 camalot or a stick clip.

Land of the Free 80' 5.11c
Greg Meyer. 1986.
The route on the left (6 b's).

Home of the Brave 80' 5.12b.
Mike Tupper. 1986.
This route starts on Land of the Free and follows the line of bolts on the right on the right (5 b's).

The Owl

WHITE ROCK SPRINGS PEAK

Ulysees

Sheep Skull
Crags

Ledger
Crags

Descent
Gully

Angel Food Wall

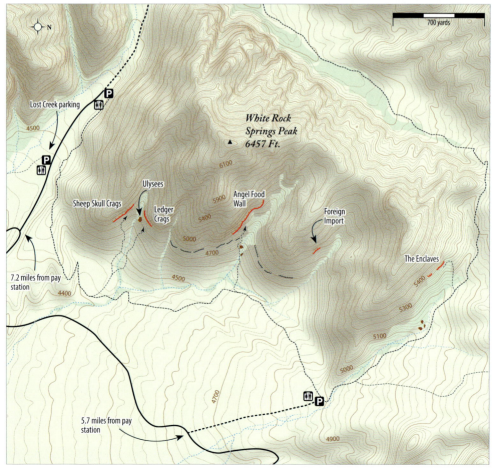

N

700 yards

Lost Creek parking

4500

*White Rock
Springs Peak
6457 Ft.*

6100

Ulysees

Sheep Skull Crags

Ledger
Crags

5900

5400

Angel Food
Wall

Foreign
Import

The Enclaves

7.2 miles from pay
station

4400

5000

4700

4500

5400

5300

5100

5000

4900

5.7 miles from pay
station

4700

The Enclaves

Foreign Import

Introduction

White Rock Springs Peak is the large mountain that is separated from the main mass of the Red Rock escarpment by Willow Springs. The main attraction from a climbing point of view is the excellent northeast face, called the Angel Food Wall, which has some great moderate routes which get a lot of shade. More recently, quite a few single pitch routes have come to light in and around White Rock Springs. In particular, The Enclaves has some very high-quality short routes on beautiful varnish.

Access

Depending on where you are climbing there are several parking places for White Rock Springs. The parking area at the end of the White Rock Springs spur road is most useful for Angel Food Wall and the Enclaves. A small pullout on the main loop directly below Sheep Skull Crags is useful for that cliff as well as Ledger Crags. If that parking is unavailable these cliffs can easily be reached from the Lost Creek parking area in Willow Springs.

Luke Olson on Saracen. Page 321.

Sheep Skull Crags

The Tipping Point. Page 313.

Sheep Skull Crags are to the left of the long gully in the south side of White Rock Peak. These walls face northeast across the gully and are shady except for some morning sun.

Approach: Park at the Lost Creek Parking area in Willow Springs and follow the White rock Springs Trail around to the southeast. The trail crosses the continuation of the obvious gully in the south face of White Rock Peak. Hike through the desert to the base of the gully and scramble up to the base of the wall on the left. 1.5 miles, 500' elevation gain, 35 minutes.

Descent: If rappelling is an option then take it, otherwise a bushy and awkward scramble leads rightwards across the top of the wall then down to the base of the far right end of the cliff.

The most obvious feature of the Sheep Skull Crags is a tall, overhanging wall of pink rock easily seen from the road.

It's a Love Thing 180' 5.9

T. Sloan. 1992.

This route sits by itself to the left of the main crag, about 100 yards left of the pink wall. Start in a large, right-facing corner with a pine tree at the base.

1. 80' 5.8 Climb the corner to a ledge.

2.100' 5.9 Climb a crack up an overhanging face, then finish up poorly-protected white rock.

Descent: To the right with one short rappel.

❶ Dust to Dust 150' 5.9

Joe Herbst, Betsy Herbst. Spring 1974.
Single rack to 4", extra finger-sized cams.

This route climbs the corner immediately to the left of the tall pink wall. Start up a white chimney, then up a thin crack in a nice, varnished corner to a large ledge. Move left and climb a nice finger-to-hand crack in a right-facing corner. Pass a dead tree with rap slings and continue more easily to the top.

Variation: Climb the big corner/chimney to the left of the normal start. 5.9.

❷ Intestinal Flu 100' 5.8

Joe Herbst, Randal Grandstaff. Spring 1974.
Single rack to 7", doubles 3"- 7".

Climb the steep chimney around to the right of the tall pink wall. Climb up the broad chimney, to get onto a large chockstone. The chimney above is blocked by a huge roof. Climb the wide crack out the left side of the roof to an anchor in the chimney above.

Variation 1: 5.11b * From below the chockstone move out around the left arete and climb an excellent, splitter crack.

Variation 2: 5.11d * From the chockstone climb the impressive right-arching roof to finish at the anchor of Tipping Point.

❸ The Tipping Point 90' 5.12d **

Single rack of cams 0.75"-2".

This route climbs the slender corner in the left arete of the smooth buttress to the right of Intestinal Flu. Start by climbing the first few feet of Intestinal Flu, then stem out right into the slanting lower corner. Climb easily up this corner, then pull over a bulge into the smooth-walled and sharply overhanging upper corner. Contort up the corner and arete above (6 b's). Precarious, pumpy and bewildering all the way to the anchor, a great piece of climbing.

❹ Black Glass 180' 5.9 *

Joe Herbst, Betsy Herbst. Spring 1974.
Single rack to 6", doubles 3"- 6".

40' to the right of Intestinal Flu is a left-facing corner with varnished walls. Climb the wide crack in the back of the corner for 60' and exit left to a ledge. Continue up the clean-cut crack in the varnished wall above the ledge to the top.

❺ Pneumonia 150' 5.8

Joe Herbst, Matt McMackin. Spring 1974.

To the right of Black Glass is a steep prow of rock. Around to the right of the prow is a huge right-facing corner. Start up the easy chimney to the right, then exit left onto a ledge below the main corner. A beautiful stem box (with a mystery anchor on the right at 20') leads up to a wild, shallow chimney, and finally a deep, easier chimney leads to the top.

To the right of Pneumonia are several long, right-slanting cracks. To reach the next route walk past these cracks and down and around a small buttress at the base of the wall. The next route is a short distance beyond the small buttress.

❻ Pencil Lead 120' 5.10b

Joe Herbst. Spring 1974.

This route climbs a right-leaning tips crack in dark rock, just to the right of a huge right-facing corner. The route finishes up a chimney with a chockstone.

Ledger Crags

On the opposite side of the gully from Sheep Skull Crags is a steep buttress which faces the road. The buttress is split by a very obvious, impressive looking offwidth crack leading to a black hole. This wall gets sun until mid-afternoon.

Approach: Park as for Sheep Skull Crags. Hike through the desert to the entrance of the gully and scramble up to the base of the wall on the right. 1.7 miles, 500' ascent, 40 minutes.

Descent: Scramble across west into the drainage. An alternative is to scramble to the right of The Ledger about 200 feet, then down a gully to a rappel tree. One rappel with two 60 meter ropes gets you back to the ground.

❶ Ulysees 40' 5.12c *

Handren, Lorenzo, Moulin, Williams. Jan 2009 after rehearsal.
This route climbs the beautiful southwest arete of the huge boulder at the base of the cliff. This old top-rope problem was led, with the addition of a bouldery direct start. Both the direct start and the upper arete are scary and serious by themselves, taken together they make for one of the more harrowing leads in Red Rocks. Start directly below the elegant arete. Boulder over the lower roof, making a precarious move to get established in the scoop on the left (V6). Pull over the next small roof *(Good blue tcu, grey camalot)* and move up to a good hold *(various tiny cams and wires, skyhook, nothing good)*. Slap up the precarious and sustained arete to the top. There is a bolt on top.

❷ The Ledger 220' 5.8

Joe & Betsy Herbst, T. Kaufman, Phil & Steve Jones. December 1974. Single rack to 3".
This route climbs a big, white corner to the left of the offwidth. A good, sunny route that is seldom busy. Start to the left of a buttress.
1. 70' 5.5 Climb an easy corner (past a bolted anchor) to a bushy ledge.
2. 100' 5.7 Climb the wide crack in the back of the huge, white corner to a big ledge at its top.
3. 50' 5.8 Start up the big corner, then follow a left-leaning crack to the top. **Variation: 5.9** Climb the stembox directly above the belay to a bolted anchor. It is possible to rap from the anchor above the variation finish to the anchor on pitch 1 with two ropes.

❸ Holed Up 230' 5.10b **

Steve Allen, Joe Herbst, Tom Kaufman. Single rack to 7", doubles 4"- 7".
This route climbs the impressive, overhanging, splitter offwidth. Start in a recess to the right of a large buttress.
1. 90' 5.6 Climb a loose, right-leaning corner crack to a bushy ledge. Belay below the offwidth.
2. 100' 5.10b Climb the offwidth to a hole. Exit the hole and follow a crack up and left to an anchor.
3. 40' 5.9 Continue up the face on the right to the top.

Angel Food Wall

Angel Food Wall is the beautiful wall of pale-colored rock at the bottom of the northeast face of White Rock Peak. It is split by many long, continuous crack systems and houses several classic moderate routes. This wall faces northeast and loses the sun by late morning in the winter, and early afternoon during the warmer months.

Approach: Drive 5.7 miles along the loop road, then turn right onto a dirt road which is followed to a parking area at its end. Hike down the old road towards the wall. After a few hundred yards a trail branches steeply down to the right into a wash. After this point the trail gradually becomes less defined and more braided, but the various options converge at the base of the wall in the vicinity of Tunnel Vision. 0.9 miles, 300' elevation gain, 25 Minutes.

Descent: The gully behind the wall, which leads steeply down to the south. Descend the gully to an obvious drop off (rappel anchors here), then cross the rib on the right (facing down) into a parallel gully which is followed down to the base of the wall.

Psychomania 365' 5.10d
Danny Meyers, Sam Hokit. 1986.
This route climbs a prominent crack system on the buttress at the left end of the wall. Start about 200' to the left of Sandy Hole and scramble up onto a ledge at the base of the wall.
1. 100' 5.5 Climb the face, heading towards a roof at the base of the crack. Belay below the roof.
2. 165' 5.10d Climb around the roof to reach the long crack system which starts as hands and gradually gets thinner. Continue to a ledge.
3. 100' 5.7 Continue up the sandy and poorly protected face above to the top.
Descent: Over the ridge into the regular descent gully.

❶ Sandy Hole 600' 5.6
Betsy Herbst, Jorge Urioste, Joanne Urioste. 1977.
Double rack to 3".
A prominent feature towards the left side of the wall is a right-facing corner that arches right at the top to form a huge, gaping chimney/roof about 150' above the ground. This route climbs the right-facing corner, then chimneys up behind the huge chimney/roof to its top. From here climb up into a huge sandy hole, then continue up until it is possible to follow an easy flake and ledge system up and left to the top of the wall.

❷ Eigerwand 700' 5.9
John Long, Randal Grandstaff, Randy Marsh. March 1981.
This route starts up Sandy Hole, but moves left to a crack system. Higher up, it follows cracks which lead onto the front side of the pillar that forms the cave of Tunnel Vision. Start at the base of Sandy Hole.
1. 180' 5.8 Climb the initial corner of Sandy Hole for 35' then move left into a crack running up a shallow corner. Follow the crack to a belay at the base of a flare.
2. 110' 5.9 Continue up the crack to its end, then climb up and right across a poorly-protected face to the flake system of Sandy Hole. Belay just below the sandy hole.
3. 90' 5.4 Climb up into the sandy hole then continue up

easy rock to the base of an obvious splitter crack.
4. 150' 5.7 Climb the widening crack, then move left to a left-curving groove which is followed to a belay at its top.
5. 100' 5.6 Climb up a left-facing corner for 20' to a bulge, then traverse left for 25' and climb up the corner above to the top of a pillar at the top of the wall.

❸ Tunnel Vision 750' 5.7+ ***
Joe Herbst, Randal Grandstaff. 1974.
Single rack to 4", optional big cam.
This is a varied and very enjoyable route up a great natural line, which includes a long, dark tunnel. The climbing is sparsely-protected in several places, including the crux chimney on the third pitch.
A prominent feature towards the left side of the wall is a right-facing corner that arches right at the top to form a huge gaping chimney / roof about 150' above the ground. This is the line of Sandy Hole. 20' to the right of the start of Sandy Hole is a short, steep corner leading to an obvious hand traverse under a roof 20' up.
Start at the base of the short, steep corner.
1. 110' 5.7+ The hand traverse on this pitch is intimidating for the second. Climb the corner to the roof, then traverse steeply to the right to reach a crack. Continue up the crack to a ledge, then continue in the crack, now a chimney, to a huge alcove.
Variation: The face to the right of this pitch is 5.9 (5 b's).
2. 100' 5.5 Climb the steep, easy rock above, then follow the left branch of the crack system, which becomes a long, smooth-walled chimney. Belay a short distance up the chimney.
3. 120' 5.7+ Continue up the beautiful chimney to a large flat ledge below a roof. It is possible to climb directly up the chimney, but in several places useful holds and some protection can be found to the left.
4. 120' 5.5 Pull around the overhang above, onto a nice varnished face covered in good holds. Continue up the face then move left and belay at the bottom of a huge chimney.
5. 150' 5.6 The tunnel. Wide stemming and chimneying on smooth rock with little protection, lead up and left into the cave. Continue until you pop out into the daylight on the opposite side of the huge flake that forms the tunnel. Continue up the corner above to a good ledge.
6. 150' 5.7 Continue up the cracks above, pulling through a steep section to reach an easy corner which leads to the top. It is possible to avoid the final steep section by traversing left below it.

Tele-Vision 400' 5.9
Keith Lober & Friends. March 2002.
Small rack to 2".
Fun climbing up a series of variations to Tunnel Vision. It ends at the base of the tunnel of that route; the final pitches of Eigerwand could make for an independent full-height route.
Start around the corner, about 50' to the right of Tunnel Vision.
1. 75' 5.9+ Climb a short, steep face (5.9+, 4 b's) on red rock, then continue past a short finger crack to a bolt and thread anchor on large ledge.
2. 120' 5.4 Climb up the chimney at the back of the ledge and move up through a chockstone to another chimney, to intersect Tunnel Vision. Climb up and keep to the left where there is a 2 bolt anchor.
3. 100' 5.7 Step onto the face on the left (b) and move left to a shallow groove, Climb the groove to just below its top then

move left onto the face and climb up (3 b's) to an anchor.
4. 150' 5.5 Head up the face above (b's) ignoring a bolted anchor, and continuing on to the cave ledge at the base of the tunnel on Tunnel Vision.

❹ Stilgar's Wild Ride 790' 5.8 *
Bob Healy, Joe Herbst. Spring 1974.
Single rack to 5".
This seldom-travelled route follows a series of variations to the right of Tunnel Vision. It has a good, natural line but is a little bold in places. Start by climbing the first pitch of Tunnel Vision to the huge alcove.
2. 60' 5.8- Start up the second pitch of Tunnel Vision but when the crack system splits follow the right branch to a good ledge with a thread anchor.
3. 210' 5.8 Climb the big chimney system above to a good ledge on the left with mid-sized cams for the anchor.
4. 100' 5.4 Follow the dwindling crack system over a little bulge with big holds (5.4) then trend left to the belay at the base of the tunnel of Tunnel Vision.
5. 100' 5.8 Continue up the huge, twisting corner above, past a series of pods and bulges, to reach a big ledge. Face holds make this easier than it looks. (Watch out for narrow spots that can pinch the rope).
6. 210' 5.8 Climb up to the roof above the belay. Turn the roof on the right and continue up the corner, passing a little bulge in white rock (5.8). Higher up, go over another bulge (5.8-) on big jugs then over a short wall to the top.

❺ Rude Rocks 220' 5.10a
Danny Meyers, Brad Stewart. 1986.
This route climbs the obvious crack in the wall to the left of the first couple of pitches of Group Therapy. Start about 50' to the left of Group Therapy, below a blocky left-facing corner.
1. 50' 5.5 Climb the corner to a bushy ledge.
2. 160' 5.10a Starting from the right side of the ledge, climb up to gain a long crack which is followed to fixed nut anchors.
Descent: Rappel with two ropes.

The next four routes are located about 100 yards to the right of Tunnel Vision. From the base of Tunnel Vision, thrash around to the right until you can see a huge chasm above a small cliff band at the base of the cliff. It is necessary to go around this small cliff band to get into the base of the chasm.

❻ Group Therapy 755' 5.7 **
Joe & Betsy Herbst, Randal Grandstaff, Matt McMackin. Spring 1974.
Single rack to 4", optional 6".
Another excellent climb up a long, continuous crack system in the face to the right of Tunnel Vision. There are several wide cracks on this route but also enough face holds to make the climbing really enjoyable. High on the wall to the right of Tunnel Vision is a large roof, Group Therapy climbs the crack system that goes through the right end of this roof.
Start on top of a block on the left edge of the chasm.
1. 140' 5.6 Climb the easy face and crack to a belay below a clean offwidth splitting the white face above.
2. 80' 5.6 Climb the offwidth to a nice ledge.
3. 100' 5.5 Climb the dwindling crack above, then face climb left into a left-facing corner which is followed to a belay ledge.
4. 80' 5.5 Weave around the slab above, using wide cracks and the faces in between. Belay on a ledge beside a tree, about 80' below the huge roof.
5. 75' 5.5 Continue up the left-facing corner above and belay

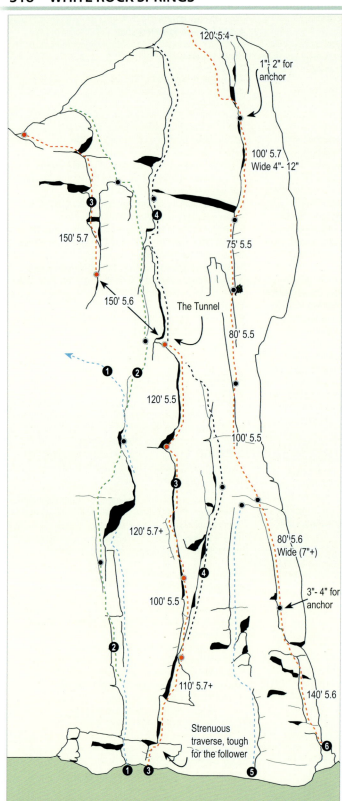

just below the huge roof.

6. 100' 5.7 Climb through the roof and continue up the widening crack to a belay.

7. 120' 5.4 From the belay, continue up the wide crack and escape out left below a roof. Continue easily to the top.

Variation: 5.8 From the belay, continue up the steep crack, pull right around a roof and continue to the top.

The next three routes start towards the back of the huge chasm to the right of Group Therapy.

Gobies for Gumbies 150' 5.11a
Paul Van Betten, Nick Nordblom, Randal Grandstaff. 1985.
Rack to 4", triple 1.25", four 1.75", 2.5".
This route climbs the very impressive right-slanting hand crack in the left wall of the huge chasm. A long, pumpy, and very sustained lead. Climb a steep crack in fragile rock to a rest, then move steeply right into the right-slanting crack. The crack starts as hands but gradually gets thinner. After an intimidating bulge it is possible to do an absurdly wide stem, across the chasm, for a much needed rest before continuing to an anchor in the left wall of the chasm. Without using the stem the route is 11d and tough to protect at the top.
Descent: Rap with two ropes from a bolt and sling anchor.

❼ Healy's Haunted House 660' 5.8
Bob Healy, Joe Herbst. Spring 1974.
Single rack to 6", optional #3 Big Bro for pitch 2.
This route has some decent climbing up wide cracks and chimneys. Start at the back of the huge chasm.

1. 130' 5.7 Face climb up the inside of the chimney at the back of the chasm on nice, water-washed rock. After pulling over a bulge, belay from an anchor on the right wall where the chimney narrows.

2. 90' 5.7+ Continue up the chimney (poor bolt and not much else unless you bring the Big Bro'), then exit right and go up and right to a belay on a big ledge at the base of a left-facing corner. A serious pitch.

3. 160' 5.6 Climb the corner, then move right to a crack which is followed past a bulge into the main corner. Continue up the wide crack to a belay.

4. 140' 5.7 Continue straight up the narrow chimney system to a good ledge inside the chimney.

5. 140' 5.8 Continue straight up the narrow chimney/off-width system. Near the top there is a bolt anchor to the right.

❽ Purblind Pillar 890' 5.8 *
Karl Wilcox, J. Urioste, Marilyn Geninatti, David Sampson. May 2006.
Wired nuts and a single rack of cams up to 4".
To the right of the chasm is an obvious buttress with a prominent crack system in its left side. Begin 30 feet left of the lower portion of this crack system, in an obvious left-facing corner. This is about 80' right of the very back of the chasm where the previous two routes start.

1. 180' 5.7 Climb the left-facing corner to a good belay stance.

2. 70' 5.8 Climb the right-facing corner above for about 25' and then head right, across rounded white rock, to a bolt. Go straight up for about 25' to a large belay ledge.

3. 100' 5.7 Traverse right for 20' to a gully. Ascend the gully for about 30', then head right (2 b's) crossing varnished plaques to reach a crack system, which is followed to a comfortable belay at an elephant's trunk.

4. 180' 5.7 Continue up the crack system to a flat belay ledge with 2 bolts.

5. 160' 5.8 Climb an open left-facing corner with a protection bolt (5.8). As the corner becomes progressively easier, head slightly right to a large belay ledge at the base of the left portion of the protruding upper buttress.

6. 200' 5.6 Climb towards the left-facing corner on the protruding buttress, but staying about 15' to its left. Two bolts show the way up this exposed and beautiful face.

5.9 Variation:
2a. 80' 5.8 Go straight up the crack system directly above the pitch 2 belay to reach a bolted belay anchor.

3a. 50' 5.7 From the anchor, traverse right on easy holds to a water groove. Climb the groove until just below a patch of scrub-oak 50' up. Belay in the groove using a couple of large cams in pockets in the base of the groove itself.

4a. 60' 5.9 The next pitch goes up the broad corner to the right of the water groove/gully. Move past a bolt into the corner. Climb to the top of the corner then traverse right around an improbable shoulder and then up easy ground to the anchor above pitch 4 of the regular route.

Descent: Head east and walk down the Angel Food Wall gully. No raps are needed.

Beheaded Burro 355' 5.7
Neal Douglas, Jason Martin. March 2010.
Single rack to 3", double 0.75" - 2".
The route climbs a crack system immediately above the start of the descent route for Purblind Pillar.

1. 160' 5.7 Make some 5.7 moves into the crack. Continue up the crack, then as it eases, scramble right to another crack. Climb up onto a bushy ledge and belay. Move the belay past the large block and set-up above a chasm. Build an anchor near the deep cave.

2. 120' 5.7 Step across the chasm and move up right toward a nice crack. Follow the 5.7 crack to a large, sandy ledge.

3. 75' 5.7 Climb up the corner from the sandy ledge to the top of the pillar. Drop down on the other side and build an anchor on the patina.

Descent: From the top of pitch three, rap 100' into a brushy gully. Descend the brushy gully (some easy 5th class) to the main Angel Food Wall descent.

Rebel Within 170' 5.9
Kevin Hogan, Scott Massey. Oct 2010.
Single rack to 4".
This route is accessed from the descent from the top of Purblind Pillar; instead of following the standard descent gully, veer into the gully to skier's right. Downclimb a class 4 chimney/slab past rap slings around a block. Across the gully from this point is a small buttress with a prominent crack. This route climbs the crack to a tree anchor at the top.

Descent: Either rap straight down the crack with two ropes or with one 60m. rope make a 50' rap off the backside of the formation, then scramble down and left to a somewhat exposed 100' rap off a scrub oak.

The next two routes are on the far right side of the wall, a couple of hundred yards to the right of the previous routes. They are reached by a bushy scramble which leads around to the right and up onto a terrace below this section of the wall. The most obvious feature of this section is a large crack system in the angle between a low-angled white face on the right and a steeper wall on the left seamed with long crack systems. Echolalia climbs the first major crack system to the left of this feature.

Echolalia 600' 5.9
Joe Herbst, Jim Rosser. 1974.
The route starts with a fourth class chimney and continues in the general line of the crack system for a total of four or five pitches. **Descent:** A long scramble leads south to the top of the regular descent gully.

Lean Lady 600' 5.7
Barbara Euser, Jineen Griffith. May 1978.
Single rack to 6", optional double on 4"-6".
This route climbs the left-most crack system on the low-angled white face. The route includes several very tight chimneys. Start by scrambling up and right on an easy ramp to a tree.

1. 140' 5.5. Follow a pocketed thin crack just left of a large, dark corner and continue up a tight chimney to a ledge.

2. 120' 5.5 Continue up the widening crack above to a belay.

3. 160' 5.7 Climb up and right into a squeeze chimney which is followed to a belay to the left of a huge block.

4. 180' 5.5 Continue up the long crack system, angling right at the top to a belay below some blocks. Another 100' of easier climbing leads to the top.

Descent: A long scramble leads south to the top of the regular descent gully.

Foreign Import 140' 5.12a *
This routes sits by itself on the left side of the first major drainage to the west of the White rock Springs parking area. Close to the entrance to the drainage, look for some steep buttresses on the left side. Foreign Import climbs the longest and steepest buttress (11 b's).

The Enclaves

These routes are on a band of scraggly buttresses on the hillside overlooking the east side of the White Rock Springs loop trail, about one mile up the trail from the White Rock Springs parking area. Although small, these buttresses contain superb varnish and some striking rock architecture. They provide a good collection of short, hardish routes in a very quiet location. The crags face almost straight north and get very little sun. They are also quite high and exposed, making this a good warm weather venue. Having said that, the harder routes tend to climb on very smooth, varnished rock and are much easier under cool, crisp conditions.

Approach: From the White Rock Springs Trailhead, hike up the main trail for about a mile. The best approach is to hike until below the right (north) end of the cliff band. Go down into the wash and hike up the short, steep hillside to the base of the crag. 1.2 miles, 500' elevation gain, 20 minutes.

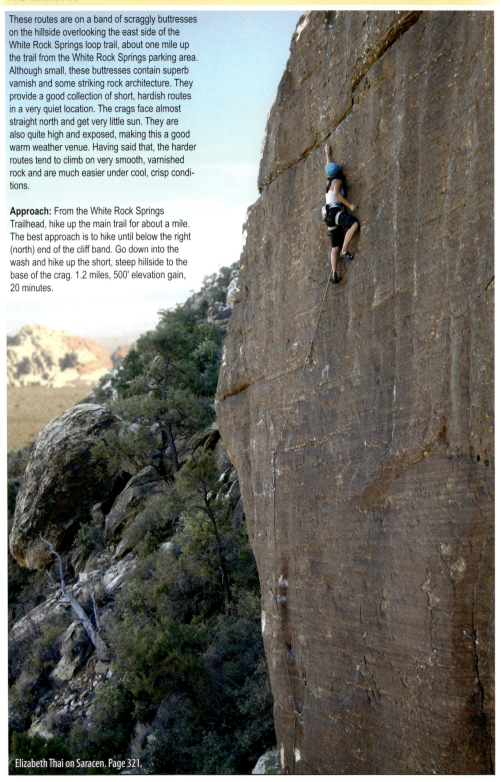

Elizabeth Thai on Saracen. Page 321.

The last major buttress at the right end of the cliff band is a sharply overhanging mushroom of rock, peppered with huecos. There is a nice flat ledge at the base of the wall.

❶ Thin Deck 35' 5.11b (Tr.)
The right edge of the wall. Start at the base of the arete. Fingery climbing on unnervingly thin, but surprisingly solid edges leads straight up the arete. 1"-2" cams for the anchor.

❷ Joker's Wild 35' 5.11b *
A few fingery pulls separated by big juggy huecos makes for an enjoyable climb. Start 10' left of the arete. Make a long reach to a pocket above the initial bulge, then move left to a big hueco. Move back right and climb straight up the wall (4 b's) to an anchor at the right edge of the final bulge.

❸ The Black Queen 45' 5.12b/c **
An enjoyable, strenuous route, with hard sequences separated by big jugs. Follow Joker's Wild to the big pocket. Move up and left to a left-leaning groove, which is followed to a junction with Blackjack at the base of the final bulge. Bouldery moves lead straight over the bulge to an anchor at the top. The anchor can be clipped before the final moves. The route finishes on a big jug up and right of the anchor.

❹ Blackjack 40' 5.11c
Mike Tupper. 1986.

This route follows the obvious line of big hueco's at the left end of the wall. Start at a pedestal. Follow the huecos up and right to the final bulge (2 b's). A burly traverse along a thin crack leads up and left (pin) to the edge of the wall.

A few yards left of the Mushroom rock is a short, flat wall which overhangs 40 degrees.

Slabby Wall 28' 5.11b
Unprotected. Start just right of the right arete of the wall. Solo the surprisingly technical wall on nice varnish.

❺ Thanks 25' 5.12a (V3/4)
Tom Moulin. Solo. November 2008.

This route climbs the right edge of the overhanging wall. Bouldery moves lead up the steep side of the arete to a horizontal at 18'. Swing around right and finish more easily. Reasonably safe with pads and a spotter. There is a bolt on top of the arete.

Directly below the overhanging wall is a small buttress of beautiful smooth rock.

❻ Stretcher Wall 30' 5.12c (Tr.)
This route climbs up through the scoop in the center of the wall. Good climbing, with the crux being a huge reach from tiny underclings in the top of the scoop. There is a bolt for top-roping at the edge of the big ledge below the 40 degree overhanging wall.

Tucked in behind the previous two buttresses is a beautiful shield of perfect varnish. Anorexic 5.14 stickmen will be able to get to the base of this wall by squeezing through a little corridor at the left end of the 40 degree wall. Burly 5.12 stompers will have to go down and around to the left.

❼ Saracen 60' 5.12c ***
A superb wall climb, technical and unrelentingly sustained. Start below a slight scoop in the left edge of the wall. Climb up (b) into the scoop (0.75" cam). Continue up the left edge of the scoop then move right into the center of the wall (4 b's). Finish direct past a good horizontal (2 gray Tcu's).

Attrition 50' 5.12a * (Tr.)
Despite being slightly escapable this is a nice route. Move onto the ledge at the start of The Bollocks. Step out left and climb to a small flake. Move up then make a long reach to an awkward slot. It is possible to escape right onto The Bollocks from here, but the route finishes slightly leftwards up the technical

The Enclaves - Right side.

Glenda Huxter on Albatross. Page 323.

headwall (crux) to a horizontal. Move back right and finish up an easy groove.

8 Knife Slits Water 60' 5.12c ** (Tr.)

This adds a hard direct start to Attrition. Start 6' left of The Bollocks, on top of a boulder. Step left off the boulder and make a long reach up and left from a small crimp/undercling, then step up to some decent holds. Make thin moves up to a rest then make a precarious traverse right into Attrition.

9 The Bollocks 45' 5.10d *

Wires, Tcu's and a couple of big cams for the pockets.
Start below the right edge of the wall. Climb up onto a ledge, then move up and right to the base of the pocketed arete. A thin move (blue and gray tcu's in a small horizontal) gains a line of huge pockets (3" - 4" cams) which leads up the crest of the arete to the top.

To the right of the previous route is a fist crack in a corner. To the right again is a short, steep slab of beautiful rock.

10 Scian Dubh 25' 5.11c

#1,2 Wild Country Z cams. Tiny wires, #1 Ballnut.
Precarious and a bit of a battle to protect, somehow the american grade just doesn't do justice to this misplaced chunk of Gritstone. Start on a big block below a slight rib in the center of the slab. Climb straight up the rib until it is possible to step right and reach up to a good hold at the base of a small, curving flake. Finish up the flake.

The next notable feature is about 100 yards around to the left of the previous routes. There is a huge overhanging block perched above a lower cliff band. Left again is a tall wall capped by roofs. The next route climbs the left-slanting crack in the wall below the roofs.

11 Landing Zone 60' 5.11d (Tr.)

The anchor can be reached by traversing out right on a sloping shelf from the gully on the left side of the formation. This route climbs the left-slanting crack below the roofs. The route starts off with some soft rock, but after a crux bulge there is some nice crack climbing. The route ends at a rap anchor on a sloping ledge below the capping overhangs.

The next routes are another fifty yards around to the left. To the left of a large, low-angled buttress is a short steep buttress of perfect varnish, on the left side of a corridor.

12 Albatross 50' 5.12b/c **

Small cams from Bd #000 to 1", double #00,#2 Tcu's.
A great short climb up the arete of the varnished buttress. Start in the corridor, 20' right of the arete. Stick clip the first bolt and make an abstract hard move to reach a line of finger holds which are followed out left to reach the arete (2 b's) above its undercut base. Continue up the arete (small cams in horizontals) to an anchor at the top.

13 Transmortifier 40' 5.11d *

Another lost piece of Gritstone. This route feels pretty bold despite some decent protection. Start 15' higher up the corridor from Albatross. Climb an easy corner in the right edge of the wall to a roof. Make hard moves over the roof, up right to a good hold. *(Tiny wires and a #1 ballnut in thin horizontal to the right).* Finish up the arete.

The Enclaves - Left side.

Chad Umbel on Monster Skank. Page 382.

The Calico Hills are the low formations of swirling red, pink and white rock, on the right, as you drive along the first few miles of the loop road. They provide a completely different style of climbing than that found in the main canyons. Although there are quite a few traditional climbs here, the majority of routes are fully-bolted sport climbs. Most of the climbing is on lightly varnished, soft sandstone which is literally covered in small edges. In the past the Calico Hills sport climbing has had a reputation for soft grades, but as the sharp edges break off and/or get more rounded with use, many of the climbs are getting steadily harder and soft touches fewer and further between. The nature of the rock is such that the climbing feels very similar from one route to the next and it is a little hard to find individual routes that really stand out, a complaint that visiting climbers sometimes voice. Nevertheless, there is a tremendous concentration of steep, fingery climbing here, with a good spread of grades, easy access, beautiful surroundings and all types of sun exposure; you'd be hard pressed to design a more user friendly climbing park.

The crags and routes in this section are grouped according to their access points. There are the three pullouts on the park road, and the Red Springs and Kraft Mountain sections in Calico Basin which lie outside the park loop road and are not subject to the same access restrictions.

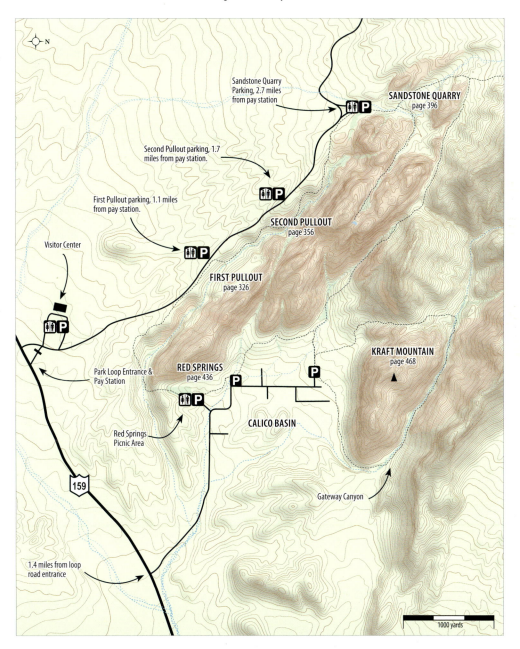

Sandstone Quarry Parking, 2.7 miles from pay station

SANDSTONE QUARRY
page 396

Second Pullout parking, 1.7 miles from pay station.

First Pullout parking, 1.1 miles from pay station.

SECOND PULLOUT
page 356

Visitor Center

FIRST PULLOUT
page 326

KRAFT MOUNTAIN
page 468

Park Loop Entrance & Pay Station

RED SPRINGS
page 436

Red Springs Picnic Area

CALICO BASIN

159

Gateway Canyon

1.4 miles from loop road entrance

1000 yards

The Oasis

Meat Puppets Wall

Fixx Cliff

Tuna and Chips

Dog Wall

Circus Wall

Introduction

Some of the cliffs in this section were among the first to be developed in the Calico Hills. Crags like Circus Wall and Fixx Cliff have never been popular because, unlike regular sport climbs, most of the routes were only partially bolted. More recently, a large number of entry-level sport climbs have been added to cliffs such as The Amusement Park, The Slab, Panty Wall and The Hamlet, and these cliffs have now become very popular. Towards the east end of the area a large number of mid-grade sport routes have been added at cliffs such as Civilization Crags and Dante's Wall.

Most of the cliffs are in the sun all day in the winter but get morning shade in the summer.

Access

The following crags and routes are all accessed from the First Pullout on the loop road. This is on the right, 1.1 miles beyond the entrance gate. The crags are described roughly from east to west.

First Pullout - Right side

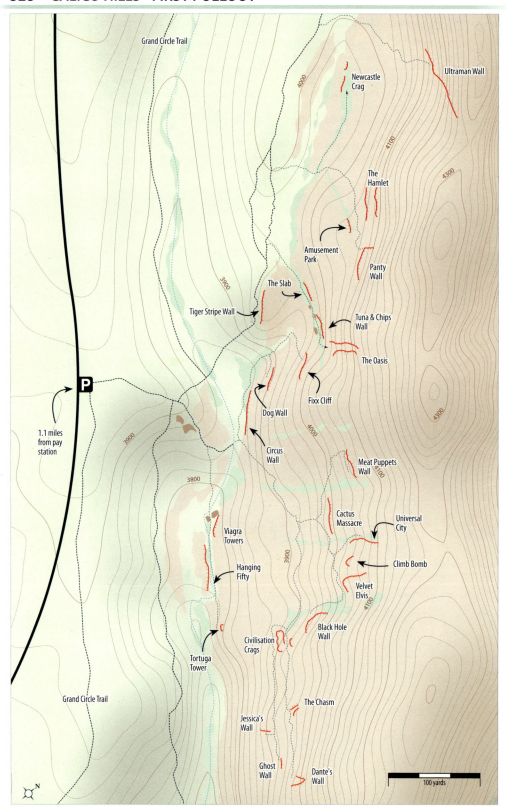

Grand Circle Trail

Ultraman Wall

Newcastle Crag

The Hamlet

Amusement Park

Panty Wall

The Slab

Tiger Stripe Wall

Tuna & Chips Wall

The Oasis

Fixx Cliff

Dog Wall

Circus Wall

Meat Puppets Wall

Cactus Massacre

Universal City

Climb Bomb

Velvet Elvis

Viagra Towers

Hanging Fifty

Black Hole Wall

Tortuga Tower

Civilisation Crags

The Chasm

Jessica's Wall

Ghost Wall

Dante's Wall

P

1.1 miles from pay station

Grand Circle Trail

N

100 yards

The fingery crux of No Dogs Allowed. Page 340.

The Chasm

At a higher level, and about 100 yards to the east of Civilization Crags (see page 332) is a 10' wide gully with vertical, varnished sidewalls. The next four routes are based around this feature. The gully walls are shady almost all the time.

Approach: Go up through the slot at the back of Civilization Crag, and continue east and up through a fairly obvious break. After continuing east for a couple of minutes on flat ground, the big gully can be seen a short distance above. 15 minutes.

The routes are described from right to left.

● Over my Depth 45' 5.9
Michael Kimm. Fall 2014.
Start at a right-facing flake in the right side of the wall on the right side of the gully. Climb the flake, then move around to the right and climb the front face of the pillar to an anchor (5 b's).

● Climhazard 60' 5.11b
Michael Kimm. Fall 2014.
Start just left of the previous route. Follow a left-curving line of bolts through nice varnish to an anchor close to the top of the gully (7 b's).

The Chasm 60' 5.6
Michael Kimm. Fall 2014.
Single rack to 3".
Climb the dirty chimney at the back of the gully.

● Into the Light 60' 5.10c *
Michael Kimm. Fall 2014.
Start near the left edge of the varnished wall on the left side of the gully. A steep, pumpy route on good rock (9 b's).

Dante's Wall

At about the same elevation as The Chasm, but around 100 yards to the east is a huge, open corner with varnished sidewalls. The side walls have some nice climbing with a couple of sections of good rock. The corner faces south-west and the main wall gets afternoon sun.

Approach: As for The Chasm. From The Chasm, scramble down to the right around the formation to reach a short, steep slot. Go up the slot and down the other side, then keep heading east a short distance to a flat area at the base of the huge, open corner. 20 minutes.

Routes are described from right to left. The first two routes are on a pillar at the bottom right end of the right wall of the corner.

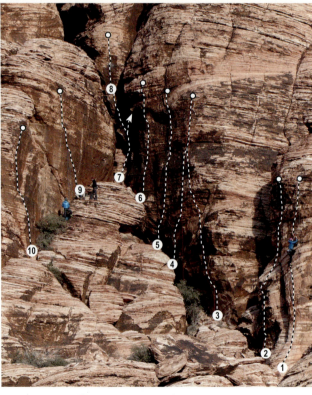

❶ The Right Road Lost 50' 5.10b
Michael Kimm. Fall 2014.
Start at the base of a left-leaning crack. Climb straight up the rounded arete to an anchor (6 b's).

❷ Virgil and Beatrice 50' 5.9+
Michael Kimm. Fall 2014.
Start 10' left of the previous route. A steep start leads to a rest then a steep, juggy finish (6 b's).

❸ Virtuous Pagans 70' 5.10c
Michael Kimm. Fall 2014.
The furthest right route on the right sidewall of the huge corner. Climb through steep rock to a rest then continue up and left to join the finish of Celestial Spheres (7 b's).

❹ Celestial Spheres 65' 5.10b *
Michael Kimm. Fall 2014.
Start 15' up and left of Virtuous Pagans. Thin climbing up nicely varnished rock leads to a break and a bulge, then a slab to the anchor (6 b's).

❺ Divine Comedy 65' 5.10a **
Michael Kimm. Fall 2014.
A very good sport route at the grade on really nice rock. Start a few feet left of the previous route. Climb up and left to join a thin seam which leads up a vertical wall to the anchors (7 b's).

❻ One Hundred Cantos 45' 5.10c
Michael Kimm. Fall 2014.
Start off the boulder just to the right of the chimney. Climb a steepening wall of varnished rock to the chains (5 b's).

At the back of the corner is a big gully. The next route climbs the steep, parallel-sided slot in the right side of the gully.

❼ Abandon all Hope 60' 5.6 *
Single rack to 2".
Very nice climbing leads up the slot to the top.

❽ Three Mouths, Three Faces 55' 5.10a
Michael Kimm. Fall 2014.
Climb the blunt rib in the back of the gully, just to the left of the slot of the previous route (6 b's).

❾ Inferno 25' 5.12a
Michael Kimm. Fall 2014.
A short, bolted boulder problem. Start 20' down and left of the gully in the back of the huge corner. Thin, sustained and fingery, it's best to preclip a draw on the third bolt (3 b's).

❿ Dis 35' 5.10c
Michael Kimm. Fall 2014.
Start 20' down and left of the previous route. Awkward moves lead up the rounded arete to the anchor (5 b's).

Ghost Wall

This is a short, steep cliff with some sandy rock. It faces south and is very sunny for most of the day. The routes were climbed by Michael Kimm in the winter, 2014.

Approach: Follow the approach to Jessica's Wall to a point directly below The Chasm. Instead of dropping down the final gully, continue east at the same elevation to the short, steep cliff on the skyline. The routes are described from right to left.

● Poltergeist 50' 5.11d *
There is a rotten, shallow cave in the center of the wall, start just to its left. Boulder up to a big hueco and continue up the steep wall to the anchor (6 b's).

Paranormal Activity 50' 5.11a
Single rack to 1", double to 0.6".
A serious route with dubious protection on the crux. Start 10' left of Poltergeist. Climb up to a left-facing flake. Up this and the seam above then move left to the anchor of Haunted.

● Haunted 45' 5.10d
Start just to the left of Paranormal Activity. Climb a thin seam, then up and right to the anchor (5 b's).

● Casper 45' 5.10b/c
A series of scoops and pillars in the left side of the wall (5 b's).

Jessica's Wall

This is a small wall of decent rock, tucked away in a gully almost directly below The Chasm. It is quite sheltered and faces east, getting morning sun. The routes were climbed by Michael Kimm in the winter, 2014.

Approach: From the south face of Civilization Crag, scramble around the right side of the crag and over a little ridge to get into a gully. Use a huge boulder to cross the top of a cavern in the gully to get into a little corridor on its far side. Go up the corridor, passing under a huge chockstone and continuing to an open gully. Continue further east to the next gully. Go down this gully for 100' to a short, varnished wall on skier's right. 15-20 minutes.
The routes are described from right to left

❶ Flying Trapeze 30' 5.10a
Climb the left-leaning seam in the right end of the wall (4 b's).

❷ Angel Tears 30' 5.10c *
A nice climb going straight up to the anchor of the previous route (4 b's). The second clip is a little sketchy.

❸ Big Head 30' 5.10a *
Another short but very nice route with good rock. Start 5' right of Light Blue. Climb up the pocketed wall (4 b's).

❹ Light Blue 30' 5.9
Small rack to 1.75".
Climb the obvious, varnished crack system in the center of the wall. Nice climbing with good protection.

❺ Here Comes the Sun 35' 5.9
Start just left of Light Blue. Pull over the initial bulge to a rest, then climb good varnish to the anchor (4 b's).

❻ Lil's Juicy Juice 30' 5.8
The leftmost route on the wall (4 b's).

Civilization Crags

This is a small group of pillars and walls near the bottom of the open gully below Velvet Elvis Crag.

Approach: From the parking area go down the main trail and scramble into the wash below Circus Cliff. From the right end of Circus Cliff, follow a terrace up and right to its top. Go down into a gully, cross over to its other side and go up to a flat area.

Go straight across the flat area and continue past another drainage. The crag is now straight ahead in a flat area on the far side of a small gully. 10-15 minutes.

At the back of the open area is a gully/slot with a south-facing, varnished slab forming its left side. The first routes are on this wall, they are described from left to right.

Civilization Crags - North side.

🔴 The Sun Never Sets 55' 5.7
Michael Kimm. April 2010.
This route starts on the left arete on the prow of rock around to the left of the gully/slot. Climb the prow then finish up an easy finger crack to the anchor (6 b's).

① Byzantium 45' 5.10b
Michael Kimm. February 2010.
This is the first route on the left as you enter the gully/slot. Climb the varnished slab to a small break, then finish up a vertical wall to the anchor (6 b's).

② Mongol Horde 40 5.10a
Michael Kimm. February 2010.
Start to the right of Byzantium in the center of the slab. Climb the slab, pulling over a small overhang to the anchor (5 b's).

③ Ming Dynasty 40' 5.9+
Michael Kimm. February 2010.
Start to the right of Mongol Horde. Reach across to two huecos and climb over a little roof up the slab to two juggy flakes. Use these to pull the overhang to the anchor (4 b's).

On the right side of the open area is a varnished, north-facing wall. The wall is split by a converging crack system in the middle. The first route starts on the right side of the short, varnished wall to the right of the crack system.

④ Conquistador 35' 5.10d
Michael Kimm. May 2010.
Climb past a couple of underclings and finish beside a thin, left-facing flake to reach the anchor (4 b's).

⑤ Evil Empire 30' 5.11a
Killis Howard. 2012.
This route starts up the right branch of the central crack system, just left of Conquistador. Climb the arching, thin, splitter crack starting up the offwidth/flare between Babylon and Conquistador. Finish at the anchor of Conquistador.

⑥ Babylon 40' 5.8
Michael Kimm. May 2010.
Start below the left branch of the central crack system. Climb straight up the rib to the right of the crack (4 b's).

The next three routes climb the nicely varnished wall to the left of the central crack.

⑦ This is Sparta 60' 5.9
Michael Kimm. May 2010.
Start below the left branch of the central crack system. Climb up the initial chimney then step left and climb the arete to the anchor (5 b's).

⑧ Manifest Destiny 70' 5.10a *
Michael Kimm. April 2010.
A nice route up the center of the wall to the left of the crack, finishing up a steep slab to the anchor (6 b's).

⑨ The Fall of Rome 70' 5.10b
Michael Kimm. April 2010.
This route climbs the left edge of the wall. Crimpy at first, then easier to the anchor. The second clip requires care (6 b's).

The next routes are on the south face of the formation containing the previous six routes. Follow the normal approach to the base of Conquistador then scramble down and around to the right to the base of the south face of the formation.

⓿ Meerkat Manor 75' 5.7
Single rack to 4".
This route climbs the left most crack system on the south face.

⓫ East India Trading Co. 50' 5.7
Michael Kimm. Fall 2014.
Start 30' up and right of Meerkat Manor. Climb the slab to a horizontal. Move left over the slight bulge above on huge jugs, then climb the scooped slab to the anchors (5 b's).

To the right of the previous route is another big crack system.

⓬ The Three Kingdoms 70' 5.7
Michael Kimm. Fall 2014.
Start 20' to the right of the big crack. Climb straight up a blunt rib to the highest point on the face (8 b's).

⓭ Super Tsardom 60' 5.5
Michael Kimm. Fall 2014.
Climb the blunt arete on the right side of the face (6 b's).

The following routes are on the east-facing wall to the right of the blunt arete of Super Tsardom.

⓮ Five Charter Oath 55' 5.8
Michael Kimm. Fall 2014.
Start 12' right of the arete. Climb the near-vertical, juggy wall to a small overhang. Make crux moves over the overhang and continue to an anchor (7 b's).

⓯ Sultans and Viziers 55' 5.9
Michael Kimm. Fall 2014.
Start 10' to the right of the previous route. Climb the face finishing at the anchor of the previous route (6 b's).

⓰ Umayyad Caliphate 60' 5.10a
Michael Kimm. Fall 2014.
Climb up the right edge of the wall, passing through a scoop on the left edge of a big overhang (8 b's).

Civilization Crags - South side.

The Black Hole

This wall is on the right side of the next gully to the east of Velvet Elvis and Climb Bomb. It is an obvious, large, varnished buttress below and to the east of Velvet Elvis.

Approach: Follow the approach to Civilization Crags. The Black hole is the next buttress up the gully from Civilization Crags. 10-15 minutes.

The routes are described from left to right. The first route climbs a left-slanting seam.

Quasar 60' 5.10c
Single rack to 1.25", Rp's, 4" cam.
Climb a seam up and left to a ledge (2 b's). Move up and right pulling over a bulge to the anchors of the next route.

⬤ Bottomless Pit 60' 5.10a
Start at the base of the seam. Follow the seam for 15' then climb straight up to an anchor (8 b's).

Black Bomber 70' 5.10c
Start 8' to the right of Bottomless Pit. Climb a face (4 b's) then head up and right to a crack which leads to the top.

The following route is around to the right of Black Bomber reached by scrambling up over a couple of large blocks to a ledge below a short, steep wall.

⬤ The End 40' 5.10c
Climb the wall (4 b's) to the top of the cliff.

Velvet Elvis

Velvet Elvis is a steep prow with an obvious, narrow gully running up its left side, and a large bushy gully to its right.

Approach: From the parking area go down the main trail and scramble down into the wash below Circus Cliff. From the right end of Circus Cliff, follow a terrace up and right to its top. Go down into a gully, cross over to its other side and go up to a flat area. Cactus Massacre is the gray and brown wall a short distance uphill. Walk up to the base of Cactus Massacre, then walk over to the gully to the right of the wall. Cross the gully and walk up a chimney on the other side for 70 feet to an area of low-angled slabs. 100 feet up and right is a steep, bulbous buttress with a large roof, facing the road. This is Climb Bomb. Just to the right of Climb Bomb is a steep prow with a deep gully to its left. This is Velvet Elvis. 15 minutes.

The first route is 70' up the gully on the left of the prow.

❶ The Bobby 40' 5.11b *
Dave Burns. 2001.
Good holds at the start give way to a thin finish on rounded knobs (5 b's).

❷ Black Tongue 50' 5.11b
Paul Van Betten, Sal Mamusia. 1989.
Single rack to 1", One 2", Rp's.
The upper seam has some surprisingly good gear, but it's hard to spot and hard to place.
Start about 60' up the gully amongst some bushes, below a seam in a very shallow corner. Climb up and right to the first bolt, then past a second bolt into the seam. Continue up the seam, then move right at its top and finish more easily. There is a bolt on top of the formation.

❸ Purple Suede 40' 5.11b
Dave Burns. 2001.
Climb over a series of bulges 25' to the left of the arete (5 b's).

❹ Isis 40' 5.11a
Sal Mamusia, Paul Van Betten. 1989.
Start at the bottom of the gully, just left of the rounded prow. Climb up a flake on the left, then move right (b) and climb the arete (2 b's). After the last bolt move right around the arete to the anchor of Backburner.

❺ Backburner 50' 5.11d
Dave Burns. 2001.
Climb the front of the prow to an anchor (6 b's).

❻ Velvet Elvis 60' 5.12a
Paul Van Betten, Don Welsh. 1989.
Single rack to 2", Rp's to do it in its original form.
This challenging mixed route has been rebolted, the fifth bolt used to be the first. Start 15' around to the right of Isis, on the south side of the buttress. Climb a steep crack and the face above (7 b's) to an anchor.

Climb Bandits 40' 5.10b
Paul Van Betten, Sal Mamusia. 1989.
This route is on the front side of a prow of rock in the next gully over to the right of the Velvet Elvis crag. Climb a steep hand crack to a small roof. Pull the roof and finish up the face.

Climb Bomb

This is a short, bulging block left of the Velvet Elvis crag

Approach: From the parking area go down the main trail and scramble down into the wash below Circus Cliff. From the right end of Circus Cliff, follow a terrace up and right to its top. Go down into a gully, cross over to its other side and go up to a flat area. Cactus Massacre is the gray and brown wall a short distance uphill. Walk up to the base of Cactus Massacre then walk over to the gully to the right of the wall. Cross the gully and walk up a chimney on the other side for 70 feet to an area of low-angled slabs. 100 feet up and right is a steep bulbous buttress, with a large roof facing the road. This is Climb Bomb. 15 minutes.

The routes are described from left to right. The first two routes start in the gully around on the left side of the crag.

❼ Climb Machine 40' 5.9
Single rack to 1.75".
Climb the curving crack in the right wall of the gully.

❽ Climb Traveler 40' 5.5
Todd Swain. July 1992.
Start 10' to the right of Climb Machine at the base of an arete. Climb the arete and the face to its left.

The next two routes climb the front face of the huge block. There is an anchor on top.

❾ Climb Warp 50' 5.11a
Paul Van Betten, Robert Finlay. December 1988.
Start near the left edge of the formation, at some big boulders. Climb up and right onto a ledge. Pull onto the steep wall, then up an overhanging seam to the anchor (5 b's).

❿ Climb Bomb 60' 5.11d
Paul Van Betten, Robert Finlay. December 1988.
Start 15' to the right of Climb Warp. Follow a left-leaning crack to a ledge. Climb the roof above and up overhanging seams to the anchor (5 b's).

Viagra Towers

This sheltered wall sits at the bottom of the main wash, down to the east of the parking area. It faces south.

Approach: Follow the main trail down towards the Circus Wall. In the vicinity of a couple of obvious, large boulders, follow a trail which heads east and drops down into the wash close to a couple of huge boulders. 5 minutes.

❶ Knocking Knees 40' 5.10b
Climb the east face of the boulder on the left. Battle past a bush, making a hard move to get established on the route. Move up into a little ramp and past a small bulge to a bolt at the top.

The rest of the routes are on the north side of the wash, just beyond (east of) the boulders. The toprope routes can be accessed by scrambling around the left side of the cliff and dropping back down to the anchors. This is also the best descent route.

❷ Viagra Corner 60' 5.6
Ninfa Cauchois and friend. 2004.
Single rack to 3".
Climb the obvious left-facing corner at the left end of the wall.

❸ The Shaft 60' 5.8 (Tr.)
Ninfa Cauchois and friend. 2004.
This route topropes the front face of the pillar to the right of the Viagra Corner. Two bolts on top of the pillar are used for the anchor.

Locate an anchor at the top of the wall, just below a bush. This anchor is used for the next two routes.

❹ Woofers 40' 5.8 (Tr.)
Ninfa Cauchois and friend. 2004.
This route starts about 15' to the right of Viagra Corner. It climbs a thin crack for 30' to a directional bolt, then traverses up and right to the anchor of Winger.

❺ Winger 40' 5.6 (Tr.)
Ninfa Cauchois and friend. 2004.
Climb the crack and face in the middle of the wall.

❻ Zig-Zag 40' 5.7 (Tr.)
Toprope the zig-zag cracks up the face 20' to the right of Winger. There is an anchor at the top of the route.

The following routes are on a couple of free-standing pillars just to the east of Viagra Towers.

To reach the first wall, from Viagra Towers walk to the east end of the cliff to enter a corridor with steep walls on either side. The first routes are on the right wall of the corridor and are shady most of the time.

Apples and Oranges 40' 5.13a (Tr.)

This route climbs a smooth section of rock at the right end of the wall. Start at the base of a right-leaning flake/ramp about 20 yards into the corridor. Climb straight up a grey bulge on tiny crimps and sloping pockets (V8) to finish on a nicely varnished wall. There is an anchor on top, reached by a short rap.

Cialis Cleft 50' 5.7+

Start about 40' to the left of the previous route on top of a medium-sized boulder. After the initial layback crux, climb straight up a twisting chimney/groove in a left-facing corner to an anchor at the top.

Priming the Pump 70' 5.10b/c (Tr.)

This route is about 40 yards to the left of Cialis Cleft. Pull through a bulge to reach a left-leaning flake. Up this and the crack above to an anchor at the top.

Deflation Dilemma 70' 5.11d (Tr.)

Start 20' left of the previous route. Climb a pocketed, bulging, orange wall just left of two short, thin left-leaning seams. Continue up the easier upper wall to an anchor.

At the left end of the wall is a steep, huecoed crack.

● Hanging Fifty 45' 5.11b/c

Jay Foley, Donna Longo, Milan Foley. Spring 2015.
Start 8' right of the crack. Climb the steep, pocketed wall until forced left into the crack. Continue over the bulge to an easier finish (7 b's).

To reach the next two routes, continue straight east from the end of the corridor, scrambling up a little gully then passing through a tunnel to emerge below a very steep pillar covered in big huecos. The pillar faces straight south towards the road.

● Turtle Track 50' 5.10d *

Jay Foley, Erin Millar. Spring 2015.
A very enjoyable climb, steep but on huge holds. Climb straight up the left side of the pillar, past a hidden bolt at the top (8 b's).

● Tortuga Tower 50' 5.11a *

Jay Foley, Erin Millar, Aloysius Leap, Hector Keeling. Spring 2015.
Climb straight up the right side of the pillar (6 b's).

Universal City

This cliff sees little traffic and some of the climbs are still fragile. It is about 50' high and faces northwest. It doesn't get much sun, just a few hours in the late afternoon, and since it sits close to the top of the hillside, it catches any wind that's blowing. A good choice for warmer weather.

Approach: From the parking area go down the main trail and scramble down into the wash below Circus Cliff. From the right end of Circus Cliff, follow a terrace up and right to its top. Go down into a gully, cross over to its other side and scramble up to a flat area. Cactus Massacre is the gray and brown wall a short distance uphill. Walk up to the base of Cactus Massacre, then walk over to the gully to the right of the wall. Cross the gully and walk up a chimney on the other side for 70 feet to an area of low-angled slabs. Up and right is a steep bulbous buttress with a large roof, facing the road. This is Climb Bomb. Universal City is the steep wall facing into the gully about 100 feet to the left of Climb Bomb. 15 minutes.

The routes are described from left to right.

❶ Ed MacMayonnaise 40' 5.8

Todd Swain. July 1992.
A trad route which climbs the clean-cut left-facing corner on the left side of the wall.

❷ Quiet on the Set 40' 5.10d

Louie Anderson, Bart Groendyke. December 1991.
The contrived arete to the right of Ed MacMayonnaise. The initial bulge has a tough move, after which the crux is avoiding sneaking into the crack to the left (5 b's).

❸ Star Search 45' 5.11d
Randy Faulk, Doug Henze. November 1991.
Start just right of the arete. Climb thin seams up the steep wall to a disconcertingly rounded crux at the top (6 b's).

❹ Celebrity Roast 50' 5.12d ✱✱
Leo Henson, Randy Faulk, Dan McQuade. November 1991.
The centerpiece of the crag. A bouldery sequence on thin holds leads through a bulge to a good shake at a horizontal. The route finishes with a pumpy headwall (7 b's).

❺ Cameo Appearance 50' 5.11d ✱
Randy Faulk. November 1991.
Climb up to a steep crack which is followed to the horizontal break. Positive, but very thin, holds lead up and left across the upper wall to the anchor (6 b's).

❻ Prime Ticket 50' 5.11b
Randy Faulk. November 1991.
This route climbs an open groove in the right edge of the wall, starting on top of a boulder (7 b's).

Cactus Massacre

This is a steep, gray wall facing the road, about 200 yards up and to the right of Dog Wall. The climbs are on steep, rounded rock and are a bit sandy and flaky at present, but would clean up with a bit of traffic. The wall gets sun from mid-morning on. Several new routes are shown on the topo but not described.

Approach: From the parking area go down the main trail and scramble down into the wash below Circus Cliff. From the right end of Circus Cliff, follow a terrace up and right to its top. Go down into a gully, cross over to its other side and go up to a flat area. Cactus Massacre is the gray and brown wall a short distance uphill. 10 minutes.
The routes are described from left to right.

❶ Cactus Massacre 50' 5.11c
Paul Van Betten, Sal Mamusia, Mike Ward. December 1987.
A few cams to 2".
Start below the gray wall in the center of the cliff. After an easy start, continue up the steep wall above (4 b's) to an anchor.

❷ Fractured Cactus 50' 5.12a/b ✱
Gary Savage. 2019.
Climb the crack in the middle of the wall (4 b's).

❸ Cactus Root 60' 5.11d
Paul Van Betten, Sal Mamusia, Jim Olsen. December 1987.
A few cams to 3".
Start 25' to the right of Cactus Massacre. Climb up pockets to a left-leaning corner. Climb the corner, then head up the steep wall (3 b's) into an overhanging seam.

❹ Cactus Head 90' 5.9
Paul Van Betten, Don Welsh. December 1989.
Single rack to 6".
Start to the right of Cactus Root and climb a left-facing corner to its top. Move right over a bulge and finish up the corner.

Cactus Wrap 80 ' 5.8
Single rack to 4".
The right-leaning crack on the east face of the formation.

Meat Puppets Wall

This short, varnished wall is a couple of hundred feet up and right of Fixx Cliff. Most of the routes on this wall now have anchors and several have been bolted into sport climbs. This will probably make the wall quite popular in the future since the climbs are good quality, although brief. For the trad routes, bring a small rack that includes Rp's, Tcu's and a couple of cams. The cliff is in the sun from mid-morning on.

Approach: From the parking area go down the main trail and scramble down into the wash below Circus Cliff. From the right end of Circus Cliff, follow a terrace up and right to its top. Go down into a gully, cross over to its other side and go up to a flat area. Cactus Massacre is the gray and brown wall a short distance uphill. From Cactus Massacre scramble up and left to a gully which is followed to the left end of the wall. 15 minutes.

The routes are described from left to right. The first route starts from a boulder in the gully to the left of the wall.

❶ Blanc Czech 45'. 5.11c *
Nick Nordblom, Paul Van Betten. 1989.
Stick clip useful. The left edge of the wall (5 b's).

Hodad starts on the ramp below the left side of the wall.

❷ Hodad 40' 5.12a *
Paul Van Betten. 1989.
Start 10' up and right of Blanc Czech. Weave up to a short crack and the anchor of Blanc Czech (5 b's).

❸ Crawdad 35' 5.11d *
Paul Van Betten. 1989.
Start 12' up and right of Hodad. Climb the wall (3 b's) finishing up a thin crack to the anchor.

The next three routes all climb the wall to a sloping ledge.

❹ Yellow Dog 30' 5.11a
Paul Van Betten. 1989.
Start 6' right of Crawdad. Climb to a thin crack which leads to an anchor on the ledge (3 b's).

❺ Danger Dawg 25' 5.10c
Climb the wall 5' right of Yellow Dog, then go past a flake to the ledge and the anchor of Yellow Dog (3 b's).

❻ Ranger Danger 20' 5.10d
Bob Conz, Mike Ward, Tom Ray. 1989.
Start 15' up and right of Yellow Dog, at the left end of a little, flat corridor below the wall. Climb the left of two cracks.

❼ Meat Puppet 25' 5.11a
Paul Van Betten, Mike Ward, Sal Mamusia. 1989.
Start 10' right of Ranger Danger. Climb the right hand of the two cracks.

❽ Gay Nazis For Christ 35' 5.12c
Paul Van Betten. 1989.
Climb the bouldery seam 10' right of Meat Puppet (4 b's).

❾ Green Eagle 35' 5.12a
Paul Van Betten. 1989.
The thin seam 12' to the right of Gay Nazis For Christ (5 b's).

❿ The Max Flex 40' 5.11c *
Craig Reason. 1989.
A nice wall climb up the right side of the wall (6 b's).

Take the Skinheads Bowling 60' 5.12a
Paul Van Betten. June 1988.
This route sits by itself in the wash a hundred yards east of the Circus Cliff. It is a gently overhanging wall which faces north across the wash. Start below the middle of the wall. A bouldery opening sequence leads to an easier finish (3 b's).

Circus Cliff

This wall sits at the bottom of the wash, facing the parking area. It only comes into view as you walk down the approach trail but is easily recognized by a huge roof in the center. Many of these routes have recently been bolted into sport climbs and will probably be quite popular going forward, which should help improve the rock quality. This is a very sheltered and warm wall; it gets sun from mid-morning to sunset.

Approach: Walk down the main trail and scramble down into the wash below the wall. 5 minutes.

The routes are described from left to right. The most obvious feature of the left end of the wall is the right-leaning crack/seam of High Wire.

❶ Human Cannonball 35' 5.10a
Kurt Maurer. 1982.
Start 5' to the left of High Wire. Climb the wall (4 b's).

❷ High Wire 45' 5.10a
Single rack to 1.25", Rp's.
Bob Finlay, Mike Ward. 1987.
The right-leaning crack/seam is a necky lead on dubious gear.

❸ Careful of Clowns 30' 5.10b
Start just left of a bush, 15' right of the finger crack of High Wire, 15' to the left of a white water streak. Climb the face to a hidden anchor (4 b's).

❹ Clown Face 30' 5.10b
Start just left of the water streak. Climb the wall to a big hole. Step right out of the hole to an anchor (3 b's).

❺ Lion Tamer 35' 5.11a
Mike Ward. 1988.
Start below the left end of the roof. Go up ledges to the roof then pull left to a thin seam which leads to the anchor (4 b's).

❻ Circus Boy 35' 5.13a
Paul Van Betten, Sal Mamusia. December 1987.
Start just right of Lion Tamer. Climb to the roof and make a really hard pull around (V7?), finishing with a couple of moves to the anchor (4 b's).

❼ Main Attraction 50' 5.12c *
Paul Van Betten, Sal Mamusia. December 1987.
Cams to 1.25" below the roof, a 4" cam for horizontal above roof.
This route climbs out through the center of the huge roof (b) and goes up the wall above, past a wide horizontal crack, to an anchor.

❽ Sideshow 50' 5.12b
Paul Van Betten, Nick Nordblom. December 1987.
Solo easily up to the right edge of the roof. Swing steeply out right on good holds, then make bouldery moves up the wall just right of a bulging seam (5 b's) until the angles eases and easier climbing leads to an anchor.

The next routes climb the tall wall to the right of the big roof. These routes have been straightened out and rebolted to create some much nicer-than-before routes.

❾ Crowd Teaser 70' 5.11d *
Paul Van Betten, Sal Mamusia. December 1987. (Gary Savage 2019).
This is a long, sustained pitch with some good climbing. Start at the bottom-right corner of the arch. Climb straight up through some shallow troughs then follow a seam over a couple of bulges to the anchor (6 b's).

❿ Tight Rope Walker 70' 5.12a *.
Paul Van Betten. 2019.
Start 10' right of the previous route at low huecos. Climb up and left along a crack/seam for 25' then head straight up the wall to an anchor above a small roof (10 b's).

⓫ Elephant Man 70' 5.11b
Jay Smith, Paul Van Betten, Sal Mamusia. 1987.
Start as forTight Rope Walker, but climb straight up into a crack. Follow this for 10' then head straight up the wall moving left at the top to the anchor ofTight Rope Walker (8 b's).

⓬ Big Top 60' 5.10d
Jay Smith, Sal Mamusia. 1987.
Start 3' to the right of Play To The Crowd, below the left side of a low roof. Climb up and right through the roof then head up the wall to an anchor under a small bulge (5 b's).

Dog Wall

This wall sits above Circus Wall, almost directly across from the parking area. It is a popular wall with good, solid rock. The routes are around 40' high, gently overhanging and mostly quite fingery. This is a very sheltered and warm wall; it gets sun from mid-morning to sunset.

Approach: Walk down the main trail and scramble into the wash below Circus Wall. Go around the left side of the Circus Wall and scramble up the gully until a ramp leads out right to the base of the wall. 10 minutes.
The routes are described from left to right.

❶ Cat Walk 40' 5.10b ★★
Don Borroughs, Alan Busby. January 1992.
The leftmost bolted line (4 b's).

❷ Pleasure Dog 40' 5.10b ★★
Rick Shull, Tim Fearn, Chris Miller. Febraury 1988.
The sustained wall to the right of the previous route (4 b's).

❸ Dog Logic 35' 5.11b
Geoff Weigand. February 1988.
Start 30' to the right of the previous route, on the left edge of a block. A hard pull past the first bolt, then easier (4 b's).

❹ No Dogs Allowed 40' 5.12b ★★
Geoff Weigand. February 1988.
Intricate moves and sustained climbing up the steepest part of the wall. Start on top of the right edge of a block (5 b's).

❺ Cujo 35' 5.11d ★★
Geoff Weigand. February 1988.
A good, pumpy route up the streak of light-colored rock just right of No Dogs Allowed (5 b's).

❻ Poodle Chainsaw Massacre 35' 5.11c
Randy Faulk, Karin Olsen. October 1991.
The rightmost route on the wall. Climb an easy right-leaning flake to the first bolt at 15'. A short bouldery crux (4 b's).

The following three routes are not on Dog Wall proper, they are on the short prow on the left side of the approach gully, a few yards above the point where the ramp leads out right to the base of Dog Wall.

Walk the Plank 35' 5.8
D. Young. March 2014.
Single rack to 3".
Start just right of the base of the prow. Climb a crack and the face above (2 b's) to an anchor.

● Burial at Sea 30' 5.10a
D. Young. March 2014.
Climb straight up to the anchor of Walk the Plank (6 b's).

Sunken Treasure 30' 5.10c
D. Young. March 2014.
Single rack to 1".
Start just right of the previous route. Climb twin cracks to a crux bulge (b) just below the anchor.

Fixx Cliff

This wall sits above and slightly to the left of Dog Wall. It is about 70 feet high at its left end and tails off to the right. This was one of the first cliffs in the Calico Hills to be developed, but the routes have never become popular. As a result the cracks tend to be sandy and the faces fragile. All the routes require gear, especially Rp's, and only Saved By Zero has an anchor. The cliff gets sun from mid-morning to sunset.

Approach: Walk down the main trail and scramble into the wash below Circus Wall. Go around the left side of Circus Wall and scramble up the gully. The Fixx wall is a short distance to the right from the top of the gully. 12 minutes.
The routes are described from left to right. The route lengths do not include some easy slab climbing at the top.

❶ The Whiff 40' 5.10b
Jay Smith, Mike Ward. March 1987.
Serious. At the left end is a short, right-leaning seam just to the left of a large, rotten hueco. Climb the seam to reach a deeper crack at 15'. Climb straight up the crack to the top.

❷ Snowblind 45' 5.11c
Paul Crawford. March 1987.
A bold route. Start 10' to the right of the Whiff, below the left end of a small overhang. Climb up and right through the overhang, then follow huecos up and left to a bolt. Step right and pull up into a slight scoop which leads to the top.

❸ Stand or Fall 50' 5.11a
Paul Van Betten, Jim Lybarger. March 1987.
Start a couple of feet to the right of Snowblind, beside a left-facing flake below the overhang. Follow huecos and varnished edges to a bolt at 20'. Follow the crack above, over a bulge, into a right-facing corner which is followed to the top.

❹ Crack 60' 5.11b *
Paul Crawford, Jay Smith. March 1987.
Single rack to 2". Rp's, double 0.4"- 1".
The obvious finger crack, which leads into a big left-facing corner, at the left end of the wall. This route can get a little sandy, but when clean it is excellent.

❺ Freebase 60' 5.11d *
Paul Crawford, Paul Van Betten, Jay Smith, Nick Nordblom. 1987.
A good route which climbs the front of the obvious pillar to the right of crack. Climb a short, steep crack (a big cam (4") is nice) then continue up the front of the pillar (3 b's) to the top.

❻ Saved by Zero 60' 5.11b **
Nick Nordblom, Danny Meyers. May 1986.
Single rack to 2.5". Rp's, double 0.4"- 1".
The obvious long, steepening hand and finger crack to the right of Freebase. When clean this is a good route.

❼ Red Skies 55' 5.11d
Paul Van Betten, Paul Crawford. March 1987.
Start 5' right of Saved by Zero. Delicate and sustained climbing up a seam leads to the first bolt at 25'. Continue up the steepening face (2 b's) to the top.

❽ The Geezer 50' 5.11b
Jay Smith, Paul Crawford. March 1987.
Start 8' to the right of Red Skies. Climb past a drilled piton to reach a crack system which is followed to the top.

The wall to the right gradually gets shorter. It is split by a series of seams which are fragile, badly protected and dangerous.

❾ Cocaine Hotline 45' 5.11b
Paul Crawford, John Rosholt, Jay Smith. March 1987.
This route starts at the left end of a horizontal seam which goes all the way across the base of the right side of the wall. Pull through the bulge to a thin seam in varnished rock which is followed (b) to the top.

❿ Reach the Beach 45' 5.11a
Nick Nordblom, Jenni Stone, Jay Smith, Paul Crawford. March 1987.
Start on top of a boulder 10' to the right of Cocaine Hotline. Climb to a varnished seam which leads past a bolt to the top.

⓫ Eight Ball 40' 5.11a
Paul Crawford, Nick Nordblom, Jenni Stone, Jay Smith. March 1987.
Start 10' to the right of Reach the Beach. A bouldery start leads to the horizontal; follow a thin seam (b) to the top.

One Thing Leads to Another 35' 5.11a
Nick Nordblom, Jenni Stone, Jay Smith, Paul Crawford. March 1987.
The scary-looking thin seam 8' to the right of Eight Ball.

The Skagg 30' 5.11b
Mike Ward, Paul Van Betten, Jay Smith, Paul Crawford. March 1987.
The 30' high seam 10' to the right of the previous route.

Running 30' 5.11b
Nick Nordblom, Jay Smith. March 1987.
The next seam, 10' to the right of The Skagg.

Outside the Envelope 20' 5.11b
Nick Nordblom. March 1987.
A 20' high route up the next seam to the right.

The Bindle 15' 5.11a
The last seam on the right.

Tiger Stripe Wall

This unusual looking wall, a white blob laced with thin bands of red rock, overlooks the hiking trail that leads west along the wash towards the Second Pullout. The rock is a bit dubious on these routes. The cliff gets the sun from mid-morning on.

Approach: From the parking area hike down the main trail for 100 yards then follow the Grand Circle trail which branches off to the left. Follow the trail to the bottom of the hill. The cliff is on the right 50 yards further along the trail. There is a small formation in front of the wall, the routes start in the corridor behind this formation. 5 minutes.

The routes are described from left to right.

A useful landmark is a long, thin seam in the middle of the wall, the line of Action by the Fraction.

Sandra Horna on The Great Red Roof. Page 352.

❶ White Tigers 70' 5.10b
Dan McQuade. 1990.
Start 30' to the left of Action by the Fraction. Climb the thin wall to an anchor (4 b's).

❷ Action by the Fraction 90' 5.10c
Danny Meyers, Jenni Stone. 1984.
Single rack to 2", Rp's.
A serious lead with poor protection. Start below and left of the central crack system. Move up and right (b) into the crack, which is followed to an anchor.

❸ A Fraction of the Action 110' 5.10a *
Paul Van Betten, Don Welsh. 1988.
Climb the wall to the right of Action by the Fraction (8 b's).

❹ Bengal 120' 5.9+
Rp's, double 4"- 7".
This route climbs the impressive offwidth crack, formed by the left edge of the huge block on the upper right side of the formation. Start 6' right of the previous route. Climb a thin seam to a ledge then finish up the offwidth.

Tigers Edge 30' 5.9
Around to the right of the previous routes facing across the gully towards Dog Wall is a short arete. Climb the arete (b).

Ultraman Wall

The Oasis

Panty Wall

The Hamlet

Newcastle Crag

Tuna & Chips

The Slab

Tiger Stripe Wall

First Pullout - Left side

Tuna and Chips Wall

The Tuna and Chips wall is the 250' high slab above and left of Dog Wall and the Fixx cliff. The upper half of the slab is split by a deep chimney/gully which drains into an obvious water streak at the bottom of the wall.

This area has a nice selection of moderate, multi-pitch routes, although the face climbs tend to be quite runout. It gets sun all day, and is very warm and sheltered.

Approach: From the parking area hike down the main trail for 100 yards then follow the Grand Circle trail which branches off to the left. Follow the trail down to the bottom of a hill and up the other side onto a dirt ridge. When the trails reaches the crest of the dirt ridge head down into the broad, bushy corridor on the right and follow it back towards the east for 250 yards to an area of blocks below the wall. 12 minutes.

Descent: Scramble off to the right.

At the left end of Tuna and Chips wall is a small buttress.

❶ The Minnow 30' 5.8 (Tr.)
This route uses a bolted anchor on top of the buttress to top rope its front face. Reach the top of the buttress by scrambling up from the left.

❷ Dolphin Safe 110' 5.7
Mark Limage, Dave Melchoir, Derek Reinig. 2001.
Start at the left edge of the wall, below the slab to the right of the small buttress. Climb the slab to a short left-facing flake/corner (2.5" cam). From the top of the corner continue up the face (5 b's) to an anchor.

❸ Tuna and Chips 200' 5.7 *
Bob Conz, Jim Lybarger. January 1987.
Single rack to 3".
Start 30' to the left of the water streak at the left edge of a block at the base of the wall.
1. 100' 5.7 Climb the slab, staying to the right of a black left-facing flake. Continue up (3 b's) and belay at a crack.
2. 100' 5.3 Continue up the easy crack and the low-angled face above to an anchor at the top.

❹ Albacore Man 100' 5.8
Mark Limage. 2000.
Start on top of the block at the base of Chips and Salsa. Climb the face to the left of Chips and Salsa (4 b's) to an anchor.

A stray anchor between Albacore Man and Chips and Salsa can be used to top rope the face between these routes (5.6).

❺ Chips and Salsa 210' 5.3 *
Single rack to 6".
One of the easiest routes in Red Rocks, a good introduction to multi-pitch climbing.
This route climbs the crack in the middle of the formation. Start just to the left of the water streak, behind a block and below a crack.
1. 60' 5.3 Climb the crack to reach an anchor at the bottom of the chimney/gully.
2. 150' 5.3 Continue up the long chimney to the top.

❻ Water Streak 50' 5.8
Jim Kessler. 1987.
Starting at the base of the water streak, zig-zag up the slab to either the anchor of Chips and Salsa or another anchor to its right. The water streak itself is quite smooth so the route uses holds on either side. Climbing up the water streak is 5.10a.

❼ Tuna Cookies 250' 5.7
Single rack to 2.5".
This route starts to the right of the water streak, beside some blocks at the base of the wall and below left-leaning seams.
1. 150' 5.7 Climb up and left for 30' to a bolt. Then continue straight up the face (b) to the left end of a roof. Climb past the roof to a ledge.
2. 100' 5.3 Climb the low-angled face to the top.

❽ Chips Ahoy 250' 5.9
Mike Ward, Paul Van Betten. 1986.
Start at the same place as Tuna Cookies.
1. 100' 5.8 Climb straight up the wall (2 b's) to an anchor below the roof.
2. 150' 5.9 Pull over the roof (b) and continue to the top.

❾ Fishbreath 120' 5.5
This route starts in a very shallow gully at the right end of the wall. Climb the gully for 15' then move left and climb a cracked wall until it is possible to move left to the anchor of Chips Ahoy.

The following routes are on the sunny wall to the right of the gully of The Oasis. From the base of Tuna and Chips, keep going up through the bushes, staying to the left until a pull over a boulder leads into a narrow corridor. The first route is at the entrance to the small corridor, on its left side.

Safe Drinking Water 65' 5.9 (Tr.)
This route uses an anchor to the left of the anchor of Reverse Osmosis to toprope a line straight up the wall.

🔴 Reverse Osmosis 70' 5.8
Mark Limage, Philip Swiny. 2007.
The well-bolted line on the left side of the wall (10 b's).

Lake Mead Funk 75' 5.8+ (Tr.)
This toprope route uses a set of anchors below and to the left of the anchors of No Hay Sequia. It climbs straight up the slabby face.

🔴 No Hay Sequia 85' 5.7+
Mark Limage, Philip Swiny. 2007.
Start 15' to the right of Reverse Osmosis below a varnished slab. The long line of bolts on the right side of the wall (10 b's).

The Oasis

The Oasis

These routes climb the walls on either side of the gully to the right of the Tuna and Chips wall. The routes are mostly shady, although those on the west wall get a little sun early in the day, and those on the east wall a little sun late in the day. The routes are quite short, but they give steep, fingery climbing on mostly good quality rock.

Approach: From the parking area hike down the main trail for 100 yards then follow the Grand Circle trail which branches off to the left. Follow the trail down to the bottom of a hill and up the other side onto a dirt ridge. When the trails reaches the crest of the dirt ridge, head down into the broad, bushy corridor on the right and follow it back towards the east for 250 yards to an area of blocks below the Tuna and Chips wall. Go around the right side of the Tuna and Chips wall and scramble up and left into the gully. 15 minutes.

The first routes described are on the east (right) wall of the approach gully and are described from right to left.

❶ Hang Ten 50' 5.11d
Brian McCray. March 1998.
The right most route on the wall climbs a thin seam into a shallow, varnished corner (5 b's).

❷ Tropicana 50' 5.12b
Brian McCray. March 1998.
Climb the bulging wall to the left of Hang Ten (7 b's).

❸ The Sands 45' 5.12b *
Brian McCray. March 1998.
The steep wall to the left of Tropicana. This route has lost some holds since it was first done, making it harder (7 b's).

❹ Pads Passion 30' 5.8
Tim Henkles. March 1998.
This route starts 15' to the left of The Sands and climbs up and left across the wall to an anchor (4 b's).

Diamond Dance 25' 5.7
Chris Lowry. March 1998.
This trad route climbs the finger crack to the left of Pads Passion. Climb the finger crack then go up and right to an anchor.

The routes on the west (left) wall of the gully are described from right to left. Towards the top, the gully bends to the right, at the bend is a short, bulging buttress with an obvious left-slanting crack, the line of Money.

● Insecure Delusions 30' 5.12b
Mike Lewis. March 1998.
The bouldery wall to the right of Money (4 b's).

● Money 30' 5.10c **
Mike Lewis. March 1998.
A fun, steep route up the left-slanting crack (3 b's).

The next routes are 50' to the left, where the left wall of the gully becomes very steep. The first route starts almost directly opposite the crack of Diamond Dance.

❺ The Warming 25' 5.10d
Brian McCray. March 1998.
Climb the short crack at the right end of the steep wall (3 b's).

❻ Snack Crack 30' 5.11d
Brian McCray. March 1998.
A bouldery crux. Climb the seam 6' left of the last route (4 b's).

❼ My Tai 35' 5.12a *
Brian McCray. March 1998.
The wall just left of Snack Crack (5 b's).

❽ Casino 35' 5.12a **
Brian McCray. March 1998.
The very steep wall to the left of My Tai (5 b's).

The next two routes start from a bolted anchor just above the drop off at the left end of the west wall.

❾ Crack Bar 100' 5.8
From the anchor, climb the right-leaning crack.

❿ Serious Libation 40' 5.8
Mark Limage. Early-2000's.
Start up Crack Bar then move left and up to an anchor (5 b's).

The Slab

This is the sunny slab, on the left side of the drainage, which is passed on the approach to the Tuna and Chips Wall. The rock is still flaky and soft, but is gradually cleaning up with use. Originally a top-roping venue, the cliff is now fully-bolted and provides some of the most moderate sport climbing in Red Rocks. The wall is in a sheltered and sunny location, getting sun from mid-morning on. A useful option for cold, windy days.

Approach: From the parking area, hike down the main trail for 100 yards then follow the trail which branches off to the left. Follow the trail down to the bottom of a hill and up the other side onto a dirt ridge. When the trails reaches the crest of the dirt ridge head down into the broad, bushy corridor on the right and follow it to the east for 50 yards. The routes are on the long slab on the left side of this drainage. 10 minutes.

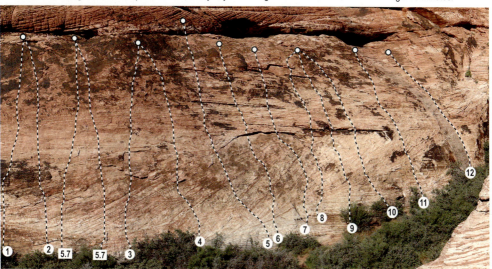

At the far left end of the slab is a left-facing, left-leaning arch.

🔴 Slabbing It 50' 5.7
Gene Scott. Winter 2018.
Not shown on the topo. Climb straight up the face starting 12' to the right of the arch (8 b's).

❶ Crab on a Slab 50' 5.8
Gene Scott. Winter 2015.
Start 20' right of the arch. Climb up and right to the first bolt, then go straight up to the anchor (6 b's).

❷ Slabracadabra 50' 5.8
Gene Scott. Winter 2015.
Start 10' right of Crab on a Slab. Climb up and slightly left to the shared anchor (6 b's).

There are two 5.7 sport routes up the slab to the right of Slabracadabra which share an anchor.

❸ Slabulous 50' 5.7
Gene Scott. Winter 2015.
Start 20' right of the previous route. Climb past the left end of a small undercling/overlap to the shared anchor (5 b's).

❹ Slab-a-dab-a-doo 50' 5.6
Gene Scott. Chere Lewis. Winter 2015.
Start 20' right of the previous route. Climb the slab to the shared anchor (5 b's).

❺ Slab One 50' 5.5
Mark Limage, J. Burkey. (T.r.) 2000's. Lead: Gene Scott. Winter 2015.
Start 10' right of the previous route. Climb left, then go straight up the slab to an anchor above the big break (5 b's).

❻ Slab Line 50' 5.5
Start as for Slab One. Climb straight up the slab, past the overlap, to an anchor below the big break (4 b's).

❼ Slab and Tickle 45' 5.6
Start a few feet right of the previous route, just right of a small left-leaning flake/ramp. Make a few thin moves past the first bolt and continue up the face to the anchor (5 b's).

❽ To Slab Or Not 50' 5.6
Gene Scott. Chere Lewis. Winter 2015.
Start at the same point as the previous route. Climb straight up the slab, past the overlap, to the shared anchor (5 b's).

❾ Slab Stick 45' 5.7
Gene Scott. Chere Lewis. Winter 2015.
Start 12' right of the previous route. After a low crux, climb the slab to the shared anchor (4 b's).

❿ Slab Happy 45' 5.7
Gene Scott. Winter 2015.
Start just left of a little dark scoop, 12' right of Slab Stick. After a low crux, climb to the shared anchor (5 b's).

⓫ Smear Campaign 50' 5.8
Jason Martin, Mark Fulmer, Glen Owen. 2007.
Start 10' right of the small scoop of Slab Happy. Climb straight up the slab, past the right end of a small overlap (5 b's).

⓬ Streak On The Slab 40' 5.9
Gene Scott. Winter 2015.
Start 10' right of Smear Campaign, below a grey water streak. Pull over the steeper bulge at the base of the slab and continue up the water streak to an anchor (6 b's).

The Hamlet

This is a multi-tiered cliff to the west of Panty Wall, sitting above the bench used to approach that cliff. The rock is quite poor quality on many of these routes, but since they are quite popular they are gradually cleaning up. The cliff is very sunny and warm, getting sun almost all day in the winter.

Approach: From the parking area hike down the main trail for 100 yards then follow the Grand Circle trail which branches off to the left. Follow the trail down to the bottom of a hill and up the other side onto a dirt ridge. Follow the ridge for 200 yards until it is easy to head down into the wash on the right. Cross the wash and scramble back east to get onto a long, slabby bench which leads back to the east. The Hamlet is the two-tiered cliff to the left of this bench. 15 minutes.

The first routes described are on a short, steep, varnished wall at the left end of the lower tier of the cliff, directly above the approach ramp.

The Hamlet

① The J Wall 40' 5.12b
This is the leftmost route on the wall. Hard moves low down lead to an easier finish to the anchors (4 b's).

② Killer Joe 50' 5.10c
Start about 20' to the right of The J Wall. Climb up and left onto a slab and continue to an anchor (5 b's).

③ Mind if I do a J 55' 5.10a
Start to the right of Killer Joe. A steep start (crux) leads to a slabby finish and the anchors (5 b's).

There are 4 anchors at the top of the wall to the right of the previous three routes. These are used to toprope a series of routes on the right side of the lower wall. The grades are 5.7, 5.6, 5.8, 5.8 going from climbers left to right. The anchors are reached from the right end of the terrace below the upper tier.

The rest of the routes on The Hamlet are on the upper tier. This is reached by scrambling around to the left of The J Wall etc. and heading up easy slabs to a terrace. The routes are described from left to right as you walk up the terrace. An obvious feature is a big arch, the first route starts below its left end.

④ The Plays the Thing 60' 5.4
Phil Bridgers, Jason Martin. 2008.
Start at a belay bolt on the slabby shelf below the left end of the arch. Climb straight up the low-angled slab (3 b's) to an anchor below the arch.

5 The Die is Cast 85' 5.9+
Start below the right side of the arch. Climb through a patch of light-colored rock and pull through the loose overhang onto the upper wall. Climb the upper wall to the anchor (5 b's).

6 Frailty, Thy Name is Sandstone 85' 5.7
Phil Bridgers, Viren & Julie Perumal, Jason Martin. 2008.
Start below the right end of the arch. Climb straight up past the right end of the arch to an anchor (8 b's).

7 Sweets to the Sweet 85' 5.7
Phil Bridgers, Jason Martin. 2008.
Start 10' right of the previous route. Climb straight up to an anchor (8 b's).

8 When the Blood Burns 85' 5.8+
To the right of the previous route there are two bushy areas. This route starts between the bushes and climbs straight up to an anchor (6 b's).

9 Thy Spirit Of A Father Lost 85' 5.10a
A. Allard, D. Young. 2017.
Start right of the previous route. Climb through the middle of the low overhang then straight up the wall to an anchor (8 b's).

Towards the right end of the terrace under the wall is a little corridor. The next route is the first bolted route on the left.

10 To Grunt to Sweat 60' 5.8
A. Reger, D. Young. 2012.
Climb straight up to an anchor (6 b's).

11 Perchance to Dream 90' 5.8-
A. Reger, D. Young. 2012.
Start in the corridor to the right of the previous route. After a low crux, the climbing is easier to the anchor (9 b's).

12 Sea of Troubles 75' 5.9
Phil Bridgers, Viren & Julie Perumal, Jason Martin, 2008.
The rightmost route in the corridor. Easy rock leads to a crux bulge then easier climbing leads to the anchor (9 b's).

To reach the next routes, walk out right on the ramp beyond the corridor. The rock on all these routes is a little dubious and since the belayer is leashed to an anchor it is best to wear a helmet.

13 Contagious Blastments 70' 5.5
Dan Young. January 2020.
Start 30' to the right of the previous route and just left of a bush. Climb the wall to the anchor (8 b's).

14 Passing Through Nature To Eternity 75' 5.5
Dan Young. January 2020.
Start just right of the bush. Climb the slabby wall (8 b's).

15 Some Strange Eruption 80' 5.6
Dan Young. January 2020.
Start 15' to the right of the previous route at two belay bolts. Climb the slabby wall to the anchor (9 b's).

16 Stand Dumb And Speak Not 80' 5.7
Dan Young. January 2020.
Start to the right of the previous route at a second anchor. Climb the slabby wall to the anchor (9 b's).

To reach the next two routes, make a 3rd class traverse right for 25' to two painted bolts in a varnished scoop.

17 Rosencrantz 85' 5.6
S. Massey, J. Wilder. 2011.
Climb straight up from the anchor, following a seam, to a set of anchors on a small stance (6 b's).

18 Guildenstern 160' 5.8
Pitch 1: Dan Young. January 2020. Pitch 2: S. Massey, J. Wilder. 2011.
This route climbs the exposed right edge of the wall, starting from the base of the cliff.
1. 80' 5.8 Start 70' up and right of the routes on J Wall at a belay bolt. After a tough move to start, climb the wall above, finishing with a mantle onto a ledge with an anchor (8 b's).
2. 80' 5.6 Step right from the anchor and climb up the prow to an anchor just below the top (8 b's).

The Panty Wall

This wall has a very good selection of moderate routes, including a few excellent, entry-level sport routes on good, well-used rock. The cliff is very popular and can get quite crowded on busy weekends and holidays. The cliff is in three sections; a long wall about 80' high with large patches of dark varnish; a smooth, red buttress at the top of the gully to the left of the main wall; and a short, steep buttress at the top of the ramp, which cuts up and right underneath the right end of the main wall. The wall gets sun from mid-morning on.

Approach: From the parking area hike down the main trail for 100 yards then follow the Grand Circle trail which branches off to the left. Follow the trail down to the bottom of a hill and up the other side onto a dirt ridge. Follow the ridge for 200 yards until it is easy to head down into the wash on the right. Cross the wash and scramble back east to get onto a long, slabby bench which leads back to the east. From the end of the bench a short scramble leads up to a big fallen pine tree at the base of the wall. 1000 yards, 15-20 minutes.

The routes are described from right to left.

The first routes are on the steep buttress at the right end of the main wall. They are reached by scrambling up and right on the ramp below the right side of the main wall.

1 Thong 30' 5.7
Todd Swain, Marion Parker. February 1994.
Start about 10' left of a flake on the right side of the buttress. Climb a crack, past steep opening moves, to easy ground.

2 Butt Floss 40' 5.10a (Tr.)
Todd Swain. December 1994.
Start 10' to the left of Thong. Climb up a right-facing flake to a roof. Pull over the roof and climb a seam to the top. There is an awkward-to-reach bolt anchor just below the top.

3 Cover my Buttress 40' 5.6
Todd Swain. February 1994.
Single rack to 4".
The crack on the left side of the buttress is climbed to an anchor at its top.

The following routes can be top-roped by scrambling up a slab above the top of the ramp and following a ledge leftwards.

Scanty Panty 30' 5.5 (Tr.)
Todd Swain, Donette Swain. February 1994.
Using the anchors of Silk Panties (there are two options), top-rope the face to the right of that route.

❹ Silk Panties 40' 5.7
Donette Swain, Todd Swain. February 1994.
The right most bolted route on the wall (5 b's).

❺ The Last Panty 45' 5.7
This route starts 35' up the ramp (6 b's).

❻ Black Lace 60' 5.8
L. Gallia, D. Young. 2013.
Climb straight up the face to the left of The Last Panty (7 b's).

❼ Boxer Rebellion 50' 5.8 *
Leo Henson, Albert Newman. November 1996.
Start 20' up the ramp. A steep start leads to enjoyable, delicate climbing, steepening for the last 20' to the anchor (6 b's).

❽ Sacred Undergarment Squeeze Job 60' 5.8 **
Mark Limage. 2005.
This route starts a short distance up the ramp. A nice, long wall climb, well-bolted (8 b's).

❾ Brief Encounter 65' 5.8 **
Albert Newman, Leo Henson. October 1998.
This is the left most bolted line on the wall, it starts 15' left of Boxer Rebellion at the base of the ramp, another long enjoyable face climb (6 b's).

The next three routes are good quality trad climbs which go through the large patch of dark varnish behind the fallen down pine tree at the base of the wall.

❿ Panty Line 70' 5.10a
Nick Nordblom, Paul Van Betten. 1987.
Single rack to 2", extra large stoppers.
Start from a couple of blocks at the base of the wall. Climb straight up the right side of the varnish to an anchor just over the top. A necky lead, but with good climbing.

Panty Wall

⓫ Panty Raid 70' 5.10a ***
Paul Van Betten, Nick Nordblom. 1987.
Single rack to 2", extra large stoppers.
An excellent route. Wander up the wall to reach the obvious crack splitting the center of the varnish. Finish up the crack to reach an anchor on the ledge at the top.

⓬ Edible Panties 70' 5.10b
Todd Swain, Donette Swain. February 1994.
Good climbing but a serious lead with fragile rock and spaced protection. Start 30' to the left of Panty Raid close to the edge of the gully at the left end of the wall. Climb a short right-slanting flake then move up onto the varnished wall, (crux). Continue up the wall to an anchor on the ledge above.

The next three routes climb the steep rock around the left side of the main wall.

⓭ Viagra Falls 60' 5.11d *
Leo Henson, Albert Newman. October 1998.
The right most route on the steep wall, it starts just around the corner from Edible Panties. A crux low down leads to easier steep climbing then a long runout to the anchors (6 b's).

⓮ Wedgie 65' 5.12b
Leo Henson, Albert Newman. November 1996.
A fingery route up the middle of the steep wall (8 b's).

⓯ Totally Clips 40' 5.11a
Scott Carson, Steve Bullock. 1990.
This route starts 40' further up the gully, at the left end of the steep rock (6 b's).

The following routes are on the steep, red buttress up and left of the main wall. They are reached by scrambling 150' up the gully to the left of the main wall, and exiting out left onto a ledge below a steep, red slab.

⓰ Panty Prow 60' 5.6 **
Donette Swain, Todd Swain. February 1994.
An enjoyable route up the rounded rib on the right edge of the red slab, (5 b's) moving left at the top to an anchor.

⓱ Victoria's Secret 40' 5.10b (Tr.)
Todd Swain, Donette Swain. February 1994.
Using the anchors of Panty Prow, top-rope the face between that route and Panty Mime, starting from a small block.

⓲ Panty Mime 40' 5.10d **
Todd Swain, Donette Swain. February 1994.
A sustained slab route with few positive holds. Climb the center of the red slab, to the anchor of Panty Prow (6 b's).

⓳ Panty Shield 50' 5.10d
Nick Nordblom, Paul Van Betten. 1987.
Start at the left end of the slab below a shallow right-facing corner. A few necky moves (10a) lead up the lower corner to a bolt. Continue up the right-leaning corner (3 b's) making a few very thin moves up the smooth right wall. A couple of large cams needed for the anchor.

Panty Raid. Page 350.

The following routes are on a series of blocks and small cliffs above and slightly to the west of Panty Wall. The first five routes are on a small cliff tucked in behind a huge block, level with and about 40 yards to the west of Panty Shield. The routes are described from right to left.

The right side of the wall is defined by a right-angled arete.

20 Office Maxx 35' 5.12a *
Jay Foley. 2015.
Climb an easy slab then launch past a hollow pistol grip to begin the steep arete. Pass a thin, short crux section midway and continue to an anchor (6 b's).

In the center of the south face of the cliff is a right-facing corner/scoop.

21 Office Expansion 40' 5.11b
David Blackburn, Dan Young. 2015.
Crimp straight up the face between the scoop and the right arete of the wall (5 b's).

22 Corner Office 40' 5.10d
Dan Young, David Blackburn. 2015.
Climb a black, slabby face into the steep right-facing corner. Climb the corner (crux) to the anchor (6 b's).

23 Office Manager 35' 5.11a *
D. Blackburn, D. Young. 2015.
Single rack to 0.5".
Start just left of the previous route. Climb a pretty, curving crack (b) in a shallow corner. Above the crack, finish up a steep face (b) to the anchor.

24 Office Party 35' 5.9
Dan Young. 2015.
Start behind a bush at the left side of the wall. Start up a shallow arete then continue up the face to the anchor (4 b's).

At the top of the gully to the right of Panty Prow is a small cliff with a huge roof, split by an impressive thin crack.

25 The Great Red Roof 50' 5.13b ***
Paul Van Betten, N. Nordblom, S. Mamusia. 1987.
FFA Tom Moulin. April 2007.
Single rack to 1.75", double 0.6" to 1.25".
A great route, following the offset crack that slashes through the huge roof. It's best to set up a belay below and slightly to the left of the roof. There is an anchor 15' above the lip

The following routes are on a short, steep block 30 yards up and left of The Great Red Roof. This formation is known as The Short Bus, the routes are described from right to left. The first two routes on the right offer fun, gymnastic climbing.

26 Get Shorty 30' 5.12b
Jay Foley, Kevin Ormerod, Kurt Burt. 2015.
Climb straight up the face a few feet to the right of a pretty, honeycombed corner. Make a tough clip and a long move at the second bolt, continue up more pumpy moves to find the anchor and clipping holds above the final bulge (4 b's).

27 Mini Me 30' 5.12a *
Jay Foley, Kevin Ormerod, Kurt Burt. 2015.
Climb straight up the pretty, honeycombed corner, pulling over the bulge at its top to a pumpy anchor clip. (4 b's). Starts easy and gets progressively harder with a dynamic move at the top.

To the left of Mini Me is a steep arete.

28 Lickn' the Window 30' 5.11a
Kurt Burt, Jay Foley. 2015.
Start a few feet to the left of the arete. Pull over the initial overhang then continue up the steep face, past a left-facing flake, to the anchor (4 b's).

29 Drool Bucket 25' 5.10c
Kurt Burt, Jay Foley. 2015.
Start 10' left of the previous route. Pull over an awkward bulge with a high hard clip and follow easier climbing up a right-leaning ramp to the anchor (3 b's). Stick clip useful.

30 Hammy The Girl 45' 5.10c
J. Kearney, J. Streit, L. Jordan, M. Schook, J. Gale. March 5, 2014.
The following route sits by itself about 30 yards around to the left of the previous routes. It is on the north side of a steep, west-facing prow. From the gully below the wall, stick clip the first bolt. Climb the smooth wall, going over a small roof to a honeycombed face then the anchor (4 b's).

Jay Foley on Get Shorty. Page 352.

The Amusement Park

The Amusement Park is a beginners sport climbing area with a collection of well-bolted 5.7 sport routes with toprope routes in between. The wall is on the south side of the little slot canyon below Panty Wall, facing straight north. The low, north-facing location means that it gets almost no sun in the winter.

Approach: From the parking area hike down the main trail for 100 yards then follow the Grand Circle trail which branches off to the left. Follow the trail down to the bottom of a hill and up the other side onto a dirt ridge. Follow the ridge for 200 yards until it is easy to head down into the wash on the right. Cross the wash and scramble back east to get onto a long, slabby bench which leads back to the east. Near the top of the bench, descend a short ramp of white rock that leads into the slot canyon below Panty Wall. The routes are on the steep slab on the south side of the canyon. 18 minutes.

The routes are described from left to right.

1 **Power Tower 35' 5.7**
L. Gallia, D. Young. 2014.
Start near the chimney on the left side of the wall.
The leftmost bolted line to an anchor (4 b's).

2 **Bumper Cars 35' 5.7**
L. Gallia, D. Young. 2014.
The second route from the left, it shares the anchor with Power
Tower (4 b's).

3 **Demon Drop 35' 5.7**
L. Gallia, D. Young. 2014.
Start to the right of Bumper Cars. Climb the face (3 b's) to a
short crack (small cam) which leads to the anchor.

4 **Haunted House 35' 5.7**
L. Gallia, D. Young. 2014.
After a slabby start, climb the face to the anchor of Demon
Drop (4 b's).

Cotton Candy 35' 5.7 (Tr.)
L. Gallia, D. Young. 2014.
Toprope straight up to the anchor of Log Flume.

5 **Log Flume 35' 5.7**
L. Gallia, D. Young. 2014.
This route is in the middle of the wall. Climb a slabby start to
the ledge above the slab. Continue up the face (4 b's) to the
anchor.

6 **Tea Cups 35' 5.7**
L. Gallia, D. Young. 2014.
Climb the face (3 b's) to a short crack (small cam or medium
nut) which leads to the anchor of Roller Coaster.

7 **Roller Coaster 35' 5.7**
L. Gallia, D. Young. 2014.
The rightmost bolted route on the wall. Climb a slabby start to
the ledge above the slab. Continue up the face (3 b's) to the
anchor.

The Amusement Park

Ultraman Wall

This is an obvious, large, red slab with a water streak coming
down from a bowl at the top. It sits above a gully several hundred yards around to the left of the Panty Wall, but at roughly
the same level. Although some of the routes are a little too
runout to be considered sport climbs, they provide good quality, moderate slab climbing. The cliff is in the sun all day. Many
of these routes are quite long, and even a single 70m is often
not enough to get down. For some of the routes on the right
side of the main slab it is possible to traverse to the anchors of
Rodan and rap that route with a single 60m rope.

Approach: From the parking area hike down the main trail for
100 yards then follow the Grand Circle trail which branches
off to the left. Follow the trail down to the bottom of a hill and
up the other side onto a dirt ridge. Follow the ridge for 200
yards until it is easy to head down into the wash on the right.
Cross the wash and scramble onto the rocks on the other side.
Head towards the cliff which is directly ahead at this point, then
scramble up and left on a big ledge and back right through a
blocky area to reach the base of the wall in the vicinity of Ultraman. 15-20 minutes.

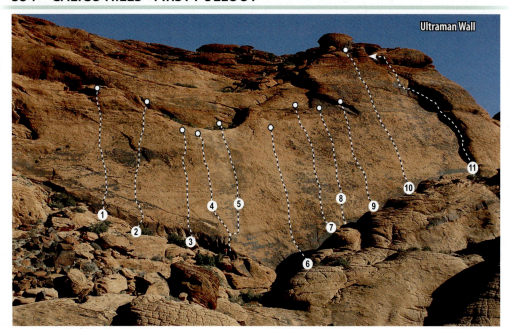

Ultraman Wall

The routes are described from left to right.

❶ Scent of the Ultraman 110' 5.7
Mark Limage, Hal Edwards. 1999.
This route climbs the slab at the left end of the cliff, starting about 70' left of Ultraman. (7 b's). A 70m rope just makes it down. **Variation:** 5.7 Top rope the zig-zag seams in the face to the right.

❷ Mothra 115' 5.7+
Killis Howard, Cassondra Long. December 2013.
Sparsely-protected but reasonably safe face climbing. Start 30' left of Clutch Cargo at a large barrel cactus, Climb up to and through two short, varnished corners before finishing up the face to an anchor on the left edge of the central scoop where several of the routes finish.

❸ Ghidorah 120' 5.8+
Killis Howard, Cassondra Long. Nathan Petrosian. December 2013.
Single rack to 1.25", Rp's.
A runout face climb with sparse protection and just two bolts. Start 15' right of Mothra, 15' left of Clutch Cargo. Step off a boulder at a good large nut placement between flakes to begin. A steep start above a slot leads to protection behind a giant flake. Continue to a bolt and climb the scary face with dubious gear to a second bolt in slabbier ground. A final runout leads to the anchor.

❹ Clutch Cargo 100' 5.9 *
Pier Locatelli, Dan McQuade. 1996.
Start at the base of the water streak on a big boulder below a short left-facing corner. Climb the corner then move left and climb the long slab to an anchor 15' below the bowl (7 b's).

❺ Ultraman 110' 5.8+ ****
Scott Gordon, John Martinet. 1977.
Nice slab climbing leads up the long water streak. Start up Clutch Cargo then move right and climb the slab (8 b's) to an anchor in the bowl at the top. A 70m rope works for the rappel.

MK Ultra 120' 5.9
Killis Howard, Howard Yang, Cassondra Long. January 2015.
A couple of tiny cams.
Start 15' down and right of Ultraman. Climb up an right (small cams) to the first bolt then go straight up (6 b's, with a well-protected crux and long, easier runouts) to reach an anchor.

❻ Speed Racer 120' 5.8+
Ed Prochaska. 1990.
A runout but very nice slab climb. This climb starts 50' to the right of Ultraman Start in a left-facing corner in black varnish. A small cam protects the moves to the first bolt. Climb the steep slab (8 b's) to an anchor.

Ultramagnetic Mc's 125' 5.8
Killis Howard, Howard Yang, Cassondra Long. January 2015.
Double to 1", Rp's.
Well-protected and enjoyable. Start 30' right of Speed Racer. Mantel up on black rock to a shallow corner. Climb the corner and the face above, zig-zaging around for protection. Higher up, a steeper wall (3 b's) leads to the anchors.

❼ Godzilla 130' 5.7
Ed Prochaska. 1990.
Start about 100' to the right of the water streak. Climb the slab (7 b's) to an anchor.

❽ Destroy All Monsters 130' 5.10a
Killis Howard, Kyle Jackson, Cassondra Long. December 2013.
This is the thinnest route on the wall, but also the best protected. The climbing is technical and thin down low, airy and mellow towards the top. Start between Godzilla and Rodan at a red, smooth, blank-looking corner with a low, red bolt. Follow the bolts (10 b's) to an anchor. Rap with two ropes or traverse right to the anchors of Rodan.

❾ Rodan 100' 5.7
This route has no protection. Solo up the slab 50' to the right of Godzilla to an anchor under an overlap.

⑩ Science Patrol 160' 5.8
Jon Martinet, Nick Nordblom. 1978.
This route starts about 200' to the right of the water streak below a short left-facing corner. It is about 50' to the left of the huge corner of the next route. Climb the slab (9 b's) to an anchor on a ledge.

⑪ The Hex Files 165' 5.6
Nick Nordblom, Jon Martinet. 1978.
Single rack to 4".
This route climbs the large left-facing corner that borders the right end of the slab. Start below the corner. Climb the corner for 80' to an alcove then traverse left to a crack which is followed to the top. Traverse left to finish at the anchor of Science Patrol.

Newcastle Crag

This area at the east end of a fin that faces north towards the Ultraman slab, it consists of two walls, a short wall on the left and a bulging buttress on the right with four sport routes.

Approach: From the parking area hike down the main trail for 100 yards then follow the Grand Circle trail which branches off to the left. Follow the trail down to the bottom of a hill and up the other side onto a dirt ridge. Follow the ridge for 200 yards until it is easy to head down into the wash on the right. Turn left and walk up the pretty wash, taking the right branch, which soon leads into a narrow corridor with a varnished left wall, this is the toprope wall. 15 minutes.

The routes are described from left to right.

The left wall of the corridor has three sets of bolts on top which are used to set up topropes. The anchors are easily reached by scrambling up from the east end of the formation.

❶ The One the Only 30' 5.9 (Tr.)
Jake Burkey, Mark Limage. 1999.
This route starts about 20' to the right of a tree in the corridor. Climb a left-facing flake and the scoop above to the anchor.

❷ The Boila 30' 5.9 (Tr.)
Jake Burkey, Mark Limage. 1999.
This route starts just to the left of some bushes at the far end of the corridor. It pulls over a slanting roof and climbs flakes to a horizontal crack, finishing up the bulge above.

❸ The Broon 25' 5.9 (Tr.)
Jake Burkey, Mark Limage. 1999.
The obvious left-facing flake/corner to the right of the previous route.

❹ Mission Accomplished 30' 5.8 (Tr.)
Mike McGlynn, Todd Lane. May 2006.
This route climbs straight up the face below the anchors of the next route.

❺ Warrantless Wiretap 30' 5.8
Mike McGlynn, Todd Lane. May 2006.
This route is at the far right end of the wall. Follow a curving flake over a bulge and up to anchors (4 b's).

The rest of the routes are on the short, steep buttress on the left about 30 yards west of the end of the corridor.

❻ Brown Ale 30' 5.11c/d
Jay Foley, Kurt Arend. 2001.
The left most route on the buttress, it starts up a left-arching flake and pulls up a bulge to reach a thin seam (6 b's).

❼ Pale Ale 40' 5.11b
Jay Foley, Kurt Arend. 2001.
This route climbs straight up the face to the right of Brown Ale finishing up an easy slab (6 b's).

❽ Guinness 40' 5.11a
Jay Foley, Kurt Arend. 2001.
The face just right of Pale Ale (6 b's).

❾ Full Sail 40' 5.10d
Jay Foley, Kurt Arend. 2001.
The rightmost route on the wall, it climbs past a big hole 20' up, then moves left to finish at the anchor of Guinness (6 b's).

The crags accessed from the Second Pullout are the most popular in Red Rocks, thanks to a large concentration of good sport routes of all grades, and a lot of very solid, well-used rock. On busy weekends parking places are hard to come by, and popular cliffs such as The Gallery and The Black Corridor can be packed with climbers.

There are some shady spots such as The Black Corridor and The Sandbox, but most of the cliffs are sunny, and are best during cooler weather. However, many of the crags face a little west, and during the late spring and early summer, with the sun high in the sky, they get shade until late morning, creating perfect redpoint conditions for the early risers. The crags are described roughly from east to west.

Access: Drive around the loop road for around 1.7 miles to a parking area on the right.

Lucas Sullivan on Glitter Gulch. Page 378.

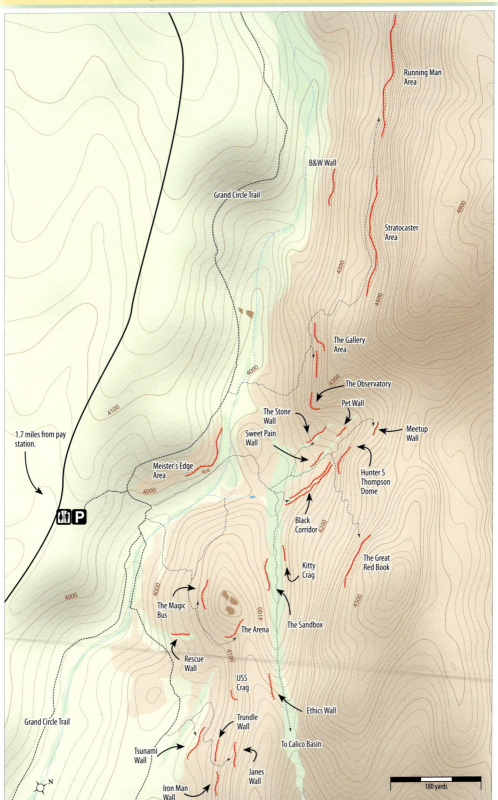

Running Man
Area

B&W Wall

Grand Circle Trail

Stratocaster
Area

4300

4400

4800

4500

The Gallery
Area

4300

The Observatory

The Stone
Wall

Pet Wall

Sweet Pain
Wall

Meetup
Wall

1.7 miles from pay
station.

Meister's Edge
Area

4100

Hunter S
Thompson
Dome

4000

Black
Corridor

4200

The Great
Red Book

P

Kitty
Crag

4500

The Magic
Bus

4000

The Arena

The Sandbox

4100

Rescue
Wall

4100

USS
Crag

Grand Circle Trail

Ethics Wall

Trundle
Wall

To Calico Basin

Tsunami
Wall

Janes
Wall

N

Iron Man
Wall

180 yards

Second Pullout - Right side

The Great Red Book Area

The Sanctuary

The Arena

Magic Bus

California 12a

Rescue Wall

Jane's Wall

This seldom visited wall has a small selection of excellent steep routes on good rock. It gets sun from mid-morning on, and its position close to the top of Calico Hills means that it will catch any wind that is blowing.

Approach: From the parking area, head down the main trail taking a right at the first fork at 170 yards. Continue to a second fork 50 yards further on. Take the trail on the right which heads down to the wash, then turns east and continues along the wash. After a couple of hundred yards the trail heads up a tiny corridor on the left. At the top of the corridor the trail turns right into a broad corridor. At the end of this corridor the trail heads up left onto a dirt ridge. Continue along the ridge for 100 yards, at which point the wildly overhanging Tsunami Wall becomes visible to the left. Go slightly past the Tsunami Wall and follow a ramp down to the wash at its base. Break through a small cliff band about 50 yards to the west (left) of the Tsunami Wall and follow slabby rock back right to the left edge of the Tsunami Wall. Scramble up the rocks above, then head right, weaving around blocks, to the base of the Trundle Wall. Scramble up a gully to the right of Trundle Wall to reach the base of Jane's Wall. 20 minutes.

The routes are described from left to right, starting with the following five routes which are on a short wall to the west, and slightly in front of the main wall.

1 Half Baked 35' 5.10a
Danny Rider, Scott Fielder. 2010.
The leftmost route on the wall is a delicate red slab (4 b's).

2 Mannish Boys 35' 5.11a
Scott Fielder, Reid Marlowe, Danny Rider. 2010.
A few feet to the right of Half Baked is a steep, left-facing flake/rib of varnish. Climb easily up to the rib then make a few technical moves to better holds and the anchor (4 b's).

3 Been Caught Stealin' 35' 5.11a
Killis Howard and Friends. 2014.
Climb straight up the face to the right of Mannish Boys (4 b's).

4 Doctors Orders 30' 5.10b
Greg Mayer. Fall 1990.
Climb a right-leaning scoop, pulling out its top and moving either left or right to the anchors of the adjacent routes (3 b's).

5 Playing Hooky 30' 5.10a
Greg Mayer. Fall 1990.
Start 6' right of Playing Hooky. Climb a shallow scoop, pulling over a little bulge at its top to reach the anchor (3 b's).

The following routes are on the main wall.

6 Every Mothers Nightmare 65' 5.12d *
Greg Mayer. Fall 1990. Originally 12b, this route became much harder when a reinforced flake broke away.
Start below an easy black slab below the left end of the crag. Climb a right-leaning crack in the black slab. Make a few very bouldery moves up the steep arete to the roof. Fun climbing on big holds and huecos leads leftwards across the roof. At the left end of the roof, pull over and up to an anchor (6 b's).

7 Stealin' 55' 5.12d
Don Welsh. Winter 1991.
Follow the previous route to the 4th bolt then move right and climb the wall past one more bolt to an anchor (5 b's).

8 Naked and Disfigured 65' 5.12b *
Don Welsh. Fall 1990.
Start at the entrance to a corridor. Climb up and right to the steep rock. Blast straight up the bulging wall (6 b's).

9 Pigs in Zen 65' 5.12c ***
Don Welsh. Fall 1990.
Solo up and left on an easy ramp to a short corner in the roof. Bouldery moves over the roof lead to long reaches on big holds up a pumpy headwall (6 b's).

10 Idiots Rule 60' 5.11d ***
Don Welsh. Fall 1990.
Another excellent route, quite varied climbing for the Calico

Hills. Start at the base of a left-leaning ramp. Scramble up 15' to the first bolt beside a large hueco. Balancy climbing past the hueco leads to a bouldery wall and a pumpy finish (6 b's).

11 See Dick Fly 55' 5.10d *

Greg Mayer. Spring 1991.

The route to the right of Idiots Rule. A good warm up with a nice, slowly building pump (5 b's).

12 Keep it Gutta 75' 5.10a

Killis Howard and Friends. 2014.
Single rack to 0.75".

Start in the corridor on the far right side of the wall, just to the right of the previous route. Climb a cracked face with good natural protection to reach a steeper headwall and the first bolt. Continue up the headwall (3 b's) to an anchor at the top.

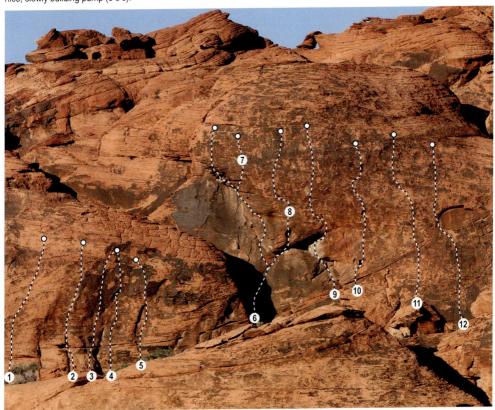

Trundle Wall

This wall provides long, vertical pitches on slightly fragile rock. It faces south and gets sun from mid-morning on.

Approach: From the parking area, head down the main trail taking a right at the first fork at 170 yards. Continue to a second fork 50 yards further on. Take the trail on the right, which heads down to the wash then turns east and continues along the wash. After a couple of hundred yards the trail heads up a tiny corridor on the left. At the top of the corridor the trail turns right into a broad corridor. At the end of this corridor the trail heads up onto a dirt ridge. Continue along the ridge for 100 yards, at which point the wildly overhanging Tsunami Wall becomes visible to the left. Go slightly past the Tsunami Wall and follow a ramp down to the wash at its base. Break through a small cliff band about 50 yards to the west (left) of the Tsunami Wall and follow slabby rock back right to the left edge of the Tsunami Wall. Scramble up the rocks above, then head right, weaving around blocks to the base of the Trundle Wall.

The routes are described from left to right.

1 **Before its Time 60' 5.12a/b**
Leo Henson. November 1994.
The leftmost route on the wall. It starts to the right of a big, rotten corner (8 b's).

2 **Standing in the Shadows 60' 5.12a**
Greg Mayer. Winter 1990.
Start to the right of Before its Time. Steep moves lead up and left to a flake which is followed to a rest below the upper wall. A hard sequence on thin holds leads onto the upper wall. Continue to the anchor (6 b's).

3 **Master Beta 55' 5.13a**
Scotty Gratton. October 1994.
A bit of a mystery route, I've never seen any chalk on this one. Start just to the right of Standing in the Shadows. Climb straight up the wall to the anchor (6 b's).

4 **Pocket Rocket 65' 5.12a ***
Mike Tupper. Winter 1990.
A good route with a variety of features. Start 15' to the right of Master Beta below a steep right-facing flake. Climb the flake then go up the wall, making a hard move to a hidden pocket in the base of a big, red scoop. Continue past a higher scoop to the anchor (6 b's).

5 **Life out of Balance 40' 5.11d**
Mike Tupper, Greg Mayer. Winter 1990.
The route to the right of Pocket Rocket. It starts with a traverse left on sloping holds to get onto a fingery wall (4 b's).

6 **Bone Machine 35' 5.11c**
Danny Meyers, Scotty Gratton. October 1994.
A short, fragile wall at the right end of the crag (4 b's).

Iron Man Wall

The Iron Man Wall is the cliff to the right (east) of Trundle Wall. A prominent feature is the big, right-curving arch of Iron Man. The rock on this cliff is still quite friable. The cliff is in the sun most of the day.

Approach: From the parking area, head down the main trail taking a right at the first fork at 170 yards. Continue to a second fork 50 yards further on. Take the trail on the right, which heads down to the wash then turns east and continues along the wash. After a couple of hundred yards the trail heads up a tiny corridor on the left. At the top of the corridor the trail turns right into a broad corridor. At the end of this corridor the trail heads up onto a dirt ridge. Continue along the ridge for 100 yards, at which point the wildly overhanging Tsunami Wall becomes visible to the left. Go slightly past the Tsunami Wall and follow a ramp down to the wash at its base. Break through a small cliff band about 50 yards to the west (left) of the Tsunami Wall and follow slabby rock back right to the left edge of the Tsunami Wall. Scramble up the rocks above, then head right, weaving around blocks to the base of the Trundle Wall. From the right end of the Trundle Wall, walk up to a little saddle and drop back down the other side to arrive at the base of Iron Man, the big, right-curving arch. 20 minutes.

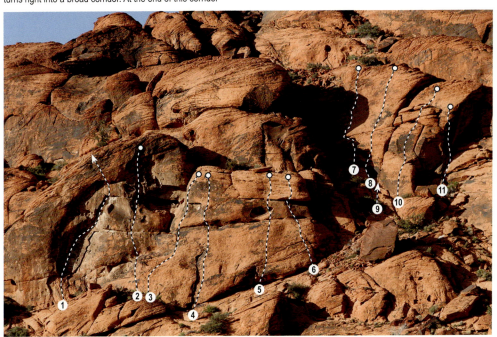

❶ Iron Man 90' 5.10d
Jay Smith, Paul Van Betten. 1983.
Single Rack to 2.5".
Follow the big arch up and right to a bolt on the lip. Pull over the arch and continue up and right to a smaller roof. Pull past this then angle back left on easier ground to the top.

❷ Iron Maiden 70' 5.11c
Michael Kimm. August 2008.
Start below the right end of the big arch of Iron Man. After an initial bulge, enjoyable climbing up big huecos leads to a steep, fingery finish to the anchors (7 b's).

To the right of Iron Man is a big scoop capped by a roof, with a crack to its right. To the right again is a slabby wall cut by a couple of long, horizontal cracks. The next route climbs the blunt arete on the left side of the slabby wall.

❸ Rust Bucket 40' 5.9
Michael Kimm. July 2008.
Start on the right side of the ledge below Iron Man. Climb easily up and right to the first bolt. Continue up the blunt arete to a thin crux just below the anchors.

❹ Test of Time 55' 5.10a
Michael Kimm, July 2008.
Start below and to the right of the previous routes at the base of a right-facing flake on the left side of the slabby wall. Climb the flake and continue through a couple of short bulges, finishing with a short runout up the final headwall to reach the chains (6 b's).

❺ Silver Surfer 55' 5.10b
Michael Kimm. July 2008.
This route climbs the face on the right side of the slabby wall. The crux comes before the first bolt so a stick clip is a good idea. Start under a small roof. Make an awkward and powerful pull off the ground (crux) and around the right side of the roof to the first bolt. Climb the slab above and then a vertical section to reach the anchors.

❻ Ferrous Wheel 45' 5.10d
Michael Kimm. November 2008.
This route climbs the far right side of the slabby wall. Straightforward 5.6 slab climbing leads to a break under a roof. Make some hard moves over the roof then continue to the anchors.

The rest of the routes are on the cliff around to the right of, and slightly behind the previous routes. The middle of the slabby wall is split by a crack, the line of Necco Waif.

7 Easiest Path 55' 5.8
Michael Kimm. July 2009.
Start below the left side of the wall. Climb an obvious crack/break to where it turns horizontal. Traverse left, and weave up the slab above. Move right around the final vertical section to the anchors (5 b's).

8 Brandi Whine 50' 5.8+
Michael Kimm. July 2009.
Climb straight up the face to the left of the Necco Waif (5 b's).

9 Necco Waif 40' 5.7
Michael Kimm. July 2009.
Single rack to 2".
Follow the thin-hands/finger crack in the middle of the wall, to the anchor of Particle Man.

10 Particle Man 30' 5.9
Michael Kimm. July 2009.
Climb the face to the right of Necco Waif (3 b's).

11 Oxosis 45' 5.11b
Michael Kimm. August 2009.
This route climbs the nice, varnished face and arete on the right side of the wall (4 b's).

USS Crag

This cliff is about 100 yards up to the west from Tsunami Wall, almost directly above the prominent roof of California 12a. The south face of the wall is a big, open slab bounded on the right by a large right-leaning roof. The routes are in the sun all day in the winter.

Approach: This cliff is probably most easily reached by following the approach to Trundle Wall, then cutting across to the west towards the right side of the cliff. Once at the buttress, go around to the left to a ledge below the slab on the south side of the buttress. 18 minutes.

The routes are described from left to right.

1 Dry Docked 75' 5.8
Michael Kimm. June 2009.
The leftmost route. Climb a flake to a break. Continue up the slab, passing to the left of the leftmost of two bushes and continuing to the anchors (7 b's).

2 Port of Call 75' 5.7
Michael Kimm. June 2009.
Climb straight up between the two bushes (7 b's).

3 Rigger Mortis 75' 5.7+
Michael Kimm. June 2009.
Climb a short corner to a break, then traverse slightly right, and continue up the slab to the anchors (7 b's).

The next route sits by itself, about 150 yards left (west) of Tsunami Wall. It faces south towards the road. It is on a terrace, about 50 feet above the same wash that runs in front of the Tsunami Wall. There are now five new routes to the left of California 12a. From left to right: 10b, 10a, 8, 11b,11d.

California 12a 35' 5.12b/c *
A classic roof problem, unique in the Calico Hills. Climb big huecos out the huge roof to reach an awkward crack. The crack leads to an anchor in a scoop (7 b's).

Tsunami Wall

This short but very impressive wall has a collection of brutally fingery routes on wildly overhanging rock. The cliff is very sunny and warm, and quite sheltered from winds.

Approach: From the parking area, head down the main trail taking a right at the first fork at 170 yards. Continue to a second fork 50 yards further on. Take the trail on the right which heads down to the wash then turns east and continues along the wash. After a couple of hundred yards the trail heads up a tiny corridor on the left. At the top of the corridor the trail turns right into a broad corridor. At the end of this corridor the trail heads up onto a dirt ridge. Continue along the ridge for 100 yards, at which point the wildly overhanging Tsunami Wall becomes visible down to the left. 15 minutes.

The routes are described from left to right, starting with the short, overhanging block to the left of the main wall.

❶ Poseidon Adventure 25' 5.12c
Chris Knuth, Leo Henson. January 1993.
The block at the left end of the main wall (4 b's).

❷ The Big Gulp 30' 5.11a
Jim Bridwell, Jay Smith, Paul Crawford. 1998.
Doubles 2.5"- 6".
The overhanging, wide crack between the big block of the previous route and the main wall.

❸ Barracuda 30' 5.13c/d ***
Chris Knuth, Leo Henson. January 1993.
This is the leftmost route on the main wall. Powerful moves and weird angles make this a real test piece.

The next three route share a start 10' right of Barracuda.

❹ Land Shark 35' 5.12c
Leo Henson. January 1992.
After the start, move to the line of bolts on the left. (6 b's).

❺ Angler 35' 5.12c
Leo Henson. January 1992.
After the common start follow the central line (6 b's).

❻ Threadfin 40' 5.12b/c ***
Leo Henson. January 1992.
A Red Rocks classic up the twin flakes in the highest part of the wall. After the shared start move right and climb the flakes to the anchor (6 b's).

❼ SOS 40' 5.13a **
Leo Henson. January 1992.
This route starts 10' to the right of the previous routes on a block under the roof. It starts with a wild swing left to a big horn on the lip of the low roof (6 b's).

❽ Man Overboard 35' 5.12d *
Leo Henson. January 1992.
Begin just right of SOS (6 b's).

❾ Aftershock 35' 5.12b **
Randy Faulk, Leo Henson. January 1992.
A good route, quite tough for the grade. Start just right of Man Overboard at the right end of the block under the roof (5 b's).

❿ Abandon Ship 30' 5.12a
Randy Faulk, Leo Henson. January 1992.
The rightmost route on the main wall. Not very good, with a one move crux (5 b's).

⓫ Women and Children First 30' 5.7
Donette Swain, Todd Swain. Spring 1993.
The crack at the right end of the main wall.

To the right of the main wall is a shorter wall with two routes.

⓬ Tremor 30' 5.10a *
Leo Henson, Karin Henson. February 1992.
The route on the left (4 b's).

⬤ Low Tide 30' 5.10b
Leo Henson, Karin Henson. February 1992.
The route on the right (4 b's).

Christa Hunter on Threadfin. Page 363.

The Arena

This is the bulging buttress at the top of the gully to the left of California 12a. It is actually the back side of the Magic Bus formation and is probably most easily reached by scrambling around to the right from the base of the Magic Bus. The routes face north and catch any wind that's going. A good choice for warm weather.

1 Gladiator 45' 5.12c
Leo Henson. April 1994.
This is the rightmost route on the wall. It is really just an alternate start to Shadow Warrior. Climb up a crack then make awkward moves left into Shadow Warrior (6 b's).

2 Shadow Warrior 50' 5.13a ★★
Leo Henson. June 1994.
A good route, low in the grade. Start below a line of shallow huecos in a smooth, varnished wall 15' left of Gladiator. A fun boulder problem start leads to a pumpy headwall (6 b's).

3 Project 55'
Start 10' left of Shadow Warrior. Climb through some big scoops to a very smooth wall. Finish up an easier face to the anchors (7 b's).

4 Project 60'
The leftmost route on the wall. Bear-hug up a steep tufa-like formation to a scoop. Make hard, fingery moves up the wall above to lower-angled rock and finish over a bulge to the anchor (7 b's).

Rescue Wall

This cliff is located in a deep, narrow gully running north to south, a couple of hundred yards to the east of the Magic Bus. The routes are on the left (west) wall of the gully, which is slightly overhanging and capped by a very steep bulge.

Approach: From the parking area, head down the main trail taking a right at the first fork at 170 yards. Continue to a second fork 50 yards further on. Take the trail on the right which heads down to the wash then turns east and continues along the wash. After a couple of hundred yards the trail heads up a tiny corridor on the left. At the top of the corridor the trail turns right into a broad corridor. Instead of turning right into the broad corridor, go left around the fin of rock in front of you. This leads into a bushy gully which goes back right behind the fin, then turns north into a narrow, steep-walled corridor. Rescue Wall is the steep wall on the left side of this corridor. 10 minutes.

The routes are described from left to right.

● Airlift 55' 5.11c
Randy Faulk, Bart Groendyke. 1992.
The leftmost route on the wall (8 b's).

● Jaws of Life 55' 5.12a
Leo Henson, Karin Henson. March 1998.
This route starts in the middle of the wall and finishes at the anchors of Airlift (7 b's).

● 911 55' 5.11d
Randy Faulk, Bart Groendyke. 1992.
This route climbs the right side of the wall (7 b's).

● Moonbeams 40' 5.12c/d
To reach this route, walk through the corridor under Rescue Wall and go up into the gully beyond. The route climbs the left edge of the wildly steep wall on the left side of the gully (5 b's).

Magic Bus

This sunny cliff is very popular thanks to several easier well-bolted sport routes, interspersed with some trad routes which can be easily toproped. The wall gets sun for most of the day, it is very exposed and will catch any wind that's blowing.

Approach: From the parking area, head down the main trail taking a right at the first fork at 170 yards. Continue to a second fork 50 yards further on. Take the trail on the left and follow it, passing under a couple of red, hueco-covered walls. After 150 yards head up a rocky wash on the right. A short distance up the wash, turn right and head up a block-filled gully for 150 feet to an obvious, sharp arete. From the arete go right and head up into a narrow corridor. At the top of the corridor go right, walking past the top of another corridor, and continue east on slabby ledges to the area below the Magic Bus. 15 minutes.

Malice Alice 35' 5.10b
Sean Ward, Chuck Carlson. April 1996.
Single rack to 1.5", double 0.6"- 1".
This route is passed on the approach to Magic Bus, after exiting the narrow corridor it can be seen on the right at the top of the next corridor to the south. Climb a finger crack in the south wall of the corridor, going over several roofs before moving right around a final roof and finishing up a face.

The routes on the main wall are described from left to right.

❶ Electric Koolaid 45' 5.9+ *
Donette Swain, Todd Swain. February 1994.
A bit fragile, but enjoyable nevertheless. Climb the left edge of the wall, moving right at the top to the anchors of the next route (5 b's).

❷ Blond Dwarf 45' 5.9
Nick Nordblom, Paul Van Betten. 1988.
Single rack to 2".
Start just right of the previous route. Climb a thin right-curving crack (5.7) then climb up and left over a short, steep wall (2 b's) to a shared anchor.

❸ Neon Sunset 45' 5.8 ***
Kevin Pogue, Craig Dobson. January 1993.
The bolt ladder in the middle of the wall (8 b's).

❹ Zipperhead 45' 5.8
Paul Van Betten, Nick Nordblom. 1988.
Single rack to 1", Rp's.
Start 10' right of Neon Sunset at a set of thin cracks. Climb the initial crack, then step right into a seam and run it out to a bolt. Continue up the wall, finishing on the anchors of either of the adjacent routes. A serious lead.

❺ Technicolor Sunrise 45' 5.8 *
Todd Swain, Donette Swain. December 1993.
Start on the left edge of a triangular cutout at the base of the cliff. Climb up the edge and the wall above to an anchor (4 b's).

❻ Queazy Sunrise 45' 5.9+
D. Young. 2013.
Climb through the right side of the cutout (crux) and continue up the face to the anchors (5 b's).

❼ Ken Queazy 45' 5.8
Todd Swain, Donette Swain. December 1993.
Single rack to 0.6".
Start on the right side of the triangular cutout. Climb a thin seam in black rock, then continue up the wall (2 b's) to the anchor. A bit sporty.

The Sanctuary

The Sanctuary is a collection of huge blocks at the top of the formation, above the Magic Bus. As well as great views and a peaceful location, this area has a good collection of technical mini-routes on excellent, varnished rock. This is quite a sunny location, although it is very exposed to any winds that may be blowing. The harder routes are very friction dependant, best during cold weather. Some of these routes have been done as boulder problems or short leads, but the landings are not very inviting.

Approach: Follow the approach to the Magic Bus. Scramble around the left side of the Magic Bus, then head up and right in a blocky gully. 18 minutes.

Approach from the left side of the Magic Bus

The first four routes climb the big boulder on the right at the top of the gully. There are anchor bolts at the top of the boulder, which can be most easily reached by soloing Blackstop.

❶ The Tickler 30' 5.11c (Tr.)
This route climbs the southwest arete of the first boulder. Start below a little scoop just left of the arete. Pull onto the wall then immediately move right and climb the right side of the arete for 20' until it is possible to make a delicate step back around to the left. A thin crack leads to the top. It is a good idea to place a directional in the final, thin crack to minimize a potentially nasty pendulum (tiny wires).

❷ Therminal 25' 10d (Tr.) *
The thin left-facing corner just left of The Tickler.

❸ Blackstop 25' 5.10b
This route is the easiest way up the boulder. It climbs the low-angled west arete after a tricky, smooth start.

❹ Quasimodo 20' 5.11d (Tr.)
This route has softer rock than the other routes here, but also some fun steep moves. Start at a couple of pockets just to the right of the steep corner in the north face of the block. The route climbs the right arete of the corner. A sit start is possible starting on some good holds very low in the corner (V4).

The next two routes are on the huge boulder with the amazing unclimbed arete. The easiest route to the top climbs the east edge of the block.

❺ Kritikator 30' 5.13a * (Tr.)
Varied and very bouldery, this route packs a lot of climbing into its meager height. Climb the left side of a black slab (crux) to reach some good holds on a rail. Follow the rail out left, then make some more hard moves to reach the top. It is possible to avoid the initial slab by starting a few feet to the right.

❻ Stepping Stone 20' 5.11a (Tr.)
This route climbs the stepped arete to the left of the unclimbed arete. Start deep in the hole and make some bouldery moves (V2/3) to the first step. Continue up the arete to a slabby mantle at the top.

The next route climbs the beautiful clean-cut arete on the opposite side of the corridor from Stepping Stone. The top of the boulder is reached by stemming up the cleft at the far end of the corridor.

❼ Workin' Man 25' 5.13a *** (Tr.)
Slap directly up the super-technical arete. A classic of its type. A tall mans' version comes in from a credit card undercling on the right and is perhaps a little easier.

Tom Hore on Workin' Man.

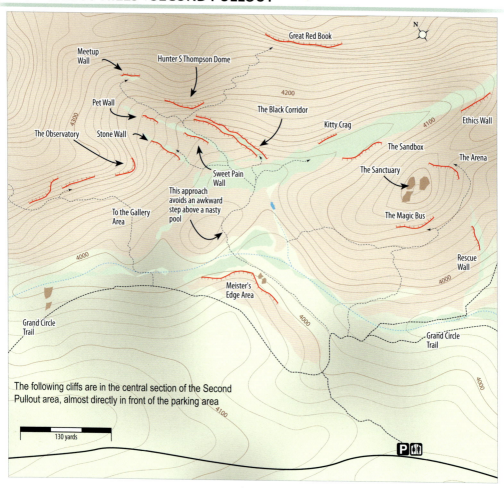

Meetup Wall

Hunter S Thompson Dome

Great Red Book

Pet Wall

The Black Corridor

Kitty Crag

Ethics Wall

The Observatory

Stone Wall

The Sandbox

The Arena

The Sanctuary

Sweet Pain Wall

This approach avoids an awkward step above a nasty pool

The Magic Bus

To the Gallery Area

Rescue Wall

Grand Circle Trail

Meister's Edge Area

Grand Circle Trail

The following cliffs are in the central section of the Second Pullout area, almost directly in front of the parking area

130 yards

Second Pullout - Central

The Great Red Book

Stratocaster Area

Meetup Wall

Stone Wall

Hunter S Thompson Dome

The Black Corridor

The Gallery Area

The Observatory

Sweet Pain wall

Meister's Edge Area

The Sandbox

This crag sits low on the right side the gully that slants up to the east under The Great Red Book. It is a very shady wall that almost never gets any sun. There is some fragile and sandy rock here, but also a few good routes.

Approach: From the parking area, head down the main trail taking a right at the first fork at 170 yards. Continue to a second fork 50 yards further on. Take the trail on the left and follow it, passing under a couple of red, hueco-covered walls. After 200 yards you will be standing under the obvious arete of Meister's Edge, a short distance to the left. Turn right, cross

the main wash and go up a shallow gully heading up to the north. About 30' below the top of the shallow gully, turn right and follow a ledge around to the right which leads down into a nice, flat area. Turn right and cross the flat area into the base of a broad, bushy gully which heads up gradually to the east. Follow a trail up the gully for 350 yards, at which point there is an obvious, very steep and shady wall on the right, The Sandbox. 20 minutes.

The crag consists of two walls. The routes are described from left to right starting with the wall on the left.

❶ Project: A partially bolted line at the left end of the wall.

❷ Public Enemy 50' 5.13a
Mike Moore. 2003.
Start just right of the previous route. This route climbs into a huge scoop and up the wall above.

❸ Project: The next route to the right (7 b's).

❹ Rubber Bullet 55' 5.13a *
Leo Henson. April 1993.
Start between two black streaks. Climb easy huecos up very steep rock then do a hard boulder problem to get onto the upper wall (7 b's).

❺ Mr Yuck 50' 5.12d
Mike Moore. 2003.
This route climbs the wall just left of the black streak on the right, past a couple of obvious pockets (6 b's).

❻ Crimson Crimp 50' 5.12b *
Leo Henson. November 1997.
Start 20' to the right of Rubber Biscuit at the right end of the wall, just to the right of the black streak on the right. Big scoops lead to thin, sustained wall climbing (6 b's).

The following routes are on the wall on the right.

❼ Generations 40' 5.13a/b
Jonathan Seigrist. February 2015.
The lower wall leads to a very hard sequence, moving right along the lip of the roof, until it is possible to pull onto the finishing slab (6 b's).

❽ Samadhi 40' 5.11d
Jarret Hunter. 2003.
Climb up between big scoops at the left end of the wall (6 b's).

❾ Sand Boxing 50' 5.12d *
Leo Henson. December 1997.
Start 50' right of the previous route. Steep climbing on good holds leads to a hard finish (7 b's).

❿ Sandblaster 50' 5.12b/c *
Leo Henson. Fall 1993.
This route became a good bit harder after it lost some holds on the crux bulge. Start beside a bush just right of Sand Boxing. Climb an open groove to the crux, moving right around a steep bulge (7 b's).

⓫ Sand Rail 50' 5.12a
Leo Henson. December 1997.
Start just right of Sandblaster. Burly moves up a steep bulge lead to a rest. Continue up the red corner above, then up to the anchor (6 b's).

⑫ Sand Buckets 50' 5.11b
Leo Henson, Karin Henson. November 1997.
Start 5' to the right of Sand Rail. A bouldery start leads to easier climbing on big hueco's (6 b's).

⑬ Sand Wedge 50' 5.11b
Leo Henson, Karin Henson. November 1997.
A chossy route. The rightmost route on the wall (6 b's).

The following routes sit in a small corridor a hundred yards around to the right of the Sandbox. It is on the left wall of the corridor formed by a huge boulder and is almost directly opposite Kitty Crag.

● Darkside Slab 30' 5.12c **
Joel Jackson. 2001.
A really good route which packs a lot of hard, varied movement into its meager height (5 b's).

● Brightside 25' 5.12c/d
The smooth wall opposite Darkside Slab, the exact difficulty depends on how far right you stray (3 b's).

Ethics Wall

This is the north-facing wall that sits above the saddle at the top of the gully that slants up to the east underneath The Great Red Book. It is a shady and exposed wall, best during warmer weather. It provides long, pumpy climbs, some of which have some interesting hueco features. The routes are seldom climbed and as a result are still a bit snappy.

Approach: From the parking area, head down the main trail taking a right at the first fork at 170 yards. Continue to a second fork 50 yards further on. Take the trail on the left and follow it, passing under a couple of red, hueco-covered walls.

After 200 yards you will be standing under the obvious arete of Meister's Edge a short distance to the left. Turn right, cross the main wash and go up a shallow gully heading up to the north. About 30' below the top of the shallow gully, turn right and follow a ledge around to the right which leads down into a nice flat area. Turn right and cross the flat area into the base of a broad, bushy gully which heads up gradually to the east. Follow a trail up the gully for 600 yards to a tall, steep wall on the right, almost at the top of the gully. 25 minutes.

The routes are described from left to right.

❶ Rafter Man 90' 5.12a
The leftmost route on the wall. It starts just to the right of a rotten left-leaning flake (8 b's).

❷ Laying Hands 90' 5.11d **
Start 15' to the right of Rafter Man. The route climbs a smooth, pocketed face then continues through the steep scoops and huecos above to an anchor (8 b's).

❸ Fast Fingers 90' 5.11d
Start 10' right of Laying Hands. Climb up and right past a series of left-facing flakes, then finish up a steep headwall to the anchors (8 b's).

❹ Mind Field 90' 5.11c
This route starts 10' to the right of the previous route. Climb a short wall covered in small, down-sloping ramps to reach a scoop. Climb the scoop to reach a steep wall which gradually eases to the anchors (7 b's).

❺ Ethical Behavior 80' 5.11c
The rightmost route on the wall is a trad route with a mixture of bolts and gear. Start 10' to the right of Mind Field. Climb up to a steep seam (small cams) and continue to an anchor (4 b's).

Retirement Plan 290' 5.7 *
Gary Sanders, Mark Limage. 1998/9.
Single rack to 1.25".
This route sits by itself on a large, south-facing slab opposite The Sandbox. It starts about 100' above the floor of the wash behind a pile of boulders and about 50' to the right of a big right-facing corner with a large water streak.

1. 180' 5.7 Go up and left to a left-facing flake. Continue to a small crescent and continue straight up to a belay at a horizontal (5 b's).
2. 110' 5.7 Continue up the face (4 b's) to reach a right-facing crack which is followed to an anchor.
Descent: Rappel with two ropes.

Kitty Crag

This small, sunny wall sits on the left side of the gully that slants up to the east below the Great Red Book, it faces south towards The Sandbox.

Approach: From the parking area, head down the main trail taking a right at the first fork at 170 yards. Continue to a second fork 50 yards further on. Take the trail on the left and follow it, passing under a couple of red, hueco-covered walls. After 200 yards you will be standing under the obvious arete of Meister's Edge a short distance to the left. Turn right, cross the main wash and go up a shallow gully heading up to the north. About 30' below the top of the shallow gully turn right and follow a ledge around to the right which leads down into a nice flat area. Turn right and cross the flat area into the base of a broad bushy gully which heads up gradually to the east. Follow a trail up the gully for 200 yards, to a small, sunny wall on the left. 18 minutes.

The route are described from left to right.

❶ Suffering Cats 60' 5.11c **
Randy Marsh. Pier Locatelli. 1994.
Climb the attractive left-leaning flake to crux moves at its top. Easier climbing leads to the anchor (6 b's).

❷ Titty Litter 50' 5.10d
Randy Marsh. Pier Locatelli. 1994.
The rounded groove just right of Suffering Cats (5 b's).

❸ Nine Lives 50' 5.11d
Leo Henson, Karin Henson. Fall 1993.
The steep groove to the right of Titty Litter (5 b's).

❹ Gatito Teiso 30' 5.12a
Jason Butts. 2004.
A short, bouldery route. Start 10' down and right of Nine Lives (5 b's).

The Great Red Book

The Great Red Book is the classic moderate route of the Calico Hills. It climbs a prominent, huge left-facing dihedral which is located on the large, red wall facing the road, at the top of the escarpment. It is north and slightly to the east from the parking area.

As well as The Great Red Book there are many moderate face climbs on the long wall to its right. On this part of the face you can pretty much climb anywhere, and it appears that some recent routes may coincide, at least in part, with older, unprotected routes.

Approach: From the parking area, head down the main trail taking a right at the first fork at 170 yards. Continue to a second fork 50 yards further on. Take the trail on the left and follow it passing under a couple of red, hueco-covered walls. After 200 yards you will be standing under the obvious arete of Meister's Edge a short distance to the left. Turn right, cross the main wash and go up a shallow gully heading up to the north. About 30' below the top of the shallow gully turn right and follow a ledge around to the right which leads down into a nice, flat area. Across the flat area, slightly to the left is a gully with a steep wall on its left side about 100 yards up. This is the Sweet Pain wall. Head up the gully until just past the Sweet Pain wall, then scramble over to the base of the obvious large wall on the right, the Hunter S. Thompson Dome. Follow the ledge to the right, under the Hunter S. Thompson Dome, then scramble up the steep, boulder-covered hillside. Reach the wall close to the base of a huge left-facing corner, the line of The Great Red Book. 30 minutes.

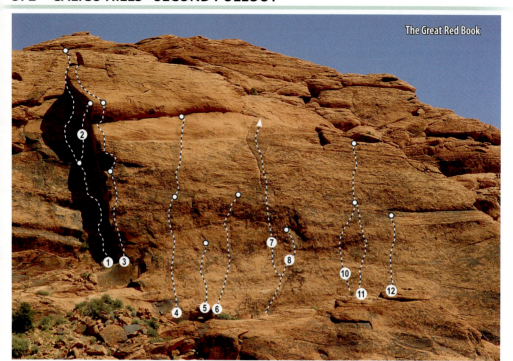

The Great Red Book

The first routes are at the far left end of the wall, about 200' left of The Great Red Book.

The Curver 50' 5.8
Single rack to 5", double 3"- 4".
This route climbs the big, right-facing flake/corner at the left end of the crag. When the corner ends, follow a left-leaning crack to the top.

The Liner 100' 5.6
Single rack to 3".
Climb the long, straight, splitter crack 10' to the right of the previous route. At the top angle right to the anchors of G. Dog.

G. Dog 100' 5.6
Gary Sanders, Mark Limage. 2000.
The runout face (3 b's) 40' to the right of the previous route is climbed to an anchor.

❶ The Great Red Book 270' 5.8 **
John Williamson, Bob Logerquist. October 1971.
Single rack to 4".
The huge, red dihedral on the left side of the cliff. The right wall of the corner keeps this route shady until late morning. Enjoyable climbing on soft but well-cleaned rock. Start on a big ledge at the base of the corner.
1. 140' 5.7 Climb up past some ledges into the corner. Go up the corner past a steep lieback then move out left and climb shallow corners to an anchor.
2. 130' 5.8 Climb the face above the anchor (2 b's.) Rejoin the corner and follow it past a wide lieback (b) into a big chasm. Continue up the face on the left to an anchor on the top of the formation.
Descent: Scramble down to the west to reach an open gully. Go down the gully then scramble back east to the base.

❷ Bury the Hatchet 50' 5.12a
Joshua Janes, Andy Hansen. November 2011.
A short, bouldery route which climbs across the right sidewall of the huge Great Red Book dihedral. Start at the anchor at the top of the first pitch of The Great Red Book. From the anchor, climb up 20' to a weakness in the steep, right wall of the huge corner. A series of burly moves (3 b's) leads to a bolt anchor on an exposed perch on the arete.

❸ Animal Boy 240' 5.11d
Don Wilson, Jack Marshall. March 1988.
A spectacular route up the right arete of the Great Red Book. Start at the base of the Great Red Book
1. 100' 5.11d Climb up and right to the base of the arete, and pull up into a thin left-leaning crack (b). Follow the crack over a bulge to easier rock which leads to an anchor in a black scoop.
2. 60' 5.10b Continue up the arete
3. 80' 5.10a Move left and follow the arete (2 b's) to the top.

The next routes are on the long, featureless wall to the right of the Great Red Book, they are generally characterized by fragile edges and long runouts, although there are also a couple of sport-bolted pitches. The first route is about 75' down and right of the Great Red Book where a large mushroom-shaped boulder sits on the ramp at the base of the wall.

❹ Tomato Amnesia 220' 5.8+
Don Wilson, Karen Wilson, Jack Marshall. March 1988.
Single rack to 1.75", Rp's.
Start just to the left of the large mushroom-shaped boulder.
1. 100' 5.8+ Climb the face to reach a curving, varnished seam which leads to an anchor (5 b's).
2. 120' 5.8 Follow the crack up the short, steep wall above then continue up the slab to an anchor with chains at a horizontal seam (2 b's).

A route starts up Tomato Amnesia and finishes on See Spot Run, a very sporty 5.10d.

❺ See Spot Run 60' 5.6
Mark Limage. 1998.
Start behind the mushroom boulder and left of some oak bushes. Climb straight up the face (3 b's) to an anchor. Easy but runout.

❻ Chips Ahoy 120' 5.9
Nick Nordblom, Jenni Stone. 1986.
Single rack to 1", Rp's.
A serious route with bad protection and poor rock. Start behind the mushroom boulder. Climb slabby rock up and right to a bolt at 40'. Continue to twin bolts below a steep, curving seam which is followed to an anchor.

Elementary Primer 70' 5.7+
Mark Limage. 1998.
Start 20' to the right of the previous routes between two bushes at a small, sandy, flat spot at the base of the cliff. Climb the runout face (3 b's) to an anchor.

❼ Stone Hammer 200' 5.8
Alan Bartlett, Eliza Moran. 1984.
Single rack to 1.75", Rp's.
Start 20' to the right of the previous route. Climb a thin, right-leaning crack for 25' (b) then move left and climb discontinuous seams (2 b's) to the top of the cliff.

❽ Seams Novel 80' 5.7+
Mark Limage. 1998.
Single rack to 0.6", Rp's.
This route climbs the right-leaning seam of Stone Hammer in its entirety (2 b's). When the seam ends, continue up to an anchor in a scoop.

The next group of routes start in a small corridor at the base of the wall, a useful landmark is a small but sturdy pine tree growing out of the top of the fin of rock that forms the corridor. The tree is about 100' to the right of the mushroom boulder.

❾ Chips Away 200' 5.10d
Single rack to 1", Rp's.
Start 50' up and right of Stone Hammer, below the small tree.

1. 100' 5.10d Climb the face to a bolt at 40', below a horizontal crack. Continue over a steeper bulge (2 b's) to an anchor.
2. 100' 5.9 Continue up the face (b) to the top.

❿ Ground up Vocabulary 190' 5.8+
Mark Limmage. 1997.
Start at the entrance to the corridor, just behind the pine tree.
1. 90' 5.8+ Scary moves reach the first bolt at 25'. Continue up the face the (5 b's) to the anchor.
2.100' 5.6 Climb the face above (b) to an anchor in a cave.

⓫ Dangling Participles 90' 5.8 *
Mark Limmage, Brady and Brady Mallory. 2004.
This route climbs straight up to the anchors of Ground up Vocabulary (14 b's).

The original route on this part of the wall, Question of Balance *(Nick Nordblom, John Martinet 1978)*, starts in the vicinity of Dangling Participles and eventually gains the horizontal break at the anchor of the next route before traversing right to the shoulder of the wall.

⓬ Subject Verb Agreement 90' 5.8 *
Mark Limage, Gary Sanders. 2000.
Start 15' to the right of the previous route, in the corridor below a patch of varnish. Climb the varnished wall (7 b's) to an anchor at a horizontal break.

● Sandstone Cowboy 180' 5.10c
Jack Marshall, Dave Wonderly. 1987.
Start at the end of the corridor to the right of a patch of smooth varnish.
1. 90' 5.10c Climb to a bolt at 30 ft. Continue up the face to a second bolt. A runout in this section was protected by lassoing a horn "far above the leaders head". From the second bolt angle left to an anchor.
2. 90' 5.8 Continue up the easier face to the top.

● Bad Grammer 60' 5.9
This route starts on top of a small fin 50' down and to the right from the end of the corridor. Climb the varnished wall to an anchor consisting of two bolts a couple of feet apart.

Hunter S. Thompson Dome

This sunny cliff is on the right side of the lower part of the wide-open gully directly opposite the pullout. It faces the road and is recognized by a white face topped by a large roof in its lower-right corner. The older routes are all mixed routes requiring various bits of gear, but more recently some sport routes have been added. A 70m rope is handy for the full-length routes since it allows the routes to be done in one long pitch, thereby avoiding some dodgy belays.

Approach: From the parking area, head down the main trail taking a right at the first fork at 170 yards. Continue to a second fork 50 yards further on. Take the trail on the left and follow it, passing under a couple of red, hueco-covered walls. After 200 yards you will be standing under the obvious arete of Meister's Edge a short distance to the left. Turn right, cross the main wash and go up a shallow gully heading up to the north. About 30' below the top of the shallow gully turn right and follow a ledge around to the right which leads down into a nice flat area. Across the flat area is an obvious gully with a steep wall on its left side about 100 yards up, this is the Sweet Pain Wall. Head up the gully until just past the Sweet Pain wall, then scramble over right to the base of the wall. 15 minutes.

The first three routes are at the top of the ramp which runs underneath the left side of the wall.

❶ Chrome Dome 60' 5.10a
Mike Ward, Danny Meyers. July 2006.
The leftmost bolted route (8 b's).

❷ Crazy Eights 80' 5.8
Mike Ward, Danny Meyers. July 2006.
The middle bolted route (9 b's).

❸ Mothers Milk 50' 5.8
Mike Ward, Danny Meyers. July 2006.
The rightmost bolted route (8 b's).

❹ Walking the Vertical Beach 220' 5.9+
Karen Wilson, Don Wilson, Jack Marshall. March 1988.
Single rack to 3", Rp's.
This route climbs the leftmost of two left-slanting cracks at
the left end of the crag, loose. Start in a small corridor. Climb
up the face (b) to reach the crack which is followed to its end.
Continue up and right up the face and over a roof (2 b's) to
a lower-angled crack. Belay below a bush on 2"- 3" cams.
Continue up the easy crack to the top.

❺ Gonzo Dogs 220' 5.10a
Jack Marshall, Dave Wonderly. December 1987.
Single rack to 2", Rp's.
This route climbs the right-hand of the two left-slanting cracks.
Climb the crack to where it ends in a big scoop (b). Continue
up a varnished face (b) to a crack in a small roof (b). Follow the
crack over the roof to a belay. Easy to the top.

❻ Runout Rodeo 220' 5.10b
Single rack to 1", Rp's.
Climb the first 10' of Gonzo Dogs then make a scary runout
right then up to the first bolt. Continue (3 b's) to easier rock
which is followed to the top.

❼ Fear and Loathing 80' 5.10d
Jack Marshall, Dave Wonderly, Warren Egbert. December 1987.
Single rack to 1".
Start at a right-facing corner 10' to the right of the previous
routes, at the entrance to the small corridor at the base of the
cliff. Climb the corner then move up and right. Continue past 2
bolts then move right to a seam which is followed to the anchor.

❽ Liquid God 80' 5.11b
Jack Marshall, Dave Wonderly, Warren Egbert. December 1987.
Start about 40' to the right of the previous route below a right-
facing corner capped by a roof. Climb the corner (b) and go
around the roof onto a varnished face with a seam, which is
followed to a roof. Pass the left side of the roof (b) and continue
to the anchor.

❾ Pretty in Pink 80' 5.12a
Paul Van Betten, Don Borroughs. 1986.
Double 0.4"- 0.75".
Start below the left end of the large roof in the lower-right corner of the crag. Climb a right-facing corner then move right to
a thin right-leaning flake which is followed (b) to a block below
the roof. Pull the roof (b) and continue to an anchor.

❿ Squire 50' 5.10c
Richard Harrison, Michelle Locatelli, Lisa Harrison. May 2006.
Climb the left side of the hueco-covered pillar of De-Nogginizer
and finish by climbing over a roof (5 b's).

⓫ The De-Nogginizer 60' 5.11a
Danny Meyers, Mike Ward. July 2006.
This route climbs a steep, hueco-covered pillar that leads up to
the right end of the roof. Pull through the roof on good holds to
reach an anchor (8 b's).

The following two routes are found a short distance up the gully
on the right side of the crag. They climb through an obvious
patch of varnished rock on the left side of the gully.

⓬ Special Guest Posers 30' 5.11a
Randy Marsh, Pier Locatelli. Fall 1990.
The line on the left (4 b's).

⓭ Tin Horn Posers 35' 5.11c
Randy Marsh, Pier Locatelli. Fall 1990.
The line on the right (5 b's).

The Black Corridor

This narrow corridor is packed with a good selection of mostly moderate sport routes on solid, well-used rock. It is a very popular area, so popular in fact that many of the rappel anchors have had to be replaced in recent years as they were getting dangerously worn down. These walls get very little sun, but they are also very sheltered and are therefore comfortable on all but the very hottest and coldest days.

Approach: From the parking area, head down the main trail taking a right at the first fork at 170 yards. Continue to a second fork 50 yards further on. Take the trail on the left and follow it, passing under a couple of red, hueco-covered walls. After 200 yards you will be standing under the obvious arete of Meister's Edge a short distance to the left. Turn right, cross the main wash and go up a shallow gully heading up to the north. About 30' below the top of the shallow gully turn right and follow a ledge around to the right which leads down into a nice flat area. Across the flat area, slightly to the right, some anchors are visible about 100 yards away, at the top of a black wall. Cross the flat area heading towards the anchors, then turn right and walk along a little rock ridge above a bushy corridor. Drop down into the corridor just before it swings to the left, turn the corner and you find yourself in a sandy-bottomed slot canyon about 15' wide with 60' high walls, the Black Corridor.
The corridor is split into an upper and a lower level by a jam of boulders. 15 minutes.

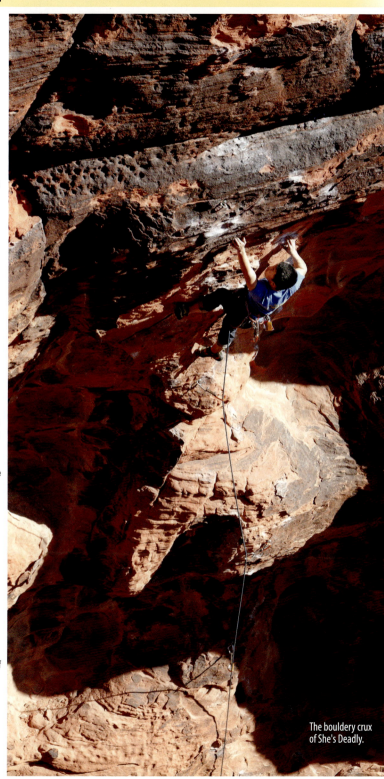

The bouldery crux of She's Deadly.

The routes are described starting with the lower level and going from left to right on the left wall, then right to left on the right wall.

Lower Level, Left Wall

1 The CEL 50' 5.9
This is the first route on the left as you enter the corridor, it starts behind the second of three small trees (6 b's).

2 L2 50' 5.9
Michelle Locatelli, Lisa Harrison. 2010.
The second route on the left (5 b's).

3 L3 60' 5.9+
The third route on the left (5 b's).

4 Bonaire 60' 5.9 *
Jim Steagall, Kevin Sandefur, Chris Werner, Dave Sobocan. Fall 1990.
Nice slabby climbing. This is the fourth route on the left as you enter the corridor, about 60' to the right of The CEL. Best to avoid the first bolt on the right (6 b's).

5 Bon EZ 50' 5.9+
Jim Steagall, Kevin Sandefur, Chris Werner, Dave Sobocan. Fall 1990.
Start 10' to the right of Bonaire, just to the left of a left-slanting ramp (7 b's).

6 Crude Boys 50' 5.10d *
Jim Steagall, Kevin Sandefur, Chris Werner, Dave Sobocan. Fall 1990
Nice rock with a delicate crux. Start 10' to the right of Bon EZ beside a small, left-leaning ramp (6 b's).

7 Black Corridor #4 50' 5.11a *
Start just right of Crude Boys. Balancy moves on smooth rock (4 b's) lead to an anchor.

8 Black Corridor #5 50' 5.11b
Jim Steagall, Kevin Sandefur, Chris Werner, Dave Sobocan. Fall 1990.
Single rack to 2", Rp's.
A serious mixed route. Start 10' right of the previous route and 20' to the left of the boulder jam. Face climb past a bolt to reach a thin crack which is followed to the top.

9 Vagabonds 55' 5.10a *
Jim Steagall, Kevin Sandefur, Chris Werner, Dave Sobocan. Fall 1990.
Start 10' left of the boulder jam. Good climbing up a slabby groove and the face above (8 b's).

10 Crude Control 50' 5.12a
Jim Steagall, Kevin Sandefur, Chris Werner, Dave Sobocan. Fall 1990.
This route climbs the short, steep wall beside the boulder jam then continues up the easier face above (6 b's).

Lower Level, Right Wall

11 Adoption 60' 5.11b
Leo Henson, Karin Henson. November 1991.
This is the first route on the right as you enter the corridor. Quite fingery at the start (7 b's).

12 Burros Don't Gamble 55' 5.10c *
Harrison Shull, Todd Hewitt. December 1994.
Start behind trees 20' to the left of Adoption. Interesting climbing on smooth huecos leads to a flake (7 b's).

13 Burros Might Fly 55' 5.10b *
Harrison Shull, Todd Hewitt. December 1994.
Start 10' left of Burros Don't Gamble. Technical climbing leads up past an undercling at 25'. Above the undercling, easier climbing leads up and right to the anchor (6 b's).

14 Psychobilly 55' 5.11b *
Michelle Locatelli, Lisa Harrison, Richard Harrison. May 2006.
This route climbs the nice-looking seam/offset 12' feet of Burros Might Fly (7 b's).

15 Michael Angelo 45' 5.11a
Michelle Locatelli. May 2006.
Start just to the right of a right-arching flake 15' to the left of Psychobilly. Climb the wall to a hard section just below the anchors (7 b's).

16 M & M 60' 5.11b
Danny Meyers, Rob Mansfield. February 2007.
Start between two trees, just left of the right-arching flake. A delicate start leads to tricky moves over the lower bulges then an easier finish (7 b's).

17 She's Deadly 65' 5.11d
Richard Harrison, Michelle Locatelli, Lisa Harrison. October 2007.
This route starts just left of M&M below a big thread/hueco 10' up. Follow edges and holes up a steep pillar to a rest in a big hueco on the right. The next bulge has a hard pull on small edges before easier moves lead to the anchor (8 b's).

18 Heavy Hitter 60' 5.10d
Mike Moore. 2006.
This route starts just left of She's Deadly, below a smooth slab to the right of a shallow, red corner. After a delicate start, enjoyable climbing on big huecos leads up a slight rib to a ledge. Finish up a short, steep wall to the anchor (10 b's).

19 Hips Don't Lie 40' 5.11c
Mike Moore. 2006.
Start 10' left of Heavy Hitter, below a long, twisting rib. Climb the rib with a bouldery crux near the top (5 b's).

20 Nightmare on Crude Street 55' 5.10d *
Jim Steagall, Kevin Sandefur, Chris Werner, Dave Sobocan. Fall 1990.
This route starts directly opposite Bonaire and about 6' to the left of the previous route. Climb up through a big groove/scoop to the final crux bulge.

21 Foe 40' 5.11a
Richard Harrison. May 2006.
Start 8' left of the previous route Climb the rib to the right of a large, rotten scoop through a bulge (5 b's).

22 Friend 40' 5.10d
Richard Harrison, Michelle Locatelli. May 2006.
Start 8' left of Foe. Climb a rib then pass the right side of a big bulge at an obvious large hueco (5 b's).

23 Idiot Parade 35' 5.10c **
Mike Moore. 2006.
Starts just below the boulder jam. Follow a right-slanting seam past some big huecos and a bulge to an anchor (5 b's).

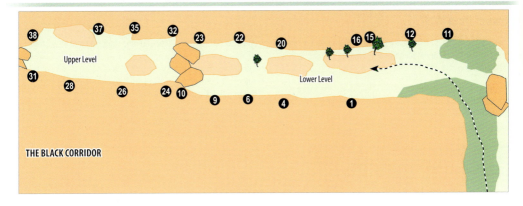

Upper Level, Left Wall

24 Thermal Breakdown 50' 5.9+
Jim Steagall, Kevin Sandefur, Chris Werner, Dave Sobocan. Fall 1990.
The first route on the left above the boulder jam. Start on top of the boulders (6 b's).

25 Crude Street Blues 45' 5.9
Jim Steagall, Kevin Sandefur, Chris Werner, Dave Sobocan. Fall 1990.
Start 10' to the right of the previous route below a low bolt (5 b's).

26 Crude Behavior 45' 5.9
Jim Steagall, Kevin Sandefur, Chris Werner, Dave Sobocan. Fall 1990.
Start below a ramp 8' to the right of the previous route (4 b's).

27 Dancin' with a God 45' 5.10a *
Jim Steagall, Kevin Sandefur, Chris Werner, Dave Sobocan. Fall 1990.
Start to the right of the previous route, about 25' to the right of the boulder jam (6 b's).

28 Live Fast, Die Young 45' 5.10d
Jim Steagall, Kevin Sandefur, Chris Werner, Dave Sobocan. Fall 1990.
Start just right of the previous route. The crux is a hard mantle low on the route (5 b's).

29 Black Gold 45' 5.10b **
Jim Steagall, Kevin Sandefur, Chris Werner, Dave Sobocan. Fall 1990.
Start at a small flake to the right of the previous route (5 b's). A bouldery start leads to very nice wall climbing.

30 Texas Tea 45' 5.10c
Jim Steagall, Kevin Sandefur, Chris Werner, Dave Sobocan. Fall 1990.
Start 8' to the right of the previous route at the left edge of a large right-leaning flake/ramp (5 b's). The moves below the first bolt are 10d. Either stick clip, or avoid this section altogether by climbing around it on the right.

31 Fool's Gold 45' 5.10b *
Jim Steagall, Kevin Sandefur, Chris Werner, Dave Sobocan. Fall 1990.
Start as for Texas Tea but move right up the ramp and climb a line of hueco's straight up, with a reachy crux at the second bolt (5 b's).

Upper Level, Right Wall

32 757 2X4 50' 5.7
This route starts immediately above the boulder Jam and climbs and a right-leaning crack/ramp (7 b's).

33 Oils Well that Ends Well 35' 5.11a
Jim Steagall, Kevin Sandefur, Chris Werner, Dave Sobocan. Fall 1990.
The second route on the right above the boulder jam. Bouldery opening moves (5 b's).

34 Sandstone Enema 45' 5.11b
Jim Steagall, Kevin Sandefur, Chris Werner, Dave Sobocan. Fall 1990.
Start 10' to the left of the previous route, below a right-leaning ramp. Climb the slabby black face with technical opening moves (6 b's).

35 Lewd, Crude, and Misconstrued 60' 5.9+ *
Jim Steagall, Kevin Sandefur, Chris Werner, Dave Sobocan. Fall 1990.
Start in the corner 10' to the left of Sandstone Enema. Climb the corner and the easier arete above (6 b's).

36 Texas Lite Sweet 35' 5.11b
Jim Steagall, Kevin Sandefur, Chris Werner, Dave Sobocan. Fall 1990.
Bouldery, thin moves up the face just left of the corner (3 b's).

37 Livin' on Borrowed Time 35' 5.11c
Jim Steagall, Kevin Sandefur, Chris Werner, Dave Sobocan. Fall 1990.
The very thin face just left of Texas Lite Sweet (4 b's).

38 Rebel without a Pause 30' 5.11b *
Jim Steagall, Kevin Sandefur, Chris Werner, Dave Sobocan. Fall 1990.
A fun, bouldery route up the short but very steep wall on the right, at the end of the corridor.

Sweet Pain Wall

This wall is a little hard to locate if its your first time, but it's a good wall with a nice selection of 5.11 routes. The cliff is very sheltered and gets sun until mid-day.

Approach: From the parking area, head down the main trail taking a right at the first fork at 170 yards. Continue to a second fork 50 yards further on. Take the trail on the left and follow it, passing under a couple of red, hueco-covered walls.

After 200 yards you will be standing under the obvious arete of Meister's Edge a short distance to the left. Turn right, cross the wash and go up a shallow gully heading up to the north. About 30' below the top of the shallow gully turn right and follow a ledge around to the right which leads down into a nice flat area. Across the flat area, slightly to the left, is an obvious bushy gully with a steep wall on its left side about 100 yards up, this is the Sweet Pain Wall. 15 minutes.

❶ Sweet Pain 35' 5.11d ★★
Leo Henson, Randy Faulk. 1991.
This route climbs a bulge at the left end of the wall, well to the left of the other routes. Short, steep and fun (5 b's).

❷ The Gambler 40' 5.11a
Michelle Locatelli, Richard Harrison, Lisa Harrison. November 2005.
This route follows a line of big edges and huecos out the bulge to the right of Sweet Pain (5 b's).

❸ Sour Pain 55' 5.11b
Valarie Heredia. 2013.
Climb a left-leaning flake to big jugs. Pull right and climb the thin wall to a set of anchors (7 b's).

The rest of the routes start from a ledge about 10' above the base of the cliff, underneath the right side of the wall.

❹ Glitter Gulch 50' 5.11a ★★
This route starts on the left side of the ledge. After a hard start a steep, enjoyable wall with good holds (6 b's).

❺ Slave to the Grind 50' 5.11b ★
This route starts just right of Glitter Gulch. A technical lower wall leads to a good rest before a steep finish (6 b's).

❻ Sister of Pain 50' 5.11b/c ★
Leo Henson, Karin Henson. Fall 1992.
Start 10' to the right of Slave to the Grind. Similar to the previous route but with a bouldery start and a steeper finish (6 b's).

Dustin Burd on The Gambler. Page 378.

The best route on the wall is a link-up which starts up Glitter Gulch, moves into Slaves to the Grind and finishes up Sister of Pain. A long, pumpy 11d.

⑦ Lee Press On 50' 5.12b/c
Leo Henson, Karin Henson. Fall 1992.
Start 10' to the right of the previous route. Tiny holds and intricate moves lead to a ledge at 25'. Easier to the anchor (6 b's).

⑧ Pain in the Neck 50' 5.10a
Start on the right side of the ledge below a right-leaning crack. Climb past 5 b's to the anchor. A loop around to the right between the first and second bolts is a little sporty. If you climb straight up this section it's 10c.

⑨ A Cute Pain 50' 5.8
T. Swain, D Swain. November 1993.
Single rack to 1".
Start to the right of the last route below a shallow, varnished left-facing corner. Climb up to a right-leaning crack which is followed for 15', then move left and climb the face to an anchor (3 b's).

⬤ The Crick 50' 5.7
Start 10' right of A Cute Pain. Go over a short wall then climb the easy slab to an anchor.

⬤ Hood Of Shame 50' 5.7
Start 12' right of The Crick. Pull over a short, steep wall then climb the easier slab to an anchor.

Pet Wall

Pet rock is the small cliff a couple of hundred feet up the gully from Sweet Pain Wall. It is on the same side of the gully as Sweet Pain, facing northeast towards the left end of the Hunter S. Thompson Dome. The rock here is still quite fragile, and the grades of the routes seem to change on a regular basis. The routes face northeast and lose the sun by mid-morning.

Approach: From Sweet Pain Cliff, scramble 50 yards up the gully to a small cliff on the left.

The routes are described from left to right.

① Desert Hamster 30' 5.11c
Michelle Locatelli, Lisa Harrison. Spring 2008.
The fragile wall to the left of Teika (5 b's).

② Teika 30' 5.12a
Michelle Locatelli, Lisa Harrison. May 2007.
This route climbs the curving, left-facing corner in the center of the wall (5 b's).

③ Turkey Brain 30' 5.10d
Michelle Locatelli, Lisa Harrison. May 2007.
Start just right of Teika. Climb out the left side of a hueco, then up to the chains (4 b's).

④ Trey Dog Boogie 30' 5.11a
Michelle Locatelli, Lisa Harrison. May 2007.
Start to the right of the previous route. Climb up through a hueco formation (5 b's).

Meetup Wall

Meetup wall is a sunny, south-west facing slab in a small corridor tucked in behind the Hunter S Thompson Dome. It contains a worthwhile selection of well-bolted, moderate sport routes, including some of the easiest described in this guidebook. Despite the out of the way location, it is quite popular.

Approach: Follow the approach to Sweet Pain Wall, then continue up the gully, passing a small, bolted wall on the left, Pet Wall. Just after Pet Wall cross to the right side of the gully and go up a short distance before heading right to a pine tree at the entrance to a small side canyon on the right. 25 minutes.

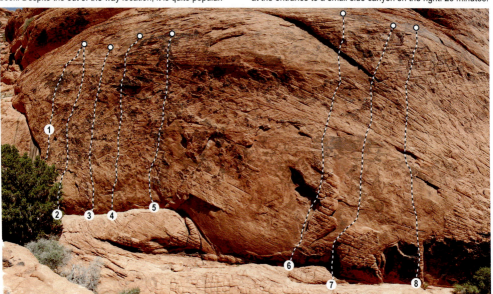

The first five routes start on a sloping ledge which slants up and right behind the pine tree.

❶ Member Profile 55' 5.7
D. Young. 2010/11.
This is the leftmost route on the wall. The first bolt is about 18' up and can be reached from directly below, but more safely by starting up Let's Meetup then moving left. Continue up the face before moving back right to finish at the anchor of Let's Meetup (4 or 5 b's).

❷ Let's Meetup 60' 5.7
Start directly behind the pine tree. Make a few bouldery moves over a short, steep section onto an easier face. Climb straight up the face to an anchor (5 b's). It's probably best to stick clip the first bolt since reaching it is the crux of the route.

❸ Safety First 55' 5.6
L. Gallia, M. Knowles, D. Young. 2010/11
Start 12' right of the tree. Make a few tricky moves off the ground then go up the pleasant face to the anchor (5 b's).

❹ Message Board 60' 5.7
L. Gallia, D. Young. 2010/11.
Start 10' right of Safety First. Climb straight up smooth rock on good, small holds, then continue up an easier face to the chains (5 b's).

❺ No Teaching! 60' 5.7
L. Gallia, M. Knowles, D. Young. 2010/11.
This route starts at the far end on the sloping ledge directly under the wall. Climb some small flakes to a high first bolt and continue to the chains (5 b's).

The next routes start from a lower ledge about 40' down and right of the previous routes. Count Me In starts on the right side of a smooth section of the wall.

❻ Count Me In 60' 5.8
D. Young. 2010/11.
Start below a big left-facing flake which begins about 8' up. Climb up the flake and over a slight bulge. Continue up the face, crossing a left-slanting fault, and continuing straight up to the anchor (6 b's).

❼ Upcoming Meetups 60' 5.10a
D. Young. 2010/11.
Start just right of the previous route. Climb creaky flakes to get up onto a ledge and the first bolt. Continue up the face to the chains (6 b's).

❽ Sponsors Wanted 60' 5.9-
D. Young. 2010/11.
The rightmost route on the wall. Climb straight up the face to the right of Upcoming Meetups (5 b's).

The next routes are on the right (south) side of the corridor. This wall faces north and gets almost no sun.

🔴 The Pumpkin King 35' 5.10a/b
Kevin Hibbert. 2013.
This is the first bolted route on the right side of the corridor. Climb through a series of huecos to the anchor (4 b's).

🔴 Sally 25' 5.9
Start just left of the previous route. Climb huecos to a flake which leads to the anchor (3 b's).

Stone Wall

This wall lies on the left side of the next gully to the west of the Sweet Pain Wall. It faces east and gets sun until late-morning. This cliff has a collection of long 5.10's which are quite enjoyable despite some soft rock.

Approach: From the parking area, head down the main trail taking a right at the first fork at 170 yards. Continue to a second fork 50 yards further on. Take the trail on the left and follow it, passing under a couple of red, hueco-covered walls. After 200 yards you will be standing under the obvious arete of Meister's Edge a short distance to the left. Turn right, cross the main wash and go up a shallow gully heading up to the north. About 30' below the top of the shallow gully turn right and follow a ledge around to the right which leads down into a nice flat area. Across the flat area, slightly to the left, is an obvious gully with a steep wall on its left side about 100 yards up, this is the Sweet Pain Wall. The Stone Wall is in the next gully to the left (west). Cross the flat area to the bottom of the Sweet Pain Gully. Just at the entrance of the gully go left past a bush into a hidden corridor which leads west. After 50 yards in the corridor head into a narrow gully on the right. The Stone wall is on the left side of this gully about 100 yards up. 15 minutes.

The routes are described from left to right.

1 Purple Haze 45' 5.10d
Don Borroughs, Alan Busby. 1993.
The leftmost route on the wall (6 b's).

2 Haunted Hooks 80' 5.10c ★★★
Don Borroughs, Alan Busby. 1993.
One of the nicer climbs of its grade in the Calico Hills. Start 15'
to the right of the last route at a small, left-leaning arch. Climb past 9 b's to the anchor.

3 Roto Hammer 50' 5.10c ★★
Daryl Ellis. August 1992.
Start 10' to the right of Haunted Hooks below a larger left-leaning arch. Climb the wall going through the left side of a small roof (7 b's).

4 Nirvana 50' 5.11a
Don Borroughs, Alan Busby. 1993.
Start below a left-facing flake to the right of Root Hammer. The crux is low down and a little sporty (7 b's).

5 Stonehenge 50' 5.11d ★
Don Borroughs, Mike Ward, Alan Busby. 1993.
Start just right of Nirvana below a left-facing flake and just left of a bush (8 b's).

6 Stone Hammer 60' 5.10c
Mike Ward, Mike Clifford. 1986.
A trad route which starts up an obvious vertical crack in the right side of the wall. Climb the crack for 30' then continue up the face (3 b's) to an anchor.

7 Birthstone 55' 5.10d
Leo Henson, Karin Henson. April 1993.
Climb straight up to the anchor on Stone Hammer (6 b's).

8 April Fools 45' 5.10b
Don Borroughs, Alan Busby. 1993.
This route climbs through some big scoops on the right side of the wall. Start about 40' to the right of stone Hammer (6 b's).

Meister's Edge Area

The following routes are on the small outcrops on the north-facing slope below the parking area. These crags face north across the wash towards the Great Red Book etc. An obvious landmark is the clean-cut arete of Meister's Edge.

Approach: From the parking area, head down the main trail taking a right at the first fork at 170 yards, continue to a second fork 50 yards further on. Take the trail on the left and follow it, passing under a couple of red, hueco-covered walls. After 200 yards you will be standing under the obvious arete of Meister's Edge a short distance to the left. 5 Minutes.

Sandman 40' 5.11c (Tr.)
Paul Van Betten, Sal Mamusia. 1986.
Top-rope a line of hueco's in the middle of the red wall.

❶ Meister's Edge 30' 5.11c *
TR. Van Betten, Mamusia. 1986. Lead, Eric Charlton. 1988.
The obvious clean-cut arete. Start on a huge block which leans against the left side of the arete. Way more awkward than it looks, with a nasty fall if you blow the crux (3 b's).

❷ The Aspirant 50' 5.13a/b *
Start around to the right of Meister's Edge at the base of the cliff. It's a good idea to pre-clip the first couple of bolts on this route. Climb the bulging wall just right of the arete to a rest. More hard moves on the upper arete lead to the anchor (8 b's).

There are a couple of random bolts in the wall to the right of the previous route.

❸ Jonny Rotten 60' 5.11a
Paul Van Betten, Sal Mamusia. 1986.
Single rack to 3.5".
The loose, right-slanting crack in the right side of the wall.

Yucca 35' 5.11d (Tr.)
Paul Van Betten. 1987.
This route climbs a short, steep wall above the ledge where Jonny Rotten ends. It follows a line of hueco's.

❹ Jonny Jamcrack 50' 5.8
Paul Van Betten, Sal Mamusia. 1986.
Single rack to 3", double 1.75"- 2.5".
Start around to the right of the overhanging wall. Climb the splitter hand crack in the left wall of a black chimney. At the top the crack angles left to a slabby ledge then continues as a thin left-leaning seam which is followed to the top.

The next route is on the other side of the wash directly opposite the Meister's Edge area.

Shut up and Dance 60' 5.10b
Danny Meyers. 1985.
Climb a thin seam, past a small roof and up the slabby, white face (2 b's) to an anchor.

The Observatory

This is the name given to the large, triangular mass of slabby rock to the right of The Gallery. The well-defined ridge that makes up the right edge of the wall is an obvious feature.

Approach: Witches' Honor is most easily reached by traversing out right from below The Gallery. Bewitched and the other routes on the right are most easily reached by following the approach to the Stone Wall then cutting out left just below the Stone Wall and scrambling up to the starting ledge.

The routes are described from left to right.

❶ Witches' Honor 160' 5.8
Danny Meyers. 1988.
A serious route with flaky rock and long run outs. Start in a body sized hole in the low-angled slabs below the left side of the formation. Climb up and right following an easy crack to reach an anchor on a ledge at the base of a vertical crack. Climb the crack past a horizontal (2 b's) then angle right to a third bolt. Follow a slab up and left to an anchor.

The next routes are best started from a flat ledge below an overhang at the base of the arete on the right side of the crag.

❷ Which Hunters 150' 5.10a
Todd Swain, Donette Swain. February 1994.
Single rack to 1.25", small tricams.
Start about 40' left of the ledge, in the middle of an easy slab. Climb the slabby wall (4 b's) then run it out, up and right to an anchor shared with the next two routes.

❸ Warlock 150' 5.9 R
Todd Swain, Donette Swain. February 1994.
Single rack to 1.25", one 3" cam.
Start about 20' to the left of the ledge. Climb up the face and

over a bulge to reach a crack which leads up between two caves to a horizontal crack. Continue to the shared anchor.

❹ Bewitched 150' 5.5 *
One of the easier bolted leads in Red Rocks. From the left end of the ledge climb the slab heading up and right (2 b's). From the second bolt move left to the right edge of a large scoop/cave. From the cave traverse right (b) to the arete which is followed (3 b's) to an anchor located just to the right of another cave.

The Gallery / Wall of Confusion

This cliff has a perfect spread of grades from 5.9 to 5.13b. The routes are basically all the same, they just get longer and steeper as the grades get higher, making The Gallery a great training cliff. The Wall of Confusion is the smaller wall tucked around to the left of The Gallery. At a higher level, between The Gallery and The Wall of Confusion, is the guano-filled cave of Resin Rose. During the winter these walls get the sun all day, and are very sheltered from the wind. In fact, the climbing here often feels a little too warm on all but the coldest days. In the late spring The Gallery gets the shade until late morning, and often these are the best redpoint conditions of the year.

Approach: From the parking area, head down the main trail for 170 yards to the first fork. Take the trail on the left and follow it for 400 yards, over a small hill and down towards the wash. Leave the main trail at a dead tree, cross the wash and head up broken slabs to a system of ramps and ledges which lead up and left. Follow the ramp, scrambling around several boulders. Continue to a huge boulder which leans across the top of a gully on the right. Step across the gully above the boulder and follow the slab up and right to the base of The Gallery. To reach the Wall of Confusion from here head around to the left for 50 yards. 15 minutes.

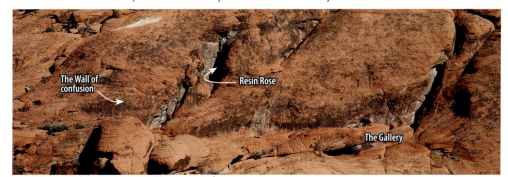

The Wall of confusion   Resin Rose   The Gallery

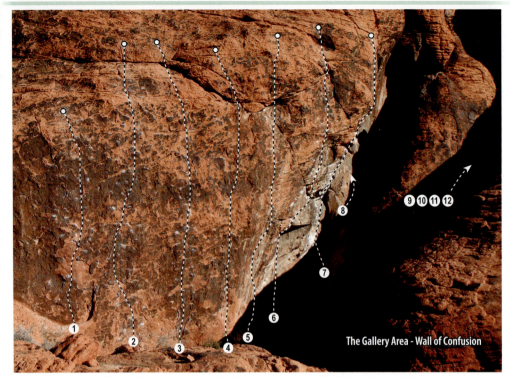

The Gallery Area - Wall of Confusion

The routes are described from left to right starting with the Wall of Confusion.

❶ The Runaway 40' 5.10c
Greg Mayer. Spring 1989.
The leftmost route on the wall (4 b's).

❷ American Sportsman 40' 5.10c **
Bone Speed, Bill Boyle. Winter 1988.
Climb the wall starting 5' to the right of The Runaway (4 b's).

❸ Desert Pickle 45' 5.11c *
Boone Speed, Bill Boyle. Winter 1988.
The next route to the right. A fingery and hard to read sequence at 20' claims a lot of scalps (4 b's).

❹ Sudden Impact 45' 5.11d
Boone Speed, Bill Boyle. Winter 1988.
The first 30' of this route has become quite fingery and sustained since several holds have broken (5 b's).

To the right of Sudden Impact the wall turns slightly to the east and becomes much steeper.

❺ Big Damage 50' 5.12b
Boone Speed. 1988.
This route feels like an extended boulder problem. Start around to the right of Sudden Impact below a very steep wall leading to a crack at 20'. Make bouldery moves with hard clips to reach the crack, then easier to the top (6 b's).

❻ Promises in the Dark 55' 5.12b **
Mike Tupper. Winter 1988.
Easy for the grade but really enjoyable. Start below a short corner leading to a roof. After a bouldery start continue over the roof and up a pumpy headwall (7 b's).

❼ Fear and Loathing 60' 5.12a ***
Bill Boyle, Boone Speed. Winter 1988.
A classic route up the sharply-overhanging, rounded arete on the right side of the wall. Great holds but a high pump factor. Start by leaning across from a boulder to the first holds (9 b's).

❽ Body English 35' 5.12c
Mike Tupper. Winter 1988.
Start from a ledge up and right, and around the corner from Fear and Loathing. Climb the steep, black corner (4 b's).

The next routes are in the big cave about 150' up and right of Fear and Loathing, reached by an easy scramble up the ramp underneath that route. These routes are seldom climbed but are quite worthwhile.

❾ The Calanque 65' 5.12a
Start at the left edge of the cave. Follow 8 bolts up varnished rock, finishing up a short, pumpy headwall.

The next three routes all end at anchors below a very steep headwall. Judging by the state of the rock, the bolts on the headwall appear to be unfinished projects.

❿ Resin Rose 60' 5.11d *
Paul Crawford, Jay Smith. April 1987.
Single rack to 5". A really big piece 8+" would be nice if you have it.
An excellent and stout trad route up the roof crack in the back of the cave.

⓫ Makulu 45' 5.11d **
A fun route up the face to the right of Resin Rose. Steep with big, awkward holds (5 b's).

⓬ Super Guide 45' 5.11a *
The rightmost route in the cave (5 b's).

Fear and Loathing. Page 384.

The next routes are all on The Gallery, the right-hand of the two walls. The first route is at the far left end of the wall, well to the left of the rest of the routes. This is almost directly above the point where the approach trail first arrives at the wall.

⑬ Range of Motion 35' 5.10d
Todd Swain, Dick Peterson, Peggy Buckey. May 1990.
Climb up a pod onto a steep wall (4 b's).

The next routes are 60' to the right.

● The Goode Dude Climb 45' 5.7
Mike Bond, Mike Moore. January 2015.
Starting a few feet to the left of a short crack, climb straight up the easy face to an anchor (5 b's).

⑭ Sport Climbing is Neither 25' 5.9
Start 10' right of the previous route beside a short crack (3 b's).

The Gallery – Left side.

⑮ Bucks Muscle World 25' 5.9
Greg Mayer. Spring 1990.
The wall 6' right of the previous route (3 b's).

⑯ Gelatin Pooch 30' 5.10a
Greg Mayer. Spring 1990.
The wall to the right of Bucks Muscle World (4 b's).

⑰ Pump First, Pay Later 35' 5.10b
Greg Mayer. Spring 1990.
The wall to the right of Gelatin Pooch and just left of Running Amuck (4 b's).

All the previous routes start from a ledge under the wall. Where the ledge fizzles out at its right end there is a short, steep left-facing flake.

⑱ Running Amuck 40' 5.10c *
Greg Mayer. Spring 1990.
Climb the flake and the wall above to a sloping finish (4 b's).

⑲ Gridlock 45' 5.11a
Greg Mayer. Spring 1990.
Start at the entrance of the sandy corridor to the right of Running Amuck. Climb the steep wall to a short crack which is

followed to the anchor (4 b's).
Variation: The original route started on Social Disorder and moved left to reach the upper crack 5.11d.

The next two routes start below a black, circular depression above a small tree in the corridor.

⑳ Social Disorder 45' 5.11d
Scott Carson, Steve Bullock, Jonathan Knight. 1991.
Bouldery. Climb up the left side of the black depression, then pull right and go up the steep wall to an easier finish (5 b's).

㉑ A Day in the Life 45' 5.11c **
Bill Boyle. Winter 1988/9.
A popular pump, but with serious enough clips that it doesn't really qualify as a sport route. Climb out of the right side of the depression and up the wall to the anchor (5 b's).

㉒ Minstrel in The Gallery 55' 5.12c *
Mike Tupper. Winter 1988/9.
No hard moves but long, steep and fingery. It is a good idea to pre-clip the first bolt. Climb straight up the wall to the right of the previous route, finishing on the final moves of Yaak Crack (5 b's). **Variation:** If you step across from the rock on the other side of the corridor it's 12a.

The Gallery – Right side.

23 Yaak Crack 50' 5.11c ***
Bill Boyle. Winter 1988/9.
This route climbs the obvious left-leaning crack just to the right of the end of the corridor. A great route with athletic climbing on big holds. Save some juice for the awkward finish (6 b's).

24 Sissy Traverse 90' 5.13b **
Don Welsh. Fall 1991.
Still one of the harder pitches in the Calico Hills. This route is usually started up the first three bolts of the Gift then climbs up and right across the wall to finish up Nothing Shocking (9 b's). The original start was on Minstrals.

25 The Gift 55' 5.12d ***
Boone Speed. Winter 1988/9
This used to be the softest 12d you could ever hope for. However after losing quite a few holds, and as the finger edges gradually get ground down and more rounded with use, it has finally achieved its original grade. Start at the base of Yaak Crack and climb straight up to a tricky finish (6 b's).

26 Where the Down Boys Go 55' 5.12d **
Mike Tupper. Winter 1988/9.
Easy for the grade, but reachy. Climb the wall to the right of the Gift passing an obvious undercling near the top (5 b's).

The next three routes all start on the Glitz which is the obvious right-slanting line of cracks and huecos on the right edge of the wall.

27 Who Made Who 55' 5.12d *
Mike Tupper. Winter 1988/9.
A hard route, much more pumpy and sustained than The Gift or Down Boys, and a little sporty to boot. Climb the initial flake of The Glitz then straight up the wall to a tough finish (5 b's).

28 Nothing Shocking 60' 5.13a **
Don Welsh. Winter 1988/9.
Climb straight up from the third bolt on The Glitz. Steep and fingery (6 b's).

29 The Glitz 60' 5.12c **
Mike Tupper. Winter 1990.
A great route with a nice variety of features. Climb the right trending flakes and cracks to a height-dependent crux past the third bolt. After the crux, enjoyable climbing on big huecos leads up and right to the anchor (6 b's).

B&W Wall

This seldom climbed wall is located below the left side of the Stratocaster Area. It is a large, slabby formation just above the main wash. It is most easily recognized by a prominent water streak. The routes are described from right to left.

Approach: From the parking area, head down the main trail for 170 yards to the first fork. Take the trail on the left and follow it for 600 yards, over a small hill and down towards the wash, then on to a huge boulder. Continue past the boulder for a couple of hundred yards. At this point the B&W wall is visible on the other side of the wash. Leave the trail and go down into the wash. Head right (east) a short distance then scramble up a slab, and follow a low-angled crack into a corridor at the base of the wall, to the right of the water streak. 15 minutes.

Descent: From the top of the formation scramble down to the west, following an easy chimney and ramp. At the bottom of the ramp follow ledges back east to the base of the wall.

❶ The Don't Come Line 210' 5.10a
Don Wilson, Karen Wilson, Jack Marshall. February 1988.
Single rack to 1.75". Extra small cams.
A bold route with good climbing. Start in a corridor below the right side of the wall.
1. 80' 5.10a Climb a shallow left-facing corner (2 b's). At its top move right (b) then make scary moves over a bulge to reach an anchor at a sloping ledge.
2. 130' 5.8 Climb up a left-leaning crack and continue up the face above (2 b's) to easier rock.

The next two routes start on top of a small buttress at the base of the wall below the water streak.

❷ Five Card Stud 190' 5.10a
Don Wilson, Karen Wilson, Jack Marshall. February 1988.
Start 5' to the right of the water streak.
1. 80' 5.10a Start by climbing a right-leaning crack for 15', step up to a bolt then make a long runout up and left to a bolt in a bulge. Continue over the steep section past a third bolt and set up an anchor.
2. 100' 5.9 Continue up the face to the top.

❸ Black Streak 170' 5.9
Wendell Broussard. 1982.
Double 0.4"- 0.75", 2"- 3" for the anchor.
This route climbs the long water streak in the middle of the wall. Fragile and runout. Start just right of some bushes. Climb up beside the water streak (4 b's). After the last bolt, good, small tcu's in horizontal slots protect the moves to an alcove at the top of the water streak. Pull over the bulge and belay on good 2-3" cams at the top of the cliff.

❹ The Negative 120' 5.10b
Jack Marshall, Dave Wonderly. February 1988.
Start in an alcove down and left of the water streak. Climb thin varnished cracks to a bolt at 15'. Continue straight up the face above (3 b's) to an anchor.

Stratocaster Wall

Pat Olson on Pablo Diablo. Page 391.

This very sunny wall is located above the huge terrace, a couple of hundred feet above the level of The Gallery. The terrace runs across to the west for nearly 800 yards, before ending well past the Running Man Area.

Approach: Follow the approach to The Gallery Area. Go around the left side of the Wall of Confusion and scramble up slabs for 200 yards to reach a huge terrace. The main Stratocaster area is a short distance to the left along the terrace.

The routes are described from right to left.

Stratocaster Wall – Left side

● Cowboy Cafe 80' 5.12b *
Don Welsh. 1990.

This route sits by itself on the very steep wall above the far right end of the terrace, several hundred yards to the right of the Stratocaster Area proper and a short distance to the right from where the approach first reaches the terrace. It is an impressive line (6 b's).

The central feature of the Stratocaster Wall is a huge cave below a tall, varnished buttress. To the right, beyond a sharply overhanging arete, is a big right-leaning corner system with an overhanging start protected by a bolt, the line of The Bristler. The next route climbs the corner system to the right again.

❶ Telecaster 100' 5.11c
Jay Smith, Paul Crawford. 1988.
Single rack to 3", double 0.5"- 1".

This route climbs the very steep corner crack 15' to the right of The Bristler. Pull over a bulge (crux) to reach the finger crack in the left-arching corner, which is followed leftwards to join The Bristler. Continue up The Bristler to the top.

❷ The Bristler 100' 5.12a
Sal Mamusia, Paul Van Betten. 1987.

The route starts on top of a block below the steep corner. Climb the initial corner (b) to reach the big right-arching corner which is followed, through a tight slot to the top. To descend either scramble over to the right and back down to the terrace or rap from a bush.

❸ Purple Haze 50' 5.12c *
Dan McQuade. February 1995. This had been started as a ground up project by Van Betten and Mamusia.

Start on top of the block at the base of The Bristler. Bouldery moves lead out right across a bulge then back left to join The Bristler above the initial corner. Move out left and climb the overhanging prow to an anchor (8 b's).

❹ Beyond Reason 45' 5.13b **
Dan McQuade. Spring 1992.

This is the sharply overhanging wall of good varnish to the right of the chimney at the start of Stratocaster. Continuous bouldery climbing for 25', then much easier. It's a good idea to stick clip the second bolt (8 b's).

❺ Stratocaster 180' 5.11d ***
Jay Smith, Nick Nordblom. Spring 1988.
Single rack to 2.5".

A classic mixed route up the central wall of the area. Start at the base of the chimney to the right of the huge roof.
1. 80' 5.10b Climb the chimney for 20' then move left and climb the face (3 b's) to an anchor.
2. 100' 5.11d Great climbing up the right edge of the wall above (5 bolts and gear) leads to an anchor.

❻ Stratocaster Direct 30' 5.12b *
Dan McQuade. Spring 1992.

Start 20' to the left of Stratocaster and boulder through a low roof to an anchor (5 b's).

❼ Ancient Aria 90' 5.11b *

Start behind Stratocaster Direct. Reach or Jump for a big hold on the lip then head up and left onto a long headwall. Climb the headwall, past a second crux, to the anchor (12 b's).

❽ Marshall Amp 105' 5.11b **
Bob Conz, Shelby Shelton, Jay Smith, Paul Van Betten. March 1991.

Start below a block underneath the left end of the huge roof. Climb a very steep right-slanting crack to the ledge on top of the block. Pull over the steep bulge on the left and continue up the long wall on big jugs and hueco's to an anchor (10 b's).
❽ₐ Variation: 5.11c After the initial crack, pull over the bulge on the right and climb the upper wall to anchors (7 b's).

❾ The Deluxe 100' 5.11b

This route climbs the wall to the left of Marshall Amp. Start at a sandstone tufa in the shallow arete just left of Marshal Amp. A sandy start leads to fun climbing higher on the route (9 b's).

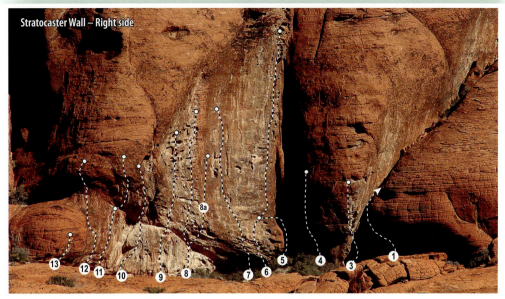

Stratocaster Wall – Right side

When the Shit Hits the Fan 200' 5.11d
This obscure route climbs the long right-arching corner system on the left side of the Stratocaster Buttress in three pitches.

10 Endless Choad 70' 5.12b
Start 20' left of The Deluxe below a corner. Pull into the corner and move right to the first bolt. Continue to a rest then climb the right edge of the upper bulge to a set of anchors (8 b's).

11 Choad Warrior 70' 5.12c *
Dan McQuade. Spring 1992.
Start around to the left of the cave. A vertical wall leads to an anchor below a huge bulge, (5.12a.) Continue out the bulge to an anchor well past the lip (11 b's).

12 Choad Hard 60' 5.12c
Tim Roberts. February 1995.
Start from a pile of rocks a few feet left of Choad Warrior. Climb the very bouldery wall to reach a rest and an anchor. Continue over the upper bulge to another anchor (10 b's).

13 Party Down 25' 5.12b
Dan McQuade. May 1995.
This boulder problem/mini route starts from low holds in a small cave just left of Choad Hard (2 b's).

14 Party Line 180' 5.10d
Nick Nordblom, Jay Smith, Joe Bentley, Jenni Stone. 1988.
Single rack to 2", Rp's.
Scramble 50' up into the base of the gully to the left of Choad Warrior and rope up at a scrub oak bush.
1. 150' 5.10d Climb up the runout, slabby face (b) to a crack. Climb the long, zig-zag crack and belay in a huge scoop.
2. 30' 5.10a Climb out the right side of the scoop to the top.
Descent: Head down to the west then scramble and rappel down the chimney to the left of Break Loose.

15 Flying V 50' 5.11b
Kelly Rich, Mark Swank. December 1993.
Start beside Party Line, 50' up the gully. Climb the face to the left of Party Line, over a bulge to an anchor (7 b's).

The following route climbs the nice, varnished wall on the left side of the big gully.

16 Footloose 60' 5.11b *
Craig Reason. 1991.
Start at the base of the gully. Climb a sharp arete onto the beautiful, varnished wall (7 b's).

17 One Eyed Jacks 40' 5.11a *
Don Borroughs, Alan Busby. 1993.
This route climbs big, rounded huecos in the front of the small pillar to the left of the gully (4 b's).

Around the corner to the left is a huge roof about 40' above the ground.

18 Cut Loose 50' 5.10d *
Jay Smith, Nick Nordblom. Spring 1998.
Single rack to 2".
Start below the right end of the huge roof. Climb the nice corner to the roof, then swing right (2 b's) and go up to an anchor just around the corner.

19 Pablo Diablo 35' 5.12d *
Paul Van Betten, Sal Mamusia. Spring 1993.
Superb technical climbing up the beautiful arete below the middle of the roof (5 b's).

20 Pablo Diablo Direct Extension 60' 5.13a
From the anchor of Pablo Diablo continue out the sandy roof above (4 b's).

Break Loose 50' 5.11a
Jay Smith, Jo Smith. 1988.
This route climbs the ugly, wide crack which breaks though the left side of the huge roof. It finishes with a long unprotected traverse (5.5) rightwards along the lip of the roof to reach the anchor above the Pablo Diablo Extension.

At the left end of the wall is an old project.

The following routes are on a tall, varnished wall between the Stratocaster and Running Man Areas.

❶ Titan Rocket 90' 5.11c
Paul Van Betten, Sal Mamusia, Bob Conz, S. Shelton. October 1991.
Start at the base of the chimney/gully to the right of the tall, varnished wall. Climb the flaky arete to the left of the gully to an anchor (8 b's).

There is a project between Titan Rocket and Tier of the Titans.

❷ Tier of the Titans 110' 5.12b
Paul Van Betten, Sal Mamusia, Bob Conz, S. Shelton. October 1991.
Small and medium wires, small cam, rp's.
Climb the initial crack of Flame Ranger (small wires) then traverse 20' up and right and climb the very impressive seam in the middle of the wall. Runout in places (7 b's).

❸ Flame Ranger 110' 5.12a **
Paul Van Betten, Sal Mamusia, Bob Conz, S. Shelton. October 1991.
Small and medium wires, small cam.
Start below a finger crack 40' to the left of the chimney/gully. Climb the finger crack (small wires) then move right 8' and climb the steep wall to the anchor of Tier of the Titans (7 b's).

❹ Flameblower 95' 5.10d **
One of the better sport routes of its grade in the Calico Hills. Start just left of Flame Ranger and climb straight up the wall to the anchors (13 b's).

❺ Swedish Erotica 120' 5.10a
Paul Van Betten, Katja Tjornman. 1988.
Single rack to 3".
Start 90' to the left of the gully at the point where the varnish ends. Climb an easy face (2 b's) to reach a crack which curves to the right around a bulge (crux). Above the bulge, the crack continues as an easy left-slanting ramp. Follow the ramp to its top then move left to the belay of Spikes and Twine.

❻ Spikes and Twine 280' 5.10c
Nick Nordblom, Jenni Stone. 1988.
Single rack to 3".
Start 10' to the left of the previous route.
1. 120' 5.9 Climb a seam for 25' then move left and climb a long crack to a belay in a horizontal break below a bulge.
2. 160' 5.10c Go over the bulge (b) then move left and climb a right-slanting crack (b) to the top. Rap from spikes & twine.

❼ Supernova 270' 5.10d
Nick Nordblom, Jay Smith. 1988.
Single rack to 2", Rp's.
Start 50' to the left of the previous route at a tiny right-facing corner in low-angled rock. A scary route with long runouts on both pitches.
1. 120' 5.9+ Climb the corner and continue up and right on a red slab to a bolt. Continue up the steepening face (2 b's) to an anchor below a bulge.
2. 150' 5.10d Pull over the bulge above the anchor to reach a seam in the impressive headwall. Climb the seam and the face above (b) to reach an anchor beside some holes.

Below the left side of the buttress containing the tall, varnished wall a huge, round boulder sits on the terrace at the base of the cliff. The next four routes start on top of this boulder.

❽ Nevada Book 240' 5.8
John Taylor, John Williamson. October 1973.
Single rack to 4".
1. 60' 5.5 From the top of the boulder climb up and right along a ramp to a fixed anchor.
2. 180' 5.8 Continue up the huge left-facing corner, past a low crux, to easier slabs.
To descend, continue to the ridge line, which is followed either west or east to reach gullies that lead back towards the road. Either option involves a lot of scrambling.

9 Split Lip 100' 5.10c
Single rack to 1", Rp's.
This route climbs the seam on the right side of the slab above the boulder. Climb the seam (4 b's) and when it finishes move right and climb another seam to the anchor.

The following two routes have a common start up a low-angled seam with two bolts.

10 Split Infinitive 80' 5.9
From the top of the boulder, climb the common start then the face on the right to an anchor (6 b's).

11 Split Ends 90' 5.10a *
From the top of the boulder, climb the common start then the face on the left to an anchor (9 b's).

12 Split Crack 500' 5.7
John Williamson, John Taylor. October 1973.
Single rack to 7".
This old route starts in the wash, a couple of hundred feet to the left of the B&W wall. It climbs a prominent chimney system in the lower wall then crosses the terrace just to the left of the huge, round boulder. The upper part of the route continues up the chimney system just left of the boulder to easier slabs. To descend, continue to the ridge line, which can be followed either west or east to reach gullies that lead back towards the road. Either option involves a lot of scrambling.

Further to the west a tall, smooth slab is reached, this is climbed by the routes Falstaff and Yodrich which, along with all the other routes further west on the terrace comprise the Running Man Area.

Running Man Area

This is the name given to the walls above the west end of the huge terrace that faces the road as you drive west from the Second Pullout. The Running Man Wall itself is the very large, varnished wall above the west end of the terrace. An obvious feature is a large roof 15' above the ground, which undercuts the left side of the wall. These routes all face south and get sun all day.

Approach: This area is most easily reached from the Sandstone Quarry pullout which is on the right 2.7 miles along the loop road. From the pullout, follow a trail, which starts in the southeast corner of the parking area, and heads around towards the east. Follow the trail for 400 yards to a point just past an obvious fin of rock on the left, called The Pier. Follow a trail on the left, down into the main wash. Go east along the wash for a hundred yards, then cross the wash and scramble up slabs and corners to reach the terrace about a hundred yards to the left of the Running Man Wall proper. 25 minutes.

The routes are described from right to left.

To reach the first routes, continue east along the terrace for a couple of hundred yards to a tall, slabby wall of red and pink rock, a short distance to the left of a huge, round boulder that sits against the base of the cliff above the terrace.

1 Yodrich 200' 5.11c
Paul Van Betten, Mike Ward. Fall 1987.
Single rack to 1.75". Rp's.
Start in the middle of the slabby wall, below and to the right of the obvious crack.
1. 100' 5.11c Climb past 2 bolts then make a long runout up and right to where the rock steepens. Climb up and right (2 b's) to reach a short crack. Climb the crack and continue over a bulge (b) to an anchor.
2. 100' 5.8 Continue up the slab (b) to the top.

Descent: Follow the gully that leads down to the west behind the formation with one short rappel.

2 Falstaff 200' 5.10a
Nick Nordblom, Paul Van Betten. 1985.
Single rack to 3".
Start beside Yodrich below some bolts in the middle of the slab. Climb the initial slab of Yodrich (2 b's) then head up left to an obvious curving crack which is followed to the top.
Descent: Follow the gully that leads down to the west behind the formation with one short rappel.

3 Northern Lights 100' 5.11d
Start about 20' to the left of Falstaff at a pile of cheater stones. Stick clip the first bolt 15' up then climb the tall face, staying to the left of the crack of Falstaff to reach an anchor where the angle eases (8 b's).

❹ Fibonacci Wall 180' 5.11d

Paul Van Betten, Don welsh. 1987.

Start in the gully around the left arete of the slabby wall. Climb up the rounded arete to the top of the formation (8 b's).

❺ Commitment to Excrement 90' 5.11c

Xavier Wasiak, Gary Fike. January 26, 2003.

Start left of Fibonacci Wall and follow a tightly-bolted line up the rounded arete, following a thin seam to an anchor (9 b's).

❻ Plastic People 80' 5.10c

Louie Anderson, Bart Groendyke. December 1990.

Start about 40' up the gully. Move out right and climb the right edge of the wall, past some flaky rock, to an anchor (8 b's).

❼ Synthetic Society 90' 5.11a

Mike Ward, Louie Anderson, Bart Groendyke. December 1990.

Climb straight up to the anchor of Plastic People (7 b's).

At the top of the gully between the Running Man wall and the big slab of Falstaff etc. is a large, flat wall with a couple of body sized hueco's near the top.

❽ Red Heat 130' 5.10d ***

Nick Nordblom, Mike Ward, Danny Meyers. Fall 1989.
Single rack to 1.25".

A superb route up the middle of the wall at the top of the gully. Climb a left-leaning corner then zig-zag up the face to an anchor in the left hand of the two hueco's (8 b's). It is possible to lower off with a 70m rope.

❾ Funk Flex 90' 5.11c

Mike Ward, Greg Mayer. 1995.

Climb the wall 30' to the left of Red Heat (9 b's).

The Running Man wall is the home of Running Man and Graveyard Waltz two of the best and longest pitches in the Calico Hills. The wall is easily recognized by a large roof which undercuts its left side. The first two routes start around on the right side, on a small ledge below a chimney.

❿ Vile Pile 50' 5.10b

Mike Ward, Danny Meyers, Jessie Baxter. Fall 1989.
0.25"- 1.75" cams.

Zig-zag up the slab to the right of the chimney (6 b's).

⓫ Galloping Gal 100' 5.11a *

A long pitch on nice, varnished rock. Climb the wall to the left of the chimney, past a reachy crux, to an anchor (10 b's).

⓬ Commando 80' 5.12b **

Louie Anderson, Bart Groendyke. 1992.

Start on top of the block that forms the small corridor at the start of Running Man. Pull over a small roof and climb the sustained wall to an anchor in a scoop (9 b's).

⓭ Graveyard Waltz 110' 5.11d **

Mike Tupper. 1989.

A long, sustained and pumpy pitch with spaced bolts. It climbs the wall to the right of Running Man (9 b's).

⓮ Running Man 110' 5.11c ***

Paul Van Betten, Mike Ward, Sal Mamusia. November 1987.
Rp's, small wires.

This route climbs the long, vertical crack/seam on the right side of the wall. It's a reasonable lead without any gear, but some of the bolts are a little spaced. Start in a small corridor below and to the right of the start of the crack. Move out left then up,

pulling through a smooth varnished section to reach the base of the crack. Follow the crack to the top. Although the hardest moves are low on the route, the pump never lets up (11 b's).

⑮ Predator 130' 5.10d
Nick Nordblom, Paul Van Betten. 1988.
Single rack to 2".
Start at the base of Running Man. Follow a horizontal crack out left and move past a bolt to the base of a long, left-slanting seam. Continue up the seam (3 b's) to an anchor where several cracks intersect.

⑯ New Traditionalists 130' 5.11d
Mike Tupper. 1989.
Start 30' down and left of Running Man. Climb a smooth varnished slab, cross Predator and continue up the long wall to an anchor (11 b's).

⑰ Second Fiddle to a Dead Man 135' 5.11d
Greg Mayer. November 1993.
25' to the left of New Traditionalists is a long, low block on the ground with a pile of cheater stones at its left end. Start at the right end of the block. Climb the wall to the top (10 b's).

⑱ There Goes The Neighborhood 135' 5.11d
Greg Mayer. 1989.
Starting on the cheater stones, climb the wall, crossing Predator and continuing up the upper wall to an anchor (1.5 friend needed at the top).

Calico Terror 110' 5.11b
Mike Ward, Paul Van Betten. December 1987.
Start at the left end of the roof. Climb a nice, varnished wall (3 b's) to reach a right-slanting seam, follow the scary seam past a fixed sling to a vertical crack which leads to an anchor.

True Lies 60' 5.10a
Single rack to 2.5".
Start 20' up the gully to the left of Calico Terror. Climb a right-facing corner for 20' then move left and climb leftwards across the face (2 b's) to an anchor.

The next major feature to the west is a huge block above the terrace, with a tall, varnished wall facing the road. This is slightly to the right of where the approach trail first reaches the terrace.

⬤ Frictiony Face, Panty Waist 80' 5.8+ **
Danny Meyers, Brad Stewart. February 1989.
This route climbs the lovely red slab to the right of the huge block. Start on a nice ledge at the base of the slab. Climb the slab to an anchor (7 b's).

Boschton Marathon 90' 5.12c
Goeff Wiegand. 1987.
This route starts in the corridor in front of the huge block. A hard boulder problem low down leads to easier climbing up the front face of the block. Runout and fragile (6 b's).

Brain Damage 100' 5.11b
Robert Findlay, Mike Ward, Paul Van Betten. 1987.
Double rack to 3", double ropes.
This route climbs beside an obvious clean-cut corner on the right side of the gully that goes up from the west end of the terrace. It is a couple of hundred feet above the level of the terrace and faces across the gully towards Americrag. Start to the right of the corner on a ramp. Climb a paper-thin, right-arching flake to reach a small ramp. Move left along the ramp then step down to the base of the upper corner. Climb the corner to the top.

The Trophy
Avian Wall
The Bull Market
Satellite Wall
Blister in the Sun
Hall of Fame
The Beach

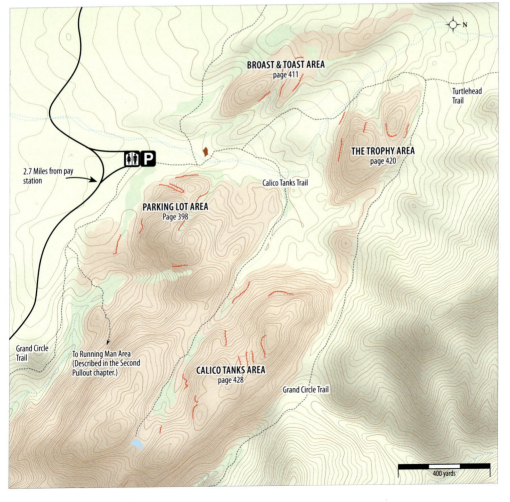

N

BROAST & TOAST AREA
page 411

Turtlehead Trail

THE TROPHY AREA
page 420

2.7 Miles from pay station

Calico Tanks Trail

PARKING LOT AREA
Page 398

Grand Circle Trail

To Running Man Area
(Described in the Second Pullout chapter.)

CALICO TANKS AREA
page 428

Grand Circle Trail

400 yards

Calico Tank

Mass Production Wall

Wake Up Wall

Sandy Corridor

Mans' Best Friend

Front Corridor

Broast and Toast Wall

Parking Lot

Introduction

The "Quarry" part of the name refers to a couple of quarried blocks a hundred yards to the north of the parking area, the remains of an old mining operation. This area has a nice selection of crags in really pleasant surroundings. Generally, these cliffs are much less crowded than those of the Second Pullout, and offer a lot of variety to boot. This section includes all the crags that are most easily accessed from this parking area, except for the Running Man area which is included with the Second Pullout.

Access

To reach the Sandstone Quarry, drive 2.7 miles along the loop road and take a right on a short road which leads to a large parking area.

Man's Best Friend, pitch 2. Page 399.

PARKING LOT AREA

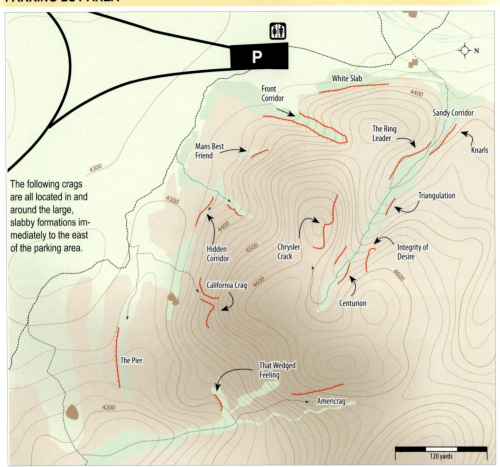

The following crags are all located in and around the large, slabby formations immediately to the east of the parking area.

White Slab

Front Corridor

Mans Best Friend

The Ring Leader

Sandy Corridor

Knarls

Triangulation

Hidden Corridor

Chrysler Crack

Integrity of Desire

California Crag

Centurion

The Pier

That Wedged Feeling

Americrag

4300
4400
4300
4400
4500
4600
4600
4200
4400

120 yards

N

There are a couple of climbs on the white slab just to the east of the parking area. The seams on either side of the White Slab route are around 5.8 and are fairly serious leads, but can be toproped from several anchors at the top of the White Slab.

❶ White Slab 90' 5.8 *
Single rack to 1.5", Rp's.
Start in the middle of the slabby face, 40' to the right of Fender Bender. Climb thin seams (4 b's) to an anchor.

❷ Fender Bender 100' 5.6 *
Matt McMackin, Jim Whitesell. May 1973.
Single rack to 4".
This route climbs the obvious right-curving flake to an anchor at its top.

❸ Pee Wee's Big Adventure 190' 5.10c R
Nick Nordblom, Danny Meyers. 1988.
Start just left of Fender Bender.
1. 70' 5.8 Follow a left-leaning seam, which turns almost horizontal. Set up an anchor in a patch of dark rock.
2. 120' 5.10c R From the belay climb up and right to a bolt. Go up to a second bolt and make a long runout up the slab above. The slab eventually gets easier and leads to the top of the formation.

Mans Best Friend

The following routes climb a face with white rock in the lower half and red rock in the upper half. It is located about 150 yards to the east of the parking area. The lower half of the face is hidden by the fin of rock which forms the east wall of the Front Corridor.

Approach: From the south end of the parking area, head straight east, climbing up the easy slabs to the top of a broad fin of rock. The wall is on the far side of the corridor beyond the fin. Either a short rappel from a well-camouflaged anchor, or a short third class descent down a trough, leads to the base of the corridor and the start of Man's Best Friend.

❶ Man's Best Friend 180' 5.7 **
Mark Limage, Ninfa Chauchois. 2005.
This is an enjoyable and well-bolted route which makes for an excellent introduction to multi-pitch climbing.
1. 90' 5.7 Start up a rounded rib, then move left and climb the face to an anchor on a varnished ledge where the rock changes color (8 b's).
2. 90' 5.7 Continue up the fragile but well-bolted face to an anchor (10 b's).
Descent: Two single rope rappels.

The next two routes start on top of a fin about 60' up the gully from the start of Man's Best Friend. There is a low first bolt which can be used for the anchor.

❷ Sea Anemone 90' 5.8
From the bolt, climb up and right, pulling over a small bulge and climbing the crest of a broad pillar to the anchor (8 b's).

❸ Crusty Creatures 140' 5.7
From the bolt, climb straight up over a small bulge (4 b's) to the base of a big right-facing flake. Climb the flake then traverse right into a left-facing corner. Climb the corner and continue to an anchor.

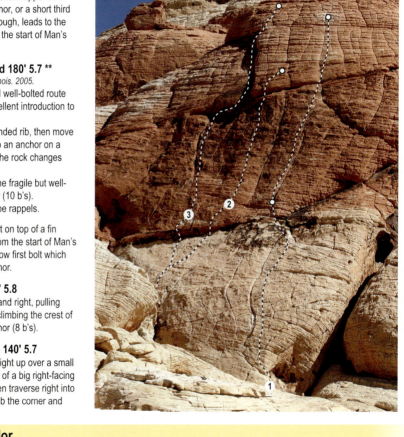

The Front Corridor

This is the impressive slot canyon just to the east of the parking area. Some of the rock is a little sandy, and can be slow to dry out, but the big sport routes in the back of the corridor are two of the most popular hard climbs in Red Rocks. The corridor is generally shady except when the sun is directly overhead. When either of the walls are getting sun the entire canyon quickly gets hot. The routes on the west wall are described first, going from left to right. The first route is about 150 feet into the corridor, above a flat, sandy clearing.

❶ Pockets of Dirt 50' 5.11b
A steep start pulls through the left side of a shallow scoop. Continue up the pocketed white wall to the chains (6 b's).

❷ Helltown 40' 5.11d
R Harrison, M. Locatelli. 2009.
Start at the right side of the shallow scoop of Pockets of Dirt. A steep start leads to a crux at half-height. Continue over a short bulge to the anchors (5 b's).

❸ Megatronic 40' 5.12c
M. Locatelli, R Harrison. 2009.
Start 10' right of Helltown. Crimpy and sustained (6 b's).

❹ Churning in the Dirt 45' 5.12b
Mike Tupper, Craig Reason. November 1988.
The leftmost bolted route on the steep wall at the back of the corridor, about 15' right of Megatronic (6 b's).

THE FRONT CORRIDOR

To Mans Best Friend

⑤ The Sound of Power 45' 5.12c **
Craig Reason, Mike Tupper. November 1988.
The beautiful flake system to the right of Churning (6 b's).

⑥ Sunsplash 70' 5.13b **
Dan McQuade. April 1995.
Start 20' to the right of Sound of Power. A fingery wall leads to an obvious undercling at 35', then a powerful yet delicate crux gains a tiny corner which leads to the anchor (9 b's).

⑦ Monster Skank 70' 5.13b ***
Dan McQuade. January 1993.
This route gets my vote for the best sport climb in Red Rocks. Powerful and sustained with very varied movement, a real rarity in the Calico Hills. Start with some easy huecos 20' to the right of Sunsplash (9 b's).

The routes on the east wall are described from left to right.

⑧ Fury 70' 5.11b
M. Locatelli, R Harrison. 2009.
Start 10' right of the chimney at the back of the corridor. Sandy and technical climbing with a sneaky chimney rest just below the anchor (7 b's).

⑨ Gun Control 100' 5.11b
Bob Conz, Shelby Shelton, Nick Nordblom. Summer 1988.
Start 10' to the right of Fury. Climb up the face into the large, black scoop. Exit out the left side of the scoop (crux) to an anchor (8 b's).

⑩ To Bolt or Toupee 70' 5.10c *
Mike Ward, Paul Van Betten. Spring 1988.
Start 8' right of Gun Control, below a corner leading to the right side of the big scoop. Climb the face to reach the corner. Tricky, thin climbing leads up the corner and past a small roof at its top to an anchor in the big scoop (7 b's).
Extension: 105' 5.11c Climb out through the right side of the big scoop above the anchor (11 b's).

● The Brawl 100' 5.11a
Dan McQuade. November 2016.
Climb straight up the face starting 20' to the right of To Bolt or Toupee, following thin seams to an anchor (11 b's).

⑪ Hair Today, Gone Tomorrow 110' 5.11a
Nick Nordblom, Paul Van Betten. Spring 1988.
This route starts about 20' to the right of The Brawl, opposite Sunsplash on a flat, red boulder. Climb up the wall to reach a long seam which trends slightly to the left (12 b's).

⑫ Shouting Match 70' 5.11b
M. Locatelli, R Harrison. 2009.
Start just right of the previous route beside a tiny, right-leaning ramp. Climb beside the ramp to the first bolt and continue up the face to the anchor (6 b's).

⑬ High Noon 110' 5.11b
Nick Nordblom, Jenni Stone. Spring 1988.
Begin 30' to the right of the previous route, below a varnished corner. Climb the corner and continue up the white seams above to an anchor (12 b's).

● Broken Tooth 80' 5.10a *
Start 40' to the right of High Noon. Climb the dark, slabby wall, crossing through the diagonal break of A Thousand New Routes to reach an anchor above (8 b's).

⑭ A Thousand New Routes 130' 5.11b
Paul Van Betten, Nick Nordblom. Summer 1986.
Single rack to 2", double 0.4"- 1", Rp's.
Start 40' to the right of the previous route, below an obvious left-leaning crack. Climb a short corner up to the crack. Follow the crack way out left (2 b's) then head up to an anchor.

⑮ Crumbling Community 100' 5.10c
Paul Van Betten, Danny Meyers. 1989.
Single rack to 2.5".
This route starts in a bushy area well to the right of the previous route. There is an empty bolt hole 10' above the ground, beside a thin seam. Climb the seam (crux- no pro) for 30' to reach a deeper crack which leads left then back right to the top. Descend to the right.

The next three routes share an anchor. They all climb the tall, slabby face to the left of a huge scoop 60 feet above the ground, at the entrance to the corridor.

⑯ Affliction for Friction 80' 5. 11a
Mike Ward, Danny Meyers. Fall 1989.
Start about 15' down the hill from Crumbling Community, in the middle of a thicket of trees. Climb up (2 b's), then make sporty moves left, then up (crux) to a bolt beside a thin seam. Continue up seams (2 b's) to an anchor on the right at the top.

⑰ Friction Addiction 90' 5.10c
Bob Conz, Shelby Shelton. Spring 1988.
Start to the right of the little thicket of trees. Weave up the wall, following thin seams to the communal anchor (6 b's).

⑱ Prescription Gription 95' 5.10c
Nick Nordblom, Jenni Stone. Spring 1988.
Start 15' to the right. Climb up and slightly to the left, following a thin corner and the seams above to the anchor (5 b's).

⑲ Siktion 60' 5.9
Nick Nordblom, Randy Marsh. Fall 1988.
Single rack to 0.75", Rp's.
This route starts below the left edge of the scoop at the entrance to the corridor. Enjoyable climbing, but the protection for the final moves into the scoop does not inspire confidence. Climb past a flake and follow a thin seam (3 b's) to the scoop. Belay on 2.5"- 3" cams. Descend to the right.

Glenda Huxter on the crux of Sunsplash. Page 400.

Sandy Corridor

The name could refer to the sandy floor of this pretty canyon, but also to the quality of most of the rock. Unfortunately, many of the anchors on top of these routes are easily accessible, and as a result hangers are often missing. The same goes for the protection bolts on some of the routes, since the area is also popular with rappelers. Hopefully, the recent installation of glue-in bolts will eliminate this problem.

Approach: The canyon entrance is about 100 yards north of the quarried blocks. From the parking area walk down the main trail to the quarry. Leave the main trail and head straight north through the bushes for about 100 yards until the corridor appears on the right. 5 minutes.

The routes on the northeast facing wall on the right side of the canyon are described first. As you walk into the canyon, the first obvious feature on the right is a long, low, black and red wall, the traverse of this wall is an excellent boulder problem (V5).

❶ The Wallow 40' 5.7
The big, left-facing offwidth corner.

The anchors on the ledge where The Wallow finishes can be used to toprope the face below (ie. to the right of The Wallow). These routes range between 5.9 and 11a. The following routes climb the slabby, red wall to the left of The Wallow.

❷ The Ring Leader 90' 5.8
Larry Moore. Late 1980's.
Single rack to 3".
Start at the base of The Wallow. Climb the face to a bolt in a band of varnish at 15'. Go up and right (2 b's) into a long crack which is followed, past a bulge, to the top.

❸ Bolt Route 100' 5.10a
Single rack to 2".
Start 20' left of The Wallow. Climb thin seams up the slabby face, passing a bolt at 30'. Continue, to reach a deeper crack 50' up. Follow the crack to the top. The top of this route can be recognized by some big metal spikes driven into the crack, where it goes over the edge of the cliff.

❹ John's Wall 100' 5.10b
Paul Van Betten. 1986.
Start 35' left of The Wallow. Boulder up a slabby face to reach a band of varnish. Continue, past a bolt into a long seam. Climb the seam, moving right at the top to finish on Bolt Route.

❺ Belay Delay 110' 5.10a
Paul Van Betten, Robert Tyler. 1988.
Start as for John's Wall. Boulder up and left to a bolt at 25'. Continue to a crack which is followed to a small ledge below a headwall. Climb past a bolt to reach a steep crack which is followed to the top.

Curtis LaBouf on
Fresh Air. Page 404.

❻ Seams to Me 110' 5.10b
Paul Crawford, Paul Van Betten. 1986.
Start 10' left of the previous route, behind a small tree. Climb past some underclings to reach a seam. Follow the seam to a small ledge then move right and finish up the previous route.

About 100 yards into the corridor, it starts to narrow. The next routes start from a large platform, 20' up on the right wall of the narrow part of the corridor. A bush at the low-point of the platform is a useful landmark.

❼ Inn Zone 80' 5.10a
Nick Nordblom, Paul Van Betten. 1986.
This route starts 20' up the ramp on the right side of the wall. Climb a thin crack and when it ends continue up the face (2 b's) to the top.

❽ Chicken Boy 100' 5.11a
Paul Van Betten, Paul Crawford. 1986.
Start 10' right of the bush. Climb past two bolts and follow a seam to its end. Continue through the steep scoops above to the top.

❾ Forbidden Zone 100' 5.11d
Paul Van Betten, Nick Nordblom. 1986.
Start just left of the bush. Climb the steep face (2 b's) to reach a crack. Follow the crack to the top.

❿ Bark at the Moon 100' 5.11b
Paul Crawford, Paul Van Betten, Mike Tupper. 1986.
Start 25' left of the bush. Pull through a varnished roof and climb (2 b's) into a shallow scoop. Climb the scoop (b) then move left at its top (b) to reach a corner/crack which leads to the top.

There are a couple of stray-looking bolts in the seams to the left of the previous route, it is unclear if these are finished routes or not.

The left side of this buttress is lower-angled and contains some fun toprope routes in the 5.7 to 5.9 range. There are four or five anchors just below the top of the wall, which can be reached by a short rappel from a couple of bolts on the top. Once again, bring your own hangers.

At the top of the corridor, on the right, is a very steep wall 150' above the floor of the canyon. This is the formation that houses the classic Chrysler Crack.

The next routes are on a steep wall directly below the Chrysler Crack formation. To reach these routes, continue up the canyon for 100 yards after scrambling out of the narrow section, then follow an easy ramp on the right side of the canyon to the base of the wall.

⓬ You Only Live Twice 50' 5.10c
Brad Stewart, Danny Meyers. 1988.
This is the route on the right. Move right past a low bolt into a seam which is followed to a steep scoop. Escape left out of the scoop and climb the wall to the top (8 b's).

⓭ Octopussy 50' 5.10c
Larry Moore.
Start 5' left. Climb straight up the wall (6 b's).

The following routes are on the Chrysler Crack formation. To reach Chrysler Crack, scramble to the top of the canyon, then go up a narrow gully on the right for 50'. Break out right onto a ledge and boulder up a short wall above a bush, onto a higher ledge. Go up the short wall above this ledge, then follow a big slabby ledge down and right to the huge, overhanging block. From the top of the formation down climb off to the left.

⑭ Chrysler Crack 100' 5.9 ***
Randal Grandstaff, Jon Martinet. 1970s.
Cams to 0.6" Rp's, 7+" cams or Big Bro's.
The offwidth that splits the north face of the formation.

⑮ Le Vent Nous Portera 90' 13b/c **
Tom Moulin. January 2014.
The beautiful and ultra-thin wall to the right of Chrysler Crack. The route starts up a thin flake then heads straight up the vertical wall past a couple of very thin crux's to a rest then a steep, bouldery finish on better holds (9 b's).

The next two routes have a common start on top of a big boulder below the undercut arete to the right of Chrysler Crack.

⑯ Fresh Air 80' 5.12b **
Tom Moulin. January 2014.
An excellent route with a powerful start. From the boulder, pull onto the rock, moving right then back left to a rest on the arete. Continue up the scalloped arete past further rests and tricky sections to an anchor (8 b's).

⑰ The Deep West 90' 5.12d *
Geoff Weigand. 1987.
From the boulder, pull onto the rock, then make hard moves up and right to better holds. Slap up the difficult arete above, making a final hard move to a good hold. Finish more easily to the anchors (9 b's).

Further to the right is an unfinished project.

The following routes are on the left wall of the corridor. They are described from left to right. The first two routes are on the long, white wall behind the bushes on the left, as you enter the corridor. The most obvious features of the wall are two long, right-arching cracks.

⑱ Mile High 40' 5.11b
Start 12' left of the start of the leftmost of the two arching cracks. Climb to a bolt at 15' and continue up the face above to a horizontal and some gear (1.75" cam). Continue to the top.

⑲ Knarls 45' 5.12a (Tr.)
Paul Van Betten, Sal Mamusia. 1981.
Climb the first 10' of the leftmost of the two arching cracks, then move left and climb the thin seam to the top. Thin and sustained.

The next routes are on a red slab which is on the left side of the canyon, just above the top of the long, narrow corridor at the top of the lower canyon.

⑳ Triangulation 50' 5.10a

Start towards the left side of the slab. Climb up and right following a line of bolts (4 b's).

㉑ Piledriver 50' 5.10a

Start below the right end of a small overlap/arch. Climb up to a bolt above the overlap then make a long runout with certain groundfall to reach a second bolt. Continue to the top.

㉒ Grounder 50' 5.9+

Follow Piledriver to the first bolt then move right and climb past two more bolts to the top.

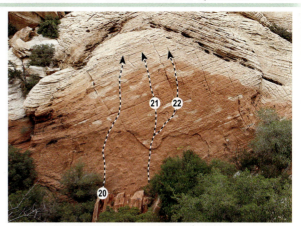

The next routes are on the Requiem Wall which is the rightmost of two steep blocks which sit on the ridge on the left side of the corridor, about 80 yards above the narrowing. From the corridor an easy scramble leads to the terrace below the huge, overhanging block.

㉓ Integrity of Desire 45' 5.12b *

Mike Tupper. Spring 1991.
Enjoyable stemming up the steep, open corner on the left side of the block (6 b's).

㉔ Flying Cowboys 45' 5.12d

Don Welsh. Spring 1991.
The central route (6 b's).

㉕ Plastic Pistol 45' 5.12b

Don Welsh. Spring 1991.
The route on the right (6 b's).

The next routes are below and to the right of the Requiem Wall, on a steep wall that forms the left side of the upper part of the canyon. This is about 120 yards above the top of the narrow corridor, on the left.

㉖ Sals Crack 70' 5.10a

Sal Mamusia. 1989.
This route climbs the crack system on the left side of the face. Two bolts at the start and one at the finish. The hangers are missing from the anchor.

㉗ Centurion 70' 5.10b

P. Van Betten, Kevin Biernacki, Sal Mamusia. Sept 1989.
The next crack, 10' to the right (2 b's).

㉘ Forced Feltch 70' 5.10d

Sal Mamusia, Paul Van Betten. October 1989.
Start 20' to the right of the previous route. Traverse up and left on an easy flake/ramp to reach the next crack system. Follow the crack, past a bolt just below the top.

㉙ Shibu Discipline 70' 5.11b

Paul Van Betten, Sal Mamusia. October 1989.
Start to the right of the previous route. Climb a steep, thin seam in brown rock to reach a long, curving crack (2 b's).

California Crags

These sunny, south facing walls are a couple of hundred yards around to the east of the parking area. They lie to the left (west) of an obvious and enormous roofed block which sits 150' above the wash. The routes here see very little action and so the rock tends to be a little flaky and sandy in places.

Approach: From the southeast corner of the parking area, follow the trail which leads around to the south side of the Calico Hills. After 350 yards a trail branches off to the left, heading towards an obvious fin of rock with a steep north face. Follow this trail down towards the wash, then cut left across the wash and scramble up slabs to a small recess below and to the left of a huge block with large roofs. 10 minutes.

The routes are described from left to right.

The first routes are about 50 yards around to the left of the recess, where there is a long, twisting arete to the left of a deep gully.

❶ Cal West 80' 5.10c
Albert Newman, Leo Henson. March 1998.
Climb the face just left of the arete (8 b's).

❷ Hurricane 80' 5.11b
Leo Henson, Albert Newman. March 1998.
Climb right of the arete to the anchor of Cal West (8 b's).

The next route starts on the left side of the recess.

❸ Quicksand 40' 5.11d
Louie Anderson. 1993.
Start 15' to the left of a smooth corner. Climb up a steep crack and over a sandy roof to the anchor (5 b's).

❹ Far Cry from Josh 35' 5.10b
Louie Anderson. 1993.
This route climbs the wall on the right side of the recess. Start on top of a block. Climb up and left to an anchor (4 b's).

❺ Just in from L.A. 35' 5.11a
Louie Anderson. 1993.
Start from the block at the base of the previous route. Climb a crack then continue up the face to an anchor (4 b's)

The next three routes climb seams in the nice, varnished wall above Quicksand. The ledge below the wall is accessed by scrambling up easy rock to the left of Quicksand.

❻ Nevadatude 40' 5.12b
Leo Henson. January 1998.
This is the leftmost route on the wall (5 b's).

❼ Serious Leisure 40' 5.12a *
Louie Anderson. 1993.
Start in the middle of the wall, below a left-leaning seam. The route starts steep and bouldery then eases towards the top (6 b's).

❽ Orange County 40' 5.11b
Leo Henson. January 1998.
The next route to the right of Serious Leisure (6 b's).

❾ The Staircase 80' 5.5
Start about 100' around to the right of the recess, just to the right of a gray cave. Climb the red slab to the right of the cave then angle up and left to the top.

The next two routes climb the huge overhanging block up and right of the recess.

❿ People Mover 40' 5.8
Single rack to 4"
This route climbs the obvious right-leaning corner to an anchor.

⓫ The Escalator 40' 5.10b
Single rack to 2", tricams useful.
Climb the right edge of the black, slabby face to the right of the previous route (2 b's).

Hidden Corridor

The following routes are all in the vicinity of a very narrow corridor just east of the parking area.

Approach: From the southeast corner of the parking area, follow the trail which leads around to the south side of the Calico Hills. After about 130 yards, scramble down a bush filled break on the left which leads to the west end of a very narrow corridor. For Little Red and The Storm, don't enter the corridor, instead scramble up the other side for 30 yards to an obvious steep, right-facing corner, the line of Little Red. The first route described in the corridor proper, Hidden Edge, goes up the arete just to skier's right of the descent gully.

Matt Kuehl on Walking on a Dream. Page 407.

Gonzo 50' 5.11d
Ryan Leigh. April 9, 2007. After Rehearsal.
Rp's & small cams to 1". 2"-4" for the anchor. Pads.
This route climbs a steep face 35' to the left of Little Red, starting just right of a boulder choke. The hard climbing is on flaky rock and all comes before the first protection, making this a very serious lead. Climb up and right to a thin, flaky seam which leads over the steep lower wall onto slabbier rock. Climb up and slightly left to the top.

Little Red 30' 5.10c
Single rack to 1.75".
Climb the pretty, right-facing corner to an anchor.

● Walking on a Dream 45' 5.11d *
Joshua Gale & Friends. February 2011.
The attractive white slab to the right of Little Red. Start 15' right of Little Red below a steep seam. Climb the seam to a rest at the base of the slab. Follow the curving micro-footledges out right until it is possible to move up to the top (7 b's). There is a somewhat useless anchor, but a slightly flimsy scrub oak about 50' back from the top can be used to clean the draws.

The Blob 40' 5.10c
Above and slightly to the left of the top of Little Red is a steep sandstone blob split by a right-facing ramp/corner. Climb the ramp (b) to a bolted anchor at its top.

The Storm 90' 5.10b
Paul Van Betten, Mike Ward.
This route climbs the right-slanting seam on the opposite side of the gully from Little Red.

The following routes are on the south wall of the Hidden Corridor proper. The rock is quite soft and sandy.

● Hidden Edge 40' 5.10b
This route climbs the arete on the right side of the wall, ie. the west edge of the south wall of the corridor. This is the route that you pass on the descent into the corridor (5 b's).

● Don't Spook the Bats 50' 5.11a
Mike Moore. December 2013.
Start about 70' left of Hidden Edge just left of two big huecos at head height. After a boulder problem crux at the bottom, easier climbing leads to the anchor (5 b's).

🔴 Q-Tip 45' 5.10b

Mike Moore. December 2013.

Start 20' left of the previous route, just past a tree. After a steep start, follow a series of big heucos to the anchor (5 b's).

🔴 Phife 40' 5.10d

Mike Moore. December 2013.

Start 10' left of the previous route where the corridor becomes very narrow. Start by stemming up to pockets then follow some shallow scoops to the anchor (6 b's).

To the left of the previous routes, the corridor becomes very narrow. The next routes are 50' further left, just as the corridor begins to open up again.

🔴 Dirty Secret 45' 5.10d

Climb straight up to a rest in a big hole. Exit right and climb the wall to the anchors (6 b's).

🔴 Sandy Secrets 45' 5.11a

Start 10' left of Dirty Secret behind a tree. Climb straight up the wall, past a shallow hole to the left of the bigger hole of Dirty Secret (6 b's).

The Pier

This wall is always in the shade and is a good choice for warmer weather. It has a dense concentration of routes, although not all are of the best quality. Nevertheless, the more popular routes are gradually cleaning up to leave some really enjoyable, steep climbing. The rock here is generally quite soft and porous, as a result these climbs become very fragile after rain. Because of the shady, low-lying location it is much slower to dry out than some of the other crags and is best avoided if there has been any recent rain. All the routes were climbed by Leo and Karin Henson in the spring of 1996.

Approach: From the southeast corner of the parking area, follow the trail which leads around to the south side of the Calico Hills. After 350 yards a trail branches off to the left, heading down towards an obvious fin of rock with a steep north face, this is The Pier. 10 Minutes.

The routes are described from right to left.

1 Scantily Clad Bimbo 30' 5.11b

The rightmost bolted route on the wall (4 b's).

2 Seventh Hour 30' 5.11a

Start 15' to the left of the previous route, just right of an oak bush. Climb a short arete and continue up seams to the anchor (5 b's).

3 This is the City 30' 5.12a

After a bouldery start, climb the seam above the bush (4 b's).

4 Desert Oasis 30' 5.12c

Start just left of the previous route and boulder up through varnished rock to reach a thin seam (4 b's).

5 How Do You Like them Pineapples 30' 5.13a/b
This route starts behind a bush and climbs up through two shallow scoops. After losing several holds, this route has become much harder and also more sustained.

6 False Alarm 30' 5.12c
Start in front of a small yucca 5' left of the previous route. Climb huecos into a thin crack then move right to a bouldery bulge (5 b's).

7 Geometric Progression 30' 5.12c *
Start just left of the previous route at a short right-facing corner. Climb the arete and huecos to a crux bulge (5 b's).

8 Drug Smelling Pot Bellied Pig 35' 5.12d
When it was first done, this route climbed a fairly direct line up the next seam to the left of Geometric Progression. It has lost so many key holds that its basically a non-route now, although it is still possible to meander up the wall in the general vicinity of the seam.

9 Thirsty Quail 40' 5.12b
Start 15' to the left of Geometric Progression. Climb a small roof into a varnished seam then a deeper crack (5 b's).

10 Cling Free 40' 5.12a *
Start just left of Thirsty Quail. This route climbs the front of a pillar, past an obvious undercling at the top.

11 Under the Boardwalk 45' 5.11a *
Start 10' to the left of the previous route and just to the right of some bushes. Enjoyable climbing on big huecos leads up a big scoop to a crux at the last bolt.

The next two routes start just to the right of a seam behind some bushes, about 10' to the left of the previous route.

12 Pier Pressure 50' 5.12c *
Climb past the first three bolts and continue up the seam until a move left leads to a decent shake. Continue up and right across a bulge to a hard crux just below the anchors (8 b's).

13 Almost but Not Quite 50' 5.12c **
Climb the first three bolts of Pier Pressure, then move around left to a rest in a big scoop. Continue straight up to a hard finish (9 b's).

14 Poco Owes Me a Concert 55' 5.12b/c
Start 20' to the left of the previous route, and just to the right of a block. A boulder problem at the start leads to easier climbing in the middle of the route then a pumpy finish (8 b's).

15 Destiny 45' 5.12c/d
Start on top of the block just left of the previous route. Climb up and slightly right to crux moves on a very steep varnished headwall just below the anchor (6 b's).

16 Basement 45' 5.11c **
From the top of the boulder, climb up left then continue up the wall just to the right of the left edge of the face (6 b's).

17 Long Walk on a Short Pier 65' 5.9
This route climbs the east-facing slab around to the left of the previous routes (8 b's).

Americrag

This impressive but seldom visited wall faces northeast across the steep gully to the west of the Running Man area.

Approach: From the pullout, follow a trail which starts in the southeast corner of the parking area and heads around towards the east. Follow the trail for four hundred yards to a point just past an obvious fin of rock on the left, The Pier. Follow a trail on the left down into the main wash. Turn left (north) and continue up the bushy wash to where it splits. Scramble up the ridge between the two gullies to the base of the wall. The first three routes are passed on the approach. 20 Minutes.

Stuck on You 50' 5.8

This route climbs the red slab on the right side of the gully on the right, a short distance after the point where the approach gully splits.

⬤ Glue Gun 50' 5.7

Chris Burton, Gary Sanders.
The slab just left of Stuck on You (3 b's).

That Wedged Feeling 120' 5.10d

Jay Smith, Leo Erickson. 1990.
Double rack to 4".
This is a stout trad route up an impressive crack. It is on a steep, red wall which faces up the hill towards Americrag proper. It is easily reached by heading over to the left, after scrambling a short way up the rock ridge on the approach to Americrag. The route starts up a hand and fist crack then goes through a bomb-bay section before finishing over a bulge.

The following routes are all on Americrag proper, they are described from left to right.

❶ Toxic Playboy 160' 5.12c/d

Paul Van Betten, Richard Harrison, Bob Conz, Sal Mamusia. April 1990.
An impressive route up the tallest part of the wall. Start below a left-leaning seam, about 50' up the gully from a pine tree.
1. 80' 5.12a Climb the seam (6 b's) to an anchor.
2. 80' 5.12c/d Continue up the wall to an anchor (6 b's).

❷ Mr. Moto 80' 5.11c

Paul Van Betten, Richard Harrison, Shelby Shelton. April 1990.
Start 15' up the gully from Toxic Playboy. Climb a curving crack to a roof at 15'. Move left (b) and pull the roof into a left-leaning seam which is followed (5 b's) to the anchor of Toxic Playboy.

❸ Jimmy Nap 60' 5.11c

Paul Van Betten, Richard Harrison, Shelby Shelton. April 1990.
Start just to the right of the previous route. Climb the face (5 b's) to an anchor.

❹ Americragger 60' 5.12a

Paul Van Betten, Richard Harrison. April 1990.
Start 20' up the gully from the previous route, directly behind a small, twisted pine tree. Climb past 6 b's to an anchor.

❺ Rebel Yell 80' 5.12a

Paul Van Betten, Danny Meyers, Jenni Stone. September 1990.
Start 40' up the gully from the previous route and 25' above a fin of rock in the gully. Climb up and left to an anchor (10 b's).

BROAST & TOAST AREA

These are the low formations about half a mile west and a little north from the parking area. Sonic Youth and Wake up Wall are quite popular, and occasionally can be crowded, the other cliffs see very little traffic. These formations seem to be a bit more exposed to the prevailing winds than the rest of the Calico Hills, which can make for much colder than expected conditions during the winter. However, if Wake Up or Sonic Youth is too cold, Numbers Crag is a warmer alternative.

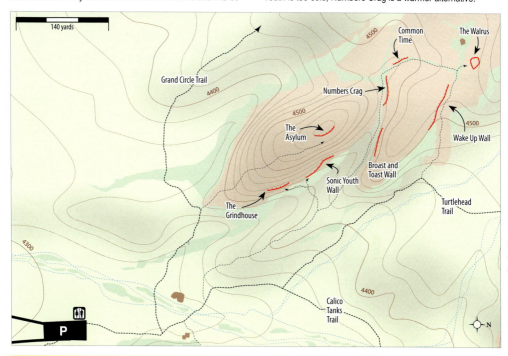

The Asylum

The Asylum can be seen from the parking area as a small block on top of the formation about half a mile northwest of the parking area. It's not as tiny as it first appears since the routes start in a corridor that cuts across the base of the wall. It is a short but very steep north-facing wall with sandy rock.

Approach: From the parking area go down he main trail to the north for 100 yards. Then turn left and follow the Grand Circle trail for a couple of hundred yards, cut right and scramble up the slabby rock on the southeast side of the formation.

● **Flip the Switch 30' 5.10d**
Chris Burton, Jeremy Taylor, Jeremy Smith. September 1997.
The rightmost route on the wall (5 b's).

● **Comforts of Madness 30' 5.11c**
Daniel Hudgins, Jeremy Smith. September 1997.
The middle route (5 b's).

● **Lounge Tomato 30' 5.12b**
Chris Burton, Jeremy Taylor, Jeremy Smith. May 1998.
The leftmost route.

The Grindhouse

Of the Toast and Broast area cliffs, this is the closest to the parking lot. The routes are in a steep alcove at the right end of a slabby ramp that cuts up the formation to the east of Sonic Youth Wall. It gets sun until early afternoon. The routes are short, fragile and bouldery.

Approach: From the north side of the parking area, follow the main trail for 200 yards to a huge, white boulder. Get onto the dirt ridge behind the boulder and follow it up the hill until it starts to level out. Continue a short distance further then drop down into the wash on the left, aiming for the left end of a ledge which slopes up to the right under the cliff. Scramble up a pocketed trough onto the ledge, and go up the ledge to the first routes. 10 minutes.
The routes are described from left to right.

❶ **Machete 50' 5.10a**
Mike Moore. 2008.
The leftmost route on the cliff. Start just left of a small corner/alcove. Pull over the initial bulge to a right-leaning crack. Follow the crack out right, then move up to a rounded crack which leads to the anchor (6 b's). Dirty at the start.

2 Hell Up In Harlem 60' 5.11a
Mike Moore. 2008.
Start 40' to the right of Machete. After a difficult start, follow sloping holds and edges up the wall to a rest on a ramp. Finish with a pull over a roof to reach to the chains (8 b's).

3 Cell Block Sisters 60' 5.11a
Mike Moore. 2008.
Start 10' right of Hell up in Harlem. A bouldery start over the initial bulge leads to easier terrain with larger holds. Pull a small roof to reach the chains (7 b's).

4 Planet Terror 55' 5.11b
Mike Moore. 2008.
Start 12' to the right of Cell Block Sisters. Climb straight up the wall, past the right end of a ramp, to reach the anchors (6 b's).

5 Death Proof 55' 5.11c
Mike Moore. 2008.
Start just right of Planet Terror just left of a small alcove/cave at the right end of the wall. The initial 25' is bouldery and sustained, then easier slab climbing leads to the anchor (7 b's).

6 Four of the Apocalypse 35' 5.10d
Mike Moore 2008.
Start on the right side of the cliff, at the right edge of a small alcove/cave . Start at a large hueco and climb the short face on pocket features to reach an anchor (4 b's).

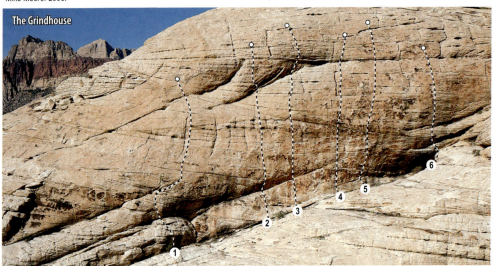

The Grindhouse

Sonic Youth Wall

This crag has a small selection of good routes offering long, pumpy pitches on solid, well-used rock. The wall faces northeast and gets very little sun for most of the year.

Approach: From the north side of the parking area, follow the main trail for 200 yards to a huge, white boulder. Get onto the dirt ridge behind the boulder and follow it for 300 yards. Sonic Youth is the steep shady wall on the left. A short scramble leads down into the wash and up to the base of the wall.

The routes are described from right to left. The first routes start from a raised platform below the right side of the wall.

1 Fearless Freaks 40' 5.11b
Steven Van Betten, Paul Van Betten. November 2006.
This route climbs the short, technical face, starting a short distance up the ramp above the platform (5 b's).

2 Gardyloo 45' 5.11a
This route climbs the steep, right-leaning trough above the right end of the platform. Climb the trough, past a steep start, to a rest. Continue to a bulge, then step left and make a couple of moves up the face to a horizontal and the anchor.

3 Everybody's Slave 45' 5.11d *
Don Welsh. April 1991.
The rightmost route on the main wall. Fingery moves low down

lead to bigger holds on the steep final wall (6 b's).

4 Sonic Youth 45' 5.11d *
Paul Van Betten, Sal Mamusia, Bob Conz. May 1989.
An excellent, pumpy wall climb. Start just left of the previous route and climb up and left to the first bolt. Continue past 4 more bolts to the anchor.

5 Agent Orange 60' 5.12b *
Paul Van Betten, Bob Conz. June 1989.
Another great route. Start 15' left of Sonic Youth. Fun climbing up excellent brown rock leads to a poor shake below a bulge. Pull over the bulge to a dissapointingly unhelpful break and make crux moves to a pumpy finish (7 b's).

6 Loki 60' 5.12b *
Don Welsh. April 1991.
This is a good route with sustained, thin climbing and a gradually building pump. Start a few feet down from the left edge of the platform. The route climbs up and left to a black streak which is followed to an anchor (8 b's).

7 Black Flag 65' 5.11c *
Paul Van Betten, Bob Conz. June 1989.
This route climbs a long seam to the left of the black streak. It starts 10' further down the ramp from Loki, to the right of a bush (8 b's).

⑧ GBH 70' 5.11d

R. Harrison, Kevin Biernacki, Paul Van Betten, Don Borroughs. 1989.
This route starts 10' left of a bush, at the left end of the ramp.
Climb up to a steep bulge. Pull over the bulge on sandy holds,
then move left and climb a thin seam to the anchor (9 b's).

⑨ Hooligans 50' 5.11d

Greg Mayer. July 1992.
This route starts just left of a bush. 6 b's to an anchor.

⑩ Last But Least 50' 5.11c

Gary Savage. Spring 2019.
The wall just left of Hooligans (7 b's).

There are several routes on the upper tier of this cliff. They are
described from right to left. They can be approached either by
climbing one of the routes on the lower tier or by making a long
exposed traverse in from the right, along a horizontal break.

⑪ Slam Dancin' with the Amish 80' 5.9+

Paul & Pauline Van Betten. June 1989.
Single rack to 1.75", 1.25"- 2.5" for the anchor.
Despite some soft rock this is an enjoyable climb. The first fea-
ture on the wall above the approach traverse is a right-facing
flake. Climb the flake and the wall above (3 b's) to the top.
Belay on mid-size cams and descend to the right.

⑫ Crankenstein 80' 5.10c

Danny Meyers. April 1988.
Almost directly above Everybody's Slave is a water streak
which goes over a big bulge. Climb the water streak (3 b's),
with a short, hard crux getting over the bulge. Belay on 2.5" to
3.5" cams and descend to the right

⑬ Seka's Soiled Panties 80' 5.11c

Richard Harrison, Paul Van Betten. September 1989.
Single rack to 0.75".
Start in the middle of the traverse ledge, below a bolt in a
big roof. This is directly above the black streak of Loki. Climb
thin seams to the roof. Pull leftwards past the bolt and over
the roof. Continue to the top. Belay on 2.5" to 3" cams and
descend to the right.

⑭ Hip Hoppin with the Hutterites 90' 5.8

Todd Swain, Donette Swain. August 1994.
Single rack to 3".
Start below a 40' high right-facing corner at the left end of the
approach ledge. Climb the corner for 20' then move left around
the arete and follow a crack. Continue to a bulge 20' higher,
pull over the bulge (crux) and continue up the easier face to
the top. Belay on small cams and descend to the right.

Broast & Toast Wall

This tall, sunny wall is clearly visible from the parking lot, half a mile to the northwest. It faces south towards the Sonic Youth Wall across a small canyon. The routes are a mixture of trad and sport on fairly soft rock.

Approach: From the north side of the parking area, follow the main trail for 200 yards to a huge, white boulder. Get onto the dirt ridge behind the boulder and follow it for 600 yards to the obvious, tall, white wall on the right. 10 minutes.

The routes are described from right to left

At the right end of the wall is a rounded prow of white rock which faces towards the parking area.

❶ Fairy Toast 70' 5.10c

R. Harrison, Paul Van Betten, Wendell Broussard. November 1989.
Single rack to 2.5".
Start at the base of the prow below a roof 20' up. Easy climbing leads to the roof. Pull over the roof at a bolt. Continue up the slabby wall then move right into a thin seam to the right of the more obvious seam of Burnt Toast. Continue up the seam (b) to the top.

❷ Burnt Toast 90' 5.10c

Bob Conz, Mike Ward, Jim Lybarger. December 1988.
Single rack to 1", Rp's.
Start at the base of a short, left-leaning arch just left of the previous route. Climb up the face, passing just to the left of the small roof of Fairy Toast, to reach an obvious left-leaning seam on the left side of the prow. Follow the seam to the top (2 b's).

❸ Rap Bolters Need to Be Famous 100' 5.11b

Richard Harrison, Paul Van Betten. November 1989.
This route starts on the left edge of the smooth varnish 25' to the left of the previous route, at the right edge of a small cave. Step right off some boulders onto the wall. Continue (b) to a band of varnish then move up and right into a scoop (b) below a left-leaning seam. Climb the steep wall to the right of the seam (3 b's) to the top.

❹ Roasted Ramen 100' 5.9+

Paul Van Betten, Don Borroughs, Sal Mamusia. November 1988.
Single rack to 1.25".
Follow the previous route to the varnished band. Traverse left (b) into a zig-zag crack which is followed (b) to the top.

❺ Calico Jack 90' 5.11b

Richard Harrison, Paul Van Betten, Don Borroughs. November 1989.
Start at the left edge of the cave. Climb straight up to a small brown roof. Climb the left-leaning crack above the roof then head straight up a varnished streak to the top (3 b's).

The next three routes climb the steep wall above the terrace at the left end of the crag.

❻ Desert Sportsman 55' 5.11c

Paul Van Betten, Sal Mamusia. December 1988.
Long, pumpy and quite enjoyable despite some soft rock. This route starts at the right end of the terrace and climbs a long, varnished streak to a strenuous, rounded crack which is followed to the anchor (7 b's).

❼ Girls Skool 50' 5.12b *

Michelle Locatelli. 2004.
The middle line of bolts. It starts at the same point as C.H.U.D. but moves right and climbs the long, intricate wall (8 b's).

❽ C.H.U.D. 55' 5.11c *

Paul Van Betten, Bob Conz, Richard Harrison, Sal Mamusia. April 1989.
The leftmost route follows a series of fragile right-facing flakes to an anchor (5 b's).

Numbers Crag

This small wall is very sunny and sheltered. It is located below and immediately to the west of Broast and Toast. The routes here have seen very little traffic over the years. Recently, extra bolts were added to some of the sportier climbs, and now that all the routes have anchors, this cliff deserves to become a bit more popular. The climbing on some of these routes is quite good, a bit like a sunny Wake Up Wall.

Approach: From the north side of the parking area, follow the main trail for 200 yards to a huge, white boulder. Get onto the dirt ridge behind the boulder and follow it for 600 yards to the Broast and Toast wall. Continue past the Broast and Toast wall for 50 yards to a small meadow under the crag. 10 minutes.

The routes are described from right to left.

On the right side of the wall, at the base, is a large varnished scoop.

❶ Number 6 30' 5.11d
Paul Van Betten, Sal Mamusia, Richard Harrison. January 1992.
Climb steeply out of the right side of the scoop on nicely varnished rock (4 b's).

❷ Number 5 45' 5.12c *
Paul Van Betten, Sal Mamusia, R. Harrison, Bob Conz. January 1992.
Climb out of the left side of the scoop to a tricky, thin seam which leads to some big holds at a bulge. A couple of long, powerfull pulls through the bulge lead to better holds beside the anchor (4 b's).

❸ Number 4 45' 5.12a?
Paul Van Betten, Sal Mamusia, Richard Harrison. January 1992.
Start 15' to the left of the scoop. Climb a thin seam into a black water streak (5 b's). This route appears to have lost some holds and may now be much harder.

❹ Number 3 45' 5.11c *
Shelby Shelton, Paul Van Betten, Richard Harrison. January 1992.
Climb the wall 10' to the left of #4 (5 b's).

❺ Number 2 45' 5.11d
Harrison, Shelby Shelton, Paul Van Betten, Sal Mamusia. Winter 1990.
Start 10' to the left of #3 below the right edge of a small shelf a few feet above the ground. Climb straight up the wall (5 b's).

❻ Number 1 40' 5.11d
Sal Mamusia, Paul Van Betten, Richard Harrison. January 1992.
Start below the shelf. Climb onto the shelf and continue up the wall past a horizontal into a bulging seam which is followed to a hard-to-see anchor in a little niche just below the top (6 b's).

❼ Number .5 40' 5.12c
Sal Mamusia, Paul Van Betten. January 1992.
On the left side of the crag is a very steep, scooped wall covered in shallow pockets. Climb a varnished slab and pull over a bulge into the thin seam in the scooped wall which is followed to the anchor (3 b's).

❽ Number 0 40' 5.10c
Paul Van Betten, Sal Mamusia, Richard Harrison. January 1992.
Start below the left edge of the scooped wall at the left end of the cliff. Follow two bolts into a thin seam which is followed to the top. There is a tree for an anchor a long way back from the edge. Descend to the left down the little corridor containing the belay tree.

Wake Up Wall

This is a good wall, packed with short, fingery sport routes on solid, well-used rock. Surprisingly, it is seldom busy, although it is probably the most popular wall in this part of the Sandstone Quarry. It faces north and is quite a cold and windy crag, best suited to warmer weather. Often the platform in front of the cliff is nice and sunny, even when the cliff is cold.

Approach: From the north side of the parking area, go down the main trail past the huge, white boulder, after 400 yards turn left onto the Turtlehead Trail. The Turtlehead Trail splits after 200 yards. Follow the left branch up onto a dirt ridge and continue to some rock slabs. Cut up and left across the slabs for 100 yards to a flat platform at the base of the wall. 10 minutes.

Wake Up Wall - Left

Monkey Rhythm 60' 5.10b

This route is not actually on the Wake Up Wall. It climbs an obvious right-leaning corner with an anchor on top. The corner is about 150 yards to the left (east) of the main wall. It is easily seen to the left of the approach trail, at the point where the trail heads up onto the dirt ridge.

The routes are described from left to right. On the left side of the crag is a steep wall, with a 10' deep trench at its base, and a big scoop about halfway up in its right side.

● The Last in Line 60' 5.10b
Mike Moore. Spring 2014.
The first fully-bolted route on the left side of the wall (7 b's).

Towards the left end of the trench is a short lower wall with two bolts leading to a long, twisting crack in the upper wall.

❶ Last Out 60' 5.10b
Single rack to 1.75", double 0.4"- 0.75".
Surprisingly well-protected. Climb past the 2 bolts to gain the thin crack system which is followed to an anchor.

❷ First Born 55' 5.10b *
Ed Prochaska. 1990.
Quite sustained and varied. Start in the trench about 20' to the

right of Last Out, below a right-leaning footledge about 10' up. Make balancy moves up the right-leaning footledge. Continue up the slab and pull over a bulge onto the upper wall. Make a few moves up the wall then move right into a rounded crack, which eventually leads to an anchor on the right (6 b's).

❸ On to the Next One 50' 5.11a
Mike & Jenny Bond, Mike Moore. November 2011.
Pull up to the right end of the footledge of First Born. After standing on the ledge, step right and climb the slab to the steeper wall. Climb the wall on flakes, making a tricky pull up to and over the final bulge to an anchor (7 b's).

The next two routes start about 20' to the right of First Born, below the left side of the scoop at a big undercling.

❹ Spanky Spangler 50' 5.10c
Richard Harrison, Michelle Locatelli. 2007.
Use the undercling to pull over the initial bulge, then follow a big flake, just left of the scoop, up a steep wall to a short, rounded crack. Up this then step right to an anchor (5 b's)

❺ Angled Dangler 50' 5.11d
Richard Harrison, Michelle Locatelli. 2007.
After the bouldery start, move right into the scoop. Exit left out of the scoop then climb the steep rib to an anchor (6 b's).

❻ Just Shut up and Climb 55' 5.11a ✶✶
Randy Faulk, Rick Denison. June 1991.
This route climbs through the roofs in the right side of the scoop. Climb up and left across slabby rock into the scoop. Fun climbing on uncharacteristically big holds leads through the roofs to an anchor (5 b's).

❼ Mic's Master 50' 5.10c ✶
Michelle Locatelli. 2007.
Start up the previous route then move right to a little, right-facing corner. After a cryptic crux, big holds lead up the rounded arete to an anchor (5 b's).

To the right is a slabby face of white rock.

❽ Poundcake 40' 5.8
Jay Meuller, Gail Meuller. May 1997.
Start just to the left of a crack system in the slab. Climb up to a ledge at 10' then continue up the slab to an anchor (3 b's).

❾ Crack of Noon 40' 5.8
Jay Meuller, Gail Meuller. April 1997.
Single rack to 1.25".
This route climbs the thin, zig-zag crack in the slab to the anchor of Poundcake, sketchy protection.

Peter Peik on Supernova. Page 427.

The right edge of the slabby face is defined by a big, left-leaning ramp which starts about 15' up, above a shelf. The following routes are on the long wall to the right of the ramp.

⑩ Too Few Years 45' 5.11a
Mike Bond, Malcolm Babbitt, Marc Dudas. 2011.
Boulder up onto the shelf below the right end of the left-leaning ramp. Step left up the ramp, then climb a thin right-leaning seam before finishing straight up to the anchor (5 b's).

⑪ The Shape of things to Come 35' 5.11a
Greg Mayer. Winter 1989.
Boulder onto the shelf below the right end of the left-leaning ramp, then zig-zag up the wall to the anchor (3 b's).

⑫ The Healer 35' 5.11d
Greg Mayer. Spring 1990.
Start 6' to the right of the previous route. This route climbs the left-facing offset past a very fingery crux (4 b's).

⑬ Rise and Whine 40' 5.12a
Mike Tupper. Spring 1990.
Start 5' right of the Healer. Boulder over a bulge to a rest. Climb past a short crux bulge to a sporty finish up a small, right-facing offset (4 b's).

⑭ Pain Check 40' 5.12a **
Bill Boyle. Spring 1990.
A good, sustained route, at the top of the grade. Climb straight up the fingery wall to the right of Rise and Whine, then make hard moves up a small left-facing offset. Another tricky move leads to a huge hold and the anchor a few feet higher (5 b's).

⑮ Good Mourning 35' 5.11c *
Bill Boyle. Spring 1990.
Start just right of Pain Check in the trough at the base of the wall, below a right-facing flake. Pull over the initial bulge to reach the flake. Climb the flake, then move right to the crux bulge and finish up a seam above (5 b's).

⑯ Native Son 35' 5.11c **
Mike Tupper. Spring 1990.
Start 10' right of Good Mourning. An excellent route with nice moves and good rock. Stretch up to some huecos then swing left to get onto a varnished wall (5 b's).

⑰ Where Egos Dare 30' 5.12a *
Greg Mayer. Summer 1991.
This short, bouldery route climbs the left edge of the steep scoop in the wall to the right of the previous route (4 b's).

On the right side of the wall is a left-slanting flared chimney.

⑱ XTZ 30' 5.9
Greg Mayer. Spring 1990.
An awkward grovel up the left-leaning chimney (3 b's).

⑲ Onsight Flight 40' 5.12b *
Don Welsh. Spring 1990.
Start just right of the chimney. A thin pull past the second bolt leads to a good shake then a pumpy finish (5 b's).

⑳ Stand and Deliver 40' 5.12c *
Mike Tupper. Spring 1990.
This is the right hand of the two routes to the right of the chimney. Stick clip the first bolt. Thin moves lead to a shake at a flake. Move right and make crux moves up a thin seam then finish over a difficult bulge (4 b's).

Wake Up Wall - Center

About 30 yards to the right of the previous routes is a shallow corridor which rises to a saddle at the right end of the wall. The following routes start at various points along this corridor.

21 The Last Drag 50' 5.10a
Mike Bond. 2011.
This is the leftmost route, which starts almost at the base of the corridor. Climb straight up the delicate face, passing just to the right of a big ledge/scoop near the top (5 b's).

22 Blame it on my ADD 45' 5.9
Mike Bond. 2011.
Start 10' right of The Last Drag and climb straight up the face on good edges to an anchor (5 b's).

23 Fall of Vegas 45' 5.10a
Mike Bond. 2011.
Start 10' right of Blame it on my ADD. After an awkward start, climb straight up the face to an anchor (5 b's).

24 Skidmark 50' 5.9+ *
Travis Graves, Phillip Swiny. March 2007.
Start 10' right of the previous route. Climb good rock with interesting pockets up a grey streak near the far right end of the wall (7 b's).

25 The Big Short 35' 5.9
Mike Bond. 2011.
Start 12' right of Skidmark. The rightmost route (5 b's).

Wake Up Wall - Right

The Walrus

The following routes are on a big boulder of nice rock (The Walrus) tucked into the rocks behind the saddle at the right end of the Wake Up Wall. The routes are mostly north-facing and shady, and exposed to winds.

Approach: From the saddle at the right end of Wake Up Wall, go down towards the wash below then scramble over the rocks on the right to a big boulder in front of a small cliff. 3 Minutes from the saddle. 15 minutes.

The first two routes are on the south face of the boulder.

I am the Walrus 30' 5.7
Mike Kellas. 2007.
This is the right of the two routes (2 b's).

They are the Eggmen 30' 5.10d
Michael Kimm. 2007.
This is the left of the two routes (2 b's).

The next routes described are on the north face of the boulder.

1 Expert Textpert 30' 5.11c
Michael Kimm. 2007.
This is the leftmost route on the north side of the Walrus. Climb the very thin, slopey seam. At the top, move right to finish at the anchors of Choking Smokers (3 b's).

2 Choking Smokers 30' 5.9
Michael Kimm. 2007.
Starts 10 feet right of Expert Textpert. Climb the right-facing flake/corner up the middle of the north face (4 b's).

3 Pornographic Priestess 30' 5.12a
Michael Kimm. 2007.
Start as for Choking Smokers. Move right at the second bolt, and make technical moves up two right-facing flakes to the anchor (4 b's).

4 Pigs from a Gun 35' 5.12b
Michael Kimm. 2007.
Climb the right arete of the north face without pulling around onto the slab on the right. Finish at the anchor of Pornographic Priestess. A little sporty and committing (4 b's).

Common Time

A short, shady wall of fragile rock, it is located on the west side of the canyon, immediately to the west of Numbers Crag. It faces east and gets morning sun.

Approach: From the north side of the parking area, follow the main trail for 200 yards to a huge, white boulder. Get onto the dirt ridge behind the boulder and follow it for 600 yards to the small canyon below the Broast and Toast Wall. Continue up the canyon past the Broast and Toast Wall and the Numbers Crag, then turn right into a narrow canyon. Common Time is 70 yards up the canyon on the left. 15 minutes.

The routes are described from left to right.

● Time Off 30' 5.11a
Leo Henson, Karin Henson, Albert Newman. March 1998.
This route climbs the wall between two cracks at the left end of the wall (5 b's).

● Paradiddle Riddle 30' 5.11b
Phil Bowden. July 1992
The wall just to the right of the previous route (4 b's).

● Myxolidian 30' 5.11b
Greg Mayer. July 1992.
Climb the wall 25' to the right of the previous route.

● One Move Number 25' 5.12a
Leo Henson, Karin Henson, Albert Newman. March 1998.
This mini-route faces west across the canyon towards Common Time. It is on a steep block 50' up the slab opposite Common Time. It climbs a steep, varnished scoop in the middle of the block. Short but good quality (2 b's).

THE TROPHY AREA

These crags are in the northwest corner of the Calico Hills, about one mile northwest from the parking area.

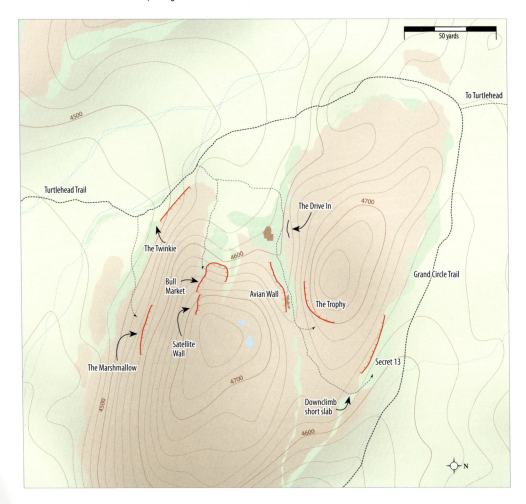

The Twinkie

This wall is a useful landmark when approaching the Trophy, Bull Market etc. It faces south towards Wake Up Wall, across a broad, open wash. It is clearly visible about 1000 yards north, and slightly to the west of the parking lot.

Approach: From the north end of the parking area, go down the main trail past the white boulder. After 400 yards turn left onto the Turtlehead Trail which is followed for 600 yards. The Twinkie is the long, low, white wall rising straight up from the flat desert a few yards to the right of the trail. 15 minutes.

The routes are described from right to left.

❶ Like Mom Used to Make 40' 5.11c *
Anthony Williams, John Day, Ralph Day. Winter 1988.
A good route which climbs the steep wall in the middle of the cliff. Fingery climbing up the lower wall leads to strenuous moves on slopers to reach the anchor (4 b's).

❷ Flake Eyes 40' 5.10d
Anthony Williams, John Day, Ralph Day. Winter 1988.
Start 10' to the left of the previous route behind a bush. Start up a short, steep flake (1.75" cam in a horizontal) and continue up the wall above (3 b's) to an anchor over the top of the formation.

❸ Short but Sweet 40' 5.10c
Anthony Williams, John Day, Ralph Day. Winter 1988.
Single rack to 0.75".
Start 30' to the left of Flake Eyes. Climb up and right across an awkward slabby ramp and move up to the first bolt. Thin climbing up the wall above (b) leads to the anchor on the top of the formation.

The Marshmallow

This is the large south-facing formation up and right of the Twinkie. It is distinguished by a long, horizontal band of varnish at 2/3 height.

Approach: From the north end of the parking area, go down the main trail past the white boulder. After 400 yards turn left onto the Turtlehead Trail which is followed for 600 yards. The Twinkie is the long, low, white wall rising straight up from the flat desert about 30 yards to the right of the trail. Skirt the right side of the Twinkie and scramble up and right to the base of the wall.

The routes are described from left to right.

Mojave Green 140' 5.8+
Jim Lybarger, Bob Conz. 1989.
Wires, Rp's. 3" cam for the anchor.
This route climbs a white slab at the left end of the formation. Start to the left of some bushes. Make some long runouts up the slab (3 b's) to a belay bolt on top. Descend to the west.

Dime Edging 170' 5.10c
Bob Conz. Mike Ward. 1989.
Single rack to 1", Rp's.
Good climbing but with a few long runouts. Start below the center of the wall, on the highest of several ledges. From the right side of the ledge step right onto varnished rock. Continue (2 b's) to a horizontal. Pull over the roof above the horizontal, at a small seam. Continue up the slab (b) to a belay.

The Trophy

This is a great crag which adds something a little different to the Calico Hills repertoire since the routes generally give steeper and less crimpy climbing than usual. The climbing is on solid, well-used, white rock with lots of flat jugs and slopers. The cliff faces east and gets morning sun, it is also quite exposed to any winds that may be blowing. Even when the cliff is in the shade the base is often sunny and warm. Despite being one of the better crags in the Calico Hills it is never crowded.

Approach: From the north end of the parking area, go down the main trail past the white boulder. After 400 yards turn left onto the Turtlehead Trail which is followed for 600 yards. The Twinkie is the long, low, white wall rising up from the flat desert about 30 yards to the right of the trail. Go past the Twinkie 30 yards and turn right to pick up a very faint trail which goes up some slabs to a nice, flat meadow behind the Twinkie. Turn left across the meadow, heading for the obvious curving shield of brown rock called the Drive In. Just below the Drive In, a trail leads northeast up a bushy corridor. The Trophy is the bulging buttress on the left, at the top of the corridor. 20 minutes.

The routes are described from left to right.

To reach the first route go around the left side of the main wall and scramble up and left along a slab for 150 feet.

Fifi Hula 45' 5.11a
Don Borroughs, Alan Busby. January 1992.
This route is about 150' to the left of the rest of the routes. It climbs a steep, south-facing wall (6 b's).

Colby Smith on Shark-walk. Page 423.

The next route is on a short, very steep buttress at the left end of the main part of the crag.

❶ Shark Walk 30' 5.13a *
Mike Tupper. February 1992.
Start just right of a cave with a bush. Short but burly (6 b's).

❷ Indian Giver 30' 5.12d
Mike Tupper. January 1992.
The seam to the right of Sharkwalk. A short bouldery crux on shallow pockets and thin crimps (5 b's).

❸ Mystery Remover 70' 5.12c
Greg Mayer. 1994.
Start to the right of the crack to the right of Indian Giver (7 b's).

The next two routes have a common start up a left-leaning handrail on the left side of the steepest part of the crag.

❹ Midnight Cowboy 50' 5.13a *
Mike Tupper. March 1992.
Climb the common start and continue leftwards along the handrail past a burly move at its end. Continue onto the easier upper wall (9 b's).

❺ Twilight of a Champion 70' 5.12d **
Mike Tupper. February 1992.
Enjoyable pumpy climbing on good holds. High in the grade. Climb the common start then go straight up the wall to a rest below the final bulge. Go over the bulge to an anchor.

❻ Pet Shop Boy 50' 5.13a ***
Mike Tupper. February 1992.
Start a few feet to the right of the previous two routes. Sustained and pumpy (6 b's).

The next two routes start at the huecoed crack at the very back of the cave.

❼ Keep your Powder Dry 75' 5.12b **
Mike Tupper. January 1992.
Climb slightly leftwards up the bulging wall to a rest ledge at 50' (12a). Continue up the technical upper wall (12b) to an anchor (11 b's).

❽ The Trophy 80' 5.12b/c ***
Mike Tupper. January 1992.
A great route, easy for the grade, and even easier than that if you know all the tricks. Follow the handrail out right and continue up the wall to a ledge at 50' with an optional anchor. Most people lower from here, although the upper wall is no giveaway (10 b's).

❾ Caught in the Crosshairs 65' 5.12a
Greg Mayer. March 1993.
Start on a block to the right of the steepest part of the crag. Climb the long, gently overhanging wall (7 b's).

❿ Dodging a Bullet 65' 5.12a *
Greg Mayer. Spring 1991.
Start 15' to the right of the previous route. A long, pumpy pitch which gradually gets harder. High in the grade, especially since the loss of some holds has made the last couple of clips harder (5 b's).

⓫ Meat Locker 25' 5.13a
The short roof at the right end of the crag (5 b's).

Secret 13

Many of the old projects on this beautiful, shady wall have now been redpointed and Secret 13 has become the best wall in Red Rocks for hard sport climbs. The cliff rises straight up from the desert to the north of the Trophy, facing north towards Turtlehead Peak. It gets almost no sun, but is also quite sheltered from the wind.

Approach: From the north end of the parking area, go down the main trail past the white boulder. After 400 yards turn left onto the Turtlehead Trail which is followed for 600 yards. The Twinkie is the long, low, white wall rising straight up from the flat desert about 30 yards to the right of the trail. Go past the Twinkie about 30 yards and turn right to pick up a very faint trail which goes up some slabs to a nice, flat meadow behind the Twinkie. Turn left across the meadow, heading for the obvious curving shield of brown rock called the Drive In. Just below the Drive In, a trail leads north up a bushy corridor. The Trophy is the bulging buttress on the left at the top of the corridor. Continue past the top of the corridor, heading north for a couple of hundred yards until a short scramble leads down to the desert floor. The wall is a short distance to the west from here. 25 minutes.

The routes are described from left to right.

❶ Inside Out 35' 5.11b
Greg Mayer. 1993.
At the left end of the wall is a short corner capped by a roof. Climb the corner, then go over the roof to the anchor (5 b's).

❷ All the Wrong Reasons 40' 5.12a
Greg Mayer. 1993.
Climb the arete to the right of the corner (6 b's).
Variation: 5.12a A few bolts up, step right and climb the face to anchors (7 b's).

Bill Ramsey on Where is my Mind?
Page 425. Photo: Tom Moulin.

❸ Sensible Shoes 40' 5.12b
Greg Mayer. 1993.
Start 15' right of the arete. Climb a grey face into a twisting seam which leads to the anchor (6 b's).

❹ DNA 50' 5.13a
Don Welsh. Spring 2006.
Start 12' right of Sensible Shoes below a steep, left-leaning seam. Climb the seam then move right and continue up the face to the top (6 b's).

❺ Recombination 55' 5.13a
Adam Harrington. 2010.
Start 20' right of DNA at a low hueco. Climb to a left-facing off-set, then continue up the face, past a bulge, to the top (7 b's).

❻ Mutation 55' 5.12d
Adam Harrington. 2010.
Start 8' right of Recombination. Climb to a right-facing offset. Up this, then head left to a seam which leads over a bulge to the anchor (7 b's).

❼ Silence 45' 5.11d *
Greg Mayer. 1993.
Start about 25' to the right of the previous route at a huecoed black crack in a right-facing corner. Climb the crack (6 b's).

To the right is a very impressive sweep of rock. These routes represent the best set of hard sport climbs in Red Rocks.

❽ Go A Hundred 60' 5.13b *
Don Welsh. Spring 2006.
This route starts about 15' to the right of Silence, it climbs a thin seam through a scoop then moves right to finish (9 b's).

❾ Ambushed 65' 5.13a/b ***
Dale Snyder. 2004.
Varied and interesting climbing. Start 15' to the right of Go A Hundred. Bouldery moves lead over a bulge to a good shake in a scoop. Hard moves gain a big hole, then a couple of fingery pulls lead to a disconcertingly rounded finish (7 b's).

❿ Youarewhatyouis 70' 5.13c ***
Don Welsh. Fall 2004.
Start 12' right of Ambushed at a little bush. Climb up and left to crux moves over a bulge, then straight up to the anchor (8 b's).

⑪ Where Is My Mind 70' 5.13c/d ***
Bill Ramsey. 2009.
A great route up the longest and steepest section of the wall. Start 10' right of Youarewhatyouis below a large hueco, the rightmost of two. Follow a long, thin seam over several bulges to the anchor (8 b's).
Variation: From the bulge, move right and finish up a seam.

⬤ Hanks Route 65' 5.13b
Nathan Rasnick. 2018.
Start 10' to the right of Where Is My Mind on a little sideways tree. Climb the red streak with some huge moves (9 b's).

⑫ Yoshimi Battles 65' 5.14a *
Don Welsh. 2009.
Start 10' right of the previous route. Climb straight up a thin seam in black rock to the anchors (8 b's).

⑬ Herbivour Dyno-soar 50' 5.14a
Steve Townshend. December 2016.
Start below an orange streak 12' to the right of Yoshimi Battles. From a basketball sized hueco, continue past a huge throw and several more big moves to reach the anchor (7 b's).
Link up: Lacerated Sky 5.13b
After 4 bolts, move right and finish up Sika 13.

⬤ Sika 13 65' 5.13a **
Nathan Rasnick. 2018.
Start 8' right of Herbivore Dyno-soar on a side pull flake. Climb the left edge of a black streak then move left and climb the wall to an anchor (7 b's).

⬤ Mescallana 60' 5.12c
Nathan Rasnick. 2018.
Start 12' right of Sika 13 at a right-leaning seam. Climb straight up over a bulge to finish up a slabbier wall (6 b's).

⬤ Pi 65' 5.12c
Greg Mayer. 1993.
This is the rightmost route on the wall. Start 5' right of Mescallana on the right side of the right-leaning seam. Climb straight up through a series of rounded bulges (7 b's).

Avian Wall

This is the slabby wall on the right side of the bushy corridor that leads up to the Trophy. It faces northwest and is shady until late afternoon.

Approach: From the north end of the parking area go down the main trail past the white boulder. After 400 yards turn left onto the Turtlehead Trail which is followed for 600 yards. The Twinkie is the long, low, white wall rising straight up from the flat desert about 30 yards to the right of the trail. Go past the Twinkie about 30 yards and turn right to pick up a very faint trail which goes up some slabs to a nice, flat meadow behind the Twinkie. Turn left across the meadow heading for the obvious curving shield of brown rock called the Drive In. Just below the Drive In a trail leads north up a bushy corridor. The Avian Wall is on the right side of the corridor. 20 minutes.

The routes are described from right to left.

❶ Spotted Owl 45' 5.11a
Don Borroughs, Alan Busby. March 1992.
This is the first route on the right as you go up the corridor, it starts at an open, sandy spot (5 b's).

❷ Thunderbird 45' 5.11b
Don Borroughs, Alan Busby. March 1992.
This route starts about 100' further up the corridor from Spotted Owl, just to the right of a huge boulder blocking the corridor. It starts up a steep wall of darker rock to reach an easier seam (6 b's).

A couple of years ago a huge boulder trundled down from the slope below the Trophy and came to rest at the base of the next route, so it's now a bit shorter!

❸ Coyote Moon 30' 5.9
Don Borroughs, Alan Busby. March 1992.
Climb the short wall above the huge boulder (3 b's).

❹ The Cat And The Bird 30' 5.10a
Pete Bresciani, Jon Cheney, Michelle Onsaga. 2012.
Start on the huge boulder just left of Coyote Moon. Climb the short wall to an anchor (6 b's).

❺ Spotted Eagle 45' 5.10a
Don Borroughs, Alan Busby. March 1992.
Start 15' to the left of the huge boulder (4 b's).

Bull Market/Satellite Wall

The rock on these walls is very flaky and soft in places, nevertheless there are a couple of very good routes. Most of the routes face south and because of the high, exposed location will catch any wind that is blowing. They are never crowded.

Approach: From the north end of the parking area go down the main trail past the white boulder. After 400 yards turn left onto the Turtlehead Trail which is followed for 600 yards. The Twinkie is the long, low, white wall rising straight up from the flat desert about 30 yards to the right of the trail. Go past the Twinkie about 30 yards and turn right to pick up a very faint trail which goes up some slabs to a nice, flat meadow behind the Twinkie. The cliff is located above the northeast corner of the meadow, between two steep gullies. 20 minutes.

The routes are described from left to right.

The first route starts a short distance up the chimney on the left side of the formation.

❶ Twentieth Century Ultra 80' 5.11c
Mike Tupper. 1992.
A long, pumpy route on the shady left wall of the formation. Start a few feet up the chimney and climb up and left up the long wall (8 b's).

2 Scudder Global 40' 5.11b
Mike Tupper. 1992.
Start below the arete to the left of the smooth rock on the front side of the formation. Climb just left of the arete to a ledge (4 b's).

3 Fidelity Select 35' 5.12b
Mike Tupper. 1992.
This route climbs the nice, orange rock on the front side of the formation, just to the right of the arete of the previous route.

The next routes are all on the southeast facing wall to the left of the gully that runs up on the right side of the formation.

4 Liar's Poker 50' 5.11b
Mike Tupper. 1992.
This is the leftmost route on the wall (7 b's).

5 Leveraged Buyout 45' 5.11d
Mike Tupper. 1992.
The next route on the right, it shares the anchor with Liar's Poker (6 b's).

6 Hostile Takeover 40' 5.11c
Mike Tupper. 1992.
The next route to the right (4 b's).

7 Pinkies for the Dean 35' 5.11c/d *
Mike Tupper. 1992.
The rightmost route on the wall follows a thin, curving crack to the anchor of Hostile Takeover. The rock is pretty good on this one (4 b's).

The Bull Market

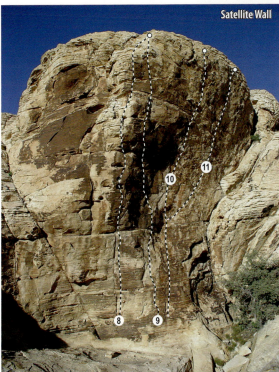

Satellite Wall

At the top of the gully that runs up underneath the previous four routes is a nice, sunny platform below a very steep buttress, called the Satellite Wall.

8 Stargazer 50' 5.12b
Leo Henson, Karin Henson. Winter 1993
The leftmost route. A bit sandy in places (7 b's).

9 Sputnik 50' 5.12a
Leo Henson, Karin Henson. Winter 1993
Start just right of Stargazer (6 b's).

10 Supernova 55' 5.12c **
R. Faulk, J. Tobish, T. Becchio. December 1991.
This is an excellent and very strenuous route, high in the grade. Start 5' to the right of Sputnik and climb straight up the highest and steepest part of the wall (8 b's).

11 Cosmos 60' 5.12d *
Leo Henson, Karin Henson. Winter 1993.
Start up the first three bolts of Supernova, then move right and climb the wall to hard moves just below the anchor (8 b's).

CALICO TANKS AREA

The following crags are all accessed from the Calico Tanks Trail

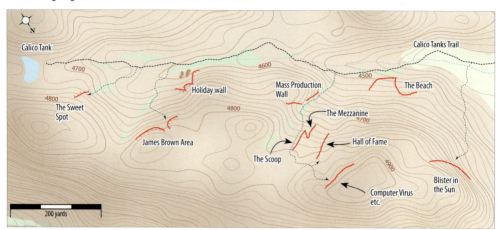

Blister in the Sun

This is the large mass of light-colored rock to the north as you first enter the wash that leads up towards Calico Tanks. The wall is easily recognized by a long, right-slanting crack. It faces southwest.

Approach: From the north side of the parking lot, follow the main trail past the huge, white boulder on the left. After 500 yards turn right on the Calico Tanks Trail. The trail leads into a narrow gravel wash. After 150 yards the trail exits right and leads into a beautiful, sandy wash which heads up to the east towards the Calico Tank. At this point the cliff is visible about 500 yards to the north. Leave the sandy wash a short distance further on and scramble over slabs and around short cliffs to the base of the wall. 20 minutes.

The routes are described from left to right. The left side of the cliff is a tall wall seamed with discontinuous cracks.

❶ Teenage Mutant Ninja Turtles 180' 5.11a
Jim Lybarger, Bob Conz, Sal Mamusia. December 1989.
Single rack to 2.5", 3"- 4" for the anchor.
Start just to the right of a right-facing corner, formed by a huge block in the lower-left corner of the wall. Climb the gradually steepening slab and go past a bolt into a long crack system which is followed to the top.

❷ Blister in the Sun 180' 5.11b
Bob Conz, S. Shelton. December 1988.
Single rack to 2.5", 3"- 4" for the anchor.
Follow High Scalin' to the base of the diagonal crack. Break out left and follow a vertical crack up the middle of the wall to a bolt. Move right and follow another crack to a bolt, then move back left to another crack which leads to the top of the wall.

❸ Tortugas Mutante 180' 5.11d
Richard Harrison, Jimmy Dunn. 1989.
Single rack to 2.5", 3"- 4" for the anchor.
Start up High Scalin', then follow a line to the right of Blister in the Sun (7 b's).

❹ High Scalin' 240' 5.7
Paul Van Betten, Nick Nordblom. 1987.
Single rack to 4", double to 3"
This route follows the long, right-slanting crack in two pitches. Start behind a dead tree on a ledge 8' up.
1. 120' 5.7 Climb thin seams up to the base of the main crack. Follow the crack up and right to a belay.
2. 120' 5.7 Continue up the crack to the top.
Descend to the right.

The Beach

This is the red wall which looms above the middle portion of the Calico Tanks trail. It is a very warm and sheltered cliff which can be comfortable on the coldest days. The rock is soft and fragile on most of the routes.

Approach: From the north side of the parking lot, follow the main trail past the huge, white boulder on the left. After 500 yards turn right on the Calico Tanks Trail. The trail leads into a narrow gravel wash. After 150 yards the trail exits right and leads into a beautiful, sandy wash which heads up to the east towards the Calico Tank. The cliff sits a few yards to the left of the trail about 300 yards further up the wash. 10 minutes.

The routes are described from left to right.

At the left end of the crag is a large block. Behind the block is a short arete of nice, varnished rock.

❶ RF Gain 35' 5.10c
Nick Nordblom. 1987.
Climb the arete past two well-spaced bolts. There is a helpful 1.75" cam placement above the second bolt. Bold but with good climbing.

❷ Squelch 35' 5.10d
Kurt Mauer. 1987.
Single rack to 1.75".
The attractive, thin crack to the right of the arete. Nice rock.

❸ Static 45' 5.6
4"- 5" cams.
This route climbs the wide corner/crack to the right.

❹ Wizard of Odds 50' 5.12a
Greg Mayer. Winter 1992.
In the center of the cliff are some red roofs, this route follows a thin seam in the steep buttress to the left of the roofs (7 b's).

❺ Southern Cross 50' 5.12b
Leo Henson. October 1994.
The steep, loose buttress to the right of the roofs (7 b's).

❻ Southern Comfort 50' 5.12d *
John Heiman. 1997.
Unlike the other sport routes here, this is an excellent, well-cleaned route. It climbs the shallow corner at the right end of the wall and finishes up the steep wall above (8 b's).

Mass Production Wall

This shady wall faces northwest, back down the Calico Tanks wash. It is a cold and windy crag with a good selection of moderate sport routes on solid, well-used rock.

Approach: From the north side of the parking lot, follow the main trail past the huge, white boulder on the left. After 500 yards turn right on the Calico Tanks Trail. The trail leads into a narrow gravel wash. After 150 yards the trail exits right and leads into a beautiful, sandy wash which heads up to the east towards the Calico Tank. Follow the trail up the wash for 600 yards. The Mass Production wall is the wall on the right side of a steep gully which cuts up the hillside to the left of the trail. 15 minutes.

The routes are described from right to left, i.e. from the bottom to the top of the gully.

❶ Some Assembly Required 50' 5.10c
Greg Mayer. Spring 1991.
This is the first route on the wall as you go up the gully. It starts behind a large pine tree and follows a thin left-slanting seam. Quite technical and sustained (6 b's).

❷ Kokopelli 50' 5.10c
Don Borroughs, Alan Busby. April 1992.
Further up the wall is a large roof. Start below a notch in the middle of the roof. Climb the thin face to the roof and make a burly pull over the lip to an anchor (5 b's).

3 Parts is Parts 35' 5.8

Todd Swain, Geoff Rickerl. April 1992.

This route starts about 50' up the gully to the left of the previous route. It starts behind a couple of trees and climbs the wall to the left of a slanting corner/roof (4 b's).

4 Battery Powered 40' 5.9

Greg Mayer. 1991.

Start a few feet to the left of the previous route and just to the right of a short right-facing corner (6 b's).

The following routes start 50 feet higher up the gully, below a large patch of smooth varnish 25 feet up the wall.

5 Foreman Ferris 50' 5.11b *

Leo Henson. October 1994.

Climb a thin seam through the right side of the varnish (5 b's).

6 Trigger Happy 50' 5.10a *

Greg Mayer. Spring 1991.

Climb the easier seam through the left side of the varnish patch (5 b's).

7 Hit and Run 40' 5.9

Greg Mayer. Spring 1991.

The leftmost route on the wall (6 b's).

Mass Production Wall

The Scoop & Vicinity

At the top of the hill, above and to the northwest of Mass Production Wall are a series of fins running down from the ridge. The Scoop is the east face of the middle of these fins and is easily seen from the main wash. The rock on this wall is very soft and dirty, but with a bit of work it could probably provide some steep and very hard climbs. The central portion of this wall is easily the most impressive chunk of unclimbed rock in the Calico Hills. Mike Tupper and Greg Mayer started work on this crag in the early 90s, but only completed a couple of routes before they got sidetracked by the better rock of The Trophy, leaving all the meaty lines unclimbed.

Approach: From the top of the Mass Production Wall gully scramble west across slabs. The Scoop is the wall on the left side of the first major corridor on the right. A short scramble leads up into the corridor. 20 minutes.

The routes are described from left to right, i.e. from the bottom to the top of the corridor.

● Turbulence 35' 5.12a

This route climbs the sharply overhanging arete on the left side of the wall, at the entrance to the corridor. The anchor is hidden on the ledge above the route (5 b's).

● Artificial Intelligence 45' 5.12a

The first bolted line to the right of the previous route (6 b's).

● Busted Brain 50' 5.12b

Start to the right of the previous route below a scoop (7 b's).

There are various anchors and partially bolted lines in the central part of the wall. The next completed routes are the last two lines on the right side of the wall, close to the top of the corridor.

● Fond Farewell 35' 5.11c

This route starts on top of some boulders and follows a crack which slants up and right (5 b's).

● First Impressions 30' 5.11d

Start just right of a short arete. Climb up and left on pockets and underclings to a short, bouldery headwall (4 b's).

The Mezzanine

This is the unusual-looking varnished wall a short distance west of The Scoop. It faces east back towards the Mass Production Wall. It is reached by continuing west past The Scoop for 75 yards.

The first route starts in the very narrow corridor below the wall.

Greg's Traverse 70' 5.12a †
Starting just inside the corridor, follow a long, right-arching line to an anchor (8 b's).

The next routes start on top of the fin that forms the right side of the narrow corridor. The top of the fin is best reached by following the Hall of Fame approach, then scrambling down the upper part of the fin to the platform below the routes.

Project 50'
The line on the left (5 b's).

28 40' 5.11c
From the top of the fin lean across the top of the corridor and climb the steep wall on the right to an anchor (5 b's).

Hall of Fame

This wall is actually the northwest face of the fin that contains the Mezzanine. It is not the easiest crag to find but has a decent set of shady routes on partially-varnished rock.

Approach: From the top of the Mass Production Gully, scramble west across slabs for 100 yards to the first major corridor on the right. Scramble up the corridor. The very impressive wall on the left side of the corridor is called The Scoop. Once you reach the flat area at the top of the corridor, start heading west again over a gully and across some slabs for around 75 yards. At this point there is a corridor heading down to your left with a steep, varnished left wall, this is the Hall of Fame. The routes are described from left to right i.e. from the top of the corridor to the bottom. 25 minutes.

● Ms Adventure 25' 5.7
Greg Mayer. Spring 1991.
The first route at the top of the corridor (3 b's).

● Innocent Bystander 40' 5.10a
Greg Mayer. Spring 1991.
This route starts 30' to the right of the previous route and climbs up, passing just to the left of a shallow cave (5 b's).

● Bad Reputation 45' 5.11b
Phil Bowden, Guy Pinjuv. Spring 1991.
Start 30' to the right. This route starts with a small roof and climbs the wall passing just to the right of the cave (6 b's).

● Armed and Dangerous 45' 5.10d *
Phil Bowden. Spring 1991.
Start about 10' to the right of Bad Reputation. Make a burly move off the ground to reach some huecos and continue up the wall to the anchor (6 b's).

The next two routes have a common start about 15 feet above the lower entrance to the corridor.

● Repeat Offender 45' 5.11a
Greg Mayer. Spring 1991.
Climb the common start then head up and left to the anchor. To keep the grade reasonable, it is necessary to make a little loop around to the left between the second and third bolts (6 b's).

● Yearnin' and Learnin' 45' 5.11a
Don Borroughs, Alan Busby. April 1992.
Climb the common start then head up and right (5 b's).

● Walk the Line 45' 5.11b
Start to the right of the common start of the previous two routes (5 b's).

● Bull Rider 30' 5.10d
The rightmost route on the wall (3 b's).

The following routes are on the long, white wall about 50 yards to the west from the top of the Hall of Fame corridor. The routes are described from right to left.

● Hero Worship 30' 5.10b
Liz Tupper. December 1993.
The short arete on the far right side of the wall (4 b's).

● Computer Virus 50' 5.12c
Mike Tupper. December 1993.
This route starts up a varnished scoop in the middle of the wall, on the tallest and steepest section of the cliff (8 b's).

Sand Illusion 35' 5.11c
Greg Mayer. Spring 1991.
This route climbs a nice-looking arete at the left end of the wall (3 b's).

● Greg's Arete 40' 5.12a
Jim Greg. Fall 1993.
This route climbs an arete that is slightly below the level of the lower entrance to the Hall of Fame and about 100 yards its west. It climbs an overhanging arete to the right of a scoop of light-brown rock. Start below a varnished slab below the arete. Climb the varnished slab and pull onto the arete which is followed to an anchor (6 b's).

Sandra Horna on Death Before Decaf.
Page 433. Photo: Tom Moulin.

Tom Moulin on Run Rabbit Run. Page 433.

Holiday Wall

Despite the relatively long approach, this is one of the most popular cliffs in the Sandstone Quarry area, thanks to a host of enjoyable 5.11 sport routes on soft, but well-used red rock. It is in the form of a large corner facing south. The right wall is shady in the morning, the left wall is shady in the afternoon.

Approach: From the north side of the parking lot, follow the main trail past the huge, white boulder on the left. After 500 yards turn right on the Calico Tanks Trail. The trail leads into a narrow gravel wash. After 150 yards the trail exits right and leads into a beautiful, sandy wash which heads up to the east towards the Calico Tank. Follow the trail up the wash for 600 yards. At this point the Mass Production Wall is just up and left of the trail. Holiday Wall is on the left another 300 yards up the trail, at the far end of a flat area in the wash. 25 minutes.

The routes are described from left to right.

❶ Presents of Mind 40' 5.12a
The leftmost route on the wall (4 b's).

❷ The Grinch 40' 5.12c
Mike Tupper. December 1990.
Stick clip the first bolt. This route starts with a hard boulder problem immediately to the right of the previous route. The upper part of the route is on bigger holds but is still pumpy (3 b's).

❸ Death Before Decaf 45' 5.12b ★★
Don Welsh. January 1991.
An excellent route. Start around to the right of The Grinch, at the right side of a low roof. In the upper part of the route the easiest line stays to the left of the bolts (6 b's).

❹ Gift Rapped 40' 5.11a
Karen Peil. December 1990.
Start a few feet to the right of the previous route, beside a small pine tree. Climb a curving crack to a rest ledge and finish up an easier headwall (6 b's).

❺ Red Sky Mining 40' 5.11b
Karen Peil. December 1990.
Climb straight up the wall just right of Gift Rapped (7 b's).

❻ Red Storm Rising 45' 5.11b/c ★
Karen Peil. December 1990.
The rightmost route on the wall. Sustained and pumpy (6 b's).

The next two routes climb the pillar in the center of the cliff.

❼ When the Cat's Away 45' 5.11b ★★★
Greg Mayer. December 1990.
An enjoyable, varied route up the front face of the pillar (6 b's).

❽ Saddam's Mom 45' 5.11d ★
Karen Peil. December 1990.
Climb the right side of the pillar. At one point it is possible to step left and get a rest before moving back right to the steep finish. If you avoid the rest it's 12a.

❾ Run Rabbit Run 40' 5.13d ★
Tom Moulin. January 2011. It took several years of sporadic attempts before Moulin convinced himself that the crux dyno was even feasible. A couple of cams to 1.5" and various tiny cams.
The sharply overhanging corner to the right of Saddams Mom. Layback the lower corner until a hard boulder problem (V9) leads to a stem rest. Stem up a few moves and somehow initiate a long dyno to a finger lock. Layback to the anchor.

The next two routes climb the arete on the right side of the cliff.

❿ Moments to Memories 30' 5.11b
Greg Mayer. December 1990.
Climb the left side of the arete, zig-zagging around the bolts in order to find the easiest line.

⓫ Fast Moving Train 30' 5.11c ★
Greg Mayer. December 1990.
A short but pumpy route up the front face of the arete.

James Brown Area

These sunny walls face south.

Approach: A few yards beyond the Holiday Wall, get onto some slabby ledges of red rock which are followed up to the east. Leave the red slabs after 150 yards and head up towards a white buttress with a prominent streak of varnish right on its prow. 30 minutes.

The routes are described from left to right.

❶ James Brown 60' 5.11d ***
Randy Marsh, Pier Locatelli. Winter 1991.
This route climbs the streak of varnished rock on the prow of the buttress. Lovely technical climbing on great rock (7 b's).

The next two routes are in the corridor to the right.

❷ Brand New Bag 30' 5.11a
Randy Marsh, Pier Locatelli. Winter 1991.
The first route in the corridor. It starts just left of a bush. Short, steep and chossy (4 b's).

❸ Soul Power 60' 5.11d ***
Randy Marsh, Pier Locatelli. Winter 1991.
Start 10' above the previous route. Steep and pumpy (8 b's).

To the right of the corridor is a tall wall above a sloping terrace. Towards the right end of the terrace is a shallow cave.

❹ External Locus 70' 5.12c
Greg Mayer. 1995.
This route climbs a long seam which starts at the left edge of the cave (10b's).

❺ Pocket Full of Kryptonite 70' 5.12b *
Greg Mayer. 1995.
Starting just right of the cave, this route climbs a long varnished streak up a line of shallow huecos and horns. This would be a good route with a bit of traffic (11b's).

The next routes start at the base of the cliff. The wall underneath the terrace is very steep and ends in a cave on its right side.

❻ They Just Don't Make Outlaws Like They Used To 80' 5.12a
Greg Mayer. Spring 1993.
Climb over the right side of the cave to a brown scoop and continue up the long wall above to the top (11b's).

❼ The Heteroclite 80' 5.11c
Greg Mayer. Spring 1993.
Start 10' to the right of Outlaws on top of a boulder. Climb the long seam to an anchor (10b's).

❽ Mirage II 80' 5.10c
Greg Mayer. Spring 1996.
This route follows a long seam 15' to the right of the previous route.

The Sweet Spot

This small shady wall is on the right side of a short, steep gully about 400 yards to the east of Holiday wall. Chossy rock.

Approach: A few yards beyond the Holiday Wall, get onto some slabby ledges of red rock which are followed to the east until they lead down into a small meadow. Go up the meadow into the steep gully on the left at its top. The first route is on the right, a few yards up the gully. 30 minutes.

● Absolute Zero 50' 5.12a
Greg Mayer. Summer 1993.
Start beside a small tree and climb a left-trending line of bolts (7 b's).

● Disposable Blues 40' 5.11c
Greg Mayer. Summer 1993.
This route follows the line of a right-facing offset just to the right of the left edge of the wall (5 b's).

Tom Moulin on Hook, Line & Sinker, Page 444.

Introduction

This is the large basin on the east side of the Calico Hills. It contains many private residences, and in the past there has been friction between climbers and homeowners. When climbing in Calico Basin, keep a low profile, park in the authorized areas, and stick to the established approaches.

The climbs in the Calico Basin are grouped into two general areas, The Red Springs area which includes all the climbing around the Red Springs parking area, and the Kraft Mountain area which includes the climbing in the vicinity of Kraft Mountain, the large hill forming the northern boundary of Calico Basin.

Access

One of the nice things about Calico Basin is that it is not necessary to drive around the loop road in order to climb here. To reach Calico Basin, turn north on a road that leaves Route 159 about 1.4 miles east of the Loop Road. Follow this road for 1.2 miles and turn left into the Red Springs parking area. The Red Spring parking area has the same hours as the loop road. For the routes in the Kraft Mountain area and also for the crags above Ash Springs, park at the Kraft Mountain Parking area which is on the left at the very end of the long, straight after passing Red Springs.

The following crags are all located close to the Red Springs parking area. Cannibal Crag and the routes Physical Graffiti and Big Bad Wolf are very popular, but most of the other cliffs see very little traffic. Surprisingly, there are a few very good crack climbs here; The Fox, Risk Brothers Roof, Allied Forces, Arms Left and Strategic Arms provide some of the best crack climbing in the Calico Hills. There are also a few obscure but outstanding sport routes that deserve a lot more action. There are also a few good bouldering areas, some of which are marked on the map. The best parking location will depend on your destination, but as stated in the introduction to Calico Basin, be aware of the current parking regulations. When approaching your crag, stick to the established trails and avoid walking across private land.

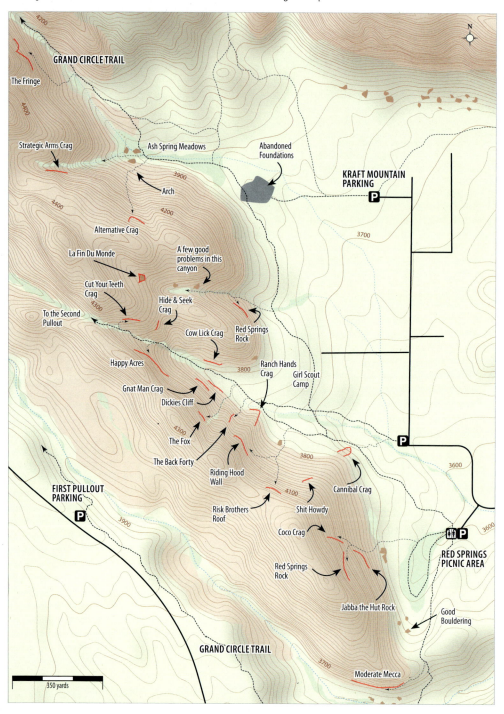

Dustin Burd on The Fox. Page 453.

The following crags are scattered around the hillside, slightly to the west of the parking area.

Moderate Mecca

This long cliff band is at the top of the ridge to the south of the Red Springs parking area; it faces south towards the loop road. Although the routes are short and the rock is not of the best quality, Moderate Mecca is quite popular thanks to a large number of easier trad and mixed routes, together with its easy access and sunny location.

Approach: Follow the trail around the left side of the park enclosure and go up an old road for 250 yards to the crest of the hill. Head down the other side for 30 yards, then follow a trail on the right onto an inobvious ledge which leads west below a short wall. All the routes, except for the first three described, are on the wall above the ledge. 10 minutes.

The routes are described from east to west, as you encounter them on the walk along the ledge. However, the first three routes are on the tier below the approach ledge.

🔴 Side Effects 60' 5.10d **
Mike Ward. 1991.
This good route climbs the southeast face of the obvious pinnacle which is below the east end of the approach ledge. Start up a short finger crack in a pink corner, then pull over a bulge onto a steep wall . Follow the big huecos up the wall to a rest below the final bulge. Pull the bulge to an anchor (7 b's).

About 80 yards to the left of Side Effects is another buttress with a couple of bolted routes. This is directly below Chicken Gumbo for your Dumbo.

❶ Baby Swiss 55' 5.11c
Leo Henson. December 2010.
The right hand of the two routes has "5.11c" scratched into a rock at its base. Climb the steep wall to a rest, then pull over the roof to an awkward bulge and the anchors (8 b's).

❷ Feelin' Groovy 50' 5.11a
Leo Henson. December 2010.
The left hand of the two routes. "5.11a Rotten" is scratched into a rock at the base. Climb the steep wall to a rest, then go over the roof to the anchor (7 b's).

The first routes on Moderate Mecca proper are found about 250 feet after the start of the ledge system, where there is an undercut arete.

❸ Bad Soup 25' 5.9
Start about 15' right of the arete, on a block below a rotten recess. Pull past the undercut start onto the face to the left of the recess. Continue up the wall, trending left to the top (3 b's).

❹ Stew on This 30' 5.10a
Kevin Campbell, Todd Swain. December 1998.
Single rack 1.75"-2.5".
This route starts at the base of the undercut arete. Pull over an overhang (b) to get off the ledge. Continue up the varnished wall (b) and easier rock above to an anchor.

❺ Is it Soup Yet 30' 5.10b
Kevin Campbell, Todd Swain. December 1998.
Single rack to 1.25".
Start on the left side of the arete. Pull over the initial bulge (b) and continue up a shallow corner in the arete to a ledge. Continue up the short wall above to the anchor.

Soup Nazi 40' 5.10a
Patrick Mulligan. 2001.
Small tcu's and brass offsets.
This route climbs the steep wall between Is it Soup Yet and Chicken Gumbo for your Dumbo. Climb out of a cave and head up a steep headwall (small microcams in the pockets) to reach an anchor on top of the tower.

Chicken Soup for the Soul 30' 5.10a (Tr.)
Theresa Krolak, Patty Gill, Todd Swain. January 1999.
Start at the base of Chicken Gumbo and climb the face to its right, past a shallow left-facing corner.

❻ Chicken Gumbo for your Dumbo 30' 5.6
Todd Swain, Patty Gill, Theresa Krolak. January 1999.
Single rack to 3".
15' around to the left of the undercut arete is a large left-facing corner. Climb the thin, varnished corner in the right wall of the main corner.

❼ Soupy Sales 30' 5.7
Patty Gill, Theresa Krolak, Todd Swain. January 1999.
Single rack to 3".
Climb twin cracks in the back of the main corner.

❽ From Soup to Nuts 30' 5.7
Todd Swain, Patty Gill, Theresa Krolak. January 1999.
Single rack to 4", save 1.75"- 2.5" for the anchor.
Start 10' to the left of the main corner. Climb through an awkward, pink scoop into a wide crack which is followed to the top.

The face just left of From Soup to Nuts is a 5.9+ top-rope.

❾ The Singing Love Pen 30' 5.9
Todd Swain, Patty Gill, Theresa Krolak. January 1999.
Single rack to 3".
The wall to the left of the big corner is undercut at its base. The only break in the overhang is a pink scoop about 30' to the left of the previous route. Climb the scoop, pulling over the bulge at its top, to an easier crack which is followed to the top.

❿ Valentines Day 40' 5.8+ *
Randal Grandstaff, Danny Rider. 1998.
Single rack to 3", double 1.75"- 2.5".
This route climbs the obvious, large left-facing corner about 40' around to the left of the previous route. It is located about 100 yards along the ledge and is one of the most prominent lines on the cliff. Enjoyable jamming and stemming lead to an anchor on the left, at the top of the corner.

⓫ Ace of Hearts 35' 5.10d
Single rack to 1.25", Rp's
This route climbs thin cracks up the left edge of the face to the left of Valentines Day. A bold lead, the pro is hard to place and not very good once it's in.

⓬ Immoral 80' 5.10d
Start below a left-facing corner 5' to the left of Ace of Hearts. Climb the corner until it is possible to hand traverse left (crux) to the finish of Immoderate (8 b's).

⓭ Immoderate 80' A0, 5.9
Start 20' left of the previous route. Stick clip the first or second bolt and winch up until it is possible to start climbing. Climb a loose flake to its top, then go over a bulge and continue up lower-angled rock to the shared anchor.

Beyond Valentines Day, the traverse ledge is covered with large boulders. About 50 yards past Valentines Day, the wall above the ledge goes back into a huge corner with a steep right wall and a slabby left wall.

⑭ Pending Disaster 60' 5.10a
Todd Swain, Kevin Campbell. December 1998.
Single rack to 4".
Start at the right edge of the wall to the right of the corner. Climb a crack, which slants leftwards through the initial overhang. Continue up a groove in the arete above to an anchor.

⑮ Not So Moderate 60' 5.11c
Joseph Smith. January 2011.
Single rack to 1", optional 4".
This route starts 10' left of Pending Disaster. Climb an offset, then move up and right following a thin seam. Make a crux traverse left along a sloping rail then climb straight up to the anchors of Pending Disaster. A bold lead.

⑯ Not So Smart 50' 5.?
Climb straight up the face to the left of the previous route, finishing at an anchor under the big roof (8 b's).

⑰ Penny Lane 100' 5.3
This route climbs up the cracks in the back of the big corner.

⑱ Goose Poop Roof 110' 5.10c
Single rack to 4".
Climb Penny Lane to the big ledge then traverse right under the roofs to below an obvious crack. Pull the roof and follow the juggy crack to the top of the cliff band.

⑲ Abbey Road 90' 5.4
This route climbs the thin crack in the slabby wall 10' to the left of the corner. Climb the crack, past a small sentry box at 50', to

a ledge 10' higher. Either go up and right to the top, or traverse left along the ledge to the anchor of Muckraker.

⑳ Fleet Street 110' 5.8
Kevin Campbell, Todd Swain. December 1998.
Single rack to 1.25".
Start 10' to the left of the previous route. Climb the slabby face to a bolt at 20', run it out to another bolt 20' higher and continue to the anchor of Muckraker on the ledge above.

㉑ Muckraker 100' 5.8
Todd Swain, Paul Ross. December 1998.
Single rack to 2.5".
Start below the large roofs at the left edge of the slabby wall. Climb the right hand of two cracks, which goes around the right edge of the roofs. Continue up the easier crack above to its top, then continue to the shared anchor on the ledge. Rappel with a 60m rope.

㉒ Scalawag 100' 5.10b
Todd Swain, Paul Ross. December 1998.
Single rack to 3.5", triple 2"- 2.5".
A very impressive line, it climbs the left hand of the two cracks through the huge roofs. Follow cracks on the upper wall to the communal anchor.

To reach the next two routes, walk 40' around the corner to the left of Scalawag, into a small overhung alcove.

㉓ Small Claims 50' 5.12b/c
Single rack to 6", double to 0.75".
This route climbs the sharply overhanging, left-facing corner that forms the right side of the alcove. Stick clip a bolt on the right arete. Pull past the bolt into a finger crack which leads past a small roof (crux) to a finish up an offwidth.

㉔ The Boodler 60' 5.9
Todd Swain, Patty Gill, Theresa Krolak. January 1999.
Single rack to 3".
Start in the alcove beside Small Claims, just as the ledge fizzles out. Climb an awkward, left-leaning break to an anchor.

To the left of The Boodler, the ledge fizzles out and reappears 70' to the west. To reach the next routes, scramble down from the vicinity of Penny Lane and walk underneath the cliff for about 150' until it is easy to scramble back up onto the ledge.

The next route starts at the right end of this ledge, below a large left-facing corner.

㉕ Carpetbagger 60' 5.6+
Todd Swain, Winston Farrar, Jake Burkey. January 1999.
Single rack to 3".
Climb the huge corner to a ledge with an anchor.

㉖ Mugwump 50' 5.10b (Tr.)
Start 10' to the left of Carpetbagger. Step off a boulder and climb the steep, pink bulge to reach easier rock which is followed to the shared anchor.

㉗ The Haj 70' 5.9
Winston Farrar, Todd Swain, Jake Burkey. January 1999.
Single rack to 2.5".
This route starts 30' left of Carpetbagger, at the left end of a pink overhang just above the ledge. It climbs a finger crack in the back of a tight, varnished corner to easier cracks, which are followed to the communal anchor.

㉘ Sir Climbalot 70' 5.7
Winston Farrar, Todd Swain, Jake Burkey. January 1999.
Single rack to 3".
Immediately to the left of The Haj is another, lower-angled corner. Climb the corner to a shared anchor.

㉙ The Route to Mecca 70' 5.7
Todd Swain, Winston Farrar, Jake Burkey. January 1999.
Single rack to 2".
Start 10' to the left of the previous route. Follow a varnished crack over a bulge to a low-angled, left-facing corner. Climb this corner and continue up easy ground to the shared anchor.

㉚ Treacherous Journey 70' 5.9
Todd Swain, Jake Burkey. January 1999.
Single rack to 2.5".
The start of this route is loose and serious. Start 10' to the left of the previous route. Climb a corner for 20' then follow an obvious crack to its end. Continue up to join the previous route just below the top.

The following route is 400 yards to the west of the last climbs on Moderate Mecca on a flat, orange wall on the north side of the wash.

Save it for a Rainy Day 50' 5.12a/b
Joseph Smith. January 24, 2011.
Single rack to 3".
Climb straight up the converging crack system to an easier finish and an anchor at the top.

Jabba The Hut Rock

This is the lowest cliffband, about 200' up the hillside and 100 yards to the west of the parking area.

Approach: From the Red Springs parking area, scramble straight up the rocky hillside to the base of the wall. The routes are described from left to right. 5 minutes.

At the left end of the wall is a steep slab split by an attractive finger crack.

❶ Hans Soloing 70' 5.4

Climb the left edge of the slab. It is possible to start this route by bouldering up through the varnish patch (5.8).

❷ Aliens Have Landed 70' 5.10a *

Single rack to 2.5", double small and medium wires.

Climb the nice crack in the center of the slab. The crux is getting established over a small roof at the start.

❸ Carrie Fissure 70' 5.8

Single rack to 2.5".

Start 10' to the right of the previous route. Climb a short right-facing corner capped by a roof. Continue up the crack above. When it ends, climb up then move right to a flake in the right edge of the wall. Follow this to the top.

The next routes are 100' to the right, in the center of the cliff.

❹ Obie-One Keone 70' 5.8

Chis Gill, Keone Kim. September 1998.
Single rack to 1.25", Rp's.

This is a serious route with little in the way of worthwhile protection and fragile rock. Start at the base of the crack of Shallow Fried Cracken. Scramble up and left on a big flake to a ledge at 20'. Boulder up the varnished wall (crux) above to a scoop. From the top of the scoop traverse up and right to join the last few feet of the Shallow Fried Cracken.

❺ Shallow Fried Cracken 70' 5.9

Larry Ferber, Leslie Tarleton. November 1991.
Single rack to 1.75".

Climb a thin seam in a steep slab in the center of the crag. With work this route can be adequately protected, but it's a challenging lead nevertheless.

❻ Gold Bikini 80' 5.10a

Todd Swain, Patty Gill. November 1998.
Single rack to 3".

Start 30' to the right of the previous route. Climb a steep start to a bolt. Step left to twin cracks, which lead into a left-facing corner. Follow the corner to the top.

Coco Crag

This is the name of the nicely-varnished walls about 100 yards up and right from Jabba the Hut Rock. The wall faces almost due north and gets very little sun. The cliff is reached by scrambling up the gully from the right edge of Jabba The Hut Rock. The routes are described from left to right as you reach them going up the gully.

The most obvious feature of the wall is a huge chimney, which separates a large pinnacle from the main mass of the buttress.

Hidden Meaning 90' 5.8 (Tr.)

Randal Grandstaff, Danny Rider. 1980's.

This route climbs the face on the right, inside the chimney.

The next routes climb very nice rock up the varnished face to the right of the huge chimney.

❶ Cocopuss 60' 5.10b **
Pier Locatelli, Randy Marsh. 1996.
The route on the left. It climbs the arete immediately to the right of the chimney (9 b's).

❷ Snagglepuss 80' 5.11a
The nicely-varnished face to the right of Cocopuss. After a contrived start, the route gains independence with height (8 b's).

❸ Stupid Cat 55' 5.10d *
Pier Locatelli, Randy Marsh. 1996.
The route on the right (8 b's).

❹ Coco Puffs 90' 5.9
Start to the right of Stupid Cat and left of Fontanar De Roja. Climb the crack left of Fontanar to the alcove of that route, then step left and continue up the face (3 b's) to an anchor.

❺ Fontanar de Rojo 160' 5.8
Single rack to 4", double 2.5"- 4".
Start 45' uphill from the chimney at a pink flake. Climb the pink flake to the ledge at 20'. Continue up the varnished corner above, to its top. Move right past a bush and follow a gully to the top.

❻ Ruta de Roja 160' 5.7
Single rack to 4", double 2.5"- 4".
Follow Fontanar de Rojo to the ledge at the top of the white flake. Step right to an obvious, varnished finger crack. Climb the crack and continue to the base of a gully which leads to the top. Descend to the right.

❼ Moon Where the Wind Blows 65' 5.9
Jonathan O'Brien, Jasmine Farro, Dustin Yager. Spring 2013.
Start 10' right of Fontanar de Rojo, below a short right-leaning scoop/corner. Climb the corner on slippery, varnished rock then continue up the face on better holds to a delicate move just below the anchor (8 b's).

❽ Adventure Guppies 120 5.8+
Jonathan O'Brien. May 25, 2010.
This route can be led as one long pitch or split into two shorter pitches. Start below the varnished right arete of the buttress, about 20' right of Fontanar de Rojo. Climb the arete, past a midway anchor on a ledge, to another anchor at the top (15 b's). One rap with a single 70m rope, 2 raps with a 60m rope.

Red Springs Rock

Above the level of Jabba the Hut Rock is a large terrace which slants up to the south. The following routes are on the buttresses above the right end of the terrace.

Approach: Scramble up the steep hillside, passing either side of Jabba The Hut Rock to get onto the terrace. 10 minutes.

Above the right end of the terrace is an obvious pinnacle. The next routes are on the first fin of rock to the left of the pinnacle.

❶ Attack Dogs 90' 5.10d
Dave Melchior. 1998.
Climb up a steep corner on the prow of the fin. Continue up the face just left of the arete, to the anchor of the next route (5 b's).

❷ Welcome to N.I.M.B.Y. Town 90' 5.8
Mark Limage, Dave Melchior. November 1998.
This route starts at the base of the bushy corner on the left side of the fin. Climb up the wall to the right of the corner, following right-facing flakes (4 b's) to an anchor.

❸ Flying Pumpkin 90' 5.9
Randal Grandstaff, Danny Rider. October 1981.
Start at the base of the bushy corner to the left of the fin. Climb a short distance up the corner then head up and left across the varnished face to white rock which is followed up and right to the top.

The next feature to the left is a very impressive arete with a varnished corner to its left.

❹ Eggs Over Sleazy 60' 5.12a *
Chris Weidner. January 23, 2013.
This route climbs the center of the varnished face to the right of the impressive arete. From the base of Classic Corner, scramble up and right onto a block below the first bolt. Climb straight up the face. The start is bouldery and the climbing thin throughout (8 b's).

❺ Classic Corner 150' 5.8 **
Single rack to 2.5".
Climb the beautiful, varnished corner, branching left at the top. Descend down the gully to the left of the formation.

❻ Badger's Buttress 100' 5.6
Todd Swain, Donette Swain, Paul Ross, Marea Ross. November 1999.
Single rack to 2.5".
This route climbs the arete to the left of Classic Corner. Start in a short gully around to the left of the arete. Traverse right onto the arete, which is climbed to the top.

The next routes are on an impressive bulging buttress, about 150 feet to the left of the Classic Corner area. To descend from the top of the buttress, scramble to the west and go down the descent gully of Classic Corner. On the right side of the buttress is a big slab topped by a steeper headwall.

❼ Mavericks 95' 5.11d
Killis Howard, Nathan Petrosian, Kyle Jackson. April 2014.
Start below the right side of the slab, about 10' left of the crack system in the right edge of the buttress. Pull up onto a black slab and climb up to and over a short headwall. Continue up and left to a crack system which splits the upper headwall. Climb this crack to an anchor at the top (13 b's).

❽ Ripcurl 110' 5.11a
Killis Howard, Nathan Petrosian, Kyle Jackson. April 2014.
Single rack to 1" including ballnutz.
Start below a wide, right-facing layback flake on the left side of the slab. Layback the flake (b) then move left along its top (2 b's). Pull over the short headwall to gain the higher slab then move right to a thin crack. Climb the thin crack to the base of a groove in the left edge of the upper headwall. Climb the groove (thread) to its capping roof, then exit right (b) and climb the varnished face (2 b's) to an anchor at the top.

❾ Rocky Road 120' 5.10a
Single rack to 5", double 3"-5".
This route climbs the corner to the right of the bulging buttress. Start on some pink boulders 10' up and right of the very toe of the buttress. Climb a short, pink corner, past an awkward bulge, and continue up the crack to a ledge. Follow the fist crack above, over the bulge, and up the lower-angled corner to some blocks at the top. Quite a pure crack for Red Rocks.

The next four routes start on a ledge 50' up Rocky Road, which can be reached either by starting up Rocky Road, or scrambling around from the right.

❿ Love on the Rocks 60' 5.12c
Mike Tupper. 1986.
1.25" cam before the first bolt.
A contrived route up the smooth, varnished face to the right of Allied Forces (5 b's).

⓫ Allied Forces 60' 5.11a *
Bob Finlay, Paul Van Betten. 1986.
Double rack to 5".
On the north face of the buttress is an impressive flare, formed by the left side of a huge flake. A good route, awkward, sustained and strenuous. Unfortunately, several of the bolts on Contempt of Court are close enough to be clipped, robbing this stout trad route of some of its oomph.

⓬ Contempt of Court 90' 5.12a
Mike Tupper. 1986.
1.75"- 2.5" cams for the anchor, 1.25" cam before the first bolt.
This route starts at the base of Allied Forces and climbs the arete to its left. Very contrived in the lower part of the route, since you are often only a couple of feet to the left of Allied Forces. Higher up, the route heads left over a roof and climbs the wall to the top (9 b's).

⓭ Hook Line and Sinker 130' 5.13a
Tom Moulin, Brian Bowman. November 2, 2010.
This route climbs straight up the front face of the buttress; long, steep and very pumpy. Start up the initial corner of Rocky Road then exit out left to a ledge below the prow (A few cams to 2" required to protect this section). Follow the bolts up and left to an anchor at the top of the prow (10 b's).

⓮ Fine Line 140' 5.12c
Spencer McCroskey. Winter 2015.
Start at the very toe of the buttress on the left side of the smooth, red wall. Climb the arete, then pull onto the easier face and climb up and right to the base of a steep corner in the upper buttress. Climb the corner to a big, flat hold and a bolt at its top. Finish up and left on a steep, fingery wall (14 b's).

The next two routes climb a pair of cracks in the back of the corner to the left of the buttress. They are reached by scrambling up 50' to an obvious ledge .

Habeas Corpus 40' 5.10b
Climb the wide crack on the right.

⓯ Haberdasher 40' 5.10d
The left hand route climbs a short, overhanging corner.

The next route climbs a thin seam up the front of the next buttress to the left.

⓰ Boulder Dash 100' 5.11b
David Parker, Raquel Speers. September 1994.
Make a burly pull over the initial bulge then climb the slabby face to a steep headwall. Follow the thin seam up the headwall to an anchor (7 b's).

⓱ The Slab Dance 100' 5.12a
Spencer McCroskey. Winter 2015.
Start on a block just left of Boulder Dash. Thin and sustained towards the top. Pull over the initial bulge and climb straight up the tall face, staying just to the right of the big, rounded prow. After the last bolt, move right to reach the anchor of Boulder Dash (8 b's).

The next route climbs the slabby pink arete on the left edge of the next buttress to the left.

Red Stringer 85' 5.10b
A few cams & wires to 1".
Climb the rounded pink arete to a small ramp (7 b's). Follow the ramp up and left to an anchor in a right-facing corner.

100 feet higher up the terrace is a buttress with an obvious crooked crack on its darkly-varnished north face.

Black Licorice 120' 5.9
Todd Swain, Donette Swain, Paul Ross, Marea Ross. November 1999. Single rack to 1.75".
Start 40' to the right of the varnished buttress and just to the right of a low ceiling. Climb to a bolt at the base of a flake which is followed to a ledge. Climb the wall above the ledge (b) pulling over a bulge at its top (b). Finish on a ledge with a tree for rapping.

Red Vines 120' 5.8
Paul Ross, Marea Ross, Todd Swain, Donette Swain. November 1999. Single rack to 5".
Start 10' to the left of the previous route, below a nice hand crack above a tree. Climb the crack to the rap tree.

Shit Howdy

Risk Brothers Roof

Riding Hood Wall

Cannibal Crag

Ranch Hands Crag

Cannibal Crag

This cliff has easy access and a good spread of grades. The southeast face of the formation gets sun until early afternoon. The northwest face only gets a little sun, in the afternoon.

Approach: From the Red Spring Parking Area, follow a trail underneath the hillside for 300 yards. Cannibal Crag is the obvious prow a few yards left of the trail. 5 minutes.

Cannibal Crag - East Face

The routes on the southeast face are described first, going from left to right. The first route starts a few feet to the right of the saddle that connects Cannibal Crag to the main hillside.

1 Maneater 25' 5.12a
Dan McQuade. Spring 1992.
The short, steep wall at the left end of the east face (4 b's).

2 Wonderstuff 30' 5.12d **
Paul Van Betten, Richard Harrison, Sal Mamusia. July 1991.
The next route to the right has some big moves, but is low in the grade (4 b's).

3 New Wave Hookers 35' 5.12c ***
Paul Van Betten, Richard Harrison, Sal Mamusia. July 1991.
An excellent route. Start as for Wonderstuff, but traverse right on a sloping shelf and continue up the bulging wall on sloping horizontals (4 b's).

4 Fear this Sport 30' 5.12c *
Paul Van Betten, Richard Harrison, Sal Mamusia. July 1991.
Start 10' down the hill to the right of the previous route. Bouldery moves at the start and finish (4 b's).

5 Nipple Fish 30' 5.12d
Mike Moore. Fall 2007.
Start 10' down and right of Fear this Sport. Stick clip the first bolt. A hard boulder problem start leads to much easier climbing up and left to the anchor of the previous route (4 b's).

6 Caliban 80' 5.8 +
Sal Mamusia, Paul Van Betten. 1993.
Start below the slab to the right of the steep wall at the left end of the southeast face. Climb the steep start to a bolt. Move

awkwardly right then step up and traverse back left to the second bolt. Continue up the slab past another bolt to the anchor.

7 Cannibal Crack 90' 5.4
The obvious left-leaning crack in the center of the east face is climbed to the anchor of Caliban.

8 Baseboy 60' 5.10d
Paul Van Betten, Richard Harrison, Sal Mamusia. August 1991.
Start at the base of Cannibal Crack. Climb Cannibal Crack for 20' then move up onto the wall on the right, traverse right then climb straight up to an anchor (4 b's).

9 Baseboy Direct 60' 5.11a **
Starting just to the right of Cannibal Crack, climb straight up to join the upper part of Baseboy (7 b's).

10 Save the Heart to Eat Later 60' 5.12a **
Sal Mamusia, R. Harrison, Paul Van Betten, Shelby Shelton. August 1991.
Climb the face to the right of Baseboy Direct. A stout route for the grade; fingery, with a technical crux up high.

11 Pickled 50' 5.11c *
Paul Van Betten, Richard Harrison, Sal Mamusia. August 1991.
This route starts up the previous route, then zig-zags up the wall on the right and finishes with a move right to the anchor.

12 Caustic 50' 5.11b ***
P. Van Betten, Dan Kruleski, S. Shelton, R. Harrison, S. Mamusia. 1991.
This route climbs the right arete of the southeast face, steep and off-balance but low in the grade. A low bolt allows the arete to be climbed directly; if the bolt is missing traverse in from the right to reach the arete (4 b's).

The following routes are on the northwest face of the formation. They are described from left to right.

⑬ Have a Beer with Fear 30' 5.11c *

Richard Harrison, Paul Van Betten. August 1992.

This route climbs the arete on the left edge of the wall (4 b's).

⑭ Fear This 30' 5.11d

Sal Mamusia, Paul Van Betten. September 1992.

Climb the wall just to the right of the previous route, past a very bouldery crux (3 b's).

⑮ Elbows of Mac and Ronnie 45' 5.11b

Todd Swain. June 1992.

Start 10' to the right of the previous route. Climb straight up to the top end of a right-leaning footledge. Step up onto the footledge and make a tricky, reachy sequence of moves over the bulge to much easier climbing. Finish up and right to an anchor (4 b's).

⑯ What's Eating You? 45' 5.10a *

Todd Swain, Randy Schenkel, Andy Schenkel. June 1992.

Start 10' to the right of the previous route. Climb a thin, left-facing flake which leads over a bulge to easier climbing (3 b's) and the anchor.

⑰ A Man in Every Pot 40' 5.8+ *

Debbie Brenchley, Todd Swain. June 1992.

Start on top of a large flake leaning against the wall. Climb straight up the wall to an anchor (3 b's).

⑱ Mac and Ronnie in Cheese 40' 5.9+

Todd Swain, Debbie Brenchley. June 1992.

Start a few feet to the right of the flake in a sandy flat spot. Climb straight up to an anchor (4 b's).

⑲ Ma and Pa in Kettle 50' 5.7

Todd Swain, Randy Schenkel, Andy Schenkel. June 1992.

Climb a tiny, varnished left-facing corner at the right end of the wall and continue up the face above (4 b's) to the top.

Cannibal Crag - West Face

The next routes are on the largest chunk of rock several hundred feet above, and a little to the west of Cannibal Crag.

Shit Howdy 50' 5.10d

Paul Van Betten, Nick Nordblom. 1986.
Single rack to 2.5", double 0.4"-0.75".

On the right side of the formation is a thin crack which goes up 15' then diagonals sharply to the right. Climb the crack.

Direct Finish 50' 5.10d

Climb the initial (crux) crack of Shit Howdy and go straight up the wall above (3 b's) to the top.

Powerfully Stupid 50' 5.11d

Richard Harrison, Michelle Locatelli. 2009.

Zig-zag up the overhanging rock on the north side of the formation.

The next two routes are on a sharply overhanging block at the top of the hill roughly halfway between Cannibal Crag and Ranch Hands Crag. A long scramble up a gully leads to the cliff. In the center of the cliff is an impressive roof crack.

Risk Brothers Roof 60' 5.11a **

Paul Van Betten, Sal Mamusia, Richard Harrison. Winter 85/86.
Single rack to 3", double 1.75"- 2.5".

A fun roof problem. Climb a steep finger crack to the roof, then jam out left to an awkward pull over the lip. There is a new anchor at the left end of the next roof.

Zona Rosa 40' 5.9

Robert Finlay. 1986.

Start in the corridor behind the formation. Climb a corner to a pink offwidth.

Ranch Hands Crag

This crag has some decent climbing on its east face. The recent addition of a couple of anchors almost brings some of these routes into the sport category, although most climbers will still want to bring a few wires and small cams for the finishes. The wall faces straight east, getting sun until early afternoon.

Approach: From the Red Springs parking area, follow a trail that heads west underneath the hillside. After passing Cannibal Crag at 300 yards, Ranch Hands is the next wall on the left, another 400 yards down the trail. 10 minutes.
The routes are described from left to right, starting at the left end of the east face of the formation.

On the left side of the wall is a huge roof.

❶ Payless Cashways 70' 5.11a
R. Harrison, Sal Mamusia, Paul Van Betten, S. Shelton. June 1991.
Start just right of the roof, climb the pillar between two large scoops and continue up the face to an anchor (5 b's).

❷ Spanky 65' 5.11a
R. Harrison, Sal Mamusia, Paul Van Betten, Shelby Shelton. June 1991.
Start 10' to the right of the previous route, at the left edge of a slabby platform underneath the wall. Climb the wall, passing just right of a large scoop, then continue up the face to a steep, thin crack which is followed to an anchor (4 b's).

❸ Mexican Secret Agent Man 65' 5.11b
Paul Van Betten, Richard Harrison. July 1991.
Start 5' to the right of Spanky, at a small, right-facing flake. Climb up and slightly right to some short, varnished cracks which are followed to an anchor (5 b's).

❹ Swilderness Experience 65' 5.12a
Paul Van Betten, Richard Harrison, Shelby Shelton. July 1991.
Start 10' to the right of the previous route. Traverse right then climb straight up the wall (5 b's). From the last bolt move right then back left to a thin seam which is followed to an anchor.

❺ Swilderness Permit 70' 5.12c
Sal Mamusia, Richard Harrison, Paul Van Betten. July 1991.
This route starts at the base of the east face, behind a bush. Follow a line of pockets, up a brown bulge and the wall above, to an undercling at 25'. Move right and make a precarious pull onto the slab above which leads more easily to the top (7 b's).

❻ Roman Meil 70' 5.11b (Tr.)
Todd Swain. December 1994.
Toprope the face 15' to the right of the previous route.

❼ Roman Hands 150' 5.4
Start on the north side of the formation and climb up and left on slabby rock, passing to the left of the steep wall at the top of the face.

The next three routes climb the overhanging block at the top of the north face of the formation. It is best to climb Roman Hands and set up a belay at the base of the block for these routes.

❽ Jack Officers 35' 5.12b
Paul Van Betten, Sal Mamusia, Richard Harrison. April 1991.
Climb the thin seam on the left side of the block (3 b's).

❾ Ranch Hands 40' 5.12c
Richard Harrison, Paul Van Betten, Sal Mamusia, Bob Conz. April 1991.
Climb up and right across the face of the block to an anchor (4 b's).

❿ Blood Stains 45' 5.10c
Richard Harrison, Paul Van Betten, Sal Mamusia. September 1990.
A serious and impressive route for the grade. From the belay, move right and climb a loose, flaky crack to a scary, overhanging block. Pull over the dangerous block and climb the steep rounded arete above (b) to another overhang. Go over this and move left to the anchor of Ranch Hands.

Big Bad Wolf, pitch 3. Page 451.

The Back Forty

This is a small, northeast-facing wall on the right side of a narrow gully about 80 yards beyond (west) of Ranch Hands Cliff. The wall gets sun for a few hours in the morning, but is generally shady. The rock is quite loose and flaky.

The routes are described from right to left.

❶ Gettin' Mavericky 65' 5.9
Michelle Locatelli, Richard and Lisa Harrison. 2009.
This route climbs the right arete of the broad pillar on the north side of the formation. Fun climbing up cream-colored, lower-angled rock (4 b's).

❷ P.A.L.S 50' 5.8
Michelle Locatelli, Richard and Lisa Harrison. 2009.
Start just inside the entrance to the raised corridor on the left side of the formation. After a steep pull on varnished crimps, climb the low-angled arete to the anchor of the previous route (4 b's).

❸ The Whistleblower 60' 5.10c
Michelle Locatelli, Richard and Lisa Harrison. 2009.
Start 30' left of the previous route. Climb past the left side of a big scoop then continue up the flaky face on edges and sidepulls. Finish up a small headwall to anchors (7 b's).

❹ It's an F'ing Nightmare 50' 5.11c
Richard and Lisa Harrison. 2009.
Start just left of the previous route. Climb past a bolt to a low-angled scoop/corner (optional small gear). Continue up the corner (3 b's) to a move left (crux). Continue to the anchors.

❺ Pandas Aren't Bears 50' 5.12a
Michelle Locatelli, Richard and Lisa Harrison. 2009.
This is the last route on the right side of the gully. Follow the left arete of the big scoop/corner then continue more easily to the anchor of the previous route. It's best to preclip the first bolt, also the proximity of a fin behind the route means that an attentive belay is required (8 b's).

Approach: From Ranch Hands Cliff, continue up the main drainage for around 80 yards to a narrow gully cutting into the rocks on the left. Scramble 150' up the gully to a small wall on its right hand side. 15 minutes.

Riding Hood Wall

This is the large, slabby buttress a couple of hundred feet above Ranch Hands Crag. It faces northeast, but is low-angled enough that it gets sun till midday or even later in the spring.

Approach: From the Red Springs parking area follow a trail that heads west underneath the hillside. After passing Cannibal Crag at 300 yards, Ranch Hands is the next wall on the left, another 400 yards down the trail. Scramble up a gully half way between Cannibal Crag and Ranch Hands. After a few hundred feet in the gully traverse out right, following slabs and ledges up and right to the base of the wall. 15 minutes.

Descent: Depending on which route you are doing, it is possible to descend on either side of the formation.

The routes are described from left to right.

❶ Riding Hood 300' 5.8+
John Williamson, Bob Logerquist. September 1970.
Single rack to 5".
High on the left side of the formation is a large, varnished corner. From the base of Physical Graffiti, scramble up and left to the base of the corner.

1. 100' 5.6 Climb the easy chimney and belay at a slung chockstone.
2. 100' 5.8+ Climb the right-facing corner above, past an awkward and ill-protected wide section to easier ground.
3. 100' 5.4 Continue up easy rock to the top.

❷ Big Bad Wolf 220' 5.9 ★★
L. Gallia, E. Allen, D. Young. 2011.
Big Bad Wolf is a very enjoyable 3-pitch sport route which climbs straight up the open face 30' left of Physical Graffiti. Scramble up the gully that leads to Riding Hood for about 20'. The route starts on a sloping ledge on top of a block.
1. 70' 5.9 Climb straight up vertical, varnished rock on good holds to reach the anchor (8 b's).
2. 80' 5.8 Climb the flaky slab, past a thin crux at mid-height. Continue to an anchor (8 b's).
3. 70' 5.8 Continue up the slab, which soon steepens to vertical. Good holds lead up the steep rock to the anchors (8 b's). Either make three raps to the ground from here with a single 60m rope or...
4. 30' 5.0 Continue up the easy slab ((2 b's) to an anchor on the walkoff ledge.

Riding Hood Wall

Scramble East into the descent gully.

60' rap into the descent gully.

5.7+

Descent: Walk off to the southeast (climbers' left) to a gully with a tree. Go down the gully.

❸ Physical Graffiti 310' 5.6 ***

Jon Martinet, Randal Grandstaff, Scott Gordon. 1973.
Single rack to 3", double 0.75"- 1.75".

A beautiful moderate route. The route starts towards the left end of the formation, at a steep, varnished corner which slants up to the right; not to be confused with steeper corners further to the right.

1. 130' 5.6 Climb the corner and the right-leaning crack above to an anchor.

2. 180' 5.6 Step right and climb the long crack system to the top of the formation.

Descent: From the belay at the top of the route, go up then around to the right for 30' where there is an anchor beside a sloping ledge on the gully wall. A single rope rappel leads down into the gully. Scramble down the gully and back east to the base of the route.

❹ Over the Hill to Grandmother's House 120' 5.9+ *

Bob Logerquist, John Williamson. September 1970.
Single rack to 3".

60' to the right of Physical Graffiti, there is a roof at the base of the cliff. This route climbs the tight corner which goes through the left end of the roof and continues up the crack system to the anchor of Physical Graffiti.

Variation: The crack on the right side of the roof can also be climbed. 5.9+.

❺ Li'l Red 150' 5.9

Single rack to 3".

Start below a right-leaning crack on the right side of the wall. The crux moves involve climbing the runout, varnished face to the crack. Once the crack is reached it is followed up and right to a belay in the gully.

❺ₐ Variation: About 70' up the route, face climb across to a long crack system on the left, which is followed to the top.

The Fox

This cliff has a collection of burly cracks and a couple of random sport routes. It faces north and gets almost no sun at any time of year.

Approach: From the Red Springs parking area, follow a trail that heads west underneath the hillside. After passing Cannibal Crag at 300 yards, Ranch Hands is the next wall on the left, another 400 yards down the trail. After another 250 yards the trail passes right underneath Dickies Cliff. If you look up the hillside from a point halfway between Ranch Hands Crag and Dickies Cliff, you will see a clean-cut, right-facing corner, slightly below the crest of the hill. A long, easy gully leads straight up to the base of the corner. 20 minutes.

Descent: Scramble around the east side of the cliff.

❶ The Fox 140' 5.10d ***
John Williamson, Bob Logerquist. 1970.
Single rack to 6", double 2"-6".
How did a beautiful Indian Creek-style corner end up in the Calico Hills? The big right-facing corner on the left side of the cliff is one of the best crack climbs of its grade in Red Rocks. The crack gradually widens from tips to offwidth, but thankfully as the crack becomes wide, face holds start to appear.

❷ Laugh with the Sinners 120' 5.10d
Celin Serbo, Chris Weidner. February 1, 2013.
Single rack to 5", double 1.25"- 3".
Start just to the right of the Fox.
1. 60' 5.7 Follow a right-arching crack to a belay below a large left-facing corner.
2. 60' 5.10d The corner is initially loose and blocky, but soon gets steep and smooth. Battle up the wide corner/crack to the top. 2"- 4" cams for an anchor under a big boulder.

To the right of the previous route is a sharp arete. Right again is another very steep corner/crack.

❸ Tooth Decay 80' 5.11b
Larry Scritchfield, Andy Norman. 1987.
Single rack to 3", double 4"- 6".
This feature has some helpful holds which keep the grade more reasonable than its appearance would suggest. Start about 100' to the right of The Fox, at the base of a chimney leading to an offwidth roof in a large, right-facing corner.
1. 40' 5.7 Squirm up a tight chimney to a small pedestal on a slab below the roof. Best to belay here because of a rope-jamming constriction at the top of the chimney (Small cams and nuts for the anchor).
2. 40' 5.11b Go up the dirty slab to the very steep offwidth. Contort out the short-but-memorable crack to the top.

❹ Bathe Hah and Bring Hah to Me 80' 5.10b
Chris Weidner, Celin Serbo. February 1, 2013.
Single rack to 5", double 1"- 2".
To the right of the previous route is a huge left-facing corner blocked by a big roof. Climb a varnished corner and dirty slab to beneath the large roof. Jam and undercling out the roof and up to the top.

The next two routes start level with the top of the Fox but a little to the west. They face north and are reached by heading up the gully to the right of the Fox. About 200' up the gully, exit out right to reach a nice platform at the base of a bulging wall.

🔴 Fox Hunt 40' 5.11b
The route on the left (5 b's).

🔴 Fox Trot 40' 5.11d
The route on the right (5 b's).

Dickies Cliff

This wall has some good rock on the harder routes, and a couple of fun, easier climbs. It faces almost straight north and only gets sun for a couple of hours in the morning.

Approach: From the Red Springs parking area follow a trail that heads west underneath the hillside. After passing Cannibal Crag at 300 yards, Ranch Hands is the next wall on the left, another 400 yards down the trail. After another 250 yards the trail passes right underneath Dickies Cliff. 15 minutes.

Descent: Scramble down the steep gully between Dickies and Gnat Man Cliff (4th class in a few spots).

The routes are described from left to right.

On the left side of the wall is a gully, blocked by a large boulder at its base.

❶ Seams Like a Butt 70' 5.7 (Tr.)
Mark Limage. 1997.
Use a bolted anchor to climb the face 10' left of Gigantor. This has been led, but it's flaky enough to be not worth the risk.

❷ Gigantor 80' 5.10c
R. Harrison, Paul Van Betten, W. Broussard, Mike Forkash. July 1991.
Single rack to 1".
Start on top of the boulder and hand traverse right (2 b's). Climb straight up the wall above (b) and continue with easier runout climbing to the top.

❸ Guys and Ghouls 100' 5.6
Donette Swain, Todd Swain, George Reid, Catriona Reid. Oct. 1994.
Single rack to 5".

In the middle of the wall is a large gully. Climb a series of short cracks up to the gully which is followed to the top.

The central feature of the crag is a nice, varnished wall with a two foot roof at 15'.

❹ Boobytrap 120' 5.12c
Sal Mamusia, Paul Van Betten. July 1991.
Climb straight up the varnished wall passing just to the left of the roof. Thin, bouldery climbing on nice rock (5 b's). Finish up an easy crack.

❺ Stukas Over Disneyland 120' 5.12b *
Paul Van Betten, Richard Harrison. July 1991.
Double rack to 1", Rp's.
Start below the right end of the roof. Climb a thin slab to the roof (2 b's) and pull over to reach nice, varnished cracks which lead up and left. Follow an easier crack back right then continue up another crack to the top.

❻ Lancaster Levels Luxor 100' 5.9+
George Reid, Todd Swain, Donette Swain. October 1994.
Single rack to 4".
This route climbs the wide crack/groove system on the right side of the crag, past an awkward bulge at 15'.

❼ Monster Island 80' 5.11b
Paul Van Betten, Sal Mamusia. July 1991.
Follow the previous route to the bulge at 15'. Pull up and right across the bulge to reach a thin crack, which is followed to its end. Easier climbing leads to the top (3 b's).

Gnat Man Crag

This is the cliff immediately above, and slightly to the right of Dickies Cliff. It has some good, moderate crack climbing. It faces almost straight north and only gets sun for a couple of hours in the morning.

Approach: Scramble up 100' of easy rock on the right side of Dickies Cliff to reach the base of the wall. 15 minutes.

Descent: Scramble down the steep gully on the right (west) side of the cliff (4th class in a few spots).

❽ Day of the Jackholes 80' 5.9+
Mark Limage, Andy Carson, Andrew Fulton. 1997.
Start in the chimney at the left edge of the wall. Climb a corner/crack, over a couple of roofs, and continue up to an anchor at the top.

❾ P-Coat Junction 120' 5.9
Todd Swain, Donette Swain. December 1994.
Single rack to 4".
Start about 20' to the left of the obvious central crack system. Climb twin cracks up a short, steep wall to reach a big, right-facing flake. At the top of the flake move right and climb up to a right-leaning corner which is climbed to the top.

❿ P-Coat Sleeve 120' 5.10a *
Paul Van Betten, Sal Mamusia. November 1991.
Single rack to 2".
Start 10' left of the central corner. Make a couple of stiff pulls

up a nice, varnished finger crack. Continue up the crack system for 40' then move right and follow the next route to the top.

⓫ Ghouls Just Wanna Have Fun 120' 5.7 **
Donette Swain, Catriona Reid. October 1994.
Single rack to 3".
Climb the central crack system to the top.

⓬ Gnat Man on Ranch Hands 100' 5.11b
Paul Van Betten, Sal Mamusia. November 1991.
Start up the steep scoop in the right wall of the previous route and climb the strenuous wall above, to finish up easier slabs (5 b's, optional Tcu above the first bolt).

⓭ Knock the Bottom Out of It 100' 5.10a
Paul Van Betten, Sal Mamusia. November 1991.
Single rack to 2.5".
Start below a patch of varnish at the base of the rounded arete to the right of Ghouls Just Wanna Have Fun. Climb the slabby wall to the top (4 b's).

⓮ Bottoms Up 100' 5.7 **
George Reid, C. Reid, Todd Swain, Donette Swain. October 1994.
Single rack to 3".
Climb the corner 10' to the right of the previous route. When the crack ends at 40' move left around a bulge, then climb up to a right-leaning flake which is followed to the top.

The Fox

Gnat Man Crag

Dickies Cliff

Cowlick Crag

This is the small, red slab directly opposite Dickies Cliff. The cliff faces straight south and is very sheltered, a good choice for a cold and/or windy day. There are several toprope anchors on either side of the established routes. Generally these anchors are easy to reach from the top of the cliff. The top-rope routes are all in the 5.5 to 5.8 range.

Approach: The cliff is best approached from the parking area at the last 90° turn in the road. From here walk up the gravel road beside the wash then follow a trail into the big drainage. The crag is very low on the right, about 100 yards after entering the main drainage. 15 minutes.

The two anchors on the left side of the crag are for two toprope routes in the 5.5/5.6 range. There is an anchor at the very

top of the formation which can be used to rap down to set up the ropes. The anchor to the left of Cow Lick Co. is for a 5.8 toprope through the middle of the slanting roof.

❶ Cow Lick Co. 50' 5.7 *
Todd Swain, Donette Swain, Mike Dimitri. November 1993.
The route on the left (4 b's).

❷ Flying Chuckwalla 45' 5.7
Mark Limage, Dave Melchior. 2000.
The route on the right, which climbs a loose seam (4 b's).

The anchor to the right of the anchor of Flying Chuckwalla is for a 5.7 toprope route. And on top of a little pillar on the right hand side of the cliff is another anchor for a pair of 5.6/7 toprope routes.

Happy Acres

This is the large, varnished slab at the far west end of the Red Springs hillside, just slightly below the top of the gully, on the left. This is a good wall for moderate routes with good climbing and a nice, exposed situation at the top of the Calico Hills. Many of these routes have seen very few ascents over the years, so crowds are not likely to be a problem, but you can expect a few fragile edges.
The wall faces northeast and is in a very windy location.

Approach: From the Red Springs parking area follow the trail that leads west underneath the hillside for 1000 yards. After

passing the Dickies Cliff, the trail continues up the left side of the broad, rocky gully that leads in the direction of the Second Pullout on the loop road (if you keep going you'll walk past The Sandbox, Black Corridor etc.) The cliff is on the left 500 yards up the gully. 25 minutes.

Descent: From the top of the wall, traverse west along the summit ridge for 100 yards then head north down a steep, bushy gully. Surprisingly fast and easy. 20 minutes. It is also possible to rap the cliff from the last anchor of Tres Hombres if you can find it.

The first route is on the far left side of the wall.

❶ Tres Hombres 270' 5.11a

D. Rider, B. Conz, L. Saca. February 27, 2009.

A three pitch route which is now fully bolted. It climbs a series of nicely-varnished walls separated by good ledges. Start directly below a small pine tree on a ledge at the top of pitch 1.

1. 115' 5.11a Sustained, technical face climbing (b's) leads to an anchor on the ledge with the tree.

2. 115' 5.11b Head up the black wall, past a low crux, to a prominent right-facing corner. Climb the corner (optional 1" to 1.25" cam) pulling over a small roof at its top to a ledge and anchor.

3. 40' 5.9+ Continue up the wall (b's) to an anchor at the top.

Descent: Three raps with a 70m rope.

The next three routes climb the tall, varnished slab to the left of the huge, right-facing corner/gully in the middle of the wall.

❷ Spontaneous Enjoyment 260' 5.9 *

Paul Van Betten, Nick Nordblom. 1984.
Single rack to 4".

Begin 30' left of Geriatric Therapy on a clean ledge 10' up.

1. 60' 5.8 Climb the scary face to an anchor on a ledge.

2. 200' 5.9 Move left (b) and climb the face (b) to reach a long crack system which is followed to the top of the wall.

❸ Greek Tragedy 220' 5.8

Chris Burton, Mike Burton. 2000's.
Single rack to 2".

Start at the top of pitch 1 of Spontaneous Enjoyment.

2. 110' 5.8 Climb up and right into a shallow, left-facing corner/crack. Follow the curving corner, and when the crack ends, face climb up and left to a bolt. Continue left and climb a short, vertical headwall (b) to an anchor on a slabby ledge.

3. 110' 5.6 From the anchor, step left and climb straight up a varnished face (b) then continue more easily to an anchor at the top of the formation.

❹ Geriatric Therapy 160' 5.8

Danny Rider, Randal Grandstaff. 1987.
Single rack to 3".

Start at the base of the broad arete to the left of the huge right-facing gully/chimney in the middle of the wall. The route starts up the slab to the left of a short, left-facing corner.

1. 50' 5.5 Climb the low-angled slab (4 b's) to an anchor.

2. 110' 5.7 Move up and right to a flake and continue to an anchor on the big ledge at the top of a pillar.

The following routes climb the face to the right of the huge corner/gully in the middle of the wall.

❺ One Hand Clapping 180' 5.9+

Nick Nordblom. 1995.

This route climbs the left side of the black slab, to the right of the huge corner/gully in the middle of the wall. From the base of the central corner/gully, scramble up about 60' onto the highest ledge below the smooth, dark wall on the right. Climb straight up the wall (3 b's).

The next four routes start from a terrace under the right side of the wall. The terrace is most easily reached from its right end.

❻ The Life Chuckle 200' 5.9

Nick Nordblom, Paul Van Betten. 1984.
Single rack to 3", triple 0.75"- 2".

This route climbs the long left-facing corner on the right side of the smooth wall of One Hand Clapping. This corner is the left side of a huge flake. Start towards the left end of the terrace, directly below the corner. Climb up into the corner and follow it all the way to the top of the wall.

Above the right end of the terrace is a left-facing corner. The next two routes climb the black slab to the left of the corner.

❼ Guys from Josh 90' 5.10c *

Randy Marsh, Peir Locatelli. 1998.
Start 30' left of the corner. Climb the black slab (7 b's).

❽ Todd's a God 90' 5.9+

Randy Marsh, Peir Locatelli. 1998.
Start 10' to the right of the previous route (8 b's).

❾ Cram It 150' 5.9 *

Randal Grandstaff, Danny Rider. 1988.
Single rack to 3".

A great pitch. Climb up and right across a varnished slab (b) to reach the clean-cut left-facing corner. Follow the corner, which jogs right at the top to finish on a shoulder. Rappel down the gully to the right. For a slightly more convenient descent, at the top of the corner follow a flake up and left to the anchor of the previous route.

❿ Happy Acres 300' 5.7

This route climbs the bushy chimney and crack system around to the right of the right edge of the wall.

Variation: Toprope the prominent crack on the right at the very top of the route.

About 120 yards higher up the gully from Happy Acres is a bulging prow on the left.

The Dividing Line 50' 5.11d

The bolts on this excellent looking route have been chopped. It starts by climbing a corner to the right of the prow then launches left onto a line of cool-looking varnished pockets just right of the prow.

Mother's Day 80' 5.10b

Randal Grandstaff, Danny Rider. 1988.
Single rack to 5".

This route climbs the right-leaning corner/ramp just to the right of the bolt holes of the previous route.

Cut Your Teeth Crag

This crag is on the opposite side of the gully, and slightly further up from Happy Acres. It faces south and has a nice sunny location with great views. The routes were first climbed by Todd Lane and Mike McGlynn in 2006.

Approach: As for Happy Acres but continue another 100 yards up the gully, then scramble up a side gully on the right. Half way up the gully scramble out right to below the wall.

❶ November Daze 100' 5.7 *
Mark Limage, Gary Sanders. 2000.
To the left of the main wall is a buttress with a well-defined right arete. Climb the wall well to the left of the arete (9 b's).

❷ September Knights 100' 5.8+
The face just right of the previous route (8 b's).

The rest of the routes here are on the main wall.

❸ Interproximal Stripper 60' 5.7
The leftmost route on the wall (7 b's).

The anchors to the right are for two toprope routes in the 5.7/8 range. Another toprope route (5.6) uses the anchor just right of the central crack.

❹ Impacted Molar 40' 5.6
This route climbs the right side of the face (4 b's).

❺ Baby Teeth 35' 5.5
Single rack to 3".
The short, right-leaning crack on the right side of the wall is climbed to an anchor.

Hide and Seek Crag

This small cliff is in a short side gully which cuts up into the rocks directly across the main drainage from Happy Acres. The routes are at the top of the side gully on a small, south-facing wall on the left side.

Approach: As for Happy Acres. Look for a gully on the right side of the drainage. The routes are on the short, varnished wall that blocks the top of the gully.

❶ Everywhere 40' 5.7 (Tr.)
To the left of the cliff there is a right-facing corner/crack. Start up an easy slab and climb the corner to an anchor.

❷ Here 45' 5.10a
Todd Lane. 2007.
Start about 15' right of Everywhere. Climb straight up to a high crux at the last bolt (5 b's).

❸ There 40' 5.9
Mike McGlynn. 2007.
Just to the right of Here. Pull over a low, small roof and climb straight up to the rightmost chains (4 b's).

The following routes and crags are located on the north side of the hill that lies northwest of the old Girl Scout Picnic area.

Little Springs Crag

A small cliff with a lot of flaky rock, but also a couple of nice slab routes. This cliff gets a couple of hours of sun in the morning and is shady for the rest of the day. The cliff is split into upper and lower tiers by a small terrace. All the climbing is on the upper tier except for the first route.

Approach: The cliff is best approached from the parking area at the last 90° turn in the road. From here walk up the gravel road beside the wash, taking a right branch which leads to the Girl Scout Camp (a grand name for a few broken picnic tables). From there, follow a trail which heads north underneath the hillside. The cliff is on the left side, at the entrance to a big gully that cuts up into the rocks about 150 yards to the north of the Girls Scout Camp. 10 minutes.

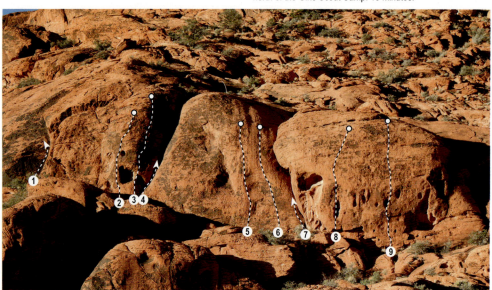

Wide Glide 50' 5.9
Danny Rider & Melanie Rider. 2000's.
Single rack to 7", double the largest cams.
The arching, left-facing corner/chimney on the lower tier.

The remaining routes are all on the upper tier. They are described from left to right. As you walk to the left on the terrace under the upper tier, the first route is about 50' to the left of the last bolted route.

❶ Ultra Glide 70' 5.5
Danny Rider, Scott Fielder, Dennis Zuniga. 27 October, 2009.
A nice, well-protected route up a left-facing corner system with a well-featured face to its left. A good beginners route.

❷ Zuni Tunes 35' 5.9+
Dennis Zuniga, Danny Rider. 12 October, 2009.
This is the leftmost bolted route. It starts below a big, shallow scoop in the lower-left corner of a narrow pillar. A hard start leads into the scoop, then up the face to the anchors (4 b's).

❸ Scotty Breaks Loose 40' 5.10a
Scott Fielder, Danny Rider. September 29, 2009.
After a tricky start, follow edges up the black face on the right side of the narrow pillar (5 b's).

❹ Electra Glide 60' 5.6
Danny Rider, Scott Fielder. 3 October, 2009.
Climb the chimney just to the right of the previous routes.

To the right of Electra Glide is a high-angle slab of decent rock.

❺ Red Nectar Rage 60' 5.10b *
Danny Rider, Scott Fielder, Dennis Zuniga. 1 October, 2009.
The leftmost of the two routes on the slab (7 b's).

❻ Red Ships of Spain 60' 5.11b *
Danny Rider, Scott Fielder. 3 October, 2009.
The rightmost of the two routes on the slab, technical and sustained (6 b's).

❼ Super Glide 60' 5.9+
Danny Rider, Dennis Zuniga. 12 October, 2009.
Single rack to 7", double the largest cams.
The chimney on the right side of the slab.

The next two routes are on the bigger wall on the right which is above the approach. These routes are quite loose and have lost some holds since they were first climbed.

❽ Red Ball Jets 55' 5.11d
Danny Rider, Scott Fielder. 22 October, 2009.
Climb up into a scoop. Hard moves lead out of the top of the scoop and up the thin face above to the anchors (6 b's).

❾ Red Rider 55' 5.10c
Danny Rider, Scott Fielder, Dennis Zuniga. 7 October, 2009.
A steep, awkward route through the scoop to the right of Red Ball Jets (6 b's).

Near the top of the drainage that runs up to the west from Little Springs Crag is a huge, mushroom-shaped block. The next routes are on this block.

● La Fin Du Monde 45' 5.13b ***
Tom Moulin. March 2007.
The northeast arete of the huge, mushroom-shaped block. If you are capable of doing the route, it's well worth taking the time to figure out the location. This is one of the nicest hard climbs in the Calico Hills. Steep and bouldery (5 b's).

● Jacks Arete 30' 5.12b
Start at the base of the left edge of the huge roof. Boulder up the lower arete to some huecos, then follow a seam to the anchor (5 b's).

● Joels Arete 40' 5.11b
This route is on a small cliff 50 yards to the south of the block. Climb the varnished prow in the center of the cliff (5 b's).

Mike Lorenzo on La Fin Du Monde. Page 461.

Alternative Crag

This small cliff has a lot of good climbing, including two of the classic sport routes in the Calico Hills. It faces northwest and is in a cold and windy location, ideal for warmer weather.

Approach: From the Kraft Rocks parking area, head straight west along the gravel road to a bushy drainage near the old foundations of an abandoned building project. Head up the drainage and short distance. Before reaching some huge boulders in the meadow, look up to your left (southwest) and you will see a natural rock bridge. Scramble up slabs and head around to the right end of the rock bridge. Walk beside the rock bridge and continue up a ramp to the base of an obvious overhanging block. 25 minutes.

Immediately to the left of the cliff is an excellent, long boulder traverse (V5) good for warming up, and a great problem in its own right.

The first two routes are on a small east-facing wall above the approach ramp, a few yards below the main Alternative Crag.

● Grunge Dyno 60' 5.12b
Leo Henson. 1997.
The route on the right (12 b's).

● Grunge 60' 5.11d
Leo Henson. 1997.
The route on the left (8 b's).

The first routes on Alternative Crag proper start below an obvious roof on the left side of the steep north face.

❶ Its All Rock 55' 5.12b
Leo Henson. 1997.
A chossy variation with a lot of fragile rock. Start up The Prophet then move left and climb the face to its left (6 b's).

❷ Stage Dive 60' 5.12c
Leo Henson. 1996.
A direct finish to the Prophet (5 b's).

❸ The Prophet 65' 5.12b *
John Heiman. 1996.
Even with the maze of crappy variations to confuse you, this is still a tremendous route. Pull over the initial roof, then continue up good huecos in the steep rib above to a rest where the rib merges with the corner on the left. Move right and pull through the steep bulge to an anchor (9 b's).

❹ Nirvana 70' 5.13a/b
John Heiman. 1997.
Start in the middle of the very impressive sweep of smooth rock in the center of the north face. The route climbs up and left to briefly join The Prophet (avoiding the rest on that route), then heads out right on very steep rock to the anchor (8 b's).

❺ Hotline 55' 5.12c *
John Heiman. 1996.
Another great route; pumpy, acrobatic and fun. It climbs the steep side of the northwest arete of the formation (7 b's).

❻ Flying Rats 50' 5.11d *
John Heiman. 1996.
Start up Hotline, then pull around to the vertical face to the right of the arete. Climb up and left across the face to the anchor (5 b's).

❼ Paralyzed 50' 5.11b **
John Heiman. 1996.
Start up Hotline then move right along a tiny ledge and continue up the varnished wall to an anchor (6 b's).

❽ Psychic Eye 40' 5.12a
John Heiman. 1996.
Start 10' to the right of the arete. A very thin direct start to Paralyzed (5 b's).

❾ Alternative Nation 35' 5.12b *
John Heiman. 1997.
The rightmost route on the west face. Technical and sustained on excellent varnished rock (5 b's).

The next route sits by itself on the left side of the gully that leads up from the west end of Ash Springs Meadow. Look for a big left-leaning trough that starts 40' up a steep slab. A short scramble leads out of the gully to the base of the slab.

Cold Sweat 160' 5.11d
Mike Tupper, Greg Mayer. 1986.
Single rack to 2".
Climbs the smooth slab to an anchor (6 b's).

Strategic Arms Wall

At the top of the gully that leads up from the west end of Ash Springs Meadow, on the left, is a tall, varnished wall with a big right-facing corner in the middle. This is the Strategic Arms Wall. The cliffs face north and east and are shady except for some morning sun.

Approach: From the Kraft Rocks parking area, head straight west along the gravel road to a bushy drainage near the old foundations of an abandoned building project. Head up the drainage a short distance to reach some huge boulders in the meadow. Continue to the far end of the meadow then head up a narrow, bushy gully on the left. The wall is on the left side of the gully about 200 yards up. 25 minutes.

As you approach the wall, the main gully is blocked by a huge boulder. Slanting up and left from this point is a blocky gully with a tall wall to its right. The first route starts a few feet up the gully.

1 Project 80'
Climb a shallow, right-facing scoop, then continue up the steep face (10 b's).

20' up the gully are two right-arching flakes.

2 Mushroom Trip 70' 5.11d
Spencer McCroskey. 2015.
Climb the rightmost flake, then move left and pull up to a roof. Go over the roof onto a steep face then up thin seams to an anchor (10 b's).

3 WildSpleef's Wildride 130' 5.11d
Spencer McCroskey. 2015.
Start 15' left of Mushroom Trip at the base of the left flake. Climb the flake then exit left and make some big moves up to and over a small bulge. Continue up the face as it narrows into a steep pillar. Finish up the pillar to an anchor (18 b's).

Beyond the previous routes the gully is blocked by bushes. Scramble up the left arete until it is possible to get back into the gully above the bushes.

4 Leaving the Nest 110' 5.11a
Jesse Adamas. 2015.
From a platform with a twisted tree, step onto the wall and start with a few fingery pulls, then climb straight up the plated face to a right-facing offset. Up this, then continue to an anchor (16 b's).

The upper face to the left of the previous route has a striking red streak of smooth rock.

5 Bohemian Club 110' 5.11a
Spencer McCroskey. 2015.
This route climbs the face right of the red streak. Start 25' left of the previous route on the right side of a block. Climb the wall to a rest then continue straight up the face, staying just right of the red streak, to reach an anchor at the top (13 b's).

6 Dancin' with Moloch 100' 5.12c
Spencer McCroskey. 2015.
Thin and sustained with good climbing. Start just left of the previous route. Climb a steep face, passing to the right of an obvious jutting flake. Continue straight up the smooth, red streak to a shallow scoop. Pull over the bulge above to reach an anchor at the top of the cliff (13 b's).

7 Mouse Bones 100' 5.11a
Jesse Adamas. 2015.
Start 20' left of the previous route below a steep, shallow, pocketed arete. Step right off a boulder and climb the arete to a sandy shelf. Make a few awkward moves to a flake and continue to the base of a thin, curving crack. Climb the crack, with some nice finger jamming, to a left-slanting ramp. Follow the ramp then continue up the face above to an anchor in the final bulge (16 b's).

8 This is Bollucks 110' 5.10b
This route starts 30' to the right of the back of the chasm, beside a right-facing flake. Climb the flake then the face above to reach a shallow right-facing corner. Climb the corner and the face above to a ledge. Continue up the right-leaning flake above to an anchor at the top (16 b's).

The following routes are on the wall above the huge boulder blocking the main gully. To reach the first five routes scramble around the right side of the boulder then back left to a ledge at its top, below the striking right-facing corner in the center of the cliff, the line of Strategic Arms.

⑨ Intercontinental Breakfast 50' 5.11b/c
Michael Kimm, Ocean Kim. September 2013.
Start at the base of the left arete of the huge corner of Strategic Arms. A steep start leads up the left side of the arete. Continue up the face to a thin crux at the last bolt (6 b's).

⑩ Arms Race 100' 5.13a
Spencer McCroskey. 2015.
Climb the right side of the arete to a rest. Continue up and right across the smooth face, crossing the traverse of Arms Left and finishing up the arete to the anchor of Strategic Arms (10 b's).

⑪ Arms Left 160' 5.10d *
Greg Mayer, Mike Tupper. 1986.
Single rack to 7", double 5"-7".
1. 100' 5.10d Climb the big corner to where it steepens. Traverse out left around the arete and set up a belay.
2. 60' 5.6 Climb the easy crack above to the top.

⑫ Strategic Arms 100' 5.12a **
Mike Tupper, Greg Mayer. 1986.
Double rack to 7"
A long, burly pitch of crack climbing with the crux right at the end. Where Arms Left traverses left, continue up the steepening corner as it curves right. Near the top, exit left to an anchor.

⑬ Project 95' 5.12d?
Unfinished. Start 40' right of Strategic Arms. Climb a smooth, left-leaning groove/scoop then continue straight up the wall following a series of wispy, thin cracks (12 b's).

The next route starts in the base of the corridor behind a tree.

⑭ SALT 95' 5.10d
Michael Kimm. August 2013.
Start behind the tree 20 feet right of Disarmament. Climb a steep, right-facing flake to its top and continue straight up, going over a bulge and up the wall above to a right-curving fault. Follow the fault for a few moves then step left and finish up a varnished wall to the anchor (13 b's).

⑮ Salted Wounds 105' 5.11b
Michael Kimm. August 2013.
Start as for SALT. Climb the initial flake of SALT to just below its top then traverse right and up to a flaky rail. Follow the rail out right to a ledge, then continue to a thin, curving crack/seam in nice varnish. Climb the crack, making a tricky move above the last bolt to reach the chains. A short crux in a long, enjoyable climb (12 b's).

⑯ Leave out the Salt 90' 5.11c/d
Spencer McCroskey. 2015.
Start just right of the initial flakes of the previous two routes. Climb straight up the steep face, crossing Salted Wounds. Continue up a thin, right-facing flake above to join SALT for a few moves. Where that route moves left, continue up and right to an anchor just left of a small roof (11 b's).

17 False Flag 90' 5.12d
Spencer McCroskey. 2015.
Start 20' right of the tree. Climb straight up the face to a left-leaning seam. Climb the seam and the varnished face above, staying just to the right of Salted Wounds. There are a choice of finishes (10 b's).

18 Honeycomb 100' 5.12a
Spencer McCroskey. 2015.
This route has lost some holds and the grade is now uncertain. Start 40' right of the tree and a few feet left of the big boulders choking the corridor. Climb up and right to a large, rotten hueco. Pull left out of the hueco and continue up the varnished face, passing a short ramp, to a short left-facing corner. Climb the corner and reach over the final roof to clip the anchor (11 b's).

19 Lost 100' 5.12a
Spencer McCroskey. 2015.
Start as for the previous route. From the hueco, climb up and right, pulling over a small, stepped roof to a shallow, left-facing flake/corner. Climb the flake and the wall above to a small ledge. Climb the thin crack on the left and the wall above to reach the anchor (12 b's).

The smooth wall to the right has a couple of random bolts marking the lines of a couple of unfinished projects.

20 Divide and Conquer 65' 5.12c
Spencer McCroskey. 2015.
Start at the top of the boulder choke. Boulder up and right into a shallow left-facing groove. Climb the groove and continue up the wall above to the anchors (8 b's).

21 Sands Trap 55' 5.12c
Spencer McCroskey. 2015.
Climb cracks in the right arete of Divide and Conquer to reach a deeper crack. Up this to an anchor on the left (8 b's).

Mike Kimm on Lunatic. Page 467.

The Fringe

This is a large, northeast facing cliff on the south side of the main drainage that runs west from Ash Spring Meadow. This is a big cliff with some long pitches and several two-pitch routes. The rock is quite flaky at present, but the routes will clean up with traffic. The walls get sun until early afternoon in the spring.

Approach: From the Kraft Rocks parking area, head west along the gravel road to a pretty meadow, called Ash Spring, near the old foundations of an abandoned building. Near the far end of the meadow, just past some big boulders, head right onto a trail on the ridge to the right of the drainage. Follow this trail to a point about 100 yards before the cliff. Drop into the drainage on the left and scramble up slabs on the other side to a big ramp leading to the base of the wall. 25-35 minutes.

The left side of the cliff is a huge corner that sits above a low-angled slab. There are two bolted lines on the lower slab which provide access to the routes on the upper walls.

❶ Approach Pitch Left 75' 5.6
This route climbs the left line of bolts up the lower slab to an anchor in a large bowl below the upper wall.

The next three routes start from the anchor at the top of the left approach pitch.

❷ Bear My Soul 100' 5.10a
Michael Kimm. Summer 2011.
From the anchor, move left and follow a line of bolts up a narrow rib of rock. The crux is a delicate sequence at the top of this rib, after which easier climbing leads to the anchor.

❸ Soul to Bear 95' 5.9
Michael Kimm. Summer 2011.
Follow the first three bolts of Bear My Soul, then break right into a left-facing corner. Climb the corner (poor rock) past a steep section (crux). Easy climbing leads to an anchor on the right, or link into Bear My Soul to finish.

❹ Grizzly 70' 5.11d
Michael Kimm. Summer 2011.
From the anchor, follow the line of bolts on the right to a standing rest below a steep, varnished wall. Climb the wall with increasing difficulty to a crux reach just below the anchor.

⑤ Approach Pitch Right 70' 5.5

This route climbs the right line of bolts up the lower slab to an anchor at the base of the huge corner in the upper wall.

The next four routes start from the anchor at the top of the right approach pitch.

⑥ Kodiac 80' 5.??

The impressive line up the steep wall and roof to the left of the huge corner is an open project.

⑦ Skullduggery 80' 5.10a
Michael Kimm. Summer 2011.
Single rack to 3".

From the anchor, climb the steep corner. The crack starts fingers to hands, then, when the wall kicks back, the crack widens abruptly to squeeze chimney. Finish up the chimney to the top. Either build an anchor and walk off, or traverse to Outlier's anchor.

⑧ Outlier 80' 5.10d
Michael Kimm. Summer 2011.

From the anchor, follow the left line of bolts up the steep right-hand wall of the huge corner. As the wall steepens, the holds get bigger.

⑨ Summer Session 90' 5.10d
Michael Kimm. Summer 2011.

From the anchor, step right and follow the right-hand line of bolts up an arete and then through an alley of ribbed huecos and horizontal pinches to a sit-down rest atop a small pillar. Pull left around the roof above and continue up the thin face to the anchor.

The next two routes start in a bowl 40 feet up, below the impressive overhanging wall that forms the lower-right side of the right wall of the huge corner.

⑩ Semantics 95' 5.11a
Michael Kimm. Spring 2012.
Single rack to 4", double 1"-3".

This route climbs the right-facing flake/corner system in the center of the wall to the right of the huge corner. From the bowl scramble up and left to the steep crack system. Climb the crack, exiting left to a rest on top of the small pillar of Summer Session. Climb up and right (2 b's) to finish at the anchor of Lunatic.

⑪ Lunatic 95' 5.11b ***
Michael Kimm. Summer 2011.

A long, pumpy pitch with some very enjoyable climbing. From the bowl, climb straight up amazing varnished pockets to a shallow, body-sized hueco. A long reach and some delicate moves up and right gain a flake on the arete. Steep, juggy rock leads up and left to the anchor (10 b's).

The next routes start at the bottom of the cliff, below the long arete that forms the right edge of the overhanging wall.

⑫ Cowboy Bebop 125' 5.11a
Michael Kimm. Summer 2011.

Start below the arete. Climb the crack and arete around onto the pillar on the left side of the slab. Continue following the bolts just right of the arete until it's possible to move left around the arete to the base of the flake of Lunatic. Finish up the last half of Lunatic.

⑬ Cowboy Curse 190' 5.10b
Michael Kimm. Summer 2011.

1. 95' 5.10b Start as for Cowboy Bebop. Where that route cuts around the arete, continue up and right on the slab, past a short, thin section to reach a line of good crimps and jugs which are followed to the anchor.
2. 95' 5.8 Head up and left, following the leftmost bolt line on the slab. Moderate climbing on good varnish holds leads to a ledge and the easing of the slab's angle. Traverse right into Hippie Vest and finish on that route.

A rickety tower leans against the wall at the base of the arete.

⑭ Hippie Vest 190' 5.9
Michael Kimm. Summer 2011.

1. 95' 5.9 Climb up the right side of the small tower to its precariously-balanced top. Make a thin move off the highest point of the tower (crux) and then follow the seams straight up to an anchor.
2. 95' 5.8 Follow the line straight up through mellow slab climbing with good varnish holds to a thin crux right below a large, sloping ledge. Take the easier terrain to the anchor.

⑮ Behavior Issues 200' 5.10b
Michael Kimm. Summer 2011.

1. 100' 5.10a Start as for Hippie Vest. From the little tower, follow the diagonal seam and the corresponding bolt line up and right to an anchor below a left-facing corner.
2. 100' 5.10b Climb the corner to a thin crux just below a large, sloping ledge. Run it out up the easy wide crack (5.3) to an anchor.

⑯ Trust Me, I Lie 190' 5.10a
Michael Kimm. Summer 2011.

1. 95' 5.10a Start in the middle of the slab to the right of the tower on a nice, flat perch. Climb the easy slab to some thin and slabby moves above a bolt (crux), or escape into the seam left. Clip one (or two) bolts on Behavior Issues, then continue up and left on a giant, hollow, varnished plate. Up and over this to an anchor.
2. 95' 5.8 Climb straight up through the mellow slab to a sloping ledge. Traverse right, and finish on the wide crack of the second pitch of Behavior Issues.

⑰ Broad Border 65' 5.7
Michael Kimm. Summer 2011.

Start on the ledge at the far right end of the slab. Step left to the first bolt, and follow the line up and slightly left until it links into Behavior Issues. Follow that route to its anchor.

Another route climbs straight up the wide pillar above the starting ledge of Broad Border.

Three Peaks Cliff

At the far west end of the south side of Kraft Mountain is a wide gully separating a rocky spur with three small, subsidiary summits from the main face of the mountain.
The following routes are scattered along a cliff band that wraps around the south and east faces of the rocky spur.

Approach: From the parking area, walk west along the gravel road a short distance, then turn right and follow a trail which heads up towards the saddle at the west end of Kraft Moun-

tain. Continue up the trail until just beyond the first cliff band on the ridge to the right, about halfway up the final hill to the saddle. Scramble up and right above the first cliff band to the base of a cracked wall at the left end of the second cliff band on the spur. 15 minutes.

The routes are described from left to right. At its left end, the cliff is split by a big, wide crack. 20' to its right is a shallow, varnished slot with a nice finger crack in the back.

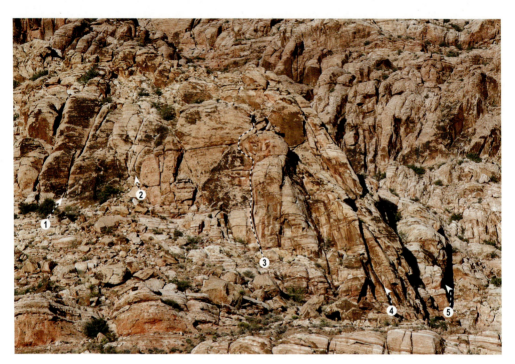

❶ Tongue Mud 50' 5.5
Luis Saca, solo. Mid-90's.
Single rack to 3".
A nice, moderate lead. Climb the varnished slot and finish up the finger crack above.

❷ Edge of Night 30' 5.5
D. Rider, A. Donnely. 21 February, 2008.
Single rack to 2".
Start 40' right of Tongue Mud at the base of a block-filled gully. Climb a right-curving finger crack and finish up the seams above.

❸ The Young and Restless 50' 5.7
D. Rider, A. Donnely. 21 February, 2008.
Single rack to 6".
Start 60' down and right of Edge of Night below a deep, left-facing corner. Jam an awkward flared crack into the corner. Continue up the corner, following it leftwards around the final bulge to reach the top.

About 80' down and right of the previous route, on the east face of the buttress are a pair of short left-facing corners.

❹ Days of Our Lives 40' 5.5
D. Rider, A. Donnely. 21 February, 2008.
Single rack to 6".
Climb the corner on the right, passing a small bulge at the top. It is also possible to start this route up the left of the two corners (5.6).

80' down and right is a steep, varnished buttress with a wide crack system on its right side.

❺ Rock Monster 80' 5.10c
D. Rider, S. Fielder, D. Zuniga. 18 December, 2009.
Single rack to 3".
Pull over the initial bulge into a short, bomb-bay chimney. Pull out of the chimney into a wide crack which is followed to the top.

Wild Thing 70' 5.6
D. Rider, M. Rider. 30 April, 2008.
60' right of Rock Monster is a small, tiger-stripped buttress. Climb the thin seams straight up the front of the buttress.

Spy Cliff

Spy cliff is on the right side of the wide gully separating the rocky spur with three small subsidiary summits from the main face of the mountain. This is quite a steep and impressive wall with long pitches and strong lines, however the rock still quite flaky on most of the routes. The cliff faces southwest and gets sun from mid-morning on.

Approach: From the parking area, walk west along the gravel road a short distance then turn right and follow a trail which heads up to the saddle at the west end of Kraft Mountain. Just as the trail begins to rise towards the saddle, head over to the right into a wide gully. Scramble almost to the top of the gully then head back right to the base of the cliff. 15 minutes.

The routes are described from left to right.

❶ The Cone of Silence 70' 5.12a
Climb past a precariously-balanced block to a steep flake. Climb the flake, then follow the thin crack above, over a bulge, to reach the anchor (9 b's).

❷ Get Smart 90' 5.11d
25' to the right is a long, shallow left-facing corner. Start below the corner and climb up to a small ledge at its base. Head up the corner, then move onto its right arete to reach a flake. Climb the flake to its top, then step right and finish up a steep varnished headwall (9 b's).

❸ Agent 99 90' 5.11d
A good route on nice rock. Start 10' right of Get Smart. Climb up to a ledge 10' up. Continue straight up a system of shallow, left-facing corners and thin cracks (9 b's).

The next route starts in a small corridor formed by a block, just to the right of the previous route.

❹ Spy Versus Spy 80' 5.11a
Move up to a ledge. Climb a thin crack to reach its left-leaning continuation. Up this for a few moves then step right and climb the right arete to the top (9 b's).

To the right of the steepest part of the buttress is a steep, varnished slab split by an attractive thin crack.

❺ Spies Like Us 150' 5.9
D. Rider, L. Saca. March 8, 2009.
Full rack to 4".
Climb the thin crack past a bulge at 50' then finish up and right.

The Lighthouse 60' 5.10d
Bob Conz, Danny Rider, Aaron Donnely. Feb. 2, 2008.
Double 2"-6".
This route is on a cliff about 100 yards up and to the left of Spy Cliff. It is easily seen from the approach to Spy Cliff. From Spy Cliff, scramble up the gully on the left, almost to its very top (cairn). Follow a terrace on the left, down and around to below a steep wall with several corners. This route climbs the wide, twisting corner on the right side of the cliff.

Kraft Crags

Kraft Crag is the lowest cliff in the middle of the south side of Kraft Mountain, a couple of hundred feet above the boulder field. This is a very sunny wall, best in the winter. Some of the rock is quite sandy and fragile.

Approach: From the parking area, hike north between two fences and follow the trail into a flat meadow covered with huge boulders. Cross the boulder field and head up and right across the steep hillside to the base of the wall. 10 minutes.

❶ California Reverse 150' 5.11b
Paul Van Betten, Randal Grandstaff. 1986.
This route starts up and left of High Roller. It climbs past a bolt to reach a crack, which is followed to the top.

On the left side of the cliff, there are two impressive offwidth cracks high on the wall. The next route starts behind some boulders below the right-hand of the two offwidths.

❷ High Roller 160' 5.11d
Paul Van Betten, Jay Smith. 1986.
1. 80' 5.11d Climb a pink left-facing corner and pull over a slight bulge into a short right-facing corner which is climbed (sketchy protection) to a belay below the offwidth.
2. 80' 5.10d The offwidth.

To the right of High Roller is a huge roof with a cavernous crack at its back. The following route climbs this feature.

❸ Shark Attack 115' 5.9+
Matt Kuehl, Jason Molina, Ken Rathcke. January 2012.
Single rack to 4", double 6" and one #5 Big Bro.
Start below the corner system leading up to the left side of the huge roof.
1. 60' 5.9 Climb loose cracks and corners to a short, clean crack which is climbed to a stance.
2. 55' 5.9+ Continue up the corner/crack into the roof. Squeeze

up and right (scary) until it is possible to exit out through a small slot, head-first. Belay a few feet higher from a slung block and micro nuts/small cam.

In the center of the cliff is an impressive pink wall, with attractive crack lines on either side of a huge flake.

❹ Shark Vegas 140' 5.11c
Paul Van Betten, Nick Nordblom. 1986.
Start to the right of two boulders, below a faint rib on the left side of a black slab. Follow a line of flaky cracks on the rib, to the base of a smooth, black slab. Climb past a bolt in the slab to reach the superb crack on the left side of the flake. Follow the flake/crack and the left-slanting corner above to the top.

❺ Viva Las Vegas 140' 5.11b
Paul Van Betten, Robert Finlay, Mike Ward, Randal Grandstaff. 1986.
Start just right of the previous route and climb the black face to reach the long, vertical crack system on the right side of the flake. The crack is followed to the top.

❻ Vegas Girls 140' 5.11b
Paul Crawford, Nick Nordblom, Paul Van Betten. 1986.
Start just right of the previous route. Climb up to a large roof at 40'. Pull the roof (thread for protection) and follow a line of huecos to a shallow arete which leads to the top (3 b's).

❼ Semi-Professional Moron 150' 5.10a
Single rack to 5", doubles from 1"- 3".
This route starts on the terrace above Kraft Rocks, about 150' to the left of the finish of High Roller etc.
The route climbs a system of corners bordering a lower-angled pillar which is recessed from the surrounding rocks.
1. 75' 5.9 Start at a finger crack in a right-facing corner. Climb the corner to a small roof, then move right to a left-facing corner/crack. Once up to a small roof, move right into the adjacent left-facing corner/crack. Pull over a bulge then move left into the obvious left-facing corner. Continue up the wide crack to a good belay stance.
2. 75' 5.10a Continue up the flaky corner, past a bulge and up easier rock to one bolt and a gear belay.
Descent: Scramble up until it is possible to traverse west to a large boulder at the top of a gully. A complicated scramble leads down the gully to reach the starting terrace. Walk east along the terrace to the base of the route.

The next route is on a big pyramid of varnished rock a couple of hundred feet up and to the right of the previous routes.

❽ Porch Pirate 160' 5.11b *
Paul Van Betten, Paul Crawford, Sal Mamusia. 1986.
Start on the right side of the wall. Scramble up a left-slanting ramp to a ledge below the smooth, varnished wall that forms the upper part of the pyramid. Follow thin seams up to a tiny corner, then make a long runout to the top (3 b's).

❾ Weasel Yeast 100' 5.10c
Paul Van Betten, Nick Nordblom. 1986.
This route starts on the ledge above Porch Pirate. It can be reached by scrambling up the gully to the left of that route. It climbs the nice crack, to the left of a smooth, varnished slab topped by a roof. Climb a left-leaning hand crack to the roof. Move left around the roof and belay on the ledge above.

Weasel Cheese 100' 5.11a (Tr.)
Nick Nordblom, Paul Van Betten. 1986.
Climb the initial crack of Weasel Yeast; move right and pull the roof into a scoop. Continue to the belay ledge.

❿ Bendylegs 150' 5.10c
Russ Ricketts, Adam Wilbur. Winter 2000.
Single to 7", double 4"-7".
This route climbs a prominent S-shaped crack at the top of the gully to the right of Porch Pirate. The first pitch climbs a steep, widening corner/crack in the right side of the gully.
1. 50' 5.10a Climb the short crack and continue to a ledge.
2. 100' 5.10c Climb a chimney and exit right, traversing under a roof to get into the S-shaped crack. Continue up the S-shaped crack to the top.

⓫ Classic Crack of Calico 310' 5.9+ *
About 50 yards to the right of Porch Pirate is a steep, shallow gully below a prominent arete 150' up the cliff.
1. 200' 5.9+ Start up the gully, then move right and climb a left-facing corner to below a roof. Move left and continue up easier ground to below a prominent varnished corner. Pull over a roof into the corner and climb it to a big ledge.
2. 110' 5.9 Move right and climb a long left-facing corner.
Descent: Traverse 150 yards northeast and go down a gully.

⓬ The Last Calico 160' 5.10b *
Single rack to 5", double 2"- 4".
This route is about 200' to the right of the previous route. It climbs a series of right-leaning cracks on a wall to the left of a steep gully. A good crack climb, sustained with a variety of sizes.

The Mall

This is the name given to a group of small walls on the south side of the east ridge of Kraft Mountain. The routes are on three separate tiers of cliff. These walls are south-facing and generally quite warm, although they tend to catch any wind thats blowing. The rock is a little flaky in places, but there are also a couple of good routes on really nice rock.

Approach: From the parking area, hike into the boulder field and follow a good trail east through the boulders for 600 yards. Just as the trail begins to go around the east ridge of Kraft Mountain, there is one last huge boulder, the Monkey Bars Boulder. The walls of the Mall are scattered around the hillside above and slightly to the west of this boulder. 15 minutes.

The first two routes climb a steep, gray prow on the lowest tier of rock, about 100 yards to the west of the Monkey Bars Boulder.

❶ Show Burro 50' 5.11a
Shelby Shelton, Danny Rider. December 1993.
Cams to 2".
The lower 20' of the prow is split by a nice finger and hand crack. Climb the crack, then move left and climb the wall (3 b's) to an anchor.

❷ Lick It 45' 5.11b *
Danny Rider, Luis Saca. December 1993.
Cams to 2".
Start up the crack of Show Burro, then move right and climb the steep wall just right of the prow (4 b's) to an anchor.

The following routes are on the next tier up. Scramble up the easy gully around to the left of Show Burro to reach the terrace below these routes.

The first route is about 60 yards around to the right along the terrace.

❸ The Figurine 50' 5.10a
Dave Kruleski, Danny Rider. 1995.
Double cams 3"- 7".
This route climbs an obvious, wide crack between two smooth

walls. An hourglass-shaped flake on the right edge of the crack is a good landmark.

❹ The Fatty 50' 5.10d
Double cams 3"- 7".
The next wide crack to the left of The Figurine.

The next routes are on the steep buttress directly above the approach gully.

❺ Repo Man 40' 5.11a
Danny Rider, Dave Kruleski. January 1994.
Start in a little corridor, formed by a boulder, on the right side of the buttress. Move out left and make scary moves up to the second bolt, continue up the slabby wall to an anchor (5 b's).

❻ Messie Nessie 45' 5.11d *
Danny Rider, Luis Saca. January 1994.
The steep wall just right of the prow of the buttress (6 b's).

❼ Dirty Little Girl 45' 5.10d
Danny Rider, Luis Saca. January 1994.
This route climbs straight up the impressive prow of the buttress on great holds (6 b's).

❽ Gold Plated Garlic Press 40' 5.11d
Paul Van Betten, Shelby Shelton. December 1993.
Climb a short, steep crack just left of the prow of the buttress.

Continue up steep rock above, then move right and finish up the previous route (6 b's).

⑨ Electric Orange Peeler 40' 5.10b
Todd Swain, Mary Hinson. October 1995.
Double 2"- 4".
This route climbs the overhanging hand and fist crack in the back of the corner to the left of the prow.

⑩ Practice Crack 60' 5.9
Single rack to 4".
This route climbs an obvious dogleg crack about 50' to the left of the previous routes. Climb the crack to a ledge, then continue up the awkward left-slanting crack to the top.

The next routes are on a very prominent block on the next tier above the previous routes. They are approached by climbing up an easy gully to the left of Practice Crack. The routes are described from left to right.

⑪ City Slickers 35' 5.11a *
Randy Marsh, Don Borroughs, Wendell Broussard. 1990.
Single rack to 2", one 4" cam.

Start at the base of the chimney high on the left side of the block. Stem up the chimney then swing right around an overhang (b) into a crack which is followed to the top.

⑫ Country Bumpkin 40' 5.11a *
Danny Rider, Dave Kruleski. January 1994.
Climb straight up the face to the right of City Slickers (4 b's).

⑬ Climb and Punishment 40' 5.12b
Richard Harrison, Michelle Locatelli. January 1994.
Start on a boulder below the south face of the block. Step left off the boulder and climb the technical wall to the right of the prow (6 b's).

⑭ Headmaster Ritual 35' 5.11c *
Paul Van Betten, Luis Saca. January 1994.
Climb the center of the south face (4 b's).

⑮ Powder Puff 30' 5.10b
A 5" cam.
Climb the 5" crack on the right side of the south face, then continue up the short but scary arete to the top.

Caligula Crag

This sunny, warm wall sits on the north side of the wash, at the entrance to Gateway Canyon. It faces southeast.

Approach: From the parking area, hike into the boulder field and follow a good trail east through the boulders for 600 yards. Just as the trail begins to go around the east ridge of Kraft Mountain, there is one last huge boulder, the Monkey Bars Boulder. Caligula crag is visible from the Monkey Bars Boulder a few hundred yards to its north, across the wash. Follow the trail past the Monkey Bars for 100 yards then heads across the wash and over to the base of the wall.

The routes are described from left to right.

❶ Ms October 50' 5.8
Todd Swain, Mary Hinson. October 1995.
Single rack to 2.5".
Climb thin cracks up a slab to a bulge. Pull the bulge, using left-slanting cracks and finish up a chimney.

The central feature of the cliff is a big, overhanging prow.

❷ Penthouse Pet 45' 5.11a
Paul Van Betten, Richard Harrison. January 1990.
Start below the corner to the left of the prow. Climb the slab to reach a pink corner with a thin crack. Climb the corner, then move right, past the third bolt of Disguise the Limit, to the anchor of Caligula.

❸ Disguise the Limit 45' 5.11d
Paul Van Betten. January 1990.
Climb the initial slab of Penthouse Pet, then move right and pull over a roof (2.5" cam). Climb the arete (3 b's) above, moving right at the top to the anchor of Caligula.

❹ Caligula 40' 5.12a
Paul Van Betten, Richard Harrison. January 1990.
Double 0.4"- 1", 2.5" cam.
An impressive trad route which climbs the thin crack system up the front face of the prow.

❺ Guccione 45' 5.11c
Richard Harrison, Paul Van Betten. January 1990.
Start in the chimney to the right of Caligula. Climb the steep wall to the top (4 b's).

The next two routes climb the north face of the formation; reached by scrambling around the right side of the crag.

Hefner 30' 5.7
Start on the left side of the wall. Step off some blocks to reach a flake. Climb the flake and continue to the top.

Bonus Pullout Section 30' 5.6
Start 8' right of Hefner. Climb right-facing flakes to the top.

Conundrum Crags

These walls are a couple of hundred yards around the corner from Monkey Bars Boulder, on the north side of Kraft Mountain. They face northeast.

Approach: From the parking area, hike into the boulder field and follow a good trail east through the boulders for 600 yards. Just as the trail begins to go around the east ridge of Kraft Mountain, there is one last huge boulder, the Monkey Bars Boulder. Follow the trail past Monkey Bars for 200 yards then leave the trail and head up the hillside on the left. 15 minutes.

The first routes are on an hourglass-shaped arete to the left of the entrance to a short gully.

❶ Hunting Party 30' 5.11a
Start 10' left of the arete. Climb the face to an anchor (5 b's).

❷ Arrowhead Arete 30' 5.11d
Leo Henson. January 1994.
Climb the front face of the arete (4 b's).

❸ Don't Laugh at me Dude 60' 5.10b
Michael Bond, Malcolm Babbitt. 2003.
This route climbs the wall on the right side of the formation to an anchor at the top (5 b's).

The next routes climb the bulging right wall of the gully to the right of Arrowhead Arete.

❹ Mr Puppy 40' 5.10c
The right most of the three routes on the wall (5 b's).

❺ Drilling Miss Daisy 40' 5.11a *
Steve Bullock. 1992.
The middle route on the wall, steep and juggy (4 b's).

❻ Satan in a Can 45' 5.12d
Jonathan Knight. 1992.
Start 20' to the left of Drilling Miss Daisy, very bouldery. Climb a thin seam (3 b's) through a bulge. An optional small cam protects a runout between the second and third bolts.

About 150' to the right of the short gully is a big buttress with a clean-cut, sharply overhanging wall at its base. The following routes are on the slabby face on the left side of the formation.

❼ Family Affair 80' 5.8
Danny Rider. Fall 1998.
Climb the right edge of the slabby face (7 b's).

❽ Family Circus 80' 5.9
Danny Rider. Fall 1998.
Start 15' to the left of Family Affair. Climb the wall (7 b's) to the top.

❾ Wayward Son 70' 5.9
Danny Rider. Fall 1998.
The next route to the left (6 b's).

❿ Black Sheep 60' 5.9
Single rack to 5".
Start just left of Wayward Son. Climb the crack to a ledge. Move around to the left into another crack which is followed to the top. Descend to the left.

The crux of Winter Heat. Page 481. Photo: Matt Kuehl.

The following crags are all in Gateway Canyon, the beautiful canyon to the north of Kraft Mountain. The cliffs are described, starting with the east end of the canyon and working west.

Swirly Cliff

This is the first major cliff on the right, as you walk west up the canyon. It is laced with swirling bands of pink and white rock. At the base of the cliff are a couple of huge boulders.

Approach: From the parking area, hike into the boulder field and follow a good trail east through the boulders for 600 yards. Just as the trail begins to go around the east ridge of Kraft Mountain there is one last huge boulder, the Monkey Bars Boulder. Continue past the Monkey Bar Boulder and follow the trail up the canyon for another 600 yards then head right, out of the wash to the base of the wall. 20 minutes.

Old School 120' 5.11a
Paul Van Betten, Danny Rider. March 1998.
This route climbs the crack system on the right side of the wall, through a small roof at the top. Two pitches.

Burns Wall

This short, steep wall is the next cliff on the right a hundred yards past the Swirly Cliff. It is a nice, steep wall with some good moderate sport routes. Its proximity to Cannabis Crag makes it a useful warm up venue for that wall. The cliff faces southwest and gets sun from mid-morning until late afternoon in the winter. In the spring it holds the shade for an extra hour or two in the morning.

Approach: From the parking area, hike into the boulder field and follow a good trail east through the boulders for 600 yards. Just as the trail begins to go around the east ridge of Kraft Mountain, there is one last huge boulder, the Monkey Bars Boulder. Continue past the Monkey Bar Boulder and follow the trail up the canyon for another 700 yards, then head right, out of the wash to the base of the wall. 25 minutes.

The routes are described from left to right.

❶ Choss to Choice 35' 5.10d
Dave Burns. 1998.
Climb through poor rock to a nice finish (5 b's).

❷ Just Shut up and Bolt 35' 5.10d
Dave Burns. 1998.
The next route to the right (5 b's).

❸ Hand Drilled Heaven 35' 5.11b *
Dave Burns. 1998.
The next route to the right (5 b's).

❹ Turkey Trot 35' 5.10c
Dave Burns. 1998.
The right most route on the wall (5 b's).

Cannabis Crag

Cannabis Crag faces back down the canyon, towards the southeast. It gets sun until mid-afternoon and is quite sheltered. It has a really good collection of mostly 5.12 routes with a good variety of climbing on steep rock.

Approach: From the parking area, hike into the boulder field and follow a good trail east through the boulders for 600 yards.

Just as the trail begins to go around the east ridge of Kraft Mountain there is one last huge boulder, the Monkey Bars Boulder. Continue past the Monkey Bar Boulder and follow the trail into Gateway Canyon. Continue up the canyon for another 800 yards then head right, out of the wash and scramble up a rocky ramp to the base of the wall. 25 minutes.

The routes are described from left to right. The first route starts from a narrow ledge underneath the left side of the wall.

❶ The Felon 35' 5.11c
Dan McQuade, Jim Greg. Spring 1993.
Bouldery and a little flaky (4 b's).

To the right of The Felon are two black water streaks which stream down a bulging wall.

❷ Cavity Search 35' 5.12c
Dan McQuade, Jim Greg. Spring 1993.
Climb pockets up the left-hand of the two water streaks, past a short, bouldery crux (5 b's).

❸ The Fiend 40' 5.12d ***
Dan McQuade, Jim Greg. Spring 1993.
An excellent route up the right-hand water streak. This is a sustained route with fingery climbing down low and a technical crux up high (5 b's).

❹ Synapse Collapse 30' 5.11d **
Dan McQuade, Jim Greg. Spring 1993.
This route climbs a line of good holds that lead leftwards across a roof in the middle of the wall (5 b's).

❺ Cannabis 30' 5.12a **
Dan McQuade, Jim Greg. Spring 1993.
Start just to the right of the previous route and just to the left of an impressive smooth water streak in the middle of the wall. Climb over a couple of bulges to the anchor (5 b's). There is

an extension which climbs up an right (3 b's) to an anchor in a black streak, 30' higher, still 12a.

The next two route have a common start about 40' to the right of the smooth water streak in the middle of the wall.

❻ KGB 60' 5.12a *
Dan McQuade, Jim Greg. Spring 1993.
Climb up to a ledge which is followed to the left. Pull past a bulge and climb the pocketed headwall to the anchor (7 b's).

❼ Freak Brothers 55' 5.12c
Paul Van Betten, Shelby Shelton. October 1994.
Start up KGB but continue straight up a very steep wall. At a bulge move left, very close to KGB, then move back right over the bulge and continue up the headwall to the anchor. Fun climbing but a little contrived (7 b's).

❽ One Man's Kokopelli 40' 5.12c *
Paul Van Betten, Richard Harrison, Michelle Locatelli. November 1993.
The small corner and thin seam to the right of the previous routes (6 b's).

❾ Good Friday 30' 5.11d
Mike Moore. 21 December, 2006.
This route starts just left of Smokin'. After a very hard start, climb up and left to an anchor (4 b's).

❿ Smokin' 30' 5.12b
The short route at the right end of the wall. No giveaway at the grade (4 b's).

Horizontal Departure 50' 5.10b *
Randy Marsh, Wendell Broussard, Pete Absolon. 1984.
Double 1"- 4" cams.
This route climbs around an impressive roof in a corner. It is on the south side of the canyon about 100 yards up the wash beyond Cannabis Crag and about 200' above the wash.

Harshwidth 50' 5.9
Single rack to 7".
A clean-cut offwidth to the left of Horizontal Departure.

The next two routes are located about 50 yards downstream from the far left end of Winter Heat Wall on an attractive slabby wall of really nice grey rock. It rises straight out of the wash,

facing north. These routes are easily top-roped from boulders and small trees at the top of the wall.

Twisting Groove 30' 5.12a (Tr.)
The curving groove in the middle of the wall requires a little bit of twisting.

Nosegrinder 30' 5.12a (Tr.)
This route climbs the attractive scoop in the right edge of the wall. Really good climbing on this one. Start in the wash and climb up to the base of the scoop, avoiding the big grey boulder (a bit contrived). Make cryptic moves up the scoop and continue to the top on thin edges.

Winter Heat Wall

This is the attractive, varnished wall on the south side of the Canyon about 200 yards past Cannabis Crag. Winter Heat Wall has an excellent collection of trad climbs on very nice, varnished rock. It faces north and is a cold and windy cliff, best suited to warmer weather.

Approach: This wall can be approached from the east end of Gateway Canyon; just follow the approach for Cannabis Crag and keep going up the canyon for a couple of hundred yards. However, it is more quickly reached by going around the west end of Kraft Mountain and dropping down into the western part of Gateway Canyon.
From the parking area, walk west along the gravel road a short distance, then turn right and follow a trail which heads up towards the saddle at the west end of Kraft Mountain. On the other side of the saddle the trail goes down to the west and after 300 yards drops into the wash. Follow the wash back to the east for 400 yards passing several walls on the left. Winter Heat Wall is the attractive, varnished wall on the right just as the wash starts to drop down more steeply to the east. Easy ledges lead out of the wash for 75 yards to the right end of the wall. 30 minutes.

Descent: Head east along the top of the wall to the anchor of Winter Heat, or go a little further and rap from a tree with webbing above the route A-OK. A single rope rap reaches the ground from here.

The routes are described from right to left.

❶ **Hole in the Pants 190' 5.7**
Gary Savage, Jake Burkey. June 1998.
Single rack to 2.5".
This route climbs the slab on the far right-hand end of the wall. Start below a crack in the middle of the slab.
1. **120' 5.3** Climb the crack, past a short wide section, to a ledge below a steeper wall. Follow a crack/ramp up and left to a belay in a right-facing corner.
2. **70' 5.7** Climb cracks in the wall to the right of the corner, past a small bulge, then step left and follow the upper part of the corner to the top. Belay on top using 1"- 2" cams.

The next routes start on a block at the right end of the tall, varnished wall in the middle of the cliff. They all begin up the short, splitter crack, which is the start of High Class Hoe.

❷ **Striptease 100' 5.12b ***
Bob Conz, Tony Yinger, Danny Rider. 2002.
A long, pumpy pitch with some good climbing. Climb the initial crack of High Class Hoe. From the ledge, climb a right-facing corner then move right over the roof to a rest. Step back left (cam) and follow thin cracks (8 b's) to an anchor over the top of the wall.

❸ **Pimpin' Da 90' (Tr.)**
This route climbs the upper face to the left of Striptease.

❹ **High Class Hoe 90' 5.10a ****
Richard Harrison, Wendell Broussard, Paul Van Betten. Spring 1983.
Single rack to 1.75".
Climb the crack to a ledge, then move left and over a bulge to a left-leaning ramp. Climb the ramp to reach an anchor.

❺ **Seasonal Controversies 80' 5.11d**
Single rack to 3".
Start below two bolts 20' to the right of Winter Heat. Climb the wall (3 b's) to the anchor of Winter Heat or High Class Hoe.

❻ **Vernal Thaw 80' 5.11d (Tr.)**
This route climbs the first 10' of Winter heat, then moves out right and climbs the smooth face. Pull over a bulge at the top to the anchor of High Class Hoe.

❼ **Winter Heat 80' 5.11b ****
Paul Crawford, R. Harrison, Jay Smith, Paul Van Betten. Spring 1983.
Single rack to 1.25", Rp's.
An excellent route on superb rock. Climb up and left into a right-facing corner. At the top of the corner, move out right to the base of another corner. Make punchy moves up this corner to an anchor over the top.

❽ **Autumnal Frost 80' 5.11d**
Todd Swain. October 1994.
Start 10' to the left of Winter Heat. Climb up and left past a bolt and a couple of huge reaches to gain a shallow corner. Climb the corner and continue with easier climbing to the top.

❾ **Couldn't be Schmooter 80' 5.9 ****
Wendell Broussard, Richard Harrison, Paul Crawford. Spring 1983.
Single rack to 3".
This route climbs the beautiful crack on the left side of the central wall. When the crack splits at 50', continue up the crack on the right to an anchor on top.

The central wall is bordered on the left by a curving chimney. This is the line of A-Ok.

⑩ Nuttin Could be Finer 70' 5.7
Bobby Knight, Donette Swain, Todd Swain. October 1994.
Start 25' to the left of the previous route at the base of the chimney of A-OK. Climb a right-leaning ramp to its top. Go straight up the wall to finish in the left-hand of two cracks.

⑪ Mo Hotta, Mo Betta 70' 5.8
Todd Swain, Donette Swain. October 1994.
Climb to the top of the ramp of the previous route. Step left and head straight up the nice, pocketed wall (runout but solid) to finish in a thin seam to the left of an overhang.

⑫ A-OK 50' 5.0
The easy chimney leads to a rappel bush.

The following two routes are on the pretty, varnished face to the left of A-OK.

⑬ Judy's Route 90' 5.10d *
Peir Marsh, Randy Marsh. 1993.
This is the right hand of the two bolted lines on the wall, a nice sustained wall climb on good varnish. Start 50" to the left of A-OK (9 b's).

⑭ The Reign of Swain 80' 5.10d *
Peir Marsh, Randy Marsh. 1993.
Start 40' to the left of the previous route at the left end of a ledge at the base of the wall (7 b's).

Sunny and Steep

This is a great crag with a dense concentration of steep and enjoyable sport routes. It gets sun until late afternoon and is very sheltered and warm. Despite the long approach, this is a popular cliff, although seldom busy enough to be a problem. The routes here were the result of a climbing trip out west for a group of Massachusetts climbers; Ward Smith, Chris Smith, Dave Quinn, Paula King and Steve Wood climbed all these routes over a two week period in February 1994.

Approach: This wall can be approached from the east end of Gateway Canyon; just follow the approach for Cannabis Crag and keep going up the canyon for a couple of hundred yards. However, it is more quickly reached by going around the west end of Kraft Mountain and dropping down into the western part of Gateway Canyon.

From the parking area, walk west along the gravel road a short distance, then turn right and follow a trail which heads up towards the saddle at the west end of Kraft Mountain. On the other side of the saddle the trail goes down to the west and after 300 yards drops into the wash. Head back east along the relatively flat wash for 350 yards past several crags. Sunny and Steep is on the left about 100 yards before the canyon starts to drop more steeply to the east. It sits above a nice, flat terrace on the left, about 50 yards from the wash. 30 minutes.

The routes are described from right to left.

Sunny and Steep

At the far right end of the cliff is a short rib, separated from the main wall by a chimney.

❶ Working For Peanuts 40' 5.9+
Climb the front face of the rib (5 b's).

❷ Cirque De Soleil 105' 5.11b *
This route climbs the tall face immediately to the left of the chimney. It starts by stemming up for few moves before launching up the wall. A long pitch with a short crux in the middle (10 b's).

❸ Mr Choads Wild Ride 105' 5.11b **
This is an excellent pitch, long, sustained and technical. Climb the wall to the left of Cirque De Soleil, starting up a left-leaning corner (10 b's).

❹ Solar Flare 45' 5.11d
Start 8' left of Mr Choads Wild Ride and follow a left-leaning seam to an anchor (7 b's).

❺ Peak Performance 45' 5.11d
Start behind a boulder 10' left of the previous route. Climb steep jugs to a hard pull onto the upper face. This route requires an attentive belayer, since the boulder is not very far behind on the crux (7 b's).

❻ Turbo Dog 45' 5.12d
A short but hard crux sequence. This route climbs through the bulge just to the left of Peak Performance and shares the anchor with that route (7 b's).

❼ Steep Thrills 45' 5.12a **
This is the third route to the right of the big chimney in the middle of the wall. An enjoyable route, very steep but with great holds all the way (6 b's).

❽ Gimme Back My Bullets 40' 5.12a **
Another excellent route which climbs the bulging wall 10 feet to the right of the sport chimney (6 b's).

⬤ Slot Machine 45' 5.12b
Louie Anderson. Fall 2010.
A steep route squeezed into the small gap between The Chimney and Gimme Back My Bullets. It finishes at the anchor of The Chimney (6 b's).

❾ Sport Chimney 70' 5.8
The big chimney in the middle of the wall (6 b's).

The next three routes all share a three bolt anchor.

❿ Tour De Pump 45' 5.12b **
Start 20' to the left of the chimney. Athletic climbing through some big roofs leads to a pumpy headwall (6 b's).

⓫ Sunny and Steep 45' 5.11d **
The steep bulge to the left of Tour de Pump (6 b's).

⓬ Turtle Wax 45' 5.11b
This route follows a line of big, awkward huecos just to the right of a crack and finishes with a couple of moves right to the shared anchor (6 b's).

⓭ Scorpions 40' 5.11a **
This route climbs the crack to the left of Turtle Wax (6 b's).

⓮ Blackened 35' 5.12a
This route climbs the right edge of the varnished bulge to the left of Scorpions. A fingery and hard-to-read crux sequence seems a bit stiff for the old 11d grade (5 b's).

⓯ Black Happy 35' 5.11d *
Climb through the middle of the varnished bulge to the left of Blackened (5 b's).

⓰ Claim Jumpers Special 35' 5.10c
The left most route on the wall. Start just to the right of a dirty chimney and climbs through a bulge into a corner (5 b's).

About 50 yards to the west is a huge boulder with two routes.

🔴 Golden Nugget 30' 5.11d
The east face of the boulder (4 b's).

🔴 Edward Silverhands 30' 5.10a
Todd Swain, Donette Swain. April 1994.
The south face of the boulder (3 b's).

The following two routes climb a steep pillar on the right side of a gully directly across the wash from the Golden Nugget Boulder.

Play with Fire 40' 5.11c
Lynn Lee. 1996.
Climb the right side of the pillar (4 b's).

Judgement Day 40' 5.12a
Lynn Lee. 1996.
Climb the left side of the pillar, starting at a thin, left-facing flake (4 b's).

The next two routes are on the varnished faces to the right of the pillar. The wall is split into two tiers.

Andy Reger on Steep Thrills. Page 482. Photo: Matt Kuehl.

Burnt Fingers 60' 5.10c.
This route climbs the upper tier. Climb a varnished face to a bush then continue up the right-leaning ramp to the top.

Singed 50' 5.10d
Climbs the crack (b) directly below the previous route.

🔴 Chunder Bolt 70' 5.12a
S. Shelton, P. Van Betten, R. Harrison, D. Rider, M. Locateli. Jan. 1994.
Climb a big scoop in the middle of a tall south-facing wall about 100 yards to the west of Sunny and Steep (9 b's).

Meyers Cracks
Theses routes are on the left side of a gully which cuts up the hillside to the north of the wash, about 200 yards to the east of where the trail first drops into the wash. Look for two corners facing each other, with a small roof spanning the gap between the two corners.

Scarred but Smarter 65' 5.10c *
Danny Meyers, Roger Morse. 1992.
Single rack to 3".
The right-facing corner on the left. An excellent clean-cut crack.

Conz Crack 65' 5.11a
Single rack to 5".
The left-facing corner on the right has a wide section in the middle, after a blocky start.

Yin and Yang

This small formation has a couple of short but really good crack climbs on splitter rock. The situation is quite exposed and windy, but the routes on the east face are often warm and sheltered.

Approach: From the parking area, walk west along the gravel road a short distance, then turn right and follow a trail which heads up towards the saddle at the west end of Kraft Mountain. Go down the trail on the north side of the saddle. After 100 yards there is a big block to the right of the trail. 20 minutes.

The first four routes are on the west face of the formation, facing the trail. They are described from left to right.

Miniwanka 30' 5.7
Single rack to 4".
The crack to the left of the smooth, bulging face in the middle of the wall.

Sport Wanker Extraordinaire 30' 5.11d
Roxanna Brock. 2000.
Single rack 2"- 7".
This route climbs the overhanging offwidth to the right of the smooth, bulging face in the middle of the wall.

Shortwank 25' 5.10c
Single rack to 1.25", double 0.75", 4"cam for the top.
The right-facing corner at the back of the recess to the right of the previous route. A nice, clean finger crack.

Bigwank 25' 5.9
Single rack 2"- 7".
The offwidth in the left-facing corner to the right of the previous route.

❶ Yin and Yang 30' 5.11a *
Single rack to 2.5", double 1.75", 2"
This route climbs a thin, right-curving crack in the smooth, east face of the block. A really nice fingers and thin-hands splitter.

❷ Zoraster 30' 5.8
The unprotected chimney to the right of the smooth wall.

❸ Atman 30' 5.10a **
Single rack 1.25"- 3".
The short-but-sweet hand crack to the right of the chimney.

❹ Controversy 30' 5.11d (Tr.)
The face to the right of Atman.

❺ Budda's Corner 45' 5.7+
Fran Baker, Jason Martin. March 2007.
Single rack to 3".
Start down and right of Controversy. Climb a flaky corner to the top of the formation.

The next two routes are on the huge block below the Yin and Yang formation.

❻ Renewal 40' 5.10c *
Tiny cams and Rp's.
This route climbs the east face of the block. Climb a crack (green alien) to a slab which is followed (3 b's) to the top.

❼ Brokedown Palace 28' 5.13a
Tom Moulin, solo. November 2007.
This route climbs the overhanging north face of the large block. A powerful and intricate sequence of moves above a terrible, jagged landing. After top rope practice, the route was soloed with protection from a large net!

Index

Graded List - Trad Routes

The following list contains the best, most popular and/or most notable trad routes in Red Rocks. An attempt was made to arrange the routes in approximate order of difficulty but don't take the order of routes too seriously.

5.13d
The Fortress ***
Dreefee ***
Run Rabbit Run *

5.13c
Crystal Dawn ***
The Pathogen **
Outrageous Fortune **

5.13b
The Unsung *
Desert Solitaire **
The Great Red Roof ***

5.13a
Atmospheres **
The Shuffle **
Hemodynamics *
Terminal Velocity *
Workin' Man *** (Tr.)

Brokedown Palace
Hook Line and Sinker
Kritikator * (Tr.)
Jet Stream ***
Feather *
Desert Gold ***

5.12d
Fuck God *
Texas Tower Direct ***
Emerald City
Hangman's House *
Gorgeous George *
Rainbow Country *
The Tipping Point **
Velvet Tongue ***

5.12c
Papillon **
The Madcap Laughs **
The Main Vein ***

Buffalo Soldiers **
Tiger Crack **
Saracen ***
Main Attraction *
Ulysees *
Fingers in the Honeypot *
Tuscarora*
Gadgers Edge *
Black Widow *
The Division Bell
Small Claims

5.12b
Albatross **
Dying Breed ***
The Bald and the Beautiful *
Decline of Man **
Venipuncture ***
Striptease *
Welcome to Red Rocks *
The Rube Goldberg *

Blood Sweat and Beers
Naysayer
The Black Queen **
K–Day *
Blue Collar Crack
Sergeant Slaughter *
Pro Life *
Stukas Over Disneyland *
Cold Front *
Kisses Don't Lie ***
Brown Recluse

5.12a
Geriatrics *
Crack Rock *
American Ghostdance *
Heinous Penis
Mustang Corner *
Parental Guidance **
The Long Riders **
Afterburner

Strategic Arms **
Gotham City ***
Flame Ranger **
Foreign Import *
Matzoland *
Velveteen Rabbit **
Time's Up **
Ancient Futures **
Tarantula *
Crowd Pleaser *
Chinese Handcuffs
Acid Jacks *
Seduction Line ***
The Original Route ***
Boondoggle
Ripcord *

5.11d
In the Red
Tri Tip **
Impact Event *

Lemon Bomb
Akido Gun Boy **
Graveyard Waltz *
Rojo *
Drifting ***
Velveeta *
Cloud Tower ***
Spring Break ***
Straight Shot **
Resin Rose *
Smears for Fears **
Dances with Beagles *
Double Sculls
Huckleberries **
Saucerful of Secrets **
West Edge Lane *
Stratocaster *
Twenty Nine Posers **
Eliminator Crack ***
Without a Paddle *
Unfinished Symphony **
Sidewinder *
Freebase *
Transmortifier *
Marijuana *
Crawdad *
My Little Pony
Resolution Arete **
Line of Addiction *
Breathing Stone
Corruption of the Jesuit **
Whiplash **
The Regatta

5.11c
Fossil Record *
Highwaymen
Cole Essence **
Dark and Long **
The Secret World of Arrietty *
Tales from the Gripped *
Dogma **
Sky Dive **
A Nasty Gash **
This Bud's For You ***
Three K *
Free Willy *
Texas Hold'Em **
Captain Hook *
Spirit Air **
Meteor *
Meister's Edge *
Levitation 29 ***
Like Mom Used to Make *
Running Man ***
Blanc Czech *
Ixtlan ***
Tooth or Consequences *
Office Manager *

5.11b
Velvet Revolver *
Voyager **
Jupiter 2 **
The Maw
Ramen Pride
Lady in Question
Short Circuit *
Right Stuff *
Blitzkrieg
Crack *
Lizard Locks *
Forget Me Knot *
Slick Willy *
Porch Pirate *
Cactus Connection
X15 *
The Delicate Sound of
Thunder ***
Winter Heat ***
Black Rose ***
Saved by Zero *

Dean's List *
Wheat Thick *
Beelzebub *
Cutting Edge **
Only the Good Die Young *
Jungle Wall ***
Spell Me
Kentucky's Finest *
Joker's Wild *
Immaculate Conception

5.11a
Sandstone Samurai
Lone Star **
Excellent Adventure ***
Go Greyhound *
The Lovely Bones *
Gobies for Gumbies
Negro Blanco *
Earth Juice *
Tiers of the Setting Sun
Clipper *
Mercedes *
Seppuku *
Yellow Rose of Texas
Risk Brothers Roof **
False Perception *
Allied Forces *
Plein Air
Plan F **
Spectrum *
Bloodline *
Woman of Mountain Dreams
Enterprise *
The Threat
Yucca Butt
Man of the People **
Bighorn Buttress **
Yin and Yang *
The Warrior **
Pro Choice *

5.10d
Challenger **
Crawford's Corner *
Left Out ***
The Undertone **
Fiddler on the Roof ***
Mai Tai ***
Sick for Toys **
Beautiful Bastard **
Return to Forever *
Tongue and Groove **
Mazatlan *
Adventure Punks **
Our Father **
Red Heat ***
Breakaway *
Red Zinger ***
Jungle Gym *
The Schwa **
Kenny Laguna *
All You Can Eat *
Mountain Beast *
Ringtail *
Orange Clonus *
Twixt Cradle and Stone
Bromancing The Stone
Celtic Cracks
Bodiddly *
Chocolate Flakes *
Five & Dime
Haul for Nothing *
Fear and Loathing **
The Next Century **
Johnny Come Lately *
Cayenne Corners *
The Fox ***
Cut Loose *
The Bollocks *
Edge of the Sun **
Gift of the Wind Gods *

Mr. Natural of the Desert
Double D
Arms Left *
Mushroom People **

5.10c
Beauty *
Risky Business ***
American Ninja *
Dense Pack *
Bro's Before Holes
Yellow Brick Road *
Renewal *
Mustang Cracks *
Eagle Dance ***
Fist or Flips *
Gin Ricky *
Out of Control ***
The Nightcrawler ***
Xyphoid Fever
Amber *
Wise Guys Off Size
Sandstone Sandwich **
Prince of Darkness **
Dog Police *
Water Dog *
Handbone *
Holed Up **
Stick Left *
High Anxiety *
OW Negative *
Unimpeachable Groping **
Miss Conception *
Raptor
Jet Stream2
Senior Dimensions
Inti Watana *
Paiute Wall, Original Route
Pink Tornado Right
Solar Flare *
The Clod Tower *

5.10b
Impulse *
Rock Warrior ***
Wholesome Fullback **
Power Failure **
N'Plus Ultra *
Gemstone **
Da Boneyard *
Cartwright Corner
OB Button *
Tri-Burro Bridge
Slot Machine **
Rob Roy **
Dubious Flirtations *
Jaws II *
La Cierta Edad *
Spark Plug *
Greased Lightning *
League of Notions
The Walker Spur *
Ice Climb **
The Last Calico *
Oakey Dokey
Edge Dressing *
Guitar Man *
Chicken Eruptus ***
The Aid Crack **
Waterboys
Triassic Sands ***
Five Pack *
Chicken Lips *
Stone the Crows

5.10a
Woodrow
The Gobbler **
Once upon a Time *
Sheep Trail *
Texas Tower Connection *
No Laughing Matter *

Cornucopia *
Rain Dance *
Small Purchase **
Back in Time *
Black Magic Panties *
This Ain't No Disco *
Sandblast *
Weenie Juice *
Panty Raid ***
Kemosabe *
Dream of Wild Turkeys ***
Dirtbaggers Compensation
Gwondonna Land Boogie
Atman **
Coffin Corner *
Slot Club *
Sour Mash **
Overhanging Hangover *
The Elephant Penis *
Aliens Have Landed *
Wax Cracks
High Class Hoe **
The Graduate *
Y2K *
Nadia's Nine *
The Minotaur
Cinnamon Hedgehog
Slippermen
Soylent Green Jeans **
Black Orpheus **

5.9
Lewd Crude and Misc...
The Wasp *
Karate Crack **
Luna
Sundog *
The Friar
Sumo Greatness *
Closed on Monday *
P,B & J
Pink Tornado Left
Trial & Terror
Lady Wilson's Cleavage *
Frigid Air Buttress **
Mister Masters *
Test Tube *
Little Big Horn **
Crabby Appleton
Hard Case *
Lucky Nuts *
Deep Space
Amazing Grace *
Straight Shooter **
Mudterm *
Black Widow Hollow *
Black Glass *
Classic Crack of Calico *
Aquarium *
Epinephrine ***
Velvet Wall - Original Route *
Blood on the Tracks
Blue Diamond Ridge
Chrysler Crack ***
Arch Enemy *
Doin' the Good Drive *
Sentimental Journey
The Misunderstanding **
Ginger Cracks *
Rabbit Stew
Leviathan
The Black Pearl *
Spontaneous Enjoyment *
Peyote Power *
Black Track **
Cadillac Crack *
Wishbone
Topless Twins *
Azkaban Jam *
Arrow Place *
Honeycomb Chímney *
The Guinness Book

Return of the Jedi *
Refried Brains *
Fine Whine *
Remote Control *
The Magic Triangle
Friendship Route
Arm Forces
First Lady of Magic
Schwalli *
Beulah's Book *
Skinny Mini
Bird Hunter Buttress
Sunflower *
Sensuous Mortician **
Hot Fudge Thursday
Above and Beyond *
Couldn't be Schmooter **
Cram It *
Clutch Cargo *
Karsten's Pyramid
Diet Delight **
Strawberry Sweat
Chuckwalla *
Vanishing Act
Armatron **
Coltrane *
Heliotrope *

5.8
Community Pillar **
Rainbow Buttress ***
Chasing Shadows *
Bourbon Street *
The Big Horn *
Crimson Chrysalis ***
Varnishing Point **
Valentines Day *
Truth
Atras *
Ultraman ***
White Slab *
Ladies Drink Free
Lotta Balls **
Ragged Edges ***
There and Back Again *
Frogland **
Head Case *
Dark Shadows ***
Classic Corner *
The Great Red Book **
Kaleidoscope Cracks
Get Rad *
Chocolate Sunday *
Cactus Flower Tower E. Ridge
Hot Flash *
The Free Crack *
Jubilant Song
Black Dagger **
Black Magic **
Cat Scratch Fever
Schaeffer's Delight **
Stilgar's Wild Ride *
Trihardral
Peaches **
Kick in the Balls
Spare Rib *
Purblind Pillar *
Cold September Corner *
Sunspot Ridge
Blockade Runner *
Dodgeball *
Fold Out **

5.7
Byrd Pinnacle: left *
Underhanging Overhang
Birdland *
Kindergarten Cop **
Pauligk Pillar *
Group Therapy **
Tunnel Vision ***
Algae on Parade *

Pillar Talk *
Ballantine Blast *
Rose Hips
Olive Oil ***
Chocolate Tranquility F.. *
Spiderline *
Fright of the Phoenix *
Bottoms Up **
The Chamber of Secrets *
Cat in the Hat **
Johnny Vegas ***

Ghouls Just Wanna Have **
Romper Room ***
Tuna and Chips *
Sunset Slab *
Shady Ladies *
Mescalito Regular Route
Lady Luck *
High Scalin'
Prime Rib
The Cookie Monster *
Slip of the Arrow

Myster Z *

5.6
Catwalk *
Physical Graffiti ***
Potso's Pudding *
Solar Slab **
Sandy Hole
Fender Bender *
Abandon all Hope *
Geronimo *

Go Ahead and Jump *
Ok Ok Ok *
Going Nuts
Doobie Dance **
Jackass Flats *
Advance Romance
Bridge Mountain, NE Arete **

5.5
Rising Moons **
Girls and Buoys

Bewitched *
Magic Mirror
Motorcycle Mama *

5.4
Black Baby
Guise and Gals *

5.3
Chips and Salsa *
Solar Slab Gully *

Graded List - Sport Routes

The following list contains all the sport routes in Red Rocks. This is the narrow definition of Sport Route; **A climb protected solely by closely spaced bolts and with a fixed anchor on top.** Routes with spaced bolts or which use one or two bits of gear, like Running Man or Prince of Darkness, are included with the trad routes. An attempt was made to arrange the routes in approximate order of difficulty, but in reality, with routes changing on a regular basis, this is an impossible task. It is not intended to be a definitive indication of the relative difficulty of the routes, just a very vague guideline.

5.14a
Yoshimi Battles **
Herbivour Dyno-Soar

5.13c/d
Where is my Mind ***
Barracuda ***

5.13c
Youarewhatyouis ***

13b/c
Le Vent Nous Portera **

5.13b
Go A Hundred *
Sissy Traverse **
Sunsplash **
Monster Skank ***
Beyond Reason **
La Fin Du Monde ***

5.13a/b
Generations
How Do You Like ...
Nirvana
The Aspirant *
Ambushed ***

5.13a
Master Beta
DNA
Nothing Shocking **
Shark Walk *
Arms Race
Recombination
Pet Shop Boy ***
Meat Locker
Public Enemy
Midnight Cowboy *
Pablo Diablo Direct Extension
Rubber Bullet *
SOS **
Shadow Warrior **

5.12d
Twilight of a Champion **
Southern Comfort **
The Deep West *
Cosmos *
Pablo Diablo ***
Celebrity Roast **
Who Made Who *
Every Mothers Nightmare *
Stealin'
Where the Down Boys Go **
Sand Boxing *
Flying Cowboys
The Gift ***

Turbo Dog
Mr Yuck
Indian Giver
The Fiend ***
Mutation
Nipple Fish
Wonderstuff **
Man Overboard *
Moonbeams
Destiny

5.12c
Supernova ***
Choad Hard
Number .5
Land Shark
Stand and Deliver *
Dancin' with Moloch
External Locus *
One Man's Kokopelli *
Hotline ***
Angler
Number 5 *
Computer Virus
Freak Brothers
Almost but Not Quite **
Desert Oasis
Cavity Search
The Sound of Power **
Choad Warrior **
The Glitz **
New Wave Hookers ***
False Alarm
The Grinch
Body English
Sandblaster *
Fear this Sport *
Pigs in Zen ***
Darkside Slab **
Poseidon Adventure
Stage Dive
Megatronic
Purple Haze *
Gladiator
Pier Pressure *
Lee Press On
Minstrel in The Gallery **
Geometric Progression **
Mystery Remover
The Trophy ***
California 12a ***
Poco Owes Me a...
Threadfin ***

5.12b
The Sands *
Smokin'
Agent Orange ***
Naked and Disfigured *
No Dogs Allowed **

Tropicana
Southern Cross
Girls Skool *
Endless Choad
Fresh Air **
Onsight Flight *
Tour De Pump **
Pigs from a Gun
Alternative Nation *
Sideshow
Stargazer
Churning in the Dirt
Death Before Decaf **
Nevadatude
Commando **
Aftershock **
Grunge Dyno
Its All Rock
Fidelity Select
The J Wall
Climb and Punishment
Big Damage
Plastic Pistol
Keep your Powder Dry **
Busted Brain
Get Shorty
Sensible Shoes
Cowboy Cafe *
Integrity of Desire *
Crimson Crimp *
Pocket Full of Kryptonite
Stratocaster Direct *
Jacks Arete
Loki **
The Prophet ***
Lounge Tomato
Slot Machine
Thirsty Quail
Promises in the Dark **
Wedgie
Party Down
Insecure Delusions
Before its Time

5.12a
Save the Heart to Eat Later **
Pain Check **
Dodging a Bullet *
Turbulence
Caught in the Crosshairs
Psychic Eye
Jaws of Life
The Cone of Silence
The Slab Dance
Wizard of Odds
Pornographic Priestess
Where Egos Dare *
Blackened
Chunder Bolt
Pocket Rocket *

Gimme Back My Bullets **
Artificial Intelligence
Eggs Over Sleazy
Gatito Teiso
Rise and Whine
Teika
KGB *
Maneater
Absolute Zero
Sputnik
Greg's Arete
The Calanque
Standing in the Shadows
Pandas Aren't Bears
One Move Number
They Just Don't Make ...
Presents of Mind
Serious Leisure *
Rafter Man
All the Wrong Reasons
Inferno
This is the City
Cling Free *
Sand Rail
Abandon Ship
Crude Control
Fear and Loathing ***
Office Maxx *
Casino **
Steep Thrills ***
My Tai *
Mini Me *
Cannabis **

5.11d
Social Disorder
Fear This
Sonic Youth ***
Cujo **
Solar Flare
Hang Ten
James Brown ***
Sudden Impact
Hooligans
Messie Nessie *
Grizzly *
Agent 99
Saddam's Mom *
Everybody's Slave *
Peak Performance
Stonehenge *
Number 6
Leveraged Buyout
Gold Plated Garlic Press
Get Smart
Life out of Balance
Synapse Collapse **
Fast Fingers
Backburner
Grunge

Poltergeist *
First Impressions
The Healer
911
Mavericks
Fox Trot
Flying Rats *
Helltown
Red Ball Jets
Number 2
Silence *
Makulu *
Star Search
Number 1
Walking on a Dream *
Nine Lives
Soul Power ***
Arrowhead Arete
Laying Hands **
GBH
Samadhi
Angled Dangler
Viagra Falls *
Golden Nugget
Idiots Rule ***
Snack Crack
Good Friday
Quicksand
She's Deadly
Cameo Appearance *
Sweet Pain **
Black Happy *
Sunny and Steep **
Pinkies for the Dean *
Brown Ale

5.11c
A Day in the Life ***
The Max Flex *
Disposable Blues
Fond Farewell
The Felon
Desert Pickle *
Bone Machine
Have a Beer with Fear *
Death Proof
Native Son **
Basement *
Baby Swiss
Number 3 *
Black Flag *
Commitment to Excrement
Titan Rocket
Fast Moving Train *
Livin' on Borrowed Time
Airlift
Mind Field
Expert Textpert
Good Mourning *
Desert Hamster

Comforts of Madness
Pickled *
Hips Don't Lie
C.H.U.D.
Poodle Chainsaw Massacre
Iron Maiden
Hostile Takeover
Twentieth Century Ultra
Tin Horn Posers
Headmaster Ritual *
Desert Sportsman *
Yaak Crack ***
The Heteroclite
Suffering Cats **
Hanging Fifty
Office Madness *
Red Storm Rising *
Intercontinental Br...
Sister of Pain

5.11b

Purple Suede
Adoption
Inside Out
Bad Reputation
Foreman Ferris *
Liar's Poker
The Bobby *
Oxosis
Boulder Dash
Fury
Myxolidian
Climhazard
Fearless Freaks
Pale Ale
M & M
Thunderbird
Sour Pain
Pockets of Dirt
Scudder Global
Walk the Line
Mr Choads Wild Ride ***
Fox Hunt
Salted Wounds
Planet Terror
Prime Ticket
Lunatic **
Marshall Amp **
Turtle Wax
Moments to Memories
Hand Drilled Heaven *
Red Ships of Spain *
Scantily Clad Bimbo
Hurricane
Slave to the Grind *
Psychobilly *
Dog Logic
Caustic ***
Rebel without a Pause *
Office Expansion
When the Cat's Away ***
Footloose **
Shouting Match
Cirque De Soleil *
Ancient Aria *
Paralyzed **
Texas Lite Sweet
Paradiddle Riddle
Orange County
Sandstone Enema
Joels Arete
Elbows of Mac and Ronnie
Flying V
The Deluxe
Red Sky Mining
Gun Control *
Sand Wedge
Sand Buckets

5.11a

Just Shut up and Climb **
Michael Angelo

Baseboy Direct **
Oils Well that Ends Well
Guinness
Too Few Years
Hell Up In Harlem
Spotted Owl
Sandy Secrets
Repeat Offender
The Shape of things to Come
Tortuga Tower *
Time Off
Seventh Hour
Super Guide *
Just in from L.A.
Cell Block Sisters
On to the Next One
Galloping Gal *
Foe
Totally Clips
Don't Spook the Bats
Drilling Miss Daisy *
Yearnin' and Learnin'
Synthetic Society
Spy Versus Spy
The Gambler
Nirvana
Black Corridor #4 *
Brand New Bag
Gridlock
Mannish Boys
Special Guest Posers
Hunting Party
Lickn' the window
Gift Rapped
One Eyed Jacks *
Trey Dog Boogie
Under the Boardwalk **
Feelin' Groovy
Been Caught Stealin'
Scorpions **
Snagglepuss
Country Bumpkin *
Gardyloo
The De-Nogginizer
Cowboy Bebop
Glitter Gulch **

5.10d

The Reign of Swain *
Range of Motion
Flameblower **
Dirty Secret
Heavy Hitter
Birthstone
Purple Haze
Full Sail
SALT
Friend
Bull Rider
Haunted
Phife
Side Effects **
Panty Mime **
Crude Boys *
Choss to Choice
Turtle Track *
Flip the Switch
Quiet on the Set
Just Shut up and Bolt
Immoral
Judy's Route *
Stupid Cat *
Outlier
Corner Office
Turkey Brain
Armed and Dangerous *
See Dick Fly *
Summer Session
Four of the Apocalypse
Titty Litter
Dirty Little Girl
Conquistador

Live Fast, Die Young
Ferrous Wheel
The Warming
Nightmare on Crude Street *
Attack Dogs

5.10c

Roto Hammer **
American Sportsman **
Burros Don't Gamble *
Mr Puppy
Killer Joe
Dis
Mic's Master *
Hammy The Girl
Into the Light *
Mirage II
Money **
Drool Bucket
Haunted Hooks ***
Turkey Trot
Virtuous Pagans
Running Amuck *
The Whistleblower
Octopussy
The End
You Only Live Twice
Angel Tears *
Squire
Spanky Spangler
Plastic People
Cal West
Red Rider
Idiot Parade **
The Runaway
Guys from Josh *
One Hundred Cantos
Claim Jumpers Special
Texas Tea
Casper

5.10b

Pleasure Dog **
Don't Laugh at me Dude
Hidden Edge
Pump First Pay Later
Cowboy Curse
The Last in Line
Burros Might Fly *
First Born *
Doctors Orders
Black Gold **
Celestial Spheres *
April Fools
Hero Worship
The Fall of Rome
Cat Walk **
Far Cry from Josh
Silver Surfer
The Right Road Lost
Q-Tip
Low Tide
Byzantium
Red Nectar Rage *
Behavior Issues
Fool's Gold *
Cocopuss **
The Pumpkin King

5.10a

Pain in the Neck
Mind if I do a J
Machete
Bottomless Pit
Tremor *
What's Eating You? *
Spotted Eagle
Destroy All Monsters
Trigger Happy *
Big Head *
Upcoming Meetups
Three Mouths, Three Faces

Scotty Breaks Loose
Test of Time
Dancin' with a God *
Edward Silverhands
Flying Trapeze
Trust Me, I Lie
Burial at Sea
A Fraction of the Action *
Divine Comedy **
Split Ends *
Innocent Bystander
Vagabonds *
Umayyad Caliphate
Gelatin Pooch
Fall of Vegas
Here
Mongol Horde
Playing Hooky
Bear My Soul
Chrome Dome
Half Baked
The Last Drag
Manifest Destiny *

5.9+

L3
Bon EZ
Mac and Ronnie in Cheese
Electric Koolaid *
Ming Dynasty
Thermal Breakdown
Virgil and Beatrice
Todd's a God
Working For Peanuts
Skidmark *
Zuni Tunes
The Die is Cast
Queazy Sunrise

5.9

Crude Street Blues
Crude Behavior
There
This is Sparta
Blame it on my ADD
Wayward Son
Long Walk on a Short Pier
Sultans and Viziers
Gettin' Mavericky
Particle Man
Big Bad Wolf **
L2
Family Circus
The CEL
Coyote Moon
Here Comes the Sun
Over my Depth
The Big Short
Hit and Run
Soul to Bear
Battery Powered
Bonaire *
Rust Bucket
Office Party
What R Streek
Sally
Hippie Vest
Sea of Troubles
Bucks Muscle World
Moon Where the Wind Blows
Choking Smokers
Sport Climbing is Neither
XTZ
Sponsors Wanted

5.8+

Brandi Whine
A Man in Every Pot *
Frictiony Face... Waist **
September Knights
Adventure Guppies
Easiest Path

5.8

To Grunt to Sweat
Serious Libation
Sacred ...squeeze Job **
Neon Sunset ***
Five Charter Oath
Sport Chimney
Black Lace
Smear Campaign
Lil's Juicy Juice
Brief Encounter **
Parts is Parts
Technicolor Sunrise *
Science Patrol
Pads Passion
Count Me In
Family Affair
Warrantless Wiretap
Poundcake
Dry Docked
Dangling Participles *
Perchance to Dream
Reverse Osmosis
Subject Verb Agreement *
Mothers Milk
P.A.L.S
Crazy Eights
Boxer Rebellion *
Babylon
Sea Anemone

5.7+

Rigger Mortis
No Hay Sequia

5.7

Ms Adventure
Flying Chuckwalla
Roller Coaster
Cow Lick Co. *
The Last Panty
Man's Best Friend **
Message Board
Tea Cups
757 2X4
Log Flume
Member Profile
No Teaching!
Broad Border
Bumper Cars
Demon Drop
Haunted House
Sweets to the Sweet
Let's Meetup
Frailty, Thy Name ...
Interproximal Stripper
The Goode Dude Climb
Silk Panties
East India Trading Co.
November Daze *
Power Tower
The Three Kingdoms
The Sun Never Sets
Port of Call
Frailty, Thy Name ...

5.6

Slab and Tickle
Safety First
Panty Prow **
Slabulous
Slab-A-Dab-A-Doo
Rosencrantz
Approach Pitch Left
Impacted Molar
Guildenstern

5.5

Super Tsardom
Slabotomy
Approach Pitch Right